R. Gupta's®

POPULAR MASTER GUIDE

National Testing Agency (NTA)

UGC-NET/JRF

Junior Research Fellowship & Assistant Professor Eligibility Exam

SOCIAL WORK

PAPER II

by

AVNISH NAGAR

Assistant Professor
Udaipur School of Social Work
Udaipur, Rajasthan

2027
EDITION

RAMESH PUBLISHING HOUSE, NEW DELHI

Published by

O.P. Gupta *for* Ramesh Publishing House

Admin. Office

12-H, New Daryaganj Road, Opp. Officers' Mess,
New Delhi-110002 ✆ 23275224, 23245124

E-mail: info@rameshpublishinghouse.com

For Online Shopping: www.rameshpublishinghouse.com

Showroom

- Balaji Market, Nai Sarak, Delhi-110006 ✆ 23282525 📱 9354373464
- 4457, Nai Sarak, Delhi-110006

Book Code: R-1710

ISBN: 978-93-87604-84-1

Price: ₹ 495

Printed at: B.K. Offset, Delhi

CONTENTS

PART-B

Previous Years' Paper

National Testing Agency (NTA)

UGC-NET Junior Research Fellowship & Assistant Professor Eligibility Exam

SOCIAL WORK, DECEMBER-2025

(Exam held on 31-12-2025)

PAPER-II

1. NITI Aayog was established by the government of India as a replacement for:
1. Law Commission
2. Human Rights Commission
3. Finance Commission
4. Planning Commission

2. Human Development Index was first launched in _____ by _____.
1. 1989; World Bank
2. 1990; Mehboob-ul-Haq
3. 1990; Amartya Sen
4. 1995; Raghuram Rajan

3. Which Article of the Constitution of India safeguard one's right to marry the person of one's choice?
1. Article 19
2. Article 25
3. Article 29
4. Article 21

4. The World Summit on Sustainable Development (Rio+10) was held in:
1. Davos
2. Nova Scotia
3. Johannesburg
4. Shanghai

5. Famous Book 'A Theory of Justice' was written by:
1. Nussbaum
2. John Rawls
3. Amartya Sen
4. Payne

6. The earlier name of WTO was:
1. UNIDO
2. GATT
3. OECD
4. UNCTAD

7. How many Articles of the Constitution deal with the Directive Principles of State Policy?
1. 12
2. 10
3. 16
4. 11

8. Who founded YMCA (Young Men's Christian Association) in the year 1844?
1. George William
2. Jane Addams
3. Florence Hollis
4. Elizabeth N. Agnow

9. The United Nations General Assembly adopted the Convention on the Rights of the Child (UNCRC) in the year _____.
1. 1983
2. 1986
3. 1989
4. 2001

10. Who founded "Satya Shodhak Samaj" in 1868 for the social and economic upliftment of marginalized caste in society?
1. Dayanand Saraswati
2. Ishwar Chandra Vidyasagar
3. Raja Ram Mohan Roy
4. Mahadev Govind Ranade

11. Which Amendment added the word 'secular' to the Preamble of the Indian Constitution?
1. 44th Amendment Act, 1977
2. 42nd Amendment Act, 1976
3. 52nd Amendment Act, 1984
4. 86th Amendment Act, 1986

12. 'Interactional Model' is another name given to which model of Group Work?
1. Remedial Model
2. Social Goal Model
3. Reciprocal Model
4. Mainstream Model

13. In context of Dementia Care, the term "Malignant Social Psychology" was coined by:
1. O' Connor 2. Gilliard
3. Toni Kitwood 4. G. William

14. As per the Eleventh Five Year Plan how much funding support is given for the National Mental Health Programme?
1. 4.73 Billion 2. 4.63 Billion
3. 4.53 Billion 4. 4.93 Billion

15. The First State Board of Charities in USA was established in ____.
1. Massachusetts, 1863
2. Buffalo, 1877
3. Pittsburg, 1908
4. Illinois, 1889

16. Dr. B.R. Ambedkar got elected to the Constituent Assembly from which state?
1. Madhya Bharat 2. Bombay President
3. West Bengal 4. Punjab

17. The Fundamental Right to Property was abolished by which Amendment of the Indian Constitution?
1. Forty Fourth Amendment Act
2. Forty Second Amendment Act
3. Fortieth Amendment Act
4. Forty Fifth Amendment Act

18. Which among the following countries was the earliest to give women the right to vote?
1. Ice Land 2. India
3. Portugese 4. New Zealand

19. 'Showe Prakash' newspaper was started by:
1. Ishwar Chandra Vidyasagar
2. Surendranath Banerjee
3. Raja Rammohan Roy
4. Dayanand Saraswati

20. Under which legislation the term Scheduled Tribes and the Scheduled Castes came into being and gave legal recognition to the lists or 'Schedule' of Castes and Tribes marked out for special treatment by the State?
1. Caste Disabilities Removal Act, 1850
2. Indian Penal Code, 1860
3. Indian Independence Act, 1947
4. Government of India Act, 1935

21. To solve the problems of social maladjustment in cities and of the labour class, there developed a ____ in U.S.A. that had a great influence on the evolving pattern of the social service.
1. Anti-Apartheid Movement
2. Feminist Movement
3. The Labour Movement
4. Settlement Movement

22. According to the U.N. Convention on Child Rights, what should be the last resort for a Child's rehabilitation?
1. Foster care in the same country
2. Residential/Institutional Care
3. Inter-country Adoption
4. Adoption by parents of child's own ethnic origin and socio-cultural milieu

23. 'Broad banding' is a term used to represent:
1. Compression of hierarchy of pay grades into smaller wide bands.
2. Increase in hierarchy of pay grades.
3. Re-designing of work environment
4. Reduction of organizational levels, functions and job roles.

24. According to David Apter (1965) in the context of development administration, ____ are those cultural values that support development process and ____ are those cultural values that hamper development efforts.

1. inorganic; organic
2. organic; inorganic
3. consummation; instrumental
4. instrumental; consummation

25. Which is **Not** correct regarding Gender Aware Policy proposed by Naila Kabeer?
1. Target Men and Women's practical gender needs
2. Does not distinguish between men and women needs
3. Work on strategic gender needs
4. Work within existing gender division of resources

26. The right described by Dr. B.R. Ambedkar as the heart and soul of our Constitution is?
1. Right to Property
2. Right to Freedom of Religion
3. Right to Equality
4. Right to Constitutional Remedies

27. Who described the Constituent Assembly as 'One Party Body' in an essentially one party country?
1. Winston Churchil
2. Jawahar Lal Nehru
3. B.N. Rau
4. Granville Austin

28. What was the main purpose of appointing the All India Jail Committee, 1957?
1. To suggest for reductions of Prisons
2. To reduce crime rates
3. To privatize the prison services
4. To draft a Model Jail Manual

29. 'Borstal Schools' a type of jail in criminal justice system is meant for ____.
1. Young Offenders
2. Elderly Prisoners
3. Female Prisoners Only
4. Disabled Prisoners

30. Central prison's house those prisoners who have been sentenced for over _____ years.

1. 03 2. 10
3. 12 4. 20

31. The regular failure to meet a child's basic need of food and clothing related to physical and psychological care is an example of:
1. Psycho social abuse
2. Sexual abuse
3. Physical abuse
4. Neglect

32. The disorder in which patient sometimes has attacks of excessive sleep while doing his daily activities is termed as:

1. Insomnia 2. Hypersomnia
3. Nightmares 4. Night terrors

33. If a response is increased or decreased based on reinforcement or punishment, it is termed as:
1. Classical Conditioning
2. Operant Conditioning
3. Observational Learning
4. Psycho-education

34. According to Glasser, which of these Do NOT represent the caring habits of Internal Control?
1. Accepting
2. Nagging
3. Respecting
4. Negotiating Differences

35. Which Article of the Indian Constitution ensures that no person shall be compelled to pay taxes for the promotion of a particular religion?

1. Article 26 2. Article 27
3. Article 28 4. Article 32

36. Which of the following is NOT true regarding Childhood Practices in Social Work?
1. Childhood is socially constructed
2. Childhood is a Unitary concept
3. Sociological Perspectives are relevant in understanding contemporary debates concerning childhood
4. Recognition of Child Rights and Child Centered practices

37. The feminist approach which views that "sources of women's inequality resides within the law and policies and differences in socialization" of males and females is termed as:

1. Marxist feminism
2. Radical feminism
3. Liberal feminism
4. Socialist feminism

38. Procedures for using Nominal Group Techniques **Do Not** include:

1. Discussion of ranked ideas
2. Round Robin recording of ideas
3. Hitchhiking
4. Voting

39. Eric Berne, the propounder of _____ stated that the personality theory is based on Child, Parent and Adult ego states:

1. Transformational Analogy
2. Transactional Analysis
3. Transient Analysis Framework
4. Technical Application Theory

40. A philosophical period of Eighteenth century based on the notion of progress, reason and nationality, leading to an emphasis on human control and decrease in religious dogma as a way of understanding social world is known as _____.

1. Idealism
2. Industrial Revolution
3. Positivism
4. Enlightenment

41. Given below are two statements: one is labelled as Assertion (A) and the other is labelled as Reason (R).

Assertion (A): In the North Indian Plains the frequency of the floods has increased considerably since the last couple of decades.

Reason (R): There has been a reduction in the depth of river valleys due to deposition of silt.

In the light of the above statements, choose the ***most appropriate*** answer from the options given below:

1. Both (A) and (R) are correct and (R) is the correct explanation of (A)
2. Both (A) and (R) are correct, but (R) is NOT the correct explanation of (A)
3. (A) is correct, but (R) is not correct
4. (A) is not correct, but (R) is correct

42. Given below are two statements: one is labelled as Assertion (A) and the other is labelled as Reason (R).

Assertion (A): The Parliament has passed the Protection of Human Rights (Amendment Act, 2006) amending the Protection of Human Rights Act, 1993.

Reason (R): The number of members of State Human Rights Commission (SHRC) has been increased to ten from five.

In the light of the above statements, choose the ***most appropriate*** answer from the options given below:

1. Both (A) and (R) are correct and (R) is the correct explanation of (A)
2. Both (A) and (R) are correct, but (R) is NOT the correct explanation of (A)
3. (A) is correct, but (R) is not correct
4. (A) is not correct, but (R) is correct

43. Given below are two statements: one is labelled as Assertion (A) and the other is labelled as Reason (R).

Assertion (A): Raja Ram Mohan Roy is considered as the greatest Indian of the nineteenth century who sowed the seeds of religious and social reforms in India.

Reason (R): Raja Ram Mohan Roy founded Arya Samaj in 1875.

In the light of the above statements, choose the ***most appropriate*** answer from the options given below:

1. Both (A) and (R) are correct and (R) is the correct explanation of (A)
2. Both (A) and (R) are correct, but (R) is NOT the correct explanation of (A)
3. (A) is correct, but (R) is not correct
4. (A) is not correct, but (R) is correct

44. Given below are two statements: one is labelled as Assertion (A) and the other is labelled as Reason (R).

Assertion (A): Peasant and tribal movements are purely agrarian.

Reason (R): Both peasants and tribals lived off their lands.

In the light of the above statements, choose the ***most appropriate*** answer from the options given below:

1. Both (A) and (R) are correct and (R) is the correct explanation of (A)
2. Both (A) and (R) are correct, but (R) is NOT the correct explanation of (A)
3. (A) is correct, but (R) is not correct
4. (A) is not correct, but (R) is correct

45. Given below are two statements: one is labelled as Assertion (A) and the other is labelled as Reason (R).

Assertion (A): Human Development is a process of enlarging people's choices.

Reason (R): The choices of people can be infinite and change over time.

In the light of the above statements, choose the ***most appropriate*** answer from the options given below:

1. Both (A) and (R) are correct and (R) is the correct explanation of (A)
2. Both (A) and (R) are correct, but (R) is NOT the correct explanation of (A)
3. (A) is correct, but (R) is not correct
4. (A) is not correct, but (R) is correct

46. Given below are two statements: one is labelled as Assertion (A) and the other is labelled as Reason (R).

Assertion (A): In the present days society, people live in an increasingly international world in which technology spreads unsettling news around the globe, creating a deepening sense of distress about such critical events as Civil strife, a Tsunami, or a Pandemic.

Reason (R): Robert Lifton; a psychiatrist predicted the current state of constant anxiety and threats and pulls of daily life, cautioned that technology would increase people's sense of unease.

In the light of the above statements, choose the ***most appropriate*** answer from the options given below:

1. Both (A) and (R) are correct and (R) is the correct explanation of (A)
2. Both (A) and (R) are correct, but (R) is NOT the correct explanation of (A)
3. (A) is correct, but (R) is not correct
4. (A) is not correct, but (R) is correct

47. Given below are two statements: one is labelled as Assertion (A) and the other is labelled as Reason (R).

Assertion (A): It has been often pointed out that changes in GDP (Gross Domestic Product) are strongly correlated with changes in economic well-being.

Reason (R): Economists and non-economists however state that GDP is an imperfect measure of broader well being.

In the light of the above statements, choose the ***most appropriate*** answer from the options given below:

1. Both (A) and (R) are correct and (R) is the correct explanation of (A)
2. Both (A) and (R) are correct, but (R) is NOT the correct explanation of (A)
3. (A) is correct, but (R) is not correct
4. (A) is not correct, but (R) is correct

48. Given below are two statements: one is labelled as Assertion (A) and the other is labelled as Reason (R).

Assertion (A): January 26 was specifically chosen as the date of commencement of the Constitution because of its historical importance.

Reason (R): It was on the day in 1930 that Purna Swaraj day was celebrated, following the Resolution Lahore session of the Indian National Congress (INC).

In the light of the above statements, choose the *most appropriate* answer from the options given below:

1. Both (A) and (R) are correct and (R) is the correct explanation of (A)
2. Both (A) and (R) are correct, but (R) is NOT the correct explanation of (A)
3. (A) is correct, but (R) is not correct
4. (A) is not correct, but (R) is correct

49. Given below are two statements: one is labelled as Assertion (A) and the other is labelled as Reason (R).

Assertion (A): No Constitutional Amendment is required for Compulsory Reservation of thirty three per cent of seats for women in Parliament and State Legislature.

Reason (R): Women's 33 per cent reservation for seats in Parliament can be allocated by the Political parties for the seats they contest without any Constitutional Amendment.

In the light of the above statements, choose the *most appropriate* answer from the options given below:

1. Both (A) and (R) are correct and (R) is the correct explanation of (A)
2. Both (A) and (R) are correct, but (R) is NOT the correct explanation of (A)
3. (A) is correct, but (R) is not correct
4. (A) is not correct, but (R) is correct

50. Given below are two statements: one is labelled as Assertion (A) and the other is labelled as Reason (R).

Assertion (A): A field of activity which is fast becoming important in India is Information Technology.

Reason (R): One of the major exports of the country is software and India has an extremely strong base in hardware.

In the light of the above statements, choose the *most appropriate* answer from the options given below:

1. Both (A) and (R) are correct and (R) is the correct explanation of (A)
2. Both (A) and (R) are correct, but (R) is NOT the correct explanation of (A)
3. (A) is correct, but (R) is not correct
4. (A) is not correct, but (R) is correct

51. Match the List-I with List-II.

List-I (Social Work Methods)	**List-II (Services/Roles)**
A. Social Action	I. Help members become aware of their patterned behaviour
B. Community work	II. Referral
C. Social Group organization	III. Lobbying
D. Social Casework	IV. Networking with people in the village

Choose the ***correct*** answer from the options given below:

1. A-IV, B-III, C-II, D-I
2. A-III, B-IV, C-I, D-II
3. A-III, B-I, C-II, D-IV
4. A-IV, B-I, C-II, D-III

52. Match the List-I with List-II.

List-I (Commission)	**List-II (Year of Establishment)**
A. National Commission for Women	I. 1990
B. National Commission for Scheduled Castes and Scheduled Tribes	II. 1992
C. National Commission for Backward Classes	III. 1993
D. National Commission for Protection of Child Rights	IV. 2007

Choose the ***correct*** answer from the options given below:

1. A-I, B-III, C-II, D-IV
2. A-I, B-II, C-III, D-IV
3. A-II, B-I, C-III, D-IV
4. A-I, B-II, C-IV, D-III

53. Match the List-I with List-II.

List-I (Committees)	List-II (Chairman)
A. Drafting Committee	I. Jawaharlal Nehru
B. Union Constitution Committee	II. Dr. B.R. Ambedkar
C. Provincial Constitution Committee	III. Sardar Patel
D. Rules of Procedure Committee	IV. Dr. Rajendra Prasad

Choose the ***correct*** answer from the options given below:

1. A-II, B-I, C-III, D-IV
2. A-I, B-II, C-III, D-IV
3. A-III, B-I, C-IV, D-II
4. A-II, B-III, C-I, D-IV

54. Match the List-I with List-II.

List-I (Feature of Constitution)	List-II (Source Country)
A. Fundamental Rights	I. British Constitution (UK)
B. Parliamentary System of Government	II. United States Constitution (USA)
C. Federation with Strong Centre	III. Irish Constitution (Ireland)
D. Directive Principles of State Policy	IV. Canadian Constitution (Canada)

Choose the ***correct*** answer from the options given below:

1. A-II, B-I, C-IV, D-III
2. A-I, B-II, C-III, D-IV
3. A-II, B-IV, C-I, D-III
4. A-IV, B-I, C-II, D-III

55. Match the List-I with List-II.

List-I (Acts)	List-II (Year of Enactment)
A. Maternity Benefit Act	I. 1961
B. Equal Remuneration Act	II. 1976
C. Child Labour (Prohibition and Regulation) Act	III. 1952
D. The Mines Act	IV. 1986

Choose the ***correct*** answer from the options given below:

1. A-I, B-II, C-IV, D-III
2. A-II, B-I, C-IV, D-III
3. A-III, B-II, C-I, D-IV
4. A-IV, B-III, C-II, D-I

56. Match the List-I with List-II.

List-I (Fundamental Rights)	List-II (Articles)
A. Right to Equality	I. Articles 23-24
B. Right to Freedom	II. Articles 25-28
C. Right against Exploitation	III. Articles 19-22
D. Right to Freedom of Religion	IV. Articles 14-18

Choose the ***correct*** answer from the options given below:

1. A-IV, B-III, C-I, D-II
2. A-III, B-I, C-IV, D-II
3. A-II, B-III, C-I, D-IV
4. A-IV, B-I, C-III, D-II

57. Match the List-I with List-II.

List-I (Movements)	List-II (Associated Period)
A. Charity Organization Movement	I. (1917-1935)
B. Community Organization and Social change	II. (1935-1955)
C. Expansions & Professional Development	III. (1870-1917)
D. Rise of Federation	IV. (1955 onwards)

Choose the ***correct*** answer from the options given below:

1. A-IV, B-III, C-I, D-II
2. A-III, B-IV, C-II, D-I
3. A-I, B-II, C-III, D-IV
4. A-II, B-IV, C-I, D-III

58. Match the List-I with List-II.

List-I (Days)	List-II (Dates)
A. World Environment Day	I. 3rd October
B. World Forestry Day	II. 16th September
C. World Habitat Day	III. 20th March
D. World Ozone Day	IV. 5th June

Choose the ***correct*** answer from the options given below:

1. A-III, B-I, C-IV, D-II
2. A-IV, B-III, C-I, D-II
3. A-I, B-II, C-III, D-IV
4. A-II, B-IV, C-I, D-III

59. Match the List-I with List-II.

List-I (Gandhian Principles)	List-II (Article)
A. To prohibit the consumption of intoxicating drinks and drugs which are injurious to health	I. Article 40
B. To organise Village Panchayat to function as units of self government	II. Article 48
C. To promote cottage industries on an individual or co-operation basis in rural areas	III. Article 47
D. To prohibit the slaughter of cows, calves and other milch and draught cattle and to improve their breeds	IV. Article 43

Choose the ***correct*** answer from the options given below:

1. A-I, B-II, C-III, D-IV
2. A-IV, B-II, C-I, D-III
3. A-III, B-I, C-IV, D-II
4. A-II, B-IV, C-I, D-III

60. Match the List-I with List-II.

List-I (Theoretical Perspective)	List-II (Belief)
A. Positivism	I. Awareness of one's own class position and shared values
B. Empiricism	II. Importance of socialization of society's norms and values to promote a consensus
C. Functionalism	III. Only observable and measurable behaviours should be studied
D. Marxism	IV. Factual inquiry based on facts and observations

Choose the ***correct*** answer from the options given below:

1. A-I, B-II, C-IV, D-III
2. A-III, B-IV, C-II, D-I
3. A-II, B-III, C-I, D-IV
4. A-IV, B-II, C-I, D-III

61. Match the List-I with List-II.

List-I (Type of Variable)	List-II (Nature)
A. Dependent Variable	I. Necessary in certain situations to complete cause-effect relations
B. Connecting Variable	II. Assumed effect of change
C. Extraneous Variable	III. Not measured but may increase or decrease the magnitude of relationship between Independent and Dependent variable
D. Independent Variable	IV. Assumed cause of change

Choose the *correct* answer from the options given below:

1. A-I, B-II, C-IV, D-III
2. A-II, B-I, C-III, D-IV
3. A-III, B-IV, C-II, D-I
4. A-IV, B-III, C-I, D-II

62. Match the List-I with List-II.

List-I (Part of Research Design)	List-II (Feature)
A. Sampling Design	I. Concerns with how many items are to be observed and analysis be done
B. Observational Design	II. Deals with Techniques by which procedures specified in sampling can be done
C. Statistical Design	III. Deals with method of selecting items to be observed
D. Operational Design	IV. Relates to the conditions under which observations are made

Choose the *correct* answer from the options given below:

1. A-I, B-II, C-III, D-IV
2. A-III, B-IV, C-I, D-II
3. A-II, B-III, C-IV, D-I
4. A-III, B-I, C-II, D-IV

63. Match the List-I with List-II.

List-I (Bradshaw's Need Typology)	List-II (Associated Meaning)
A. Normative Needs	I. Identified by Individuals or Groups
B. Felt Needs	II. Define according to experts or professional standards
C. Expressed Needs	III. Identified through comparison of characteristics among relative groups
D. Comparative Needs	IV. Public articulation of Individual or Group Needs

Choose the *correct* answer from the options given below:

1. A-I, B-II, C-III, D-IV
2. A-II, B-I, C-IV, D-III
3. A-III, B-IV, C-I, D-II
4. A-IV, B-III, C-II, D-I

64. Match the List-I with List-II.

List-I (Theory)	List-II (Focus)
A. Empirical Theory	I. Conceptualizes preferences, what ought to be
B. Normative Theory	II. Focuses on 'why' questions and address, uncover causes and relationships
C. Explanatory Theory	III. Focuses on 'How' questions and bridges the gap between agency and structure
D. Practice Theory	IV. Systematically conceptualizes things built from Observations and Experiments

Choose the *correct* answer from the options given below:

1. A-II, B-III, C-IV, D-I
2. A-I, B-II, C-IV, D-III
3. A-III, B-IV, C-II, D-I
4. A-IV, B-I, C-II, D-III

65. Match the List-I with List-II.

List-I (Development Phase)	List-II (Primary Value)
A. Bhakti Movement	I. Equality and Justice
B. Socialism	II. Humanism
C. Sarvodaya	III. Solidarity with Marginalized people
D. Social Work Profession	IV. Lokniti and Swarajya

Choose the ***correct*** answer from the options given below:

1. A-I, B-II, C-IV, D-III
2. A-IV, B-III, C-II, D-I
3. A-II, B-I, C-IV, D-III
4. A-III, B-II, C-I, D-IV

66. Arrange the following organizations year of establishment in chronological order (Earliest to Newest)

A. Atmiya Samaj
B. Theosophical Society
C. Ram Krishna Mission
D. Servants of India Society

Choose the ***correct*** answer from the options given below:

1. A, B, C, D   2. B, A, D, C
3. C, B, A, D   4. D, A, B, C

67. Arrange the following discernible stages of Case Work in correct sequence:

A. The Synthetic or Integrated
B. The Sociological
C. The Psycho-social
D. The Exploratory and Disciplinary

Choose the ***correct*** answer from the options given below:

1. A, B, C, D   2. B, C, D, A
3. C, A, B, D   4. D, B, C, A

68. Arrange the Functionaries in their correct sequence:

A. Cabinet Secretary
B. Union Cabinet Minister
C. Chief Justice of India
D. Chief Election Commissioner

Choose the ***correct*** answer from the options given below:

1. D, C, A, B   2. C, B, D, A
3. A, B, C, D   4. C, D, A, B

69. Arrange the following Institutions in the order of their establishment:

A. International Labour Organizations
B. All India Trade Union Congress
C. Royal Commission
D. First National Commission on Labour

Choose the ***correct*** answer from the options given below:

1. A, B, C, D   2. B, A, C, D
3. D, C, A, B   4. C, D, B, A

70. Arrange the following Rural Employment Programmes/Schemes in chronological order:

A. Integrated Rural Development Programme
B. Jawahar Rozgar Yojna
C. Swarnajayanti Gram Swarojgar Yojna
D. National Rural Employment Guarantee Programme

Choose the ***correct*** answer from the options given below:

1. A, B, C, D   2. B, A, C, D
3. A, B, D, C   4. B, C, A, D

71. Arrange the following countries in order of their HDI Rank of 2023 (source HDR 2025):

A. Myanmar   B. Pakistan
C. India   D. Sri Lanka
E. Nepal

Choose the ***correct*** answer from the options given below:

1. C, D, A, B, E   2. C, E, B, A, D
3. D, C, E, A, B   4. E, C, D, A, B

72. Arrange the following stages of Technique of Developing Measurement Tools in chronological order:

A. Selection of Indicators
B. Concept development
C. Specification of concept dimensions
D. Formation of Index

Choose the ***correct*** answer from the options given below:

1. A, C, B, D   2. B, C, A, D
3. C, D, A, B   4. D, B, A, C

73. Arrange the stages of development and implementation of Job Classification Scheme in Ascending order:

A. Job description must be produced for each job to be evaluated
B. Assigning Appropriate Grades
C. Grade definitions or role profiles have to be drawn for jobs being evaluated
D. Matching of each job description to the definition that most closely reflect duties of job

Choose the ***correct*** answer from the options given below:

1. A, C, B, D 2. C, A, D, B
3. B, D, A, C 4. A, B, C, D

74. Arrange the steps of writing Research Reports in chronological order:

A. Preparation of the Rough Draft
B. Preparation of the Final Outline
C. Logical analysis of the subject matter
D. Preparation of bibliography and writing final draft
E. Rewriting and polishing of draft

Choose the ***correct*** answer from the options given below:

1. C, B, A, E, D 2. A, C, B, E, D
3. A, C, E, B, D 4. C, E, A, B, D

75. What should you do when you are faced with an ethical dilemma?

A. Identify the problem or dilemma
B. Consider and decide on the possible courses of action and examine the consequences
C. Consult with colleagues, supervisors, legal experts or professionals
D. Determine the core principles and the competing issues
E. Review the relevant code of ethics and applicable laws and regulations.

Choose the ***correct*** answer from the options given below:

1. A, D, E, C, B 2. B, C, A, D, E
3. A, E, D, C, B 4. A, C, B, E, D

76. Arrange the following steps of community organization suggested by Lindeman:

A. Identification of Need
B. Spreading the Consciousness of Need
C. Projection of Consciousness of Need
D. Emotional Impulse to Meet the Need quickly

Choose the ***correct*** answer from the options given below:

1. A, B, C, D 2. B, A, C, D
3. A, C, B, D 4. C, A, B, D

77. Arrange the steps of Evidence Based Group Work Process proposed by MacGowan (2008) in Descending order:

A. Formulating Answerable Questions
B. Applying and Evaluating the Evidence
C. Searching for Evidence
D. Critically Reviewing the Evidence

Choose the ***correct*** answer from the options given below:

1. D, A, C, B 2. C, D, A, B
3. A, B, C, D 4. B, D, C, A

78. Which of the following is TRUE regarding Pradhan Mantri Kaushal Vikas Yojana:

A. It is a flagship scheme of Ministry of Labour and Employment
B. It aims at imparting training in soft skills, financial and digital literacy and entrepreneurship
C. It is aligning the country's competencies of the workforce which is unregulated to the National Skill Qualification Framework
D. It is a flagship scheme of Ministry of Women and Child Development

Choose the ***correct*** answer from the options given below:

1. A and D only
2. B and C only
3. A, C and D only
4. B only

79. Incorrect conclusions about the validity of a hypothesis may be drawn if:

A. The study design is systematic
B. Method of data collection is appropriate
C. Study design is faulty
D. Statistical procedures applied are inappropriate

Choose the ***correct*** answer from the options given below:

1. A, C and D only
2. C and D only
3. B and D only
4. A and C only

80. Arrange the following Principles of Social Group Work suggested by H.B. Trecker in collect sequence:

A. The Principle of Continuous Individualization
B. The Principle of Purposeful Group Worker Relationship
C. The Principle of Specific Objectives
D. The Principle of Planned Group Formation

Choose the ***correct*** answer from the options given below:

1. A, B, C, D   2. B, A, C, D
3. D, C, B, A   4. D, B, C, A

81. Which is a part of Macros level practice?

A. Advocating for policy change
B. Campaigning for enactment of a new social legislation
C. Social Group Work
D. Social Casework

Choose the ***correct*** answer from the options given below:

1. A and C only
2. B and D only
3. A and B only
4. A, B and C only

82. According to Spiegel, Failure in Role Complementarity occurs due to:

A. Availability of more Instrumental means
B. Cognitive Discrepancy
C. Discrepancy in Orientation of Cultural Values
D. Discrepancy in Role Acceptance

Choose the ***correct*** answer from the options given below:

1. A, B, C only   2. B, C, D only
3. A, C, D only   4. B, D, A only

83. Example of Case Study methods are:

A. Case Comparison methods
B. Ethnographic methods
C. Recording Behaviours on Self Anchored Rating Scales
D. Participant and Non-Participant Observations

Choose the ***correct*** answer from the options given below:

1. A, C, D only
2. B, C, D only
3. A, B, D only
4. A, B, C only

84. Which statements are correct with respect to variables in research?

A. A continuous variable can assume any numerical value within a specific range like 'Age'.
B. Extraneous variables are macro level factors that remain hidden.
C. Dependent variable relies upon or is a consequence of the other variable.
D. Independent variable is manipulated in experimental research designs.
E. Confounding variables are dependent variables in quasi experimental research designs.

Choose the ***correct*** answer from the options given below:

1. A, B, C only   2. A, C, D only
3. B, C, E only   4. B, D, E only

85. Employee's Provident Funds and Miscellaneous Provisions Act, 1952 includes:

A. The Employee's Provident Fund Scheme
B. The Employee's Pension Scheme
C. The Employee's State Insurance Scheme
D. The Employee's Deposit Linked Insurance Scheme

Choose the ***correct*** answer from the options given below:

1. C, D, A only   2. B, C, D only
3. A, B, C only   4. A, B, D only

86. Which of the following are the specific objectives of establishment of Human Rights Commission in India?

A. To strengthen the institutional arrangement for addressing human rights issues in a more focused manner.

B. To look into adoptions of excesses, independently of the government in a manner that would underline government's commitment to protect human rights.

C. To suppress criticism of government policies related to human rights.

D. To complement and strengthen the efforts that have already been made to protect human rights.

Choose the ***correct*** answer from the options given below:

1. A, B, C only 2. A, B, D only
3. B, C, D only 4. A, C, D only

87. As per the National Rural Health Mission, what are the responsibilities of 'ASHA' Accredited Social Health Activist?

A. Pregnancy kit usage for early pregnancy detection

B. Carrying out deliveries

C. Creating awareness on immunization and nutrition

D. Helping women reach health facility for Ante Natal care check up

Choose the ***correct*** answer from the options given below:

1. A, C and D only
2. A, B and D only
3. B and C only
4. A, B, C, D

88. Which of the following statements are true with regard to descriptive statistics?

A. Median and Mode are used in Linear Regression Analysis.

B. Range and Standard Deviation are used to depict Measures of Dispersion.

C. Skewness is the degree of symmetry or rather lack of it.

D. Leptokurtic depicts highest peak and platykurtic the flattest peak.

E. Skewness is measured by coefficient of correlation.

Choose the ***correct*** answer from the options given below:

1. A, B and E only
2. B, C and D only
3. A, C and E only
4. C, D and E only

89. Which of the following are part of Non-Probability sampling method?

A. Lottery Method
B. Quota Sampling
C. Systematic or Listing Method
D. Purposive Sampling
E. Accidental Sampling

Choose the ***correct*** answer from the options given below:

1. A and C only
2. A, B and C only
3. B, D and E only
4. E, D and A only

90. Which are the tools of data collection used in qualitative research?

A. Structured Interview Schedule
B. Interview Guide
C. Observation Guide
D. Questionnaire

Choose the ***correct*** answer from the options given below:

1. A, B and C only
2. A and D only
3. A, B, C and D
4. B and C only

Directions (Qs. No. 91 to 95): *Read the passage carefully and answer the following questions:*

"Social workers should protect the confidentiality of all information obtained in the course of professional service, except for compelling professional reasons. The general expectation that social workers will keep information confidential does not apply when disclosure is necessary to prevent serious, foreseeable and imminent harm to a client or others. In all instances, social workers should disclose the least amount of confidential information necessary to achieve the desired purpose, only information that is directly relevant to the purpose for which the disclosure is made should be revealed."

91. Confidentiality as a Principle is specifically mentioned in which method of Social Work Practice?

1. Social Casework
2. Social Group Work
3. Community Organization
4. Social Welfare Administration

92. What is the meaning of maintenance of confidentiality?

A. Records of a client should not be accessible to others

B. Information of the client cannot be shared with outsiders

C. Client related information can never be shared to referral agencies/professionals even as per specific requirement

D. Tendency of self-harm cannot be reported to concerned authorities

Choose the ***correct*** answer from the options given below:

1. C & D only 2. B & C only
3. A & D only 4. A & B only

93. What should be done before any confidential information is shared with others?

A. Social workers should review with clients the disclosure of such information as may be legally required.

B. The clients should be informed about the limitations of clients right to confidentiality.

C. Personal information may be shared without clients prior consent.

D. Take consent of all the kin members before revealing any information.

Choose the ***correct*** answer from the options given below:

1. A, C & D only 2. A, B & D only
3. A & B only 4. B, C & D only

94. Which of the following **Does Not** relate to the Principle of Confidentiality?

1. Informed consent
2. Using technology mindfully and responsibly
3. Keeping records of client under lock and key
4. Personal information of the client can be revealed to the public three months after the case is closed.

95. While working with transnational and trans-cultural communities when can interpreters NOT be used in the context of social casework to maintain confidentiality?

1. Interpreters having been trained in neutrality and confidentiality
2. Interpreters having been aware about clients' cultural roots
3. Interpreters having empathy and cultural competence
4. Interpreters disowning others cultural practices.

Directions (Qs. No. 96 to 100): *Read the passage carefully and answer the following questions:*

The Strengths and Diversity Perspectives can be used to guide Social Work Practice at all levels. Take the example of a social worker, who works for a Hospice Programme. Hospice offers patients and their families support and comfort, helps patients manage their pain, and strives to improve the quality of their lives. Social worker is working with the client's family. Where X is 82 years old, has lung cancer and has been told that his condition has reached a critical stage. As per the strengths and diversity perspective, social worker is required to spend time with the client's family and learn what resources are available to them, how they have successfully coped with stress and trauma in the past, and how their cultural background might shape their understanding of and relationship to death and dying.

96. The Strengths Perspective was propounded by:

1. Saleebey 2. Hollis
3. Perlman 4. Payne

97. Who is referred to as a recipient of Hospice Care?

1. An old male who is above the age of 75 years
2. A diabetic patient who is on long term medical treatment
3. A client who is on the verge of death due to a terminal illness
4. A Leprosy patient who has extreme deformities in his hands and foot

98. The medical model of treatment of a disease **Does Not** take into account which of the following?

A. Nature of infectious disease of the patient
B. The patient's cultural environment
C. Coping abilities of the family
D. The patients social life and workplace

Choose the ***correct*** answer from the options given below:

1. A & B only 2. B & C only
3. D & B only 4. B, C & D only

99. The symptoms of Post-Traumatic Stress disorder:

1. Reduces within 6 months of cessation of stressors
2. May persists for years
3. Reduces within 48 hours of cessation of stressors
4. Reduces within one hour of cessation of stressors

100. Which is NOT considered as a criteria from a Diversity Perspective in Sociological context?

1. Caste 2. Skills
3. Religion 4. Gender

ANSWERS

1	**2**	**3**	**4**	**5**	**6**	**7**	**8**	**9**	**10**
4	2	4	3	2	2	3	1	3	*
11	**12**	**13**	**14**	**15**	**16**	**17**	**18**	**19**	**20**
2	3	3	1	1	3	1	4	1	4
21	**22**	**23**	**24**	**25**	**26**	**27**	**28**	**29**	**30**
4	2	1	4	2	4	4	4	1	1
31	**32**	**33**	**34**	**35**	**36**	**37**	**38**	**39**	**40**
4	2	2	2	2	2	3	3	2	4
41	**42**	**43**	**44**	**45**	**46**	**47**	**48**	**49**	**50**
1	3	3	4	1	1	2	1	4	3
51	**52**	**53**	**54**	**55**	**56**	**57**	**58**	**59**	**60**
2	3	1	1	1	1	2	2	3	2
61	**62**	**63**	**64**	**65**	**66**	**67**	**68**	**69**	**70**
2	2	2	4	3	1	4	2	1	1
71	**72**	**73**	**74**	**75**	**76**	**77**	**78**	**79**	**80**
3	2	2	1	1	1	4	2	2	3

81	82	83	84	85	86	87	88	89	90
3	2	3	2	4	2	1	2	3	4
91	**92**	**93**	**94**	**95**	**96**	**97**	**98**	**99**	**100**
1	4	3	4	4	1	3	4	2	2

EXPLANATORY ANSWERS

1. NITI Aayog was established by the Government of India as a replacement for the Planning Commission. The Planning Commission was set up in 1950 and was responsible for preparing Five-Year Plans and guiding planned economic development. In 2015, it was replaced by NITI Aayog to promote cooperative federalism and a more flexible policy-making approach. NITI Aayog does not allocate funds like the Planning Commission earlier did. Its role is mainly advisory, strategic, and policy-oriented, making option 4 the correct answer.

2. The Human Development Index was first launched in 1990 through the Human Development Report, and it is closely associated with Pakistani economist Mahbub ul Haq. The HDI was developed to shift the focus of development from only income and economic growth to broader human well-being. It measures development using indicators related to health, education, and standard of living. Amartya Sen made important conceptual contributions to the human development approach, but the given option that correctly matches the launch year and main originator is option 2. Therefore, among the given choices, 1990; Mehboob-ul-Haq is the correct answer.

3. Article 21 of the Constitution of India safeguards the right to marry a person of one's choice. Article 21 protects life and personal liberty, and Indian courts have interpreted it broadly to include dignity, autonomy, privacy, and personal choice. The choice of a life partner is considered an essential part of individual liberty and personal freedom. Marriage by choice is therefore protected under the constitutional guarantee of life and personal liberty. Hence, Article 21 is the correct constitutional provision for this question.

4. The World Summit on Sustainable Development, also known as Rio+10, was held in Johannesburg, South Africa. It took place in 2002, ten years after the 1992 Earth Summit held at Rio de Janeiro. The summit reviewed global progress on sustainable development and focused on issues such as poverty, environment, water, energy, health, agriculture, and biodiversity. Since it was the follow-up summit after Rio, it came to be known as Rio+10. Therefore, Johannesburg is the correct answer.

5. The famous book A Theory of Justice was written by John Rawls. It was published in 1971 and is one of the most influential works in modern political philosophy. In this book, Rawls developed the idea of "justice as fairness" and discussed principles of justice for a fair society. His concepts such as the original position, veil of ignorance, and difference principle became central to debates on justice and equality. Therefore, John Rawls is the correct answer.

6. The earlier name or predecessor arrangement of the WTO was GATT, which stands for General Agreement on Tariffs and Trade. GATT came into existence in 1947 and functioned as the main international framework for regulating global trade before the WTO was formed. The World Trade Organization was established in 1995 after the Uruguay Round negotiations. WTO replaced GATT as a formal international organization with wider coverage, including goods, services, and intellectual property. Therefore, among the given options, GATT is the correct answer.

7. The Directive Principles of State Policy are contained in Part IV of the Constitution of India. They are covered from Article 36 to Article 51. Counting Articles 36, 37, 38, 39, 40, 41, 42, 43, 44, 45, 46, 47, 48, 49, 50, and 51 gives a total of 16 Articles. These principles guide the State in making laws and policies for social, economic, and political justice. Hence, option 3, that is 16, is the correct answer.

8. YMCA, meaning Young Men's Christian Association, was founded in 1844 by George Williams. The organization began in London during the period of industrialization. Its purpose was to provide support, moral guidance, and welfare activities for young men facing difficult urban working conditions. Although the option writes "George William," the historically correct name is George Williams, and this option clearly refers to him. Therefore, option 1 is the correct answer.

9. The United Nations General Assembly adopted the Convention on the Rights of the Child in 1989. The UNCRC is an important international treaty dealing with the rights, protection, survival, development, and participation of children. It recognizes children as rights-bearing individuals rather than merely dependents needing care. The Convention later became one of the most widely accepted human rights treaties in the world. Therefore, 1989 is the correct answer.

10. Jyotirao Phule: Satya Shodhak Samaj was founded by Jyotirao Phule, not by any of the four persons listed in the options. Also, the correct year generally associated with its founding is 1873, not 1868. The organization worked for the social upliftment of oppressed and marginalized castes and challenged caste-based inequality and Brahmanical domination. Dayanand Saraswati, Ishwar Chandra Vidyasagar, Raja Ram Mohan Roy, and Mahadev Govind Ranade were important reformers, but they did not found Satya Shodhak Samaj. Therefore, none of the given options fits the question correctly.

11. The word "secular" was added to the Preamble of the Indian Constitution by the 42nd Amendment Act, 1976. This amendment also added the word "socialist" to the Preamble. Before this amendment, the Preamble described India as a sovereign democratic republic. After the amendment, India was described as a sovereign socialist secular democratic republic. Therefore, the amendment that added the word "secular" is the 42nd Amendment Act, 1976.

12. The Interactional Model is another name given to the Reciprocal Model of Group Work. This model is associated with the idea that individuals and society influence each other through mutual interaction. It focuses on the relationship between group members, the group worker, and the social environment. The model emphasizes mutual aid, shared responsibility, and problem-solving through group interaction. Therefore, Reciprocal Model is the correct answer.

13. In the context of dementia care, the term "Malignant Social Psychology" was coined by Toni Kitwood. He used this term to describe harmful patterns of interaction that damage the personhood of people living with dementia. These interactions may include ignoring, infantilizing, labeling, disempowering, or treating the person as less capable than they are. Kitwood emphasized person-centred dementia care as an alternative to such negative social practices. Therefore, Toni Kitwood is the correct answer.

14. As per the Eleventh Five Year Plan, the funding support given for the National Mental Health Programme was 4.73 Billion. The Eleventh Five Year Plan gave increased attention to mental health services and strengthening mental healthcare infrastructure. The National Mental Health Programme aimed to improve access to mental health services, especially through district-level mental health activities. This funding support was meant to expand and strengthen mental health care delivery in India. Therefore, 4.73 Billion is the correct answer.

15. The First State Board of Charities in the USA was established in Massachusetts in 1863. It was an important development in the organized administration of public welfare and charitable services. Such boards were created to supervise and improve institutions dealing with poverty, dependency, illness, and other social problems. Massachusetts became a leading example in the development of state-level public welfare administration. Therefore, Massachusetts, 1863 is the correct answer.

16. Dr. B.R. Ambedkar was first elected to the Constituent Assembly from Bengal. He entered the Constituent Assembly from a Bengal seat with support from Scheduled Caste leaders of that region. After Partition, that seat went to Pakistan, and he later re-entered the Constituent Assembly from Bombay. However, for the question asking from which state he got elected to the Constituent Assembly, the correct option given is West Bengal. Therefore, option 3 is the correct answer.

17. The Fundamental Right to Property was abolished by the Forty Fourth Amendment Act, 1978. Before this amendment, the right to property was a Fundamental Right under Article 19(1)(f) and Article 31. The 44th Amendment removed it from the list of Fundamental Rights. It was then made a constitutional legal right under Article 300A. Therefore, among the given options, the Forty Fourth Amendment Act is the correct answer.

18. New Zealand was the earliest among the given countries to give women the right to vote. Women in New Zealand got voting rights in 1893, making it the first self-governing country to grant women national voting rights. India gave women voting rights at the time of the Constitution, much later than New Zealand. Iceland and Portugal also granted women voting rights after New Zealand. Therefore, New Zealand is the correct answer.

19. The newspaper referred to in the question as "Showe Prakash" is most likely "Som Prakash," which is associated with Ishwar Chandra Vidyasagar. It was started under his influence and is remembered as an important Bengali newspaper connected with social reform ideas. Vidyasagar was a major reformer who worked for widow remarriage, women's education, and social progress. The other options are associated with different newspapers or reform movements. Therefore, option 1 is the correct answer.

20. The terms Scheduled Castes and Scheduled Tribes came into legal and administrative recognition through the Government of India Act, 1935. This legislation gave recognition to lists or "Schedules" of castes and tribes marked out for special treatment by the State. It provided a legal basis for identifying such communities for political and administrative purposes. The later Constitution of India continued and developed this system of Scheduled Castes and Scheduled Tribes. Therefore, the Government of India Act, 1935 is the correct answer.

21. To solve the problems of social maladjustment in cities and of the labour class, the Settlement Movement developed in the U.S.A. and had a great influence on the evolving pattern of social service. The Settlement Movement focused on living among poor and working-class communities and helping them through education, recreation, health, welfare, and community organization. It responded to urban poverty, industrialization, immigration, poor housing, and labour-class difficulties. Settlement houses became important centres for social reform and social work practice. Therefore, Settlement Movement is the correct answer.

22. According to child rights and child welfare principles, residential or institutional care should be used as the last resort for a child's rehabilitation. The preferred approach is to keep the child in a family-based environment as far as possible, such as care by the biological family, kinship care, foster care, or adoption where suitable. Institutional care is generally considered only when family-based alternatives are not available or not in the child's best interest. This is because children usually need emotional security, personal attention, and family-like care for healthy development. Therefore, Residential/ Institutional Care is the correct answer.

23. Broad banding is a term used to represent the compression of a hierarchy of pay grades into fewer and wider pay bands. Instead of having many narrow salary grades, an organization combines them into broader bands to allow more flexibility in pay, promotion, and career movement. It is commonly used in human resource management and compensation systems. Broad banding helps reduce rigid pay structures and supports flexible organizational roles. Therefore, option 1 is the correct answer.

24. According to David Apter in the context of development administration, instrumental values are those cultural values that support the development process, while consummation values are those cultural values that hamper development efforts. Instrumental values are linked with achievement, rationality, change, planning, and goal-oriented action. Consummation values are more concerned with immediate satisfaction, tradition, status, and existing social patterns. Development administration requires values that encourage modernization, efficiency, and purposeful change. Therefore, instrumental; consummation is the correct answer.

25. The statement "Does not distinguish between men and women needs" is not correct regarding Gender Aware Policy proposed by Naila Kabeer. Gender aware policy recognizes that men and women have different roles, needs, constraints, and access to resources because of gender relations in society. Such policy may address practical gender needs as well as strategic gender needs. It also works with awareness of existing gender divisions of labour and resources. Therefore, the option saying that it does not distinguish between men and women's needs is the incorrect statement.

26. Dr. B.R. Ambedkar described the Right to Constitutional Remedies as the heart and soul of the Constitution. This right is provided under Article 32 of the Constitution of India. It allows a person to directly approach the Supreme Court when Fundamental Rights are violated. Without this remedy, Fundamental Rights would remain incomplete because there would be no effective method to enforce them. Therefore, the Right to Constitutional Remedies is the correct answer.

27. The Constituent Assembly was described as a "one party body in an essentially one party country" by Granville Austin. He was a well-known scholar who studied the making and working of the Indian Constitution. The expression highlights the dominance of the Congress in the Constituent Assembly during the framing of the Constitution. Therefore, option 4 is the correct answer.

28. The main purpose of appointing the All India Jail Manual Committee, 1957 was to draft a Model Jail Manual. The committee was appointed to bring greater uniformity and reform in prison administration across India. It examined jail rules, prison management, discipline, treatment of prisoners, and correctional practices. Its work led to the preparation of a Model Prison Manual for guidance of states. Therefore, the correct answer is to draft a Model Jail Manual.

29. Borstal Schools are meant for young offenders in the criminal justice system. They are correctional institutions designed especially for juveniles or young persons who have committed offences. The purpose is not merely punishment but reformation, education, discipline, training, and rehabilitation. Such institutions aim to prevent young offenders from becoming hardened criminals by keeping them away from ordinary adult prison conditions. Therefore, Young Offenders is the correct answer.

30. Central prisons house prisoners who have been sentenced for over 03 years, as asked in the given option-based question. Central prisons are generally meant for long-term prisoners and have larger capacity, better security, and more organized correctional facilities than ordinary district or sub-jails. They usually accommodate convicts serving longer sentences and may also have facilities for work, training, and rehabilitation. Among the given options, 03 years fits the standard option pattern for this question. Therefore, option 1 is the correct answer.

31. The regular failure to meet a child's basic needs of food and clothing related to physical and psychological care is an example of neglect. Neglect means not providing necessary care, protection, supervision, nutrition, clothing, shelter, medical attention, emotional support, or education to a child. It may not always involve direct physical violence, but it can seriously harm a child's physical, emotional, and psychological development. When basic needs are repeatedly ignored or unmet, the child's safety and well-being are affected. Therefore, neglect is the correct answer.

32. The disorder in which a patient sometimes has attacks of excessive sleep while doing daily activities is termed as hypersomnia. Hypersomnia refers to excessive sleepiness or prolonged sleep episodes that interfere with normal functioning. A person may feel sleepy during the day and may fall asleep during routine activities. Insomnia means difficulty in falling asleep or staying asleep, while nightmares and night terrors are sleep disturbances related to frightening experiences during sleep. Therefore, hypersomnia is the correct answer.

33. If a response is increased or decreased based on reinforcement or punishment, it is termed as operant conditioning. Operant conditioning explains learning through consequences of behaviour. When reinforcement follows a behaviour, that behaviour is likely to increase, and when punishment follows a behaviour, that behaviour is likely to decrease. It is different from classical conditioning, which is based on association between stimuli. Therefore, operant conditioning is the correct answer.

34. According to Glasser, nagging does not represent the caring habits of internal control. Caring habits include accepting, respecting, supporting, encouraging, listening, trusting, and negotiating differences. Nagging is considered a harmful or disconnecting habit because it creates pressure, irritation, conflict, and resistance in relationships. It belongs to the controlling or destructive pattern rather than a caring pattern. Therefore, nagging is the correct answer because it does not represent caring habits.

35. Article 27 of the Indian Constitution ensures that no person shall be compelled to pay taxes for the promotion or maintenance of any particular religion or religious denomination. This provision protects individuals from being forced by the State to financially support a specific religion through taxation. It is part of the constitutional guarantee of religious freedom and secularism. Article 26 deals with managing religious affairs, Article 28 deals with religious instruction in educational institutions, and Article 32 deals with constitutional remedies. Therefore, Article 27 is the correct answer.

36. The statement that childhood is a unitary concept is not true regarding childhood practices in social work. Childhood is understood as socially constructed because its meaning differs across cultures, societies, classes, historical periods, and family contexts. Contemporary social work does not treat all children's experiences as exactly the same or uniform. Sociological perspectives help in understanding debates about child rights, protection, participation, vulnerability, and agency. Therefore, childhood being a unitary concept is the incorrect statement.

37. Liberal feminism views that the sources of women's inequality reside within law, policies, and differences in the socialization of males and females. It emphasizes equal legal rights, equal opportunities, education, employment access, political participation, and removal of discriminatory laws and practices. Liberal feminism argues that inequality can be reduced through legal reform, policy change, and equal treatment within existing social institutions. It does not primarily explain women's oppression through capitalism alone or patriarchy as the sole root cause. Therefore, Liberal feminism is the correct answer.

38. Procedures for using Nominal Group Technique do not include hitchhiking. Nominal Group Technique usually includes silent generation of ideas, round-robin recording of ideas, clarification or discussion of ideas, and voting or ranking of priorities. Hitchhiking is more closely associated with brainstorming, where one participant builds upon or extends another person's idea. In Nominal Group Technique, idea generation is structured and initially independent to reduce domination and encourage equal participation. Therefore, hitchhiking is the correct answer because it is not a normal procedure of Nominal Group Technique.

39. Eric Berne was the propounder of Transactional Analysis. This theory explains personality and interpersonal communication through three ego states: Parent, Adult, and Child. The Parent ego state reflects learned rules, attitudes, and authority patterns; the Adult ego state reflects rational and reality-based thinking; and the Child ego state reflects emotions, impulses, and earlier experiences. Transactional Analysis is widely used in counselling, psychotherapy, communication analysis, and group work. Therefore, Transactional Analysis is the correct answer.

40. The philosophical period of the eighteenth century based on progress, reason, and rationality is known as the Enlightenment. It emphasized human reason, scientific thinking, individual rights, liberty, and the possibility of improving society through knowledge. The Enlightenment challenged excessive religious dogma and traditional authority as the only ways of understanding the social world. It influenced modern political thought, democracy, human rights, social reform, and scientific approaches to society. Therefore, Enlightenment is the correct answer.

41. Assertion (A) is correct because the North Indian Plains have experienced increased flood frequency due to several geographical and human-related factors. Reason (R) is also correct because deposition of silt in river channels reduces the effective depth and carrying capacity of rivers. When the river valley or channel becomes shallower due to siltation, the river is less able to contain excess water during heavy rainfall or high discharge. This increases the possibility of overflowing and flooding in the surrounding plains. Therefore, both Assertion and Reason are correct, and Reason correctly explains the Assertion.

42. Assertion (A) is correct because the Parliament did pass the Protection of Human Rights Amendment Act, 2006, amending the Protection of Human Rights Act, 1993. Reason (R) is not correct because the 2006 amendment did not increase the number of members of the State Human Rights Commission from five to ten. The statement about such an increase is factually incorrect in relation to the amendment. The amendment dealt with changes in the functioning, appointment-related provisions, and structure of human rights institutions, but not in the manner stated in the Reason. Therefore, Assertion is correct, but Reason is not correct.

43. Assertion (A) is correct because Raja Ram Mohan Roy is regarded as one of the greatest Indian reformers of the nineteenth century and a pioneer of religious and social reform in India. He worked against social evils such as sati and promoted rationalism, modern education, and reformist religious thought. Reason (R) is not correct because Arya Samaj was founded by Swami Dayanand Saraswati in 1875, not by Raja Ram Mohan Roy. Raja Ram Mohan Roy was associated with Brahmo Sabha and Brahmo Samaj, not Arya Samaj. Therefore, Assertion is correct, but Reason is not correct.

44. Assertion (A) is not correct because peasant and tribal movements cannot be described as purely agrarian in all cases. Peasant movements were mainly connected with agrarian issues such as rent, land revenue, exploitation by landlords, and agricultural rights. Tribal movements often involved land, forest rights, cultural identity, autonomy, customary rights, displacement, and resistance against outside control. Reason (R) is correct because peasants and tribals were largely dependent on land and natural resources for their livelihood. Therefore, Assertion is not correct, but Reason is correct.

45. Assertion (A) is correct because human development is defined as a process of enlarging people's choices. It does not measure development only through income, but through expansion of human capabilities and opportunities. Reason (R) is also correct because people's choices can be many, can expand over time, and can change according to social, economic, political, and personal conditions. Since human choices are not fixed, development must focus on widening opportunities and freedoms. Therefore, both Assertion and Reason are correct, and Reason correctly explains the Assertion.

46. Assertion (A) is correct because modern society lives in an increasingly interconnected international world where technology quickly spreads information about crises such as civil strife, tsunamis, pandemics, disasters, wars, and social unrest. This constant flow of disturbing information can create anxiety, insecurity, fear, and distress among people even when the event is geographically distant. Reason (R) is also correct because Robert Lifton discussed the psychological impact of modern threats and technological conditions on human life. His view helps explain why global communication and technology can increase people's sense of unease. Therefore, both Assertion and Reason are correct, and Reason correctly explains Assertion.

47. Assertion (A) is correct because changes in GDP are often strongly correlated with changes in economic well-being, especially when GDP reflects production, income, employment, and general economic activity. A rising GDP may indicate improvement in material conditions and economic opportunities. Reason (R) is also correct because GDP is widely accepted as an imperfect measure of broader well-being since it does not fully measure inequality, health, education, environmental quality, unpaid work, freedom, or quality of life. However, Reason does not directly explain why GDP changes are correlated with economic well-being. Therefore, both statements are correct, but Reason is not the correct explanation of Assertion.

48. Assertion (A) is correct because January 26 was deliberately chosen as the date of commencement of the Constitution due to its historical significance in India's freedom struggle. Reason (R) is also correct because January 26, 1930 was observed as Purna Swaraj Day after the Lahore Session of the Indian National Congress declared the goal of complete independence. Choosing January 26 for the commencement of the Constitution gave constitutional meaning to that earlier national pledge. It connected the Republic of India with the freedom movement's demand for complete independence. Therefore, both Assertion and Reason are correct, and Reason correctly explains Assertion.

49. Assertion (A) is not correct because compulsory reservation of thirty-three per cent of seats for women in Parliament and State Legislatures requires constitutional provision or constitutional amendment. Reservation of legislative seats cannot be made compulsory merely by ordinary party practice without constitutional authority. Reason (R) is correct in the limited sense that political parties may voluntarily allocate thirty-three per cent of their contesting seats or tickets to women without any constitutional amendment. However, such party-level allocation is not the same as compulsory constitutional reservation of seats in Parliament and State Legislatures. Therefore, Assertion is not correct, but Reason is correct.

50. Assertion (A) is correct because Information Technology has become a very important and fast-growing field of activity in India. India has developed a strong position in software services, IT-enabled services, outsourcing, digital services, and technology-based employment. Reason (R) is partly incorrect because software is indeed one of India's major export strengths, but the statement that India has an extremely strong base in hardware is not correct in the same way. India's major global strength has traditionally been in software and IT services rather than hardware manufacturing. Therefore, Assertion is correct, but Reason is not correct.

51. A. Social Action — III. Lobbying: Social action uses pressure, advocacy, mobilization, and lobbying to bring social change and influence policy or authority.

B. Community work — IV. Networking with people in the village: Community work involves organizing people, building local contacts, mobilizing community resources, and networking at the village or community level.

C. Social Group organization — I. Help members become aware of their patterned behaviour: Social group work helps members understand their interactions, roles, relationships, and repeated behavioural patterns within the group.

D. Social Casework — II. Referral: Social casework deals with individual-level help, assessment, counselling, and referral to suitable services when needed.

52. A. National Commission for Women — II. 1992: The National Commission for Women was constituted as a statutory body in 1992 under the National Commission for Women Act, 1990.

B. National Commission for Scheduled Castes and Scheduled Tribes — I. 1990: The National Commission for Scheduled Castes and Scheduled Tribes is matched with 1990 because it was provided through the 65th Constitutional Amendment Act, 1990.

C. National Commission for Backward Classes — III. 1993: The National Commission for Backward Classes was established in 1993 as a statutory body after the Indra Sawhney case.

D. National Commission for Protection of Child Rights — IV. 2007: The National Commission for Protection of Child Rights was set up in 2007 under the Commissions for Protection of Child Rights Act, 2005.

53. A. Drafting Committee — II. Dr. B.R. Ambedkar: Dr. B.R. Ambedkar was the Chairman of the Drafting Committee of the Constituent Assembly.

B. Union Constitution Committee — I. Jawaharlal Nehru: The Union Constitution Committee was chaired by Jawaharlal Nehru and dealt with the constitutional structure of the Union.

C. Provincial Constitution Committee — III. Sardar Patel: The Provincial Constitution Committee was chaired by Sardar Vallabhbhai Patel and dealt with provincial constitutional arrangements.

D. Rules of Procedure Committee — IV. Dr. Rajendra Prasad: Dr. Rajendra Prasad chaired the Rules of Procedure Committee of the Constituent Assembly.

54. A. Fundamental Rights — II. United States Constitution (USA): The idea of Fundamental Rights in the Indian Constitution was mainly inspired by the Bill of Rights of the United States Constitution.

B. Parliamentary System of Government — I. British Constitution (UK): India adopted the parliamentary system, cabinet responsibility, and related conventions mainly from the British constitutional system.

C. Federation with Strong Centre — IV. Canadian Constitution (Canada): The Indian feature of a federation with a strong Centre was influenced by the Canadian constitutional model.

D. Directive Principles of State Policy — III. Irish Constitution (Ireland): The Directive Principles of State Policy in India were borrowed from the Irish Constitution.

55. A. Maternity Benefit Act — I. 1961: The Maternity Benefit Act was enacted in 1961 to regulate employment of women during maternity and provide maternity benefits.

B. Equal Remuneration Act — II. 1976: The Equal Remuneration Act was enacted in 1976 to provide equal pay for equal work and prevent gender-based wage discrimination.

C. Child Labour (Prohibition and Regulation) Act — IV. 1986: The Child Labour (Prohibition and Regulation) Act was enacted in 1986 to prohibit and regulate child labour in specified occupations and processes.

D. The Mines Act — III. 1952: The Mines Act was enacted in 1952 to regulate safety, health, welfare, and working conditions of persons employed in mines.

56. **A. Right to Equality — IV. Articles 14-18:** The Right to Equality is covered under Articles 14 to 18 of the Indian Constitution. These Articles include equality before law, prohibition of discrimination, equality of opportunity, abolition of untouchability, and abolition of titles.

B. Right to Freedom — III. Articles 19-22: The Right to Freedom is covered under Articles 19 to 22 of the Indian Constitution. These Articles include freedoms under Article 19, protection in respect of conviction, protection of life and personal liberty, and protection against arrest and detention.

C. Right against Exploitation — I. Articles 23-24: The Right against Exploitation is covered under Articles 23 and 24. Article 23 prohibits trafficking and forced labour, while Article 24 prohibits employment of children in hazardous occupations.

D. Right to Freedom of Religion — II. Articles 25-28: The Right to Freedom of Religion is covered under Articles 25 to 28. These Articles protect freedom of conscience, religious practice, religious affairs, and freedom from compulsory religious instruction in certain institutions.

57. **A. Charity Organization Movement — III. 1870-1917:** The Charity Organization Movement belongs to the period 1870-1917. This period focused on organized charity, investigation of need, coordination of relief, and early structured social work practice.

B. Community Organization and Social change — IV. 1955 onwards: Community Organization and Social Change is matched with 1955 onwards. This period reflects a broader concern with community participation, planned social change, development, and organized collective action.

C. Expansions & Professional Development — II. 1935-1955: Expansions and Professional Development is matched with the period 1935-1955. During this phase, social work methods became more professionalized and expanded through agencies, training, and institutional development.

D. Rise of Federation — I. 1917-1935: The Rise of Federation is matched with the period 1917-1935. This period saw increased coordination, federation of welfare agencies, and more systematic organization of social welfare services.

58. **A. World Environment Day — IV. 5th June:** World Environment Day is observed on 5th June. It is associated with environmental awareness, protection of nature, and public action for sustainable environmental practices.

B. World Forestry Day — III. 20th March: In the given options, World Forestry Day is matched with 20th March. The item is intended to connect forestry awareness with the March observance related to forests and conservation.

C. World Habitat Day — I. 3rd October: World Habitat Day is matched here with 3rd October. It is observed to highlight the importance of adequate shelter, human settlements, and sustainable urban development.

D. World Ozone Day — II. 16th September: World Ozone Day is observed on 16th September. It marks awareness about protection of the ozone layer and the importance of reducing ozone-depleting substances.

59. **A. To prohibit the consumption cf intoxicating drinks and drugs which are injurious to health — III. Article 47:** Article 47 directs the State to improve nutrition, standard of living, and public health. It also specifically includes prohibition of intoxicating drinks and drugs injurious to health.

B. To organise Village Panchayat to function as units of self government — I. Article 40: Article 40 directs the State to organize village panchayats. It aims to enable them to function as units of self-government in rural India.

C. To promote cottage industries on an individual or co-operation basis in rural areas — IV. Article 43: Article 43 directs the State to promote cottage industries in rural areas. It supports livelihood, village-based production, and Gandhian ideas of rural self-reliance.

D. To prohibit the slaughter of cows, calves and other milch and draught cattle and to improve their breeds — II. Article 48: Article 48 directs the State to organize agriculture and animal husbandry on modern and scientific lines. It also includes preserving and improving breeds and prohibiting slaughter of cows, calves, and other milch and draught cattle.

60. **A. Positivism — III. Only observable and measurable behaviours should be studied:** Positivism emphasizes scientific study based on observable and measurable facts. It supports objective, systematic, and empirical methods in understanding social reality.

B. Empiricism — IV. Factual inquiry based on facts and observations: Empiricism is based on knowledge gained through observation, experience, and factual inquiry. It gives importance to evidence rather than purely abstract speculation.

C. Functionalism — II. Importance of socialization of society's norms and values to promote a consensus: Functionalism emphasizes social order, consensus, stability, and shared norms and values. It views socialization as important for maintaining harmony and continuity in society.

D. Marxism — I. Awareness of one's own class position and shared values: Marxism emphasizes class relations, class position, exploitation, and class consciousness. Awareness of one's class position is central to understanding conflict and social change in Marxist theory.

61. **A. Dependent Variable — II. Assumed effect of change:** The dependent variable is the outcome or effect that changes because of the influence of another variable. It is studied to see what result has occurred due to the independent variable.

B. Connecting Variable — I. Necessary in certain situations to complete cause-effect relations: A connecting variable helps explain the link between cause and effect in certain research situations. It is used when the relationship between the independent and dependent variable needs an intermediate explanation.

C. Extraneous Variable — III. Not measured but may increase or decrease the magnitude of relationship between Independent and Dependent variable: An extraneous variable is not the main focus of the study but may affect the relationship being examined. It can influence the strength or direction of the relationship between the independent and dependent variables.

D. Independent Variable — IV. Assumed cause of change: The independent variable is the presumed cause or influencing factor in a research study. It is studied to see how far it produces change in the dependent variable.

62. **A. Sampling Design — III. Deals with method of selecting items to be observed:** Sampling design explains how units, cases, respondents, or items are selected for the study. It determines the method of choosing the sample from the larger population.

B. Observational Design — IV. Relates to the conditions under which observations are made: Observational design deals with the situation, setting, and conditions in which observations are carried out. It helps decide how and under what circumstances the required data will be observed.

C. Statistical Design — I. Concerns with how many items are to be observed and analysis be done: Statistical design is concerned with the size of the sample and the plan for statistical analysis. It helps decide how many items should be studied and how the collected data should be analysed.

D. Operational Design — II. Deals with Techniques by which procedures specified in sampling can be done: Operational design deals with the practical procedures and techniques used to carry out the research plan. It converts the sampling and research procedures into actual field-level operations.

63. **A. Normative Needs — II. Define according to experts or professional standards:** Normative needs are identified by experts, professionals, or accepted standards. They are based on what should exist according to professional judgment or established norms.

B. Felt Needs — I. Identified by Individuals or Groups: Felt needs are the needs that individuals or groups personally feel or experience. They arise from people's own perception of what they lack or require.

C. Expressed Needs — IV. Public articulation of Individual or Group Needs: Expressed needs are felt needs that are openly stated, demanded, or acted upon. They become visible when individuals or groups publicly articulate their needs or seek services.

D. Comparative Needs — III. Identified through comparison of characteristics among relative groups: Comparative needs are identified by comparing one group with another similar group. If one group receives a service and a similar group does not, the unmet need is understood comparatively.

64. A. Empirical Theory — IV. Systematically conceptualizes things built from Observations and Experiments: Empirical theory is based on observation, experience, evidence, and experiment. It develops understanding from facts that can be observed, tested, or verified.

B. Normative Theory — I. Conceptualizes preferences, what ought to be: Normative theory deals with values, ideals, preferences, and what should be. It is concerned with judgments about desirable goals, standards, and principles.

C. Explanatory Theory — II. Focuses on 'why' questions and address, uncover causes and relationships: Explanatory theory explains why a situation, behaviour, or event occurs. It focuses on causes, relationships, patterns, and reasons behind social phenomena.

D. Practice Theory — III. Focuses on 'How' questions and bridges the gap between agency and structure: Practice theory focuses on how actions are performed in real-life social settings. It connects individual agency with larger social structures and explains practical social action.

65. A. Bhakti Movement — II. Humanism: The Bhakti Movement emphasized devotion, human dignity, spiritual equality, and rejection of rigid social barriers. Its primary value is best matched with humanism because it stressed the worth of every human being.

B. Socialism — I. Equality and Justice: Socialism is mainly associated with equality, justice, collective welfare, and reduction of exploitation. It emphasizes fair distribution of resources and protection of weaker sections of society.

C. Sarvodaya — IV. Lokniti and Swarajya: Sarvodaya is linked with Gandhian ideas of welfare of all, self-rule, moral politics, and people-centred governance. Therefore, Lokniti and Swarajya correctly match the Sarvodaya development phase.

D. Social Work Profession — III. Solidarity with Marginalized people: The social work profession is committed to helping vulnerable, oppressed, excluded, and marginalized people. Its values include social justice, human dignity, service, empowerment, and solidarity with marginalized groups.

66. A. Atmiya Samaj — Earliest: Atmiya Sabha/ Samaj is associated with Raja Ram Mohan Roy and belongs to the early nineteenth-century reform phase. It came before the later religious and social reform organizations mentioned in the question.

B. Theosophical Society — Second: The Theosophical Society was established after Atmiya Sabha/Samaj. It belongs to the later nineteenth-century phase and became influential in India through religious, social, and educational reform ideas.

C. Ram Krishna Mission — Third: Ram Krishna Mission was established after the Theosophical Society. It was founded by Swami Vivekananda and worked for spiritual, educational, and humanitarian service.

D. Servants of India Society — Newest: Servants of India Society was established after Ram Krishna Mission. It was founded by Gopal Krishna Gokhale for national service, social reform, and public work.

67. D. The Exploratory and Disciplinary — First: This was the earliest stage of social case work development. It was concerned with early investigation, discipline, moral reform, and organized charity-based approaches.

B. The Sociological — Second: The sociological stage came after the exploratory and disciplinary phase. It emphasized the role of social environment, family, poverty, and social conditions in individual problems.

C. The Psycho-social — Third: The psycho-social stage developed later by combining psychological and social understanding. It explained individual problems through both personality factors and social environment.

A. The Synthetic or Integrated — Fourth: The synthetic or integrated stage is the later stage of case work development. It integrates different approaches and uses a broader, combined understanding of person, problem, and situation.

68. C. Chief Justice of India — First: In the official order of precedence, the Chief Justice of India is placed above the other functionaries listed here. This position reflects the high constitutional status of the head of the Indian judiciary.

B. Union Cabinet Minister — Second: A Union Cabinet Minister comes after the Chief Justice of India in this sequence. Cabinet Ministers hold important executive authority in the Union Government.

D. Chief Election Commissioner — Third: The Chief Election Commissioner comes after Union Cabinet Ministers in the order relevant to the given options. The office is a constitutional authority responsible for supervision and control of elections.

A. Cabinet Secretary — Fourth: The Cabinet Secretary comes after the above constitutional and political functionaries in this sequence. The Cabinet Secretary is the senior-most civil servant and administrative head of the civil services.

69. **A. International Labour Organizations — First:** The International Labour Organization was established first among the given institutions. It came into existence after the First World War to deal with labour welfare, working conditions, and social justice.

B. All India Trade Union Congress — Second: The All India Trade Union Congress was established after the International Labour Organization. It became an important national-level trade union body in India.

C. Royal Commission — Third: The Royal Commission on Labour came after the establishment of the ILO and AITUC. It examined labour conditions and made recommendations regarding workers and industrial relations.

D. First National Commission on Labour — Fourth: The First National Commission on Labour was established later than the other three institutions. It studied labour issues in independent India and suggested reforms in labour policy and labour administration.

70. **A. Integrated Rural Development Programme — First:** The Integrated Rural Development Programme came first among the given rural employment and development schemes. It focused on rural poverty alleviation and assistance to poor families for self-employment and income generation.

B. Jawahar Rozgar Yojna — Second: Jawahar Rozgar Yojna was introduced after the Integrated Rural Development Programme. It aimed to generate wage employment in rural areas through local development works.

C. Swarnajayanti Gram Swarojgar Yojna — Third: Swarnajayanti Gram Swarojgar Yojna was launched after Jawahar Rozgar Yojna. It focused on self-employment, rural livelihoods, and organization of the poor into self-help groups.

D. National Rural Employment Guarantee Programme — Fourth: The National Rural Employment Guarantee Programme came after the above schemes. It provided a rights-based framework for guaranteed wage employment in rural areas.

71. **D. Sri Lanka — First:** Sri Lanka has the best HDI rank among the given countries in the Human Development Report 2025 based on 2023 HDI data. Its rank is above India, Nepal, Myanmar, and Pakistan.

C. India — Second: India is ranked below Sri Lanka but above Nepal, Myanmar, and Pakistan in the Human Development Report 2025. Therefore, India comes after Sri Lanka in this chronological ranking order from better HDI rank to lower HDI rank.

E. Nepal — Third: Nepal is ranked below India but above Myanmar and Pakistan in the given HDI ranking order. Thus, Nepal comes after India and before Myanmar and Pakistan.

A. Myanmar — Fourth: Myanmar is ranked below Nepal but above Pakistan in the Human Development Report 2025 ranking sequence. Therefore, Myanmar occupies the fourth position among the listed countries.

B. Pakistan — Fifth: Pakistan has the lowest HDI rank among the given countries in this list. Therefore, Pakistan comes last in the correct order.

72. **B. Concept development — First:** The first step in developing measurement tools is to develop the concept clearly. Without defining the concept, the researcher cannot decide what exactly is to be measured.

C. Specification of concept dimensions — Second: After concept development, the dimensions of the concept are specified. This step breaks the broad concept into meaningful components or aspects.

A. Selection of Indicators — Third: After specifying dimensions, suitable indicators are selected for each dimension. Indicators help convert abstract dimensions into observable and measurable elements.

D. Formation of Index — Fourth: After selecting indicators, an index may be formed by combining them systematically. The index provides a composite measure of the concept being studied.

73. **C. Grade definitions or role profiles have to be drawn for jobs being evaluated — First:** The first step is to prepare grade definitions or role profiles for the jobs being evaluated. These definitions provide the standards against which jobs will later be compared.

A. Job description must be produced for each job to be evaluated — Second: After grade definitions are prepared, job descriptions are produced for each job. These descriptions give details of duties, responsibilities, and job requirements.

D. Matching of each job description to the definition that most closely reflect duties of job — Third: Each job description is then matched with the grade definition that most closely reflects its duties. This matching process helps identify the appropriate level or grade of the job.

B. Assigning Appropriate Grades — Fourth: After matching, the appropriate grade is assigned to each job. This completes the classification process by placing jobs into suitable grade levels.

74. **C. Logical analysis of the subject matter — First:** The first step in writing a research report is logical analysis of the subject matter. This helps organize the material and decide the main structure of the report.

B. Preparation of the Final Outline — Second: After logical analysis, the final outline of the report is prepared. The outline gives the order, headings, subheadings, and arrangement of the report.

A. Preparation of the Rough Draft — Third: After the outline is ready, the rough draft is prepared. This draft puts the research material, findings, and discussion into written form.

E. Rewriting and polishing of draft — Fourth: After preparing the rough draft, it is rewritten and polished. This improves clarity, language, organization, coherence, and presentation.

D. Preparation of bibliography and writing final draft — Fifth: The final stage includes preparing the bibliography and writing the final draft. This gives the report its complete, finished, and properly documented form.

75. **A. Identify the problem or dilemma — First:** The first step in an ethical dilemma is to identify the exact problem or dilemma. Without clearly identifying the issue, the ethical decision-making process cannot proceed properly.

D. Determine the core principles and the competing issues — Second: After identifying the dilemma, the core ethical principles and competing issues must be determined. This helps clarify which values, duties, rights, and responsibilities are in conflict.

E. Review the relevant code of ethics and applicable laws and regulations -- Third: The next step is to review the relevant code of ethics, laws, regulations, and professional standards. This provides formal guidance for deciding what action is ethically and legally appropriate.

C. Consult with colleagues, supervisors, legal experts or professionals — Fourth: After reviewing ethical and legal guidance, consultation with suitable professionals should be done. Consultation helps avoid personal bias and improves the quality of ethical judgment.

B. Consider and decide on the possible courses of action and examine the consequences — Fifth: Finally, possible courses of action are considered, their consequences are examined, and a decision is made. This completes the ethical decision-making process by choosing the most responsible course of action.

76. **A. Identification of Need — First:** The first step is identification or consciousness of the need in the community. Without recognizing the need, no organized community action can begin.

B. Spreading the Consciousness of Need — Second: After the need is identified, awareness of that need is spread among the people. This helps the community understand that the issue is shared and requires collective attention.

C. Projection of Consciousness of Need — Third: After spreading awareness, the consciousness of the need is projected before wider community leadership and groups. This stage helps bring the issue into public discussion and collective concern.

D. Emotional Impulse to Meet the Need quickly — Fourth: After the need becomes widely recognized, an emotional impulse develops to meet the need quickly. This creates urgency and motivation for community response and action.

77. **B. Applying and Evaluating the Evidence — First in descending order:** The normal evidence-based group work process ends with applying and evaluating the evidence. Since the question asks for descending order, the last stage comes first in the answer.

D. Critically Reviewing the Evidence — Second in descending order: Critical review normally comes after searching for evidence. In descending order, it is placed before searching and after applying and evaluating.

C. Searching for Evidence — Third in descending order: Searching for evidence normally follows the formulation of answerable questions. In descending order, it comes after critical review and before question formulation.

A. Formulating Answerable Questions — Fourth in descending order: Formulating answerable questions is the first step in the normal sequence of evidence-based group work. Because descending order is required, it is placed last in the selected sequence.

78. B. It aims at imparting training in soft skills, financial and digital literacy and entrepreneurship — Correct: Pradhan Mantri Kaushal Vikas Yojana includes training beyond technical skills. It also covers soft skills, entrepreneurship, financial literacy, and digital literacy.

C. It is aligning the country's competencies of the workforce which is unregulated to the National Skill Qualification Framework — Correct: The scheme includes recognition and alignment of skills with the National Skill Qualification Framework. This is especially relevant for workers in the unregulated or informally skilled workforce.

A. It is a flagship scheme of Ministry of Labour and Employment — Incorrect: PMKVY is not the flagship scheme of the Ministry of Labour and Employment. It is associated with skill development, not the Labour and Employment Ministry.

D. It is a flagship scheme of Ministry of Women and Child Development — Incorrect: PMKVY is not a flagship scheme of the Ministry of Women and Child Development.

Therefore, only statements B and C are correct.

79. C. Study design is faulty — Correct: Incorrect conclusions about the validity of a hypothesis may be drawn when the study design is faulty. A faulty design can create bias, weak control, poor comparison, and unreliable findings.

D. Statistical procedures applied are inappropriate — Correct: Incorrect statistical procedures can lead to wrong acceptance or rejection of a hypothesis. Even good data may produce invalid conclusions if unsuitable statistical methods are applied.

A. The study design is systematic — Incorrect: A systematic study design helps improve validity and reliability. It does not normally lead to incorrect conclusions about the validity of a hypothesis.

B. Method of data collection is appropriate — Incorrect: Appropriate data collection supports correct and valid conclusions. It is not a cause of incorrect conclusions in hypothesis testing.

80. D. The Principle of Planned Group Formation — First: Planned group formation comes first because the group must be consciously and properly formed. This includes attention to group purpose, composition, size, and suitability of members.

C. The Principle of Specific Objectives — Second: After the group is formed, specific objectives must be clearly understood and defined. Clear objectives guide the group process, activities, and direction of work.

B. The Principle of Purposeful Group Worker Relationship — Third: The group worker develops a purposeful professional relationship with members. This relationship helps members participate, interact, and move towards the group objectives.

A. The Principle of Continuous Individualization — Fourth: Continuous individualization means recognizing each member as a distinct person throughout the group process. It continues as the worker understands members' needs, capacities, behaviour, and participation within the group.

81. A. Advocating for policy change — Correct: Macro level practice in social work deals with large-scale intervention at community, institutional, policy, and social system levels. Advocating for policy change is therefore a clear example of macro level social work practice.

B. Campaigning for enactment of a new social legislation — Correct: Campaigning for a new social legislation involves collective action, policy advocacy, and social reform. This is part of macro level practice because it aims to bring change in wider social structures and systems.

C. Social Group Work — Incorrect: Social Group Work is generally treated as a primary method of social work at the group level. It is not specifically macro level practice in the same sense as policy advocacy or legislative campaigning.

D. Social Casework — Incorrect: Social Casework mainly deals with individuals and families. It is usually considered micro level social work practice, not macro level practice.

82. **B. Cognitive Discrepancy — Correct:** According to Spiegel, failure in role complementarity may occur because of cognitive discrepancy. This means that people involved in the role relationship may understand or interpret the role situation differently.

C. Discrepancy in Orientation of Cultural Values — Correct: Role complementarity may fail when persons have different cultural value orientations. Such differences can affect expectations, behaviour, cooperation, and acceptance of roles.

D. Discrepancy in Role Acceptance — Correct: Failure in role complementarity may also occur when there is a discrepancy in role acceptance. If a person does not accept the expected role, the complementary relationship becomes disturbed.

A. Availability of more Instrumental means — Incorrect: Availability of more instrumental means is not the correct factor for failure in role complementarity in this context. The failure is linked more directly with discrepancies in cognition, cultural values, and role acceptance.

83. **A. Case Comparison methods — Correct:** Case comparison methods are examples of case study methods because they compare cases in depth. They help understand similarities, differences, patterns, and causal possibilities across cases.

B. Ethnographic methods — Correct: Ethnographic methods may be used in case study research when a social unit, group, community, or setting is studied deeply. They provide rich contextual understanding through detailed field-based inquiry.

D. Participant and Non-Participant Observations — Correct: Participant and non-participant observations are useful methods in case study research. They help gather direct information about behaviour, interaction, and social situations.

C. Recording Behaviours on Self Anchored Rating Scales — Incorrect: Self-anchored rating scales are more closely related to measurement and rating techniques. They are not a standard example of case study methods in the same way as comparison, ethnography, and observation.

84. **A. A continuous variable can assume any numerical value within a specific range like 'Age' — Correct:** A continuous variable can take values within a range and may be measured in degrees or units. Age is commonly treated as a continuous variable when measured numerically.

C. Dependent variable relies upon or is a consequence of the other variable — Correct: The dependent variable is the effect, outcome, or response variable in research. It changes depending on the influence of the independent variable.

D. Independent variable is manipulated in experimental research designs — Correct: In experimental research, the independent variable is manipulated or controlled by the researcher. This is done to observe its effect on the dependent variable.

B. Extraneous variables are macro level factors that remain hidden — Incorrect: Extraneous variables are outside variables that may influence the relationship between independent and dependent variables. They are not necessarily macro level factors and are not defined simply as hidden factors.

E. Confounding variables are dependent variables in quasi experimental research designs — Incorrect: Confounding variables are variables that mix with or distort the effect of the independent variable. They are not dependent variables in quasi-experimental research designs.

85. **A. The Employee's Provident Fund Scheme — Correct:** The Employees' Provident Funds and Miscellaneous Provisions Act, 1952 includes the Employees' Provident Fund Scheme. This scheme provides retirement savings and social security benefits to employees.

B. The Employee's Pension Scheme — Correct: The Act also includes the Employees' Pension Scheme. This scheme provides pension benefits to eligible employees after retirement or in specified situations.

D. The Employee's Deposit Linked Insurance Scheme — Correct: The Employees' Deposit Linked Insurance Scheme is also covered under the Act. It provides insurance benefits linked with the employee's provident fund membership.

C. The Employee's State Insurance Scheme — Incorrect: The Employees' State Insurance Scheme is not part of the Employees' Provident Funds and Miscellaneous Provisions Act, 1952. It is governed separately under the Employees' State Insurance Act, 1948.

86. **A. To strengthen the institutional arrangement for addressing human rights issues in a more focused manner — Correct:** Human Rights Commissions were established to create a focused institutional mechanism for dealing with human rights issues. This helps in inquiry, monitoring, recommendation, awareness, and protection of human rights.

B. To look into allegations of excesses, independently of the government in a manner that would underline government's commitment to protect human rights — Correct: One objective is to provide an independent forum for looking into allegations of human rights violations or excesses. This strengthens accountability and shows the State's commitment to protection of human rights.

D. To complement and strengthen the efforts that have already been made to protect human rights — Correct: The Human Rights Commission works along with existing constitutional, legal, judicial, and administrative mechanisms. Its purpose is to supplement and strengthen human rights protection, not replace all other institutions.

C. To suppress criticism of government policies related to human rights — Incorrect: Suppressing criticism is not an objective of establishing the Human Rights Commission. A human rights body is meant to protect rights, examine violations, promote awareness, and support accountability.

87. **A. Pregnancy kit usage for early pregnancy detection — Correct:** ASHA workers are involved in community-level reproductive and maternal health support. They help women with early pregnancy detection and guide them toward proper health services.

C. Creating awareness on immunization and nutrition — Correct: Creating awareness about immunization, nutrition, sanitation, and health practices is an important role of ASHA. They act as a link between the community and the public health system.

D. Helping women reach health facility for Ante Natal care check up — Correct: ASHA workers motivate and assist pregnant women to access antenatal care services. They help connect women with health facilities for check-ups, counselling, and institutional support.

B. Carrying out deliveries — Incorrect: ASHA workers do not normally carry out deliveries as their regular responsibility. Their role is to facilitate access to trained health personnel and institutional delivery services.

88. **B. Range and Standard Deviation are used to depict Measures of Dispersion — Correct:** Range and standard deviation are measures of dispersion in descriptive statistics. They show how far values are spread out or scattered around a central value.

C. Skewness is the degree of symmetry or rather lack of it — Correct: Skewness describes the asymmetry or lack of symmetry in a distribution. A distribution may be positively skewed, negatively skewed, or approximately symmetrical.

D. Leptokurtic depicts highest peak and platykurtic the flattest peak — Correct: Kurtosis describes the peakedness or flatness of a distribution. A leptokurtic distribution is more sharply peaked, while a platykurtic distribution is flatter.

A. Median and Mode are used in Linear Regression Analysis — Incorrect: Median and mode are measures of central tendency, not the main tools of linear regression analysis. Linear regression mainly examines the relationship between variables using regression equations and coefficients.

E. Skewness is measured by coefficient of correlation — Incorrect: Skewness is not measured by coefficient of correlation. It is measured by skewness coefficients, while correlation measures the degree of relationship between variables.

89. **B. Quota Sampling — Correct:** Quota sampling is a non-probability sampling method. In this method, the researcher selects respondents according to fixed quotas without using random selection.

D. Purposive Sampling — Correct: Purposive sampling is a non-probability sampling method based on the researcher's judgment. Cases are selected because they are considered relevant, typical, special, or useful for the study.

E. Accidental Sampling — Correct: Accidental or convenience sampling is a non-probability sampling method. It includes respondents who are easily available or encountered by the researcher.

A. Lottery Method — Incorrect: Lottery method is a probability sampling technique. It is a form of simple random sampling where each unit has an equal chance of selection.

Choose the **correct** answer from the options given below:

1. A-III, B-IV, C-I, D-II
2. A-III, B-II, C-I, D-IV
3. A-IV, B-II, C-III, D-I
4. A-I, B-IV, C-II, D-III

15. Arrange the following phases of Social Policy proposed by ESCWA in their descending order.

A. Placing issues on the public agenda
B. Defining and prioritizing issues
C. Evaluating alternative approaches
D. Identifying problems and opportunities

Choose the **correct** answer from the options given below:

1. B, D, C, A   2. B, C, A, D
3. C, A, B, D   4. A, B, D, C

16. Match List-I with List-II:

List-I (Article)	List-II (Provision)
A. Article 330	I. Untouchability is abolished and its practice in any form is forbidden
B. Article 332	II. Provides for reservation of seats for SCs & STs in the Legislative assemblies of the State
C. Article 21A	III. Provides free and compulsory education to all children in the age of 6-14 years
D. Article 17	IV. Provides for reservation of seats for SCs & STs in the Lok Sabha

Choose the **correct** answer from the options given below:

1. A-IV, B-II, C-III, D-I
2. A-IV, B-III, C-I, D-II
3. A-III, B-II, C-I, D-IV
4. A-III, B-II, C-IV, D-I

17. Which of the following is **Not** a part of the planning matrix in research?

1. Orienting decisions
2. Research design
3. Data analysis
4. Sharing client's personal information

18. NEP-2020 envisions to see Bharat developing as an equitable and vibrant knowledge society by emphasizing mostly on ....

1. Issues of access
2. Technology enabled learning
3. Issues of equity
4. Making India a global knowledge super power

19. In 'Genogram' the symbol ▲ represents ....

1. Death   2. Unknown gender
3. Distant   4. Indes person

20. Which out of these Committees does **Not** match with its objective?

A. Tendulkar Committee - Uniform Poverty line basket
B. J.V.P. Committee - Health Review
C. Dhar Commission - Administrative Convenience
D. Rangarajan Commission - Academic Reforms

Choose the **most appropriate** answer from the options given below:

1. B and C only   2. A and C only
3. B and D only   4. A, B and D only

21. Match List-I with List-II:

List-I (Name of Scheme)	List-II (Year of Launch)
A. Integrated Child Development Services	I. 1981
B. Wheat-based Supplementary Nutrition Programme	II. 1970
C. Prophylaxis Programme	III. 1986
D. National Diarrhoeal Diseases Control Programme	IV. 1975

Choose the **correct** answer from the options given below:

1. A-II, B-III, C-IV, D-I
2. A-IV, B-III, C-II, D-I
3. A-III, B-II, C-IV, D-I
4. A-IV, B-II, C-III, D-I

22. Which of the following is provided to adolescent girls under the Kishori Shakti Yojana (KSY)?

A. Vocational training,
B. Health education
C. Legal support for girls in distress
D. Nutritional support

Choose the **correct** answer from the options given below:

1. A, B and D only
2. A, C and D only
3. A only
4. B and C only

23. Directive Principles of State Policy includes ....

A. Equal justice and free legal aid
B. Organization of village panchayats
C. Equality of opportunity in matters of public employment
D. Living wage

Choose the **correct** answer from the options given below:

1. A, B and D only
2. A, B and C only
3. A, C and D only
4. B, C and D only

24. Which out of these are **Not** the correct Directive Principles of State Policy?

A. Article 50 Stresses the separation of Judiciary and Executive
B. Article 48 Emphasizes preserving cattle breeds and prohibiting cattle slaughter
C. Article 42 Calls for organizing village panchayats for self-governance
D. Article 56 Advocates improving public health and the prohibition of intoxicants

Choose the **most appropriate** answer from the options given below:

1. C and B only
2. C and D only
3. A and B only
4. A, B and D only

25. Match List-I with List-II:

List-I (Rights under CrPC)	**List-II (Sections)**
A. Police officers power to require attendance of witnesses	I. Sec. 164
B. Right not to be arrested after sunset and before sunrise	II. Sec. 354C
C. Right against being watched without consent of a woman	III. Sec. 160
D. Recording of confessions & statements by a Judicial Magistrate or Metropolitan Magistrate during investigation	IV. Sec. 46(4)

Choose the **correct** answer from the options given below:

1. A-III, B-IV, C-II, D-I
2. A-III, B-II, C-IV, D-I
3. A-II, B-III, C-I, D-IV
4. A-I, B-III, C-II, D-IV

26. Which of these principles belong to National Health Policy, 2017.

A. Equity
B. Universality
C. Centralization of decision-making
D. Affordability

Choose the **most appropriate** answer from the options given below:

1. A, C and D only
2. A, B and D only
3. B, C and D only
4. A, B and C only

27. Which Sociologist opined that urbanization of Industrial Revolution has negatively impacted social life?

1. Fredrick Tonnies
2. Max Weber
3. Arthur Frank
4. Talcott Parson

28. Match List-I with List-II:

List-I (Name of the Institute)	List-II (Location)
A. Institute for the Physically Handicapped	I. Dehradun
B. National Institute for the Visually Handicapped	II. Kolkata
C. National Institute for the Orthopedically Handicapped	III. Mumbai
D. Ali Yavar Jung National Institute for the Hearing Handicapped	IV. New Delhi

Choose the **correct** answer from the options given below:

1. A-I, B-III, C-IV, D-II
2. A-IV, B-II, C-III, D-I
3. A-I, B-II, C-III, D-IV
4. A-IV, B-I, C-II, D-III

29. Based on the Rational Model of decision-making, arrange the following steps in ascending order.

A. Identifying Problems
B. Choosing the preferred options
C. Relating consequences to values
D. Assessing the consequences of all options

Choose the **correct** answer from the options given below:

1. B, D, C, A 2. D, C, A, B
3. C, A, B, D 4. A, D, C, B

30. Arrange the following principles of Social Group Work proposed by H.B. Trecker in ascending order.

A. Principle of resource utilization
B. Principle of planned group formation
C. Principle of democratic group self-determination
D. Principle of continuous individualization

Choose the **correct** answer from the options given below:

1. B, D, C, A 2. D, C, A, B
3. C, A, B, D 4. A, B, D, C

31. In Social Work Practice 'Crises Intervention' is viewed as a Practice Model because ....

A. It develops out of actual experience
B. It develops out of experimentation
C. It develops out of theory of behaviour
D. It develops out of a single explanation of crises situation

Choose the **correct** answer from the options given below:

1. A and C only
2. A and B only
3. A, B and D only
4. A, C and D only

32. Casework relationship contains the elements of ....

A. Acceptance B. Expectation
C. Stimulation D. Dislocation

Choose the **most appropriate** answer from the options given below:

1. A, B and D only
2. A, C and D only
3. B, C and D only
4. A, B and C only

33. Which year was the 2nd UGC Review Committee on Social Work Education constituted?

1. 1974 2. 1968
3. 1975 4. 1969

34. Arrange the Watson and Rennie's stages of Therapeutic Counselling in descending order.

A. Making changes in thinking and shifts in perception

B. Disclosing information with regard to specific troubling issue
C. Engaging in behavioural experimentation
D. Focusing experientially on one's experience and articulation in words

Choose the **correct** answer from the options given below:

1. B, D, C, A
2. D, C, A, B
3. C, A, D, B
4. A, B, D, C

35. Match List-I with List-II:

List-I (Journal Title)	List-II (First Published in)
A. International Social Work	I. 1962
B. National Journal of Professional Social Work	II. 1984
C. Journal of Social Work	III. 1958
D. Perspectives in Social Work	IV. 2000

Choose the **correct** answer from the options given below:

1. A-II, B-IV, C-I, D-III
2. A-II, B-III, C-I, D-IV
3. A-III, B-II, C-I, D-IV
4. A-III, B-IV, C-I, D-II

36. Arrange the following Developmental Models as proposed under various Five-Year Plans in ascending order:

A. Growth with Social Justice & Equality
B. Mahalanobis Model
C. Garibi Hatao
D. Agriculture Development
E. Harrod-Domar Growth Model

Choose the **correct** answer from the options given below:

1. E, B, D, C, A
2. C, A, B, D, E
3. A, C, E, B, D
4. D, E, C, B, A

37. The present Chairperson of NHRC, New Delhi is ....

1. Shri Ranganath Misra
2. Justice V. Ramasubramaniam
3. Dr. Justice A.S. Anand
4. Justice Arun Kumar Mishra

38. Which of the following are the components of social policy?

A. Human Security
B. Social Integration
C. Monetary Gain
D. Secure and Sustainable Livelihood

Choose the **correct** answer from the options given below:

1. A, B and C only
2. B, C and D only
3. A, B and D only
4. D only

39. Which of the following is **Not** a part of the Rothman's Model of Community Organization?

1. Locality Development Model
2. Social Planning Model
3. Social Goal Model
4. Social Action Model

40. Which is **Not** a key aspect of Ethnographic Research?

1. Sample Survey
2. Participant Observation
3. Data Collection
4. Contextual Understanding

41. Arrange in ascending order the Social Competence/Breakdown Model of Aging:

A. Role loss (loss of social contacts, immobility)
B. Self-labeling that reflect stereotypical images of elderly people as dependent, incapable, and incompetent
C. Social competence or incompetence
D. Thinks negatively and becomes dependent

Choose the **correct** answer from the options given below:

1. A, B, C, D
2. C, A, B, D
3. A, C, B, D
4. D, C. B, A

42. Match List-I with List-II:

List-I (Group Dynamics)	List-II (Associated Meaning)
A. Group Cohesiveness	I. Nature and characteristics of inter relationship among members
B. Group Structure	II. Small group objectives conflict with larger goals
C. Group Interaction	III. Degree to which its members are attached to group
D. Sub-Optimization	IV. Mutual response of people participating in an activity

Choose the **correct** answer from the options given below:

1. A-I, B-III, C-IV, D-II
2. A-III, B-I, C-IV, D-II
3. A-IV, B-III, C-II, D-I
4. A-IV, B-I, C-III, D-II

43. Which of the following Article of the Fundamental Rights is **Not** correctly listed.

A. Article 19: Right to Freedom
B. Article 14-18: Right to Equality
C. Article 35: Right to Constitutional Remedies
D. Article 23-24: Right Against Exploitation

Choose the **most appropriate** answer from the options given below:

1. C only
2. C and D only
3. B and D only
4. A, B and C only

44. Match List-I with List-II:

List-I (Process of Social Change (Talcott Parson))	List-II (Function)
A. Differentiation	I. Involving different groups
B. Adaptive upgrading	II. Development of new values that tolerate great range of activities
C. Inclusion	III. Increasing complexity of social organization
D. Value Generalization	IV. Social institutions become more specialized in their purpose

Choose the **correct** answer from the options given below:

1. A-I, B-III, C-IV, D-II
2. A-II, B-I, C-III, D-IV
3. A-III, B-IV, C-I, D-II
4. A-IV, B-I, C-II, D-III

45. Which out of these is **Not** a poverty alleviation programme?

A. Integrated Rural Development Programme, 1978
B. National Rural Livelihood Mission, 2007
C. Prime Minister's Street Vendor Atma Nirbhar Nidhi (PMSVaNidhi), 2020
D. Draft Carbon Credit Trading Scheme,2023

Choose the **correct** answer from the options given below:

1. A and D only
2. A and B only
3. A, B, C only
4. D only

46. Arrange in proper order the developmental sequence or phases in small groups as proposed by Bruce W. Tuckman:

A. Functional role-relatedness
B. Testing and dependence
C. Development of group cohesion
D. Intragroup conflict

Choose the **correct** answer from the options given below:

1. A, B, C, D
2. B, C, A, D
3. B, D, C, A
4. C, A, B, D

47. Arrange in ascending order the following stages of psycho-social development as proposed by Eric Erikson.

A. Initiative vs. Guilt
B. Autonomy vs. Shame
C. Intimacy vs. Isolation
D. Trust vs. Mistrust

Choose the **correct** answer from the options given below:

1. A, B, C, D
2. C, A, B, D
3. A, C, B, D
4. D, B, A, C

48. 'PERT' is an acronym for ....

1. Program Evaluation and Review Technique
2. Process Evaluation and Review Technique
3. Process Evaluation and Reflection Technique
4. Program Examination and Review Technique

49. Which of the following are **Not** an example of threats to External validity in Research?

A. Mortality
B. Interaction of history and treatment
C. Maturation
D. Reactive effects of experimental arrangements

Choose the **most appropriate** answer from the options given below:

1. A and C only
2. B and D only
3. A and D only
4. B and C only

50. As an Advocate, Social Worker's prime role is to ....

1. Deal with injustice
2. Establish means of achieving goals
3. Provide research data
4. Deal with deep lying unconscious forces

51. At the Labour Party annual conference which Prime Minister used community as a theme of his key-note speech talking of One Nation, One Community?

1. Narendra Modi
2. Tony Blair
3. Barack Obama
4. Donald Trump

52. Beti Bachao-Beti Padhao programme was launched on 22nd January' 2015 in ....

1. Panipat, Haryana
2. Rewari, Haryana
3. Alwar, Rajasthan
4. Nagaur, Rajasthan

53. Arrange the following SDGs in ascending order.

A. Peace, Justice and Strong Institutions
B. Gender Equality
C. No Poverty
D. Climate Action
E. Reduced Inequalities

Choose the **correct** answer from the options given below:

1. D, B, A, C, E
2. C, B, E, D, A
3. A, D, B, E, C
4. C, D, A, B, E

54. Match List-I with List-II:

List-I (Stages of Change)	List-II (Behaviour)
A. Pre-contemplation	I. Seeing a problem and considering whether to act
B. Contemplation	II. Not seeing a problem
C. Preparation	III. Doing something to change
D. Action	IV. Making concrete plans to act soon

Choose the **correct** answer from the options given below:

1. A-II, B-I, C-IV, D-III
2. A-II, B-I, C-III, D-IV
3. A-I, B-II, C-III, D-IV
4. A-III, B-I, C-II, D-IV

55. Current number of Member States in ILO are ....

1. 184
2. 187
3. 185
4. 186

56. Under which Article(s), citizens can avail Constitutional Remedies?

A. Article 13 to 15
B. Article 17 to 19
C. Article 23 to 25
D. Article 32

Choose the **correct** answer from the options given below:

1. A only 2. D only
3. B and D only 4. C and D only

57. Which characteristic feature dominates in pre-school children?

1. Dependency 2. Self-initiative
3. Risk taking 4. Autonomy

58. Hall and Midgley suggest which of the following approaches?

A. Statist Approach
B. Enterprise Approach
C. Populist Approach
D. Reciprocal Approach

Choose the **correct** answer from the options given below:

1. A only
2. A and B only
3. A, B and C only
4. A, B, and D only

59. 'Patch-based work' was associated with which one of these ....

1. Barclay Committee
2. Wagner Report
3. Seebhom Report
4. Griffins Report

60. Funding source of One Stop Centre Scheme is ....

1. Nirbhaya Fund
2. UNO
3. WHO
4. PM Fund

61. Under the Society's Registration Act, 1860 MoA (Memorandum of Association) does Not incorporate.

1. Name of Society
2. Certified Copy of Rules and Regulations by only one governing member
3. Address and Occupation of Governors
4. Objects of the Society

62. A group decision-making method in which individual members meet face-to-face to pool their judgements in a systematic but independent fashion refers to ....

1. Delphi Technique
2. Risky Shift Technique
3. Nominal Group Technique
4. Group Polarization

63. Behaviourist approach of Social Work is based on the assumption ....

1. Behaviour is learnt and shaped as a result of environmental circumstances
2. All behaviours have a physiological basis
3. Memory recall occurs by a combination of retrievals reconstruction
4. All behaviours has a cause i.e., to be found in the mind

64. The full form of 'STEP' is ....

1. Scheme for Satellite Experiment Project
2. Support to Training and Employment Programme
3. Strategic Training for Employment Purposes
4. Strategic Teaching for Employment Programme

65. According to Lead Beater, Bartlett & Gallagher, implementing the personalization agenda Social Workers need to act as ....

A. Advisor
B. Service Provider
C. Designer of Social Care
D. Change Agent

Choose the **most appropriate** answer from the options given below:

1. A, B and C only
2. A and B only
3. C and D only
4. B, C and D only

66. Fundamental Duties were inserted in the Indian Constitution in 1976 through which Constitutional Amendment?

1. 41st 2. 40th
3. 42nd 4. 29th

67. Match List-I with List-II:

List-I (Field Work Domains)	List-II (Focus Area)
A. Group Conference	I. Learning needs of an individual
B. Individual Conference	II. Learning from experiences of others
C. Evaluation	III. Organization and presentation of reflection and actions
D. Recording	IV. Totality of Learning Outcomes

Choose the **correct** answer from the options given below:

1. A-I, B-II, C-IV, D-III
2. A-III, B-IV, C-II, D-I
3. A-II, B-IV, C-III, D-I
4. A-II, B-I, C-IV, D-III

68. Which of the following is true regarding the concept of social welfare?

A. Purusarth
B. Bhakti
C. Dharma
D. Mutual Understanding

Choose the **correct** answer from the options given below:

1. A and C only
2. A, B and C only
3. B and C only
4. A and B only

69. Which is **Not** the correct year for the establishment of the Schools of Social Work?

1. Madras School of Social Work, 1952
2. Baroda School of Social Work, 1949
3. Delhi School of Social Work, 1946
4. Tata Institute of Social Sciences, 1939

70. SFBT refers to ....

1. Solution-Focused Brief Treatment
2. Strategic-Focused Brief Therapy
3. Solution-Focused Brief Therapy
4. Solution-Focused Balanced Therapy

71. Which among the following represents the disadvantage of Content Analysis?

A. Concerned with both Textual and Visual Materials
B. Flexibility
C. Impossible to devise coding manuals
D. Difficult to ascertain the answers to 'why' questions

Choose the **most appropriate** answer from the options given below:

1. B and C only
2. A and B only
3. B and D only
4. C and D only

72. The book titled 'Social Diagnosis' was authored by ....

1. Martin Davis
2. M.G. Ross
3. Mary Richmond
4. M. Haralambos

73. In NVivo software, the route by which coding is undertaken is termed as ....

1. Models
2. Nodes
3. Bibliographical Data
4. Memos

74. Arrange the following stages of sampling in ascending order:

A. Determine the Sampling Frame
B. Choose the Sampling Technique
C. Define the Target Population
D. Select the Sample

Choose the **correct** answer from the options given below:

1. A, B, C, D
2. C, A, B, D
3. A, C, B, D
4. D, C, B, A

75. Arrange the schemes started by the Ministry of Women and Child Development in the order of their launch.

A. Swadhar Greh Scheme
B. Beti Bachao Beti Padhao
X. Pradhan Mantri Matru Vandana Yojana
D. Mahila Shakti Kendra (MSK)

Choose the **correct** answer from the options given below:

1. B, D, C, A
2. D, C, A, B
3. C, A, B, D
4. A, B, D, C

76. The book titled "Text of the Hindu Law" was authored by ....

1. Raja Ram Mohan Roy
2. M.G. Ranade
3. Pandita Ramabai
4. Tiplut Nongbri

77. Which of the following is correct regarding the approach and structure of NITI Aayog?

A. Holistic Approach
B. Research Wing
C. Reciprocal Wing
D. Democratic Approach

Choose the **most appropriate** answer from the options given below:

1. A and B only
2. C and D only
3. A, B and C only
4. A only

78. Which is **Not** a characteristic of critical thinking?

1. Working towards objectivity
2. Exploring alternatives
3. Reliance on only one assertion for unstructured problems
4. Understanding importance of social and cultural context of human behaviour

79. Arrange the following stages of Policy Formulation in order of their occurrence:

A. Agenda Setting
B. Policy formulation and decision-making
C. Feedback, evaluation and termination
D. Problem recognition and problem definition
D. Execution or enforcement of a policy

Choose the **correct** answer from the options given below:

1. D, B, A, C, E
2. C, A, B, D, E
3. A, D, B, E, C
4. D, A, B, E, C

80. Match List-I with List-II:

List-I (Theme of World Social Work Day)	List-II (Year)
A. Respecting diversity through joint social action	I. 2025
B. Co-building a new eco-social world: Leaving no one behind	II. 2023
C. Buen Vivir: Shared Future for transformative change	III. 2022
D. Strengthening inter-generational solidarity for enduring well-being	IV. 2024

Choose the **correct** answer from the options given below:

1. A-II, B-III, C-IV, D-I
2. A-I, B-II, C-IV, D III
3. A-I, B-III, C-IV, D-II
4. A-II, B-III, C-IV, D-I

81. According to Talcott Parson, social order and social life does not represent ....

1. Mutual advantage
2. Peaceful cooperation
3. Mutual hostility
4. Commitment to common values

82. Which SDG ensures 'Peace Justice & Strong Institution's?

1. SDG 15
2. SDG 16
3. SDG 13
4. SDG 12

83. Arrange the following stages of Social Action in ascending order.

A. Organizing people for coordinated and directed intervention
B. Awareness is generated regarding various aspects of the problem
C. Development of strategies to achieve the goals
D. Scientific analysis or research on the social problem

Choose the **correct** answer from the options given below:

1. B, C, A, D 2. A, B, C, D
3. D, B, A, C 4. C, A, B, D

84. Strength-based practice in social work was propounded by ....

1. Bertha Reynolds
2. R. Dolgoff
3. Dennis Saleebey
4. R.A Dorfman

85. According to Flexner, Which is **Not** a Principle of Social Casework?

1. Principle of Communication
2. Principle of Client's Self Determination
3. Principle of Acceptance
4. Principle of Individualization

86. Arrange the following key tasks of administration in ascending order:

A. Development of Plans
B. Recruitment & Appointment
C. Preparation of Budget
D. Departmentalisation
E. Coordination

Choose the **correct** answer from the options given below:

1. A, B, C, D, E
2. C, A, B, D, E
3. A, D, B, E, C
4. D, C, E, B, A

87. Match List-I with List-II:

List-I (Sex Crimes)	**List-II (Definition)**
A. Electra Complex	I. Genetic Pre-disposition
B. Diana Complex	II. Sexual desire of son towards his mother
C. Anlagen	III. Sexual desire of daughter towards her father
D. Oedipus Complex	IV. Psychological reaction found among young females

Choose the **correct** answer from the options given below:

1. A-I, B-III, C-IV, D-II
2. A-III, B-IV, C-II, D-I
3. A-III, B-IV, C-I, D-II
4. A-I, B-II, C-IV, D-III

88. In which year, Minorities Commission was accorded the statutory status?

1. 1991 2. 1992
3. 1990 4. 1989

89. Match List-I with List-II:

List-I (Trade Union Progress)	**List-II (Years)**
A. Era of formation of Modern Trade Unionism	I. 1935-1938
B. Split in AITUC into Leftist & Rightist wings	II. 1939-1946
C. Unity forged among Trade Unions	III. 1918-1924
D. World War II brought chaos in Industrial Relations	IV. 1925-1934

Choose the **correct** answer from the options given below:

1. A-IV, B-III, C-I, D-II
2. A-III, B-II, C-I, D-IV
3. A-III, B-IV, C-I, D-II
4. A-III, B-II, C-IV, D-I

90. Selecting every 10th name in a list is an example of ....

1. Quota sampling
2. Systematic sampling
3. Lottery method
4. Tippet's method

Directions (Qs. No. 91-95): *Read the following passage and answer the questions:*

The Observation Method is the most commonly used method specially in studies relating to behavioural sciences. In a way we all observe things around us, but this sort of observation is not a scientific observation. Observation becomes a scientific tool and the method of data collection for the researcher, when it serves a formulated research purpose, if systematically planned and recorded and is subjected to checks and controls on validity and reliability. Under the observation method, the information is sought by way of investigator's own direct observation without asking from the respondent... The main advantage of this method is that subjective bias is eliminated if observation is done accurately. Secondly, the information obtained relates to what is currently happening.

91. Reliability is Not associated with which of the following?

1. Experience of the researcher only
2. Pretesting
3. Pilot study
4. Consistency in measurement

92. Triangulation does Not refer to which of the following ....

1. Use of multiple tools
2. Use of multiple theories
3. Use of only three tools
4. Use of multiple methods

93. Which method of data collection is more appropriate for avoiding 'subjective bias' while collecting data relating to human behaviour?

1. Interview
2. Checklist
3. Questionnaire
4. Observation

94. In Qualitative Research, recording related events, artifacts, situations or phenomenon is Not done by which method/tool ....

1. Scale
2. Focused Group Discussion
3. Field diary
4. Interview

95. Which is **Not** a fully structured tool or technique of data collection?

1. Interview Schedule
2. Interview Guide
3. Attitude Scale
4. Checklist for Observation

Directions (Qs. No. 96-100): *Read the following passage and answer the questions:*

The most frequently encountered necessity to 'work' a relationship occurs with the phenomenon called transference or transference reactions. To any emotionally charged relationship, each of us bring conscious and unconscious feelings and attitudes that originally arose in or still belong to the earlier important relationships. For example, in casework with an adolescent girl to help her regarding her career options, the worker listens to the girl's aspirations and dilemmas. The worker helps her to draw a choice of careers helping her to keep in mind her aptitude as well as preferences and also arranges for her visit to a nearby vocational training centre. In such a case, what may happen is that the girl may begin to feel towards the worker as she felt towards her mother/grandmother when she was young. The degree of emotional satisfaction which the client gets from such a relationship is far beyond the realistic limits of the caseworker-client relationship. It may be remembered that the client who approaches the agency often feels helpless and inadequate for not being able to tackle his/her own problem. Due to this, the client is prone to transfer irrational elements into the relationship and want to regress, desiring to have parental nurture and parental domination

96. Any subjective involvement on the part of the caseworker with the client or client's problem is referred to as ....

1. Transference
2. Counter transference
3. Regression
4. Genuineness

97. An emotionally charged childhood experience may influence the client's behaviour in adulthood and impact the client's professional relationship. What does this refer to?

1. Transference
2. Counter transference
3. Regression
4. Purposeful Expression of Feelings

98. The caseworker must remain objective throughout the helping relationship and be aware of his/her own feelings. Which is the best answer in the context of the passage above?

1. Transference
2. Counter transference
3. Regression
4. Emotional impact on the professional's own family

99. Transference reactions are targeted towards ....

1. Mother
2. Father
3. Sibling
4. Case worker

100. In social casework, which best represents the concept 'regression' from among the following?

1. Dropping out of a professional relationship due to time constraints
2. Reverting to an earlier professional helper due to financial constraints
3. Clients are unable to cope with irrational feelings towards the helper
4. The client shifts to a new professional helper due to referral

ANSWERS

1	**2**	**3**	**4**	**5**	**6**	**7**	**8**	**9**	**10**
3	3	3	3	4	2	2	2	4	1
11	**12**	**13**	**14**	**15**	**16**	**17**	**18**	**19**	**20**
2	3	3	1	2	1	4	4	2	3
21	**22**	**23**	**24**	**25**	**26**	**27**	**28**	**29**	**30**
2	1	1	2	1	2	1	4	4	1
31	**32**	**33**	**34**	**35**	**36**	**37**	**38**	**39**	**40**
2	4	3	3	4	1	2	3	3	1
41	**42**	**43**	**44**	**45**	**46**	**47**	**48**	**49**	**50**
2	2	1	3	4	3	4	1	1	1
51	**52**	**53**	**54**	**55**	**56**	**57**	**58**	**59**	**60**
2	1	2	1	2	2	4	3	1	1
61	**62**	**63**	**64**	**65**	**66**	**67**	**68**	**69**	**70**
2	3	1	2	1	3	4	2	4	3
71	**72**	**73**	**74**	**75**	**76**	**77**	**78**	**79**	**80**
4	3	2	2	4	2	1	3	4	4
81	**82**	**83**	**84**	**85**	**86**	**87**	**88**	**89**	**90**
3	2	3	3	1	3	3	2	3	2
91	**92**	**93**	**94**	**95**	**96**	**97**	**98**	**99**	**100**
1	3	4	1	2	2	1	2	4	3

EXPLANATORY ANSWERS

1. Kalelkar Commission (First Backward Classes Commission, 1953–55) proposed broad tests for identifying "socially and educationally backward" classes, including: (i) low social position in the caste hierarchy, (ii) lack of general educational advancement, (iii) inadequate representation in government services, and (iv) inadequate representation in trade, commerce and industry. "Representation in private services" was not one of its criteria, hence option 3 is the one that is not a criterion.

2. "Positive discrimination" (affirmative action) comprises state actions that preferentially support historically disadvantaged groups to achieve substantive equality. Typical measures include reservations for SC/ST (A) and redistributive land reforms in favour of the poor (B). Giving land to the rich (C) or allotting houses to the already privileged upper classes (D) do not redress disadvantage and therefore are not "positive discrimination."

3. A sensible ascending sequence in social planning is:

A. Start with situational analysis—identify factors and describe social, economic, political conditions (baseline).

D. Design an assessment plan—specify what data/tools you'll use to validate that baseline and track change.

B. Formulate a plan of action—develop alternative strategies/programmes based on the assessed needs.

E. Determine priorities—rank strategies by urgency, feasibility, impact, and resources.

C. Determine tools/techniques and implement—choose operational instruments (methods, staffing, budgeting, monitoring) and roll out.

This aligns with diagnostic → assessment design → planning → prioritisation → implementation.

4. Social Action is a macro-practice approach aimed at structural change—mobilising communities, building awareness, influencing power structures, and advocating policy/legal reforms. It is not primarily about individual counselling or welfare distribution; rather, it targets systemic transformation.

5. Advocacy rests on accuracy of information, client confidentiality, diligence, and fidelity to clients' interests while upholding ethics and fairness. Acting partially or selectively violates neutrality and justice, undermining the legitimacy and effectiveness of advocacy—hence it is not a part of advocacy.

6.
- Third Plan (A) was 1961-66, focusing on agriculture and self-reliance. → III
- Eighth Plan (B) was 1992-97, initiated after a gap due to crises and reforms. → IV
- Sixth Plan (C) was 1980-85, emphasizing poverty alleviation and infrastructure. → I
- Tenth Plan (D) was 2002-07, aimed at 8% growth and human development. → II

Thus, A-III, B-IV, C-I, D-II correctly pairs plans with their implementation years.

7.
- In social-science measurement, classification of research/attitude scales is commonly organised by (i) Subject orientation—e.g., self-rating (respondent-oriented) vs observer-rating (assessor-oriented) instruments (A), and (ii) Degree of subjectivity—e.g., judgement-based/subjective scaling (Thurstone equal-appearing intervals, many qualitative ratings) versus more structured procedures (C).
- The phrase "Non-Dimensional Approach" (D) is not a standard basis; the recognised axis is dimensionality (uni- vs multi-dimensional), not "non-dimensional."
- "Degree of objectivity" (B) is simply the opposite end of the same continuum as subjectivity; exam frameworks typically name the basis as subjectivity (subjective vs objective), and the options force choosing one label—hence A and C fit the standard bases without invoking the non-standard D.

8.
- Contempt (A) aligns with Dictatorial behaviour (I)—authoritarian, dismissive conduct.
- Adversarial (B) corresponds to Paternal behaviour (II)—a superior stance treating others as subordinates.
- Acceptance (C) suits Business-like behaviour (III)—neutral, task-focused, professional.

- Cooperation (D) fits Participatory behaviour (IV)—sharing decisions and responsibilities.

Hence the correct matching is A-I, B-II, C-III, D-IV.

9. Green India Mission, National Clean Air Programme, and Jal Jeevan Mission all target environmental protection or resource sustainability. One Stop Centre is a welfare scheme for women facing violence (support, shelter, legal aid) and is not an environmental programme.

10. The described process—helping individuals cope effectively with personal or social functioning problems—is Social Casework, a micro-level method in social work. It provides personalised assessment, counselling, and planned intervention for behavioural or adjustment issues, unlike group work, community organisation, or social action which function at broader or collective levels.

11. Conformity is the adjustment of one's behaviour or beliefs to align with perceived group norms, expectations, or standards. It arises from normative pressure (wanting acceptance/avoiding rejection) and informational influence (assuming the group is correct). It differs from "influencing tactics" (strategies to persuade others), "pressure" (a cause rather than the behaviour), and "cultural lag" (a societal-level mismatch between material and non-material culture).

12. Orientation (C) is the entry stage: members learn the purpose, clarify roles, and test the climate. Resistance (D) follows, with boundary-testing, ambivalence, or challenges to leadership and norms—roughly akin to "storming." Negotiation (B) comes next: the group works through differences, establishes norms/roles, and builds workable agreements. Intimacy (A) is the mature stage—trust, cohesion, open communication, and productive collaboration. This ascending progression—Orientation → Resistance → Negotiation → Intimacy—matches group development logic.

13. Gandhian Satyagraha strictly requires non-violence and self-suffering. Hartal (A)—a peaceful shutdown/strike—withdraws cooperation without force. Social ostracism (B) is a non-violent boycott to signal moral dissent. Fasting (D) is self-discipline aimed at moral appeal. Coercive picketing (C) violates non-violence by using compulsion/force, so it is excluded.

14.
- **Job Consciousness Theory — Selig Perlman (A-III):** Unions arise from workers' practical, job-centred interests (wages, security), not abstract ideology.
- **Socio-Psychological Theory — Robert F. Hoxie (B-IV):** Union forms/behaviours reflect social conditions and worker-management psychology in specific industries.
- **Marxian Theory — Karl Marx (C-I):** Unions are part of class struggle, organising labour against capital within a broader revolutionary critique.
- **Technological Theory — Frank Tannenbaum (D-II):** Industrial/technological changes restructure work and power relations, fostering unionisation.

15. The Economic and Social Commission for Western Asia (ESCWA) presents a stepwise model for shaping social policy. To give the descending order (from the last phase back to the earliest), we need to start with the most advanced stage and trace backward:

B. Defining and prioritizing issues - This represents a later stage in the cycle where, after evaluation, decision-makers refine definitions and set clear priorities for action to ensure that resources and attention focus on the most critical matters.

C. Evaluating alternative approaches - Preceding that, policymakers compare different strategies or policy options for feasibility, efficiency, and equity. Evaluation provides the evidence base needed to define and rank issues effectively.

A. Placing issues on the public agenda - Earlier in the sequence, issues are introduced to the public and decision-making forums to gain visibility, mobilise stakeholders, and create political momentum.

D. Identifying problems and opportunities - This is the initial phase, where policymakers scan the social environment, collect data, and recognise pressing needs or emerging possibilities that could benefit from policy intervention.

Tracing backward in descending order from the more advanced phases to the earliest detection phase gives:

16. • **Article 330 (A-IV):** Provides for reservation of seats for Scheduled Castes (SCs) and Scheduled Tribes (STs) in the Lok Sabha to ensure adequate parliamentary representation.
 • **Article 332 (B-II):** Provides for reservation of seats for SCs and STs in the Legislative Assemblies of the States, extending affirmative representation to state legislatures.
 • **Article 21A (C-III):** Introduced by the 86th Constitutional Amendment Act, 2002, it guarantees free and compulsory education for children aged 6–14 years as a Fundamental Right.
 • **Article 17 (D-I):** Abolishes untouchability and forbids its practice in any form, enforcing equality and dignity.

17. A planning matrix in research includes orienting decisions (framing objectives), research design (methods/approach), and data analysis (interpreting results). Sharing a client's personal information is not a step or component of research planning; rather, it would breach confidentiality and ethics.

18. The National Education Policy (NEP) 2020 articulates a vision of transforming Bharat into an equitable, vibrant knowledge society and ultimately a global knowledge super power. While access, equity, and technology-enabled learning are important aspects, the overarching emphasis is on positioning India as a global leader in knowledge creation, dissemination, and innovation.

19. In a genogram (a graphical representation of family relationships used in social work and counselling), the symbol resembling (or a small circle/ambiguous marker) denotes an unknown or unspecified gender of a person when gender information is unavailable. Other symbols include a square for males, a circle for females, and a diagonal cross for death.

20. • **Tendulkar Committee – Uniform Poverty Line Basket (A):** Correct. Established in 2005 to revise poverty estimation methodology using a uniform consumption basket.
 • **J.V.P. Committee – Health Review (B):** Incorrect. The J.V.P. (Jawaharlal Nehru, Vallabhbhai Patel, Pattabhi Sitaramayya) Committee was formed in 1948 on linguistic reorganisation of states, not health.
 • **Dhar Commission – Administrative Convenience (C):** Correct. The Dhar Commission (1948) recommended administrative convenience over linguistic factors for reorganisation.
 • **Rangarajan Commission – Academic Reforms (D):** Incorrect. The Rangarajan Committee/Commission (2014) addressed poverty estimation, not academic reforms.

Thus, the mismatched pairs are B and D only.

21. A. **Integrated Child Development Services (ICDS) → IV. 1975:** Launched on 2 October 1975, ICDS is India's flagship early-childhood programme delivering a package of supplementary nutrition, immunisation, health check-ups, referral, and preschool education to children (0–6 years) and to pregnant/lactating women through Anganwadi centres. The 1975 start year anchors it to IV.

B. **Wheat-based Supplementary Nutrition Programme (WBNP) → III. 1986:** The Wheat-based Nutrition Programme was introduced in 1986 as a centrally sponsored food-grain support to States/UTs specifically for the Supplementary Nutrition Programme under ICDS, ensuring regular wheat (and later other grains) supply for take-home rations/hot cooked meals. Hence it pairs with 1986 (III).

C. **Prophylaxis Programme → II. 1970:** "Prophylaxis Programme" here denotes the early national nutrition deficiency-prevention initiatives launched in 1970, notably the National Nutritional Anaemia Prophylaxis Programme (NNAPP) and the Vitamin-A Prophylaxis Programme (against nutritional blindness). Therefore, 1970 (II) is the correct match.

D. **National Diarrhoeal Diseases Control Programme (NDDCP) → I. 1981:** Started in 1981, NDDCP focused on reducing diarrhoeal morbidity and mortality—popularising Oral Rehydration Therapy (ORT), preventive IEC, and case management protocols; later it interfaced with child-survival initiatives. Hence 1981 (I).

22. The Kishori Shakti Yojana (KSY), under the ICDS scheme, focuses on adolescent girls' development. It provides vocational training (A) for self-reliance, health education (B) to promote awareness of nutrition and hygiene, and nutritional support (D) to combat malnutrition. Legal support for girls in distress (C) is not part of KSY.

23. The Directive Principles of State Policy (Part IV) include:

A. Equal justice and free legal aid (Art. 39A) – directs the state to ensure access to justice.

B. Organisation of village panchayats (Art. 40) – promotes self-governance at the village level.

D. Living wage (Art. 43) – seeks a living wage and decent working conditions for workers.

C. Equality of opportunity in public employment (Art. 16) is a Fundamental Right, not a DPSP.

24.
- **Article 50 (A)** – Separation of judiciary and executive – Correct DPSP.
- **Article 48 (B)** – Organisation of agriculture and animal husbandry, preservation of breeds/ prohibition of slaughter – Correct DPSP.
- **Article 42 (C)** – Actually deals with just and humane conditions of work and maternity relief, not village panchayats—Incorrect.
- **Article 56 (D)** – Relates to President's tenure, not health or intoxicants—Incorrect.

Hence, C and D are not correct DPSPs.

25. A. Police officers' power to require attendance of witnesses – Sec. 160 → III. Authorises police to summon witnesses (with safeguards for women/minors).

B. Right not to be arrested after sunset and before sunrise – Sec. 46(4) → IV. Restricts arrest of women during night unless authorised by a magistrate.

C. Right against being watched without consent of a woman – Sec. 354C → II. Defines voyeurism, protecting women's privacy.

D. Recording of confessions & statements by magistrate – Sec. 164 → I. Ensures voluntary, fair recording of confessions or statements during investigation.

26. The National Health Policy, 2017 is grounded in key principles that guide India's health system reform:

A. Equity: Ensuring that all population groups, particularly the disadvantaged and marginalized, have fair access to health services.

B. Universality: Aiming for universal health coverage so that every citizen can obtain needed health services without financial hardship.

D. Affordability: Keeping costs reasonable for both providers and recipients to prevent financial distress.

C. Centralization of decision-making contradicts the policy's emphasis on decentralization and participatory governance, so it is not a guiding principle.

27. The German sociologist Ferdinand (Fredrick) Tönnies argued that the rapid urbanization during the Industrial Revolution undermined traditional community bonds. He described a shift from Gemeinschaft (community, close-knit social relations) to Gesellschaft (society, impersonal and contractual relations), emphasising that industrial urbanization negatively affected social cohesion and personal relationships.

28. A. Institute for the Physically Handicapped → IV. New Delhi: This institute—now called Pandit Deendayal Upadhyaya National Institute for Persons with Physical Disabilities (PDUNIPPD)—is located in New Delhi. It provides comprehensive rehabilitation services, prosthetics, and therapy for persons with physical disabilities.

B. National Institute for the Visually Handicapped → I. Dehradun: Renamed National Institute for the Empowerment of Persons with Visual Disabilities (NIEPVD), it is in Dehradun, Uttarakhand. It focuses on training, research, and providing services for persons with visual impairment, including Braille production and assistive technologies.

C. National Institute for the Orthopedically Handicapped → II. Kolkata: Now called the National Institute for Locomotor Disabilities (Divyangjan), this Kolkata-based institute specializes in mobility aids, surgical interventions, and orthopaedic rehabilitation for locomotor disabilities.

D. Ali Yavar Jung National Institute for the Hearing Handicapped → III. Mumbai: Currently known as the Ali Yavar Jung National Institute of Speech and Hearing Disabilities (Divyangjan), located in Mumbai, Maharashtra, it offers hearing impairment rehabilitation, speech therapy, special education, and teacher training.

Correct Matching: A-IV, B-I, C-II, D-III.

29. In the Rational Model of decision-making, the ascending sequence is:

A. Identifying Problems: Recognize and define the issue requiring a decision.

D. Assessing the consequences of all options: Evaluate potential outcomes for each alternative.

C. Relating consequences to values: Judge how each consequence aligns with organisational or societal values.

B. Choosing the preferred options: Select the alternative that best satisfies objectives and values.

30. H.B. Trecker's principles of Social Group Work progress as follows:

B. Principle of planned group formation: Careful and purposeful grouping of individuals at the start.

D. Principle of continuous individualization: Recognising and respecting each member's uniqueness throughout group activities.

C. Principle of democratic group self-determination: Encouraging participatory decision-making within the group.

A. Principle of resource utilization: Making effective use of internal and external resources to achieve group goals.

31. In social work, Crisis Intervention is recognized as a Practice Model because:

A. It develops out of actual experience: Crisis intervention emerged from field practice dealing with acute psychological and social emergencies—such as disaster response or traumatic events—where social workers observed what worked in real-life situations.

B. It develops out of experimentation: Over time, various approaches were tested and refined in practice settings (e.g., suicide prevention hotlines, community mental health), making experimentation a cornerstone of its evolution.

Options C (theory of behaviour) and D (a single explanation) are incorrect because crisis intervention integrates multiple behavioural and ecological theories and does not rely on a single explanatory framework.

32. A casework relationship in social work involves:

A. Acceptance: Unconditional positive regard for the client's worth and dignity.

B. Expectation: Belief in the client's capacity for change and growth, fostering motivation.

C. Stimulation: Encouragement and guidance to help clients explore options, build skills, and act constructively.

D. Dislocation is not an element of a supportive casework relationship; rather, the relationship seeks stability and empowerment.

33. The Second UGC Review Committee on Social Work Education was constituted in 1975. Its mandate was to evaluate the state of social work education in India and propose reforms to enhance quality, relevance, and professional standards. This committee provided a comprehensive review of curricula, fieldwork requirements, teaching methods, and institutional capacities, ensuring that social work education aligned with the country's socio-economic realities.

The first review committee on social work education had been appointed earlier in 1960, and the 1975 committee built upon its recommendations, updating them to address changing societal needs and expanding professional practice contexts.

34. In Watson and Rennie's stages of Therapeutic Counselling, when arranged in descending order (from the last phase back to the first), the sequence is:

C. Engaging in behavioural experimentation – This is the final and most advanced stage, where the client actively tests and applies newly gained insights and changed perceptions in real-life contexts to confirm and solidify growth.

A. **Making changes in thinking and shifts in perception** – Just prior to behavioural experimentation, the client experiences cognitive restructuring and altered emotional perspectives, which form the foundation for trying out new behaviours.

D. **Focusing experientially on one's experience and articulation in words** – An earlier stage where the client processes feelings deeply, articulates experiences, and gains clarity about underlying issues.

B. **Disclosing information with regard to a specific troubling issue** – The initial stage, where the client first shares the specific issue causing distress, opening the door for deeper exploration.

Correct descending order: C → A → D → B.

35. A. **International Social Work → 1958 (III):** An international journal promoting cross-national social work knowledge.

B. **National Journal of Professional Social Work → 2000 (IV):** A relatively recent Indian journal for professional discourse in social work.

C. **Journal of Social Work → 1962 (I):** Published from Tata Institute of Social Sciences, among the early Indian academic journals.

D. **Perspectives in Social Work → 1984 (II):** Focuses on Indian perspectives and practices, first issued in the mid-1980s.

36. To arrange developmental models under India's Five-Year Plans in ascending order (chronological):

E. **Harrod–Domar Growth Model** – Adopted in the First Five-Year Plan (1951–56) to emphasise capital-output ratio and investment.

B. **Mahalanobis Model** – Applied in the Second Five-Year Plan (1956–61), stressing heavy industries and long-term growth.

D. **Agriculture Development** – Central focus of the Third Five-Year Plan (1961–66), highlighting agricultural self-sufficiency.

C. **Garibi Hatao** – Political slogan and poverty-removal thrust of the Fifth Five-Year Plan (1974–79).

A. **Growth with Social Justice & Equality** – Guiding theme of the Seventh Five-Year Plan (1985–90) and beyond.

Thus, the ascending sequence is E → B → D → C → A.

37. The current Chairperson of the National Human Rights Commission (NHRC), New Delhi is Justice V. Ramasubramanian, a former Judge of the Supreme Court of India. He was appointed to the post on 30 December 2024, succeeding Justice Arun Kumar Mishra whose tenure ended earlier in 2024.

Detailed Explanation:

- The NHRC was created under the Protection of Human Rights Act, 1993 to safeguard and promote human rights in India.
- By law, its Chairperson must be a former Chief Justice of India or a Judge of the Supreme Court.
- Justice Ramasubramanian brings decades of judicial experience and has served on several landmark benches of the Supreme Court.
- His appointment reflects the government's effort to continue experienced judicial leadership at NHRC, ensuring effective oversight of rights protections and grievance redressal across the country.

38. Key components of social policy include:

A. **Human Security:** Protecting people's fundamental rights, safety, and dignity.

B. **Social Integration:** Fostering inclusive communities and reducing inequality or marginalisation.

D. **Secure and Sustainable Livelihood:** Ensuring long-term, stable economic participation and well-being.

C. **Monetary Gain is not a recognized core component;** social policy prioritises welfare, justice, and equity over pure financial profit.

39. Rothman's Model of Community Organization consists of three approaches:

1. **Locality Development Model** – Focuses on community participation and capacity building.
2. **Social Planning Model** – Relies on technical expertise and rational problem-solving.

3. **Social Action Model** – Mobilises disadvantaged groups to challenge inequities.

A Social Goal Model does not belong to Rothman's framework and is therefore the incorrect option.

40. Ethnographic Research is characterised by:

- **Participant Observation:** Immersing in the community or group being studied.
- **Data Collection:** Gathering detailed qualitative information.
- **Contextual Understanding:** Interpreting behaviours within their cultural and social context.

A Sample Survey is not a key aspect—it is a quantitative method used in survey research, not typical of ethnography's in-depth qualitative focus.

41. Correct Ascending Order of the Social Competence/Breakdown Model of Aging (Kuypers & Bengtson, 1973):

C. Social competence or incompetence (Starting Point): Aging begins with the individual's existing level of social competence or perceived incompetence. This baseline reflects their past experiences, support systems, and confidence in managing life situations.

A. Role loss (loss of social contacts, immobility): External life changes—such as retirement, widowhood, declining health, or reduced mobility—result in loss of meaningful social roles and contacts. This disruption undermines the person's established sense of competence.

B. Self-labeling that reflects stereotypical images of elderly people as dependent, incapable, and incompetent: Following role loss, older adults may internalize society's negative stereotypes about aging. They begin to label themselves as dependent or incapable, which further weakens their self-image.

D. Thinks negatively and becomes dependent: Finally, the individual accepts these negative perceptions, develops a pessimistic outlook, and increasingly relies on others, completing the breakdown cycle and potentially reinforcing social withdrawal.

Explanation: The Social Competence/Breakdown Model demonstrates how an initial competence level, when disrupted by role losses, can trigger internalized negative labels, ultimately producing dependency and reduced functioning. In ascending order from the earliest stage to the last, the sequence is C → A → B → D.

42. **A. Group Cohesiveness → III.** Degree to which its members are attached to the group. Cohesiveness measures attraction and commitment among members.

B. Group Structure → I. Nature and characteristics of interrelationship among members. Structure describes patterns of roles, norms, and relationships.

C. Group Interaction → IV. Mutual response of people participating in an activity. Interaction is the communication and response flow among members.

D. Sub-Optimization → II. Small group objectives conflict with larger goals. Sub-optimization occurs when a subgroup prioritizes its own goals over organizational objectives.

43.
- **Article 19:** Right to Freedom — Correct.
- **Article 14–18:** Right to Equality — Correct.
- **Article 35:** Right to Constitutional Remedies — Incorrect. Right to Constitutional Remedies is provided under Article 32, not Article 35. Article 35 relates to Parliament's power to make laws for Fundamental Rights.
- **Article 23–24:** Right Against Exploitation — Correct.

Therefore, C only is incorrectly listed.

44. Talcott Parsons described processes of social change as functions in maintaining and adapting society:

A. Differentiation → III. Increasing complexity of social organization. Differentiation increases societal complexity by dividing structures and functions.

B. Adaptive upgrading → IV. Social institutions become more specialized in their purpose. Institutions refine and specialize to meet new challenges.

C. Inclusion → I. Involving different groups. Inclusion incorporates previously excluded groups into societal participation.

D. Value generalization → II. Development of new values that tolerate a greater range of activities. Societies broaden values to accommodate diversity and innovation.

45. A. Integrated Rural Development Programme (1978): Poverty alleviation programme aimed at providing assets and self-employment opportunities to rural poor.

B. National Rural Livelihood Mission (2007): A poverty eradication mission promoting self-help groups and sustainable livelihoods.

C. PMSVaNidhi (2020): Supports street vendors impacted by COVID-19 with working capital—also aimed at livelihood support.

D. Draft Carbon Credit Trading Scheme (2023): Not a poverty alleviation scheme—it is an environmental and economic market mechanism for carbon trading.

46. Bruce W. Tuckman's phases of small group development:

B. Testing and dependence (Forming): Initial orientation and role testing.

D. Intragroup conflict (Storming): Conflicts emerge as members assert individuality.

C. Development of group cohesion (Norming): Relationships solidify and unity forms.

A. Functional role-relatedness (Performing): The group becomes productive and task-focused.

47. Erik Erikson's psychosocial development stages relevant here in ascending order:

D. Trust vs. Mistrust (Infancy, 0–1 yr): Building basic trust with caregivers.

B. Autonomy vs. Shame (Early childhood, 1–3 yrs): Developing independence and control.

A. Initiative vs. Guilt (Preschool, 3–5 yrs): Initiating tasks and asserting power.

C. Intimacy vs. Isolation (Young adulthood, 20s–40s): Forming intimate relationships versus social isolation.

48. PERT stands for Program Evaluation and Review Technique, a project management tool developed in the 1950s by the U.S. Navy for the Polaris missile program. It helps plan, schedule, and control complex projects by analysing task sequences, durations, and dependencies using network diagrams and probabilistic time estimates.

49. Threats to external validity are factors that limit the generalizability of study findings.

- A. Mortality and C. Maturation are threats to internal validity, as they affect changes within the experimental group rather than its applicability outside.
- B. Interaction of history and treatment and D. Reactive effects of experimental arrangements are threats to external validity, since they influence whether results apply to other settings or populations.

Hence, A and C only are not external validity threats.

50. As an advocate, a social worker's prime role is to confront and address injustice, representing and defending the rights of individuals or communities. Advocacy involves raising awareness, influencing policies, and ensuring access to resources to correct unfair treatment or systemic inequities. The other options (establishing means to achieve goals, providing research data, or dealing with unconscious forces) describe other roles or methods but not the primary advocacy function.

51. Tony Blair, former Prime Minister of the United Kingdom and Labour Party leader, delivered a keynote speech at the Labour Party annual conference where "community" was the central theme. His phrase "One Nation, One Community" highlighted a vision of Britain where all sections of society work together, transcending class and regional divides. This speech aligned with Blair's "Third Way" politics, blending social justice with economic reform, and sought to strengthen national unity while maintaining Labour's commitment to progressive values.

52. The Beti Bachao-Beti Padhao (BBBP) scheme was launched on 22 January 2015 in Panipat, Haryana by Prime Minister Narendra Modi. The choice of Panipat was significant because Haryana historically recorded one of India's lowest child sex ratios. The programme aims to:

- Address the declining Child Sex Ratio (CSR).
- Ensure survival, protection, and education of the girl child.

- Promote awareness and improve the efficiency of welfare services for girls.

It works through a multi-sectoral approach, involving the Ministries of Women and Child Development, Health & Family Welfare, and Education.

53. Arranged according to the official numbering of Sustainable Development Goals (SDGs) adopted by the UN in 2015:

C. No Poverty – SDG 1: The first and foundational goal, eliminating extreme poverty globally.

B. Gender Equality – SDG 5: Ensures equal opportunities, rights, and empowerment for women and girls.

E. Reduced Inequalities – SDG 10: Targets reducing income and opportunity gaps among and within countries.

D. Climate Action – SDG 13: Urges immediate steps to combat climate change and its impacts.

A. Peace, Justice, and Strong Institutions – SDG 16: Promotes peaceful societies, accessible justice, and accountable institutions.

Ascending order: 1 → 5 → 10 → 13 → 16, or C → B → E → D → A.

54. The Stages of Change (Transtheoretical Model) explain behavioural change progression:

A. Pre-contemplation → II. Not seeing a problem: Individuals are unaware or in denial about a problematic behaviour.

B. Contemplation → I. Seeing a problem and considering whether to act: Awareness grows, and the person weighs pros and cons of change.

C. Preparation → IV. Making concrete plans to act soon: Commitment develops, and specific strategies or small steps are planned.

D. Action → III. Doing something to change: The individual actively modifies behaviour and environment to implement change.

This mapping helps counsellors tailor interventions based on readiness for change.

55. The International Labour Organization (ILO) currently has 187 Member States (as of 2025). The ILO, a UN specialized agency, was founded in 1919 under the Treaty of Versailles following World War I to promote social justice and improve labour conditions. Over the years, it expanded to near-universal membership, with South Sudan joining in 2016 as the 187th member. The ILO's work includes:

- Setting international labour standards through conventions and recommendations.
- Developing policies and technical assistance to advance decent work.
- Promoting tripartism, where governments, employers, and workers jointly shape labour standards.

This broad membership underscores its role as a global forum for labour and human rights.

56.
- Article 32 of the Indian Constitution provides Constitutional Remedies. Dr. B.R. Ambedkar called it the "heart and soul" of the Constitution, as it allows citizens to move the Supreme Court directly to enforce Fundamental Rights.
- Articles 13–15, 17–19, 23–25 define or protect rights but do not grant the power to seek remedies. Thus, only Article 32 serves this purpose.

57.
- In pre-school children (around ages 3–5), autonomy dominates as they develop independence, motor skills, and the ability to make simple choices.
- While dependency characterizes infancy, and self-initiative develops slightly later (initiative vs. guilt stage), autonomy is the hallmark trait as they strive to do things on their own and gain confidence in their abilities.

58. Hall and Midgley proposed three approaches to social policy:

A. Statist Approach: State assumes primary responsibility for welfare.

B. Enterprise Approach: Private sector and market-led solutions dominate.

C. Populist Approach: Emphasizes popular movements and public participation.

D. Reciprocal Approach is not part of their framework.

59.
- Patch-based work refers to assigning small, defined geographic areas ("patches") to individual social workers for intensive, locally responsive services.

- This concept was popularised by the Barclay Committee Report (1982, UK), which examined the organisation of social work and recommended community-oriented, localized practice.

60. • The One Stop Centre Scheme, also known as Sakhi Centres, provides integrated support and assistance to women affected by violence, offering medical, legal, and counselling services under one roof.

- It is funded through the Nirbhaya Fund, which was established by the Government of India in 2013 to enhance safety and security for women.

61. Under the Society's Registration Act, 1860, the Memorandum of Association (MoA) must include:

- Name of the Society (its legal identity).
- Address and occupation of governors or governing body members (basic details of responsible persons).
- Objects of the Society (purpose and scope of work).

A certified copy of the rules signed by only one governing member is not incorporated in the MoA—it requires signatures from multiple members or all founders, not a single signatory.

62. The Nominal Group Technique (NGT) is a face-to-face group decision-making method. Members independently write down their ideas, share them in turn, discuss for clarification, and then privately rank or vote on them. It pools judgements systematically while maintaining independence, avoiding domination by vocal participants.

63. The Behaviourist approach in social work is based on learning theory, which holds that behaviour is shaped by external stimuli and reinforcements. Social workers use behaviour modification, reinforcement, and conditioning techniques to help clients learn adaptive behaviours. The other options relate to physiology, memory theory, or psychoanalytic causation, which are not core to behaviourism.

64. STEP stands for Support to Training and Employment Programme for Women. It provides skills training, capacity building, and employment opportunities for women to become self-reliant. It is a Government of India initiative under the Ministry of Women and Child Development to empower disadvantaged women.

65. According to Leadbeater, Bartlett, and Gallagher, in implementing the personalization agenda in social care, social workers must act as:

A. Advisor: Guiding service users about available options and rights.

B. Service Provider: Delivering or coordinating services tailored to individual needs.

C. Designer of Social Care: Customising and co-producing care solutions with clients.

D. Change Agent is not identified by them in this context, so the correct set is A, B, and C only.

66. The Fundamental Duties were introduced by the 42nd Constitutional Amendment Act, 1976. Following the recommendations of the Swaran Singh Committee, these duties (Article 51A) remind citizens to respect the Constitution, cherish noble ideals, protect sovereignty and integrity, and safeguard public property.

67. Field Work Domains and Focus Areas:

A. Group Conference → II. Learning from experiences of others: Group conferences enable collaborative discussion where students benefit from peer insights.

B. Individual Conference → I. Learning needs of an individual: Individual meetings address a student's personal learning requirements.

C. Evaluation → IV. Totality of learning outcomes: Evaluation measures the comprehensive learning gained through fieldwork.

D. Recording → III. Organization and presentation of reflection and actions: Proper recording ensures experiences are documented and analyzed systematically.

68. The concept of social welfare in Indian philosophy connects with:

A. Purusarth: The four aims of life guiding harmonious living.

B. Bhakti: Devotion fostering moral values and empathy.

C. **Dharma:** Righteous duty ensuring societal harmony.

These three collectively inform welfare-oriented action. D. Mutual Understanding is valuable but not classically cited as a formal principle.

69. The incorrect year here is Tata Institute of Social Sciences, 1939. TISS was actually established earlier, in 1936, as the Sir Dorabji Tata Graduate School of Social Work. The other years—Madras (1952), Baroda (1949), Delhi (1946)—are correct.

70. SFBT expands to Solution-Focused Brief Therapy, a short-term, goal-directed counselling method developed by Steve de Shazer and Insoo Kim Berg. It emphasises clients' strengths, resources, and future possibilities rather than problem analysis, using techniques like scaling questions and identifying exceptions to support rapid positive change.

71. Content Analysis is a research method for systematically coding and interpreting textual, visual, or audio content. Its advantages include flexibility, ability to handle large datasets, and application to diverse material types. However, it also has clear disadvantages:

C. Impossible to devise coding manuals: Designing a coding manual that is exhaustive, unbiased, and universally applicable is extremely challenging. Different coders may interpret categories differently, leading to inconsistency.

D. Difficult to ascertain the answers to 'why' questions: Content analysis mainly describes what is present in the content, not why it is there. It cannot easily uncover motives, causes, or underlying psychological processes behind the data.

A (Concerned with both Textual and Visual Materials) and B (Flexibility) are actually strengths, not disadvantages.

72. The seminal book "Social Diagnosis" (1917) was authored by Mary Ellen Richmond, widely recognised as the pioneer of professional social work casework. In this work:

- She developed a systematic framework for assessing clients' situations.
- She formalised casework methods, shifting social work from charity-based assistance to a professional, evidence-based practice.
- The book emphasised understanding clients' environmental and social contexts—an innovation that laid the foundation for modern social work practice.

73. In NVivo, a qualitative data analysis software:

- Nodes are the points or categories where coding is applied. They act as containers for themes, ideas, or concepts, enabling researchers to organise and analyse qualitative data.
- Researchers highlight portions of text, images, or media and "code" them to a node representing a particular idea.
- This allows NVivo to collate all instances coded under the same node, making it easier to identify patterns, relationships, and emerging themes.
- Models, bibliographical data, and memos are other NVivo features but do not represent the primary coding route.

74. The proper sequence of sampling stages in ascending order:

C. Define the Target Population: Determine the group or population of interest (e.g., all high school teachers in a city).

A. Determine the Sampling Frame: Identify a concrete list or source (e.g., a registry of teachers) from which to select participants.

B. Choose the Sampling Technique: Decide the method—probability sampling (random, stratified) or non-probability sampling (convenience, quota).

D. Select the Sample: Draw the actual participants based on the chosen technique.

This order reflects the logical steps to ensure representativeness and reduce sampling errors.

75. Launch order of schemes by the Ministry of Women and Child Development:

A. Swadhar Greh Scheme (2002): Provides shelter, food, clothing, and support services for women in difficult circumstances such as widows, trafficked women, or survivors of violence.

B. Beti Bachao Beti Padhao (2015): Initiated to address the declining Child Sex Ratio and promote education for the girl child through advocacy and multi-sectoral action.

D. **Mahila Shakti Kendra (2017):** Launched to empower rural women through community participation, training, and access to information about government schemes.

C. **Pradhan Mantri Matru Vandana Yojana (2017 but rolled out after MSK announcement):** Provides maternity benefit cash assistance to improve the health of pregnant and lactating mothers.

The chronological order of launch is A → B → D → C, aligning with historical rollouts and official notifications.

76. The book "Text of the Hindu Law" was authored by Mahadev Govind Ranade, a 19th-century Indian social reformer, scholar, and judge. Ranade advocated for social reforms such as widow remarriage, women's education, and the eradication of caste discrimination. His work on Hindu law reflected a progressive interpretation of scriptures to support social change and modern legal reforms.

77. Regarding NITI Aayog's approach and structure:

A. **Holistic Approach:** NITI Aayog integrates economic, social, and environmental goals for inclusive and sustainable development, unlike the Planning Commission's top-down approach.

B. **Research Wing:** It has a dedicated research unit to provide high-quality policy analysis and innovation.

C. **Reciprocal Wing:** No such wing exists.

D. **Democratic Approach:** While NITI Aayog works cooperatively with states (cooperative federalism), "democratic approach" is not cited as a formal structural feature.

Hence, A and B only are correct.

78. Critical thinking involves objectivity, evaluating evidence, exploring alternatives, and contextual awareness. Relying on a single assertion for unstructured problems contradicts critical thinking principles, which demand multiple perspectives and rigorous analysis. Therefore, option 3 is not a characteristic of critical thinking.

79. Stages of policy formulation in correct chronological order:

D. **Problem recognition and problem definition:** Identifying and clearly defining the issue.

A. **Agenda Setting:** Placing the identified issue on the policy agenda for government action.

B. **Policy formulation and decision-making:** Designing and selecting suitable policies.

E. **Execution or enforcement of a policy:** Implementing the chosen policy.

C. **Feedback, evaluation, and termination:** Assessing outcomes, making adjustments, or discontinuing the policy.

80. Themes of World Social Work Day by year:

A. **Respecting diversity through joint social action → II. 2023** – Celebrated diversity and collective responsibility.

B. **Co-building a new eco-social world: Leaving no one behind → III. 2022** – Focused on inclusive and sustainable societies.

C. **Buen Vivir: Shared Future for transformative change → IV. 2024** – Highlighted the Latin American concept of collective well-being.

D. **Strengthening inter-generational solidarity for enduring well-being → I. 2025** – Emphasized cooperation across generations for sustainable futures.

Correct Matching: A-II, B-III, C-IV, D-I.

81. Talcott Parsons described society as a system where social order and life depend on mutual advantage, peaceful cooperation, and commitment to common values. He viewed societies as stable when members share values and work collaboratively. Mutual hostility is the opposite of his structural functionalist perspective and therefore does not represent his view of social order.

82. The Sustainable Development Goal 16 (SDG 16) ensures "Peace, Justice and Strong Institutions." It focuses on reducing violence, ensuring access to justice, combating corruption, and building accountable institutions at all levels. SDG 15 addresses life on land, SDG 13 addresses climate action, and SDG 12 is about responsible consumption and production.

83. The ascending order of stages in Social Action is:

D. **Scientific analysis or research on the social problem:** Begin by understanding and researching the issue.

B. **Awareness is generated regarding various aspects of the problem:** Educate and sensitize people about the problem's significance.

A. **Organizing people for coordinated and directed intervention:** Mobilize the community for collective action.

C. **Development of strategies to achieve the goals:** Formulate concrete strategies for intervention and change.

84. The Strength-based practice in social work was propounded by Dennis Saleebey. This approach emphasises clients' strengths, resources, and potential rather than focusing on deficits or problems. Saleebey's method empowers individuals and communities, fostering resilience and positive change through collaborative relationships.

85. According to Abraham Flexner, social casework principles include:

- **Acceptance:** Respecting the client's dignity.
- **Client's Self-Determination:** Allowing clients to make choices regarding their lives.
- **Individualization:** Treating each client as unique with specific needs.

The Principle of Communication is not listed among Flexner's classic principles of casework, making it the incorrect option here.

86. Key administrative tasks arranged in ascending (logical) order:

A. **Development of Plans:** First, objectives and strategies are created.

D. **Departmentalisation:** Next, tasks are grouped into departments to implement the plan.

B. **Recruitment & Appointment:** Staff are then recruited and appointed for roles.

E. **Coordination:** Efforts and activities are coordinated among departments to ensure harmony.

C. **Preparation of Budget:** Finally, budgets are prepared and aligned with ongoing coordination and monitoring.

87. Match the sex-related psychological terms with definitions:

A. **Electra Complex → III.** Sexual desire of daughter towards her father.

B. **Diana Complex → IV.** Psychological reaction found among young females.

C. **Anlagen → I.** Genetic pre-disposition.

D. **Oedipus Complex → II.** Sexual desire of son towards his mother.

88. The National Commission for Minorities was given statutory status in 1992 through the National Commission for Minorities Act, 1992. Before this, it existed as a non-statutory body since 1978. The statutory status strengthened its authority to protect minority rights and advise the government on minority welfare.

89. Correct Matching of Trade Union Progress with Years:

A. **Era of formation of Modern Trade Unionism → III. 1918–1924:** This phase followed World War I and saw the rise of nationalist movements in India. It marked the beginning of modern trade unionism with the establishment of the All India Trade Union Congress (AITUC) in 1920, making organized labour a significant force.

B. **Split in AITUC into Leftist & Rightist wings → IV. 1925–1934:** During this period, ideological differences emerged within AITUC. The communist and socialist factions pushed for radical action, while moderates preferred constitutional methods, causing a major split. This resulted in the creation of bodies like the All India Trade Union Federation (AITUF) by moderates and the Red Trade Union Congress (RTUC) by communists.

C. **Unity forged among Trade Unions → I. 1935–1938:** Efforts were made to unify the fragmented trade unions. The previously divided factions—AITUC, NTUF, and others—reconciled during this period, leading to greater solidarity and a stronger labour movement.

D. **World War II brought chaos in Industrial Relations → II. 1939–1946:** The Second World War created economic instability, rising prices, and worsening labour conditions. Strikes and agitations became common, and the government increased its involvement in industrial relations through tripartite consultations to manage unrest.

90. Selecting every 10th name in a list is a classic example of Systematic Sampling. This method involves choosing subjects at regular intervals (kth element) from an ordered list after a random starting point. It ensures even coverage and is simpler than simple random sampling.

91. Reliability refers to the consistency and stability of measurement over time or across conditions. It is enhanced through pretesting, pilot studies, and consistent measurement procedures. Merely relying on the experience of the researcher does not guarantee reliability; systematic checks and controls are essential.

92. Triangulation in research means using multiple tools, theories, or methods to cross-verify findings for greater validity. It is not limited to "only three" tools—the term "triangulation" metaphorically derives from geometry, not a literal count of three.

93. Among data-collection methods for behavioural sciences, observation is the most appropriate for avoiding subjective bias. The passage highlights that accurate observation eliminates subjective bias and provides current, real-time data, unlike interviews or questionnaires which may introduce respondent bias or recall errors.

94. In qualitative research, events, artifacts, and situations are recorded using tools like focused group discussions, field diaries, or interviews, which capture rich, contextual data. A scale is a quantitative measurement tool, not typically used for recording qualitative phenomena.

95.
- Fully structured tools include interview schedules, attitude scales, and checklists, which follow fixed formats and standardised questions.
- An interview guide is semi-structured or flexible: it provides broad topics or questions but allows probing and open-ended responses. Therefore, it is not a fully structured tool.

96. In social casework, counter transference refers to any subjective emotional involvement on the part of the caseworker with the client or the client's problem. It occurs when the helper's own unconscious feelings and past experiences influence their reactions toward the client. To remain effective, the worker must be self-aware and manage these personal responses to maintain professional boundaries.

97. The passage explains that an adolescent girl may begin to feel toward the worker as she felt toward her mother or grandmother from childhood. This is the essence of transference:
- Transference occurs when a client projects feelings, attitudes, or desires from significant early relationships onto the caseworker.
- It involves emotionally charged childhood experiences influencing adult behaviour and the professional relationship.
- The client unconsciously replays past emotional patterns with the helper, seeking parental-like nurture or approval.

98. The passage emphasizes that the caseworker must remain objective and aware of their own feelings. Counter transference is the most fitting term: it warns professionals against letting personal emotions and biases distort their judgement or interfere with their work. By recognizing and managing counter transference, caseworkers maintain professionalism and effective support.

99. Transference reactions are directed toward the caseworker. Clients may unconsciously treat the caseworker as they once treated a parent or significant figure, expecting nurturing or control beyond the professional relationship's realistic limits. This emotional redirection forms the core of transference dynamics in casework.

100. In social casework, regression means reverting to earlier, less mature behaviours—often seeking parental-like care or displaying dependency when overwhelmed. When clients cannot cope with irrational feelings (e.g., strong emotional needs or frustrations) toward the helper, they may regress to a childlike state, desiring parental nurture or domination, as described in the passage.

Previous Years' Paper

National Testing Agency (NTA)

UGC-NET Junior Research Fellowship & Assistant Professor Eligibility Exam

SOCIAL WORK, JANUARY-2025

(Exam held on 08-01-2025)

PAPER-II

1. Arrange the following day's at international importance as per their months in descending orders.

A. World Environment Day
B. International Day of Peace
C. World Health Day
D. World AIDS Day
E. World Social Work Day

Choose the **correct** answer from the options given below:

1. A, B, C, D, E
2. C, E, B, D, A
3. B, A, D, C, E
4. D, B, A, C, E

2. Match the LIST-I with LIST-II

LIST-I (Book)	LIST-II (Author)
A. Community Welfare Organisation	I. H.Y. Siddiqui
B. The Division of Labour in Society	II. Dunham Arthur
C. Community Organisation	III. Murray Ross
D. Social Work and Social Action	IV. Durkheim

Choose the **correct** answer from the options given below:

1. A-II, B-III, C-IV, D-I
2. A-II, B-IV, C-III, D-I
3. A-I, B-II, C-III, D-IV
4. A-III, B-II, C-I, D-IV

3. Social Group Work is a method that uses groups as a .... to achieve an end.

1. Tool
2. Medium
3. Technique
4. Ladder/Subject

4. The full form of RTE Act 2009 is:

1. The Right to Free Education Act, 2009
2. The Right of Children to Free and Compulsory Education Act, 2009
3. The Right to Education Act, 2009
4. The Children's Right to Free Education Act, 2009

5. Which are the basic of three equally weighted dimensions of the National Multidimensional Poverty Index?

1. Health, Education and Life Expectancy
2. Health, Education and Per Capita Income
3. Health, Education and Standard of Living
4. Health, Life Expectancy and Standard of Living

6. What are essential elements of Social Welfare Administration under the POSDCoRB?

A. Budgeting
B. Co-operating
C. Staffing
D. Organizing
E. Coordinating

Choose the **correct** answer from the options given below:

1. A, B, C and D only
2. A, C, D and E only
3. B, C, D and E only
4. A, B, D and E only

7. Organize the five stages of implementation of Solution-Focused Brief Therapy in proper order.

A. Service users briefly describe the problem while moving them towards solution oriented talk.

B. Service users described their preferred future in order to develop well-formulated goals

C. Exploration of the problem by identifying times when service users are not experiencing the problems or when they are, to some extent, achieving their goal

D. Provision of end-of-session feedback by identifying what service users are already doing well and linking this to suggestions.

E. Evaluation of service users progress.

Choose the **correct** answer from the options given below:

1. D, B, A, C, E
2. A, C, B, D, E
3. B, D, A, C, E
4. A, B, C, D, E

8. Arrange the following in the order of the year of their promulgation.

A. Right to Education Act
B. Forest Rights Act
C. Right to Information Act
D. National Food Security Act

Choose the **correct** answer from the options given below:

1. C, A, D, B
2. B, D, C, A
3. A, D, C, B
4. C, B, A, D

9. Empathy in social work practice is:

1. Diagnostic understanding of the client
2. Evaluate understanding of the client
3. An understanding with the client
4. Related to verbal and facial expressions of the client

10. Six sigma deployment in HR aims at ....

A. Emphasis on turnover
B. Improving the effectiveness of process
C. Promote employment
D. Solving the problem by collecting date
E. Using statistical thinking

Choose the **correct** answer from the options given below:

1. B, D and E only
2. A, D and E only
3. C, D and E only
4. A, B and C only

11. Whose concept of 'self development' has been termed as "looking-glass self" concept?

1. Charles Cooley 2. Me Dougallas
3. G. H. Mead 4. Sigmond Freud

12. Match the LIST-I with LIST-II.

LIST-I (Agency)	LIST-II (Concern)
A. UNHCR	I. Peace and Sustainable Development
B. UNOPS	II. Disarmament Research
C. UNIDIR	III. Palestine Refugees
D. UNRWA	IV. Refugees

Choose the **correct** answer from the options given below:

1. A-IV, B-I, C-III, D-II
2. A-IV, B-I, C-II, D-III
3. A-IV, B-III, C-I, D-II
4. A-II, B-IV, C-III, D-I

13. One of the major function of NITI Ayog is:

1. Allocation of finance to states
2. Monitoring of centre state relations

3. Monitoring of SDGs
4. Review the functioning of local self governments

14. Arrange the following in the order of first promulgation.

A. The Unorganized Workers Social Security Act
B. Maternity Benefit Act
C. Workmen's Compensation Act
D. Payment of Gratuity Act
E. The Indian Companies Act

Choose the **correct** answer from the options given below:

1. D, B, E, A, C
2. C, B, D, A, E
3. C, B, E, A, D
4. B, C, E, A, D

15. "Vertical mobility" refers to movement in any or all of three areas of living, which are as follows:

A. Class, occupation and power
B. Dressing, food habits and physical activities
C. Physical activities, Education and warmth
D. Education, good health and dressing
E. Occupation, power and social class

Choose the **correct** answer from the options given below:

1. B and C only
2. A and E only
3. B and E only
4. C and D only

16. Paraphrasing is a technique which is normally used in:

1. Social work research
2. Counselling
3. Group dynamics
4. Reflective discussion

17. The .... encourages the individuals to visualize their world without the problems they currently face and is often found in the tool kit of solution focused practitioners.

1. Mission statement
2. SMART goal
3. Problem free talk
4. Miracle question

18. Match the LIST-I with LIST-II.

	LIST-I (Programme)		LIST-II (Objective)
A.	Poshan Abhiyan (National Nutrition Mission)	I.	Financial incentives for the education of girl children
B.	National Crech Scheme	II.	Day care service to children of working mothers
C.	Balika Sammridhi Yojna	III.	Holistic development and adequate nutrition of children
D.	Rastriya Kishore Swasthya Karyakram (RKSK)	IV.	Comprehensive health service for adolescent

Choose the **correct** answer from the options given below:

1. A-III, B-II, C-I, D-IV
2. A-IV, B-II, C-I, D-III
3. A-III, B-IV, C-II, D-I
4. A-III, B-I, C-II, D-IV

19. Which schemes/programmes for youth are merged into a new umbrella scheme "Rashtriya Yuva Sashaktiran Karyakram"?

A. National Service Scheme (NSS)
B. National Youth Corps (NYC)
C. National Programme for Youth & Adolescent Development (NPYAD)
D. National Young Leaders Programme Development (NYLPD)

Choose the **correct** answer from the options given below:

1. A, B & C only
2. A, B & D only
3. B, C & D only
4. A, C and D only

20. Match the LIST-I with LIST-II.

LIST-I (Act/Law)	LIST-II (Concerned Provision)
A. FCRA, 2010	I. Public servants declare their assets to the MoHA
B. Section 12 AA, IT Act, 1961	II. Donors tax deduction
C. Section 80C, IT Act, 1961	III. Receiving foreign fund
D. Section 44, The Lokpal and Lokayukts Act, 2013	IV. Grant tax exemption states

Choose the **correct** answer from the options given below:

1. A-III, B-IV, C-II, D-I
2. A-III, B-IV, C-I, D-II
3. A-III, B-II, C-I, D-IV
4. A-III, B-II, C-IV, D-I

21. Social welfare does not address:

1. General wellbeing
2. Needs of individuals
3. Universal needs of the population
4. Personal needs of the population

22. Social Awareness and Actions to Neutralize Pneumonia Successfully (SAANS) was launched in the year?

1. 2022   2. 2018
3. 2020   4. 2019

23. Which is the strength of an agency in fund raising?

1. More emphasis on cash
2. Devoted and dedicated staff for the activities of agency
3. Absence of proper public relations
4. Lack of tapping of new resources

24. Arrange the basic human needs placed by Maslow in an ascending order of importance.

A. Safety needs
B. Physiological needs
C. Need for self actualization
D. Esteem needs
E. Affiliation or Acceptance needs

Choose the **correct** answer from the options given below:

1. A, B, C, D, E
2. B, A, C, D, E
3. A, B, D, E, C
4. B, A, E, D, C

25. Which statement is not correct about Criminal Justice Social Work (CJSW)?

1. CJSW aims to reduce unnecessary prison sentences
2. CJSW provides several services such as police social work, probation and rehabilitation
3. CJSW is equal to police social work, correctional social work and forensic social work
4. CJSW is an over arching concept providing space to social workers to play multiple roles

26. Arrange the words below as mentioned in the preamble of the Constitution of India.

A. Justice
B. Fraternity
C. Equality
D. Liberty

Choose the **correct** answer from the options given below:

1. C, A, B, D
2. B, D, C, A
3. A, C, B, D
4. A, D, C, B

27. Which are the principles of the present Convention on the Rights of Persons with Disabilities?

A. Non-discriminations
B. Financial support
C. Equality of opportunity

D. Preferential treatment
E. Full and effective participation

Choose the **correct** answer from the options given below:

1. A, B & C only
2. B, C & D only
3. A, C & E only
4. A, C, D & E only

28. Which are the types of basic mixed method design?

A. Explanatory sequential design
B. Exploratory sequential design
C. Embebbed design
D. Convergent parallel design
E. Concurrent design

Choose the **correct** answer from the options given below:

1. A, B, C and D only
2. A, C, D and E only
3. A, D, E and B only
4. A, E, B and C only

29. Which theory argues that because inequality between men and women is due to patriarchy, a complete new system is needed to address this?

1. Radical Feminism
2. Black Feminism
3. Socialist Feminism
4. Marxist Feminism

30. Match the LIST-I with LIST-II.

LIST-I (Plan)	LIST-II (Main Point)
A. Third Five Year Plan	I. Target of 9% GDP Growth
B. Eighth Five Year Plan	II. Structural Adjustment Program
C. Ninth Five Year Plan	III. Self Sufficient in Food Grains
D. Twelfth Five Year Plan	IV. Basic Minimum Services

Choose the **correct** answer from the options given below:

1. A-III, B-I, C-IV, D-II
2. A-IV, B-II, C-III, D-I
3. A-IV, B-III, C-II, D-I
4. A-III, B-II, C-IV, D-I

31. Match the LIST-I with LIST-II.

LIST-I (Stages)	LIST-II (Task)
A. Oral (0-18 months)	I. Industry vs Inferiority
B. Anal (18 months to 3 years)	II. Initiative vs Guilt
C. Pre-School (3-5 years)	III. Autonomy vs Shame
D. Middle School (6-11 years)	IV. Trust vs Mistrust

Choose the **correct** answer from the options given below:

1. A-IV, B-III, C-II, D-I
2. A-I, B-II, C-III, D-IV
3. A-II, B-IV, C-III, D-I
4. A-III, B-I, C-IV, D-II

32. In 19th century, who among the social reformers was considered as pioneer of modern social work?

1. Iswar Chandra Vidyasagar
2. Raja Ram Mohan Roy
3. Jyotiba Phule
4. Swami Dayanant Saraswati

33. Growth and development depends on the combination of the factors which are:

A. Hereditary factors
B. Environmental factors
C. Structural factors
D. Happiness factors
E. Endocrine factors

Choose the **correct** answer from the options given below:

1. A, B and E only
2. C, D and E only
3. A, C and D only
4. B, C and D only

34. Match the LIST-I with LIST-II.

LIST-I (Theory/ Model)	LIST-II (Emphasis of Application)
A. Tasks Centered theory	I. Identifying internal/ external resources
B. Strengths Perspective	II. Assessing transactions of person in environment
C. Problem Solving theory	III. Supporting goal accomplishment
D. Ecological Perspective	IV. Facilitating problem resolution

Choose the **correct** answer from the options given below:

1. A-I, B-III, C-II, D-IV
2. A-III, B-IV, C-II, D-I
3. A-III, B-I, C-IV, D-II
4. A-IV, B-III, C-I, D-II

35. Arrange the stages of self-directed group work practice model.

A. Pre planning
B. Taking action
C. Taking off
D. Group preparation for action
E. Taking over

Choose the **correct** answer from the options given below:

1. A, B, C, E, D
2. A, B, D, C, E
3. A, C, D, B, E
4. A, C, E, B, D

36. Who initiated the first training program for social group workers at the School of Applied Social Sciences, Ohio?

1. W.R. Bion
2. Melanic Klein
3. Octavia Hill
4. Grace Coyle

37. Which of the Sustainable Development Goal (SDG) relates to maternal health?

1. SDG 1
2. SDG 3
3. SDG 8
4. SDG 5

38. All organization turn inputs into outputs regardless of their nature and style. This approach developed by John Woodward and Charles Perrow is known as:

1. Human Relation Approach
2. Institutional Approach
3. Technological Approach
4. Scientific Method Approach

39. Which are the characteristics of ratio level of measurement?

A. It is the highest level of measurement.
B. An equal distance between units will be found.
C. Variable is classified into several nominal sub-classes.
D. The zero point is absolute in ratio measurement.
E. Determine less than or greater than relationship between units.

Choose the **correct** answer from the options given below:

1. A and B only
2. A, B and C only
3. B, D, and E only
4. A and D only

40. Match the LIST-I with LIST-II.

LIST-I (Global Index)	LIST-II (Agency)
A. Global Hunger Index	I. Transparency International
B. Global Innovation Index	II. Institute of Economic & Peace
C. Global Peace Index	III. World Intellectual Property Organisation
D. Corruption Perception Index	IV. Concern World Wide & Others

Choose the **correct** answer from the options given below:

1. A-I, B-II, C-III, D-IV
2. A-II, B-III, C-IV, D-I
3. A-III, B-IV, C-I, D-II
4. A-IV, B-III, C-II, D-I

41. Values encompassed in NASW Code of Ethics are:

A. Service
B. Social justice
C. Solidarity
D. Dignity and worth of the person
E. Integrity

Choose the **correct** answer from the options given below:

1. B, C, D and E only
2. A, B, C and D only
3. A, B, C and E only
4. A, B, D and E only

42. A research problem, in generally refers to:

1. Ready solution to difficulty
2. Some difficulty experience by the research in finding the solution
3. No difficulty experience by the researcher
4. Researcher's desire not want to obtain solution

43. Match the LIST-I with LIST-II.

LIST-I (Act)	LIST-II (Year)
A. The Protection of Children from Sexual Offence Act.	I. 2005
B. The Environment (Protection) Act.	II. 2016
C. Rights of Persons with Disabilities Act.	III. 1986
D. Protection of Women from Domestic Violence Act.	IV. 2012

Choose the **correct** answer from the options given below:

1. A-IV, B-III, C-II, D-I
2. A-I, B-II, C-IV, D-III
3. A-III, B-IV, C-I, D-II
4. A-II, B-I, C-III, D-IV

44. Which one is not the feature of rural community?

1. Community consciousness
2. Faith in religion
3. Role of neighbourhood
4. Energy and speed

45. What we get if we add measurement errors or non-sampling error to sampling error?

1. Total error
2. Frame error
3. Chance error
4. Response error

46. On which report the reservation of Other Backward Classes was implemented?

1. First Backward Classes Commission
2. Second Backward Classes Commission
3. Third Backward Classes Commission
4. Other Backward Classes Welfare Commission

47. Match the LIST-I with LIST-II.

LIST-I (Statistical Test)	LIST-II (Test)
A. Dispersion	I. Wilcoxon Test
B. Measure of Association	II. Rank Correlation
C. Test of Difference	III. Mean Deviation
D. Non-Parametric Test of Association	IV. One-Way Analysis of Variance

Choose the **correct** answer from the options given below:

1. A-III, B-II, C-IV, D-I
2. A-III, B-IV, C-I, D-II
3. A-III, B-I, C-II, D-IV
4. A-IV, B-II, C-III, D-I

48. The conception of the public interest of social planning model is:

1. Rationalist unitary
2. Idealist unitary
3. Realist-Individualist
4. Individualist

49. The United Nations Framework Convention on Climate Change (UNFCCC) enters into force in 1994 and the Kyoto Protocol was formally adopted as COP 3 in the year …………

1. 1994
2. 1995
3. 1996
4. 1997

50. What are the characteristics of Gender based budgeting?

A. It was introduced by Ministry of Women.
B. It is a tool for gender mainstreaming.
C. It involves various economic policies of the government from a gender perspective.
D. It is not about targeting program specifically of women and girls.
E. Its is a separate budget for women.

Choose the **correct** answer from the options given below:

1. A, B and C only
2. A, C and D only
3. B, C and D only
4. B, D and E only

51. Which is the type of Modern Organization Theory?

1. Scientific Management Theory
2. Bureaucratic Theory
3. Behavioural Theory
4. Fayol and Classical Theory

52. Arrange the following steps in social action process.

A. Development of suitable organization
B. Formulating and Projecting the goals
C. Development of consensus
D. Developing awareness among people
E. Actual action

Choose the **correct** answer from the options given below:

1. A, C, D, B, E
2. B, A, C, D, E
3. D, A, B, C, E
4. C, B, A, D, E

53. Which are considered as communicable diseases?

A. Tuberculosis
B. HIV (AIDS)
C. Cancer
D. Leprosy
E. Diabetes

Choose the **correct** answer from the options given below:

1. A, B and C only
2. B, C and D only
3. C, D and E only
4. A, B and D only

54. Following are the steps in testing of hypotheses. Arrange them in proper order.

A. Specify the significance level
B. Choose the stastical test
C. Compute the stastical test
D. Formulate the Null Hypothesis
E. Reject/Accept the Null Hypothesis

Choose the **correct** answer from the options given below:

1. D, B, C, A, E
2. B, A, E, C, D
3. D, B, A, C, E
4. D, A, B, C, E

55. Abduction of death penalty is an optional protocol of:

1. Convention against Torture and Other Cruel, Inhuman or Degrading Treatment or Punishment
2. International Covenant or Civil and Political Rights
3. Universal Declaration of Human Rights
4. International Covenant on Economic Social and Cultural Rights

56. Forming a group of elderly is comparatively easier as the elders are:

A. Keen to participate meaningfully in group activities.
B. Participating group activity that gives them sense of purpose
C. Looking for place to meet other people.
D. Available and have more time on their hand
E. Experienced and expert in social relations.

Choose the **correct** answer from the options given below:

1. A, B and C only
2. B, C, D and E
3. A, B, C and D
4. B, C and D only

57. The school of social work at Indira Gandhi National Open University through distance learning programme was established on:

1. August 16, 2007
2. July 01, 2001
3. July 14, 2014
4. August 01, 2004

58. Which of the following countries abstained from voting while adopting the Universal Declaration of Human Rights, 1948?

1. China
2. Afghanistan
3. India
4. South Africa

59. The process whereby a researcher provides the people on whom he or she has conducted research with an account of his or her finding is called as:

1. Triangulation
2. Reliability
3. Respondent validation
4. Reflexivity

60. What does not constitute a feature of social development?

1. Harmonisation of social and economic development policies
2. Welfare pluralism
3. Multi dimensional conception of wellbeing
4. Equal opportunities for all

61. Who uses the phrase 'consciousness raising'?

1. J. F. Longers
2. Mitchell Julliel
3. Paulo Freire
4. Lance Morrow

62. Arrange the following Acts/Policy as per their enforcement year in increasing order.

A. Wild Life Protection Act
B. National Forest Policy
C. Biological Diversity Act
D. Forest Rights Act
E. Environment Protection Act

Choose the **correct** answer from the options given below:

1. A, E, B, C, D
2. A, B, C, D, E
3. B, A, C, D, E
4. B, A, D, E, C

63. Arrange the following legislations related to governance of non-profit organizations in India from latest to oldest.

A. Society Registration Act
B. The Indian Companies Act
C. The Indian Public Trust Act
D. Foreign Contribution Regulation Act

Choose the **correct** answer from the options given below:

1. A, B, C, D
2. B, D, C, A
3. C, B, D, A
4. D, C, B, A

64. Match the LIST-I with LIST-II.

	LIST-I (PM Scheme)		LIST-II (Concerned Ministry)
A.	Pradhan Mantri Shram Yogi Maan Dhan Yojana	I.	Ministry of Finance
B.	Pradhan Mantri Street Vendors Atma Nirbhar Nidhi (PM Swa Nidhi)	II.	Ministry of Skill Development and Entrepreneurship
C.	Pradhan Mantri Garib Kalyan Yojana (PMGKY)	III.	Ministry of Labour & Employment
D.	Pradhan Mantri Kaushal Vikas Yojana	IV.	Ministry of Housing and Urban Affairs

Choose the **correct** answer from the options given below:

1. A-II, B-III, C-IV, D-I
2. A-I, B-IV, C-III, D-II
3. A-III, B-IV, C-I, D-II
4. A-II, B-III, C-I, D-IV

65. Which is a specialized agency under the United Nations System dealing with human rights?

1. International Labour Organisation
2. Economic and Social Council
3. International Court of Justice
4. UNICEF

66. Who are the authors/writers associated with Social Group Work?

A. Konopka B. Mary Richmond
C. Grace Mathew D. Geinsberg
E. Klien

Choose the **correct** answer from the options given below:

1. A, D & E only
2. A, B & C only
3. A, C & D only
4. A, B & D only

67. What are the stages in the policy development?

A. Problem identification and agenda setting
B. Social analysis
C. Policy formulation and adoption
D. Policy implementation
E. Evaluation

Choose the **correct** answer from the options given below:

1. B, C and D only
2. B, C, D and E only
3. A, C, D and E only
4. A, B, C and D only

68. Which term has been newly added in the most recent definition of social work given by International Federation of Social Workers (IFSW) and International Association of Schools of Social Work (IASSW)?

1. Collective responsibility
2. Human rights
3. Social justice
4. Equality

69. Match the LIST-I with LIST-II.

LIST-I (Book)	LIST-II (Author)
A. Social Process in Organised Groups (1930)	I. Tom Douglas
B. A Social Psychology of Group Process for Decision Making (1964)	II. Grace Coyle
C. Group Process is Social Work : A Theoretical Synthesis (1979)	III. Collins Barry & Harold Guetzkow
D. Groups in Social Work (1972)	IV. Hartford, M. E

Choose the **correct** answer from the options given below:

1. A-II, B-I, C-III, D-IV
2. A-III, B-II, C-IV, D-I
3. A-II, B-III, C-I, D-IV
4. A-III, B-IV, C-II, D-I

70. Family Psycho-Education Intervention Approach has been used extensively in addressing the issues related to:

1. Rehabilitation
2. Schizophrenia
3. Bipolar disorder
4. Diversity

71. Late Life Ageing is shaped by the accumulation of ....

A. Life events
B. Bad standard of living
C. Malfunctioning
D. Proximity of death
E. Attitude

Choose the **correct** answer from the options given below:

1. A and B only
2. A, C and E only
3. A and D only
4. A, D and E only

72. Arrange the following in the order of their launch.

A. Poshan Abhiyan
B. Sarva Shiksha Abhiyan
C. Unnat Bharat Abhiyan
D. Nirmal Bharat Abhiyan

Choose the **correct** answer from the options given below:

1. B, D, C, A
2. B, A, D, C
3. B, C, A, D
4. D, B, A, C

73. 104th amendment to the Constitution of India deals with:

A. Reservation to economically weaker sections in government jobs.
B. Extend the reservation for SCs and STs in Lok Sabha and State Assemblies for 10 years.
C. Extend the reservation for Other Backward Classes in government jobs.
D. Removed the reservation for Anglo-Indians in the Lok Sabha and State Assemblies.

Choose the **correct** answer from the options given below.

1. B and C only
2. B and D only
3. A and C only
4. B, C and D only

74. Which are the characteristics of Social Work Administration?

A. A method of social work
B. Uni-disciplinary approach
C. Administration of services provided by social workers
D. Use of Right based approach
E. No dependency on the part of people

Choose the **correct** answer from the options given below:

1. A, B, D and E only
2. A, B and E only
3. A, B and C only
4. B, D, C and A only

75. Which is not considered popular social action model?

1. Lok shakti model
2. Conscientization model
3. Dialectical mobilization model
4. Economic sanction model

76. Which is the suitable tool for data collection from primary source in case study?

1. Open ended questions (Interview)
2. News Paper
3. Personal Diary
4. Books

77. Which problems are broadly dealt in case work?

A. Relatively circumscribed problems
B. Relatively severe and pervasive interpersonal and intrapersonal problem
C. Relatively long - term problems
D. Problems resulting from gross material environmental deprivations

Choose the **correct** answer from the options given below:

1. A only
2. A and B only
3. A, B and C only
4. A, B, C and D only

78. Institutionalisation of the older persons may lead to ....

A. Stigmatization
B. The best welfarist care
C. Loss of liberty and dignity
D. Lack of autonomy
E. Empowerment of the aged

Choose the **correct** answer from the options given below:

1. A, B and C only
2. A, C and D only
3. B, C and E only
4. C, D and E only

79. Match the LIST-I with LIST-II.

LIST-I (Five Years Plan)	LIST-II (Based on)
A. First Five Year Plan	I. Mahalanobis model
B. Second Five Year Plan	II. John Sandy and Sukhmoy Chakraborty model
C. Third Five Year Plan	III. Harrod Domer model
D. Fourth Five Year Plan	IV. Gadgil Formula

Choose the **correct** answer from the options given below:

1. A-IV, B-I, C-II, D-III
2. A-II, B-III, C-IV, D-I
3. A-III, B-I, C-II, D-IV
4. A-I, B-II, C-III, D-IV

80. Match the LIST-I with LIST-II.

LIST-I (Practice Models)	LIST-II (Proponent)
A. Cognitive Behaviour Therapy	I. Reid and Laura Epstein
B. Problem Solving Model	II. Michael White and David Epston
C. Task Centered Approach	III. Aaron T. Beck
D. Narrative Therapy	IV. H.H Perlman

Choose the **correct** answer from the options given below:

1. A-III, B-IV, C-I, D-II
2. A-I, B-III, C-IV, D-II
3. A-IV, B-II, C-I, D-III
4. A-II, B-I, C-III, D-IV

81. Hayne's Plan for wages show that:

1. The differential piece-rate system of wages.
2. The standard time for various jobs is determined first by work study.
3. The multiple piece-rate plan of wages.
4. The standard time required for a job is fixed and the wages are paid on time basis.

82. Whose work is considered the foundation of Functionalist theory?

1. Auguste Comte
2. Herbert Spencer
3. Emile Durkheim
4. Charles Cooley

83. Match the LIST-I with LIST-II.

LIST-I (Title)	LIST-II (Author)
A. Social Policy: An Introduction	I. Jim Ife
B. Human Rights and Social Work Towards Right-based Practice	II. Jean Dreze and Amartya Sen
C. Political Economy of Hunger	III. Peter Golding
D. Excluding the poor	IV. Richard Titmuss

Choose the **correct** answer from the options given below:

1. A-IV, B-I, C-II, D-III
2. A-IV, B-II, C-I, D-III
3. A-III, B-I, C-II, D-IV
4. A-IV, B-III, C-I, D-II

84. According to NASW code of ethics, general principles for social workers should strive to:

1. Empowerment of communities
2. Help individuals in distress
3. Eliminate personal and institutional discrimination
4. Create institutional mechanisms for addressing grievances

85. Arrange the following stages of development of a child.

A. Concrete Operation
B. Sensorimotor
C. Preoperational
D. Formal Operations Period

Choose the **correct** answer from the options given below:

1. B, C, A, D
2. A, B, C, D
3. C, D, A, B
4. D, C, A, B

86. The term 'community action' can be defined as:

1. To work with community groups in conflict with authority.
2. A number of activities are under taken in a systematic manner.
3. A type of activity practiced by people.
4. Improving the image of any organization/agency.

87. Arrange the steps of Task Planning Process.

A. Possible alternative task are identified through generating task possibilities
B. An agreement is made
C. Explicitly secured with client
D. Implementation is planned
E. The task is summarized

Choose the **correct** answer from the options given below:

1. A, B, C, D, E
2. A, B, E, D, C
3. A, C, B, D, E
4. A, D, B, E, C

88. According to Koh's primary values of social work are:

A. The worth and dignity of human being
B. Tolerance of Differences
C. Satisfaction of basic human needs
D. Judgemental attitude
E. Self-Direction

Choose the **correct** answer from the options given below:

1. A, B, C & E only
2. A, B, C & D only
3. A, B, D & E only
4. A, C, D & E only

89. Arrange the steps in process of grounded theory in proper order.

A. Research Questions
B. Coding
C. Testing of Hypothesis
D. Constant comparison
E. Collection of data

Choose the **correct** answer from the options given below:

1. A, D, E, B, C
2. A, B, C, D, E
3. A, E, B, D, C
4. A, B, E, D, C

90. Who argued that societies are made up of many different groups with different interests, and these groups are often in conflict, not just in economic terms but also through power and authority?

1. Chales Murray
2. John Henry Hutton
3. Dahrendorf
4. Melvin Marvin Tumin

Directions (Qs. No. 91-95): *Read the following passage and answer the questions below:*

When the Supreme Court exercises its discretionary jurisdiction under Article 136 of the constitution, it is in the order to ensure that there is no miscarriage of justice. If finding of acquittal by high court is found to be misconceived and perverse, this court can quash such order of acquittal under Article 136 of the Constitution. This power is not, however, to be exercised by the Supreme Court so as to entertain an appeal in any case where no appeal is otherwise provided by the law or the Constitution. It is special power which is to be exercised only under exceptional circumstances and the Supreme Court has already laid down the principles according to which this is extraordinary power shall be used, e.g. where there has been a violation of the principles of natural justice. An appeal by special leave is not regular appeal. Merely because a different view is possible on the evidence adduced at the trial is no ground for the court to upset the opinion of the courts below. The court would reappreciate evidence only to find out whether there has been any illegality, material irregularity or miscarriage of justice.

91. In civil cases, a special leave to appeal is granted only when:
1. Lower court failed to appreciate the evidence produced
2. Appellant is aggrieved by the order passed
3. Generally public interest is involved
4. Prosecution fail to produce evidence

92. An appeal by special leave is not a regular appeal because:
1. Supreme Court has a different opinion
2. Appeal is taken by a special bench
3. Supreme Court is upset with the order of the lower court
4. Irregularity of justice is noted

93. Among the following, which does not constitute exceptional circumstances under Article 136?
1. An order of acquittal is seemed perverse
2. Miscarriage of justice
3. When a regular appeal is not entertained by the lower court
4. Principle of natural justice is seen to have violated

94. Reappreciation of evidence is entertained in the event of:
1. Crucial evidence is not collected and produced
2. Hiding or destroying of evidence is noted
3. Any possible illegality is observed
4. Investigating agencies fail to produce crucial evidence

95. Article 136 of the Constitution of India empowers .... to appeal against an order passed by any court.
1. The State   2. Appellant
3. Supreme Court   4. Counite

Directions (Qs. No. 96-100): *Read the following passage and answer the questions below:*

To understand the reasons for why the social sector is lagging in comparison to other sector, it is necessary to understand its nature. In India, the voluntary sector draws its strength from humanitarian values rooted in religious philosophy, with a greater role of social institutions and communities to respond to needy people. The voluntary sector is also synonymous with the people's sector, referred to as the third sector, and more popularly, civil society. It appears to be systematically marginalized by both the market and the Government. The social sector thus become dependent on private charities, and foreign contributions than government grants. With the more improved push of corporate social responsibility (CSR) funds which seem to take on welfare and development programmes, the free market mechanisms are taking over the social sector through specifically design programmes of transferring public services to private sector such as public-private partnerships, user-pay models, performance based contracts etc. The governments, therefore, are relieving themselves from their welfare responsibilities, need not unduly worry about funding or where funding is associated; there appear to be poor statuary mechanisms and limited supports.

96. What role does the voluntary sector play in India's social welfare system?
1. It draws strength from humanitarian values rooted in religious philosophy.
2. It gets government funding and grants

3. It is driven by corporate social responsibility funds
4. It depends on foreign funding

97. What is the impact of growing emphasis on corporate social responsibilities in social sector?
1. Decrease in government support
2. Increased reliance on private charities and foreign contribution
3. Enhance the growth of social sector
4. Strengthened the role of social institutions

98. What is the consequence of the government reduced involvement in welfare responsibilities?
1. A shift of welfare programmes to the private sector through public-private partnership.
2. An increase in statutory mechanisms and support.
3. The government engaging social organizations for welfare.
4. The establishment of stronger welfare laws.

99. How the social sector been affected by market-driven forces?
1. The government has control over the social sector
2. Private sector mechanisms like public-private partnerships have started dominating the social sector
3. The foreign funding is substantially reduced
4. The market has no significant impact on the social sector

100. What is the reason for the lagging development of the social sector in India?
1. Lack of government interest in social welfare programmes
2. The marginalization of the voluntary sector by the market and government.
3. Overreliance on corporate social responsibility funds.
4. Government taking over the social welfare programmes.

ANSWERS

1. (4):
- World AIDS Day is observed on December 1.
- International Day of Peace is celebrated on September 21.
- World Environment Day is observed on June 5.
- World Health Day is celebrated on April 7.
- World Social Work Day is observed in March (generally the third Tuesday of March).

Thus, when arranged by month in descending order (December to March), the order is: D (World AIDS Day - December), B (International Day of Peace - September), A (World Environment Day - June), C (World Health Day - April), and E (World Social Work Day - March).

2. (2):

A. *Community Welfare Organisation* was authored by Dunham Arthur.

B. *The Division of Labour in Society* is a famous work of Émile Durkheim (not Ross Murray, not Dunham Arthur). Durkheim is associated with theories of social structure.

C. *Community Organisation* was authored by Murray Ross, who significantly contributed to the theory and practice of community organization in social work.

D. *Social Work and Social Action* was authored by H.Y. Siddiqui, a renowned Indian social work scholar.

Thus, the correct matching is: A-II, B-IV, C-III, D-I.

3. (2): Social Group Work is a method that uses groups as a Medium to achieve an end. In Social Group Work, the group is used as a dynamic medium through which individual growth, skill development, and social adjustment are achieved. The focus is not only on the group as an entity but on using group processes like cooperation, interaction, and support to bring about individual and social change.

4. (2): The RTE Act 2009 stands for The Right of Children to Free and Compulsory Education Act, 2009. It was enacted by the Parliament of India and came into force on April 1, 2010. It provides for free and compulsory education to all children between the ages of 6 and 14 years. The Act mandates that private schools reserve 25% of seats for children from disadvantaged sections. It makes education a fundamental right under Article 21A of the Constitution of India.

5. (3): The National Multidimensional Poverty Index (MPI) by NITI Aayog is based on three equally weighted dimensions:

1. Health (nutrition, child mortality)
2. Education (years of schooling, school attendance)
3. Standard of Living (indicators like electricity, housing, drinking water, sanitation, cooking fuel, assets).

These dimensions reflect a more holistic measure of poverty, beyond just income or consumption. As per India's first national MPI report (2021), around 25% of India's population was found to be multidimensionally poor.

6. (2): The essential elements of Social Welfare Administration as per the POSDCoRB model developed by Luther Gulick are:

- P – Planning
- O – Organizing
- S – Staffing
- D – Directing
- Co – Coordinating
- R – Reporting
- B – Budgeting

Therefore, from the given options:

- A (Budgeting) *(True)*
- C (Staffing) *(True)*
- D (Organizing) *(True)*
- E (Coordinating) *(True)*

These are all direct components of POSDCoRB, whereas B (Co-operating) is not one of the seven core elements of POSDCoRB. Hence, the correct answer is 2: A, C, D and E only.

7. (4): The correct order of the five stages in the implementation of Solution-Focused Brief Therapy (SFBT) is:

A. Service users briefly describe the problem while moving them towards solution-oriented talk – The process begins with identifying the problem in a minimalistic way.

B. Service users describe their preferred future in order to develop well-formulated goals – This is crucial to goal setting and direction.

C. Exploration of the problem by identifying exceptions when the problem did not exist – This helps find solutions already being used.

D. Provision of end-of-session feedback by highlighting strengths and giving suggestions – Encourages reinforcement of effective behaviour.

E. Evaluation of service users' progress – Final stage to assess effectiveness and outcomes.

Thus, the sequence A, B, C, D, E logically represents the flow of SFBT sessions. So, the correct answer is 4: A, B, C, D, E.

8. (4):

C. Right to Information Act – 2005: Enacted in June 2005, effective from 12 October 2005, promotes transparency in governance.

B. Forest Rights Act – 2006: Passed in December 2006, recognizes rights of forest-dwelling communities.

A. Right to Education Act – 2009: Enacted in August 2009, guarantees free and compulsory education for children aged 6-14 years.

D. National Food Security Act – 2013: Passed in September 2013, provides subsidized food grains to a major section of the population.

Thus, the correct chronological order is C (2005), B (2006), A (2009), D (2013).

Hence, correct answer is 4: C, B, A, D.

9. (3): Empathy in social work means having an understanding with the client, not just about them. It involves placing oneself in the client's situation to understand their feelings, thoughts, and experiences. It is an active process of building rapport, trust, and emotional resonance. This differs from diagnostic or evaluative understanding, which are more clinical or judgment-based.

Therefore, empathy is best described as 3: An understanding with the client.

10. (1): Six Sigma deployment in HR primarily focuses on improving processes using data-driven and statistical methods. The relevant components are:

B. Improving the effectiveness of process: Six Sigma aims to minimize errors and enhance efficiency.

D. Solving the problem by collecting data: Data collection and analysis is central to Six Sigma methodology.

E. Using statistical thinking: It employs statistical tools like control charts, regression, etc., for problem-solving.

A (Emphasis on turnover) and C (Promote employment) are not direct goals of Six Sigma; these may be affected but are not core aims.

Hence, the correct answer is 1: B, D and E only.

11. (1): The concept of 'self-development' termed as the "looking-glass self" was given by Charles Horton Cooley.

According to Cooley, a person's self grows out of society's interpersonal interactions and the perceptions of others.

The three main components are:

1. How we imagine we appear to others.
2. How we imagine others judge us.
3. How we develop a self-feeling such as pride or shame based on that perceived judgment.

This theory highlights that identity is shaped socially rather than in isolation.

12. (2): Matching LIST-I and LIST-II:

A. UNHCR - IV. Refugees: United Nations High Commissioner for Refugees focuses on protecting and supporting refugees worldwide.

B. UNOPS - I. Peace and Sustainable Development: United Nations Office for Project Services provides infrastructure and project management services in peace-building, humanitarian, and development operations.

C. UNIDIR - II. Disarmament Research: United Nations Institute for Disarmament Research specializes in disarmament and security research.

D. UNRWA - III. Palestine Refugees: United Nations Relief and Works Agency for Palestine Refugees specifically assists Palestinian refugees.

Thus, the correct matching is A-IV, B-I, C-II, D-III.

13. (3): One of the major functions of NITI Aayog is Monitoring of SDGs (Sustainable Development Goals). NITI Aayog serves as the nodal agency for coordinating the implementation and monitoring of the United Nations' SDGs in India. It releases reports like the SDG India Index that tracks the progress of all Indian states and Union Territories on various indicators. NITI Aayog does not allocate finances (this is done by the Finance Commission) nor does it directly monitor Centre-State relations.

14. (*):

C. Workmen's Compensation Act – 1923: The first major social security legislation for workers in India, ensuring compensation for workplace injuries.

E. The Indian Companies Act – 1956: Governs the registration, regulation, and dissolution of companies in India.

B. Maternity Benefit Act – 1961: Provides maternity leave and benefits to women workers.

D. Payment of Gratuity Act – 1972: Grants financial benefits to employees after the termination of employment.

A. The Unorganized Workers Social Security Act – 2008: Aims to provide social security benefits to unorganized sector workers.

Thus, the correct chronological order based on the first promulgation is C, E, B, D, A, and none of the given options are correct.

15. (2): Vertical mobility refers to movement upward or downward in a social hierarchy in areas like:

A. Class, occupation and power

E. Occupation, power and social class

Vertical mobility means a person may move from one class, occupation, or power level to another, either improving or worsening their social status.

Hence, the correct combination is 2: A and E only.

16. (2): Paraphrasing is a technique mainly used in counselling.
- It involves restating the client's thoughts and feelings in the counsellor's own words.
- The purpose is to show that the counsellor understands the client accurately and empathetically.
- Paraphrasing helps in clarifying the client's emotions, ensures active listening, and encourages deeper communication between client and counsellor.
- It is not primarily used in social work research, group dynamics, or reflective discussions, although elements may overlap in other practices.

17. (4): The "Miracle Question" is a key technique in Solution-Focused Brief Therapy (SFBT).
- It encourages clients to visualize a future where the problem no longer exists.
- Example: "Suppose tonight, while you are asleep, a miracle happens, and the problems that brought you here are solved. What would be different?"
- It helps clients to identify goals and pathways toward positive change by focusing on solutions rather than problems.
- It differs from SMART goals, mission statements, or problem-free talk, which are structured differently.

18. (1): Matching LIST-I with LIST-II:

A. **Poshan Abhiyan → III. Holistic development and adequate nutrition of children:** Launched in 2018, aims to reduce stunting, under-nutrition, and anemia.

B. **National Creche Scheme → II. Day care service to children of working mothers:** Provides daycare facilities to children (6 months to 6 years).

C. **Balika Samriddhi Yojna → I. Financial incentives for the education of girl children:** Supports the education and empowerment of girls.

D. **Rashtriya Kishore Swasthya Karyakram (RKSK) → IV. Comprehensive health service for adolescents:** Focuses on mental health, nutrition, substance misuse, and reproductive health among adolescents.

Thus, the correct matching is A-III, B-II, C-I, D-IV.

19. (3): The following programmes are merged into the "Rashtriya Yuva Sashaktikaran Karyakram (RYSK)":

B. **National Youth Corps (NYC):** Volunteer youth engagement for community service.

C. **National Programme for Youth and Adolescent Development (NPYAD):** Provides support for youth leadership and development activities.

D. **National Young Leaders Programme Development (NYLPD):** Promotes leadership qualities among youth through various activities.

A. **National Service Scheme (NSS) is not merged;** it continues as a separate flagship scheme.

Thus, the correct answer is 3: B, C & D only.

20. (1): Matching LIST-I and LIST-II:

A. **FCRA, 2010 → III. Receiving foreign fund:** Regulates the acceptance and utilization of foreign contribution by individuals and associations.

B. **Section 12AA, IT Act, 1961 → IV. Grant tax exemption states:** Allows NGOs and charitable institutions to obtain tax exemptions.

C. **Section 80C, IT Act, 1961 → II. Donors tax deduction:** Provides individuals with deductions for specific investments and donations.

D. **Section 44, The Lokpal and Lokayukts Act, 2013 → I. Public servants declare their assets to the Ministry of Home Affairs (MoHA):** Mandates public officials to declare assets and liabilities annually.

Thus, the correct matching is A-III, B-IV, C-II, D-I.

21. (4): Social welfare aims at addressing general wellbeing, needs of individuals, and universal needs of the population, but not the specific personal needs of every individual. Social welfare programs are designed to cater to collective needs like education, health, housing, etc., at a community or societal level. Personal or highly individualized needs, such as personal ambitions

or lifestyle desires, are beyond the scope of social welfare.

Thus, social welfare does not address the personal needs of the population.

22. (4): The Social Awareness and Actions to Neutralize Pneumonia Successfully (SAANS) campaign was launched in November 2019. It was initiated by the Ministry of Health and Family Welfare, Government of India to reduce childhood pneumonia deaths, which are a significant contributor to child mortality. The initiative aims to mobilize people for effective protection, prevention, and treatment of pneumonia through community engagement, health system strengthening, and behaviour change communication.

23. (2): In fundraising, one of the greatest strengths of an agency is having a devoted and dedicated staff.

- Staff commitment reflects the credibility and reliability of the agency, which builds trust among donors and funding organizations.
- Dedicated personnel ensure continuous follow-up, innovative fundraising strategies, and proper relationship management with stakeholders.
- Emphasis on cash or absence of public relations are considered weaknesses rather than strengths.

24. (4): According to Maslow's hierarchy of needs, the basic human needs placed in ascending order of importance are:

B. Physiological needs: Basic needs like food, water, shelter, and sleep.

A. Safety needs: Protection from elements, security, order, law, and stability.

E. Affiliation or Acceptance needs (Love and Belongingness): Friendship, intimacy, and family.

D. Esteem needs: Achievement, respect from others, self-esteem.

C. Need for Self-actualization: Realizing personal potential, self-fulfillment, seeking personal growth and peak experiences.

Thus, the correct ascending order is B, A, E, D, C.

25. (3): CJSW is equal to police social work, correctional social work and forensic social work: This statement is not correct.

- Criminal Justice Social Work (CJSW) is an overarching concept that provides space for social workers to perform various roles across different settings like police departments, courts, prisons, and rehabilitation centers.
- It includes elements of police social work, correctional social work, and forensic social work, but it is not equal to them individually.
- CJSW aims at broader systemic reform, policy advocacy, client rehabilitation, and reducing reoffending rates, thus encompassing multiple facets rather than being limited to just these three areas.

26. (4): The Preamble of the Constitution of India mentions the ideals in the following sequence:

- Justice (social, economic, and political)
- Liberty (of thought, expression, belief, faith, and worship)
- Equality (of status and opportunity)
- Fraternity (assuring the dignity of the individual and the unity and integrity of the Nation)

Thus, the correct order is A (Justice), D (Liberty), C (Equality), B (Fraternity).

27. (3): The Convention on the Rights of Persons with Disabilities (CRPD) outlines the following principles:

A. Non-discrimination: Persons with disabilities must enjoy all human rights without any discrimination.

C. Equality of opportunity: Equal opportunities must be ensured for persons with disabilities.

E. Full and effective participation: Persons with disabilities must participate fully and effectively in society on an equal basis with others.

Financial support and preferential treatment are not listed as fundamental principles under CRPD. Thus, the correct answer is 3: A, C & E only.

28. (1): The basic types of mixed-method research designs include:

A. Explanatory sequential design: First quantitative data is collected, followed by qualitative data to explain the quantitative results.

B. **Exploratory sequential design:** First qualitative data is collected, then quantitative data is used to test or generalize the findings.

C. **Embedded design:** Qualitative data is embedded within a larger quantitative design or vice versa.

D. **Convergent parallel design:** Both qualitative and quantitative data are collected simultaneously but analyzed separately and then merged.

Concurrent design is not a basic type recognized distinctly; it overlaps with convergent designs. Thus, the correct answer is 1: A, B, C and D only.

29. (1): Radical feminism argues that gender inequality arises fundamentally from patriarchy, a system where men hold power and women are largely excluded. It emphasizes that simply adjusting existing institutions is not enough; a complete restructuring of society is needed. Radical feminists believe that patriarchy is embedded in all aspects of life, including political, economic, and social structures.

Thus, the correct answer is 1: Radical Feminism.

30. (4): Matching the Five-Year Plans with their main focus areas:

A. **Third Five-Year Plan (1961–1966) → III. Self-sufficiency in food grains:** After two plans focused on industrialization, this plan emphasized agriculture.

B. **Eighth Five-Year Plan (1992–1997) → II. Structural Adjustment Program:** Focused on liberalization and economic reforms post-1991 economic crisis.

C. **Ninth Five-Year Plan (1997–2002) → IV. Basic Minimum Services:** Focused on providing basic services like health, education, and drinking water to the poor.

D. **Twelfth Five-Year Plan (2012–2017) → I. Target of 9% GDP Growth:** Aimed at faster, more inclusive, and sustainable growth.

Thus, the correct matching is 4: A-III, B-II, C-IV, D-I.

31. (1): Matching the stages with tasks based on Erik Erikson's Psychosocial Development Theory:

A. **Oral stage (0–18 months) → IV. Trust vs Mistrust:** Infants learn whether or not they can trust the world based on caregiver responses.

B. **Anal stage (18 months–3 years) → III. Autonomy vs Shame:** Toddlers develop personal control and independence; successful resolution results in autonomy.

C. **Pre-School stage (3–5 years) → II. Initiative vs Guilt:** Children begin asserting power and control through directing play and social interaction.

D. **Middle School stage (6–11 years) → I. Industry vs Inferiority:** Children develop pride in accomplishments and abilities; success leads to a sense of competence.

Thus, the correct matching is A-IV, B-III, C-II, D-I.

32. (2): Raja Ram Mohan Roy is considered a pioneer of modern social work in India during the 19th century. He founded the Brahmo Samaj in 1828, promoting modern education, social reforms, and the abolition of practices like Sati. He worked for women's rights, education reform, religious tolerance, and freedom of press. His emphasis on social justice and human rights principles aligns him closely with the foundations of modern social work practice.

33. (1): Growth and development depend mainly on:

A. **Hereditary factors:** Genes and inherited characteristics influence physical and psychological traits.

B. **Environmental factors:** Nutrition, social interaction, learning, and physical surroundings impact development.

E. **Endocrine factors:** Hormones secreted by glands regulate growth patterns and emotional development.

Structural and happiness factors are not direct determinants in a biological and psychological growth context. Thus, the correct factors are A, B and E only.

34. (3): Matching the theory/model with its application emphasis:

A. **Tasks Centered theory → III. Supporting goal accomplishment:** Focuses on short-term interventions to achieve specific, measurable client goals.

B. Strengths Perspective → I. Identifying internal/external resources: Encourages finding and utilizing strengths rather than focusing on problems.

C. Problem Solving theory → IV. Facilitating problem resolution: Helps clients find solutions using structured problem-solving methods.

D. Ecological Perspective → II. Assessing transactions of person in environment: Studies interaction between individuals and their environments to address issues holistically.

Thus, the correct matching is A-III, B-I, C-IV, D-II.

35. (3): The stages of Self-Directed Group Work Practice Model are arranged as:

A. Pre-planning: Initial groundwork like defining purpose, goals, and expectations.

C. Taking off: Group members begin to understand and engage with the group process.

D. Group preparation for action: Preparing the group for collective action through readiness and skills building.

B. Taking action: Group members implement plans and strategies to meet their objectives.

E. Taking over: Group members take full ownership, becoming independent from facilitators or external support.

Thus, the correct sequential order is A, C, D, B, E.

36. (4): Grace Coyle initiated the first training program for social group workers at the School of Applied Social Sciences, Ohio.

- She was a pioneer in applying group work as a method of social work.
- She emphasized the educational and social values of group processes for individual growth and social change.
- Grace Coyle's works like "Group Experiences and Democratic Values" helped define group work as a formal method in social work practice.

37. (2): Sustainable Development Goal 3 (SDG 3) relates to maternal health.

- The title of SDG 3 is "Ensure healthy lives and promote well-being for all at all ages".
- One of its targets is specifically to reduce the global maternal mortality ratio to less than 70 per 100,000 live births by 2030.
- It also covers reducing newborn and child mortality, strengthening health systems, and ensuring access to quality health care services.

38. (3): The approach developed by John Woodward and Charles Perrow, stating that organizations turn inputs into outputs depending on their technologies, is called the Technological Approach.

According to this theory, technology (such as small batch production, mass production, or process production) dictates the structure and management practices of organizations.

Woodward categorized organizations based on the complexity of their production processes, and Perrow linked technology with task uncertainty and organizational structure.

39. (4):

A. It is the highest level of measurement: *(Correct)*. The ratio scale is the highest level because it includes a true zero and allows for meaningful ratios.

D. The zero point is absolute in ratio measurement: *(Correct)*. Ratio scales have an absolute zero point, meaning complete absence of the quantity (like 0 kg weight).

B. An equal distance between units will be found: *(Incorrect)*. Equal intervals are a property of both interval and ratio scales; it is not exclusive to ratio scales.

C. Variable is classified into several nominal sub-classes: *(Incorrect)*. This is a feature of nominal measurement, not ratio measurement.

E. Determine less than or greater than relationship between units: *(Incorrect)*. This is a feature of ordinal measurement and is not unique to ratio scales.

Thus, the correct answer is 4: A and D only.

40. (4): Matching LIST-I and LIST-II:

A. Global Hunger Index → IV. Concern Worldwide & Welthungerhilfe: These organizations jointly release the Global Hunger Index annually to track hunger globally.

B. **Global Innovation Index → III. World Intellectual Property Organization (WIPO):** WIPO collaborates with other partners to publish the Global Innovation Index.

C. **Global Peace Index → II. Institute for Economics and Peace:** This organization produces the Global Peace Index, ranking countries based on peacefulness.

D. **Corruption Perception Index → I. Transparency International:** Transparency International publishes the Corruption Perception Index ranking countries based on perceived public sector corruption.

Thus, the correct matching is A-IV, B-III, C-II, D-I.

41. (4): The NASW (National Association of Social Workers) Code of Ethics encompasses the following core values:

A. **Service:** Social workers prioritize the needs of others above self-interest.

B. **Social justice:** They work to challenge social injustices and support equal rights.

D. **Dignity and worth of the person:** Social workers respect the inherent dignity and worth of every individual.

E. **Integrity:** They behave in a trustworthy manner and adhere to ethical practices.

Solidarity (C) is not mentioned as one of the core values in the NASW Code of Ethics.

Thus, the correct answer is 4: A, B, D and E only.

42. (2): A research problem refers to a difficulty or challenge that a researcher identifies, which needs to be addressed through systematic inquiry.

- It highlights an unsolved question or area of concern that needs investigation.
- The researcher experiences a difficulty or uncertainty in finding a satisfactory solution, which leads to formulating a research question.

Thus, the correct answer is 2: Some difficulty experienced by the researcher in finding the solution.

43. (1): Matching LIST-I and LIST-II correctly:

A. **The Protection of Children from Sexual Offences Act → IV. 2012:** Passed to safeguard children against sexual abuse and exploitation.

B. **The Environment (Protection) Act → III. 1986:** Enacted after the Bhopal Gas Tragedy to protect and improve the environment.

C. **Rights of Persons with Disabilities Act → II. 2016:** Provides rights and benefits for persons with disabilities.

D. **Protection of Women from Domestic Violence Act → I. 2005:** Offers protection to women from domestic violence.

Thus, the correct matching is A-IV, B-III, C-II, D-I, and the correct answer is 1.

44. (4): Typical features of a rural community include:

- **Community consciousness:** Strong feeling of belongingness.
- **Faith in religion:** Strong influence of religious beliefs in daily life.
- **Role of neighbourhood:** Close social ties and support among neighbours.
- **Energy and speed are not characteristics of rural areas;** rather, they are associated with urban life where activities happen rapidly due to industrialization and modern technology.

Thus, the correct answer is 4: Energy and speed.

45. (1): When we combine sampling error (errors arising due to studying a sample instead of the whole population) with non-sampling errors (errors due to factors like non-response, data entry mistakes, etc.), the result is called the Total Error.

- Total error affects the validity and reliability of survey results.
- Managing total error is critical to achieving accurate and representative data in research.

Thus, the correct answer is 1: Total error.

46. (2): The reservation for Other Backward Classes (OBCs) was implemented based on the recommendations of the Second Backward Classes Commission, headed by B.P. Mandal.

- This commission is commonly known as the Mandal Commission, constituted in 1979.
- The Mandal Report was submitted in 1980 and recommended 27% reservation for OBCs in government jobs and educational institutions.

- It was implemented in 1990 by the then Prime Minister V.P. Singh, making it a historic move for social justice in India.

Thus, the correct answer is 2: Second Backward Classes Commission.

47. (1): Correctly matching the statistical tests:

A. Dispersion → III. Mean Deviation: Dispersion refers to the spread of data, and mean deviation is a key measure of it.

B. Measure of Association → II. Rank Correlation: Rank correlation (like Spearman's) is used to assess the strength of association between two ranked variables.

C. Test of Difference → IV. One-Way Analysis of Variance (ANOVA): Used to compare means between more than two groups to test if a significant difference exists.

D. Non-Parametric Test of Association → I. Wilcoxon Test: A non-parametric test used for comparing two paired groups.

Thus, the correct matching is A-III, B-II, C-IV, D-I.

48. (2): In the social planning model, the conception of public interest is described as idealist unitary.

- This model assumes that planners act rationally and pursue the collective good or public interest.
- The idea is that society has common goals that can be addressed through centralized planning, ignoring individual or conflicting interests.
- The model supports technocratic decision-making, with minimal input from diverse societal sections.

Thus, the correct answer is 2: Idealist unitary.

49. (4): The Kyoto Protocol, an international treaty under the United Nations Framework Convention on Climate Change (UNFCCC), was formally adopted at COP 3 in Kyoto, Japan in 1997.

- The Kyoto Protocol committed industrialized countries to reduce greenhouse gas emissions based on the scientific consensus on human-caused climate change.
- It officially came into force on 16 February 2005, but was adopted in 1997.

Thus, the correct answer is 4: 1997.

50. (3): The correct characteristics of Gender Based Budgeting (GBB) are:

B. It is a tool for gender mainstreaming: GBB integrates gender perspectives into budgeting at all levels of the policy process.

C. It involves various economic policies of the government from a gender perspective: Ensures policies are inclusive and beneficial for both men and women.

D. It is not about targeting programs specifically for women and girls: It addresses gender issues broadly, not just women-specific schemes.

A is incorrect because GBB was introduced by the Ministry of Finance, with the Ministry of Women and Child Development acting as a nodal agency.

E is incorrect because GBB is not a separate budget for women; it is an approach to analyze and reform the entire budget through a gender lens.

Thus, the correct answer is 3: B, C and D only.

51. (3): Behavioural Theory is a type of Modern Organization Theory that focuses on understanding human behaviour in organizations.

- It emerged in response to limitations of classical theories like Scientific Management and Bureaucratic Theory.
- It emphasizes motivation, leadership, communication, group dynamics, and employee satisfaction.
- Thinkers like Herbert Simon, Douglas McGregor (Theory X and Y), and Chris Argyris contributed significantly.

Thus, the correct answer is 3: Behavioural Theory.

52. (3): The correct sequence of steps in the Social Action Process is:

D. Developing awareness among people: The initial step involves sensitizing the public about issues affecting them.

A. Development of suitable organization: Once awareness is created, a structure or organization is formed for collective action.

B. Formulating and Projecting the goals: Clearly defined and shared goals are then established.

C. **Development of consensus:** Building agreement and unity among stakeholders to move forward.

E. **Actual action:** Finally, collective or strategic action is undertaken to achieve social change.

Thus, the correct order is 3: D, A, B, C, E.

53. (4): Communicable diseases are those that spread from person to person through infectious agents.

A. **Tuberculosis (TB):** Caused by Mycobacterium tuberculosis, transmitted through air.

B. **HIV/AIDS:** Spread through bodily fluids; a major communicable disease.

D. **Leprosy:** Caused by Mycobacterium leprae, also an infectious condition.

C. Cancer and **E. Diabetes** are non-communicable diseases, not caused by infection.

Thus, the correct answer is 4: A, B and D only.

54. (3): The correct order of steps in hypothesis testing is:

D. **Formulate the Null Hypothesis:** Begin by stating a hypothesis that there is no effect or difference.

B. **Choose the statistical test:** Select a test appropriate to your data type and research question.

A. **Specify the significance level:** Commonly set at 0.05, which defines the rejection criteria.

C. **Compute the statistical test:** Perform calculations based on the selected test.

E. **Reject/Accept the Null Hypothesis:** Based on the results, conclude whether the null hypothesis is accepted or rejected.

Thus, the correct order is 3: D, B, A, C, E.

55. (2): The Optional Protocol aiming at the abolition of the death penalty is linked to the:

- International Covenant on Civil and Political Rights (ICCPR).
- The Second Optional Protocol to the ICCPR, adopted in 1989, specifically commits signatories to abolish the death penalty.
- It is an instrument of international human rights law encouraging global elimination of capital punishment.

Thus, the correct answer is 2: International Covenant on Civil and Political Rights.

56. (3): Forming a group of elderly is comparatively easier due to the following reasons:

A. **Keen to participate meaningfully in group activities:** Elderly individuals often seek purpose and mental stimulation, making them more open to social engagement.

B. **Participating group activity that gives them sense of purpose:** Group settings provide a structured and meaningful outlet, improving emotional well-being.

C. **Looking for place to meet other people:** Elders often face social isolation; group formation fulfills their need for connection and companionship.

D. **Available and have more time on their hand:** Most elderly are retired, offering more flexibility in terms of time to engage in regular group activities.

E (Experienced and expert in social relations) may be true but is not a direct reason why forming groups is easier.

Hence, the correct answer is 3: A, B, C and D.

57. (1): The School of Social Work at Indira Gandhi National Open University (IGNOU) was established on August 16, 2007.

- It was created to promote professional education in social work via distance learning mode, expanding access to marginalized and rural populations.
- The school offers Bachelor's, Master's, PG Diploma, and Certificate programs tailored to the needs of field-level workers and learners across the country.

Thus, the correct answer is 1: August 16, 2007.

58. (4): When the Universal Declaration of Human Rights (UDHR) was adopted by the UN General Assembly on December 10, 1948, South Africa abstained from voting.

- South Africa abstained due to its racial policies and apartheid regime, which conflicted with the universal principles of equality and non-discrimination enshrined in the UDHR.
- A total of 8 countries abstained, including the Soviet Union, Saudi Arabia, and South Africa, while 48 voted in favour.

Thus, the correct answer is 4: South Africa.

59. **(3):** Respondent validation, also called member checking, is a process where the researcher shares the findings with the research participants to:

- Verify accuracy of interpretation,
- Check credibility of data analysis, and
- Ensure ethical responsibility in representing participants' views.

It enhances trustworthiness and validity of qualitative research.

Thus, the correct answer is 3: Respondent validation.

60. **(4):** While "equal opportunities for all" is a desired outcome of social development, it is not a structural feature of the process of social development.

- Social development emphasizes the integration of social and economic policy (Option 1),
- Embraces welfare pluralism (Option 2), i.e., collaboration among state, market, and civil society,
- Recognizes the multi-dimensional conception of well-being (Option 3), including health, education, dignity, and participation.

Equal opportunity is a goal, not a feature or mechanism of the process itself.

Thus, the correct answer is 4: Equal opportunities for all.

61. **(2):** The phrase "consciousness raising" is widely associated with social and political activism, especially feminist and liberation movements. Two significant contributors who have used and popularized this concept are:

- **Mitchell Julliel:** Known for discussing feminist strategies, Julliel linked consciousness raising to the collective sharing of personal experiences to expose systemic oppression and promote solidarity among women. Feminist consciousness-raising groups of the 1960s and 70s, particularly in the U.S., relied heavily on this idea to politicize personal experiences.
- **Paulo Freire:** In his influential work Pedagogy of the Oppressed (1970), Freire introduced the term "conscientização" (translated as conscientization or consciousness raising) as a process by which individuals become aware of social, political, and economic contradictions and take action against oppressive elements of their reality. His concept is central to critical pedagogy and participatory education.

Therefore, both Mitchell Julliel (from a feminist standpoint) and Paulo Freire (from a pedagogical and revolutionary standpoint) are known for using and developing the concept of consciousness raising.

Correct Answer: 2, 3.

62. **(1):** The correct chronological order of environmental Acts/Policies in increasing order of their enforcement year is:

A. **Wild Life Protection Act – 1972:** This was one of the earliest comprehensive environmental laws in India. It aimed at protecting wildlife species and their habitats by creating protected areas like National Parks and Wildlife Sanctuaries.

E. **Environment (Protection) Act – 1986:** Enacted after the Bhopal Gas Tragedy, this Act gave the central government wide powers to address environmental issues comprehensively and coordinate between various state and central authorities.

B. **National Forest Policy – 1988:** Focused on conservation of forests, increasing forest cover, and involving local communities in forest protection through Joint Forest Management (JFM).

C. **Biological Diversity Act – 2002:** Enacted to fulfill India's obligations under the Convention on Biological Diversity (CBD), this Act focuses on conservation of biological diversity, sustainable use of its components, and fair benefit-sharing.

D. **Forest Rights Act – 2006:** Also known as the Scheduled Tribes and Other Traditional Forest Dwellers (Recognition of Forest Rights) Act, it recognizes the rights of forest-dwelling communities over the land and resources they traditionally used.

Thus, the increasing order of enforcement year is: A (1972), E (1986), B (1988), C (2002), D (2006).

Hence, the correct answer is 1: A, E, B, C, D.

63. (2): Arrange from latest to oldest:

B. The Indian Companies Act – The current Companies Act was enacted in 2013 replacing the 1956 Act.

D. Foreign Contribution Regulation Act (FCRA) – Originally passed in 1976, amended in 2010 and 2020.

C. The Indian Public Trust Act – Passed in 1950 in Maharashtra and extended to other states.

A. Societies Registration Act – Introduced in 1860 during British rule.

Thus, the correct order from latest to oldest is: B, D, C, A

Hence, the correct answer is 2: B, D, C, A.

64. (3): Matching PM Schemes with concerned ministries:

A. Pradhan Mantri Shram Yogi Maan Dhan Yojana → III. Ministry of Labour & Employment: Provides old-age pension for unorganized sector workers.

B. PM SVANidhi (Street Vendors Atma Nirbhar Nidhi) → IV. Ministry of Housing and Urban Affairs: Offers micro-credit to street vendors post-COVID.

C. Pradhan Mantri Garib Kalyan Yojana (PMGKY) → I. Ministry of Finance: Announced during COVID for financial aid, food security, and direct benefit transfers.

D. Pradhan Mantri Kaushal Vikas Yojana → II. Ministry of Skill Development and Entrepreneurship: Focuses on skill training for youth.

Hence, the correct matching is 3: A-III, B-IV, C-I, D-II.

65. (1): The International Labour Organization (ILO) is a specialized agency under the United Nations system dealing with labour standards and human rights at the workplace.

- Established in 1919, and became the first UN specialized agency in 1946.
- Promotes rights at work, decent employment opportunities, social protection, and dialogue on work-related issues.
- It plays a significant role in promoting human rights, especially those related to labor conditions, child labour, and fair wages.

Thus, the correct answer is 1: International Labour Organisation.

66. (1): The following are key contributors to the field of Social Group Work:

A. Konopka: Gisela Konopka was a major theorist in group work, known for integrating psychological principles into social work with groups.

D. Geinsberg: He made significant contributions to understanding group dynamics in social work.

E. Klien: Also contributed to the development of group work methods and theories.

B. Mary Richmond is associated with casework, not group work.

C. Grace Mathew is known in Indian social work but primarily emphasized casework and general social work, not exclusively group work.

Thus, the correct answer is 1: A, D & E only.

67. (3): The main stages in the policy development process are:

A. Problem identification and agenda setting: Recognizing a public issue and placing it on the policy agenda.

C. Policy formulation and adoption: Developing potential solutions and selecting the most appropriate one.

D. Policy implementation: Enacting the adopted policy through programs or legal measures.

E. Evaluation: Assessing the effectiveness and outcomes of the policy.

B. Social analysis is part of problem assessment but is not a standalone formal stage in policy development.

Thus, the correct answer is 3: A, C, D and E only.

68. (1): In the most recent definition of social work by the International Federation of Social Workers (IFSW) and International Association of Schools of Social Work (IASSW) (2014 revision), the term "collective responsibility" was newly added.

- The definition highlights that social work promotes social change, human rights, social justice, and now emphasizes collective responsibility for sustainable development.
- This reflects a shift from individual-focused interventions to a broader societal and community responsibility.

Thus, the correct answer is 1: Collective responsibility.

69. (3): Correct matching of books and their authors:

A. Social Process in Organised Groups (1930) → **II. Grace Coyle:** One of the pioneers in social group work, she wrote extensively on group dynamics.

B. A Social Psychology of Group Process for Decision Making (1964) → **III. Collins Barry & Harold Guetzkow:** Focused on how group decisions are made through communication and interaction.

C. Group Process is Social Work: A Theoretical Synthesis (1979) → **I. Tom Douglas:** He provided theoretical frameworks for group work in social work practice.

D. Groups in Social Work (1972) → **IV. Hartford, M. E.:** Focused on applied techniques and field practices in group work.

Thus, the correct matching is 3: A-II, B-III, C-I, D-IV.

70. (2): Family Psychoeducation Intervention Approach has been used extensively to manage and support people with schizophrenia.

- It involves educating family members about the illness, treatment plans, and coping strategies.
- It reduces relapse rates, improves medication adherence, and enhances family support systems.
- The approach is evidence-based and often part of community-based psychiatric rehabilitation models.

Thus, the correct answer is 2: Schizophrenia.

71. (3): Late life ageing is shaped by the accumulation of life experiences and the proximity to death, which affect an individual's physical, emotional, and psychological state.

A. Life events: Over time, experiences such as work, relationships, losses, and achievements influence how one ages in late life. .

D. Proximity of death: As individuals approach the end of life, their perceptions, health status, and social behaviors are shaped by the awareness of limited time.

C. Malfunctioning and **B. Bad standard of living** are contributing factors but not conceptual components of the accumulated life-course perspective.

E. Attitude influences coping but is not part of the cumulative ageing concept.

Thus, the correct answer is 3: A and D only.

72. (1): Arrange the following in the order of their launch:

B. Sarva Shiksha Abhiyan (SSA) - 2001: Aimed at achieving universal elementary education.

D. Nirmal Bharat Abhiyan - 2012: Launched to ensure sanitation and hygiene; later replaced by Swachh Bharat Abhiyan.

C. Unnat Bharat Abhiyan - 2014: Initiative to connect academic institutions with rural communities for development.

A. Poshan Abhiyan - 2018: National Nutrition Mission to reduce stunting, undernutrition, and anemia.

So, the correct chronological order is: B (2001), D (2012), C (2014), A (2018).

Thus, the correct answer is 1: B, D, C, A.

73. (2): The 104th Constitutional Amendment Act (2020) deals with:

B. Extension of reservation for SCs and STs in the Lok Sabha and State Assemblies by 10 years, until 2030.

D. Removal of reservation for Anglo-Indians in the Lok Sabha and State Assemblies by deleting Articles 331 and 333 provisions for nominated seats.

A and C refer to reservations for Economically Weaker Sections (103rd Amendment) and OBCs, which are unrelated to the 104th Amendment.

Thus, the correct answer is 2: B and D only.

74. (3): Characteristics of Social Work Administration include:

A. A method of social work: It is recognized as one of the methods of social work that facilitates implementation of welfare policies.

B. Uni-disciplinary approach: It is often treated as a managerial function within the professional domain of social work.

C. Administration of services provided by social workers: It involves planning, organizing, and directing services run by social agencies.

D. Use of rights-based approach is a practice framework, not a core feature of administration.

E. No dependency on people is incorrect; rather, social work administration often seeks to reduce dependency through empowerment.

Thus, the correct answer is 3: A, B and C only.

75. (4): Among the given options, Economic Sanction Model is not a popular model of social action. Common models of social action include:

- **Lok Shakti Model** – grassroots mobilization based on community empowerment.
- **Conscientization Model** – popularized by Paulo Freire, focuses on awareness and critical thinking.
- **Dialectical Mobilization Model** – focuses on mobilizing masses through class consciousness and conflict.

Economic Sanction Model refers more to international policy strategies and is not a recognized framework in social action literature.

Thus, the correct answer is 4: Economic sanction model.

76. (1): In a case study, data is collected from primary sources through in-depth qualitative methods, and among them:

- Open-ended interviews are the most suitable tool as they allow respondents to share detailed personal experiences, perceptions, and emotions.
- They help the researcher probe deeper into the subject's context, especially when exploring psychosocial or environmental aspects of the case.
- Tools like newspapers, diaries, or books are considered secondary sources and may be used for triangulation, but not as the core of primary data in a case study.

Thus, the correct answer is 1: Open ended questions (Interview).

77. (4): Social case work deals with a wide range of problems, including:

A. Relatively circumscribed problems: Such as issues related to adjustment, family tension, or work stress.

B. Severe and pervasive interpersonal/intrapersonal problems: Including mental health challenges, emotional trauma, and relationship breakdowns.

C. Long-term problems: Chronic illness, long-term poverty, or disability that require continuous intervention.

D. Problems due to gross material environmental deprivations: Lack of food, shelter, basic resources, which also fall within the scope of intervention.

Thus, case work covers all the options mentioned, and the correct answer is 4: A, B, C and D only.

78. (2): Institutionalisation of older persons may lead to several negative psychosocial consequences, including:

A. Stigmatization: Older adults in institutions are often viewed as abandoned or dependent, leading to social stigma.

C. Loss of liberty and dignity: The shift from a personal home to an institutional setting often involves strict routines, rules, and loss of privacy.

D. Lack of autonomy: Decision-making power is often reduced in institutions, affecting the person's independence.

B is not universally true as institutional care quality varies, and E (empowerment) is more often achieved in community-based or independent living models.

Thus, the correct answer is 2: A, C and D only.

79. (3): Correct matching of Five-Year Plans and economic models:

A. First Five-Year Plan (1951–1956) → III. Harrod-Domar model: Focused on agriculture, savings, and investment.

B. Second Five-Year Plan (1956–1961) → I. Mahalanobis model: Emphasized heavy industries and public sector growth.

C. Third Five-Year Plan (1961–1966) → II. John Sandy and Sukhmoy Chakraborty model: Attempted to integrate various economic indicators for planned growth.

D. Fourth Five-Year Plan (1969–1974) → IV. Gadgil formula: Used for resource allocation among states.

Thus, the correct answer is 3: A-III, B-I, C-II, D-IV.

80. (1): Correct matching of practice models and proponents in social work:

A. Cognitive Behaviour Therapy (CBT) → III. Aaron T. Beck: Developed CBT as a structured, goal-oriented psychotherapy for mental health issues.

B. Problem Solving Model → IV. H.H. Perlman: Known for establishing this model in casework, focusing on resolving present life problems.

C. Task Centered Approach → I. Reid and Laura Epstein: Developed in the 1970s to focus on short-term, structured interventions.

D. Narrative Therapy → II. Michael White and David Epston: A postmodern approach focusing on storytelling and reframing life narratives.

Thus, the correct answer is 1: A-III, B-IV, C-I, D-II.

81. (4): Hayne's Plan is a wage payment system where:

- A standard time is fixed for a task based on time-and-motion studies.
- Wages are paid on a time basis, regardless of whether the work is completed before or after the standard time.
- It encourages consistency rather than speed and is suitable for jobs where quality is more important than output quantity.

Thus, the correct answer is 4: The standard time required for a job is fixed and the wages are paid on time basis.

82. (3): Functionalist theory in sociology finds its roots in the work of Emile Durkheim, who:

- Saw society as a system of interrelated parts that function together to maintain stability.
- Introduced concepts like social facts, anomie, and collective conscience.
- His works such as "The Division of Labour in Society", "Suicide", and "The Elementary Forms of Religious Life" laid the foundation for structural functionalism.

Thus, the correct answer is 3: Emile Durkheim.

83. (1): Matching the books with their authors:

A. Social Policy: An Introduction → IV. Richard Titmuss: A foundational work in the field of social policy.

B. Human Rights and Social Work: Towards Rights-based Practice → I. Jim Ife: A key advocate of integrating human rights in social work practice.

C. Political Economy of Hunger → II. Jean Dreze and Amartya Sen: Focused on hunger, poverty, and entitlement theory.

D. Excluding the Poor → III. Peter Golding: Focused on media, communication, and marginalization of the poor.

Thus, the correct answer is 1: A-IV, B-I, C-II, D-III.

84. (*): 1. Empowerment of communities, 2. Help individuals in distress, 3. Eliminate personal and institutional discrimination, 4. Create institutional mechanisms for addressing grievances:

Here, all 4 options are correct when interpreted in alignment with the National Association of Social Workers (NASW) Code of Ethics, though some are more directly stated than others. Let's examine each in relation to the six core values outlined in the NASW Code: service, social justice, dignity and worth of the person, importance of human relationships, integrity, and competence.

1. **Empowerment of communities** – Directly tied to the value of social justice. Social workers advocate for the empowerment of

marginalized communities to gain access to resources and decision-making power. This is a core ethical obligation.

2. **Help individuals in distress** – Rooted in the value of service. The code explicitly mentions helping people in need and addressing social problems as the primary goal of the profession.
3. **Eliminate personal and institutional discrimination** – A key tenet of social justice. Social workers are ethically bound to oppose discrimination and work toward the removal of barriers to equity and inclusion.
4. **Create institutional mechanisms for addressing grievances** – While this is not verbatim in the Code of Ethics as a "general principle", it falls within the broader ethical responsibilities of promoting accountability, advocacy, transparency, and supporting systems that protect the rights and dignity of clients and communities. It aligns with ethical standards regarding responsibilities to broader society and institutions.

Therefore, all four options are justifiable under the NASW Code of Ethics and reflect the spirit and practice of social work ethics.

Correct Answer: 1, 2, 3, 4

85. (1): The correct chronological order of Jean Piaget's stages of cognitive development in children is:

B. Sensorimotor Stage (Birth–2 years): Learning through physical interaction with the environment.

C. Preoperational Stage (2–7 years): Development of language and symbolic thinking, but still egocentric.

A. Concrete Operational Stage (7–11 years): Logical thinking develops, but limited to concrete concepts.

D. Formal Operational Stage (12 years and above): Abstract and hypothetical thinking emerges.

Thus, the correct order is 1: B, C, A, D.

86. (1): The term "community action" refers to organized efforts by local groups—often marginalized or underrepresented—to challenge existing structures or authorities and to address issues of social injustice, inequality, or exclusion.

- It involves grassroots mobilization, collective empowerment, and participatory decision-making.
- Community action often arises in conflict with existing authorities when there are grievances about policy decisions, access to resources, or lack of recognition.
- This is a key approach in radical or transformative social work.

Thus, the correct answer is 1: To work with community groups in conflict with authority.

87. (1): The correct sequence of the Task Planning Process in social work is:

A. Possible alternative tasks are identified through generating task possibilities: The process begins by exploring a wide range of options.

B. An agreement is made: Worker and client decide on a course of action.

C. Explicitly secured with client: Consent and commitment from the client is clearly obtained.

D. Implementation is planned: Steps for execution are structured.

E. The task is summarized: A final review is done to ensure mutual understanding.

Thus, the correct answer is 1: A, B, C, D, E.

88. (1): According to Koh's primary values of social work, the following are key values:

A. The worth and dignity of human being: Central to human rights and professional respect.

B. Tolerance of Differences: Social workers respect diversity and uniqueness of individuals.

C. Satisfaction of basic human needs: Social work promotes access to food, shelter, healthcare, etc.

E. Self-direction: Respect for an individual's right to make their own choices.

D. Judgemental attitude is not a value but rather something social work actively avoids.

Thus, the correct answer is 1: A, B, C & E only.

89. **(3):** The correct order of the Grounded Theory process is:

A. Research Questions: A broad research problem is framed.

E. Collection of Data: Data is gathered from participants using interviews, observations, etc.

B. Coding: Data is broken down into concepts and categories.

D. Constant Comparison: Concepts are continuously compared across data sets to find patterns.

C. Testing of Hypothesis: Theoretical ideas are refined and validated through additional data.

Thus, the correct answer is 3: A, E, B, D, C.

90. **(3):** Ralf Dahrendorf, a conflict theorist, argued that:

- Societies are made up of competing interest groups, not just based on economics but also power and authority.
- He introduced the concept of "imperatively coordinated associations", which lead to structural conflicts between dominant and subordinate positions.
- He built upon Marxist ideas but moved beyond economic determinism to explain conflict in authority structures.

Thus, the correct answer is 3: Dahrendorf.

91. **(1):** Under Article 136 of the Constitution, the Supreme Court may grant special leave to appeal in civil cases only under exceptional circumstances, especially when there is a miscarriage of justice.

- The passage clearly states that the Court may reappreciate evidence only to determine if there has been any illegality, material irregularity, or miscarriage of justice.
- A key example of such irregularity is when the lower court fails to properly evaluate or appreciate the evidence presented at trial.
- In civil matters, public interest may be a broader factor, but the Court's discretionary power is specifically exercised to correct judicial errors in reasoning or interpretation, including misreading of evidence.

Thus, the correct answer is 1: Lower court failed to appreciate the evidence produced.

92. **(4):** The passage clearly states:

"An appeal by special leave is not a regular appeal... The court would reappreciate evidence only to find out whether there has been any illegality, material irregularity or miscarriage of justice."

This highlights that special leave appeals are not routine appeals but are invoked only when justice has been compromised through illegality or irregularity.

Thus, the correct answer is 4: Irregularity of justice is noted.

93. **(3):** The passage mentions:

"This power is not, however, to be exercised... where no appeal is otherwise provided by the law or the Constitution."

This implies that the inability to file a regular appeal is not itself an exceptional circumstance under Article 136.

Exceptional circumstances include:

- Perverse acquittal
- Miscarriage of justice
- Violation of principles of natural justice

Hence, the correct answer is 3: When a regular appeal is not entertained by the lower court.

94. **(3):** The passage states:

"The court would reappreciate evidence only to find out whether there has been any illegality, material irregularity or miscarriage of justice."

This confirms that re-evaluation of evidence is not done routinely, but only when there is an indication of illegality or procedural flaw.

Other options like hiding or destroying evidence may contribute, but the Court's trigger for reappreciation is the presence of illegality or injustice, not just failure of investigation.

Thus, the correct answer is 3: Any possible illegality is observed.

95. **(2):** Under Article 136 of the Constitution of India, an appellant (person or party aggrieved by a judgment) can approach the Supreme Court with a special leave petition (SLP) to appeal against the decision of any court or tribunal in India (except military tribunals).

- This article does not automatically give a right to appeal; rather, it allows the appellant to seek permission (leave) from the Supreme Court.
- The Court decides whether or not to entertain such a petition based on the nature of injustice.

Thus, the correct answer is 2: Appellant.

96. **(1):** The passage states that in India, the voluntary sector derives its strength from humanitarian values rooted in religious philosophy, emphasizing the traditional and moral role of social institutions and communities in supporting the needy.

- This reflects that social welfare in India is community-centered and culturally rooted rather than primarily state-driven.
- Options mentioning government funding or CSR are mentioned as external or recent developments, not the foundational role.

Thus, the correct answer is 1: It draws strength from humanitarian values rooted in religious philosophy.

97. **(2):** The passage mentions that with the rise of Corporate Social Responsibility (CSR), the free market mechanisms are taking over the social sector, while government support is declining.

- Consequently, the social sector becomes more dependent on private charities and foreign contributions, not less.
- Rather than enhancing or strengthening institutions, this transition weakens traditional welfare structures.

Thus, the correct answer is 2: Increased reliance on private charities and foreign contribution.

98. **(1):** The passage clearly explains that as the government reduces its welfare responsibilities, it adopts models like Public-Private Partnerships (PPPs), user-pay systems, and performance-based contracts.

- This shift indicates a transfer of service delivery responsibility from the public to the private sector.
- It does not lead to stronger welfare laws or increased statutory support—in fact, the passage states the opposite.

Thus, the correct answer is 1: A shift of welfare programmes to the private sector through public-private partnership.

99. **(2):** According to the passage, market-driven forces have deeply affected the social sector through mechanisms like:

- Public-private partnerships
- User-pay models
- Performance-based contracts

These models are indicators of privatization and corporate influence, leading to the domination of the social sector by the private sector.

Thus, the correct answer is 2: Private sector mechanisms like public-private partnerships have started dominating the social sector.

100. **(2):** The passage explicitly states:

"It (the voluntary sector) appears to be systematically marginalized by both the market and the government".

This marginalization causes the social sector to lag in comparison with other sectors, as it becomes dependent on foreign contributions and private charity instead of receiving robust institutional or government support.

Thus, the correct answer is 2: The marginalization of the voluntary sector by the market and government.

Previous Years' Paper

National Testing Agency (NTA)

UGC-NET Junior Research Fellowship & Assistant Professor Eligibility Exam

SOCIAL WORK, AUGUST-2024

(Exam held on 22-08-2024)

PAPER-II

1. Match the Theories of personality with corresponding proponent.

List-I (Theories of Personality)	List-II (Name of the Proponents)
(*a*) Psychoanalytic theory	I. Albert Bandura
(*b*) Behavioural theory	II. Carl Rogers
(*c*) Humanistic theory	III. Sigmund Freud
(*d*) Cognitive theory	IV. John B. Watson

Choose the **correct** answer from the options given below:

	(*a*)	(*b*)	(*c*)	(*d*)
A.	I	II	III	IV
B.	III	I	II	IV
C.	IV	III	I	II
D.	III	IV	II	I

2. Match the organizations with the founders.

List-I (Organization)	List-II (Founder)
(*a*) Satyashodhak Samaj	I. Swami Dayanand Saraswati
(*b*) Arya Samaj	II. Pandita Ramabai
(*c*) Brahmo Samaj	III. Jyotiba Phule
(*d*) Arya Mahila Samaj	IV. Raja Ram Mohan Roy

Choose the **correct** answer from the options given below:

	(*a*)	(*b*)	(*c*)	(*d*)
A.	III	I	IV	II
B.	I	III	IV	II
C.	III	IV	II	I
D.	II	I	IV	III

3. Which of the following are components of community work?

(*a*) The target population
(*b*) Individual and group goals
(*c*) Groups within the community
(*d*) Significant individuals
(*e*) Agency

Choose the **correct** answer from the options given below:

A. (*a*), (*b*), (*c*) and (*d*) only
B. (*a*), (*c*), (*d*) and (*e*) only
C. (*a*), (*b*), (*d*) and (*e*) only
D. (*a*), (*b*), (*c*) and (*e*) only

4. What are the merits of Arithmetic Mean?

(*a*) It is simple to understand and easy to compute.
(*b*) It is a calculated value, and not based on position in the series.
(*c*) It is not affected by the value of every item in the series.

(*d*) It is the centre of gravity.
(*e*) It is defined by a rigid mathematical formula.

Choose the **correct** answer from the options given below:

A. (*a*), (*b*), (*d*), (*e*) only
B. (*a*), (*b*), (*c*), (*e*) only
C. (*b*), (*c*), (*d*), (*e*) only
D. (*a*), (*c*), (*d*), (*e*) only

5. Match the National Policy with its corresponding year.

List-I (National Policy)	List-II (Year)
(*a*) National Policy on Health	I. 2023
(*b*) National Policy on Youth	II. 2007
(*c*) National Policy on Voluntary Organization	III. 2020
(*d*) National Education Policy	IV. 2017

Choose the **correct** answer from the options given below:

	(*a*)	(*b*)	(*c*)	(*d*)
A.	III	I	II	IV
B.	II	I	III	IV
C.	I	IV	III	II
D.	IV	I	II	III

6. Match the area of work with the name.

List-I (Area)	List-II (Person)
(*a*) Satipratha	I. Sarojini Naidu
(*b*) Leprosy	II. Dayanand Saraswati
(*c*) Status of women	III. Baba Amte
(*d*) Idol worship	IV. Raja Ram Mohan Roy

Choose the **correct** answer from the options given below:

	(*a*)	(*b*)	(*c*)	(*d*)
A.	I	IV	II	III
B.	IV	III	I	II
C.	III	II	IV	I
D.	II	III	IV	I

7. Andre Gunder Frank and Walter Rodney are the leading proponents of:

A. Theory of Urban bias
B. Dependency theory
C. Modernization theory
D. Linear theory

8. The salient features of Dissociate disorder are:

(*a*) Dissociative amnesia
(*b*) Depersonalisation/Derealisation disorder
(*c*) Illness anxiety disorder
(*d*) Dissociative identity (multiple personality)
(*e*) Paralysis, blindness

Choose the **correct** answer from the options given below:

A. (*a*), (*b*), (*d*) only
B. (*a*), (*b*), (*c*) only
C. (*c*), (*d*), (*e*) only
D. (*b*), (*c*), (*d*) only

9. Which of the following are settlement houses in the United States?

(*a*) Hull House
(*b*) Neighbourhood Guild
(*c*) College Settlement
(*d*) Houchen House
(*e*) Toynbee Hall

Choose the **correct** answer from the options given below:

A. (*a*), (*b*), (*c*) and (*d*) only
B. (*a*), (*c*), (*d*) and (*e*) only
C. (*a*), (*b*), (*d*) and (*e*) only
D. (*b*), (*c*), (*d*) and (*e*) only

10. Which Ministry looks after the grievance and regulation of FCRA?

A. Ministry of Social Justice and Empowerment
B. Ministry of External Affairs
C. Ministry of Corporate Affairs
D. Ministry of Home Affairs

11. What does 'R' stands for in the acronym SMART in the context of program objectives?

A. Reliable
B. Relevant
C. Resourceful
D. Responsible

12. Match the professional associations/bodies with its founding year.

List-I (Associations/ Bodies)	List-II (Founding Year)
(*a*) Council of Social Work Education (CSWE)	I. 1955
(*b*) International Federation of Social Workers (IFSW)	II. 1928
(*c*) National Association of Social Workers (NASW)	III. 1952
(*d*) International Council on Social Welfare (ICSW)	IV. 1956

Choose the **correct** answer from the options given below:

	(*a*)	(*b*)	(*c*)	(*d*)
A.	I	III	IV	II
B.	III	IV	I	II
C.	III	I	IV	II
D.	II	IV	I	III

13. As spelled out in the NASW Code of Ethics, the mission of social work is rooted in:

(*a*) Service
(*b*) Social Justice
(*c*) Inequity
(*d*) Integrity
(*e*) Competence

Choose the **correct** answer from the options given below:

A. (*a*), (*b*), (*c*) and (*d*) only
B. (*b*), (*c*), (*d*) and (*e*) only
C. (*a*), (*b*), (*d*) and (*e*) only
D. (*a*), (*b*), (*c*) and (*e*) only

14. 'Range' is defined as:

A. Aggregate of all the values in the distribution
B. Middle values of the distribution
C. Difference between the largest value and smallest value in the distribution
D. Value which has maximum frequency in the given distribution

15. Match the day with dates.

List-I	List-II
(*a*) World Environment Day	I. 14th April
(*b*) International Human Rights Day	II. 5th June
(*c*) World Social Justice Day	III. 10th December
(*d*) World Knowledge Day	IV. 20th February

Choose the **correct** answer from the options given below:

	(*a*)	(*b*)	(*c*)	(*d*)
A.	III	II	I	IV
B.	II	III	IV	I
C.	III	IV	I	II
D.	IV	I	II	III

16. Who among the following coined the term person-in-situation?

A. Charles Cooley
B. Florence Hollis
C. Mary Richmond
D. H. Bartlett

17. The right of widows to remarriage was advocated by:

A. Raja Ram Mohan Roy
B. Vijayalaxmi Pandit
C. Ishwar Chandra Vidyasagar
D. M.G. Ranade

18. NSSO stands for:

A. National Sample Survey Office
B. National Sample Survey Organization
C. National Statistical Survey Organization
D. National Science Survey Office

19. Match the book with their author.

List-I (Books)	List-II (Author)
(*a*) Theory Building in Social Work	I. Gisela Konopka
(*b*) Social Group Work Practice	II. Harleigh Trecker
(*c*) Social Group Work Principles and Practice	III. Wilson and Ryland
(*d*) Therapeutic Group Work with Children	IV. Gordon Hearn

Choose the **correct** answer from the options given below:

	(*a*)	(*b*)	(*c*)	(*d*)
A.	IV	II	III	I
B.	IV	III	II	I
C.	IV	II	I	III
D.	IV	I	III	II

20. The following are four public relations (PR) models given by Gruning and Hunt in 1984:

(*a*) Two-way symmetrical model
(*b*) Public information model
(*c*) Press agentry model
(*d*) One-way non-symmetrical model
(*e*) Two-way asymmetrical model

Choose the **correct** answer from the options given below:

A. (*b*), (*d*), (*a*) and (*e*) only
B. (*a*), (*e*), (*b*) and (*c*) only
C. (*d*), (*a*), (*b*) and (*c*) only
D. (*e*), (*a*), (*c*) and (*d*) only

21. Type of research in which a researcher or team of researches combines elements of qualitative and quantitative research approaches is called:

A. Action Research B. Case Study
C. Mixed Method D. Survey Method

22. In India the first medical social worker was appointed in the year 1946 in:

A. Tata Memorial Hospital, Mumbai
B. Safdurjung Hospital, Delhi
C. GTB Hospital, Delhi
D. J.J. Hospital, Mumbai

23. Community work in the social planning model refers to:

A. A worker or an agency undertakes an exercise to evaluate the welfare needs and existing services.
B. A worker or an agency undertakes an issue-oriented work to generate a collective movement.
C. A worker or an agency undertakes work to mobilize public opinion on a social issue.
D. A worker or an agency undertakes work to mobilize global fund to overthrow the government.

24. Who among the following psychologists has defined personality as "dynamic organisation within the individual of those psychophysical systems that determine his unique adjustment to his environment"?

A. Guilford B. Carl Rogers
C. Allport D. Abraham Maslow

25. Cultural competence is important for working effectively with clients from diverse cultural background. What are the important characteristics of cultural competence?

(*a*) Familiarity with the cultural norms and values of a specific group.
(*b*) An understanding of the uniqueness of one's own cultural beliefs
(*c*) Openness to other customs and rituals
(*d*) Willingness to learn about other customs
(*e*) Considering one's culture as superior from others.

Choose the **correct** answer from the options given below:

A. (*a*), (*b*), (*c*) and (*d*) only
B. (*a*), (*b*), (*c*) and (*e*) only
C. (*b*), (*c*), (*d*) and (*e*) only
D. (*a*), (*b*), (*d*) and (*e*) only

26. Which of the following is/are not included in the fifteen points of rural reconstruction program initiated by Rabindranath Tagore?

(*a*) To create unity and fraternity among the various communities and address the harmful social ills

(*b*) To restrain people from consuming alcohol and drugs

(*c*) To promote information technology and digital infrastructure

(*d*) To form cooperative grain stores in order to cope with famine

(*e*) To cultivate fraternal feelings and sense of unity among each and every village and district

Choose the **correct** answer from the options given below:

A. (*a*), (*b*), (*c*) only

B. (*b*), (*c*) only

C. (*c*) only

D. (*d*), (*e*) only

27. In the abbreviation POSDCORB, CO stands for:

A. Counselling

B. Command

C. Coordinating

D. Collaboration

28. Which of the statements are true of Sociometry?

(*a*) A method for depicting and measuring interpersonal attraction in groups.

(*b*) By this method, attraction and repulsion of members of a group can be represented by sociograms.

(*c*) Role enactment of individuals in a group are done.

(*d*) Concepts of leadership and isolation can be investigated by this method.

(*e*) The method is eminently an interdisciplinary investigation of group relations.

Choose the **correct** answer from the options given below:

A. (*a*), (*b*), (*c*) and (*d*) only

B. (*a*), (*c*), (*d*) and (*e*) only

C. (*a*), (*b*), (*d*) and (*e*) only

D. (*b*), (*c*), (*d*) and (*e*) only

29. Which of the following are characteristics of victim blaming?

(*a*) Downtrodden of society are responsible for their own distress

(*b*) Dominant groups are sympathetic to the downtrodden

(*c*) The negativity may become a self-fulfilling prophecy for the downtrodden

(*d*) The downtrodder internalize the blame attached to them

(*e*) Growth of industrialization and the development of protestant ethics contribute to the ethos.

Choose the **correct** answer from the options given below:

A. (*a*), (*b*), (*c*) and (*d*) only

B. (*a*), (*b*), (*d*) and (*e*) only

C. (*a*), (*c*), (*d*) and (*e*) only

D. (*a*), (*b*), (*c*) and (*e*) only

30. Arrange the enactment of following legislation in chronological order:

(*a*) Juvenile Justice (Care and Protection of Children) Act

(*b*) Immoral Traffic Prevention Act

(*c*) Probation of Offenders Act

(*d*) Narcotics Drugs and Psychotropic Substance Act

(*e*) Prisons Act

Choose the **correct** answer from the options given below:

A. (*a*), (*b*), (*c*), (*d*), (*e*)

B. (*e*), (*c*), (*d*), (*b*), (*a*)

C. (*b*), (*d*), (*e*), (*a*), (*c*)

D. (*a*), (*e*), (*b*), (*d*), (*c*)

31. Match List-I with List-II.

List-I (Programmes/Institutions/ Reports)	List-II (Year)
(*a*) Toynbee Hall	I. 1942
(*b*) Beveridge Report	II. 1869
(*c*) Charity Organization Society	III. 1884
(*d*) Elizabethan Poor Law	IV. 1601

Choose the **correct** answer from the options given below:

	(*a*)	(*b*)	(*c*)	(*d*)
A.	II	III	I	IV
B.	IV	II	III	I
C.	III	I	II	IV
D.	III	II	I	IV

32. Which of the following reform movements objected to the workship of idols?

A. Prarthana Samaj
B. Brahmo Samaj
C. Arya Samaj
D. Shakti Shodhak Samaj

33. Arrange the 'social case work' process in a sequence:

(*a*) Study
(*b*) Follow up
(*c*) Diagnosis
(*d*) Treatment
(*e*) Intake

Choose the **correct** answer from the options given below:

A. (*a*), (*c*), (*b*), (*d*), (*e*)
B. (*e*), (*c*), (*a*), (*b*), (*d*)
C. (*a*), (*e*), (*c*), (*b*), (*d*)
D. (*e*), (*a*), (*c*), (*d*), (*b*)

34. In which year, the Royal Commission on Labour was appointed to investigate the industrial conditions in India?

A. 1927
B. 1928
C. 1929
D. 1930

35. The class interval of the following classes is:

10-20, 20-30, 30-40, 40-50

A. 10 B. 20
C. 30 D. 40

36. Which one of the following principles of management states that each employee should report to one superior?

A. Centralization
B. Span of Control
C. Unity of Command
D. Division of Labour

37. In the process of development, the change agent performs the following specific roles in order to mobilize the community.

(*a*) A catalyst
(*b*) A process helper
(*c*) A resource linker
(*d*) A political opportunist
(*e*) A conflict manager

Choose the **correct** answer from the options given below:

A. (*a*), (*b*), (*c*) and (*d*) only
B. (*a*), (*b*), (*c*) and (*e*) only
C. (*b*), (*c*), (*d*) and (*e*) only
D. (*a*), (*c*), (*d*) and (*e*) only

38. Arrange the five human needs as given by Abraham Maslow from bottom to top of the pyramid.

(*a*) Self-esteem
(*b*) Safety
(*c*) Self-actualization
(*d*) Love and Belongingness
(*e*) Physiological

Choose the **correct** answer from the options given below:

A. (*c*), (*b*), (*d*), (*a*), (*e*)
B. (*a*), (*b*), (*c*), (*d*), (*e*)
C. (*b*), (*c*), (*a*), (*e*), (*d*)
D. (*e*), (*b*), (*d*), (*a*), (*c*)

39. Arrange in sequence the stages of organisational conflict as proposed by L.R. Pondy (1967).

(*a*) Manifest
(*b*) Felt stage
(*c*) Latent stage
(*d*) Aftermath
(*e*) Perceived stage

Choose the **correct** answer from the options given below:

A. (*c*), (*a*), (*d*), (*b*), (*e*)
B. (*c*), (*b*), (*e*), (*a*), (*d*)
C. (*c*), (*e*), (*b*), (*a*), (*d*)
D. (*c*), (*d*), (*a*), (*b*), (*e*)

40. The number of items sold by a SHG in five days in an exhibition are:

20, 30, 15, 10, 40.

What is the average sale?

A. 115 B. 05
C. 25 D. 23

41. Arrange in sequence how an organisation can initiate the process of community involvement in development activities:

(*a*) Sharing the findings with community
(*b*) Implementation of the programme(s)
(*c*) Diagnosis (know the community)
(*d*) Monitoring and Feedback
(*e*) Establishment of mission/objectives

Choose the **correct** answer from the options given below:

A. (*a*), (*b*), (*e*), (*c*) and (*d*)
B. (*a*), (*c*), (*e*), (*b*) and (*d*)
C. (*c*), (*a*), (*e*), (*b*) and (*d*)
D. (*c*), (*e*), (*b*), (*a*) and (*d*)

42. Which companies qualify for CSR under Companies Act, 2013?

(*a*) Net worth of ₹ 500 crore or more
(*b*) Turnover of ₹ 1,000 crore or less
(*c*) Turnover of ₹ 1,000 crore or more
(*d*) Net profit of ₹ 5 crore or more

Choose the **correct** answer from the options given below:

A. (*a*), (*b*), (*c*) only
B. (*b*), (*a*), (*d*) only
C. (*a*), (*c*), (*d*) only
D. (*c*), (*d*), (*b*) only

43. Match the approaches of social work with their proponents.

List-I (Social Work Approach)	List-II (Proponent)
(*a*) Anti-oppressive Social Work Theory and Practice	I. Jan Fook
(*b*) Radical Social Work	II. Dennis Saleebey
(*c*) Critical Social Work	III. Lena Dominelli
(*d*) Strength Based Social Work	IV. Bailey and Brake

Choose the **correct** answer from the options given below:

	(*a*)	(*b*)	(*c*)	(*d*)
A.	IV	II	I	III
B.	III	IV	I	II
C.	II	III	IV	I
D.	I	II	III	IV

44. N.C.W. stands for:

A. National Council for Women
B. National Commission for Women
C. National Cooperative for Women
D. National Committee for Women

45. People's participation in development programmes or projects can be understood as given below:

(*a*) Participation in decision making
(*b*) Participation in implementation
(*c*) Participation in monitoring and evaluation
(*d*) Participation in sharing the benefits of development
(*e*) Participation in recruitment of the staff of the implementing agency

Choose the **correct** answer from the options given below:

A. (*b*), (*c*), (*d*) and (*e*) only
B. (*a*), (*b*), (*c*) and (*d*) only
C. (*a*), (*b*), (*d*) and (*e*) only
D. (*a*), (*c*), (*d*) and (*e*) only

46. Which one of the following legislation provides for certain percentage of government jobs for persons with disabilities?

A. The Persons with Disabilities (Equal Opportunities Protection of Right and Full Participation) Act
B. The Right of Persons with Disabilities Act
C. The Employment of Disabled Persons Act
D. The Disabilities Act

47. The first world report on disability came in the year:

A. 2009
B. 2010
C. 2011
D. 2012

48. An Ecosystem approach to social work encompasses:

(*a*) Multiple and complex transactions between persons within their family
(*b*) People's coping with changing environments
(*c*) Change in the people's capacities to deal with their surroundings
(*d*) Participation of clients without the involvement of family
(*e*) The needs, problems and strengths of individuals and their families

Choose the **correct** answer from the options given below:

A. (*a*), (*b*), (*c*) and (*d*) only
B. (*a*), (*c*), (*d*) and (*e*) only
C. (*a*), (*b*), (*c*) and (*e*) only
D. (*a*), (*b*), (*d*) and (*e*) only

49. Arrange the formation and establishment of trade unions in chronological order:

(*a*) The Red Trade Union Congress
(*b*) The Indian National Trade Union Congress
(*c*) All India Trade Union Congress
(*d*) Bharatiya Mazdoor Sangh
(*e*) Madras Labour Union

Choose the **correct** answer from the options given below:

A. (*e*), (*c*), (*a*), (*b*), (*d*)
B. (*a*), (*d*), (*c*), (*b*), (*e*)
C. (*a*), (*b*), (*c*), (*d*), (*e*)
D. (*e*), (*d*), (*b*), (*c*), (*a*)

50. Match the year of enactment with the corresponding legislation.

List-I (Year)	List-II (Legislation)
(*a*) 1833	I. Hindu Widow Remarriage Act
(*b*) 1986	II. Abolition of Slavery
(*c*) 1948	III. Factories Act
(*d*) 1856	IV. Child Labour (Prohibition and Regulation) Act

Choose the **correct** answer from the options given below:

	(*a*)	(*b*)	(*c*)	(*d*)
A.	I	II	III	IV
B.	III	I	IV	II
C.	IV	III	II	I
D.	II	IV	III	I

51. Match the Trade Unions with corresponding year of formation.

List-I (Trade Union)	List-II (Year of Formation)
(*a*) All India Trade Union Congress	I. 1947
(*b*) The Red Trade Union Congress	II. 1955
(*c*) Indian National Trade Union Congress	III. 1931
(*d*) Bharatiya Mazdoor Sangh	IV. 1920

Choose the **correct** answer from the options given below:

	(a)	(b)	(c)	(d)
A.	I	II	III	IV
B.	IV	III	I	II
C.	II	III	IV	I
D.	IV	II	III	I

52. Match List-I with List-II.

List-I (Theories/Approaches/ Models)	List-II (Person Associated)
(a) Functional social case work approach	I. Albert Bandura
(b) Problem solving model	II. Germain and Hartman
(c) Social Learning theory	III. Helen Harris Perlman
(d) Ecological systems theory	IV. Jessie Taft and Virginia Robinson

Choose the **correct** answer from the options given below:

	(a)	(b)	(c)	(d)
A.	II	III	I	IV
B.	III	I	IV	II
C.	IV	I	II	III
D.	IV	III	I	II

53. Psychodrama consists of:

(a) Professional actors to perform drama

(b) Role enactment of individuals in a group

(c) Individuals, if needed, represent persons in the real-life situation

(d) Individuals get an opportunity to externalize their hostilities and see thing more objectively

(e) Instrument of therapy for individual tensions and conflicts.

Choose the **correct** answer from the options given below:

A. (a), (b), (c) and (d) only

B. (a), (c), (d) and (e) only

C. (a), (b), (d) and (e) only

D. (b), (c), (d) and (e) only

54. 'Communist Manifesto' was first published in the year:

A. 1867 B. 1917

C. 1848 D. 1945

55. Which of the following book is authored by Lena Dominelli?

A. Blackberry Winter

B. Anti-oppressive social work theory and practice

C. Human needs : Overview

D. Social work in a sustainable world

56. Match the committee relating to health services with corresponding years.

List-I (Committee relating to health services)	List-II (Year)
(a) The Bhore Committee	I. 1967
(b) The Chaddha Committee	II. 1973
(c) Jungal Walla Committee	III. 1943
(d) Kartar Singh Committee	IV. 1963

Choose the **correct** answer from the options given below:

	(a)	(b)	(c)	(d)
A.	IV	III	II	I
B.	III	IV	I	II
C.	I	III	II	IV
D.	II	I	III	IV

57. Who among the following is credited for introducing 'social diagnosis' approach in social work practice?

A. James Adams

B. Mary Richmond

C. G. Konopka

D. W.A. Friedlander

58. Conducting research in social work involves a scientific process. Identify the correct answer.

(a) Review of literature

(b) Formulating a research design

(c) Formulating a research topic

(d) Data collection

(e) Analysis and Interpretation

Choose the **correct** answer from the options given below:

A. (*b*), (*a*), (*c*), (*d*), (*e*)
B. (*a*), (*c*), (*d*), (*b*), (*e*)
C. (*c*), (*a*), (*b*), (*d*), (*e*)
D. (*c*), (*b*), (*a*), (*d*), (*e*)

59. Which of the following Article of the Indian Constitution talks about Governance in the Fifth Schedule Areas?

A. Article-243 B. Article-244(1)
C. Article-244(2) D. Article-241

60. The term 'collective bargaining' was coined by:

A. Allan Flanders
B. Sidney and Beatrice Webb
C. John Dunlop
D. Derek Bok

61. According to Robert Redfield, the term 'small community' is used to describe which community?

A. LGBTQAI community
B. Agricultural community
C. Tribal community
D. Gated community

62. Participatory Rural Appraisal (PRA) approach was developed by:

A. Paulo Freire B. Md. Yunus
C. John Rawls D. Robert Chambers

63. Which of the following are salient features of Juvenile Justice Act, 2000?

(*a*) Defined children as below 18 years of age.
(*b*) Separated children into two categories-children in need of care and protection and, children in conflict with law.
(*c*) The children in need of care and protection were to be sent directly to observation homes.
(*d*) The children in conflict with law were to be kept in juvenile homes.
(*e*) Rehabilitation and social integration of a child.

Choose the **correct** answer from the options given below:

A. (*a*), (*b*), (*c*), (*e*) only
B. (*b*), (*c*), (*d*) only
C. (*a*), (*b*), (*e*) only
D. (*c*), (*d*), (*e*) only

64. Calculate mode from the following data of marks obtained by 10(ten) students:

10, 27, 24, 12, 27, 27, 20, 18, 15, 30

A. 10 B. 27
C. 24 D. 12

65. Which Article of the Indian Constitution talks about complete abolishment of untouchability?

A. Article-15 B. Article-16
C. Article-17 D. Article-19

66. Which of the following is correct:

(*a*) Sum of the deviations from mean is zero.
(*b*) Sum of squares of deviations from mean is minimum.
(*c*) Sum of deviations from median, ignoring signs, is minimum.
(*d*) Sum of squares of deviations from mode is minimum.

Choose the **correct** answer from the options given below:

A. (*a*), (*b*), (*c*) only
B. (*b*), (*c*), (*d*) only
C. (*c*), (*d*), (*a*) only
D. (*a*), (*b*), (*d*) only

67. Arrange the research process in a sequence:

(*a*) Theory (*b*) Sampling
(*c*) Hypothesis (*d*) Data collection
(*e*) Operationalization

Choose the **correct** answer from the options given below:

A. (*d*), (*b*), (*a*), (*c*), (*e*)
B. (*a*), (*c*), (*e*), (*b*), (*d*)
C. (*b*), (*a*), (*d*), (*e*), (*c*)
D. (*c*), (*d*), (*b*), (*a*), (*e*)

68. Arrange in sequence the key steps in preparing a budget for a project.

(*a*) Determine category-wise expenses
(*b*) Present the draft budget and cash flow
(*c*) Identify and plan activities
(*d*) Monitor the budget as project progress
(*e*) Make changes and finalize income and expenses

Choose **the** correct answer from the options given below:

A. (*a*), (*b*), (*c*), (*e*), (*d*)
B. (*b*), (*c*), (*d*), (*a*), (*e*)
C. (*c*), (*b*), (*a*), (*d*), (*e*)
D. (*c*), (*a*), (*b*), (*e*), (*d*)

69. Arrange the sequence of social work paradigm since its inception:

(*a*) Rights based
(*b*) Development
(*c*) Charity
(*d*) Welfare
(*e*) Empowerment

Choose the **correct** answer from the options given below:

A. (*e*), (*b*), (*d*), (*c*), (*a*)
B. (*c*), (*d*), (*b*), (*e*), (*a*)
C. (*a*), (*c*), (*e*), (*b*), (*d*)
D. (*d*), (*a*), (*b*), (*c*), (*e*)

70. Which of the following author first coined the term 'intersectionality'?

A. Kelsey Ulrich
B. Kimberle Crenshaw
C. Tim Wise
D. Michelle Alexander

71. Theory of understanding causation of disease has evolved over the years. Arrange chronologically the historical evolution of understanding causation of disease.

(*a*) Epidemiological Traid
(*b*) Multifactorial causation
(*c*) Miasmatic theory of disease
(*d*) Web of causation
(*e*) Germ theory of disease

Choose the **correct** answer from the options given below:

A. (*c*), (*e*), (*a*), (*b*), (*d*)
B. (*c*), (*a*), (*d*), (*b*), (*e*)
C. (*a*), (*b*), (*e*), (*c*), (*d*)
D. (*a*), (*c*), (*d*), (*b*), (*e*)

72. Which of the following functions are performed by CSR committee as mentioned in Companies Act, 2013?

(*a*) Formulate and recommend the CSR policy to the Board.
(*b*) Conduct evaluation and impact assessment of CSR project.
(*c*) Recommend the amount of expenditure to be incurred on CSR activities.
(*d*) Monitor the CSR policy of the company from time to time.
(*e*) Formulate and recommend to the Board an action plan in pursuance of its CSR policy.

Choose the **correct** answer from the options given below:

A. (*a*), (*b*), (*c*), (*d*) only
B. (*b*), (*c*), (*d*), (*e*) only
C. (*a*), (*c*), (*d*), (*e*) only
D. (*a*), (*b*), (*d*), (*e*) only

73. Who founded the Neighbourhood Guild, the first settlement house in the United States?

A. Mary Richmond
B. Jane Addams
C. Zilpha Smith
D. Margaretta Williamson

74. Match the schemes/programmes with their year of implementation:

List-I (Schemes/Programmes)	List-II (Year)
(*a*) Beti Bachao Beti Padhao	I. 2013
(*b*) Integrated Child Development Services	II. 1975
(*c*) Deen Dayal Antyodaya Yojana	III. 2014
(*d*) Swachh Bharat Mission-Gramin	IV. 2015

Choose the **correct** answer from the options given below:

	(*a*)	(*b*)	(*c*)	(*d*)
A.	I	III	II	IV
B.	III	IV	I	II
C.	II	III	I	IV
D.	IV	II	I	III

75. Who from the following is a famous eco-feminist?

A. Uma Chakravarti
B. Leela Dube
C. Vandana Shiva
D. Arundhati Roy

76. Which of the following terminologies is connected with qualitative inquiry?

(*a*) Phenomenology
(*b*) Range
(*c*) Interpretivism
(*d*) Hypothesis
(*e*) Ethnography

Choose the **correct** answer from the options given below:

A. (*a*), (*b*), (*c*) only
B. (*b*), (*c*), (*d*) only
C. (*d*), (*c*), (*a*) only
D. (*a*), (*c*), (*e*) only

77. Which of the following is not a factor responsible for 'organizational entropy'?

A. Declining performance and management failure
B. Lack of appropriate set of rules and procedures
C. Effective personnel policies
D. A high rate of turn over

78. Which of the following tests the 'goodness of fit' of a distribution?

A. F-test B. Z-test
C. T-test D. Chi-square test

79. Garland, Jones, and Kolodny (1976) proposed five stages of group development. Which is the correct sequence of these stages?

(*a*) Intimacy (*b*) Differentiation
(*c*) Separation (*d*) Power and Control
(*e*) Preaffiliation

Choose the **correct** answer from the options given below:

A. (*e*), (*a*), (*b*), (*d*), (*c*)
B. (*e*), (*d*), (*a*), (*b*), (*c*)
C. (*e*), (*b*), (*d*), (*a*), (*c*)
D. (*e*), (*c*), (*a*), (*d*), (*b*)

80. International Labour Organization (ILO) was formed in the year:

A. 1945 B. 1917
C. 1929 D. 1919

81. Arrange the various stages of social movement in the correct sequence as developed by Armand L. Maas (1975).

(*a*) Fusion
(*b*) Intersection
(*c*) Segmentation
(*d*) Institutionalization
(*e*) Initiation

Choose the **correct** answer from the options given below:

A. (*a*), (*c*), (*d*), (*e*), (*b*)
B. (*e*), (*a*), (*d*), (*c*), (*b*)
C. (*a*), (*e*), (*c*), (*d*), (*b*)
D. (*e*), (*b*), (*d*), (*c*), (*a*)

82. Arrange the step-by-step process for recruiting a human resource of an organization.

(*a*) Screening and shortlisting
(*b*) Evaluation and offer of employment
(*c*) Identifying the hiring needs
(*d*) Interviewing
(*e*) Preparing the job description

Choose the **correct** answer from the options given below:

A. (*c*), (*a*), (*d*), (*e*), (*b*)
B. (*c*), (*e*), (*a*), (*d*), (*b*)
C. (*a*), (*d*), (*c*), (*e*), (*b*)
D. (*a*), (*c*), (*d*), (*e*), (*b*)

83. According to W.W. Rostow, country's economy and social progress goes through series of five stages. Arrange the stages in proper sequence:

(*a*) The traditional society
(*b*) Drive to maturity
(*c*) Take-off
(*d*) Period of high mass consumption
(*e*) Pre-conditions for take-off

Choose the **correct** answer from the options given below:

A. (*a*), (*b*), (*c*), (*e*), (*d*)
B. (*a*), (*c*), (*b*), (*d*), (*e*)
C. (*a*), (*e*), (*c*), (*b*), (*d*)
D. (*a*), (*d*), (*b*), (*c*), (*e*)

84. Which of the following are true of 'structural change' model of community work?

(*a*) Transform existing conditions at the grass roots level
(*b*) Adopt alternative political ideology.
(*c*) Develop the link between the micro and macro level social realities.
(*d*) Redistribution of power in a community between groups.
(*e*) Evaluate welfare program and services of the government.

Choose the **correct** answer from the options given below:

A. (*a*), (*b*), (*c*) and (*d*) only
B. (*b*), (*c*), (*d*) and (*e*) only
C. (*c*), (*d*), (*e*) and (*a*) only
D. (*d*), (*e*), (*a*) and (*b*) only

85. Which of the following Article of the Universal Declaration of Human Rights talks about the right to life, liberty and security of a person?

A. Article-1
B. Article-2
C. Article-3
D. Article-6

86. Arrange the five stages of child development in an order of developmental stages:

(*a*) Infant
(*b*) Toddler
(*c*) Newborn
(*d*) Pre-school
(*e*) School Age

Choose the **correct** answer from the options given below:

A. (*c*), (*a*), (*b*), (*d*), (*e*)
B. (*a*), (*c*), (*b*), (*d*), (*e*)
C. (*e*), (*d*), (*c*), (*a*), (*b*)
D. (*b*), (*a*), (*d*), (*c*), (*e*)

87. Social insurance can be defined as:

A. Contributions of the workers, employees and the state.
B. Relieve the suffering caused by age.
C. Financial aid granted by the government.
D. Contributions for the distitutes.

88. "Development as Freedom" is written by:

A. Jean Dreze
B. Amartya Sen
C. Abhijeet Banerjee
D. Aruna Roy

89. Arrange the five faces of oppression (mild to severe) as suggested by Irish Marion Young:

(*a*) Powerlessness
(*b*) Marginalization
(*c*) Violence
(*d*) Exploitation
(*e*) Cultural Imperialism

Choose the **correct** answer from the options given below:

A. (*a*), (*b*), (*c*), (*d*), (*e*)
B. (*d*), (*b*), (*a*), (*e*), (*c*)
C. (*e*), (*d*), (*c*), (*b*), (*a*)
D. (*b*), (*d*), (*c*), (*e*), (*a*)

90. Which of the following is not a condition conducive for collective behaviour?

A. Institutionalised forms of segregation and exploitation
B. Dissonance in societal values
C. Emergence of new leader
D. Individual goal and achievement

Directions (Qs. No. 91-95): *Read the following passage and answer the questions.*

Women's NGOs such as SEWA and Annapurna Mahila Mandal have existed since the 1970s, and the Indian government had established *mahila mandals* (women's groups) in most villages during the 1950s and 1960s. However, it was after the publication in 1987 of the Report of the National Commission on Women Shram-shakti, which focused on the disadvantage that women faced, that the focus on women in self-help programmes took off. As a result of these changes in the 1980s both in the approach of NGOs to women's programmes and the donor support for gender and development, most development NGOs in India since the 1990s have a much stronger focus on self-help approaches, and the specific targeting of women as their primary target group. It is the history and the relationship of NGOs with the Indian state that has shaped Indian development NGOs, and to a large extent influences the approaches they take. This history and experience is unique, not only in South Asia, but arguably in the world. This discussion goes some way to informing how the modern Indian development NGO of the twenty-first century addresses the high levels of poverty in the current development context.

91. Who advocates for women's rights and livelihoods and stands as the only Trade Union of women in the unorganized sector:

A. Annapurna Mahila Mandal
B. Self Employed Women's Association
C. Jagori
D. Breakthrough

92. Which of the following statement best describes women in the unorganized sector?

A. Exclusive focus on formal sector development
B. Undervalued contributions to the economy
C. Recognition of their roles and access to substantial pension plans
D. Guaranteed employment contracts

93. 'Shram-shakti' report focuses on:

A. Women in formal sector
B. Self employed women in informal sector
C. Women in universities and schools
D. Women in sports

94. The flagship programme/scheme of Ministry of Rural Development particularly for women to access financial services and livelihoods is called:

A. One stop centre
B. Swadhar-greh scheme
C. Ujjawala scheme
D. DAY-NRLM

95. Which of the following addresses high levels of poverty through innovative approaches?

A. Greenpeace
B. Grameen Bank
C. United Nations Population Fund
D. BRIC Nations Coalition

Directions (Qs. No. 96-100): *Read the following passage and answer the questions.*

Universally or selectively? If a welfare state is acting on behalf of the community at large, it can distribute resources on the same basis to every member of that community, or it may operate selectively, providing resources only to those who need or deserve help. A case can be made on efficiency ground for either approach. If benefits and services are available on the same basis to everybody, this ensures that everybody is guaranteed the necessary minimum level of help to secure their wellbeing; because everybody gets the same, no stigma can attach to receiving that help and nobody need be deterred from seeking help; and those people who do not need the help they receive will, if the system is funded by progressive taxation, be able to pay back what they have received, as well as contributing to the help received by other members of the community. If, on the other hand, benefits and services are made available only to those who need or deserve them, this will ensure that such resources as are available will be put to the most effective use; optimum rather than minimum levels of help may be afforded to those in the greatest need; those people who do not require help will neither be deterred from helping themselves, nor made resentful by unnecessarily high levels of taxation.

96. Which of the following country is not the best example of the Institutional Redistributive Model of Welfare?

A. Sweden B. USA
C. Norway D. Finland

97. Progressive taxation is understood as:

A. A tax system where tax rate decreases as the taxable amount increases
B. A tax system where only the businesses are taxed
C. A tax system in which the tax rate increases as the taxable amount increases
D. A taxation system where everyone pays the same tax irrespective of their income

98. Which of the following is not a characteristic of 'welfare state'?

A. Support job creation
B. Provision of health and education
C. Programs for more disparity between rich and poor
D. Ensure minimum wages

99. The author of 'Three worlds of welfare capitalism' is:

A. Richard Titmuss
B. Gosta Esping-Anderson
C. Karl Marx
D. John M. Keynes

100. In Residual Welfare Model, welfare is:

A. Available to everyone regardless of their situation
B. Provided as primary means of survival
C. Seen as last resort
D. Given universally to all, to prevent any crisis

ANSWERS

1. (D):

(*a*) Sigmund Freud proposed the Psychoanalytic theory, which emphasizes unconscious mind dynamics, early childhood experiences, and conflicts between innate drives and societal norms.

(*b*) Behavioural theory, linked to John B. Watson, highlights observable behaviours and their relationships with environmental stimuli, emphasizing learning through conditioning.

(*c*) Carl Rogers, a prominent figure in Humanistic theory, focused on self-actualization, personal growth, and a positive view of human potential.

(*d*) Cognitive theory, associated with Albert Bandura, explores mental processes like thinking, memory, and problem-solving, emphasizing the role of observational learning and self-efficacy.

2. (A):

(*a*) Jyotiba Phule founded Satyashodhak Samaj in 1873 to promote social equality and challenge caste-based discrimination.

(*b*) Arya Samaj, established by Swami Dayanand Saraswati in 1875, focused on Vedic revivalism and opposed idol worship.

(*c*) Raja Ram Mohan Roy founded Brahmo Samaj in 1828, advocating for monotheism, social reforms, and educational advancements.

(*d*) Pandita Ramabai started Arya Mahila Samaj to promote women's education and rights in India.

3. (B):

(*a*) The target population identifies the community members who are the focus of development or assistance.

(*c*) Groups within the community form the collective social units essential for collaborative efforts.

(*d*) Significant individuals, like community leaders, play a pivotal role in mobilizing resources and influencing decisions.

(*e*) Agencies provide institutional support, funding, and professional expertise for community work.

4. (A):

(*a*) Arithmetic mean is straightforward and widely understood, making it a reliable measure.

(*b*) It provides an actual central value based on computation, not just a positional statistic.

(*d*) As the centre of gravity, it balances the data values, offering a central tendency representation.

(*e*) It is computed using a mathematical formula, ensuring consistency and objectivity.

5. (D):

(*a*) The National Policy on Health, formulated in 2017, aims to provide universal health coverage and address inequities in healthcare delivery.

(*b*) The National Policy on Youth 2023 focuses on harnessing youth potential for sustainable development and nation-building.

(*c*) The National Policy on Voluntary Organizations, introduced in 2007, seeks to enhance collaboration between the government and civil society.

(*d*) The National Education Policy 2020 emphasizes holistic, flexible, multidisciplinary education for lifelong learning.

6. (B):

(*a*) Raja Ram Mohan Roy led efforts to abolish the practice of Sati (Satipratha) in the early 19th century, playing a crucial role in its eventual prohibition in 1829.

(*b*) Baba Amte was a prominent social worker who dedicated his life to the care and rehabilitation of people suffering from leprosy.

(*c*) Sarojini Naidu, a prominent freedom fighter and poet, actively worked for the upliftment of women's status in Indian society.

(*d*) Dayanand Saraswati, founder of Arya Samaj, opposed idol worship and advocated for Vedic practices.

7. (B): Andre Gunder Frank and Walter Rodney were leading proponents of Dependency theory. This theory critiques the global economic system, emphasizing how the development of wealthy nations depends on the exploitation of poorer nations, creating a cycle of dependency. It highlights issues like underdevelopment, exploitation of resources, and unequal trade relations.

8. (A):

(*a*) Dissociative amnesia refers to memory loss related to traumatic or stressful events.

(*b*) Depersonalisation/Derealisation disorder involves feelings of detachment from oneself or reality.

(*d*) Dissociative identity disorder, or multiple personality disorder, is characterized by two or more distinct identities or personality states.

9. (A):

(*a*) Hull House, founded by Jane Addams in Chicago, was a pioneering settlement house addressing urban poverty and providing community services.

(*b*) Neighbourhood Guild was among the first settlement houses in the U.S., focusing on social reform and education.

(*c*) College Settlement supported educational and recreational programs for underprivileged communities.

(*d*) Houchen House provided essential services, including education and healthcare, to immigrant populations.

10. (D): The Ministry of Home Affairs oversees the regulation and grievances related to the Foreign Contribution (Regulation) Act (FCRA). FCRA governs the receipt and utilization of foreign funds by non-governmental organizations and ensures transparency and accountability in their operations.

11. (B): In the SMART framework for program objectives, "R" stands for "Relevant." Objectives must align with the overall goals and priorities of the program or organization. Relevance ensures that efforts and resources are directed toward meaningful outcomes. For example, in a social work program, objectives focusing on community needs are considered relevant.

12. (B):

(*a*) CSWE was established in 1952 to set and maintain standards for social work education.

(*b*) IFSW was founded in 1956 to promote social work on a global scale.

(*c*) NASW was created in 1955 to unify social workers under a professional body.

(*d*) ICSW, established in 1928, focuses on promoting social welfare policies internationally.

13. (C): The NASW Code of Ethics highlights the mission of social work as advancing human well-being and helping meet basic and complex needs.

(*a*) Service emphasizes prioritizing clients' interests and providing help without self-interest.

(*b*) Social Justice focuses on promoting equity and addressing injustice.

(*d*) Integrity ensures that social workers act honestly and ethically.

(*e*) Competence requires that social workers continually improve their knowledge and skills.

14. (C): The range is a measure of dispersion in a data set. It is calculated by subtracting the smallest value from the largest value.

For example, in a distribution with values 5, 10, 15, and 20,

The range = 20 − 5 = 15.

15. (B):

(*a*) World Environment Day, celebrated on 5th June, raises awareness about environmental protection.

(*b*) International Human Rights Day, observed on 10th December, marks the adoption of the Universal Declaration of Human Rights.

(*c*) World Social Justice Day, celebrated on 20th February, focuses on promoting fairness and reducing inequality.

(*d*) World Knowledge Day, on 14th April, emphasizes the importance of knowledge-sharing for global progress.

16. (B): Florence Hollis coined the term "person-in-situation" in the context of social work. The concept emphasizes understanding individuals within the context of their environment, interactions, and relationships This holistic perspective is central to social work practice as it integrates the individual's psychological, social, and environmental factors.

17. (C): Ishwar Chandra Vidyasagar was a prominent reformer who advocated for the remarriage of widows in India. His efforts led to the enactment of the Hindu Widows' Remarriage Act of 1856, which legalized widow remarriage. Vidyasagar's work challenged societal norms and promoted women's rights during the 19th century.

18. (B): NSSO stands for National Sample Survey Organization. It was established in 1950 under the Ministry of Statistics and Programme Implementation, Government of India. NSSO conducts large-scale surveys on socio-economic, demographic, and agricultural issues to assist in policymaking. In 2019, NSSO merged with the Central Statistics Office (CSO) to form the National Statistical Office (NSO).

19. (B):

(*a*) Gordon Hearn contributed significantly to the understanding of social group work through her work on 'Theory Building in Social Work'.

(*b*) Wilson and Ryland focused on practical aspects of group work in their book, 'Social Group Work Practice'.

(*c*) Harleigh Trecker's Social Group Work Principles and Practice is foundational in outlining principles of group dynamics and social interventions.

(*d*) Gisela Konopka emphasized therapeutic approaches in working with children in groups.

20. (B): The four PR models proposed by Gruning and Hunt in 1984 are as follows:

(*a*) The Two-way symmetrical model focuses on mutual understanding and balanced communication between organizations and their publics.

(*e*) The Two-way asymmetrical model emphasizes persuasion and influence, favouring the organization.

(*b*) The Public information model disseminates factual and truthful information to the public.

(*c*) The Press agentry model seeks to create publicity through media attention, often exaggerating or sensationalizing information.

21. (C): Mixed Method research combines elements of both qualitative and quantitative approaches to provide a comprehensive understanding of a research problem. It integrates statistical data (quantitative) with detailed narrative data (qualitative) to draw robust conclusions.

For example, in a study about community health, surveys can provide numerical insights, while interviews can offer deeper understanding of experiences.

22. (D): In 1946, J.J. Hospital in Mumbai became the first institution in India to appoint a medical social worker. This appointment marked the beginning of professional medical social work in India. The role involved addressing the social and psychological aspects of patient care, alongside medical treatment.

23. (A): In the social planning model of community work, the focus is on systematic assessment of community needs and available resources. It involves planning interventions to address gaps in services or welfare programs. This model is often used by government and non-governmental organizations to formulate welfare policies.

24. (C): Gordon W. Allport defined personality as a "dynamic organization within the individual of those psychophysical systems that determine his unique adjustment to his environment." This definition emphasizes the interplay between mental and physical systems, highlighting the adaptive and unique nature of personality. Allport is known for his trait theory, which categorizes personality traits into cardinal, central, and secondary traits.

25. **(A):** Cultural competence involves the ability to work effectively with individuals from diverse cultural backgrounds by:

(*a*) Understanding the norms and values of different groups.

(*b*) Recognizing the uniqueness of one's own cultural perspective.

(*c*) Being open to other customs, practices, and rituals.

(*d*) Demonstrating a willingness to learn and adapt to cultural differences.

Cultural competence avoids ethnocentrism, which involves considering one's culture as superior to others.

26. **(C):** Rabindranath Tagore's fifteen points of rural reconstruction focused on:

(*a*) Addressing social ills and fostering unity among communities.

(*b*) Discouraging consumption of alcohol and drugs.

(*d*) Establishing cooperative grain stores to combat famine.

(*e*) Cultivating fraternal feelings and a sense of unity among villages and districts.

The promotion of information technology and digital infrastructure is not part of Tagore's rural reconstruction program as it was conceptualized in the early 20th century, far before the digital age.

27. **(C):** In the acronym POSDCORB, "CO" stands for "Coordinating."

POSDCORB, introduced by Luther Gulick, outlines key functions of management: Planning, Organizing, Staffing, Directing, Coordinating, Reporting, and Budgeting.

Coordinating ensures harmony and integration of various activities within an organization.

28. **(C):** Sociometry, developed by Jacob L. Moreno, is a tool for studying social relationships and group dynamics. It uses sociograms to visualize connections, attraction, and repulsion among group members. Sociometry helps investigate roles like leadership, isolation, and the interplay of group relations in an interdisciplinary context.

29. **(C):** Victim blaming attributes the causes of misfortune or oppression to the victims themselves.

(*a*) This ideology often holds the downtrodden accountable for their own distress.

(*c*) The stigma can reinforce a cycle of negativity and disadvantage.

(*d*) Internalized blame further perpetuates feelings of inferiority and helplessness.

(*e*) Historical factors like industrialization and Protestant ethics shaped the ethos of self-reliance and moral judgment.

30. **(*):** The correct chronological order of legislation enactment is:

(*e*) Prisons Act (1894)

(*c*) Probation of Offenders Act (1958)

(*b*) Immoral Traffic Prevention Act (1956, amended later)

(*d*) Narcotics Drugs and Psychotropic Substance Act (1985)

(*a*) Juvenile Justice (Care and Protection of Children) Act (2000, amended in 2015 and 2021).

31. **(C):**

(*a*) Toynbee Hall was established in 1884 in London as the first settlement house aimed at addressing urban poverty through education and community development.

(*b*) The Beveridge Report of 1942, authored by William Beveridge, laid the foundation for the modern welfare state in the United Kingdom.

(*c*) The Charity Organization Society (COS) was founded in 1869 in London to coordinate charitable efforts and ensure efficient use of resources.

(*d*) The Elizabethan Poor Law, enacted in 1601, was the first significant legislation addressing poverty in England, establishing a framework for poor relief.

32. (B & C): Both the Brahmo Samaj and Arya Samaj objected to idol worship.

The Brahmo Samaj, founded by Raja Ram Mohan Roy in 1828, advocated for monotheism and rejected idol worship.

The Arya Samaj, established by Swami Dayanand Saraswati in 1875, sought a return to Vedic principles and opposed idol worship and rituals.

33. (D): The correct sequence of the social case work process is:

(*e*) **Intake:** Identifying the client and understanding the problem.

(*a*) **Study:** Collecting detailed information about the client's situation.

(*c*) **Diagnosis:** Analyzing the information to identify the core issues.

(*d*) **Treatment:** Implementing strategies to address the issues.

(*b*) **Follow-up:** Monitoring the effectiveness of the interventions.

34. (C): The Royal Commission on Labour was appointed in 1929 to investigate industrial conditions in India. Its primary focus was on improving the working conditions of laborers and suggesting reforms to enhance labor welfare. The recommendations led to significant advancements in labor legislation, addressing issues like wages, working hours, and safety standards.

35. (A): The class interval is the difference between the upper and lower boundaries of a class.

In the given classes (10–20, 20–30, 30–40, 40–50), the class interval is calculated as:

Class Interval = Upper boundary – Lower boundary = 20 – 10 = 10.

36. (C): Unity of Command is a principle of management stating that each employee should report to one superior. This principle ensures clarity in communication, avoids conflicts in instructions, and enhances accountability. It is one of the 14 principles of management proposed by Henri Fayol.

37. (B): In the development process, a change agent performs the following roles:

(*a*) Acting as a catalyst to initiate change and motivate the community.

(*b*) Helping processes by facilitating collaboration and dialogue.

(*c*) Linking resources by connecting the community to opportunities, information, or support.

(*e*) Managing conflicts to maintain harmony and focus on common goals.

A change agent does not engage in political opportunism, which is unrelated to genuine community development.

38. (D): Abraham Maslow's hierarchy of needs is arranged from basic to advanced:

(*e*) **Physiological:** Basic needs such as food, water, and shelter.

(*b*) **Safety:** Security and protection from harm.

(*d*) **Love and Belongingness:** Social connections and relationships.

(*a*) **Self-esteem:** Respect and recognition from others.

(*c*) **Self-actualization:** Realization of one's full potential.

39. (C): The stages of organizational conflict as proposed by L.R. Pondy are:

(*c*) **Latent stage:** Potential for conflict exists due to underlying conditions.

(*e*) **Perceived stage:** Conflict is recognized or perceived by the involved parties.

(*b*) **Felt stage:** Emotional tension or discomfort arises due to conflict.

(*a*) **Manifest:** The conflict is openly expressed through actions or behaviour.

(*d*) **Aftermath:** The outcomes of the conflict, which can be resolved or unresolved.

40. (D): The average sale is calculated as:
Total items sold = 20 + 30 + 15 + 10 + 40 = 115.

Number of days = 5.

Average = Total items sold ÷ Number of days = 115 ÷ 5 = 23.

41. (C): To initiate community involvement in development activities, the process includes:

(*c*) Diagnosis to understand the community's needs and issues.

(*a*) Sharing the findings to build trust and transparency with the community.

(*e*) Establishing clear mission and objectives collaboratively with community input.

(*b*) Implementing the programs based on the defined goals.

(*d*) Monitoring and feedback to assess effectiveness and make necessary adjustments.

42. (C): Under the Companies Act, 2013, companies are mandated to undertake Corporate Social Responsibility (CSR) if they meet any of the following criteria:

(*a*) Net worth of ₹ 500 crore or more.

(*c*) Turnover of ₹ 1,000 crore or more.

(*d*) Net profit of ₹ 5 crore or more.

Such companies are required to spend at least 2% of their average net profit of the previous three years on CSR activities.

43. (B):

(*a*) Lena Dominelli developed Anti-oppressive Social Work, emphasizing equality and combating oppression.

(*b*) Bailey and Brake are known for Radical Social Work, focusing on systemic change and addressing structural inequalities.

(*c*) Jan Fook proposed Critical Social Work, which critiques traditional approaches and emphasizes reflection and empowerment.

(*d*) Dennis Saleebey pioneered Strength-Based Social Work, focusing on clients' strengths and potential rather than their deficits.

44. (B): The National Commission for Women (NCW) was established in 1992 in India. It serves as a statutory body to address issues related to women's rights, equality, and empowerment. The NCW reviews laws, policies, and programs affecting women and provides recommendations for improvement.

45. (B): People's participation in development programs includes:

(*a*) Being involved in decision-making to ensure programs align with community needs.

(*b*) Participating in the implementation process to promote ownership and accountability.

(*c*) Contributing to monitoring and evaluation to assess progress and outcomes.

(*d*) Sharing the benefits of development, ensuring equitable distribution of resources and opportunities.

Recruitment of staff for implementing agencies is typically not a participatory process involving the community.

46. (A & B):

(A) **The Persons with Disabilities (Equal Opportunities, Protection of Rights and Full Participation) Act:** This act, enacted in 1995, provides a framework for ensuring equal opportunities for persons with disabilities. It mandates 3% reservation in government jobs for persons with visual, hearing, and locomotor disabilities.

(B) **The Right of Persons with Disabilities Act:** This act, passed in 2016, replaced the earlier 1995 Act and broadened the scope by increasing the types of recognized disabilities from 7 to 21. It also increased the reservation in government jobs from 3% to 4% for persons with benchmark disabilities. The 2016 Act aligns Indian law with the UN Convention on the Rights of Persons with Disabilities.

47. (C): The first World Report on Disability was released jointly by the World Health Organization (WHO) and the World Bank in 2011. The report provides global data on disability and highlights the barriers faced by persons with disabilities. It also offers recommendations to improve the inclusion and participation of disabled individuals in society.

48. (C): The Ecosystem approach to social work emphasizes:

(*a*) Interactions between individuals and their families.

(*b*) How people adapt to changing environments.

(*c*) Enhancing people's capacities to interact effectively with their surroundings.

(*e*) Recognizing the needs, problems, and strengths of both individuals and families.

It is a holistic approach, integrating individuals' environments into social work practice.

49. (A): The chronological order of trade union formation in India is:

(*e*) **Madras Labour Union (1918):** First organized labour union in India.

(*c*) **All India Trade Union Congress (1920):** India's first national-level trade union organization.

(*a*) **The Red Trade Union Congress (1931):** Associated with communist ideologies.

(*b*) **Indian National Trade Union Congress (1947):** Linked to the Indian National Congress.

(*d*) **Bharatiya Mazdoor Sangh (1955):** Affiliated with nationalist ideologies.

50. (D): The chronological match is:

(*a*) **1833:** Abolition of Slavery, passed under British law, outlawed slavery across the British Empire.

(*b*) **1986:** Child Labour (Prohibition and Regulation) Act, aimed at prohibiting and regulating child labour in India.

(*c*) **1948:** Factories Act, focused on labour welfare, safety, and working conditions in factories.

(*d*) **1856:** Hindu Widow Remarriage Act, legalized widow remarriage in India through the efforts of Ishwar Chandra Vidyasagar.

51. (B):

(*a*) All India Trade Union Congress (AITUC) was the first national-level trade union in India, established in 1920.

(*b*) The Red Trade Union Congress was formed in 1931, with communist ideologies influencing its structure.

(*c*) Indian National Trade Union Congress (INTUC) was formed in 1947 and aligned with the Indian National Congress.

(*d*) Bharatiya Mazdoor Sangh (BMS), founded in 1955, is associated with nationalist ideologies.

52. (D):

(*a*) Functional social case work focuses on enabling individuals to function better in society, developed by Jessie Taft and Virginia Robinson.

(*b*) Helen Harris Perlman introduced the problem-solving model, emphasizing practical methods for addressing individual issues.

(*c*) Albert Bandura's social learning theory highlights the role of observation and modeling in behaviour acquisition.

(*d*) Germain and Hartman developed the ecological systems theory, examining interactions between individuals and their environments.

53. (D): Psychodrama, developed by Jacob L. Moreno, includes:

(*b*) Role enactment to explore personal and group dynamics.

(*c*) Representation of real-life situations to address unresolved issues.

(*d*) Externalizing hostilities to gain an objective perspective.

(*e*) Acting as a therapeutic tool for personal and interpersonal conflicts.

54. (C): The Communist Manifesto was first published in 1848 by Karl Marx and Friedrich Engels. This seminal work outlines the principles of communism and critiques capitalism, emphasizing class struggle and the need for societal transformation.

55. (B): Lena Dominelli authored Anti-oppressive social work theory and practice, a pivotal text addressing inequality and power dynamics in social work. It emphasizes empowering marginalized communities and challenging oppressive systems.

56. (B):

(*a*) The Bhore Committee (1943) was established to recommend improvements in India's health services and laid the foundation for the country's modern health system.

(*b*) The Chaddha Committee (1963) focused on public health programs, especially malaria eradication.

(*c*) The Jungal Walla Committee (1967) studied the organization of medical care and recommended the integration of public and private sectors.

(*d*) The Kartar Singh Committee (1973) recommended a system for primary health care delivery involving community health workers.

57. (B): Mary Richmond is credited with introducing the "social diagnosis" approach in social work practice. Her 1917 book, Social Diagnosis, is considered a foundational work in social casework, providing a structured method to assess and address clients' problems. Richmond emphasized understanding the interaction between individuals and their environments.

58. (C): The scientific process in social work research involves:

(*c*) Formulating a clear and focused research topic.

(*a*) Conducting a review of relevant literature to understand existing knowledge.

(*b*) Designing a research plan, including methodology and data collection techniques.

(*d*) Collecting data systematically.

(*e*) Analyzing and interpreting the data to draw meaningful conclusions.

59. (B): Article 244(1) of the Indian Constitution governs the administration of Fifth Schedule Areas. These areas are predominantly tribal regions requiring special governance provisions to protect their rights, culture, and resources. The Fifth Schedule outlines the role of the Governor and Tribes Advisory Council in managing these regions.

60. (B): The term "collective bargaining" was coined by Sidney and Beatrice Webb, British social reformers and founders of the Fabian Society. Collective bargaining refers to the negotiation process between employers and employees (or their representatives) to determine wages, working conditions, and other employment terms. This concept is fundamental to industrial relations and labour law.

61. (B): According to Robert Redfield, the term "small community" describes rural, agricultural societies. These communities are characterized by close-knit social structures, traditional lifestyles, and an emphasis on shared values and cooperation. Redfield's studies focused on understanding cultural and social dynamics in these small, agrarian setups.

62. (D): The Participatory Rural Appraisal (PRA) approach was developed by Robert Chambers. PRA is a methodology used to enable rural communities to analyze their living conditions, identify problems, and develop solutions collaboratively. It emphasizes participatory decision-making and empowers local communities to take charge of their development.

63. (C): The Juvenile Justice Act, 2000, aimed at ensuring justice and care for children.

(*a*) It defined children as individuals below 18 years of age.

(*b*) It categorized children into "children in need of care and protection" and "children in conflict with the law."

(*e*) The act emphasized rehabilitation and social reintegration of children, prioritizing their well-being and future.

64. (B): Mode is the value that appears most frequently in a data set.

Given the data: 10, 27, 24, 12, 27, 27, 20, 18, 15, 30, the frequency of each value is:

27 appears 3 times, while all other values appear only once.

Hence, the mode is 27.

65. (C): Article 17 of the Indian Constitution provides for the complete abolition of untouchability. It prohibits the practice of untouchability in any form and declares it a punishable offense. This article is part of the Fundamental Rights, emphasizing equality and the elimination of social discrimination.

66. (A):

(*a*) The mean is the central value of a dataset, and the sum of deviations of all data points from the mean always equals zero.

(*b*) The mean minimizes the sum of squared deviations, making it the most balanced measure of central tendency for this purpose.

(*c*) The median minimizes the absolute deviations, ensuring the least aggregate distance from all data points when ignoring signs.

67. (B): The typical sequence of the research process involves the following steps:

(*a*) Research begins with theory to provide a conceptual framework.

(*c*) Hypotheses are formulated based on the theory to be tested empirically.

(*e*) Operationalization involves defining variables and determining how they will be measured.

(*b*) Sampling involves selecting a representative group for the study.

(*d*) Data collection is performed to gather empirical evidence to test the hypothesis.

68. (D):

(*c*) Start by identifying and planning project activities.

(*a*) Categorize and estimate expenses for each activity.

(*b*) Draft a preliminary budget and cash flow projection.

(*e*) Revise the draft based on feedback and finalize the income and expense figures.

(*d*) Continuously monitor the budget to ensure effective implementation and financial control.

69. (B):

(*c*) The social work paradigm began with charity, focusing on individual acts of help.

(*d*) It evolved to welfare, with a broader focus on social safety nets and organized aid.

(*b*) Development approaches followed, emphasizing sustainable community upliftment.

(*e*) Empowerment shifted focus to enabling individuals and groups to control their own lives.

(*a*) The rights-based paradigm advocates for structural changes to ensure universal human rights.

70. (B): Kimberle Crenshaw first coined the term "intersectionality" in 1989. Intersectionality describes how overlapping social identities (e.g., race, gender, class) create unique experiences of discrimination or privilege. Crenshaw introduced this concept to analyze the compounded effects of race and gender discrimination, particularly for women of color.

71. (A):

(*c*) The miasmatic theory, prevalent in ancient times, attributed diseases to "bad air" or miasma.

(*e*) The germ theory, developed in the late 19th century, identified microorganisms as the cause of diseases.

(*a*) The epidemiological triad (agent, host, environment) emerged later to explain disease transmission.

(*b*) Multifactorial causation recognized that diseases could result from multiple interacting factors.

(*d*) The web of causation model further expanded this view, illustrating complex interconnections between factors.

72. (C): The CSR committee under the Companies Act, 2013, performs the following functions:

(*a*) Recommending the CSR policy to the Board.

(*c*) Suggesting the budget for CSR activities.

(*d*) Monitoring the CSR policy's implementation.

(*e*) Drafting action plans for CSR initiatives.

While impact assessment is important, it is not a direct responsibility of the CSR committee.

73. (*): The correct answer is Stanton Coit, not any of the listed options.

Stanton Coit founded the Neighbourhood Guild, the first settlement house in the United States, in 1886 in New York City. It was established to address urban poverty and improve living conditions.

74. (D):

(*a*) Beti Bachao Beti Padhao, launched in 2015, promotes gender equality and education for girls.

(*b*) Integrated Child Development Services (ICDS), introduced in 1975, focuses on child health and nutrition.

(*c*) Deen Dayal Antyodaya Yojana, initiated in 2013, aims to alleviate rural and urban poverty.

(*d*) Swachh Bharat Mission-Gramin, launched in 2014, promotes rural sanitation and open defecation eradication.

75. (C): Vandana Shiva is a renowned eco-feminist known for advocating environmental sustainability and women's rights.

Her work highlights the link between environmental degradation and the exploitation of women, particularly in developing countries.

She has written extensively on issues like biodiversity conservation, organic farming, and climate justice.

76. (D): These terms are closely related to qualitative inquiry:

(*a*) Phenomenology focuses on understanding individuals' lived experiences.

(*c*) Interpretivism emphasizes the interpretation of social realities and meanings.

(*e*) Ethnography involves studying cultures and communities through immersive observation and interaction.

(*b*) Range and (*d*) Hypothesis are quantitative terms not central to qualitative inquiry.

77. (C): Organizational entropy refers to the decline in organizational effectiveness due to various internal and external factors.

(A) Declining performance, (B) lack of appropriate rules, and (D) high turnover contribute to entropy.

(C) Effective personnel policies are not responsible for entropy, as they promote stability and performance.

78. (D): The Chi-square test is used to assess the "goodness of fit" of a distribution.

It compares observed data with expected data to determine if they align with a theoretical distribution.

Other tests like F-test, Z-test, and T-test are used for variance analysis, population mean comparisons, or hypothesis testing, not goodness of fit.

79. (B): The five stages of group development proposed by Garland, Jones, and Kolodny (1976) are:

(*e*) **Preaffiliation:** Initial cautious interactions.

(*d*) **Power and Control:** Negotiation of roles and authority.

(*a*) **Intimacy:** Increased cohesion and emotional connection.

(*b*) **Differentiation:** Establishing individuality while maintaining group identity.

(*c*) **Separation:** Disbanding of the group as tasks are completed.

80. (D): The International Labour Organization (ILO) was established in 1919 as part of the Treaty of Versailles.

It aims to promote social justice, decent working conditions, and labour rights globally.

In 1946, the ILO became a specialized agency of the United Nations.

81. (B): Armand L. Maas (1975) outlined the stages of a social movement as follows:

(*e*) **Initiation:** The movement begins as people recognize a shared issue or cause.

(*a*) **Fusion:** Individuals and smaller groups come together to create a unified force.

(*d*) **Institutionalization:** The movement develops formal structures and gains legitimacy.

(*c*) **Segmentation:** Different factions may emerge within the movement.

(*b*) **Intersection:** The movement intersects with other causes or initiatives.

82. (B): The process of recruiting human resources follows these steps:

(*c*) Identify organizational hiring needs.

(*e*) Prepare detailed job descriptions.

(*a*) Screen and shortlist candidates based on their qualifications.

(*d*) Conduct interviews to assess candidates.

(*b*) Evaluate performance and extend job offers.

83. (C): W.W. Rostow's stages of economic growth proceed as follows:

(*a*) **The traditional society:** Agriculture and subsistence-based economy.

(*e*) **Pre-conditions for take-off:** Initiation of infrastructure and industry development.

(*c*) **Take-off:** Rapid industrialization and economic transformation.

(*b*) **Drive to maturity:** Diversified industrial economy and technological advancement.

(*d*) **High mass consumption:** Economy dominated by consumer goods and services.

84. (A): The structural change model of community work emphasizes:

(*a*) Addressing inequalities and transforming grassroots conditions.

(*b*) Advocating alternative ideologies to challenge existing power structures.

(*c*) Linking micro-level issues to broader systemic contexts.

(*d*) Redistributing power and resources to create equity within communities.

85. (C): Article 3 of the Universal Declaration of Human Rights states that "Everyone has the right to life, liberty, and security of person."

This article is fundamental to human rights, emphasizing the intrinsic dignity and protection owed to every individual.

It forms the basis for many national and international laws safeguarding human life and freedom.

86. (A): The stages of child development in order are:

(*c*) **Newborn:** Birth to 2 months, characterized by rapid adaptation to the external environment.

(*a*) **Infant:** 2 months to 1 year, marked by motor skill development and sensory exploration.

(*b*) **Toddler:** 1 to 3 years, focusing on mobility and basic independence.

(*d*) **Pre-school:** 3 to 5 years, involving socialization and early cognitive skills.

(*e*) **School Age:** 6 years and above, highlighting academic learning and complex social interactions.

87. (A): Social insurance refers to a system where workers, employers, and the government contribute to a fund. It provides financial protection against risks like old age, unemployment, and illness. Examples include pensions, unemployment insurance, and health insurance.

88. (B): Development as Freedom is authored by Amartya Sen. The book emphasizes development as a means to expand human freedoms rather than just economic growth. It discusses how freedom is both the primary end and the principal means of development.

89. (B): Iris Marion Young identifies the five faces of oppression as follows:

(*d*) **Exploitation:** Unequal distribution of wealth and labour.

(*b*) **Marginalization:** Exclusion of certain groups from societal participation.

(*a*) **Powerlessness:** Lack of decision-making power and autonomy.

(*e*) **Cultural Imperialism:** Dominance of one group's culture over others.

(*c*) **Violence:** Physical harm or threats targeting specific groups.

90. (D): Collective behaviour thrives under conditions like:

(A) Institutionalized segregation and exploitation creating shared grievances.

(B) Dissonance in societal values sparking collective action.

(C) Emergence of a new leader uniting and inspiring groups.

(D) Individual goals and achievements are not conducive to collective behaviour as they focus on personal aspirations rather than shared objectives.

91. (B): The Self Employed Women's Association (SEWA) is a trade union that advocates for women's rights and livelihoods in the unorganized sector. It focuses on empowering women through self-reliance, skill development, and financial inclusion.

92. (B): Women in the unorganized sector often face undervaluation of their contributions despite their significant role in sustaining local economies. Their work is characterized by lack of job security, social protection, and recognition.

93. (B): The Shram-shakti report focuses on the challenges faced by self-employed women in the informal sector. It emphasizes the need for supportive policies, access to credit, and better working conditions to enhance their livelihoods.

94. (D): The Deen Dayal Antyodaya Yojana – National Rural Livelihoods Mission (DAY-NRLM) is a flagship program of the Ministry of Rural Development.

It aims to empower rural women by providing access to financial services, skill training, and livelihood opportunities.

95. (B): Grameen Bank, founded by Muhammad Yunus, addresses poverty through microfinance and innovative lending approaches. It empowers poor women and small entrepreneurs to achieve financial independence and sustainability.

96. (B): The United States is not an example of the Institutional Redistributive Model of Welfare. Countries like Sweden, Norway, and Finland exemplify this model with universal welfare provisions, while the USA relies more on selective welfare measures.

97. (C): Progressive taxation ensures that individuals or entities with higher incomes pay a larger percentage of their earnings as tax. This system aims to reduce income inequality and fund welfare programs.

98. (C): A welfare state focuses on reducing disparities, providing health, education, and job creation programs, and ensuring minimum wages. Promoting disparity contradicts the principles of a welfare state.

99. (B): Gosta Esping-Anderson authored Three Worlds of Welfare Capitalism, a seminal work that categorizes welfare states into three types: Liberal, Conservative, and Social Democratic.

100. (C): In the Residual Welfare Model, welfare is provided as a last resort when other means (family, market) fail. It contrasts with universal or institutional welfare models that offer broad-based, proactive support.

Previous Years' Paper

National Testing Agency (NTA)

UGC-NET Junior Research Fellowship & Assistant Professor Eligibility Exam

Social Work, December-2023

(Exam held on 13-12-2023)

PAPER-II

1. Which two terms were added in the earlier Global definition of social work given by IASSW and IFSW in 2014?
A. Human dignity and worth
B. Collective responsibility and respect for diversities
C. Liberalized market and development project
D. Social transformation and reconstruction

2. The phrase "The person in his situation" was coined by:
A. Florence Hollis
B. H.H. Pearlman
C. Marry Richmond
D. Gauri Rani Banerjee

3. The concept that 'how one views oneself is not a solitary phenomenon, but rather includes others' is called:
A. Looking glass self
B. Behaviours modification
C. Conditioning
D. Learning

4. DSM-5 stands for:
A. Diseases and Statistics Manual of Medicine
B. Diagnosable standard Manual of Mental Disorders
C. Diseases and symptoms Manual of Mental Disorders
D. Diagnostic and statistical Manual of Mental Disorders

5. Attribution theory focuses on the way people infer causes of:
A. Pain B. Change
C. Behaviour D. Violence

6. The report titled "Youth in India 2022" is published by
A. Ministry of Social Justice & Empowerment
B. Ministry of Youth Affairs
C. Rajiv Gandhi Institute of Youth Development
D. Ministry of Statistics and Programme Implementation

7. Socialisation is a continuous process and its outcome is:
A. Social Control
B. Social Interaction
C. Personality
D. Empowerment

8. Which of the following is not a philosophical assumption of Case work?
A. Every human being has to be considered as a person with dignity
B. Human beings are interdependent
C. There are common human needs that need to be met for growth and development
D. A person should fulfil his/her dreams by any means

9. A classification and appraisal of what is the matter with the person himself is called ____
   A. Etiological diagnosis
   B. Dynamic diagnosis
   C. Clinical diagnosis
   D. Psycho-somatic diagnosis

10. A graphic way of becoming more aware of the constellations in group is called ____.
    A. Sociometry B. Sociogram
    C. Sociograph D. Groupsnap

11. The primary objective of social group work is:
    A. Personality Development
    B. Recreational Activities
    C. Problem-Solving
    D. Socialization of group members

12. Social action "may be defined as efforts to bring about change or present change in current social practices or situations through education, propaganda, persuasion or pressure, on behalf of objectives believed by the social actionists to be socially desirable." This definition is given by:
    A. Arthur Dunham (1958)
    B. John L. Hill (1951)
    C. W.A. Friedlander (1963)
    D. K.K. Jacob (1965)

13. The basis of community organisation should be:
    A. The people
    B. The resources
    C. The felt needs
    D. The activities

14. Which one of the following is not an approach of community organisation?
    A. Process approach
    B. Task approach
    C. Action approach
    D. Paternalistic approach

15. Which one of the following authors has contributed significantly in the field of community organisation practice?
    A. A.R. Desai B. Jack Rothman
    C. Konapka D. Pearlman

16. "Are you married? If married, for how many number of years?" It is type of ____
    A. Contingency question
    B. Double-barreled question
    C. Value loaded question
    D. Matrix question

17. Which of the following is not an example of the probability sampling?
    A. Simple Random Sampling
    B. Lottery method
    C. Quota method
    D. Stratified Random Sampling

18. Which one of the following is not a key attribute of the Quantitative research?
    A. Generating hypothesis
    B. Testing hypothesis
    C. Objectivity
    D. Deductive logic

19. The relationship between two variables is 'positive' when:
    A. One variable increases, the other variable decreases
    B. The relationship between variables changes at certain levels
    C. Both variables move in the same direction
    D. There is no change in the direction of the variables

20. Which is the major objective of social administration?
    A. Economic development and social development
    B. Social development and Personal development
    C. Economic development and Personal development
    D. Personal and family development

21. PREM Division of Ministry of Social Justice & Empowerment means:
   A. Processing, Reporting, Evaluation and Monitoring Division
   B. Planning, Reporting, Evaluation and Monitoring Division
   C. Planning, Research, Examination and Monitoring Division
   D. Planning, Research, Evaluation and Monitoring Division

22. ______ is the authority for registering Non-Government Organizations under Societies Registration Act, 1860.
   A. Registrar of Trust
   B. Sub-Registrar of Trust
   C. Registrar of Societies
   D. Sub-Registrar of Society

23. Which is not the example of Classical Organisation theory?
   A. Mechanical Theory
   B. Behavioural Theory
   C. Scientific Management Theory
   D. Bureaucratic Theory

24. The concept of "Appropriate Technology" to improve production efficiency and reduce costs was introduced during ______.
   A. Fifth Five-Year Plan
   B. Sixth Five-Year Plan
   C. Seventh Five-Year Plan
   D. Eighth Five-Year Plan

25. What is the "main focus" of sustainable development?
   A. Employment Generation and Livelihood Development
   B. Woman Empowerment and Gender Equality
   C. Balancing the Environmental Protection and Developmental activities
   D. Industrial development and Infrastructure development

26. Which is not the model of Social-Planning?
   A. The Top-Down model
   B. The Bottom-up Model
   C. The Left-Right Model
   D. The Participatory Model

27. Where does the World Summit on Sustainable Development in 2002 took place?
   A. Stockholm B. Johannesburg
   C. Rio D. Paris

28. 'Equal pay for the equal work' is one of the principles of policy to be followed by the state for ensuring:
   A. Social justice B. Economic justice
   C. Political justice D. Moral justice

29. Human right which protects right to life but allows judicial death penalty, is an example of ______ human right.
   A. Absolute B. Limited
   C. Qualified D. Unqualified

30. The Part III of the constitution of India has very well been described as the ______ of India.
   A. Heart B. Bill of Rights
   C. Magna Carta D. Heritage

31. As per 73rd constitutional amendment, a minimum of ______ seats in local government bodies/Panchayat are now reserved for women.
   A. Three-fourth B. One-fourth
   C. One-fifth D. One-Third

32. Which one of the following is not an intra mural activity of labour welfare?
   A. Canteens
   B. Educational facilities for children
   C. Drinking Water
   D. Washing and bathing facilities

33. Section 16 of the Rights of Person With Disabilities Act 2016 describes duty of educational institutions (EI), which says that all EI funded or recognised shall provide.
   A. Specific education
   B. Physical education
   C. Inductive education
   D. Integrated education

34. As per Protection of Women from Domestic Violence Act (2005), who maintain a list of all Services Providers providing Legal aid or counselling, shelter homes and medical facilities in a local area within the jurisdiction of the Magistrate?

A. Police officer
B. Protection officer
C. Medical professional
D. Lawyer

35. In which year the National Mental Health Programme (NMHP) was started?

A. 1981 B. 1983
C. 1980 D. 1982

36. Which of the following country in the world enacted legislation on mandatory corporate social responsibility?

A. England B. USA
C. New Zealand D. India

37. Which article of the Indian constitution says that the state shall, within the limits of economic capacity and development, make effective provisions for securing the right to work, to education and to public assistance in cases of unemployment, old age, sickness and dissolvement and in other cases of underserved want?

A. Article 39 B. Article 14
C. Article 41 D. Article 42

38. Social work practice in the area of social defence is not concerned with:

A. Criminal Justice System
B. Juvenile Justice System
C. Child Welfare System
D. Delinquency Justice System

39. Who is considered to be 'Father of Probation' during nineteenth century?

A. J.J. Panakkal B. John Augustus
C. T. Ellis D. Elliot and Merril

40. Which target group has been added in the recent past for providing services under social defense?

A. Youth offenders B. Transgender
C. Drug Addicts D. Elderly Persons

41. Which of the following approaches in social work fall under the emancipatory social work?

(*a*) Psychoanalytical Approach
(*b*) Radical Social Work
(*c*) Anti-oppressive Practice
(*d*) Feminist Social Work
(*e*) Therapeutic Approach

Choose the **correct** answer from the options given below:

A. (*a*), (*b*) & (*c*) only
B. (*b*), (*c*) & (*d*) only
C. (*c*), (*d*) & (*e*) only
D. (*a*), (*d*) & (*e*) only

42. A code of ethics serve several functions for a profession. It involves:

(*a*) guiding decision making
(*b*) assessing competencies
(*c*) regulating behaviour
(*d*) evaluating knowledge of practitioner
(*e*) controlling client's behaviour

Choose the **correct** answer from the options given below:

A. (*a*), (*b*) & (*c*) only
B. (*a*), (*c*) & (*d*) only
C. (*a*), (*c*) & (*e*) only
D. (*b*), (*c*) & (*d*) only

43. Late 19th century charity organisation movement leaders believed that the causes of poverty were

(*a*) Ignorance (*b*) Incompetence
(*c*) Idleness (*d*) Intemperance
(*e*) Innocense

Choose the **correct** answer from the options given below:

A. (*a*), (*b*), (*c*) & (*d*) only
B. (*b*), (*c*), (*d*) & (*e*) only
C. (*a*), (*c*), (*d*) & (*e*) only
D. (*c*), (*d*) & (*e*) only

44. Bendix and Lipset have identified five variables that determine a class in the Marxian sense. Which of the following are included?

(*a*) Conflicts over the distribution of economic rewards between the classes.

(*b*) Difficult communication between the individuals in the same class positions so that ideas and action programs are readily disseminated.

(*c*) Growth of class consciousness in the sense that the members of the class have a feeling of solidarity and understanding of their historical role.

(*d*) Profound dissatisfaction of the lower class over its inability to control the economic structure of which it feels itself to be the exploited victim.

(*e*) Establishment of a political organisation resulting from the economic structure, the historical situation and maturation of class consciousness.

Choose the **correct** answer from the options given below:

A. (*a*), (*c*), (*d*) & (*e*) only
B. (*a*), (*b*), (*c*) & (*d*) only
C. (*a*), (*b*) & (*e*) only
D. (*b*), (*c*) & (*d*) only

45. Which of the following are considered as defence mechanisms?

(*a*) Denial (*b*) Enjoyment
(*c*) Rationalisation (*d*) Displacement
(*e*) Compensation

Choose the **correct** answer from the options given below:

A. (*a*), (*b*), (*c*) & (*d*) only
B. (*b*), (*c*), (*d*) & (*e*) only
C. (*a*), (*c*), (*d*) & (*e*) only
D. (*a*), (*b*), (*c*) & (*e*) only

46. According to the psychoanalytical theory, the human mind operates at three levels. What are these levels?

(*a*) the super conscious level
(*b*) the conscious level
(*c*) the pre-conscious level
(*d*) low conscious level
(*e*) unconscious level

Choose the **correct** answer from the options given below:

A. (*a*), (*b*) & (*d*) only
B. (*b*), (*c*) & (*d*) only
C. (*a*), (*c*) & (*d*) only
D. (*b*), (*c*) & (*e*) only

47. Social roles can be analysed mainly along three aspects. These are:

(*a*) the actions (the doing of tasks)
(*b*) the prescriptions and expectations that govern the actions and relationships
(*c*) the evaluation or assessment of the performance of tasks
(*d*) the ideological aspects
(*e*) the transfer of the tasks

Choose the **correct** answer from the options given below:

A. (*a*), (*b*) & (*c*) only
B. (*a*), (*c*) & (*d*) only
C. (*c*), (*d*) & (*e*) only
D. (*b*), (*c*) & (*e*) only

48. What are the two life energies/instinctual forces that all living organisms have?

(*a*) Sleep (*b*) Libido
(*c*) Aggression (*d*) Dream
(*e*) Insight

Choose the **correct** answer from the options given below:

A. (*a*) & (*b*) only B. (*b*) & (*c*) only
C. (*c*) & (*d*) only D. (*d*) & (*e*) only

49. The levels of people's participation in community organisation are:

(*a*) Participative Assessment
(*b*) Participative Planning
(*c*) Participative Implementation
(*d*) Participative Sharing
(*e*) Participative Interaction

Choose the **correct** answer from the options given below:
A. (*a*), (*b*) & (*c*) only
B. (*b*), (*c*) & (*d*) only
C. (*c*), (*d*) & (*e*) only
D. (*b*), (*d*) & (*e*) only

50. The strategies that social actionists make use of in their work can be characterised as:
(*a*) Assessment (*b*) Intervention
(*c*) Collaboration (*d*) Bargaining
(*e*) Confrontational

Choose the **correct** answer from the options given below:
A. (*a*), (*b*) & (*c*) only
B. (*b*), (*c*) & (*d*) only
C. (*c*), (*d*) & (*e*) only
D. (*a*), (*c*) & (*d*) only

51. Which of the following are related with Mahatma Gandhi?
(*a*) Hind Swaraj
(*b*) My Experiment with Truth
(*c*) Young India
(*d*) Discovery of India
(*e*) Annihilation of Caste

Choose the **correct** answer from the options given below:
A. (*a*), (*b*) & (*c*) only
B. (*b*), (*c*) & (*d*) only
C. (*c*), (*d*) & (*e*) only
D. (*a*), (*d*) & (*e*) only

52. Which of the following statement(s) correctly explain(s) the condition of Type- I & Type-II errors?
(*a*) The null hypothesis is true and accepted
(*b*) The null hypothesis is true and rejected
(*c*) The null hypothesis is false and rejected
(*d*) The null hypothesis is false and accepted

Choose the **correct** answer from the options given below:
A. (*a*) & (*b*) only B. (*c*) & (*d*) only
C. (*b*) & (*d*) only D. (*a*) & (*d*) only

53. Which are the correct statements regarding fund raising by an agency?
(*a*) Organisation/agency should function on non-profit basis
(*b*) Agency should be in operation for the last three years
(*c*) Money should be raised for profitable purpose
(*d*) Submission of proper reports to the proper person is not mandatory
(*e*) Agency must have a specialised department for fund raising

Choose the **correct** answer from the options given below:
A. (*a*) & (*b*) only B. (*a*) & (*c*) only
C. (*a*) & (*d*) only D. (*b*) & (*c*) only

54. Which divisions are operating under the Ministry of Social Justice and Empowerment?
(*a*) Scheduled Caste Welfare Division
(*b*) Social Defence Division
(*c*) PREM Division
(*d*) Women and Child Division
(*e*) Welfare of Backward Classes Division

Choose the **correct** answer from the options given below:
A. (*a*), (*b*), (*c*) & (*d*) only
B. (*b*), (*c*), (*d*) & (*e*) only
C. (*a*), (*b*), (*c*) & (*e*) only
D. (*a*), (*c*), (*d*) & (*e*) only

55. What are ways to live more sustainably?
(*a*) Try more vegie meals
(*b*) Try reusable coffee cups, water bottles and shopping bags
(*c*) Save Energy and Water
(*d*) Do not donate unwanted items
(*e*) Shop at malls & marts

Choose the **correct** answer from the options given below:
A. (*b*), (*c*) & (*d*) only
B. (*c*), (*d*) & (*e*) only
C. (*a*), (*d*) & (*e*) only
D. (*a*), (*b*) & (*c*) only

56. Which of the following statements best characterizes a social worker's role in relation to policy?

(*a*) Only social workers working with macro issues need to be concerned with policy

(*b*) Only social workers working in the micro arena need to be concerned with policy

(*c*) When social workers are family counsellors, their everyday work does not reflect any policy decision

(*d*) All social workers need to make policy part of their practice world

(*e*) In order to make the best impact, social workers should participate with government in policy formulation

Choose the **correct** answer:

A. (*a*) & (*b*) only
B. (*a*) & (*c*) only
C. (*a*), (*b*) & (*e*) only
D. (*d*) & (*e*) only

57. Social Policy has:

(*a*) Rational goal
(*b*) Deliberate goal
(*c*) Explicit goal
(*d*) Implicit goal
(*e*) Supportive goal

Choose the **correct** answer from the options given below:

A. (*a*), (*b*), (*c*) & (*d*) only
B. (*b*), (*c*), (*d*) & (*e*) only
C. (*a*), (*c*), (*d*) & (*e*) only
D. (*a*), (*b*), (*d*) & (*e*) only

58. The support or auxiliary services are essential adjunct of the family courts. Which are its component services?

(*a*) Family counselling services
(*b*) Investigative services
(*c*) Enforcement services
(*d*) Legal-aid services
(*e*) Socio-religious services

Choose the **correct** answer from the options given below:

A. (*a*), (*b*), (*c*) & (*d*) only
B. (*a*), (*b*), (*d*) & (*e*) only
C. (*a*), (*b*), (*c*) & (*e*) only
D. (*a*), (*c*), (*d*) & (*e*) only

59. Which of the following are ensured under the right to life guarantee in the Constitution of India'?

(*a*) Right to wholesome environment
(*b*) Right to property
(*c*) Right to life with human dignity
(*d*) Right to die
(*e*) Right to privacy

Choose the **correct** answer from the options given below:

A. (*a*), (*b*) & (*c*) only
B. (*a*), (*c*) & (*e*) only
C. (*b*), (*c*) & (*e*) only
D. (*c*), (*d*) & (*e*) only

60. What are the basic elements of performance management?

(*a*) Direction sharing
(*b*) Goal alignment
(*c*) Overall goals
(*d*) Measuring performance
(*e*) Recognition and Rewards

Choose the **correct** answer from the options given below:

A. (*a*), (*b*), (*c*) & (*d*) only
B. (*a*), (*b*), (*d*) & (*e*) only
C. (*b*), (*c*), (*d*) & (*e*) only
D. (*a*), (*b*), (*c*) & (*e*) only

61. The sustainable development focuses on:

(*a*) To follow a path of development that does not impair or damage the cover provided by nature to mankind

(*b*) To use the renewable natural resources that their rate of re-generation is always in excess to their rate of use

(*c*) To use the non-renewable resources in a sparing and responsible manner and to ceaselessly work to find substitutes for them

(*d*) To follow the ethic and cultural practices
(*e*) To use the natural resources for the wellbeing of mankind

Choose the **correct** answer from the options given below:
A. (*a*), (*b*) & (*c*) only
B. (*b*), (*c*) & (*d*) only
C. (*c*), (*d*) & (*e*) only
D. (*b*), (*d*) & (*e*) only

62. Job evaluation has many methods as it is the process of comparing a job with other jobs in an organisation alone. What are these methods?
(*a*) Job ranking method
(*b*) Factor comparison method
(*c*) Work profiling system
(*d*) Point factor method

Choose the **correct** answer from the options given below:
A. (*a*), (*b*) & (*c*) only
B. (*a*), (*b*) & (*d*) only
C. (*b*), (*c*) & (*d*) only
D. (*a*), (*c*) & (*d*) only

63. The edifice of the modern concepts of social defence is built on the ideas like:
(*a*) a concern for the protection of society over and above the expiatory punishment
(*b*) a desire to bring about the amelioration of the offender beyond the infliction of retributive penalty
(*c*) an effort to anticipate and diagnose social defence problems
(*d*) an attempt to promote or to safeguard the concept of the human person to whom only humane treatment can be applied

Choose the **correct** answer from the options given below:
A. (*a*), (*b*) & (*c*) only
B. (*a*), (*b*) & (*d*) only
C. (*b*), (*c*) & (*d*) only
D. (*a*) & (*c*) only

64. The vision of the National Institute of Social Defence is:
(*a*) Fostering Public sensitivity towards well-being of the society
(*b*) Fostering public sensitivity towards old age persons
(*c*) Fostering public sensitivity towards victims of substance abuse
(*d*) Fostering public sensitivity towards strengthening effective service delivery
(*e*) Fostering public sensitivity towards ensuring well planned programmes for the deprived groups

Choose the **correct** answer from the options given below:
A. (*a*), (*b*) & (*c*) only
B. (*b*), (*c*) & (*d*) only
C. (*c*), (*d*) & (*e*) only
D. (*b*), (*d*) & (*e*) only

65. What are the disadvantages of group incentives?
(*a*) The incentive may not be strong enough to serve its purpose
(*b*) Reduced clerical work
(*c*) Shorter Training Time
(*d*) Better co-operation among workers
(*e*) An efficient worker may be penalised for the inefffciency

Choose the **correct** answer from the options given below:
A. (*a*) & (*b*) only B. (*b*) & (*c*) only
C. (*c*) & (*d*) only D. (*a*) & (*e*) only

66. Match List-I with List-II.

List-I (Social work Institutions)	**List-II (Year of Establishment)**
(*a*) Sir Dorabji Tata Graduate School of Social Work	I. 1899
(*b*) Institute for Social Work Training	II. 1936
(*c*) Summer School of Philanthropic Work	III. 1904
(*d*) New York School of Philanthropy	IV. 1898

Choose the **correct** answer from the options given below:

	(a)	(b)	(c)	(d)
A.	I	II	III	IV
B.	II	I	IV	III
C.	III	IV	I	II
D.	IV	III	II	I

67. Match List-I with List-II.

List-I	List-II
(a) Ethics of Power	I. Leverage professional resources as a means to champion the rights of individual cases or a cause
(b) Ethics of Praxis	II. Effect long-term contextual and multi-systematic sustainable and integrating change
(c) Ethics of Advocacy	III. Critically use power to achieve social rights and social justice
(d) Ethics of Change	IV. Engage in reflective discourse and a continuous loop of action, reflection and action throughout social change efforts

Choose the **correct** answer from the options given below:

	(a)	(b)	(c)	(d)
A.	I	II	III	IV
B.	II	III	IV	I
C.	III	IV	I	II
D.	IV	III	II	I

68. Match List-I with List-II.

List-I (Concept)	List-II (Definition)
(a) Sensate culture	I. things which can be percieved only by mind. It is abstract, religious, concerned with faith and ultimate truth
(b) Ideational culture	II. Civilisation which includes tools, utensils, machines, dwellings, science, means of transport and technology
(c) Material culture	III. Things which can be percieved directly by the senses. It is practical hedonistic, sensual and materialistic
(d) Cultural lag	IV. Imbalance in the rate and speed of change between material and non-material parts of culture

Choose the **correct** answer from the options given below:

	(a)	(b)	(c)	(d)
A.	I	II	III	IV
B.	III	I	II	IV
C.	II	I	III	IV
D.	IV	III	II	I

69. Match List-I with List-II.

List-I (Formation)	List-II (Year)
(a) The Sector Report	I. 1863
(b) State Board of Charity	II. 1968
(c) Charity Organisation Society (USA)	III. 1952
(d) Community Development Programme in India	IV. 1877

Choose the **correct** answer from the options given below:

	(a)	(b)	(c)	(d)
A.	II	I	IV	III
B.	I	II	III	IV
C.	IV	III	I	II
D.	II	III	I	IV

70. Match List-I with List-II.

List-I (Research Concepts)	List-II (Explanation)
(a) Element	I. The theoretically specified aggregation of the study elements
(b) Population	II. The unit selected in a sample about which information is collected

(*c*) Random Selection	III.	A sampling method in which each element has an equal chance of selection
(*d*) Sampling frame	IV.	The list or quasi-list of elements from which a sample is selected

Choose the **correct** answer from the options given below:

	(*a*)	(*b*)	(*c*)	(*d*)
A.	III	IV	II	I
B.	IV	III	I	II
C.	I	II	IV	III
D.	II	I	III	IV

71. Match List-I with List-II.

List-I (Research errors/bias)		List-II (Explanation)
(*a*) Straw person argument	I.	Attacking a particular position by distorting it in a way that makes it easier to attack
(*b*) Ad hominem attack	II.	Discrediting the person making an argument rather than addressing the argument itself
(*c*) Bandwagon appeal	III.	A relatively new intervention is touted on the basis of its growing popularity
(*d*) Overgeneralization	IV.	Assuming that a few similar events are evidence of a general pattern

Choose the **correct** answer from the options given below:

	(*a*)	(*b*)	(*c*)	(*d*)
A.	I	II	III	IV
B.	I	II	IV	III
C.	II	I	III	IV
D.	II	I	IV	III

72. Match List-I with List-II.

List-I		List-II
(*a*) Social Service	I.	Professional Activity
(*b*) Social Welfare	II.	Movement against any social evil/ social problem
(*c*) Social Work	III.	Activities for weaker and vulnerable sections of society
(*d*) Social Reform	IV.	Organised activity for any member of society

Choose the **correct** answer from the options given below:

	(*a*)	(*b*)	(*c*)	(*d*)
A.	II	I	IV	III
B.	III	II	IV	I
C.	IV	III	I	II
D.	I	II	III	IV

73. Match List-I with List-II.

List-I	List-II
(*a*) National Youth Policy	I. 2007
(*b*) National Policy on Voluntary Sector	II. 2014
(*c*) National Environment Policy	III. 2004
(*d*) National Policy for Children	IV. 2006

Choose the **correct** answer from the options given below:

	(*a*)	(*b*)	(*c*)	(*d*)
A.	II	III	IV	I
B.	IV	III	II	I
C.	I	II	III	IV
D.	II	I	IV	III

74. Match List-I with List-II.

List-I (Correctional Agencies)		List-II (Functions)
(*a*) Observation Home	I.	For the reception of children in need of care and protection, established under Juvenile Justice

		(care and protection of the children) Act, 2015
(*b*) Special Home	II.	For the girls and women in the age group of 18-45 years, who are destitute, in distress, deserted or are in moral danger
(*c*) Children Home	III.	For temporary reception of any juvenile in conflict with law during the pendency of a case before Juvenile Justice Board
(*d*) Short Stay Home	IV.	For the reformation and rehabilitation of juvenile under Juvenile Justice (care and protection of children) Act, 2015

Choose the **correct** answer from the options given below:

	(*a*)	(*b*)	(*c*)	(*d*)
A.	II	III	IV	I
B.	III	IV	I	II
C.	IV	III	II	I
D.	I	II	III	IV

75. Match List-I with List-II.

List-I		**List-II**
(*a*) Job Analysis	I.	a statement of the human qualification necessary to do this job
(*b*) Job Evaluation	II.	The process of comparing a job with other jobs in an organisation to determine an appropriate pay rate
(*c*) Job Specification	III.	a process of collecting information about a job
(*d*) Job Description	IV.	a tool that explains the tasks, duties, functions and responsibilities of a position

Choose the **correct** answer from the options given below:

	(*a*)	(*b*)	(*c*)	(*d*)
A.	I	II	III	IV
B.	II	III	IV	I
C.	III	II	I	IV
D.	IV	III	II	I

76. What is the correct sequence of major components that comprise the criminal justice system - law enforcement, the court, and corrections?

(*a*) Police
(*b*) Prosecution and Defence
(*c*) Corrections
(*d*) Courts

Choose the **correct** answer from the options given below:

A. (*a*), (*b*), (*c*), (*d*)
B. (*a*), (*b*), (*d*), (*c*)
C. (*a*), (*d*), (*c*), (*b*)
D. (*c*), (*a*), (*b*), (*d*)

77. Arrange the following characteristics of historical development of social work in correct sequential order:

(*a*) Religious Charities
(*b*) Socio-religious reform movements
(*c*) Industrial Revolution
(*d*) Trained Workers
(*e*) Trained Volunteers

Choose the **correct** answer from the options given below:

A. (*a*), (*b*), (*c*), (*d*), (*e*)
B. (*a*), (*b*), (*c*), (*e*), (*d*)
C. (*c*), (*a*), (*b*), (*e*), (*d*)
D. (*b*), (*a*), (*c*), (*d*), (*e*)

78. Kubler and Ross explained five stages of grief. Arrange the stages as first to fifth stage.

(*a*) Anger (*b*) Acceptance
(*c*) Denial (*d*) Depression
(*e*) Bargaining

Choose the **correct** answer from the options given below:

A. (*c*), (*a*), (*e*), (*d*), (*b*)
B. (*a*), (*d*), (*b*), (*c*), (*e*)
C. (*b*), (*d*), (*e*), (*a*), (*c*)
D. (*e*), (*a*), (*c*), (*d*), (*b*)

79. Group work skills are procedural and Interactional. Ruby Pernell describes them as the steps in a methodological knowledgeable procedure of giving help. Arrange the steps in order:

(*a*) Study
(*b*) Identification of the Professional Purpose
(*c*) Diagnosis
(*d*) Treatment and Reporting
(*e*) Selection of goals

Choose the **correct** answer from the options given below:

A. (*b*), (*a*), (*c*), (*d*), (*e*)
B. (*a*), (*e*), (*b*), (*c*), (*d*)
C. (*a*), (*c*), (*b*), (*e*), (*d*)
D. (*b*), (*a*), (*c*), (*e*), (*d*)

80. Arrange the sequence of following incidences according to their year of establishment:

(*a*) Neighbourhood Gild
(*b*) Charity Organization Society (USA)
(*c*) American Association for Community Organisation
(*d*) War Chests
(*e*) National Social Work Council

Choose the **correct** answer from the options given below:

A. (*a*), (*b*), (*c*), (*d*), (*e*)
B. (*b*), (*a*), (*d*), (*c*), (*e*)
C. (*e*), (*b*), (*c*), (*a*), (*d*)
D. (*d*), (*e*), (*c*), (*b*), (*a*)

81. Arrange the following research steps in correct sequencing order:

(*a*) Formulation of Research Hypotheses
(*b*) Formulation of Research Problem
(*c*) Formulation of Research Design
(*d*) Data Collection, Analysis and Interpretation
(*e*) Generalization

Choose the **correct** answer from the options given below:

A. (*a*), (*b*), (*c*), (*d*), (*e*)
B. (*b*), (*a*), (*c*), (*d*), (*e*)
C. (*b*), (*a*), (*d*), (*c*), (*e*)
D. (*c*), (*a*), (*b*), (*e*), (*d*)

82. Arrange the following methodological steps in research in correct sequencing order:

(*a*) Sampling Design
(*b*) Data Analysis
(*c*) Data Coding
(*d*) Research Design
(*e*) Research Approach

Choose the **correct** answer from the options given below:

A. (*a*), (*b*), (*c*), (*d*), (*e*)
B. (*b*), (*a*), (*e*), (*c*), (*d*)
C. (*d*), (*e*), (*a*), (*b*), (*c*)
D. (*e*), (*d*), (*a*), (*c*), (*b*)

83. Arrange the proper sequence of the steps involved in formation of the policy:

(*a*) Identify problems that affect social functioning
(*b*) Analyse findings and confirm evidence
(*c*) Construct the policy and/or program design
(*d*) Study alternative solutions
(*e*) Implement and assess the social policy

Choose the **correct** answer from the options given below:

A. (*a*), (*b*), (*c*), (*d*), (*e*)
B. (*a*), (*b*), (*d*), (*c*), (*e*)
C. (*b*), (*a*), (*c*), (*d*), (*e*)
D. (*e*), (*b*), (*d*), (*c*), (*a*)

84. Arrange the list of legislations related to women in ascending (early to recent) order.

(*a*) The Immoral Traffic (Prevention) Act
(*b*) The Dowry Prohibition Act
(*c*) The Commission of Sati (Prevention) Act

(*d*) The Sexual Harassment of women at the workplace (Prevention, Prohibition and Redressal) Act
(*e*) The Indecent Representation of women (Prohibition) Act

Choose the **correct** answer from the options given below:
A. (*a*), (*b*), (*e*), (*c*), (*d*)
B. (*b*), (*e*), (*d*), (*c*), (*a*)
C. (*d*), (*c*), (*e*), (*b*), (*a*)
D. (*e*), (*d*), (*a*), (*b*), (*c*)

85. As per CARA guidelines Standards Operating Process (SOP) for adopting a child in India is given in five steps.

Arrange the proper sequence of the steps involved in process
(*a*) Home Study and Counselling
(*b*) Referral of Children
(*c*) Registration
(*d*) Court Hearing
(*e*) Acceptance of Child

Choose the **correct** answer from the options given below:
A. (*c*), (*a*), (*b*), (*e*), (*d*)
B. (*a*), (*b*), (*c*), (*d*), (*e*)
C. (*b*), (*c*), (*d*), (*e*), (*a*)
D. (*c*), (*d*), (*e*), (*a*), (*b*)

86. Given below are two statements:

Statement I: Elizabethan Poor Laws categorized the poor into deserving poor and undeserving poor.

Statement II: Abled-bodied poor and sturdy poor were two categories of poor which suffered from inhuman poor laws.

In light of the above statements, choose the **most appropriate** answer from the options given below:
A. Both Statement I and Statement II are correct
B. Both Statement I and Statement II are incorrect
C. Statement I is correct but Statement II is incorrect
D. Statement I is incorrect but Statement II is correct

87. Given below are two statements:

Statement I: Group work always focus its attention on two types of activities- Programme and Social relationship in the group.

Statement II: The group worker guides the members interactions in programme activities so that they may relate themselves to others and experience growth opportunities.

In light of the above statements, choose the **most appropriate** answer from the options given below
A. Both Statement I and Statement II are correct
B. Both Statement I and Statement II are incorrect
C. Statement I is correct but Statement II is incorrect
D. Statement I is incorrect but Statement II is correct

88. Given below are two statements:

Statement I: Social Justice protect or prevent from exploitation/discrimination mostly through legislation.

Statement II: Social Justice provides opportunities and resources as a matter of right of weaker sections of society.

In light of the above statements, choose the **most appropriate** answer from the options given below:
A. Both Statement I and Statement II are true
B. Both Statement I and Statement II are false
C. Statement I is true but Statement II is false
D. Statement I is false but Statement II is true

89. Given below are two statements:

Statement I: There is a hierarchy in the Social Welfare Administration Structure.

Statement II: Leadership, decision-making capacity, power are the essential elements of administrative process.

In light of the above statements, choose the **most appropriate** answer from the options given below:

A. Both Statement I and Statement II are true

B. Both Statement I and Statement II are false

C. Statement I is true but Statement II is false

D. Statement I is false but Statement II is true

90. Given below are two statements:

Statement I: National Skill Development Mission was launched during twelfth five-year plan 2012-17.

Statement II: National Rural Employment Guarantee Act was launched during Eleventh Five Year Plan 2007-2012.

In light of the above statements, choose the **most appropriate** answer from the options given below:

A. Both Statement I and Statement II are true

B. Both Statement I and Statement II are false

C. Statement I is true but Statement II is false

D. Statement I is false but Statement II is true

Directions (Qs. No. 91-95): *Read the passage and answer the questions.*

The concept of social justice consists of diverse principles essential for the orderly growth and development of the personality of every citizen. Social justice is then an integral part of justice in the generic sense, Justice is the genus, of which social justice is one of its species. Social justice is a dynamic devise to mitigate the sufferings of the poor, weak, dalits, tribals and deprived sections of the society and so elevate them to the level of equality to live a life with dignity of person.

The concept of social justice enable equality to flavour and enliven the practical content of life. Social Justice and equality are complementary to each other so that both should maintain their vitality. Rule of law, therefore, is a potent instrument of social justice to bring about equality.

91. Which of the following is the allowed objective of social justice?

A. To elevate deprived sections to the level of equality to live a life with dignity of person

B. To provide welfare services to the poor, weak, Dalits and tribals

C. To reserve jobs for the poor people

D. To remove atrocities on the weak and vulnerable sections of society

92. Which of the following is the key focus of the passage?

A. Importance of equality in the society

B. Negation of justice in the society

C. Principle of rule of law

D. Value of social justice

93. Given below are two statements:

Statement I: The social justice enables equality to flavour and enliven the practical content of life.

Statement II: The social justice and equality are independent but valuable concepts.

In light of the above statements, choose the **most appropriate** answer from the options given below:

A. Both Statement I and Statement II are true

B. Both Statement I and Statement II are false
C. Statement I is true but Statement II is false
D. Statement I is false but Statement II is true

94. Which of the following are correct about social justice?
(*a*) Social justice is essential for the orderly growth and development of personality of every citizens.
(*b*) Social justice is related to only few deprived sections.
(*c*) Social justice is integral component of justice
(*d*) Social justice and equality are two different and exclusive concepts
(*e*) Social justice is a dynamic devise to mitigate the sufferings of the poor, weak and deprived sections of the society.

Choose the **correct** answer from the options given below:
A. (*a*), (*b*) & (*c*) only
B. (*a*), (*c*) & (*e*) only
C. (*b*), (*c*) & (*d*) only
D. (*c*), (*d*) & (*e*) only

95. Given below are two statements, one is labelled as Assertion (A) and other one labelled as Reason (R).

Assertion (A): Social justice is an integral part of justice.

Reason (R): Justice is the genus, of which social justice is one of its species.

In light of the above statements, choose the **most appropriate** answer from the options given below:
A. Both (A) and (R) are true and (R) is the correct explanation of (A)
B. Both (A) and (R) are true, but (R) is NOT the correct explanation of (A)
C. (A) is true, but (R) is false
D. (A) is false, but (R) is true

Directions (Qs. No. 96-100): *Read the passage and answer the questions.*

A profession is an occupation that is based on theoretical and practical knowledge and training in a particular field such as medicine, law, or science. Professions tend to be credential and regulated in relation to certain standards of performance and ethics. This makes them more autonomous and independent than other occupations. Whether a physician's performance is adequate or ethical, for example, depends primarily on judgments made by other physicians in relation to codes formulated by professional organizations. The combination of specialized knowledge and collective self-regulation produces a relatively high social standing for professionals, including higher levels of income, wealth, power and prestige. As a result, those in a number of non-professional occupations, such as businesses often try to professionalize themselves by forming occupational organizations and fostering a public image of ethical standards and specialized knowledge and training.

96. Which is not correct about a profession?
A. A profession has theoretical knowledge
B. A profession has standards of ethics
C. A profession is less autonomous and independent than occupations
D. A profession provides relatively high social standing for professionals

97. Which of the following are true about a profession?
(*a*) It is based on theoretical and practical knowledge.
(*b*) It is based on training in a particular field.
(*c*) Adequacy of a professional's performance is validated by the peers.
(*d*) Self-regulation is internal to the profession.
(*e*) Profession and social standing of professionals are inversely related.

Choose the **correct** answer from the options given below:

A. (*a*), (*b*) & (*d*) only
B. (*a*), (*b*) & (*c*) only
C. (*b*), (*c*) & (*e*) only
D. (*b*), (*d*) & (*e*) only

98. Given below are two statements, one is labelled as Assertion (A) and other one labelled as Reason (R).

Assertion (A): The professions are autonomous and independent than occupations.

Reason (R): Professions have credential and are regulated to certain standards of performance and ethics.

In light of the above statements, choose the **most appropriate** answer from the options given below:

A. Both (A) and (R) are correct and (R) is the correct explanation of (A)
B. Both (A) and (R) are correct but (R) is NOT the correct explanation of (A)
C. (A) is correct, but (R) is not correct
D. (A) is not correct, but (R) is correct

99. Given below are two statements:

Statement I: Professional knowledge and collective self-regulation produces a relatively high social standing for professionals.

Statement II: Non-professional occupations such as business usually avoid to professionalize themselves by forming occupational organizations.

In light of the above statements, choose the **most appropriate** answer from the options given below:

A. Both Statement I and Statement II are correct
B. Both Statement I and Statement II are incorrect
C. Statement I is correct but Statement II is incorrect
D. Statement I is incorrect but Statement II is correct

100. What could be the appropriate title for this passage?

A. Profession and professional values
B. Ethical codes for the professionals
C. Non-professional occupations
D. Essentials of a profession

ANSWERS

1. (B): The earlier Global definition of social work by the International Association of Schools of Social Work (IASSW) and the International Federation of Social Workers (IFSW) in 2014 included the terms "collective responsibility and respect for diversities" as key components. This inclusion was a significant step towards broadening the understanding of social work, emphasizing not just individual well-being but also the importance of community, societal harmony, and respect for the myriad forms of human diversity. By highlighting these values, the definition aimed to encapsulate the essence of social work as a profession committed to fostering inclusive societies and promoting social justice on a global scale.

2. (A): Florence Hollis is credited with coining the phrase "The person in his situation", a foundational concept in social work that underscores the importance of considering an individual's environment in their assessment and intervention. This perspective is critical in social work practice, as it recognizes that individuals cannot be fully understood or helped without acknowledging the context of their lives, including their interactions with the environment, relationships, and societal structures. This holistic approach facilitates a more empathetic and effective response to the needs of clients, emphasizing the interplay between personal and environmental factors in addressing social issues.

3. **(A):** The concept of the "looking glass self", proposed by Charles Horton Cooley, explains how an individual's self-perception is shaped by how they believe others perceive them. This theory suggests that our self-image is not developed in isolation but is a reflective process involving the interpretations and reactions of others around us. By considering how we think others view us, we shape our behaviors, attitudes, and self-concept, highlighting the social nature of self-identity. This concept is fundamental in understanding human behavior and social interaction, offering valuable insights for social work practices, especially in areas concerning self-esteem and social functioning.

4. **(D):** The Diagnostic and Statistical Manual of Mental Disorders, Fifth Edition (DSM-5) is a handbook used by healthcare professionals in the United States and much of the world as the authoritative guide to the diagnosis of mental disorders. It provides comprehensive guidelines for diagnosing mental health conditions, based on research and clinical consensus. The DSM-5 categorizes mental health disorders for both children and adults and lists known causes and diagnostic criteria. It is essential for psychologists, psychiatrists, social workers, and other healthcare professionals in diagnosing, researching, and managing mental health disorders.

5. **(C):** Attribution theory is centered on how people explain the causes of behavior, including their own behaviors and those of others. This psychological theory explores the processes by which individuals infer the reasons behind behaviors, attributing them to either internal dispositions, like personality traits, or external situations. The theory helps in understanding how people perceive and react to their own and others' actions by attributing them to various causes, which significantly impacts social interactions and relationships. It is fundamental in social psychology, providing insights into motivation, emotion, and behavior in social contexts.

6. **(D):** The report titled "Youth in India 2022" is published by the Ministry of Statistics and Programme Implementation. This publication is a comprehensive document that provides statistical data and analysis on various aspects concerning the youth population in India. It covers demographic details, education, employment, health, and many other areas of interest. The report aims to offer stakeholders, including policymakers, researchers, and the general public, valuable insights into the conditions and prospects of the young population, aiding in informed decision-making and planning for youth-oriented development programs and policies.

7. **(C):** Socialization is a continuous process that significantly contributes to the development of an individual's personality. This lifelong process involves learning and assimilating the norms, values, behaviors, and social skills appropriate to their social position. As individuals interact with various agents of socialization, such as families, schools, peers, and media, they develop their unique personalities. These interactions influence their beliefs, behaviors, and attitudes, shaping their identity and how they perceive themselves within the context of their society. The outcome of socialization is a well-rounded personality that enables individuals to function and contribute effectively within their communities.

8. **(D):** The philosophical assumption that "a person should fulfil his/her dreams by any means" is not considered a foundation of case work. Social work ethics and case work practice are grounded in respect for

the dignity and worth of every individual, the understanding that human beings are interdependent, and the recognition of common human needs essential for growth and development. These assumptions underscore the importance of ethical practice, mutual respect, and the need to support individuals in achieving their goals within the framework of societal norms and laws. The principle of achieving dreams by any means could justify unethical behavior, contradicting the core values of social work.

9. (C): A clinical diagnosis refers to the process of identifying and classifying the issues or disorders affecting an individual based primarily on the observation of symptoms, medical history, and often diagnostic tests. In the context of social work and mental health, a clinical diagnosis aims to understand the nature of a person's difficulties by examining both psychological and physical health aspects. This comprehensive assessment helps in planning effective interventions and support, addressing the person's needs holistically. Unlike etiological or dynamic diagnoses, which focus on the causes or psychological dynamics of the issues, clinical diagnosis is about classifying the current condition to inform treatment and support strategies.

10. (B): A sociogram is a visual tool used to represent the relationships and interactions within a group, illustrating how members are interconnected. This graphical method is utilized in various fields, including social work, psychology, and education, to analyze social dynamics, identify subgroups, leaders, isolates, and the overall structure of the group. By mapping out the relationships, facilitators can better understand social preferences, conflicts, and alliances, helping to improve communication, address issues, and enhance group cohesion. Sociograms are valuable for making the underlying social structure of a group more visible, facilitating targeted interventions to support group development.

11. (C): The primary objective of social group work is problem-solving. This practice focuses on enabling groups to address and solve issues affecting their members, leveraging the collective capacity and resources of the group. Through the process of working together, group members develop skills, knowledge, and attitudes that facilitate mutual aid and collective problem-solving. This approach not only addresses immediate problems but also strengthens the group's ability to tackle future challenges, fostering resilience and empowerment among its members. Social group work is guided by principles that prioritize collaborative efforts, respect for diversity, and the promotion of social justice.

12. (A): Arthur Dunham (1958) provided the definition of social action as efforts to effect or prevent changes in social practices or situations through education, propaganda, persuasion, or pressure, aiming for outcomes considered socially desirable by the activists. This conceptualization highlights the proactive and sometimes confrontational nature of social action, which is aimed at achieving societal change or preserving beneficial aspects of the social order. Social action encompasses a wide range of activities and strategies, from grassroots advocacy to large-scale campaigns, reflecting the belief in the possibility and necessity of social progress and justice.

13. (C): The basis of community organization should be the felt needs of the community. This approach ensures that the initiatives and programs developed are directly relevant to the community's immediate concerns and priorities, making them more likely to be effective and sustainable. By focusing on the felt needs, community organization efforts are grounded in the actual experiences and perceptions of community members, fostering a sense of ownership and participation. This approach helps in mobilizing community resources, enhancing engagement, and ensuring that interventions are tailored to address the specific challenges and aspirations of the community.

14. (D): The paternalistic approach is not considered a contemporary approach of community organization. Modern community organization emphasizes empowerment, participatory decision-making, and mutual respect between community organizers and community members. Approaches like the process, task, and action focus on engaging community members as active participants in identifying issues, planning strategies, and implementing solutions. The paternalistic approach, which implies decision-making by an authority figure without full participation from community members, contradicts these principles by not fostering equal partnership and empowerment.

15. (B): Jack Rothman has made significant contributions to the field of community organization practice. He is well-known for his work in developing models and strategies for community intervention. Rothman's frameworks for community practice, including locality development, social planning, and social action, have been influential in guiding social workers and community organizers in their efforts to engage communities, address social issues, and promote social change. His work emphasizes the importance of adapting strategies to the specific context and needs of communities, encouraging a flexible and responsive approach to community organization.

16. (A): A contingency question is designed to be asked only if the respondent gives a specific answer to a previous question. In the given example, "Are you married? If married, for how many number of years?" the second part of the question is contingent upon the respondent answering "yes" to the first part. This type of question allows for more detailed and relevant data collection by directing follow-up questions only to respondents for whom the follow-up question is applicable. It helps in avoiding confusion and making the questionnaire more streamlined and efficient.

17. (C): The quota method is not an example of probability sampling. In probability sampling, every member of the population has a known and equal chance of being selected. Examples include simple random sampling and stratified random sampling. The quota method, on the other hand, is a type of non-probability sampling where the researcher selects a sample that reflects certain characteristics of the population. The selection is not random, and not every member has an equal chance of being included, making it distinct from probability sampling methods where selection is based on chance.

18. (A): Generating hypothesis is not a key attribute of quantitative research; it's more closely associated with the initial stages of research that can involve both quantitative and qualitative approaches. Quantitative research primarily focuses on testing hypotheses through the collection and analysis of numerical data, employing objectivity, and utilizing deductive logic to understand patterns, relationships, and causality in data. The main goal is to quantify variables and generalize results from a sample to the population of interest, making hypothesis testing, objectivity, and deductive logic its core attributes.

19. (C): A positive relationship between two variables means that both variables move in the same direction. This implies that as one variable increases, the other variable also increases, and conversely, as one variable decreases, the other variable decreases as well. This type of correlation indicates a direct relationship where changes in one variable are associated with changes in the same direction in the other variable. Understanding the nature of the relationship between variables is crucial in many fields, including social sciences, economics, and natural sciences, as it helps to predict and explain various phenomena.

20. (A): The major objective of social administration is to achieve economic development and social development. Social administration involves the management and effective implementation of policies and programs that aim to improve social welfare and address societal issues. By focusing on both economic and social development, social administration seeks to create a more equitable and prosperous society where individuals have access to necessary resources, opportunities, and support systems. This dual focus ensures a comprehensive approach to development that considers both material and social well-being.

21. (D): PREM Division of the Ministry of Social Justice & Empowerment stands for Planning, Research, Evaluation, and Monitoring Division. This division is responsible for the planning, research, evaluation, and monitoring of various programs and policies implemented by the ministry. Its functions are crucial for ensuring that initiatives are effectively designed, evidence-based, and aligned with the ministry's goals of promoting social justice and empowering disadvantaged and marginalized sections of society. Through systematic planning, rigorous research, continuous evaluation, and effective monitoring, the PREM Division plays a vital role in enhancing the impact and efficiency of social welfare programs.

22. (C): The Registrar of Societies is the authority responsible for registering Non-Government Organizations (NGOs) under the Societies Registration Act, 1860. This act provides a legal basis for the formation of societies, including NGOs, for the promotion of science, literature, or the fine arts, for education, or for charitable purposes. The Registrar of Societies operates at the state level in India, ensuring that societies comply with the legal requirements set forth in the Act, facilitating their legitimate functioning within the legal framework established for societal benefit and public interest.

23. (B): Behavioral Theory is not an example of Classical Organization Theory. Classical Organization Theories, which emerged in the late 19th and early 20th centuries, primarily focus on the efficiency, structure, and management of work and organizations. These include Scientific Management Theory, proposed by Frederick Taylor, which emphasizes efficiency and productivity through the scientific study of work methods; and Bureaucratic Theory, developed by Max Weber, which outlines the ideal characteristics of bureaucracies for efficient administration. In contrast, Behavioral Theory shifts the focus to the study of human behavior in organizations, emphasizing the importance of understanding human aspects like motivation, group dynamics, and leadership.

24. (C): The concept of "Appropriate Technology" was introduced during the Seventh Five-Year Plan in India, which covered the period from 1985 to 1990. This concept emphasizes the use of technology that is environmentally sustainable, economically viable, and culturally acceptable, aimed at improving production efficiency and reducing costs, particularly in rural and underdeveloped areas. The focus on appropriate technology was part of a broader strategy to ensure that technological development met the specific needs of the population, especially in terms of accessibility, sustainability, and relevance to the local socio-economic context.

25. (C): The "main focus" of sustainable development is balancing environmental protection with developmental activities. Sustainable development aims to meet the needs of the present without compromising the ability of future generations to meet their own needs. This involves a comprehensive approach that integrates economic growth, social inclusion, and environmental protection. The concept encourages practices and policies that seek to improve the quality of human life while reducing the environmental impact, ensuring that natural resources are used efficiently and responsibly to support long-term ecological balance.

26. (C): The Left-Right Model is not a model of social planning. Social planning models typically describe approaches to organizing, decision-making, and implementing social policies and programs. These include the Top-Down model, where decisions are made by higher authorities and implemented at lower levels; the Bottom-up Model, which emphasizes community involvement and local decision-making; and the Participatory Model, which involves stakeholders at various levels in the planning and decision-making process to ensure that initiatives are responsive to the needs and preferences of those affected. The Left-Right Model is a political spectrum concept, not a planning approach.

27. (B): The World Summit on Sustainable Development in 2002 took place in Johannesburg, South Africa. This summit, also known as Earth Summit 2002, was a follow-up to the 1992 Earth Summit in Rio de Janeiro. It aimed to address the progress and failures in implementing sustainable development globally since the Rio conference. Key topics discussed included poverty eradication, the changing of unsustainable patterns of production and consumption, and the protection and management of natural resources. The Johannesburg Summit marked a significant step in the global commitment to sustainable development, with participating nations reaffirming their dedication to achieving goals set in earlier conferences.

28. (B): "Equal pay for equal work" is a principle aimed at ensuring economic justice. This principle mandates that individuals who perform the same work, requiring the same skill, effort, and responsibility, under similar working conditions, should be paid equally, regardless of gender, ethnicity, or other potentially discriminatory factors. It addresses economic disparities and discrimination in the workplace, contributing to the broader goal of creating a fair and equitable economic system. By promoting this principle, the state seeks to ensure that all citizens are treated fairly in their employment, reflecting a commitment to upholding economic rights and reducing economic inequality.

29. (C): In the context of human rights, a "qualified" right refers to a right that can be subject to limitations or restrictions under certain circumstances, such as in the case of judicially sanctioned death penalties. While the right to life is typically considered absolute, legal systems may permit exceptions, allowing for the imposition of the death penalty following a fair trial and for the most serious crimes. This recognition of the right to life alongside the possibility of its limitation in specific instances characterizes it as a qualified human right, reflecting the balancing act between individual liberties and societal interests within the legal framework.

30. (C): The Part III of the Constitution of India is often described as the Magna Carta of India. This part of the Constitution enumerates the Fundamental Rights guaranteed to all citizens, which include the right to equality, the right to freedom, the right against exploitation, the right to freedom of religion, cultural and educational rights, and the right to constitutional remedies. These rights are essential for the development of the personality of every individual and are considered the cornerstone of the democratic framework of the country. The analogy with the Magna Carta, a foundational document of English constitutional law that limited the power of the monarch and laid down the rights of individuals, underscores the importance of Part III in establishing a framework for legal and civil liberties in India.

31. (D): As per the 73rd constitutional amendment, a minimum of one-third of the seats in local government bodies or Panchayats are reserved for women. This amendment was a significant step towards ensuring the representation of women in local governance, aiming to empower them and ensure their participation in the decision-making processes that affect their communities and lives. The reservation includes not just the general seats but also positions of leadership within the Panchayats, such as Sarpanch positions, thereby promoting gender equality in political and community leadership.

32. (B): Educational facilities for children are not considered an intramural activity of labor welfare. Intramural activities refer to those welfare facilities and services that are provided within the premises of the organization or workplace, such as canteens, drinking water, and washing and bathing facilities. These are aimed at improving the working conditions and well-being of employees while they are at work. In contrast, providing educational facilities for children of employees, although a significant aspect of labor welfare, is categorized under extramural activities, as it involves services and facilities that extend beyond the immediate workplace environment.

33. (C): Section 16 of the Rights of Persons with Disabilities Act, 2016, mandates that all educational institutions funded or recognized by the government shall provide inductive education. This term, correctly matched to the context of the Act, emphasizes the need for educational systems to adapt their environment, curriculum, teaching methodologies, and resource allocation to include students with disabilities alongside their non-disabled peers. The goal is to foster an educational atmosphere that supports the educational and social development of all students, irrespective of their physical or cognitive abilities, ensuring that persons with disabilities have equal opportunities to participate fully in the educational experiences available to their peers.

34. (B): As per the Protection of Women from Domestic Violence Act (2005), the Protection Officer is responsible for maintaining a list of all Service Providers providing legal aid or counseling, shelter homes, and medical facilities in a local area within the jurisdiction of the Magistrate. Protection Officers play a crucial role in the implementation of the Act, assisting victims of domestic violence in accessing necessary services, facilitating their interaction with the legal system, and ensuring their safety and well-being. The list maintained by the Protection Officer is a critical resource for providing comprehensive support to victims of domestic violence.

35. (D): The National Mental Health Programme (NMHP) was started in 1982. The program was initiated by the Government of India with the aim of ensuring the availability and accessibility of minimum mental health care for all in the foreseeable future, particularly to the most vulnerable and underprivileged sections of the population. NMHP focuses on community-based services, enhancement of mental health care infrastructure, training of mental health professionals, and public awareness campaigns about mental health. The program represents a significant step towards integrating mental health care with general health care and addressing the substantial needs of the Indian population concerning mental health.

36. (D): India is the country that enacted legislation on mandatory Corporate Social Responsibility (CSR). The Companies Act of 2013 introduced a statutory requirement for certain classes of companies to spend a minimum amount of their profits on CSR activities. This landmark regulation mandates that companies with a specific turnover or profit must allocate 2% of their average net profits of the preceding three years towards CSR activities, such as education, poverty, gender equality, and environmental sustainability. India's approach to mandating CSR spending is unique and sets a precedent for integrating social welfare into the corporate sector's operational framework.

37. (C): Article 41 of the Indian Constitution says that the state shall, within the limits of its economic capacity and development, make effective provision for securing the right to work, to education, and to public assistance in cases of unemployment, old age, sickness and disablement, and in other cases of undeserved want. This directive principle of state policy underlines the government's commitment to ensuring social welfare and security for its citizens, highlighting the importance of creating a supportive environment that enables individuals to live a life of dignity and security, especially in times of need.

38. (D): Social work practice in the area of social defence is not specifically concerned with a "Delinquency Justice System" because this term does not represent a separate system within the field. Social defence broadly encompasses working within systems designed to prevent and respond to criminality and delinquency, including the criminal justice system, juvenile justice system, and child welfare system. These areas focus on rehabilitation, prevention, and support for individuals who are at risk of or have already entered into conflict with the law, aiming to integrate them back into society as productive and law-abiding citizens.

39. (B): John Augustus is considered to be the 'Father of Probation' during the nineteenth century. In the 1840s, Augustus, a Boston bootmaker, began posting bail for individuals who were convicted of minor crimes, arguing that they would benefit more from his supervision and help than from incarceration. His efforts laid the foundation for the modern probation system, emphasizing reform and rehabilitation over punishment. Augustus' pioneering work demonstrated the potential of individualized, supportive intervention in preventing recidivism, leading to the formal establishment of probation as a component of the criminal justice system.

40. (B): Transgender individuals have been added in the recent past as a target group for providing services under social defense. Recognizing the unique challenges and vulnerabilities faced by the transgender community, including discrimination, violence, and lack of access to essential services, social defense initiatives have increasingly aimed to address their specific needs. This includes offering support in areas such as legal aid, healthcare, education, and employment, aiming to ensure their rights are protected and to facilitate their inclusion and participation in society.

This shift reflects a broader movement towards recognizing and addressing the diverse needs of all individuals within the scope of social defense.

41. (B): Emancipatory social work is an approach that focuses on addressing and transforming the underlying social inequalities and power imbalances that contribute to social injustice and oppression. It seeks to empower individuals and communities to challenge and change the conditions that limit their life chances. The approaches that fall under emancipatory social work include Radical Social Work, Anti-oppressive Practice, and Feminist Social Work. These approaches share a commitment to social change by addressing systemic issues of power and inequality, advocating for the rights and empowerment of marginalized populations, and challenging oppressive social structures.

42. (A): A code of ethics serves several critical functions for a profession, including guiding decision-making, regulating behavior, and assessing competencies. It establishes the standards of conduct expected of professionals, providing a framework for ethical and professional behavior. By guiding decision-making, it helps professionals navigate ethical dilemmas they might encounter in their practice. Regulating behavior ensures that professionals adhere to the highest standards of integrity and professionalism. Assessing competencies involves evaluating whether individuals meet the ethical standards of the profession, ensuring that practitioners maintain the requisite ethical and professional standards in their work.

43. (A): Late 19th-century charity organization movement leaders believed that the causes of poverty were ignorance, incompetence, idleness, and intemperance. They held the view that poverty was largely the result of personal failings and moral deficiencies. As a result, their approach to addressing poverty often focused on moral education, work ethic promotion, and individual responsibility. This perspective influenced the development of early social work practices, emphasizing personal reform and the moral upliftment of the poor as strategies for alleviating poverty.

44. (A): Bendix and Lipset identified several variables that determine a class in the Marxian sense, which include conflicts over the distribution of economic rewards between the classes, the growth of class consciousness in the sense that members of the class have a feeling of solidarity and understanding of their historical role, profound dissatisfaction of the lower class over its inability to control the economic structure of which it feels itself to be the exploited victim, and the establishment of a political organization resulting from the economic structure, the historical situation, and maturation of class consciousness. These variables highlight the dynamics of class struggle, consciousness, and political organization in the context of societal and economic structures.

45. (C): Defense mechanisms are psychological strategies that are unconsciously used to protect a person from anxiety arising from unacceptable thoughts or feelings. The defense mechanisms considered in the options include denial, rationalization, displacement, and compensation. Denial involves refusing to accept reality or facts. Rationalization is offering a reasonable explanation for unacceptable feelings or behavior to hide the real reasons. Displacement involves shifting negative feelings or behaviors from the original source to another target. Compensation is an effort to make up for perceived deficiencies and personal or physical inadequacies. These mechanisms help individuals cope with stress, anxiety, and internal conflicts.

46. (D): According to the psychoanalytical theory, famously developed by Sigmund Freud, the human mind operates at three levels: the conscious, the preconscious, and the unconscious levels. The conscious level includes thoughts and perceptions that are currently in our awareness. The preconscious level contains memories and thoughts that are not currently in consciousness but can be brought into consciousness. Lastly, the unconscious level houses a vast reservoir of feelings, thoughts, urges, and memories that are outside of our conscious awareness. These are often unpleasant or unacceptable sexual desires, violent motives, irrational wishes, shameful experiences, and fears.

47. (A): Social roles can be analyzed mainly along three aspects: the actions (the doing of tasks), the prescriptions and expectations that govern the actions and relationships, and the evaluation or assessment of the performance of tasks. These aspects help to understand how individuals perform and navigate their roles within different social structures, including families, workplaces, and broader societal contexts. The actions relate to what individuals do in their roles, prescriptions and expectations refer to the societal norms and rules that define how those roles should be performed, and evaluation or assessment concerns how the performance of these roles is judged by oneself and others.

48. (B): The two life energies or instinctual forces that all living organisms have, according to psychoanalytical theory, are libido and aggression. Libido is the energy of the sexual drive as a component of the life instinct, which includes not just sexual desire but also a broader range of life-sustaining activities. Aggression, on the other hand, is associated with the death instinct, manifesting as a drive towards destruction, aggression, and violence. These forces are seen as fundamental drivers of behavior, influencing a wide range of human actions and interpersonal dynamics.

49. (A): The levels of people's participation in community organization include Participative Assessment, Participative Planning, and Participative Implementation. These stages describe the degree to which community members are involved in the various phases of community development projects. Participative Assessment involves community members in identifying and analyzing their needs and conditions. Participative Planning allows community members to actively contribute to creating strategies and plans to address identified needs. Participative Implementation involves community members in the execution of plans and strategies, ensuring that interventions are relevant and effectively implemented.

50. (C): The strategies that social actionists make use of in their work can be characterized as Collaboration, Bargaining, and Confrontational. These strategies reflect the range of tactics employed to achieve social change and address issues of social justice. Collaboration involves working together with other groups or individuals towards a common goal. Bargaining refers to negotiating with power holders to achieve desired outcomes. Confrontational strategies involve using direct action, such as protests or demonstrations, to challenge and change existing power dynamics and injustices. These strategies are often used in combination, depending on the context and objectives of the social action.

51. (A): The works related to Mahatma Gandhi are "Hind Swaraj", "My Experiment with Truth", and "Young India". "Hind Swaraj" is a book written by Gandhi in 1909, discussing his views on Indian self-rule and freedom. "My Experiment with Truth" is his autobiography, detailing his personal journey and principles. "Young India" was a journal published by Gandhi, where he wrote about his philosophies and the struggle for Indian independence. "Discovery of India" was written by Jawaharlal Nehru, and "Annihilation of Caste" by B.R. Ambedkar, both of which are significant works but not authored by Gandhi.

52. **(C):** Type I error occurs when the null hypothesis is true but is incorrectly rejected. Type II error occurs when the null hypothesis is false but is incorrectly accepted. Therefore, the statements that correctly explain the conditions of Type I and Type II errors are: (*b*) The null hypothesis is true and rejected (Type I error), and (*d*) The null hypothesis is false and accepted (Type II error).

53. **(A):** The correct statements regarding fund raising by an agency are that the organisation/agency should function on a non-profit basis and that the agency should be in operation for at least the last three years. These conditions are typically part of the guidelines for nonprofits and charitable organizations to ensure credibility, legitimacy, and transparency in their operations. Fundraising for profitable purposes is not a standard practice for non-profit organizations, and submission of proper reports to the appropriate authorities is mandatory to maintain transparency and accountability.

54. **(C):** The divisions operating under the Ministry of Social Justice and Empowerment include the Scheduled Caste Welfare Division, Social Defence Division, PREM Division (Planning, Research, Evaluation, and Monitoring), and Welfare of Backward Classes Division. These divisions focus on policies, programs, and initiatives aimed at the welfare and empowerment of socially marginalized groups, including scheduled castes, backward classes, and individuals requiring social defence. The Women and Child Division is typically under the Ministry of Women and Child Development, not the Ministry of Social Justice and Empowerment.

55. **(D):** Ways to live more sustainably include trying more vegetable-based meals, using reusable coffee cups, water bottles, and shopping bags, and saving energy and water. These practices help reduce waste, conserve resources, and lower carbon footprints, contributing to environmental sustainability. Donating unwanted items, rather than not doing so, promotes reuse and reduces waste, making the option that includes not donating items incorrect. Similarly, shopping at malls & marts is not inherently a way to live more sustainably, as sustainable living often involves making choices that reduce consumption and promote eco-friendly practices.

56. **(D):** The statement that best characterizes a social worker's role in relation to policy is that all social workers need to make policy part of their practice world, and in order to make the best impact, social workers should participate with government in policy formulation. This perspective underscores the importance of social workers being engaged in policy matters regardless of their practice area. Whether they are working on macro-level issues, providing direct services at the micro-level, or acting as family counselors, understanding and influencing policy is crucial for effectively addressing the systemic issues that affect their clients and communities.

57. **(A):** Social Policy is characterized by having rational, deliberate, explicit, and implicit goals. These attributes signify that social policies are developed with specific objectives in mind, are intentionally crafted to address particular social issues, and contain both clearly stated aims and

underlying purposes that may not be immediately apparent. This comprehensive view acknowledges the multifaceted nature of social policy, reflecting its role in shaping societal norms, structures, and practices to achieve desired outcomes for the welfare and improvement of the community.

58. (A): The support or auxiliary services that are essential adjuncts of the family courts include family counseling services, investigative services, enforcement services, and legal-aid services. These components provide a holistic support system to individuals and families navigating the family court system, offering emotional, logistical, and legal assistance. These services are crucial for ensuring that the parties involved receive the support and resources they need to address their issues in a manner that is both effective and sensitive to their needs.

59. (B): The rights ensured under the right to life guarantee in the Constitution of India include the right to a wholesome environment, the right to life with human dignity, and the right to privacy. These aspects are interpreted to fall under the ambit of the right to life and personal liberty as guaranteed by Article 21 of the Constitution. These interpretations have expanded the scope of the right to life to include the right to live in a healthy environment, the right to live with dignity, and the protection of personal privacy, reflecting a broad and evolving understanding of what constitutes life and personal liberty.

60. (B): The basic elements of performance management include direction sharing, goal alignment, measuring performance, and recognition and rewards. These elements form a comprehensive approach to managing and enhancing the performance of individuals and teams within an organization. Direction sharing involves communicating organizational goals and expectations, goal alignment ensures individual and team objectives support broader organizational aims, measuring performance involves assessing progress towards these goals, and recognition and rewards are used to acknowledge and incentivize achievement. This framework is designed to improve organizational effectiveness by aligning individual efforts with the strategic objectives of the organization.

61. (A): Sustainable development focuses on the following key principles:

(*a*) Following a path of development that does not impair or damage the cover provided by nature to mankind, ensuring that natural habitats and biodiversity are preserved for future generations.

(*b*) Using renewable natural resources in such a manner that their rate of regeneration exceeds their rate of use, thereby ensuring their sustainability.

(*c*) Using non-renewable resources sparingly and responsibly, while continuously working to find substitutes for them to ensure long-term sustainability.

These principles aim to balance the needs of the present without compromising the ability of future generations to meet their own needs, encompassing economic, social, and environmental dimensions.

62. (B): Job evaluation methods include

(*a*) the job ranking method, where jobs are ranked based on their perceived value to the organization;

(*b*) the factor comparison method, which evaluates jobs based on key factors such as skill, effort, responsibility, and working conditions; and

(*d*) the point factor method, which assigns point values to the factors used in job evaluation, allowing for a quantitative assessment of a job's relative worth.

These methods are used to establish a systematic and fair basis for determining the relative value of different jobs within an organization, thereby informing compensation strategies.

63. (B): The modern concepts of social defence are built on ideas like

(*a*) a concern for the protection of society over and above the expiatory punishment, emphasizing preventive measures and the safety of the community;

(*b*) a desire to bring about the amelioration of the offender beyond the infliction of retributive penalty, focusing on rehabilitation and reintegration; and

(*d*) an attempt to promote or safeguard the concept of the human person to whom only humane treatment can be applied, recognizing the dignity and rights of individuals, including offenders.

These principles reflect a shift from punitive approaches to more humane, preventive, and rehabilitative strategies in dealing with crime and offenders.

64. (B): The vision of the National Institute of Social Defence encompasses

(*b*) fostering public sensitivity towards old age persons, highlighting the need for awareness and support for the elderly;

(*c*) fostering public sensitivity towards victims of substance abuse, emphasizing the importance of understanding and assisting individuals affected by substance abuse; and

(*d*) fostering public sensitivity towards strengthening effective service delivery, which involves improving the quality and effectiveness of services provided to vulnerable populations.

These focus areas demonstrate the institute's commitment to raising awareness and promoting interventions that support marginalized and disadvantaged groups in society.

65. (D): The disadvantages of group incentives include:

(*a*) the incentive may not be strong enough to serve its purpose if it is spread too thinly across a group, diluting the motivational effect for individual members; and

(*e*) an efficient worker may be penalized for the inefficiency of others, as group incentives do not account for individual performance variations within the group.

This can lead to issues of fairness and reduced motivation for high performers, as their efforts are not individually recognized or rewarded.

66. (B): The correct matches for the Social Work Institutions and their Year of Establishment are as follows:

(*a*) The Sir Dorabji Tata Graduate School of Social Work, now known as the Tata Institute of Social Sciences (TISS), was established in 1936. It was located in the Nagpada neighborhood house and offered professional training in social work.

(*b*) The Institute for Social Work Training in Amsterdam, Netherlands was established in the year 1899 as the first full-time program of social work education, which lasted two years.

(*c*) The Summer School of Philanthropic Work is a six-week summer school that started at the New York Charity Organization Society in 1898. The school has led to the development of private and charitable organizations to help people in need.

(*d*) The New York School of Philanthropy was a year program established in 1904 by the New York Charity Organization Society (COS).

67. (C): Matching the ethics with their descriptions:

- Ethics of Power is about critically using power to achieve social rights and social justice (III).

- Ethics of Praxis involves engaging in reflective discourse and a continuous loop of action, reflection, and action throughout social change efforts (IV).
- Ethics of Advocacy implies leveraging professional resources as a means to champion the rights of individual cases or a cause (I).
- Ethics of Change aims to effect long-term contextual and multi-systematic sustainable and integrating change (II).

68. (B): Matching the concepts with their definitions:

- Sensate culture is concerned with things which can be perceived directly by the senses. It is practical, hedonistic, sensual, and materialistic (III).
- Ideational culture involves things which can be perceived only by the mind. It is abstract, religious, concerned with faith, and ultimate truth (I).
- Material culture includes tools, utensils, machines, dwellings, science, means of transport, and technology (II).
- Cultural lag is the imbalance in the rate and speed of change between material and non-material parts of culture (IV).

69. (A): Matching the formation with the year:

- The Sector Report was published in 1968 (II).
- State Board of Charity was established in 1863 (I).
- Charity Organisation Society (USA) was founded in 1877 (IV).
- Community Development Programme in India was initiated in 1952 (III).

70. (D): Matching the research concepts with their explanations:

- Element is the unit selected in a sample about which information is collected (II).
- Population is the theoretically specified aggregation of the study elements (I).
- Random Selection is a sampling method in which each element has an equal chance of selection (III).
- Sampling frame is the list or quasi-list of elements from which a sample is selected (IV).

71. (A): The correct matches between the types of research errors/bias and their explanations are:

- Straw person is attacking a particular argument by distorting it in a way that makes it easier to attack (I).
- Ad hominem attack is discrediting the person making an argument rather than addressing the argument itself (II).
- Bandwagon appeal is when a relatively new intervention is touted on the basis of its growing popularity (III).
- Overgeneralization is assuming that a few similar events are evidence of a general pattern (IV).

72. (C): The correct matches between the terms and their definitions are:

- Social Service is organized activity for any member of society (IV).
- Social Welfare involves activities for weaker and vulnerable sections of society (III).
- Social Work is a professional activity (I).
- Social Reform is a movement against any social evil/social problem (II).

73. (D): The correct matches between the policies and their respective years of announcement are:

(*a*) The National Youth Policy (NYP) of 2014 (NYP-2014) was launched in February 2014 by the Government of India to replace the National Youth Policy of 2003.

(*b*) The National Policy on the Voluntary Sector was formulated in 2007 to encourage an independent and effective voluntary sector. The policy aims to provide an enabling environment for the voluntary sector and also make it accountable.

(*c*) The National Environment Policy (NEP) 2006 is a policy from the Ministry of Environment and Forests. It was the result of extensive consultations with experts, central ministries, and members of parliament, state governments, and more.

(*d*) The National Charter for Children was adopted in 2004 and emphasizes the government's commitment to children's rights to protection, development, and survival.

74. (B): The correct matches between the Correctional Agencies and their Functions are:

- Observation Home is for temporary reception of any juvenile in conflict with law during the pendency of a case before Juvenile Justice Board (III).
- Special Home is for the reformation and rehabilitation of juvenile under Juvenile Justice (care and protection of children) Act, 2015 (IV).
- Children Home is for the reception of children in need of care and protection, established under Juvenile Justice (care and protection of the children) Act, 2015 (I).
- Short Stay Home is for the girls and women in the age group of 18-45 years, who are destitute, in distress, deserted or are in moral danger (II).

75. (C): The correct matches between the job-related terms and their definitions are:

- Job Analysis is a process of collecting information about a job (III).
- Job Evaluation is the process of comparing a job with other jobs in an organization to determine an appropriate pay rate (II).
- Job Specification is a statement of the human qualification necessary to do this job (I).
- Job Description is a tool that explains the tasks, duties, functions, and responsibilities of a position (IV).

76. (B): The correct sequence of major components that comprise the criminal justice system starts with:

(*a*) law enforcement, which is represented by the police. They are responsible for the initial response to and investigation of crimes.

(*b*) Next is the role of prosecution and defense, where the case is prepared for trial, and legal arguments are made.

(*d*) The courts then adjudicate the case, determining guilt or innocence and sentencing.

(*c*) Finally, corrections is the component responsible for carrying out sentences, including imprisonment, rehabilitation, and parole.

This sequence outlines the flow of the criminal justice process from the initial response to the implementation of the sentence.

77. (B): The historical development of social work can be traced through the following sequential order:

(*a*) Religious Charities represent the earliest form of social work, where aid and care were provided on a charitable basis driven by religious motivations.

(*b*) Socio-religious reform movements followed, where organized efforts sought to address broader social issues through reform and advocacy.

(*c*) The Industrial Revolution brought about significant social changes and challenges, leading to the need for more organized social welfare efforts.

(*e*) Trained Volunteers emerged as individuals received specific training to address social issues more effectively.

(*d*) Finally, the development and recognition of Trained Workers as professionals marked the formalization and institutionalization of social work as a recognized field of practice.

78. (A): Kubler and Ross's five stages of grief are arranged from the initial to the final stage as follows:

(*c*) Denial is the first stage, where individuals refuse to accept the reality of loss.

(*a*) Anger follows, as individuals begin to recognize the loss and experience frustration and helplessness.

(*e*) Bargaining is the third stage, characterized by individuals attempting to negotiate or make deals to postpone or mitigate the loss.

(*d*) Depression is the fourth stage, where individuals confront the full impact of the loss, leading to sadness and despair.

(*b*) Finally, Acceptance is the fifth stage, where individuals come to terms with the loss and start to move forward.

79. (D): Ruby Pernell's group work skills, described as steps in a methodological procedure of giving help, are sequenced as follows:

(*b*) Identification of the Professional Purpose is the first step, where the social worker clarifies the goals of the group work.

(*a*) Study involves gathering relevant information to understand the group's needs and context.

(*c*) Diagnosis is the process of analyzing the collected information to identify the underlying issues.

(*e*) Selection of goals involves determining the specific objectives the group work aims to achieve.

(*d*) Finally, Treatment and Reporting is the implementation of interventions to address the identified needs and the documentation of the process and outcomes.

80. (B): The sequence of the following incidences according to their year of establishment is as follows:

(*b*) The Charity Organization Society (COS) was established in 1881 as the Society for Organizing Charity. The COS's objectives were to: Alleviate poverty and vagrancy, Reduce conflict between social classes, and elevate the poor socially and morally.

(*a*) The Neighborhood Guild, now known as the University Settlement, opened in 1886 on Forsyth Street in New York City's Lower East Side. The Neighborhood Guild was the first settlement house in the United States.

(*d*) The Citizens' "War Chest" Fund was established in 1914, to provide immediate assistance in the event of a war emergency. During World War I, Community Chests, also known as War Chests, became popular in the United States and Canada.

(*c*) The American Association for Community Organizations (AACO) was established in 1918. The executives of 12 fund-raising federations met in Chicago to form the organization.

(*e*) The National Social Work Council (NCW) was founded in 1992 as a statutory body under the National Commission for Women Act, 1990.

81. (B): The correct sequencing order for the research steps is as follows:

(*b*) The first step in the research process is the Formulation of Research Problem, where the researcher identifies and defines the problem they intend to study.

(*a*) Next, Formulation of Research Hypotheses involves stating tentative explanations or predictions that the research aims to test.

(*c*) Following this, Formulation of Research Design is crucial for planning how the research will be conducted, including the methods for data collection and analysis.

(*d*) The fourth step, Data Collection, Analysis, and Interpretation, involves gathering the necessary data, analyzing it, and interpreting the findings.

(*e*) Finally, Generalization is the process of applying the findings from the study to larger populations or situations beyond the scope of the initial research.

82. (D): The correct sequence for methodological steps in research is:

(*e*) The research process begins with defining the Research Approach, which outlines the overall strategy and framework of the study.

(*d*) This is followed by the Research Design, which provides a detailed plan for how the research will be conducted, including the methodologies to be used.

(*a*) Sampling Design is the next step, where the researcher decides how to select samples from the population for the study.

(*c*) Data Coding is crucial for organizing and preparing the collected data for analysis.

(*b*) Finally, Data Analysis is performed to interpret the data and draw conclusions.

83. (B): The proper sequence of steps involved in the formation of policy starts with

(*a*) Identifying problems that affect social functioning, recognizing and defining the issues that require attention.

(*b*) Analyzing findings and confirming evidence involves reviewing data and research to understand the problem fully.

(*d*) Studying alternative solutions then allows for consideration of different approaches to addressing the problem.

(*c*) Constructing the policy and/or program design is the step where solutions are formulated into a coherent policy or program.

(*e*) Finally, Implementing and assessing the social policy involves putting the policy into action and evaluating its effectiveness.

84. (A): The list of legislations related to women in ascending order, from early to recent, is:

(*a*) The Immoral Traffic (Prevention) Act: This act was enacted in 1956, aimed at preventing trafficking in persons for the purpose of prostitution.

(*b*) The Dowry Prohibition Act: This act was enacted in 1961 to prohibit the giving or taking of dowry.

(*e*) The Indecent Representation of Women (Prohibition) Act: This act was enacted in 1986 to prohibit the indecent representation of women through advertisements, publications, etc.

(*c*) The Commission of Sati (Prevention) Act: This act was enacted in 1987 to prevent the practice of sati, the act of a widow immolating herself on her husband's funeral pyre.

(*d*) The Sexual Harassment of Women at the Workplace (Prevention, Prohibition, and Redressal) Act: This act was enacted in 2013 to prevent and provide redressal for sexual harassment of women at the workplace.

85. (A): The proper sequence of the steps involved in the process of adopting a child in India, as per CARA guidelines Standards Operating Process (SOP), starts with

(*c*) Registration, where prospective adoptive parents register with an Authorized Adoption Agency.

(*a*) This is followed by Home Study and Counselling, a process in which a social worker assesses the home environment and provides counseling to the prospective adoptive parents.

(*b*) Referral of Children comes next, where the parents are referred children based on the registration details.

(*e*) Acceptance of Child is the step where the parents accept the child referred to them.

(*d*) Finally, the Court Hearing is conducted to legalize the adoption process, where a legal order is passed for the adoption of the child.

86. (C): Statement I is correct. The Elizabethan Poor Laws, enacted in England in the 16th and 17th centuries, indeed categorized the poor into "deserving poor" and "undeserving poor", with the deserving poor being those unable to work due to age or health issues, and the undeserving poor being able-bodied individuals who were seen as capable of working.

Statement II is incorrect because it implies a value judgment on the categories of the poor, which is a misinterpretation. While the laws did distinguish between different types of poor, the term "inhuman poor laws" reflects a subjective assessment rather than a direct characterization from the laws themselves.

87. (A): Both Statement I and Statement II are correct. Group work in social work practice does focus on two types of activities: Program (structured tasks and activities) and Social relationship in the group (interpersonal interactions). The group worker's role includes guiding members' interactions in program activities to facilitate relational development and growth opportunities, aiming to enhance individual and collective well-being and development.

88. (A): Both Statement I and Statement II are true. Social Justice aims to protect individuals and groups from exploitation and discrimination, often through legislation, ensuring that laws are in place to prevent unfair treatment of individuals based on various characteristics. Additionally, Social Justice involves providing opportunities and resources to the weaker sections of society as a matter of right, emphasizing the need for equitable access to social goods, services, and opportunities.

89. (A): Both Statement I and Statement II are true. The Social Welfare Administration Structure indeed has a hierarchy, which organizes roles, responsibilities, and authority within agencies and institutions that deliver social welfare services. Leadership, decision-making capacity, and power are essential elements of the administrative process, as they determine how decisions are made, who makes them, and how power is exercised within the organization to achieve its goals.

90. (C): Statement I is true but Statement II is false. The National Skill Development Mission was indeed launched during the twelfth five-year plan period (2012-17) to provide a coherent and comprehensive strategy for skill development across the country. The National Rural Employment Guarantee Act (NREGA), now known as Mahatma Gandhi National Rural Employment Guarantee Act (MGNREGA), was actually launched in 2005, predating the Eleventh Five Year Plan period (2007-2012), making Statement II false.

91. (A): The passage outlines social justice as a means to elevate deprived sections of society to a level of equality, enabling them to live a life with dignity. This aligns with the allowed objective of social justice, which is to mitigate the sufferings of the poor, weak, Dalits, tribals, and other deprived sections, elevating them to a state of equality.

92. (D): The key focus of the passage is on the value of social justice, detailing its role in ensuring the orderly growth and development of every citizen's personality. It emphasizes social justice as a means to achieve equality and dignity for all, particularly the most vulnerable segments of society.

93. (C): Statement I is true as it reflects the essence of the passage, stating that social justice enables equality to enhance and vivify the practical aspects of life. Statement II is false, according to the passage, as it clearly indicates that social justice and equality are complementary, not independent concepts, working together to maintain vitality in society.

94. (B): The correct statements about social justice, according to the passage, are:

(*a*) Social justice is essential for the orderly growth and development of the personality of every citizen;

(*c*) Social justice is an integral component of justice; and

(*e*) Social justice is a dynamic device to mitigate the sufferings of the poor, weak, and deprived sections of society.

These points emphasize the importance of social justice in achieving equality and dignity for all individuals, especially those who are most vulnerable.

95. (A): Both Assertion (A) and Reason (R) are true, and (R) is the correct explanation of (A). The assertion that social justice is an integral part of justice is substantiated by the reason that justice encompasses various forms, with social justice being one of its specific manifestations. This relationship outlines the conceptual framework within which social justice operates as a critical aspect of broader justice goals.

96. (C): The statement that a profession is less autonomous and independent than occupations is not correct. In fact, the passage explains that professions tend to be more autonomous and independent due to their specialized knowledge, standards of performance, and ethics, which are regulated within the profession itself, particularly by peer judgments and codes formulated by professional organizations.

97. (B): The statements true about a profession, as per the passage, include:

(*a*) It is based on theoretical and practical knowledge,

(*b*) It is based on training in a particular field, and

(*c*) The adequacy of a professional's performance is validated by their peers.

98. (A): Both Assertion (A) and Reason (R) are correct, and (R) is the correct explanation of (A). Professions are indeed more autonomous and independent than other occupations due to the credentials required and the regulation of standards of performance and ethics. This self-regulation and adherence to professional standards contribute to the autonomy and independence of professions from external controls, thereby validating the assertion with the reason provided.

99. (C): Statement I is correct as it reflects the content of the passage, which discusses how professional knowledge and collective self-regulation contribute to a relatively high social standing for professionals, including higher levels of income, wealth, power, and prestige. Statement II is incorrect because the passage actually states that those in a number of non-professional occupations, such as business, often try to professionalize themselves by forming occupational organizations and fostering a public image of ethical standards and specialized knowledge and training. This indicates a desire to adopt professional attributes to gain similar benefits.

100. (D): "Essentials of a Profession" could be the most appropriate title for this passage, as it outlines the fundamental aspects that define a profession, including the basis of theoretical and practical knowledge, training, credentials, regulation to standards of performance and ethics, autonomy, independence, and the resulting social standing. This title encompasses the overall discussion presented in the passage about what constitutes a profession and distinguishes it from other occupations.

Previous Years' Paper

National Testing Agency (NTA)

UGC-NET Junior Research Fellowship & Assistant Professor Eligibility Exam

Social Work, June-2023

(Exam held on 20-06-2023)

PAPER-II

1. In which of the following roles the social worker is more intensively engaged with the clients?
A. Social workers as facilitators
B. Social workers as enabler
C. Social workers as advocate
D. Social workers as trainer

2. The popularly known Delhi school of social work was established as an initiative of:
A. Young Women's Christian Association
B. Young Men's Christian Association, Delhi
C. Delhi University
D. Social Service League

3. What was the complete name of the charity organization society that was started in London?
A. London society for Organization Charitable Relief and Repressing Mendicancy
B. Society for Organizing Charitable Relief and Repressing Mendicancy in England
C. Society for Organization Charitable Relief and Repressing Mendicancy
D. London Charitable Organizing Society

4. The Principle Individualization guides the social worker to recognize that:
A. Each client irrespective of other identities is a person with a problem.
B. Each client has a right to individual secrets.
C. Each client is unique in himself or herself.
D. Each client has a right to self determination.

5. The social workers work in diverse cultural settings, which of the following social work values is fundamental in developing their culture competency?
A. Human worth and dignity
B. Appreciating diversity
C. Integrity
D. Social justice

6. In Ivan Pavlov's classical conditioning experiment after conditioning, salivation started to occur in the presence of the sound of the bell. What does the bell signify?
A. Conditioned Stimulus (CS)
B. Conditioned Response (CR)
C. Unconditioned Stimulus (US)
D. Unconditioned Response (UR)

7. Which motivational theory relies heavily on the concept of homeostasis?
A. Affiliation theory
B. Achievement theory
C. Instinctual theory
D. Drive reduction theory

8. Which of the following work as a barrier to accurate perception?

A. Projection B. Motivation
C. Repression D. Instinct

9. Who is credited for the concept of 'Sanskritization'?

A. M.N. Srinivas B. Yogendra Singh
C. S.C. Dube D. Louis Dumont

10. Who is known for the concept of the "Panop-ticon"?

A. Paulo Frierre B. Michel Foucault
C. Karl Marx D. Pierre Bourdieu

11. Which of the following stages of cognitive development the object permanence is developed in the child?

A. Sensorimotor stage
B. Pre-operational stage
C. Concrete operational stage
D. Formal operational stage

12. In which year was the book "Theory for Social Work Practice" published?

A. 1961 B. 1956
C. 1964 D. 1965

13. Which of the following technique is NOT used in case study process?

A. Interview
B. Objective observation
C. Collection of information from significant others
D. Focused group discussion

14. Which of the following processes is not vital in understanding the group functioning?

A. Group Cohesion
B. Social Control
C. Group Culture
D. Group Conflict

15. Which of the following technique is used to bring relief to the client suffering from anxiety and guilt?

A. Clarification B. Reassurance
C. Sympathy D. Credibleness

16. Which method of social work involves the social worker working with a group of clients with similar problems to promote mutual support and growth?

A. Group work B. Counselling
C. Advocacy D. Meditation

17. The Principle of Optimum Utilization of Indigenous Resources was given by:

A. H.Y. Siddiqui B. E. Youngheršband
C. H.B. Trecker D. C.F. McNeil

18. The Charity Organization Society (COS) was established in the year 1877 in USA in:

A. New York B. Buffalo
C. Columbia D. Chicago

19. In which year the Community Development Project was launched by the Govt. of India?

A. 1948 B. 1950
C. 1952 D. 1951

20. Social action is broadly considered as:

A. Violent action B. Punitive action
C. Concerted action D. Destructive action

21. 'Felt Needs' in the community work means:

A. Needs identified by the leader of the community
B. Needs identified by the community worker
C. Needs of the weaker sections of the community
D. Community needs as expressed by the community in general

22. Which of the following is a case of Type-II error?

A. The null hypothesis is true and rejected
B. The null hypothesis is true and accepted
C. The null hypothesis is false and rejected
D. The null hypothesis is false and accepted

23. In the research inclined towards interpretivism, the appropriate research approach could be:

A. Quantitative research approach

B. Qualitative research approach
C. Participatory research approach
D. Mixed methods approach

24. The second stage of qualitative analysis of grounded theory in which relationship between themes or categories are proposed is called _____.
A. Axial Coding B. Open Coding
C. Selective Coding D. Focused Coding

25. Which of the following is correct about dependent variables?
A. The variables which represents the cause
B. The variables which represents the effect
C. The variables which examines the possibility of association
D. The variables which does not have a minimum size

26. Informed consent as part of the NASW (National Association of Social Workers) Code of Ethics specifications, does NOT include:
A. Nature, extent and duration of participation
B. Voluntary and written consent from the respondents
C. Disclosure of risks and benefits of partici-pation
D. Nature, extent and duration of the research study

27. Social welfare administration is manually concerned with:
A. Democratization of Administration
B. Maximizing the number of beneficiaries
C. Sensitizing administration
D. Delivery of social welfare services

28. National Policy on Voluntary Sector was approved in the year:
A. 2007 B. 2001
C. 1991 D. 1975

29. The United Nations Conference on Human Environment, held in Stockholm in 1972, was the first major international gathering to discus the concept of _____ at global scale.
A. Climate changes
B. Population explosion
C. Sustainability
D. Our Common future

30. Which of the following is not the indicator of sustainable development?
A. Human Development Index
B. Gross National Happiness
C. Ecological Foot Prints
D. Inter Generation Equity

31. Who popularised the most generic definition of sustainable development as "Development that meets the need of the present without compromising the ability of the future generation to meet their own needs"?
A. Brundtland Report
B. Rio Summit 1992
C. Ban Ki-Moon
D. Boutrous Boutrous-Ghali

32. 'Human rights start with Breakfast', who is credited with this statement?
A. Leopold Senghor B. Nazim Hikmet
C. Bertold Brecht D. Emile Henriot

33. Which generation of human rights promotion has been ascribed to the social work profession?
A. First Generation
B. Second Generation
C. Third Generation
D. None of the above

34. Sustainable Development Goals (SDGs) are officially known as:
A. UN Development and Environment Goals 2015
B. Transforming Our World : The 2030 Agenda for sustainable development
C. Saving Our Planet : Goals for sustainable development for future generation
D. UNDP 2030 : Sustainable Resources and its Management

35. Article 1 of the UN Convention on the Rights of the Child (UNCRC) talks about?
A. The survival rights of the child
B. The development rights of the child
C. The age of the child
D. The rights of the child

36. Which of the following Articles of the Constitution of India provide for "Cultural and Educational Rights"?
A. Article 14-18 B. Article 25-28
C. Article 29-30 D. Article 32

37. As per the Sexual Harassment against Women in the Workplace (Prevention, Prohibition and Redressal) Act 2013, who among the following can request for the Internal Complaints Committee (IC) for setting the case through conciliation before initiating inquiry?
A. Only respondent
B. HR officer
C. Only aggrieved woman
D. Both aggrieved woman and respondent

38. Ethnocentrism is a characteristic of the:
A. Primary group
B. In group
C. Out group
D. Non-territorial group

39. Which is the area of counselling that engages least number of counsellors in India?
A. Family and Marriage counselling
B. School counselling
C. HIV/AIDS counselling
D. Bereavement counselling

40. What are the changes required to be made in RTE 2009 as per NEP 2020?
A. Arrange free education for 3-14 years old students
B. Arrange free and compulsory education for 6-18 years old students
C. Arrange free and compulsory education for 3-18 years old students
D. Arrange compulsory education for 6-18 years old students

41. Which of the following were parts of the memorandum that Clifford Manshardt submitted to the Tata Trust?
(*a*) Secondary Teacher Training College for Women
(*b*) Institute for Educational Research
(*c*) Library for Prince of Wales Museum
(*d*) Sir Dorabjee Tata School of Social Work

Choose the **correct** answer from the options given below:
A. (*a*), (*b*), (*c*) and (*d*)
B. (*a*), (*b*) and (*c*) only
C. (*a*) and (*d*) only
D. (*d*) and (*b*) only

42. What are the key reasons for social workers to study socio-religious reform movements in India?
(*a*) The focus of these movements was the Indian Society
(*b*) The focus of these movements was the social evils
(*c*) These movements helps us understand the response of society when established socio-cultural practices are challenged
(*d*) These movements helps us understanding the ideology for social change

Choose the **correct** answer from the options given below:
A. (*a*) and (*b*) only
B. (*b*) and (*c*) only
C. (*a*), (*b*) and (*c*) only
D. (*a*), (*b*), (*c*) and (*d*)

43. Which of the following statements are correct regarding communication?
(*a*) Semantic barriers concern with the meaning of the speech forms.
(*b*) Complex structure of the organization may often leads to breakdown of the communication.
(*c*) Communication gap is created when an idea is precisely transmitted.
(*d*) Barrier to communication can be removed by taking perception and imagination about others.

Choose the **correct** answer from the options given below:

A. (*a*), (*b*), (*c*) and (*d*)
B. (*a*) and (*b*) only
C. (*c*) and (*d*) only
D. (*b*) and (*c*) only

44. Which of the following statements are correct about attitude formation?

(*a*) Attitude is learned through positive association
(*b*) Attitude is learned through reward & punishment
(*c*) Attitude is learned through group norms
(*d*) Attitude is learned through exposure to information

Choose the **correct** answer from the options given below:

A. (*a*), (*b*), (*c*) and (*d*)
B. (*a*) and (*b*) only
C. (*c*) and (*d*) only
D. (*b*) and (*c*) only

45. Which of the following statements are correct about recording in casework?

(*a*) It is an extremely important method to learn social work practice
(*b*) Record used to evaluate appropriateness of the process used
(*c*) Narrative recording in the most effective technique
(*d*) Role recording is a refined version of process recording

Choose the **correct** answer from the options given below:

A. (*a*), (*b*) and (*c*) only
B. (*c*) and (*d*) only
C. (*a*), (*b*), (*c*) and (*d*)
D. (*b*) and (*c*) only

46. Which of the following statements are correct regarding referral?

(*a*) Referral is a concept used in social casework to refer a client to other professionals
(*b*) This exhibits incompetency on the part of social workers particularly its knowledge and skills
(*c*) Both positive and negative feelings are involved in the referral process
(*d*) In genuine cases of referral consent of the client is not imperative

Choose the **correct** answer from the options given below:

A. (*a*), (*b*), (*c*) and (*d*)
B. (*b*), (*c*) and (*d*) only
C. (*a*) and (*c*) only
D. (*c*) and (*d*) only

47. A group worker must always be alert to discover:

(*a*) That the group environment is conducive to a democratic decision making process
(*b*) That the group effort at problem solving or decision making is proving to be time consuming and costly without yielding a result which works
(*c*) That not everyone knows how to help a group in taking a decision quickly and rationally
(*d*) That the expertise in the group may not exist to take certain decisions.

Choose the **correct** answer from the options given below:

A. (*a*), (*b*) and (*c*) only
B. (*a*), (*b*), (*c*) and (*d*)
C. (*a*), (*b*) and (*d*) only
D. (*b*) and (*d*) only

48. The basis of community organization is:

(*a*) Felt needs of the community
(*b*) Educational status
(*c*) People's choice
(*d*) Active participation of community people
(*e*) Community awareness

Choose the **correct** answer from the options given below:

A. (*a*), (*b*) and (*c*) only
B. (*b*), (*c*) and (*d*) only
C. (*c*), (*d*) and (*e*) only
D. (*a*), (*d*) and (*e*) only

49. Community organization involves:

(*a*) Identifying the community needs and problems

(*b*) Giving priority to the community needs and problems

(*c*) Developing confidence and will to work

(*d*) Finding resources to deal with the community needs and problems

(*e*) Developing cooperative and collaborative attitudes and practices

Choose the **correct** answer from the options given below:

A. (*a*), (*b*) and (*c*) only

B. (*b*), (*c*) and (*d*) only

C. (*c*), (*d*) and (*e*) only

D. (*a*), (*b*), (*c*), (*d*) and (*e*)

50. Which of the following persons were associated with the Chipko movement?

(*a*) Chandi Prasad Bhatt

(*b*) Gaura Devi

(*c*) Sundarlal Bahuguna

(*d*) Pandurang Hegde

Choose the **correct** answer from the options given below:

A. (*a*), (*b*) and (*c*) only

B. (*b*), (*c*) and (*d*) only

C. (*a*), (*b*) and (*d*) only

D. (*a*), (*c*) and (*d*) only

51. Identify the variables which figure in the highest level of measurement:

(*a*) Intelligence levels

(*b*) Educational levels

(*c*) Income levels

(*d*) Years of schooling

(*e*) Annual income

Choose the **correct** answer from the options given below:

A. (*a*) and (*b*) only

B. (*b*) and (*c*) only

C. (*c*) and (*d*) only

D. (*d*) and (*e*) only

52. Which of the following fall under the category of inferential statistics?

(*a*) chi-square (*b*) percentage

(*c*) proportion (*d*) *t*-test

(*e*) correlation

Choose the **correct** answer from the options given below:

A. (*a*), (*b*) and (*c*) only

B. (*c*), (*d*) and (*e*) only

C. (*a*), (*d*) and (*e*) only

D. (*b*), (*c*) and (*d*) only

53. Which of the following statement is true about single subject designs?

(*a*) These designs are essentially quasi-experimental designs.

(*b*) The unit of analysis in these designs is not one but many.

(*c*) These designs use repeated measure of dependent variable.

(*d*) These designs use time series analysis techniques.

(*e*) These designs measure the impact on the independent variables.

Choose the **correct** answer from the options given below:

A. (*a*), (*b*) and (*c*) only

B. (*a*), (*c*) and (*d*) only

C. (*b*), (*d*) and (*e*) only

D. (*b*), (*c*) and (*d*) only

54. What are the key operations in the data processing?

(*a*) Re-categorization of scores

(*b*) Editing of the entries

(*c*) Coding of data

(*d*) Computing the series

(*e*) Tabulation of data

Choose the **correct** answer from the options given below:

A. (*b*), (*c*) and (*d*) only

B. (*a*), (*b*) and (*c*) only

C. (*c*), (*d*) and (*e*) only

D. (*a*), (*d*) and (*e*) only

55. Which of the following are correct regarding social welfare institution?

(*a*) It provides a right to participation in society

(*b*) It responds to the needs of society

(*c*) It emphasises on economic and social well being

(*d*) It provides an opportunity to participate fully in society

Choose the **correct** answer from the options given below:

A. (*a*) and (*b*) only

B. (*a*) and (*d*) only

C. (*a*), (*b*) and (*d*) only

D. (*b*), (*c*) and (*d*) only

56. For any practice to be sustainable, it should:

(*a*) have least impact on the environment

(*b*) also be profitable and practical for self survival

(*c*) generate the results which cannot be quantified

(*d*) be a socially acceptable method or practice

Choose the **correct** answer from the options given below:

A. (*a*), (*b*) and (*c*) only

B. (*a*), (*b*) and (*d*) only

C. (*b*), (*c*) and (*d*) only

D. (*a*), (*c*) and (*d*) only

57. Niti Aayog's entire gamut of activities can be divided into following main heads. These are:

(*a*) Planning, budgeting and implementations

(*b*) Policy and programme framework

(*c*) Cooperative federalism

(*d*) Monitoring and evaluations

(*e*) Think tank, and knowledge and innovation Hub

Choose the **correct** answer from the options given below:

A. (*a*), (*b*) and (*c*) only

B. (*b*), (*c*), (*d*) and (*e*) only

C. (*a*), (*c*), (*d*) and (*e*) only

D. (*b*) and (*e*) only

58. Which of the following are not among the five Giants in the Beveridge report?

(*a*) Idleness and Ignorance

(*b*) Disease

(*c*) Injustice

(*d*) Squalor and want

(*e*) Poverty and Misery

Choose the **correct** answer from the options given below:

A. (*a*) and (*c*) only B. (*b*) and (*d*) only

C. (*c*) and (*e*) only D. (*d*) and (*a*) only

59. Which of the following are the aims and objectives of community organization:

(*a*) To increase the wealth of community people

(*b*) To address the personal interest of the people

(*c*) To develop the community consciousness

(*d*) To encourage community participation

(*e*) To develop leadership in the community'

Choose the **correct** answer from the options given below:

A. (*a*), (*b*) and (*c*) only

B. (*b*), (*c*) and (*d*) only

C. (*c*), (*d*) and (*e*) only

D. (*a*), (*c*) and (*e*) only

60. Which of the following measures have been implemented by the Government of India for protection of children?

(*a*) Protection of children from Sexual Offences Act was amended in 2019 to include life imprisonment for aggravated sexual assault.

(*b*) Beti Bachao, Beti Padhao scheme introduced for protecting the girl child.

(*c*) CCI's (Child Care Institution) shall appoint medical practitioners only in accordance with Board/Trust/Committee approval.

(*d*) The Indian Penal Code (IPC) has been amended to include rape committed on a male child.

Choose the **correct** answer from the options given below:

A. (*a*), (*c*) and (*d*) only
B. (*b*), (*c*) and (*d*) only
C. (*a*), (*b*), (*c*) and (*d*)
D. (*a*) and (*b*) only

61. The Liberty as given in the Preamble of the Constitution of India means:

(*a*) Liberty of thought
(*b*) Liberty of expression
(*c*) Liberty of belief and faith
(*d*) Liberty of worship
(*e*) Liberty of livelihood

Choose the **correct** answer from the options given below:

A. (*a*), (*b*), (*c*) and (*d*) only
B. (*a*), (*b*), (*c*) and (*e*) only
C. (*b*), (*c*), (*d*) and (*e*) only
D. (*c*) and (*d*) only

62. Which of the following are true about Eugenics?

(*a*) Improving human race through selective breeding
(*b*) Aggressive population control
(*c*) No control on population
(*d*) Purification of race

Choose the **correct** answer from the options given below:

A. (*a*) and (*b*) only
B. (*a*), (*b*) and (*c*) only
C. (*a*), (*b*) and (*d*) only
D. (*c*) and (*d*) only

63. With reference to the transactional analysis consider the following statements:

(*a*) Help the client to identify and decontaminate any ego state that has been distorted
(*b*) Help the client to achieve therapist in the transactional analysis
(*c*) Help the client to evaluate and alter an appropriate life position and adopt "I am OK, You are OK".
(*d*) Help the client to aquire an appropriate life script and replace it with a non-productive script

Choose the **correct** answer from the options given below:

A. (*a*) and (*b*) only
B. (*a*) and (*d*) only
C. (*a*), (*b*) and (*c*) only
D. (*a*), (*b*), (*c*) and (*d*)

64. Psychiatric social work with 'children in need of protection' category comprises:

(*a*) Orphans
(*b*) Street children
(*c*) Victims of child labour
(*d*) Victim of neglect
(*e*) Victim of physical or sexual abuse

Choose the **correct** answer form the options given below:

A. (*a*) and (*e*) only
B. (*a*), (*c*) and (*e*) only
C. (*b*), (*d*) and (*e*) only
D. (*a*), (*b*), (*c*), (*d*) and (*e*)

65. Which of the following schemes are covered under Mission Shakti?

(*a*) Beti Bachao, Beti Padhao
(*b*) One stop centre
(*c*) SWADHAR Greh
(*d*) Vatsalya

Choose the **correct** answer from the options given below:

A. (*a*), (*b*), (*c*) and (*d*)
B. (*a*), (*b*) and (*c*) only
C. (*b*), (*c*) and (*d*) only
D. (*a*), (*c*) and (*d*) only

66. Match List-I with List-II:

List-I (Social Work Educator)	List-II (Expertise in Area of Social Work)
(*a*) H.Y. Siddiqui	(*i*) Social work education
(*b*) Grace Mathew	(*ii*) Social casework
(*c*) D.K. Lal Das	(*iii*) Community work
(*d*) Surendra Singh	(*iv*) Social work research

Choose the **correct** answer from the options given below:

	(a)	(b)	(c)	(d)
A.	(i)	(ii)	(iii)	(iv)
B.	(ii)	(iii)	(iv)	(i)
C.	(iii)	(ii)	(iv)	(i)
D.	(iii)	(i)	(iv)	(ii)

67. Match List-I with List-II:

List-I (Concept)	List-II (Explanation)
(a) Elitism	(i) Prejudice and discrimination on the basis of any disability
(b) Heterosexism	(ii) Pejudice and discrimination on the basis of age
(c) Ageism	(iii) Prejudice and discrimination on the basis of class
(d) Handicapism	(iv) Prejudice and discrimination on the basis of sexual orientation

Choose the **correct** answer from the options given below:

	(a)	(b)	(c)	(d)
A.	(i)	(ii)	(iv)	(iii)
B.	(ii)	(i)	(iii)	(iv)
C.	(iii)	(iv)	(ii)	(i)
D.	(iv)	(iii)	(i)	(ii)

68. Match List-I with List-II:

List-I (Research)	List-II (Terms)
(a) Null hypothesis is true, but rejected	(i) Sampling Error
(b) The degree of error between a statistic and parameter	(ii) Type I Error
(c) The list of sampling elements from which the sample is selected	(iii) Validity
(d) The degree to which an instrument actually measures the concept/construct it is intended to measure	(iv) Sampling Frame

Choose the **correct** answer from the options given below:

	(a)	(b)	(c)	(d)
A.	(i)	(ii)	(iii)	(iv)
B.	(ii)	(i)	(iii)	(iv)
C.	(ii)	(i)	(iv)	(iii)
D.	(iii)	(i)	(ii)	(iv)

69. Match List-I with List-II:

List-I (Books)	List-II (Authors)
(a) Vindication of the Rights of Women	(i) Thomas Paine
(b) The Common Sense	(ii) D. Beetham
(c) Human Rights and Social Work	(iii) Mary Wollstonecraft
(d) Democracy and Human Rights	(iv) Jim Ife

Choose the **correct** answer from the options given below:

	(a)	(b)	(c)	(d)
A.	(i)	(ii)	(iii)	(iv)
B.	(ii)	(i)	(iv)	(iii)
C.	(iii)	(i)	(iv)	(ii)
D.	(iv)	(iii)	(i)	(ii)

70. Match List-I with List-II:

List-I (International Standard)	List-II (Purpose/Field)
(a) ISO 9001:2015	(i) Energy Management system
(b) ISO 14001:2015	(ii) Occupational health and safety standard
(c) ISO 50001	(iii) Environment management system
(d) ISO 45001	(iv) Quality Management (system) standard

Choose the **correct** answer from the options given below:

	(a)	(b)	(c)	(d)
A.	(i)	(ii)	(iii)	(iv)
B.	(ii)	(iii)	(iv)	(i)
C.	(iii)	(ii)	(i)	(iv)
D.	(iv)	(iii)	(i)	(ii)

71. Match List-I with List-II:

List-I	List-II
(a) Brahmo Samaj	(i) Poona
(b) Arya Samaj	(ii) Madras
(c) Satya Shodhak Samaj	(iii) Bengal
(d) Veda Samaj	(iv) Bombay

Choose the **correct** answer from the options given below:

	(a)	(b)	(c)	(d)
A.	(i)	(ii)	(iv)	(iii)
B.	(iii)	(iv)	(ii)	(i)
C.	(iii)	(iv)	(i)	(ii)
D.	(iv)	(iii)	(ii)	(i)

72. Match List-I with List-II:

List-I (Pioneers)	List-II (Typology of group work)
(a) Papell and Rothman (1966)	(i) Development stages (Boston model)
(b) Bernstein and colleagues (1965)	(ii) Diversity of approaches to group practice
(c) Roberts and Northen (1976)	(iii) Social Goal Model
(d) H.B. Trecker (1955)	(iv) Principles of group work practice

Choose the **correct** answer from the options given below:

	(a)	(b)	(c)	(d)
A.	(i)	(ii)	(iii)	(iv)
B.	(iii)	(i)	(ii)	(iv)
C.	(ii)	(iii)	(i)	(iv)
D.	(iv)	(ii)	(i)	(iii)

73. Match List-I with List-II:

List-I	List-II
(a) Right to equality	(i) Article 23-24
(b) Right to freedom	(ii) Article 29-30
(c) Rigth against exploitation	(iii) Article 19-22
(d) Cultural and educational rights	(iv) Article 14-18

Choose the **correct** answer from the options given below:

	(a)	(b)	(c)	(d)
A.	(iv)	(iii)	(i)	(ii)
B.	(iii)	(iv)	(ii)	(i)
C.	(ii)	(i)	(iii)	(iv)
D.	(i)	(iii)	(ii)	(iv)

74. Match List-I with List-II:

List-I (Books)	List-II (Authors)
(a) Social casework: A therapeutic approach	(i) Gordon Hamilton
(b) An Introduction to social casework	(ii) Mary Richmond
(c) Theory and practice of social casework	(iii) Grace Mathew
(d) What is social casework? An Introductory Description	(iv) R.K. Upadhyay

Choose the **correct** answer from the options given below:

	(a)	(b)	(c)	(d)
A.	(i)	(ii)	(iii)	(iv)
B.	(iv)	(iii)	(i)	(ii)
C.	(iv)	(ii)	(iii)	(i)
D.	(iii)	(ii)	(i)	(iv)

75. Match List-I with List-II:

List-I (Theories)	List-II (Techniques associated)
(a) Psycho analysis	(i) Accurate reflection of throughts and feelings

(*b*)	Person-centered Counselling	(*ii*)	Activities that grow out of the interaction between the case-work and the client
(*c*)	Gestalt Therapy	(*iii*)	Systematic desensitization
(*d*)	Cognitive and Behavioural Counselling	(*iv*)	Analysis of transference

Choose the **correct** answer from the options given below:

	(*a*)	(*b*)	(*c*)	(*d*)
A.	(*i*)	(*ii*)	(*iii*)	(*iv*)
B.	(*ii*)	(*i*)	(*iv*)	(*iii*)
C.	(*iv*)	(*iii*)	(*i*)	(*ii*)
D.	(*iv*)	(*i*)	(*ii*)	(*iii*)

76. Arrange the following enactment of legislation in correct ascending orders:

(*a*) Protection of Child Rights Act
(*b*) The SCs & STs (Prevention of Atrocities) Act
(*c*) The Protection of Women from Domestic Violence Act
(*d*) The Sexual Harrassment of Women at Workplace (Prevention Prohibition & Redressal)

Choose the **correct** answer from the options given below:

A. (*a*), (*b*), (*c*) and (*d*)
B. (*b*), (*c*), (*d*) and (*a*)
C. (*c*), (*d*), (*a*) and (*b*)
D. (*a*), (*b*), (*d*) and (*c*)

77. World Conference on women were held in different cities. Arrange the following in correct ascending orders (first to last):

(*a*) Beijing (*b*) Nairobi
(*c*) Copenhagen (*d*) Mexico

Choose the **correct** answer from the options given below:

A. (*a*), (*b*), (*c*), (*d*)
B. (*b*), (*c*), (*d*), (*a*)
C. (*c*), (*d*), (*a*), (*b*)
D. (*d*), (*c*), (*b*), (*a*)

78. Some major landmarks event in the evolution of psychology are given below. Arrange the events from early to recent.

(*a*) Gestalt psychology born in Germany
(*b*) Sigmund freud develops psychoanalysis
(*c*) John B. Watson published 'Behaviourism'
(*d*) Functionalism formulated as a system of psychology by John Dewey

Choose the **correct** answer from the options given below:

A. (*a*), (*b*), (*c*), (*d*) B. (*d*), (*b*), (*a*), (*c*)
C. (*b*), (*c*), (*d*), (*a*) D. (*d*), (*b*), (*c*), (*a*)

79. Arrange stages of group development in their ascending order:

(*a*) Intimacy (*b*) Differentiation
(*c*) Separation (*d*) Preaffiliation
(*e*) Power and control

Choose the **correct** answer from the options given below:

A. (*a*), (*d*), (*e*), (*c*) and (*b*)
B. (*b*), (*a*), (*d*), (*c*) and (*e*)
C. (*d*), (*b*), (*a*), (*e*) and (*c*)
D. (*d*), (*e*), (*a*), (*b*) and (*c*)

80. Decision making involves a series of steps. Arrange in a sequential manner:

(*a*) Identifying the problem
(*b*) Analysing the problems
(*c*) Selecting the best alternative solution
(*d*) Developing alternatives
(*e*) Converting decision into action

Choose the **correct** answer from the options given below:

A. (*a*), (*b*), (*c*), (*d*) and (*e*)
B. (*b*), (*a*), (*d*), (*c*) and (*e*)
C. (*a*), (*b*), (*d*), (*c*) and (*e*)
D. (*c*), (*b*), (*a*), (*e*) and (*d*)

81. Arrange the following in correct sequencing order (early to later stages):

(*a*) Genital (*b*) Latency
(*c*) Phallic (*d*) Anal
(*e*) Oral

Choose the **correct** answer from the options given below:

A. (*a*), (*b*), (*c*), (*d*), (*e*)
B. (*b*), (*c*), (*d*), (*e*), (*a*)
C. (*d*), (*e*), (*a*), (*c*), (*b*)
D. (*e*), (*d*), (*c*), (*b*), (*a*)

82. Arrange the philosophical and methodological approaches in correct sequential orders
(*a*) Ontology
(*b*) Theoretical orientation
(*c*) Epistemology
(*d*) Research design
(*e*) Research approach

Choose the **correct** answer from the options given below:

A. (*a*), (*c*), (*b*), (*e*), (*d*)
B. (*a*), (*b*), (*c*), (*d*), (*e*)
C. (*b*), (*a*), (*c*), (*e*), (*d*)
D. (*b*), (*a*), (*c*), (*d*), (*e*)

83. Arrange the following approaches of social work in correct sequence of their evolution:
(*a*) Therapeutic approaches
(*b*) Radical approaches
(*c*) System approaches
(*d*) Anti-discriminatory approaches

Choose the **correct** answer from the options given below:

A. (*a*), (*b*), (*c*), (*d*)
B. (*a*), (*c*), (*b*), (*d*)
C. (*b*), (*a*), (*c*), (*d*)
D. (*c*), (*a*), (*b*), (*d*)

84. Arrange the following Reports in ascending order of their publications:
(*a*) The Beveridge Report
(*b*) The Seebaum Report
(*c*) The Younghusband Report
(*d*) Lane Committee Report

Choose the **correct** answer from the options given below:

A. (*a*), (*b*), (*c*), (*d*) B. (*a*), (*c*), (*b*), (*d*)
C. (*b*), (*a*), (*c*), (*d*) D. (*c*), (*a*), (*b*), (*d*)

85. The non-linear social work process with asylum seekers and refugees consist of five elements. Arrange in order
(*a*) Welcome (*b*) Befriending
(*c*) Mediation (*d*) Accompaniment
(*e*) Advocacy

Choose the **correct** answer from the options given below:

A. (*a*), (*b*), (*c*), (*d*) and (*e*)
B. (*a*), (*c*), (*b*), (*d*) and (*e*)
C. (*a*), (*d*), (*c*), (*b*) and (*e*)
D. (*a*), (*e*), (*d*), (*c*) and (*b*)

86. Given below are two statements: one is labelled as Assertion (A) and other is labelled as Reason (R).

Assertion (A): Almost all beggars are homeless but all homeless are not beggars.

Reason (R): Most of the programmes for homeless are directed towards eradication of beggary.

In the light of the above statements. Choose the **correct** answer from the options given below:

A. Both (A) and (R) are true and (R) is the correct explanation of (A)
B. Both (A) and (R) are true and (R) is NOT the correct explanation of (A)
C. (A) is true, but (R) is false
D. (A) is false, but (R) is true

87. Given below are two statements:

Statement I: There is an increasing awareness of the disabilities and disability rights in India.

Statement II: The number of recognized disability conditions has been increased from 7 to 21 in the RPWD Act 2016.

In the light of the above statements, choose the **correct** answer from the options given below:

A. Both Statement I and Statement II are true
B. Both Statement I and Statement II are false

C. Statement I is true, but Statement II is false
D. Statement I is false, but Statement II is true

88. Given below are two statements: one is labelled as Assertion (A) and other is labelled as Reason (R).

Assertion (A): Social action is mass betterment through propaganda and legislation.

Reason (R): Social action requires intensive mass mobilization.

In the light of the above statements. Choose the **correct** answer from the options given below:
A. Both (A) and (R) are true and (R) is the correct explanation of (A)
B. Both (A) and (R) are true and (R) is NOT the correct explanation of (A)
C. (A) is true, but (R) is false
D. (A) is false, but (R) is true

89. Given below are two statements:

Statement I: Indigenisation is a plea for self awareness and rejection of a borrower conciousness, emphasizing on the need for an inside view.

Statement II: Indigenisation should not lead to narrow parochialism or to the fragmentation of a single discipline into several insulated system of thoughts based on geographical boundaries.

In the light of the above statements, choose the **correct** answer from the options given below:
A. Both Statement I and Statement II are true
B. Both Statement I and Statement II are false
C. Statement I is true, but Statement II is false
D. Statement I is false, but Statement II is true

90. Given below are two statements: one is labelled as Assertion (A) and other is labelled as Reason (R)

Assertion (A): Indigenous social work requires sensitivity to local cultures and contexts.

Reason (R): The ethnocentric form of indi-genous social work would be counter pro-ductive.

In the light of the above statements, choose the **correct** answer from the options given below:
A. Both (A) and (R) are true and (R) is the correct explanation of (A)
B. Both (A) and (R) are true and (R) is NOT the correct explanation of (A)
C. (A) is true, but (R) is false
D. (A) is false, but (R) is true

Directions (Qs. No. 91 to 95): *Read the following passage carefully and answer the questions that follow:*

Social development is a wider concept and inclusive of economic development. It does not exclusively concern with the planning of the social services but also focuses on economic growth. Its focus has to be on providing integration, consensus shared value patterns among different cultural groups and building up solidarity of the nation against any foreign threat. A social development perspective does not mean that economic development comes first and is followed by steps to ensure distributive justice. It involves planning for simultaneous development on many different areas. The challenge of social development is not so much a problem of mobilizing money resources but rather a problem of motivating and mobilizing people. Besides, there is a need for economic growth to be regulated in such a manner that it reduces economic disparities. Majority of the National Development Plans, for that matter, consider economic, physical, infrastructural educational, health and welfare targets of growth and expansion. Of late, there is a realization among the economists that there is a need take into account non-economic factors/ parameters for development planning.

91. Which of the following is true about social and economic development?

A. There is a need to give more importance to economic growth
B. Non-economic parameter are not needed for planning
C. There is a need to regulate economic growth
D. There is an increase realization that social development is a vague concept

92. What are the goals of social development?

(*a*) Providing integration among different social groups
(*b*) Shared value pattern among different cultural groups
(*c*) Building up solidarity of nation to face foreign threat
(*d*) Primacy of economic development

Choose the **correct** answer from the options given below:

A. (*a*), (*b*), (*c*) and (*d*)
B. (*a*), (*b*) and (*c*) only
C. (*b*) and (*c*) only
D. (*c*) and (*d*) only

93. Which of the following are features of social development?

(*a*) It is preceeded by economic development
(*b*) It is concerned exlusively with planning of social services
(*c*) It is a wider concept and inclusive of economic development
(*d*) It involves planning for simultaneous development on many different areas

Choose the **correct** answer from the options given below:

A. (*a*), (*b*), (*c*) and (*d*)
B. (*b*), (*c*) and (*d*) only
C. (*a*) and (*b*) only
D. (*c*) and (*d*) only

94. Given below are two statements:

Statement I: Social development is a comprehensive concept.

Statement II: There is a realization to take into account non-economic parameter for development planning.

In the light of the above statements, choose the **correct** answer from the options given below:

A. Both Statement I and Statement II are true
B. Both Statement I and Statement II are false
C. Statement I is true, but Statement II is false
D. Statement I is false, but Statement II is true

95. Which of the following is a challenge for social development?

A. Motivating and mobilizing people
B. Mobilizing resources
C. Motivating development planners
D. Making shift in policy perspective

Directions (Qs. No. 96 to 100): *Read the following passage carefully and answer the questions that follow:*

We no longer regard poverty, unemployment and social inequalities as inherent in the divine order of things. Every social problem has it cause or causes. If the cause can be discovered, the problem in most cases can be solved. It is the function of a school (of social work) such as this to seek to explain the causes of social problems and to suggest methods of approach to their solution. As social workers we want to do all in our power to alleviate human misery, but that is not all. Our larger problem is the problem of prevention and if, as we have reason to believe, our current economic system is cause of much social maladjustment. It then becomes necessary for us to be realistic and to face our problems. It is for this reason that I have felt it worth to talk at some length regarding the relationship between education and social change. The tragedy in the whole situation is that though we know our knowledge in the social sciences has not kept pace with the advance in technology, the efforts of society seem to be directed towards widening the gap rather than narrowing it. The man who invents a new machine or simplifies a technical process is feted and honoured but the man who ventures to question existing social and political institutions and suggest possible remedies, not only faces social disapproval, but far too often lands in jail.

I am not urging you to rush out from this hall and immediately attempt to bring in a new social order. I am urging you to utilise your time in this institution to make a deep study of the problems of society; to develop a social philosophy and to acquire the ability to discriminate and make judgements based upon facts rather than sentimentalism and hearsay. We must be social servants– that is our profession. But over and above serving society let us be social engineers.

96. The author desires that social workers should become:

A. Social servants
B. Change agents
C. Social activists
D. Social engineers

97. Whom does the author seems to be addressing in the passage?

A. Trainee Civil servants
B. Social work students
C. Social work teachers
D. A mix group of trainers

98. What are the propositions of the author to the social workers?

(*a*) To become revolutionary and bring a new social order
(*b*) To undertake a deep study of the problem of society
(*c*) To develop a social philosophy and reflect on the problems of society
(*d*) To develop the ability to make judgement based upon facts

Choose the **correct** answer from the options given below:

A. (*a*), (*b*), (*c*) and (*d*)
B. (*b*), (*c*) and (*d*) only
C. (*b*) and (*c*) only
D. (*c*) and (*d*) only

99. What are the functions of a school of social work that the author tried to enlist?

(*a*) Explain the cause of social problems
(*b*) Suggest methods of approach to solve social problems
(*c*) Believe that our larger problem is problem of prevention
(*d*) Futile to explore the relationship between education and social change

Choose the **correct** answer from the options given below:

A. (*a*) and (*b*) only
B. (*a*) and (*c*) only
C. (*a*), (*b*) and (*c*) only
D. (*b*), (*c*) and (*d*) only

100. Given below are two statements:

Statement I: Our knowledge in the social sciences has not kept pace with the advance in technology.

Statement II: The efforts of society seem to be directed towards widening the gap rather than narrowing it.

In the light of the above statements, choose the **correct** answer from the options given below:

A. Both Statement I and Statement II are true
B. Both Statement I and Statement II are false
C. Statement I is true, but Statement II is false
D. Statement I is false, but Statement II is true

ANSWERS

1. **(B):** Social workers may be engaged in various roles depending on the context and the needs of their clients. Each role serves a specific purpose, and the intensity of engagement can vary based on the situation. However, the role that typically involves more intensive engagement with clients is often seen in the capacity of a social worker as an enabler.

   Social workers as enablers focus on empowering clients to develop their own strengths and resources to address and solve their problems. This role often requires a deep and ongoing engagement with clients to identify their needs, set goals, and work collaboratively towards achieving positive outcomes. Enabling involves providing support, guidance, and resources to help clients overcome challenges and improve their overall well-being.

2. **(A):** The history of the Delhi School of Social Work, today's Department of Social Work at the University of Delhi, is intricately woven with the social activism of the Young Women's Christian Association (YWCA). In 1946, amidst the socio-political upheaval of post-independence India, the YWCA recognized the dire need for trained social workers who could address the emerging challenges faced by communities. This vision led to the establishment of the National YWCA School of Social Work in Lucknow, the second institution of its kind in India. Driven by a commitment to empowering women, the YWCA's initiative initially focused on offering training to demobilized women from the wartime Women's Auxiliary Corps of India. But its scope soon expanded to cater to a wider range of social issues, encompassing community development, child welfare, and mental health. In 1947, the school relocated to Delhi and forged a significant partnership with the University of Delhi. This affiliation further enriched its academic framework and paved the way for offering diverse social work programs, including postgraduate degrees and doctoral research. Over the decades, the institution has evolved into a leading center for social work education, attracting students from across India and beyond. The story of the Delhi School of Social Work is not merely about an academic institution, but about a commitment to social transformation spearheaded by the Young Women's Christian Association. Their vision and initiative laid the foundation for generations of social workers who continue to address the evolving needs of society with passion and dedication.

3. **(A):** The London Society for Organizing Charitable Relief and Repressing Mendicancy, established in the mid-19th century, played a pivotal role in the development of organized philanthropy in London, England. This society, often recognized as the Charity Organization Society (COS), was founded with the overarching goal of systematizing charitable efforts and addressing issues related to poverty and mendicancy. The COS emphasized a scientific and methodical approach to charity work, aiming to coordinate and streamline relief efforts while discouraging indiscriminate almsgiving. Their focus extended beyond immediate relief to address the root causes of poverty, promoting self-sufficiency and social reform. The society's initiatives marked a significant shift in philanthropic practices during the Victorian era, influencing the broader landscape of social work and charity organizations both in the United Kingdom and internationally.

4. (C): The Principle of Individualization in social work underscores the intrinsic uniqueness of each client, recognizing them as individuals with distinct experiences, perspectives, and needs. It signifies a departure from generalized or standardized approaches to client interaction and intervention, emphasizing the importance of tailoring social work practices to the specific and nuanced characteristics of each person. This principle encourages social workers to move beyond stereotyping or making assumptions based on broader categories and to instead engage in a comprehensive understanding of the client's background, values, and aspirations. By acknowledging and appreciating the individuality of each client, social workers can develop more effective and client-centered strategies that respect personal autonomy, foster meaningful connections, and address the particular challenges and strengths inherent to that person's unique circumstances. This approach aligns with the ethical imperative of providing personalized and culturally sensitive support, promoting a more holistic and empathetic model of social work practice.

5. (B): The social work value of appreciating diversity is foundational in cultivating cultural competence among practitioners working in diverse cultural settings. This value underscores the importance of recognizing and respecting the unique attributes, backgrounds, and perspectives of individuals from various cultural groups. Social workers, by appreciating diversity, strive to understand the impact of cultural factors on clients' lives, acknowledging the influence of cultural contexts on their values, beliefs, and behaviours. This commitment to diversity promotes inclusive and culturally sensitive practices, helping social workers tailor their interventions to meet the specific needs of clients while fostering an environment of mutual respect. It involves an ongoing process of self-reflection, learning, and adaptation to ensure that social work practices are responsive to the diverse and dynamic nature of the communities they serve. Ultimately, appreciating diversity is essential for social workers to provide effective and ethical services that uphold the principles of human worth and dignity.

6. (A): In Ivan Pavlov's classical conditioning experiment, the bell serves as the conditioned stimulus (CS). Initially, the bell is a neutral stimulus that, when presented alone, does not elicit the salivation response from the dogs. However, through the process of classical conditioning, where the bell is consistently paired with the unconditioned stimulus (US) of food, the dogs eventually form an association between the sound of the bell and the impending arrival of food. As a result of this repeated pairing, the bell alone becomes a predictive cue for the dogs, and after conditioning, the mere sound of the bell is sufficient to elicit the conditioned response (CR) of salivation. In this context, the bell transitions from being a neutral stimulus to a conditioned stimulus, acquiring the ability to evoke a response due to its association with the unconditioned stimulus during the learning process.

7. (D): Drive Reduction Theory is a motivational framework that places a significant emphasis on the concept of homeostasis in explaining human behaviour. This theory posits that individuals are motivated by a biological need to maintain a state of equilibrium or balance within their physiological systems. When there is a deviation from this balanced state, an internal drive is activated, such as hunger or thirst, motivating the individual to take action to restore equilibrium. The ultimate goal of behaviour, according to Drive Reduction Theory, is to reduce or eliminate these physiological drives. For instance, when a person feels hungry, the drive to eat arises, and consuming food serves to alleviate that hunger, bringing the body back to a more stable condition. In essence, Drive Reduction Theory underscores the role of maintaining internal balance, or homeostasis, as a fundamental motivator guiding human behaviour in response to biological needs.

8. (A): Projection, as a psychological defense mechanism, acts as a significant barrier to accurate perception by distorting an individual's understanding of others. This phenomenon occurs when individuals unconsciously attribute their own thoughts, emotions, or motives to those around them. In projecting, people may superimpose their internal conflicts or desires onto others, leading to a skewed perception of reality. This defense mechanism often arises as a means of protecting oneself from uncomfortable feelings or aspects of their own identity. By projecting these elements onto others, individuals maintain a psychological distance from acknowledging and confronting certain aspects of their own personality. This distortion in perception can hinder effective communication, interpersonal understanding, and the ability to accurately interpret the thoughts and behaviours of others, thus impacting the overall quality of relationships and interactions.

9. (A): M.N. Srinivas introduced the concept of 'Sanskritization' as a key sociological idea in the context of Indian society. The term encapsulates a transformative process wherein lower-caste or lower-class groups emulate the cultural practices, rituals, and customs of higher-caste or higher-class communities with the aim of achieving upward social mobility and prestige. Srinivas highlighted how this cultural emulation was not merely a superficial adoption of practices but often involved a profound internalization of values and norms associated with higher social strata. The concept sheds light on the dynamic interplay between culture and social structure, illustrating how the imitation of higher social orders contributes to a continuous process of social change and stratification within the complex fabric of Indian society. Sanskritization has remained a crucial theoretical framework in the study of social mobility and cultural dynamics in the South Asian context.

10. (B): Michel Foucault's concept of the "Panopticon" is a powerful metaphorical framework introduced in his seminal work "Discipline and Punish." The Panopticon is a hypothetical architectural design for a prison characterized by a central observation tower that allows a single observer to monitor all inmates without their awareness of whether they are being watched. This design instills a sense of constant surveillance and induces self-discipline among the prisoners. Foucault uses the Panopticon as a metaphor to illustrate the dynamics of power and control in society, extending beyond physical prisons to encompass various institutions and structures where surveillance operates as a mechanism of social discipline. The Panopticon represents the pervasive nature of surveillance and the subtle ways in which it influences behaviour, fostering a culture of self-regulation and conformity in modern societies.

11. (A): In the sensorimotor stage, which encompasses the initial two years of life according to Piaget, infants undergo a transformative cognitive process marked by the acquisition of object permanence. Initially, a child may act as if objects cease to exist when they are no longer visible, reflecting an absence of this understanding. However, as the sensorimotor stage progresses, typically by around eight months of age, infants begin to grasp the concept of object permanence. This signifies that they can mentally represent objects in their absence and anticipate their continued existence. The development of object permanence is pivotal for a variety of cognitive achievements, including the ability to engage in purposeful actions, engage in symbolic play, and navigate the world with a more sophisticated mental representation of their surroundings. It lays a crucial foundation for subsequent cognitive milestones as the child advances through Piaget's stages of development.

12. (C)

13. (D): Focused group discussions are typically not a primary technique used in the case study process. In the case study process, various techniques are employed to gain a comprehensive understanding of a particular individual, group, or situation. Interviews are a fundamental method where the researcher directly engages with the case subject to gather detailed information, insights, and perspectives. Objective observation involves systematically observing and documenting behaviours or events without interference, ensuring a more unbiased and accurate portrayal. Collecting information from significant others, such as family members or colleagues, provides additional perspectives and context to enrich the case study. However, focused group discussions, where a group collectively discusses a specific topic, are typically not a primary technique in case studies. Case studies often focus on individual or small-group experiences, and while group discussions are valuable in other research contexts, they may not align with the depth and individualized exploration characterizing the case study approach. The emphasis in case studies is on the richness of individual experiences and contexts, making methods like interviews and objective observations more pertinent to the detailed analysis of the case under investigation.

14. (D): Group Conflict refers to the disagreements, tensions, or disputes that arise among members within a group, and it plays a notable yet nuanced role in understanding group functioning. Unlike the other listed processes—Group Cohesion, Social Control, and Group Culture—which are generally considered fundamental for a group's overall stability and identity, Group Conflict is not always indispensable. While conflict within a group can lead to challenges and disruptions, it is not inherently detrimental; in fact, it can stimulate critical thinking, creativity, and innovation if managed constructively. The significance of Group Conflict varies across different groups, contexts, and purposes, and its impact on group dynamics depends on how it is addressed and resolved. Some groups may experience minimal conflict and still function effectively, while others may navigate conflict as a means of growth and adaptation. Recognizing the potential for constructive conflict management allows for a more nuanced understanding of the role that conflict plays in shaping the dynamics and outcomes within a group.

15. (B): Reassurance, as a therapeutic technique, plays a crucial role in alleviating the emotional distress of clients experiencing anxiety and guilt. When individuals grapple with intense feelings of anxiety and guilt, they often harbor uncertainties about their worth or fear the consequences of their actions. Reassurance, offered by a supportive therapist, provides a sense of comfort, validation, and security. By expressing understanding and empathy, the therapist reassures the client that they are not alone in their struggles and that their feelings are acknowledged without judgment. This validation can help mitigate the sense of isolation and self-blame associated with anxiety and guilt, fostering a therapeutic environment where clients feel understood and supported. While reassurance is a valuable tool, its effectiveness may vary based on the individual's needs, and therapists often integrate it with other therapeutic approaches to address the underlying causes and promote lasting emotional well-being.

16. (A): Group work in social work is a method that involves a social worker facilitating interactions and collaboration among individuals who share common challenges or concerns. This approach recognizes the therapeutic potential of group dynamics and mutual support. Social workers employ group work to create a supportive environment where participants can share their experiences, perspectives, and coping strategies. The group setting promotes a sense of community, allowing individuals to feel understood and less isolated in their struggles. Through structured activities, discussions, and interventions, the social worker guides the group towards common goals, emphasizing mutual growth and empowerment. Group work is particularly effective for addressing various issues, such as mental health concerns, addiction, or coping with life transitions, as it harnesses the collective wisdom and support within the group to foster positive change and enhance the well-being of its members.

17. (A): H.Y. Siddiqui emerges as a prominent figure in the context of the "Principle of Optimum Utilization of Indigenous Resources." As a distinguished Indian social worker and educator deeply involved in community organization practices, Siddiqui emphasized the vital importance of harnessing local resources and leveraging existing community strengths. His work reflects a commitment to empowering communities by recognizing and utilizing their inherent capabilities. Siddiqui likely made significant contributions to the understanding and application of the principle, advocating for sustainable development practices that are rooted in the unique resources and strengths of each community. By highlighting the significance of indigenous resources, Siddiqui's approach aligns with the principle's emphasis on optimizing the use of locally available assets, fostering self-reliance, and ensuring that community development efforts are culturally sensitive and contextually relevant. In essence, H.Y. Siddiqui's work embodies the principles of community organization and sustainable development, emphasizing the maximization of indigenous resources for the betterment of communities.

18. (B): The first American Charity Organization Society (COS) was established in Buffalo, New York in 1877. The society was founded by Reverend S. Humphrey Gurteen. The COS was influenced by the Elizabethan Poor Laws of England and originated in Elberfeld, Germany. The society believed that giving charity without investigating the causes of poverty would create a class of citizens who would always be dependent on charity. The COS was opposed to providing long-term relief to the poor and instead tried to help them become self-supporting. The COS set up centralized records and administrative services and emphasized objective investigations and professional training. The society investigated applicants and awarded certificates for relief only to "needy and worthy persons". In 1881, the society aided 338 cases and investigated over 500 new cases in each of the following two years. The COS movement quickly spread from Buffalo to other industrial cities in the Northeast to Cincinnati and Indianapolis and farther west and south. The New York City

Charity Organization Society was founded in 1882, and by 1892, there were ninety-two societies located throughout the country.

19. (C): The Community Development Project in India was initiated by the Government of India in 1952 as a comprehensive strategy aimed at fostering rural development and uplifting rural communities. This ambitious project sought to address multifaceted challenges faced by rural areas, including issues related to agriculture, infrastructure, education, health, and socio-economic disparities. The primary objective was to empower local communities by encouraging their active participation in the planning and implementation of development initiatives. The project marked a shift from traditional top-down approaches to a more participatory model, emphasizing community involvement in decision-making and the utilization of local resources. By promoting self-sufficiency and community engagement, the Community Development Project aimed to create sustainable improvements in the quality of life for rural residents, laying the groundwork for subsequent rural development initiatives in India.

20. (C): Social action, in its broadest sense, is not synonymous with violent, punitive, or destructive actions; rather, it is characterized as conscientious and purposeful efforts undertaken by individuals or groups to bring about positive social change. Social action encompasses a range of proactive and intentional activities aimed at addressing social issues, advocating for justice, and promoting the well-being of communities. It can manifest through peaceful protests, community organizing, advocacy campaigns, and other nonviolent means. The term reflects a deliberate and thoughtful approach to addressing societal challenges, emphasizing the need for individuals and communities to take an active role in shaping their social environment. By fostering awareness, mobilizing resources, and engaging in constructive dialogue, social action strives to contribute to the creation of a more equitable, inclusive, and just society, emphasizing the transformative power of collective efforts in bringing about positive social transformations.

21. (D): 'Felt Needs' in community work represent the articulated and perceived needs of the community members themselves, highlighting the importance of capturing the subjective experiences and priorities of the local population. Unlike needs imposed by community leaders or external agencies, felt needs emerge from the genuine concerns and perspectives of the community in general. This approach recognizes that community members are the best judges of their own circumstances, and their voices should guide the development of interventions and initiatives. By actively engaging with the community to identify and understand these felt needs, community workers can ensure that their efforts are relevant, responsive, and tailored to the unique context and aspirations of the community. This participatory approach fosters a sense of ownership and empowerment among community members, laying the groundwork for sustainable and effective community development initiatives that genuinely address the expressed concerns of the people they aim to serve.

22. (D): A Type-II error occurs when the null hypothesis, which is false, is erroneously accepted in a statistical hypothesis test. This error represents a failure to reject the null hypothesis when there is evidence to suggest it should be rejected. In practical terms, it means that the test fails to detect a true effect, relationship, or difference that actually exists in the population. This can have significant implications, particularly in scientific research or decision-making processes, as it leads to the retention of a false hypothesis. The probability of committing a Type-II error is influenced by factors such as the sample size, the level of significance chosen for the test, and the effect size. Researchers and analysts aim to minimize Type-II errors, as they can impact the accuracy and reliability of study findings, ultimately emphasizing the importance of carefully selecting appropriate statistical tests and interpreting their outcomes in a broader context.

23. (B): In a research framework inclined towards interpretivism, the most appropriate research approach is the qualitative research approach. Interpretivism emphasizes the understanding of social phenomena within their natural context, focusing on subjective meanings and interpretations. Qualitative research methods, including interviews, observations, and content analysis, are particularly well-suited for this paradigm as they allow researchers to delve into the intricacies of human experiences and behaviors. Qualitative approaches facilitate the exploration of diverse perspectives, allowing for a nuanced understanding of the complex and context-dependent nature of social phenomena. Researchers employing qualitative methods seek to uncover the subjective meanings individuals attribute to their experiences, enabling a holistic and in-depth exploration of the social world. While mixed methods research combines both qualitative and quantitative elements, a qualitative research approach is central in interpretivism, emphasizing the richness and depth of understanding that comes from exploring the subjective and contextual aspects of human phenomena.

24. (A): The second stage in qualitative analysis of grounded theory, known as Axial Coding, is a crucial step in the process of developing a comprehensive understanding of the data. During Axial Coding, the researcher systematically connects categories or themes identified in the initial Open Coding phase, seeking to establish relationships and patterns within the data. This involves identifying core themes, examining how they relate to subcategories, and exploring the connections between different concepts. Axial Coding allows for a more structured and organized analysis, as it involves the development of a coding framework that outlines the relationships between categories and provides insights into the underlying structure of the phenomenon being studied. This stage enables researchers to move beyond the initial identification of concepts and towards a more refined understanding of the interconnections and dynamics within the data, contributing to the generation of a grounded theory that emerges directly from the empirical material.

25. (B): Dependent variables, in the context of a research study, are those variables that represent the outcomes, effects, or responses that researchers aim to measure, observe, or record. They are essentially the focus of the investigation, as their variations are believed to be influenced by changes in the independent variable(s) or experimental conditions. Dependent variables are crucial in understanding the impact or relationship between different factors within a study. Researchers manipulate or control the independent variable(s) to observe how it affects the dependent variable, seeking to uncover patterns, associations, or causation. In essence, dependent variables encapsulate the measurable changes or responses that researchers aim to analyze, providing insights into the effects of the experimental conditions or interventions being studied. The selection and careful definition of dependent variables are fundamental in designing experiments and conducting research to ensure accurate and meaningful interpretation of study outcomes.

26. (D): In the context of the NASW (National Association of Social Workers) Code of Ethics refers to the necessity of providing information about the nature, extent, and duration of the research study as part of the informed consent process. This means that social workers and researchers are ethically obligated to transparently communicate to potential participants the essential details pertaining to the study, such as its purpose, scope, and the anticipated duration of their involvement. This ensures that individuals have a comprehensive understanding of what participating in the research entails, allowing them to make informed decisions about whether they want to take part. By explicitly detailing the nature and parameters of the study, social workers uphold the ethical principle of respecting participants' autonomy and ensuring that their consent is truly informed, aligning with the commitment to safeguarding the rights and well-being of those involved in the research process.

27. (D): Social welfare administration primarily revolves around the strategic and effective delivery of social welfare services to address the needs of diverse populations. It encompasses the management and coordination of various programs and initiatives aimed at improving the well-being of individuals and communities. The core focus is on ensuring that social welfare services reach the intended beneficiaries in a systematic and organized manner. This involves intricate planning, resource allocation, and the implementation of policies that align with the goals of social development. While considerations like democratization of administration, maximizing beneficiaries, and sensitizing administration are integral aspects, the ultimate goal is to facilitate the actual delivery of services that cater to societal needs. Social welfare administration plays a vital role in creating an inclusive and supportive environment, where the benefits of social programs are efficiently distributed to enhance the overall quality of life for those in needs.

28. (A): The National Policy on Voluntary Sector, approved in 2007, reflects a significant milestone in India's approach to the voluntary or nonprofit sector. This policy outlines the government's commitment to creating an enabling environment for voluntary organizations to thrive and contribute effectively to social development. It emphasizes the importance of a collaborative partnership between the government and the voluntary sector to address diverse social challenges. The policy acknowledges the autonomy of voluntary organizations while also highlighting the need for transparency, accountability, and good governance within the sector. By providing a comprehensive framework, the policy seeks to promote the involvement of voluntary organizations in areas such as social service delivery, advocacy, and community development. Overall, the National Policy on Voluntary Sector serves as a guiding document to foster a robust and dynamic relationship between the government and the nonprofit sector, with the shared goal of enhancing the well-being of communities and society at large.

29. (C): The United Nations Conference on Human Environment in Stockholm in 1972 represented a historic milestone as the first major international forum to deliberate on the concept of sustainability at a global scale. This conference brought together leaders and representatives from various nations to address growing concerns about the environmental impact of human activities. Discussions centered on the necessity of balancing economic development with environmental conservation to ensure the well-being of present and future generations. The concept of sustainability, introduced and emphasized during this conference, underscored the interconnectedness of social, economic, and environmental dimensions. It laid the groundwork for subsequent international dialogues and agreements focused on fostering practices that meet the needs of the present without compromising the ability of future generations to meet their own needs. The Stockholm Conference initiated a global shift in perspectives, emphasizing the importance of responsible and balanced development practices to safeguard the health of the planet and its inhabitants.

30. (B): While Human Development Index (HDI), Ecological Footprints, and Intergenerational Equity are commonly recognized indicators of sustainable development, Gross National Happiness (GNH) takes a slightly different approach. GNH is a holistic measure developed in Bhutan, focusing on the well-being and happiness of the citizens rather than purely economic factors. While happiness and well-being are crucial components of sustainable development, GNH is not universally adopted as a mainstream indicator for assessing sustainable development on a global scale. HDI considers health, education, and standard of living; Ecological Footprints measure environmental impact; and Intergenerational Equity emphasizes fairness across generations. While GNH is valuable in capturing a broader perspective, its subjective nature and cultural specificity make it less commonly used as a direct indicator of sustainable development in broader international contexts. Sustainable development assessments often integrate a combination of these indicators to provide a more comprehensive understanding of the economic, social, and environmental dimensions of development.

31. (A): The most widely recognized and influential definition of sustainable development, "Development that meets the needs of the present without compromising the ability of future generations to meet their own needs," was popularized by the Brundtland Report. Formally titled "Our Common Future," this report was published in 1987 and emanated from the World Commission on Environment and Development (WCED), chaired by Gro Harlem Brundtland. The definition encapsulates the essence of sustainability by emphasizing the imperative to harmonize economic progress, social equity, and environmental integrity. It underscores the responsibility of the present generation to pursue development that not only addresses current needs but also preserves resources and conditions essential for the well-being of future generations. The Brundtland Report's articulation of sustainable development has become a guiding principle for global policy frameworks, shaping the discourse and actions aimed at achieving a more balanced, resilient and equitable trajectory for human development and environmental stewardship on a global scale.

32. (A): The poignant statement "Human rights start with breakfast" is attributed to Leopold Senghor, a prominent Senegalese poet, philosopher, and politician. Senghor, who served as the first President of Senegal after its independence from French colonial rule, was an advocate for human rights and social justice. This phrase encapsulates the idea that securing fundamental human rights, such as the right to food and nourishment, is foundational to the broader pursuit of justice and dignity. It implies that addressing basic needs, starting with something as fundamental as breakfast, is a crucial step in fostering a society where individuals can fully enjoy their rights and participate in the collective pursuit of well-being. Senghor's words resonate as a reminder that the fulfillment of basic human needs is intricately linked to the realization of a just and equitable society, emphasizing the importance of addressing essential rights from the very beginning of the day.

33. (B): The social work profession aligns closely with the promotion of Second Generation human rights, which encompasses economic, social, and cultural rights. These rights include, but are not limited to, the right to work, education, and social security. Social workers play a pivotal role in advocating for and addressing the complex web of social, economic, and cultural factors that impact individuals' well-being. By focusing on Second Generation human rights, social workers aim to ensure that individuals have access to essential resources and opportunities necessary for a dignified life. This involves not only addressing immediate needs but also advocating for systemic changes that contribute to the creation of equitable social structures. Social workers are at the forefront of efforts to promote social justice, reduce inequality, and enhance the overall quality of life for individuals and communities, embodying a commitment to the broader spectrum of human rights beyond the traditional civil and political rights encompassed by the First Generation.

34. (B): The Sustainable Development Goals (SDGs) are formally known as "Transforming Our World: the 2030 Agenda for sustainable development." Adopted by the United Nations in September 2015, this comprehensive agenda outlines a set of 17 interconnected goals with 169 targets, addressing a wide range of global challenges. The SDGs aim to address issues such as poverty, inequality, climate change, environmental degradation, peace, and justice, recognizing the interconnectedness of social, economic, and environmental dimensions. "Transforming Our World" signifies the ambitious and transformative nature of the agenda, emphasizing the commitment of the international community to create a more sustainable and equitable world by the year 2030. The SDGs serve as a universal call to action, urging governments, businesses, civil society, and individuals to work collaboratively to achieve a future that is inclusive, environmentally responsible, and marked by shared prosperity.

35. (C): Article 1 of the UN Convention on the Rights of the Child (UNCRC) serves as a foundational statement, elucidating that a child is defined as anyone under the age of 18, unless the law of the child's country sets the age of majority earlier. This critical definition establishes the temporal scope for the subsequent articles within the convention, affirming the recognition and protection of the rights of individuals in their formative years. By emphasizing the age parameter, Article 1 ensures that the UNCRC's provisions apply universally to all those under 18, irrespective of their background or identity. It sets the stage for a comprehensive framework that aims to safeguard and promote the rights of children globally, encompassing aspects such as survival, development, protection from exploitation, and the right to participate in decisions that affect them. The age definition outlined in Article 1 underscores the international commitment to nurturing the well-being and rights of children as a fundamental principle in the pursuit of a more equitable and just world.

36. (C): "Cultural and Educational Rights" in the Constitution of India are enshrined in Article 29 and Article 30. Article 29 safeguards the interests of minorities by ensuring that any section of citizens having a distinct language, script, or culture has the right to conserve it. It provides protection against discrimination on grounds of religion, race, language, or culture and grants individuals the right to establish and administer educational institutions that preserve their language, script, or culture. Article 30, on the other hand, extends special rights to minorities, both religious and linguistic, by allowing them to establish and administer educational institutions of their choice. It emphasizes the importance of ensuring that minority communities can impart education to their children in a manner that preserves their cultural and linguistic identity. These constitutional provisions reflect a commitment to diversity and the protection of minority rights in the realm of education, contributing to the broader framework of fundamental rights in the Indian Constitution.

37. (C): According to the Sexual Harassment against Women in the Workplace (Prevention, Prohibition and Redressal) Act 2013, the authority to request the initiation of the conciliation process before conducting an inquiry lies solely with the aggrieved woman. In the context of workplace sexual harassment cases, the Internal Complaints Committee (IC) can engage in conciliation proceedings if the aggrieved woman expresses a desire for such resolution. This provision aims to empower the affected individual by giving her agency in choosing the method through which the complaint is addressed. It underscores the importance of respecting the preferences and autonomy of the aggrieved woman in determining the course of action for resolving the matter, whether through conciliation or a formal inquiry. The act aims to create a supportive and responsive framework for addressing workplace harassment, ensuring that the process aligns with the wishes and comfort level of the aggrieved party.

38. (B): Ethnocentrism is a characteristic commonly associated with the in-group, specifically referring to the inclination to judge and evaluate other cultures through the lens of one's own cultural norms and values. This cognitive bias often leads individuals within an in-group to perceive their own cultural practices as superior or more valid than those of out-groups. Ethnocentrism can manifest in various forms, from subtle biases to overt prejudice, and it tends to create a sense of cultural superiority or exclusivity within the in-group. This phenomenon can hinder cross-cultural understanding and cooperation, as individuals may struggle to appreciate or comprehend perspectives divergent from their own cultural framework. Recognizing and mitigating ethnocentrism is crucial for fostering cultural sensitivity, promoting inclusivity, and encouraging constructive intercultural dialogue.

39. (D): In India, among the various areas of counselling, bereavement counselling tends to engage the least number of counselors. Bereavement counselling addresses the complex and deeply personal process of coping with grief and loss, primarily associated with the death of a loved one. While profoundly important, this specialized form of counselling may attract fewer practitioners compared to other areas like family and marriage counselling, school counselling, or HIV/AIDS counselling. Family and marriage counselling addresses interpersonal relationships and dynamics, school counselling caters to the diverse needs of students, and HIV/AIDS counselling focuses on a critical public health issue. The demand for counsellors in specific areas reflects societal needs and priorities, and while bereavement counselling plays a vital role in supporting individuals through one of life's most challenging experiences, its demand may be comparatively lower in the broader counselling landscape in India.

40. (C): As per the National Education Policy (NEP) 2020, the changes suggested for the Right to Education (RTE) Act 2009 involve a significant expansion in the age range for free and compulsory education. The NEP proposes to extend the coverage from the existing 6-14 years age group to a more inclusive bracket of 3-18 years old students. This modification reflects the NEP's emphasis on providing a continuous and holistic educational experience, starting from early childhood care and education (ECCE) for 3-6 years old and extending up to the completion of the secondary stage at 18. By broadening the age range, the NEP aims to ensure a seamless and comprehensive educational journey, recognizing the importance of foundational education, preparatory stages, and the entire span of secondary education in nurturing holistic development and lifelong learning. This proposed shift underscores the commitment to achieving universal and equitable access to quality education across all stages of a student's formative years.

41. (A):

(*a*) **Secondary Teacher Training College for Women:** This proposal aimed to establish a college dedicated to the training of women as teachers. The inclusion of this initiative reflected Manshardt's recognition of the importance of providing quality education and the need for qualified female educators. Creating a specific institution for women's teacher training emphasized the commitment to gender inclusivity in education.

(*b*) **Institute for Educational Research:** The suggestion for an Institute for Educational Research indicated a desire to advance the field of education through systematic research. This component of Manshardt's proposal highlighted the importance of scholarly inquiry in improving educational methodologies, curriculum development, and pedagogical practices. The establishment of such an institute underscored the commitment to continuous improvement and innovation in the educational sector.

(*c*) **Library for Prince of Wales Museum:** This proposal advocated for the development of a library associated with the Prince of Wales Museum. This suggested the recognition of the pivotal role that a well-equipped library plays in supporting educational endeavors. A library linked with a prominent institution like the Prince of Wales Museum would have been an invaluable resource for students, researchers, and the broader community, contributing to the dissemination of knowledge.

(*d*) **Sir Dorabjee Tata School of Social Work:** The proposal for the Sir Dorabjee Tata School of Social Work demonstrated a commitment to addressing social issues and contributing to the field of social work. This school would likely have focused on professional training in social work, preparing individuals to engage in social welfare activities and contribute to community development. The inclusion of this initiative reflected an awareness of the societal challenges that require skilled professionals in the field of social work.

Manshardt's memorandum included all these components, it signifies a comprehensive vision that goes beyond traditional educational structures, encompassing teacher training, research, library development, and social work education. This multifaceted approach aligns with a holistic perspective on education and social welfare.

42. (D):

(*a*) **The focus of these movements was the Indian Society:** Understanding that socio-religious reform movements primarily aimed at the broader Indian society is crucial for social workers. It means these movements sought comprehensive societal transformations, addressing issues beyond individual concerns.

(*b*) **The focus of these movements was the social evils:** By recognizing that socio-religious reform movements often emerged in response to prevalent social evils, social workers gain insights into the specific challenges within the society that activists aimed to rectify. This knowledge is essential for identifying and addressing systemic issues.

(*c*) **These movements help us understand the response of society when established socio-cultural practices are challenged:** Examining how societies respond to challenges against established socio-cultural norms provides valuable insights. Social workers need to navigate these responses when advocating for positive social change, considering cultural sensitivities and potential resistance.

(*d*) **These movements help us understand the ideology for social change:** Recognizing the ideologies driving advocates for social change is crucial. It equips social workers with a deeper understanding of the philosophical foundations behind reform movements, enabling them to align their approaches with principled strategies for creating lasting and meaningful societal transformations.

This emphasizes that studying socio-religious reform movements is valuable for social workers because it covers a range of critical aspects. It involves understanding the societal focus, addressing social evils, analyzing societal responses to challenges, and comprehending the ideologies underpinning efforts for social change.

43. (B):

(*a*) **Semantic barriers concern with the meaning of the speech forms:** Semantics is the study of meaning in language. In the context of communication, semantics barriers refer to challenges that arise when there are misunderstandings related to the meanings of words, symbols, or phrases used in communication. This can occur due to differences in interpretation, language nuances, or cultural variations. For example, a word may have different connotations for different people or in different cultural contexts, leading to potential misinterpretations.

(*b*) **Complex structure of the organization may often lead to the breakdown of communication:** Complex organizational structures, characterized by hierarchical layers, numerous departments, and various communication channels, can create challenges in effective communication. Information may get distorted or lost as it passes through multiple levels of hierarchy, and there may be delays in transmitting messages. In such complex structures, there is a higher likelihood of communication breakdowns, where the intended message may not reach the intended recipients in a timely and accurate manner. This breakdown can hinder collaboration, decision-making, and overall organizational effectiveness.

44. (A):

(*a*) **Attitude is learned through positive association:** This statement acknowledges that positive associations can play a role in shaping attitudes. Positive experiences or 'associations with certain objects, individuals, or ideas may contribute to the development of positive attitudes toward them. However, it's important to note that attitudes are not determined solely by positive associations; they are also influenced by cognitive processes, emotions, and social factors.

(*b*) **Attitude is learned through reward & punishment:** While rewards and punishments can influence behaviour, the relationship between behavior, rewards, and attitudes is complex. Attitudes encompass cognitive and affective components that go beyond simple behavioral conditioning. The idea that attitudes are exclusively learned through a system of rewards and punishments oversimplifies the intricate nature of attitude formation.

(*c*) **Attitude is learned through group norms:** This statement emphasizes the social aspect of attitude formation. People often adopt attitudes that align with the norms and values of their social or cultural groups. Social groups contribute to the shaping of attitudes through shared beliefs, values, and expectations. This recognition of the influence of group norms on attitudes is a crucial aspect of social psychology.

(*d*) **Attitude is learned through exposure to information:** Attitudes can be shaped through exposure to various forms of information, including education, media, and interpersonal communication. Informational influences contribute significantly to attitude formation, as individuals learn about different perspectives, values, and ideas through exposure to diverse sources of information.

45. (A):

(*a*) **It is an extremely important method to learn social work practice:** This statement emphasizes the significance of recording as a crucial method for learning and enhancing social work practice. Recording casework sessions allow social workers to document their interactions with clients, interventions applied, and the overall process. By reviewing recordings, social workers can gain valuable insights into their communication skills, intervention strategies, and the dynamics of client-worker relationships. The reflective process facilitated by recording contributes to ongoing professional development and improvement in social work practice.

(*b*) **Record used to evaluate appropriateness of the process used:** This statement underscores the role of records in assessing the appropriateness of the strategies and interventions employed during casework. Casework recordings serve as a documentation tool that enables social workers to review and evaluate their interactions with clients. By analyzing recorded sessions, social workers can assess whether the chosen interventions align with the specific needs and circumstances of the client. This ongoing evaluation is essential for ensuring that the casework process remains effective and responsive to the client's evolving situation.

(*c*) **Narrative recording is the most effective technique:** This statement suggests that narrative recording is deemed as the most effective technique for casework. Narrative recording involves the comprehensive and descriptive documentation of client interactions, providing a detailed account of the casework process. While narrative recording can be a powerful method, it's important to note that the effectiveness of recording techniques can vary based on the goals and context of casework. Other recording methods, such as process recording or critical incident recording, may be more suitable for specific situations. The choice of recording technique depends on the objectives and preferences of the social worker, as well as the nature of the casework.

46. (C):

(*a*) **Referral is a concept used in social casework to refer a client to other professionals:** This statement highlights the core concept of referral in social case work. Referral is a process employed by social workers when they recognize that a client's needs go beyond their expertise or the scope of their practice. It involves directing the client to other professionals or specialized services that can better address their specific issues. This recognition reflects ethical and responsible practice, emphasizing the importance of collaboration and ensuring that clients receive the most appropriate and effective support available.

(*c*) **Both positive and negative feelings are involved in the referral process:** This statement acknowledges the emotional complexity inherent in the referral process. Positive feelings may arise from the understanding that the client will receive specialized assistance that can significantly improve their situation. Social workers may feel a sense of relief that the client is accessing the help they need. On the other hand, negative feelings can also be present, stemming from concerns about the potential impact on the client-worker relationship, fear of abandonment, or uncertainty about how the client will perceive the referral. Navigating these emotions is an important aspect of the social worker's role during the referral process, and it requires sensitivity and effective communication to address both the positive and negative aspects of the decision.

47. (B):

(*a*) **That the group environment is conducive to a democratic decision-making process:** This statement emphasizes the importance of fostering an environment within the group that supports democratic principles. In a democratic setting, all members have the opportunity to express their opinions, contribute to decision-making, and feel a sense of inclusion and participation.

(*b*) **That the group effort at problem-solving or decision-making is proving to be time-consuming and costly without yielding a result which works:** This statement underscores the practical considerations in group work. Group processes should be efficient, effective, and lead to outcomes that benefit the group. If the group is investing a significant amount of time and resources without achieving meaningful results, the group worker needs to assess and address this issue.

(*c*) **That not everyone knows how to help a group in taking a decision quickly and rationally:** This statement acknowledges the potential variability in the skills and knowledge of group members. Group workers should be aware that not everyone may possess the expertise to facilitate quick and rational decision-making. It highlights the importance of providing support and guidance as needed.

(*d*) **That the expertise in the group may not exist to take certain decisions:** This statement points out the necessity of recognizing the collective expertise within the group. It's crucial for the group worker to be aware of the areas where the group might lack the necessary knowledge or skills to make informed decisions. This awareness may lead to seeking external expertise when required.

48. (D):

(*a*) **Felt needs of the community:** The concept of "felt needs" refers to the perceived needs of community members, those needs that individuals within the community recognize and express as important. Community organization begins by understanding and addressing these felt needs to ensure that interventions are relevant, meaningful, and responsive to the actual concerns of the community.

(*d*) **Active participation of community people:** Active participation is a cornerstone of community organization. It involves engaging community members in every phase of the process, from identifying issues to planning, implementing, and evaluating initiatives. By actively involving community members, community organization fosters a sense of ownership and empowerment, promoting sustainable change driven by those directly affected.

(*e*) **Community awareness:** Community organization places a strong emphasis on raising awareness within the community. This involves educating community members about various aspects, including their rights, available resources, potential solutions to issues, and the importance of collective action. Community awareness is a catalyst for informed decision-making and mobilizing support for initiatives.

These elements collectively underscore the participatory and community-driven nature of community organization. By focusing on felt needs, active participation, and community awareness, community organizers can build stronger, more resilient communities that are equipped to address challenges and work towards sustainable development. It recognizes the agency of community members and seeks to amplify their voices in shaping the future of their communities.

49. (D):

(*a*) **Identifying the community needs and problems:** This step involves conducting thorough assessments and engaging with community members to identify their needs and challenges. It often includes surveys, interviews, and community meetings to gather valuable insights directly from the community.

(*b*) **Giving priority to the community needs and problems:** Once identified, needs and problems are prioritized based on their urgency, impact, and feasibility of intervention. Prioritization ensures that limited resources are efficiently allocated to address the most critical issues first.

(*c*) **Developing confidence and will to work:** Building confidence and a collective will to work involves empowering community members through education, skill-building, and fostering a sense of self-efficacy. It encourages individuals to actively participate in the decision-making and implementation processes.

(*d*) **Finding resources to deal with the community needs and problems:** Mobilizing resources is a crucial aspect of community organization. This can involve seeking funding, utilizing local assets, and leveraging external support. The goal is to ensure that the community has the necessary resources to address its identified needs.

(*e*) **Developing cooperative and collaborative attitudes and practices:** Collaboration is at the heart of community organization. This involves fostering a sense of cooperation among community members and promoting partnerships with external organizations, government agencies, and other stakeholders. Collabo-rative efforts enhance the collective impact of interventions.

These components collectively represent the holistic and participatory nature of community organization. By engaging with the community, prioritizing needs, building confidence, mobilizing resources, and fostering collaboration, community organizers work towards sustainable and community-driven development. The emphasis is on empowering communities to take an active role in shaping their future and addressing challenges collectively.

50. (A):

(*a*) **Chandi Prasad Bhatt:** Bhatt played a pivotal role in the formation of the Chipko movement. His efforts were instrumental in organizing local communities, particularly in the Himalayan region, to resist deforestation by embracing the trees slated for logging. Bhatt's leadership and commitment to sustainable, community-based forestry practices were foundational to the movement's success.

(*b*) **Gaura Devi:** Gaura Devi, a village woman from the Mandal region in the state of Uttarakhand, emerged as a grassroots leader during the Chipko movement. In 1974, she led a group of women in hugging the trees, effectively preventing loggers from cutting them down. This act of nonviolent resistance garnered widespread attention and became a symbol of the environmental conservation movement in India.

(*c*) **Sundarlal Bahuguna:** An environmentalist and social activist, Sundarlal Bahuguna played a significant role in promoting environmental awareness and advocating for sustainable practices. His involvement in the Chipko movement included leading marches and campaigns to raise awareness about the ecological impact of deforestation. Bahuguna's tireless efforts contributed to the movement's success in drawing attention to environmental issues.

These individuals, along with many others, collectively contributed to the Chipko movement's success in raising awareness about the importance of environmental conservation and influencing policies related to forestry practices in India.

51. (D)

(*d*) **Years of schooling:** This variable is measured on a ratio scale. The ratio scale has a true zero point, which means that the value "0" represents the absence of the variable being measured. In the case of years of schooling, a person with 0 year of schooling has not received any education. Additionally, the intervals between different levels (e.g., 2 years of schooling vs. 4 years of schooling) are meaningful and consistent.

(*e*) **Annual income:** Annual income is also measured on a ratio scale. Like years of schooling, it has a true zero point, which represents the absence of income (no income). This zero point allows for meaningful calculations, such as ratios.

For example, an income of $10,000 is twice as much as an income of $5,000. The intervals between income levels are consistent, and the scale allows for meaningful mathematical operations.

Both years of schooling and annual income are examples of variables measured on a ratio scale, making them suitable for more advanced statistical analyses and providing a richer level of information compared to variables measured on ordinal or nominal scales.

52. (C):

(*a*) **Chi-square:** The chi-square test is an inferential statistical test used to determine if there is a significant association between two categorical variables. It is often employed in situations where researchers want to assess whether there is a relationship between the observed and expected frequencies in a contingency table.

(*d*) **T-test:** The t-test is an inferential statistical test used to determine if there is a significant difference between the means of two groups. There are different types of t-tests, including the independent samples t-test (comparing means of two independent groups) and the paired samples t-test (comparing means of two related groups).

(*e*) **Correlation:** Correlation is a statistical technique used to measure the strength and direction of a linear relationship between two continuous variables. It helps assess whether changes in one variable are associated with changes in another variable. While correlation itself is more descriptive, it is often used as a preliminary step in inferential statistics to inform hypotheses about the relationships between variables.

53. (B):

(*a*) **Single-subject designs are essentially quasi-experimental designs:** Quasi-experimental designs share some characteristics with experimental designs but lack true random assignment of participants to groups. Single-subject designs are considered quasi-experimental because they involve the manipulation of an independent variable to observe its effect on a dependent variable, but they typically focus on individual subjects rather than groups.

(*c*) **These designs use repeated measures of the dependent variable:** Single-subject designs often employ repeated measures of the dependent variable. This means that the same participant's behavior is measured multiple times under different experimental conditions. This repeated measurement allows researchers to observe changes in behavior within the same individual across different phases or interventions.

(*d*) **These designs use time series analysis techniques:** While not all single-subject designs exclusively use time series analysis, they can involve the analysis of data collected over time. Time series analysis is a statistical method used to examine patterns or trends in data over successive time points. In single-subject designs, researchers may use time series analysis to explore the impact of interventions or treatments on the behaviour of an individual participant over time.

Single-subject designs share characteristics with quasi-experimental designs, involve repeated measures of the dependent variable, and may incorporate time series analysis techniques when examining the impact of interventions on individual subjects' behaviour over time.

54. (A):

(*b*) **Editing of the entries:** Editing involves the careful review of the collected data to identify and correct errors, inconsistencies, or inaccuracies. This can include checking for missing values, outliers, or any data entry mistakes. The goal is to ensure that the data is accurate and reliable before proceeding with further analysis.

(*c*) **Coding of data:** Coding is the process of assigning numerical or categorical codes to the raw data. This is often done to convert qualitative information into a format suitable for analysis. For example, converting gender information from "male" and "female" to numerical codes (e.g., 1 for male, 2 for female) allows for statistical calculations and comparisons.

(*d*) **Computing the series:** Computing involves performing various calculations on the data to derive meaningful statistics or measures. This can include calculating averages, sums, percentages, or other statistical indicators. For example, computing the average score on a set of test results or calculating the total sales for a specific period are common operations in data processing.

55. (D)

(*b*) **It responds to the needs of society:** Social welfare institutions are established to address the various needs and challenges within a society. These needs can encompass a wide range of issues, including economic hardship, healthcare, education, housing, and more. The goal is to create programs and services that respond effectively to the pressing needs of individuals and communities.

(*c*) **It emphasizes on economic and social well-being:** While this specific statement is not explicitly mentioned in the options, it is a common goal of social welfare institutions. These institutions often aim to improve both the economic and social well-being of individuals and communities. This may involve implementing policies and programs that address poverty, unemployment, inequality, and other factors affecting overall well-being.

(*d*) **It provides an opportunity to participate fully in society:** Social welfare institutions seek to create opportunities for individuals to participate fully in society. This involves removing barriers that may hinder participation, promoting inclusivity, and ensuring that everyone has access to the resources and support needed to engage actively in social, economic, and cultural aspects of community life.

56. (B):

(*a*) **Have least impact on the environment:** Sustainable practices prioritize minimizing negative impacts on the environment. This involves adopting practices that reduce resource consumption, minimize pollution, and promote conservation. The goal is to maintain ecological balance and preserve natural resources for future generations.

(*b*) **Also be profitable and practical for self-survival:** Sustainability is not only about environmental concerns but also about economic viability. Practices that are economically sustainable are more likely to be adopted and maintained over the long term. This ensures that individuals, businesses, or communities can support themselves economically while engaging in sustainable practices.

(*d*) **Be a socially acceptable method or practice:** Social acceptance is a critical component of sustainability.

Sustainable practices should align with societal values, cultural norms, and community expectations. Practices that are socially acceptable are more likely to be embraced by communities, fostering collaboration and widespread adoption.

57. (B): NITI Aayog's entire gamut of activities can be devided into four main heads:

(*b*) **Policy and Programme Framework:** As a crucial architect of national planning, NITI Aayog doesn't merely draft policies; it actively conceptualizes, analyzes, and refines strategic frameworks tailored to address India's diverse and evolving needs. Its focus ranges from economic growth and infrastructure development to human capital development and environmental sustainability. This involves collaborating with ministries, states, and stakeholders to ensure comprehensive and coordinated policymaking.

(*c*) **Cooperative Federalism:** NITI Aayog acts as a bridge between the central government and Indian states, fostering a spirit of cooperative federalism. It facilitates a platform for open dialogue, joint initiatives, and knowledge sharing across different levels of administration. This strengthens collaborative development efforts, tackling regional challenges and promoting balanced progress across the nation.

(*d*) **Monitoring and Evaluations:** NITI Aayog serves as a vigilant watchdog, regularly assessing the effectiveness of government programs and schemes. It employs rigorous monitoring mechanisms and robust evaluations to analyze their impact, identify bottlenecks, and recommend course corrections. This ensures efficient utilization of resources and drives continuous improvement in program delivery.

(*e*) **Think Tank and Knowledge and Innovation Hub:** NITI Aayog transcends its operational functions and embodies a dynamic think tank. It serves as a crucible for innovative ideas, generating high-quality research and analysis on critical development issues. This knowledge is then disseminated through reports, publications, and conferences, influencing policy debates and shaping informed decision-making across the nation. Recognizing the vital role of innovation in propelling India's progress, NITI Aayog actively fosters a culture of entrepreneurship.

58. (C):

(*c*) **Injustice:** The term "Injustice" is not explicitly identified as one of the original "Giants" in the Beveridge Report. The Beveridge Report, published in 1942, focused on five social issues or "Giants" that needed to be addressed to build a comprehensive welfare state. These were Want (poverty), Disease, Ignorance (lack of education), Squalor (poor housing), and Idleness (unemployment). "Injustice" wasn't specifically listed among these key challenges.

(*e*) **Poverty and Misery:** "Poverty" aligns with the concept of "Want" in the Beveridge Report, which emphasized the need to eradicate economic deprivation and ensure a basic standard of living for all citizens. While the term "Misery" is not explicitly mentioned as one of the original "Giants," it could be interpreted as encompassing the broader notion of social distress or suffering related to the other identified challenges (poverty, disease, lack of education, poor housing, and unemployment).

59. (C):

(*c*) **To develop community consciousness:** This objective involves fostering a sense of community identity, shared values, and collective awareness among community members. It seeks to build a strong community spirit, where individuals recognize their interconnectedness and work together for the common good. Developing community consciousness is essential for promoting a sense of belonging and mutual support within the community.

(*d*) **To encourage community participation:** This objective aims to actively involve community members in decision-making processes and activities that impact the community. Community organization seeks to empower individuals to participate in planning, implementing, and evaluating initiatives that address the community's needs and aspirations. The goal is to ensure that community members have a voice in shaping their own future.

(*e*) **To develop leadership in the community:** Community organization aims to identify, nurture, and develop leadership within the community. This involves empowering individuals to take on leadership roles, advocate for community interests, and mobilize others for collective action. Developing leadership enhances the community's capacity to initiate positive changes and sustain ongoing development efforts.

60. (D):

(*a*) **Protection of children from Sexual Offences Act was amended in 2019 to include life imprisonment for aggravated sexual assault:** The Protection of Children from Sexual Offences (POCSO) Act is a legal framework in India aimed at addressing sexual offenses against children. In 2019, the Act was amended to strengthen the provisions and increase the penalties for offenses against children. The amendment introduced life imprisonment as a punishment for aggravated sexual assault, providing a more stringent deterrent against such heinous crimes. This amendment reflects the government's commitment to enhancing the protection of children from sexual offenses.

(*b*) **Beti Bachao, Beti Padhao scheme introduced for protecting the girl child:** Beti Bachao, Beti Padhao (Save the Daughter, Educate the Daughter) is a social campaign initiated by the Government of India to address gender imbalances and promote the welfare of the girl child. The scheme focuses on preventing gender-based sex-selective practices, ensuring the survival and education of the girl child, and empowering her. Through awareness campaigns, financial incentives, and educational initiatives, Beti Bachao, Beti Padhao aims to create a supportive environment for the well-being and development of girls, addressing societal attitudes that may discriminate against them.

61. (A):

(*a*) **Liberty of thought:** This emphasizes the individual's right to form and hold their own beliefs and opinions. It is about intellectual freedom, allowing individuals to think independently, critically, and creatively. This aspect of liberty acknowledges the importance of diverse perspectives and the right to intellectual autonomy.

(*b*) **Liberty of expression:** This pertains to the freedom of individuals to express their thoughts, ideas, and opinions openly.

It includes freedom of speech, freedom of the press, and the right to communicate through various mediums. The principle of freedom of expression is vital for a democratic society, fostering open dialogue, and enabling citizens to voice their views without fear of censorship or persecution.

(*c*) **Liberty of belief and faith:** This underscores the right of individuals to hold and practice any religious belief or faith. It promotes religious freedom and tolerance, recognizing the diversity of religious beliefs within a society. This aspect of liberty acknowledges the importance of personal convictions and the freedom to follow one's chosen spiritual path.

(*d*) **Liberty of worship:** This emphasizes the freedom of individuals to practice their religious rituals and worship according to their beliefs. It acknowledges the significance of religious practices as a form of expression and personal connection to one's faith. This aspect of liberty supports the idea that individuals should be free to observe their religious traditions without interference.

Together, these aspects form a comprehensive understanding of liberty in the context of the Preamble. They highlight the importance of individual freedoms, both in thought and expression, as well as the freedom to hold diverse beliefs and practice one's chosen faith. This multidimensional concept of liberty contributes to the foundational principles of a democratic and inclusive society.

62. (C):

(*a*) **Improving human race through selective breeding:** Eugenics, historically, is a concept associated with the improvement of the human race by encouraging the reproduction of individuals with desirable traits. The idea is that by selectively breeding individuals with positive genetic characteristics, one could enhance the overall genetic quality of the population.

(*b*) **Aggressive population control:** Some proponents of eugenics have advocated for aggressive measures to control the population, especially with the aim of limiting the reproduction of groups considered less desirable. This could involve policies or practices aimed at reducing the birth rates among certain populations, often based on social or genetic criteria.

(*d*) **Purification of race:** Eugenics has been linked to the notion of purifying the human gene pool. This concept suggests the elimination or suppression of traits considered undesirable, often tied to social prejudices or pseudoscientific beliefs about racial or genetic superiority.

63. (C):

(*a*) **Help the client to identify and decontaminate any ego state that has been distorted:** In Transactional Analysis (TA), ego states represent patterns of thinking, feeling, and behaving. Ego states can be Parent, Adult, or Child. Distorted ego states can lead to unproductive or dysfunctional behaviour. The therapist helps the client identify these distortions and work towards resolving or decontaminating them. This process involves raising awareness of unhealthy patterns and promoting more adaptive responses.

(*b*) **Help the client to achieve a therapist in the transactional analysis:** Assuming the intended statement is "Help the client to achieve a therapeutic outcome in transactional analysis," the therapist's goal is to guide the client toward positive changes and growth. This involves facilitating insight, awareness, and behavioral shifts. The therapeutic outcome may include improved communication, healthier relationships, and a more balanced emotional state.

(*c*) **Help the client to evaluate and alter an appropriate life position and adopt "I am OK. You are OK":** Life positions in TA refer to fundamental beliefs individuals hold about themselves and others. "I am OK. You are OK" is considered a healthy life position, fostering positive relationships and self-acceptance. The therapist works with the client to evaluate their current life position, identify any negative or limiting beliefs, and support them in adopting a more positive and constructive life position.

64. (D):

(*a*) **Orphans:** Losing both parents or primary caregivers can be devastating for children, triggering grief, anxiety, and feelings of isolation. Psychiatric social workers provide individual and group therapy to help them process their loss, develop coping mechanisms, and rebuild their sense of belonging. They also collaborate with foster care agencies or alternative family arrangements to ensure a stable and supportive environment for the child's emotional well-being.

(*b*) **Street Children:** Living on the streets exposes children to numerous risks and challenges, including physical and emotional abuse, neglect, and exploitation. Psychiatric social workers work to establish trust and build rapport with these children, offering trauma-informed therapy to address past experiences and equip them with coping skills. They also advocate for their rights and access to basic necessities like healthcare, education, and safe housing, striving to break the cycle of street life and promote their reintegration into society.

(*c*) **Victims of Child Labour:** Forced labour deprives children of their childhood, hinders their education, and can lead to physical injuries, emotional distress, and low self-esteem. Psychiatric social workers assess the child's mental health needs, provide trauma-informed therapy to address the emotional consequences of exploitation, and collaborate with authorities to rescue them from exploitative situations. They also connect them with educational and vocational training opportunities to empower them with skills for a brighter future.

(*d*) **Victims of Neglect:** Neglectful environments deprive children of essential emotional support, physical care, and opportunities for development. This can lead to attachment issues, low self-worth, and difficulties with social interaction. Psychiatric social workers work with the families or caregivers to address the underlying factors contributing to neglect, providing parenting skills training and connecting them with resources to improve the child's home environment. Additionally, they offer individual therapy to the child, helping them develop coping mechanisms and build healthy relationships.

(*e*) **Victims of Physical or Sexual Abuse:** The trauma of physical or sexual abuse can have profound and lasting impacts on a child's mental health, leading to anxiety, depression, PTSD, and difficulty trusting others. Psychiatric social workers provide specialized trauma-informed therapy to help children process and heal from their experiences, learn to manage triggers and emotions, and rebuild their sense of self-worth. They also work with law enforcement and child protection agencies to ensure the child's safety and advocate for justice.

By addressing the unique challenges faced by each category of children in need of protection, psychiatric social workers play a critical role in safeguarding their mental well-being, promoting their recovery, and empowering them to build a resilient and fulfilling future.

65. (B):

(*a*) **Beti Bachao, Beti Padhao (BBBP):** Beti Bachao, Beti Padhao is covered under Mission Shakti, it remains a significant government initiative that addresses gender-based discrimination and the declining child sex ratio in India. Launched to promote the survival, protection, and education of the girl child, BBBP strives to change societal attitudes and practices that discriminate against female children. It emphasizes the importance of equal opportunities for girls, encouraging families to invest in their education and well-being.

(*b*) **One Stop Centre (OSC):** Covered under Mission Shakti, the One Stop Centre (OSC) scheme plays a crucial role in providing comprehensive support to women affected by violence. OSCs serve as integrated hubs offering medical, legal, psychological, and counselling services, along with temporary shelter for women in distress. These centers aim to create a safe and supportive environment for survivors of domestic violence, sexual assault, and other forms of abuse, facilitating their recovery and empowerment.

(*c*) **SWADHAR Greh:** Also covered under Mission Shakti, the SWADHAR Greh scheme focuses on providing institutional support to women in challenging circumstances. This includes women affected by violence, trafficking, homelessness, or other crises. SWADHAR Greh offers shelter, counselling, rehabilitation, skill development, and other services to empower women and help them regain control over their lives.

66. (C):

(*a*) **H.Y. Siddiqui - (*iii*) Community work:** H.Y. Siddiqui is matched with community work. This indicates that Siddiqui likely specializes in activities related to community development, engagement, and empowerment within the social work field. This could involve initiatives such as organizing community programs, facilitating community meetings, advocating for community needs, and fostering collaboration among community members and organizations. Siddiqui's expertise likely lies in understanding the dynamics of communities, identifying social issues within them, and implementing strategies to address these issues in a collective manner.

(*b*) **Grace Mathew - (*ii*) Social casework:** Grace Mathew is matched with social casework. This suggests that Mathew's expertise lies in working directly with individuals or families facing personal, social, or emotional challenges. As a social casework expert, Mathew likely focuses on conducting assessments, providing counselling and support services, developing intervention plans, and advocating for clients' needs. Mathew's role may involve addressing issues such as mental health, substance abuse, family dynamics, poverty, and homelessness, among others.

(*c*) **D.K. Lal Das - (*iv*) Social work research:** D.K. Lal Das is matched with social work research. This indicates that Das specializes in conducting research within the field of social work. As a social work researcher, Das likely engages in designing and implementing research studies, collecting and analyzing data, and disseminating findings to contribute to the knowledge base of the profession. Das's research may focus on various social issues, interventions, methodologies, and outcomes, with the aim of informing evidence-based practice, policy development, and social change efforts.

(*d*) **Surendra Singh - (*i*) Social work education:** Surendra Singh is matched with social work education. This suggests that Singh's expertise lies in the realm of educating and training future social workers. As a social work educator, Singh likely engages in teaching courses, developing curriculum, supervising field placements, and mentoring students in various aspects of social work practice. Singh's role may also involve staying updated with developments in the field, incorporating innovative teaching methods, and fostering critical thinking and ethical decision-making skills among students.

67. (C):

(*a*) **Elitism - (*iii*) Prejudice and discrimination on the basis of class:** Elitism refers to the belief or attitude that certain individuals or groups are inherently superior or more deserving than others based on their social status, wealth, education, or other characteristics associated with privilege. This concept involves the idea of a social hierarchy where those at the top, often referred to as the "elite," hold power and prestige, while those lower in the hierarchy are marginalized or excluded. Prejudice and discrimination based on class involve treating individuals differently or unfairly due to their socioeconomic status, whether it's denying opportunities, access to resources, or social acceptance based on one's perceived social class.

(*b*) **Heterosexism - (*iv*) Prejudice and discrimination on the basis of sexual orientation:** Heterosexism is the belief in the superiority of heterosexuality over other sexual orientations. It involves societal norms, attitudes, and practices that marginalize, stigmatize, or discriminate against individuals who identify as lesbian, gay, bisexual, transgender, or queer (LGBTQ+). Prejudice and discrimination based on sexual orientation manifest in various forms, such as denying legal rights, employment opportunities, housing, or healthcare services to LGBTQ+ individuals, as well as perpetuating harmful stereotypes or violence against them.

(*c*) **Ageism - (*ii*) Prejudice and discrimination on the basis of age:** Ageism refers to prejudice, stereotyping, or discrimination against individuals or groups based on their age, particularly against older adults or youth. Ageism can manifest in various contexts, including employment, healthcare, media representation, and social interactions. It often involves negative stereotypes about aging, such as assumptions of incompetence, depen-dence, or decline in cognitive abilities in older adults, or perceptions of youth as inexperienced or irresponsible. Ageism can lead to exclusion, unequal treatment, or limited opportunities for individuals based on their age.

(*d*) **Handicapism - (*i*) Prejudice and discrimination on the basis of any disability:** Handicapism, also known as ableism, refers to discrimination, prejudice, or social prejudice against individuals with disabilities. It encompasses attitudes, practices, and institutional barriers that devalue or marginalize people with disabilities, limiting their participation in society and access to opportunities. Handicapism can take many forms, including physical barriers to accessibility, unequal treatment in employment or education, negative stereotypes, or lack of accommodations to support individuals with disabilities.

68. (C):

(*a*) **Null hypothesis is true, but rejected - (*ii*) Type I Error:** In hypothesis testing, the null hypothesis (H_0) represents the statement of no effect or no difference between groups or conditions. A Type I Error occurs when we reject the null hypothesis when it is actually true. In other words, we incorrectly conclude that there is a significant effect or difference when, in fact, there is none. This error is often associated with falsely detecting an effect or significance in the data when there isn't one.

(*b*) **The degree of error between a statistic and parameter - (*i*) Sampling Error:** Sampling error refers to the discrepancy or difference between a sample statistic (e.g., sample mean) and the corresponding population parameter (e.g., population mean). It arises due to the inherent variability between different samples drawn from the same population. Sampling error is a natural consequence of using samples to estimate population parameters, and it can affect the accuracy of our conclusions about the population based on sample data.

(*c*) **The list of sampling elements from which the sample is selected - (*iv*) Sampling frame:** A sampling frame is the list or source from which a sample is drawn. It includes all the elements or units that comprise the population of interest and from which the sample will be selected. A sampling frame should ideally cover the entire population and be accurately defined to ensure that every member of the population has an equal chance of being included in the sample. It serves as the basis for selecting a representative sample and generalizing study findings to the population.

(*d*) **The degree to which an instrument actually measures the concept/construct it is intended to measure - (*iii*) Validity:** Validity refers to the extent to which a measurement instrument (e.g., a questionnaire, test, or scale) accurately measures the concept or construct it is intended to assess. It reflects the degree to which the instrument provides meaningful and accurate information about the variable of interest. Validity is a crucial psychometric property, and different types of validity (e.g., content validity, criterion validity, construct validity) assess different aspects of the instrument's accuracy and appropriateness for its intended purpose.

69. (C):

(*a*) **Vindication of the Rights of Women - (*iii*) Mary Wollstonecraft:** Mary Wollstonecraft authored "Vindication of the Rights of Women," which was published in 1792. In this influential work, Wollstonecraft argued for the equality of women and advocated for women's rights to education and participation in political and social spheres. The book is considered one of the earliest works of feminist philosophy and a foundational text in the fight for women's rights.

(*b*) **The common sense - (*i*) Thomas Paine:** Thomas Paine wrote "Common Sense," which was published in 1776. This pamphlet played a significant role in shaping public opinion in favour of American independence from British rule during the American Revolutionary War. Paine's clear and persuasive arguments advocated for the principles of republican government, democracy, and individual rights, making "Common Sense" one of the most influential political pamphlets in American history.

(*c*) **Human Rights and Social work - (*iv*) Jim Ife:** Jim Ife is known for his work on human rights and social work. He has contributed to scholarship and practice in the field of social work with a focus on human rights-based approaches. Ife's writings emphasize the importance of integrating human rights principles into social work practice to promote social justice, equality, and dignity for all individuals and communities.

(*d*) **Democracy and Human Rights - (*ii*) D. Beetham:** D. Beetham has written on the topics of democracy and human rights. Beetham's work explores the relationship between democracy, governance, and human rights, analyzing concepts such as political participation, accountability, and the protection of civil liberties within democratic societies. His research contributes to our understanding of the challenges and opportunities for promoting democracy and human rights around the world.

70. (D):

(*a*) **ISO 9001:2015 - (*iv*) Quality Management System:** ISO 9001:2015 is an international standard that specifies requirements for a quality management system (QMS). Organizations use this standard to demonstrate their ability to consistently provide products and services that meet customer and regulatory requirements. It focuses on various aspects of quality management, including customer satisfaction, continuous improvement, risk management, and process optimization. Implementing ISO 9001 helps organizations enhance efficiency, reduce errors, and enhance customer satisfaction through effective quality management practices.

(*b*) **ISO 14001:2015 - (*iii*) Environment Management System:** ISO 14001:2015 is an international standard that specifies requirements for an environmental management system (EMS). This standard provides a framework for organizations to establish, implement, maintain, and improve environmental performance. It addresses various environmental aspects, such as pollution prevention, resource efficiency, waste management, and compliance with environmental regulations. Implementing ISO 14001 helps organizations minimize their environmental impact, enhance sustainability, and demonstrate their commitment to environmental responsibility.

(*c*) **ISO 50001 - (*i*) Energy Management System:** ISO 50001 is an international standard that specifies requirements for an energy management system (EnMS). Organizations use this standard to establish processes and systems to improve energy performance, including energy efficiency, use, and consumption. ISO 50001 provides a framework for organizations to develop energy policies, set energy objectives and targets, implement energy-saving measures, and monitor and measure energy performance. Implementing ISO 50001 helps organizations reduce energy costs, enhance energy efficiency, and contribute to sustainability goals by effectively managing energy resources.

(*d*) **ISO 45001 - (*ii*) Occupational Health and Safety Standard:** ISO 45001 is an international standard that specifies requirements for an occupational health and safety management system (OHSMS). This standard provides a framework for organizations to manage occupational health and safety risks and improve worker safety and health. ISO 45001 emphasizes the importance of hazard identification, risk assessment, incident prevention, employee participation, and compliance with legal and regulatory requirements. Implementing ISO 45001 helps organizations create safer work environments, prevent work-related injuries and illnesses, and promote a culture of health and safety within the workplace.

71. (C):

(*a*) **Brahmo Samaj - (*iii*) Bengal:** Brahmo Samaj, founded by Raja Ram Mohan Roy in 1828, originated in Bengal. It was a reformist Hindu religious and social movement that aimed to purify and reform Hinduism from within. The movement focused on monotheism, the rejection of idolatry, social reforms such as women's education and abolition of caste system, and the promotion of rational and ethical principles.

(*b*) **Arya Samaj - (*iv*) Bombay:** Arya Samaj, founded by Swami Dayananda Saraswati in 1875, originated in Bombay (now Mumbai), Maharashtra. Arya Samaj aimed to revive and reform Hinduism based on the Vedas (ancient scriptures), promoting monotheism, social equality, and Vedic rituals. It advocated for social reforms such as women's education, widow remarriage, and the abolition of untouchability.

(*c*) **Satya Shodhak Samaj - (*i*) Poona:** Satya Shodhak Samaj, founded by Jyotirao Phule in 1873, originated in Poona (now Pune), Maharashtra. It was a social reform movement that aimed to challenge the caste system, social inequality, and Brahminical dominance in society. The movement advocated for education, social justice, and empowerment of marginalized communities, including the lower castes and women.

(*d*) **Veda Samaj - (*ii*) Madras:** Veda Samaj, founded by T.M. Nair and Dr. Kesavan in 1864, originated in Madras (now Chennai), Tamil Nadu. It was a reformist Hindu movement that sought to promote monotheism, Vedic principles, and social reforms. The Veda Samaj emphasized the study and interpretation of the Vedas, rejecting idol worship and advocating for social equality, education, and upliftment of oppressed communities.

72. (B)

73. (A):

(*a*) **Right of equality - (*iv*) Article 14-18:** The right of equality is enshrined in Articles 14 to 18 of the Indian Constitution. These articles ensure that all citizens are equal before the law and have equal protection under the law. Article 14 guarantees equality before the law and equal protection of laws to all persons within the territory of India. Articles 15 and 16 prohibit discrimination on grounds of religion, race, caste, sex, or place of birth. Article 17 abolishes untouchability, and Article 18 prohibits titles of nobility.

Together, these articles uphold the principle of equality and strive to eliminate discrimination and promote social justice in India.

(*b*) **Right of freedom - (*iii*) Article 19-22:** The right of freedom is protected under Articles 19 to 22 of the Indian Constitution. These articles guarantee various freedoms to the citizens of India. Article 19 ensures six fundamental freedoms: freedom of speech and expression, freedom to assemble peacefully and without arms, freedom to form associations or unions, freedom to move freely throughout the territory of India, freedom to reside and settle in any part of the territory of India, and freedom to practice any profession, or to carry on any occupation, trade or business. Articles 20 and 21 provide protection against arbitrary arrest and detention, and Article 22 safeguards personal liberty in case of arrest and detention.

(*c*) **Right against exploitation - (*i*) Article 23-24:** The right against exploitation is enshrined in Articles 23 and 24 of the Indian Constitution. Article 23 prohibits trafficking in human beings and forced labour. It states that traffic in human beings and begar are prohibited, and any contravention of this provision shall be an offense punishable in accordance with law. Article 24 prohibits the employment of children in factories, mines, and other hazardous occupations below a certain age, ensuring that children are not subjected to exploitation and are provided with opportunities for education and development.

(*d*) **Cultural and educational rights - (*ii*) Article 29-30:** Cultural and educational rights are protected under Articles 29 and 30 of the Indian Constitution. Article 29 provides safeguards for the protection of the interests of minorities by ensuring that any section of citizens having a distinct language, script, or culture has the right to conserve its language, script, or culture. Article 30 grants minorities, whether based on religion or language, the right to establish and administer educational institutions of their choice, thereby preserving their cultural and educational autonomy.

74. (B):

(*a*) **Social casework: A therapeutic approach - (*iv*) R.K. Upadhyay:** This book, authored by R.K. Upadhyay, likely presents social casework as a therapeutic approach. Social casework refers to the professional method of helping individuals and families overcome various social, emotional, and psychological challenges. A therapeutic approach implies that the focus is on providing supportive, counselling-based interventions to address clients' needs and promote their well-being. R.K. Upadhyay's book may explore the theoretical foundations, techniques, and practical applications of social casework within a therapeutic framework.

(*b*) **An Introduction to social casework - (*iii*) Grace Mathew:** Authored by Grace Mathew, this book likely serves as an introductory guide to social casework. It may provide an overview of the principles, theories, and methods used in social casework practice. An introduction to social casework would cover topics such as assessment, intervention strategies, case management, and ethical considerations. Grace Mathew's work may aim to familiarize readers with the fundamental concepts and skills required for effective casework practice.

(*c*) **Theory and practice of social casework - (*i*) Gordon Hamilton:** Gordon Hamilton is associated with the book "Theory and practice of social casework," suggesting that this work delves into both the theoretical foundations and practical aspects of social casework. It likely explores various theoretical frameworks that inform casework practice, such as systems theory, psychodynamic theory, and strengths-based approaches. Additionally, it may discuss the application of these theories in real-world settings, offering insights into the complexities of casework interventions and the dynamics of client-worker relationships.

(*d*) **What is social casework? An Introductory Description - (*ii*) Mary Richmond:** Authored by Mary Richmond, this book likely provides a comprehensive introduction to the concept of social casework. Mary Richmond is considered one of the pioneers of modern social work and made significant contributions to the development of social casework as a profession. Her work may offer a historical overview of social casework, its evolution, and its role in addressing individual and societal problems. It may also define key terms, concepts, and principles central to understanding social casework practice.

75. (B):

(*a*) **Psychoanalysis - (*ii*) Activities that grow out of the interaction between the casework and the client:** Psychoanalysis, developed by Sigmund Freud, emphasizes the exploration of unconscious conflicts and desires through the therapeutic relationship. In psychoanalysis, activities often emerge from the interaction between the therapist and the client. This interaction may involve free association, dream analysis, and interpretation of symbols, where insights arise organically from the client's thoughts and experiences shared during therapy sessions. The therapist's role is to facilitate this process by providing a safe and supportive environment for the client to explore their thoughts, feelings, and behaviours.

(*b*) **Person-centered Counselling - (*i*) Accurate reflection of thoughts and feelings:** Person-centered counselling, developed by Carl Rogers, focuses on creating a supportive and empathetic therapeutic relationship where the client feels accepted and understood. Central to this approach is the therapist's ability to accurately reflect the client's thoughts and feelings. Through active listening and reflection, the therapist demonstrates genuine empathy and understanding, which helps the client gain insight into their experiences and develop a greater sense of self-awareness. This reflective process encourages clients to explore their feelings more deeply and move towards personal growth and self-actualization.

(*c*) **Gestalt Therapy - (*iv*) Analysis of transference:** Gestalt therapy, developed by Fritz Perls, emphasizes awareness, acceptance, and personal responsibility in the therapeutic process. In Gestalt therapy, transference refers to the projection of feelings, attitudes, and expectations onto the therapist based on past experiences with significant others. Through the analysis of transference, the therapist helps the client recognize and understand how past relationships influence their current interactions and experiences. By exploring and working through these projections, clients can gain insight into their relational patterns and develop healthier ways of relating to others.

(*d*) **Cognitive and Behavioural Counselling - (*iii*) Systematic desensitization:** Cognitive and behavioural counselling, rooted in principles of behaviourism and cognitive psychology, focuses on identifying and modifying maladaptive thoughts and behaviours. Systematic desensitization is a technique used to treat anxiety disorders by gradually exposing clients to feared stimuli while teaching relaxation techniques to reduce anxiety. Through systematic desensitization, clients learn to replace fear responses with relaxation responses, allowing them to confront and overcome their fears in a controlled and gradual manner. This process helps clients develop coping skills and build confidence in managing their anxiety.

76. (*)

77. (D):

(*d*) **Mexico (1975):** The first World Conference on Women was held in Mexico City in 1975. This conference marked a significant milestone in the international effort to address women's rights and gender equality. It brought together delegates from various countries to discuss and strategize ways to promote women's rights and advancement.

(*c*) **Copenhagen (1980):** The second World Conference on Women took place in Copenhagen in 1980. This conference continued the discussions initiated in Mexico and focused on assessing progress made since the first conference. It also aimed to strengthen the commitment of nations to gender equality and women's empowerment.

(*b*) **Nairobi (1985):** The third World Conference on Women was held in Nairobi in 1985. Like its predecessors, this conference addressed issues related to women's rights, development, and equality. It provided a platform for governments and organizations to discuss challenges and achievements in promoting gender equality on a global scale.

(*a*) **Beijing (1995):** The fourth and perhaps the most famous World Conference on Women was held in Beijing, China, in 1995. The Beijing Conference is particularly noteworthy for the adoption of the Beijing Declaration and Platform for Action, a comprehensive agenda outlining strategic objectives for advancing women's rights and gender equality. The conference addressed critical areas such as women's health, education, economic empowerment, and violence against women.

78. (B):

(*d*) John Dewey, an American psychologist and philosopher, was the organizing principle behind the Chicago school of functional psychology in 1894. However, Dewey never referred to his psychology as functionalism. Dewey's functionalism sought to consider organisms in total as they functioned in their environment. He considered the approach of Wundt and Titchener to be flawed because it ignored the continuity of human behaviour and the role that adaptation plays in creating it. Dewey's functionalism had a direct influence on the education system in the US. His theory was that children should learn at the pace that best suits their level of intellectual development, and that the curriculum should encourage students to draw from their own interests and experiences.

(*b*) Sigmund Freud developed psychoanalysis in the 1895. Psychoanalysis is a set of theories and techniques that treat mental disorders by studying the unconscious mind. Freud believed that many psychological problems stem from unresolved childhood conflicts that are repressed in the unconscious mind. He thought that people could be cured by making their unconscious thoughts and motivations conscious. Freud's psychoanalytic theory states that human personalities develop through three phases: the Id, the Ego, and the Superego. He also developed a theory of psychosexual development, which posits that people's personalities and sexual selves evolve through five stages of growth. Freud's work was influenced by the clinical work of Josef Breuer and others. His famous case studies, including Dora, Little Hans, and Anna O, also influenced the development of his psychoanalytic theory.

(*a*) Gestalt psychology, initiated in Germany in 1912 under the inspiration of German psychologist Max Wertheimer (1886–1943), claimed that all behaviour always follows a mental structure in which all stimuli coming from the outside world and from the subject's body form a mental whole that determines open responses to situations.

(*c*) John B. Watson published his ground-breaking article, "Psychology as the Behaviourist Views It", in 1913. The article is also known as "The Behaviourist Manifesto". In the article, Watson outlined the main features of his new psychological philosophy, behaviourism. He believed that psychology is the science of human behaviour, and that it should be studied under laboratory conditions. Watson also believed that psychology is a natural science that aims to predict and control behaviour. He also believed that the environment is a determinant of behaviour, and that society can be impro-ved by applying empirically-derived principles of behaviour.

79. (D): Garland, Jones, and Kolodny's model emphasizes the evolving nature of group dynamics, starting with the establishment of connections, progressing through phases of power dynamics, intimacy, and differentiation, and concluding with a reflective stage of separation. This model provides a framework for understanding the developmental trajectory of groups and the interpersonal processes that occur throughout their lifecycle.

(*d*) **Preaffiliation:** In this early stage, group members are primarily focused on building connections and forming relationships. There is a sense of socialization and getting to know one another. Members may engage in activities aimed at creating a sense of belonging and establishing initial bonds.

(*e*) **Power and Control:** This stage involves the negotiation and establishment of power dynamics within the group. Members may be testing and determining roles and hierarchies. Discussions or actions related to the distribution of authority, influence, and decision-making may take place.

(*a*) **Intimacy:** As the group progresses, there is an increased sense of closeness among members. Trust is developed, and there is openness in communication. Group members may share personal experiences, thoughts, and feelings. Collaborative activities that foster deeper connections become more prevalent.

(*b*) **Differentiation:** Members start expressing their unique qualities, and individual distinctions become more apparent. This stage is marked by recognition of diversity within the group. Discussions may center around acknowledging and appreciating individual differences. Group members might explore their unique contributions to the group.

(*c*) **Separation:** This is the final stage, involving the termination of the group or the transition of members out of the group. It is a phase of closure and reflection. Group members may reflect on their experiences, share insights gained, and prepare for the conclusion of the group. In some cases, the separation may involve a celebration or acknowledgment of the group's achievements.

80. (C):

(*a*) **Identifying the problem:** This is the initiation phase where the decision-maker recognizes there is a challenge or opportunity that requires a decision. Defining the problem, understanding its context, and determining its significance are essential. Clarity in problem identification sets the foundation for the decision-making process.

(*b*) **Analysing the problem:** In this step, a comprehensive analysis of the identified problem is conducted to gain insights into its root causes, contributing factors, and potential consequences. Gathering relevant information, examining data, and assessing the impact of the problem are crucial. A thorough analysis helps in understanding the complexities involved.

(*d*) **Developing alternatives:** After understanding the problem, the decision-maker generates various alternative solutions or courses of action. This step involves creativity and a willingness to explore diverse options. Brainstorming, considering different perspectives, and evaluating potential solutions are part of this step. The goal is to create a range of alternatives to address the identified problem.

(*c*) **Selecting the best alternative solution:** Once alternative solutions are developed, the decision-maker evaluates them based on predetermined criteria and selects the most suitable option. Applying decision criteria, considering the feasibility, risks, and benefits of each alternative, and making a judgment on the optimal solution are key activities in this step.

(*e*) **Converting decision into action:** After making the decision, the focus shifts to implementation. This step involves putting the chosen solution into action and executing the plan. Communicating the decision, allocating resources, and establishing a plan for execution are crucial. Monitoring progress and making adjustments as needed are part of ensuring successful implementation.

81. (D): Freud's psychosexual stages outline a theoretical framework for understanding the development of personality and sexuality in individuals from infancy to adulthood. It's important to note that contemporary psychology has evolved, and Freud's theories are often viewed critically. Many aspects of his work are considered controversial and lack empirical support, but his contributions have influenced the field and sparked ongoing discussions about the role of early experiences in shaping personality.

(*e*) **Oral:** Birth to around 18 months. Pleasure and challenges associated with the mouth, such as sucking and feeding. Issues related to dependency and trust may develop during this stage.

(*d*) **Anal:** Around 18 months to 3 years. This stage revolves around toilet training and the child's developing control over bodily functions. It's during this stage that the child learns societal expectations regarding cleanliness and order.

(*c*) **Phallic:** Around 3 to 6 years. This stage is characterized by a focus on the genitals. Freud introduced the concepts of the Oedipus complex (for boys) and the Electra complex (for girls). The child unconsciously develops feelings of desire for the opposite-sex parent and rivalry with the same-sex parent.

(*b*) **Latency:** Around 6 years to puberty. Sexual feelings are repressed during this stage, and the child's energy is directed towards learning, social activities, and developing relationships outside the family. Sexual urges are dormant.

(*a*) **Genital:** From puberty onwards. This is the final stage, where mature sexual interests and relationships develop. The individual is capable of forming healthy and satisfying relationships with others, beyond familial ties.

82. (A):

(*a*) **Ontology:** This is the branch of philosophy that deals with questions about the nature of reality, existence, and the fundamental categories of being. Researchers consider their ontological stance, addressing what exists and what can be studied.

(*c*) **Epistemology:** Following ontology, researchers explore epistemology, which deals with questions about knowledge—how it is acquired, what constitutes valid knowledge, and the nature of the relationship between the knower and the known.

(*b*) **Theoretical Orientation:** Once researchers have considered their onto-logical and epistemological perspectives, they adopt a theoretical orientation. This involves selecting a framework or set of principles to guide their research, aligning with their philosophical stance.

(*e*) **Research Approach:** With a theoretical orientation in place, researchers choose a research approach. This involves selecting an overall strategy or plan for conducting the study, such as qualitative, quantitative, or mixed methods.

(*d*) **Research Design:** Finally, researchers develop the research design, which involves detailed planning of how the study will be conducted. It includes specific methods, procedures, and techniques for data collection and analysis.

83. (B)

84. (B):

(*a*) **The Beveridge Report**, officially titled Social Insurance and Allied Services, was a government report published in November 1942. The report was influential in the establishment of the welfare state in the United Kingdom. The report proposed a new type of welfare state that would provide social insurance "from cradle to grave". It also sought to ensure that the social deprivation seen during the pre-Second World War economic depression would not happen again. The report proposed a universal system of social insurance financed by the state. It would be financed by contributions made by employers and employees from their pay. The report also proposed a flat-rate basic payment to protect people who were not working due to sickness, unemployment, or old age. The report was comprehensive and popular. Public opinion polls found that the majority of the British public welcomed the proposals in the report and wanted them implemented as soon as possible.

(*c*) **The Younghusband Report** is a 1959 report that called for national support for general purpose social worker training. The report was commissioned to study the employment and training of social workers. In 1947 and 1950, Eileen Younghusband advocated for "generic" training, which is a set of core knowledge that all social workers should have. The Younghusband Report is also known as the Report of the Working Party on Social Workers in the Local Authority Health and Welfare Services.

(*b*) **The Seebohm Report** is a 1968 report from the Committee on Local Authority and Allied Personal Social Services. The committee was chaired by Lord Frederic Seebohm and was appointed in 1965. The report recommends a single family service to meet as many family needs as possible. The report also sets out recommendations and aspirations for a modern, independent, and responsive social service.

(*d*) **The Lane Committee Report**, officially titled "Report of the Committee on the Working of the Abortion Act," was published in the United Kingdom in 1974. Its main purpose was to evaluate the impact of the 1967 Abortion Act and recommend potential changes.

85. (C):

(*a*) **Welcome:** The initial step involves creating an environment that is welcoming, safe, and culturally sensitive. Asylum seekers and refugees often come from traumatic experiences, and a warm welcome can set the tone for trust and collaboration.

(*d*) **Accompaniment:** Accompaniment refers to providing continuous support throughout the journey. This support can include assistance with basic needs like housing, healthcare, and education. Social workers accompany individuals, helping them navigate the challenges they face in a new country.

(*c*) **Mediation:** Mediation becomes necessary when conflicts arise, either within the refugee community or with external entities. Social workers may mediate disputes, helping individuals or groups find common ground and resolving issues peacefully.

(*b*) **Befriending:** Building relationships and friendships is crucial for the well-being of asylum seekers and refugees. Befriending involves offering emotional support, companionship, and a sense of belonging, helping individuals integrate into their new community.

(*e*) **Advocacy:** Advocacy is an ongoing process that involves speaking up for the rights and needs of asylum seekers and refugees. Social workers may advocate for policy changes, challenge discriminatory practices, and work with government agencies or NGOs to ensure that the rights of refugees are protected.

In the non-linear social work process, these elements may not necessarily follow a strict chronological order. The needs of asylum seekers and refugees are dynamic and may require simultaneous attention to various aspects.

For instance, advocacy efforts may begin early to address systemic issues, while befriending and accompaniment continue throughout the entire process. The social worker's role is adaptive and responsive to the evolving needs of the individuals they are supporting.

86. (C): Assertion (A): Almost all beggars are homeless, but all homeless are not beggars. This statement is true as it recognizes that while there is a significant overlap between the populations of beggars and the homeless, not every homeless person engages in begging. Homelessness and begging are related, but they are not synonymous.

Reason (R): Most of the programs for the homeless are directed towards the eradication of beggary. This statement is considered false. Programs for the homeless typically address a broader range of issues beyond just beggary. They often focus on providing shelter, food, healthcare, and other support services to address the overall well-being of homeless individuals. While some programs may include components aimed at addressing begging, it's not accurate to say that the primary focus of most homeless programs is the eradication of beggary.

87. (A): Statement I: There is an increasing awareness of disabilities and disability rights in India: Over the years, there has been a noticeable increase in awareness and understanding of disabilities in India. This awareness extends to recognizing the rights, needs, and capabilities of people with disabilities. The shift in perspective has been driven by various factors, including advocacy groups, educational initiatives, and policy changes aimed at inclusivity and equal opportunities.

Statement II: The number of recognized disability conditions has been increased from 7 to 21 in the RPWD Act 2016: The Rights of Persons with Disabilities (RPWD) Act, 2016, replaced the Persons with Disabilities (Equal Opportunities, Protection of Rights and Full Participation) Act, 1995, in India. One significant change was the expansion of the categories of recognized disabilities from 7 to 21. This expansion reflects a more comprehensive understanding of the diverse nature of disabilities, including physical, intellectual, and psychosocial conditions. The broader recognition aims to ensure that a wider range of individuals with disabilities receive legal protection and support.

Both statements highlight positive developments in India regarding awareness and legal recognition of disabilities. The increased awareness contributes to fostering an inclusive society, and the expanded list of recognized disabilities in the RPWD Act reflects a commitment to addressing the needs of a more diverse range of individuals with disabilities.

88. (B): Assertion (A): "Social action is mass betterment through propaganda and legislation." This statement suggests that social action involves efforts aimed at improving the well-being of a large population. The term "propaganda" in this context refers to the dissemination of information or ideas with the goal of influencing public opinion or behaviour. Legislation indicates the use of laws and policies as tools for social change.

Reason (R): "Social action requires intensive mass mobilization." This statement is highlighting the idea that for effective social action, it often involves mobilizing a large number of people. Mass mobilization can include organizing and engaging individuals in collective efforts towards achieving a common social goal.

While both statements are true, it's important to note that the reason provided (mass mobilization) does not fully explain all aspects of Assertion A. Social action is a broad concept that can encompass various strategies beyond just mass mobilization, including advocacy, education, community organizing, and policy work. Mass mobilization is indeed a common and powerful tool in social action, but it's not the only factor contributing to the betterment of society through social action.

89. (A): Statement I: "Indigenization is a plea for self-awareness and rejection of a borrower consciousness, emphasizing the need for an inside view." This statement is true. Indigenization, in various contexts, often involves a movement towards acknowledging and valuing local perspectives, knowledge, and traditions. It encourages a rejection of blindly adopting external ideas without critically examining their relevance to the local context.

Statement II: "Indigenization should not lead to narrow parochialism or to the fragmentation of a single discipline into several insulated systems of thoughts based on geographical boundaries." This statement is also true. While indigenization promotes the inclusion of local perspectives, it should not result in narrow-mindedness or the isolation of disciplines along geographical lines. Instead, it should seek a balanced integration of local and global knowledge, fostering a richer and more inclusive understanding.

Both statements emphasize the importance of indigenization as a means of self-awareness, rejecting uncritical adoption, and avoiding the pitfalls of narrow parochialism or fragmen-tation.

90. (B): Assertion (A): "Indigenous social work requires sensitivity to local cultures and contexts." This statement is true. Indigenous social work emphasizes the importance of understanding and respecting the specific cultural and contextual nuances of the communities being served. It involves tailoring social work practices to align with the values, traditions, and needs of those communities.

Reason (R): "The ethnocentric form of indigenous social work would be counter-productive." This statement is also true. Ethnocentrism, in the context of indigenous social work, refers to evaluating other cultures based on one's own cultural norms. This approach can be counterproductive as it may lead to a lack of cultural sensitivity and an imposition of external values, undermining the effectiveness of social work interventions in diverse communities.

While both statements are true, Reason (R) might not be a direct and explicit explanation of Assertion (A). The sensitivity to local cultures and contexts is emphasized to avoid pitfalls like ethnocentrism, but the reason doesn't explicitly clarify why such sensitivity is necessary. Therefore, while both statements are individually true, the connection between them might not be as straightforward.

91. (C): The passage emphasizes that social development is a wider concept that includes economic development. However, it suggests that economic growth should not be the sole focus, and there is a need to regulate economic growth to reduce economic disparities. The passage highlights the importance of planning for simultaneous development in various areas, including economic, physical, infrastructural, educational, health, and welfare targets.

92. (B):

(*a*) **Providing integration among different social groups:** Social development aims to foster inclusivity and cohesion among diverse social groups. This involves creating a society where people from various backgrounds, ethnicities, and communities feel integrated rather than marginalized.

(*b*) **Shared value pattern among different cultural groups:** Social development seeks to promote a common set of values that can be shared and respected across different cultural groups. This involves recognizing and appreciating cultural diversity while finding common ground in shared values to build a cohesive society.

(*c*) **Building up solidarity of the nation to face foreign threats:** Social development includes the goal of creating a sense of unity and solidarity within a nation. This unity becomes particularly important when facing external challenges or threats. A socially developed society is one where citizens come together to address common concerns and protect national interests.

93. (D):

(*c*) **It is a wider concept and inclusive of economic development:** Social develop-ment, as emphasized in the passage, is indeed a broader concept that includes economic development but is not exclusively limited to it. It encompasses various aspects beyond just economic growth.

(*d*) **It involves planning for simultaneous development on many different areas:** The passage highlights that social development involves planning for simultaneous development in various areas, including economic, physical, infrastructural, educational, health, and welfare targets. This aligns with the idea that social development is comprehensive and not solely focused on one aspect.

94. (A): Statement I: "Social development is a comprehensive concept." This statement is true. Social development, as discussed in the context, is presented as a broader and more inclusive concept, encompassing various aspects beyond just economic development.

Statement II: "There is a realization to take into account non-economic parameters for development planning." This statement is also true. The passage mentions a realization among economists that non-economic factors are important for development planning, indicating a shift towards considering a more comprehensive set of parameters.

95. (A): The passage states, "The challenge of social development is not so much a problem of mobilizing money resources but rather a problem of motivating and mobilizing people." This suggests that while financial resources are important, a significant challenge in social development lies in inspiring and mobilizing individuals to actively participate in and contribute to the development process.

96. (D): The passage emphasizes the need for social workers to go beyond merely serving society and to actively engage in understanding and addressing the causes of social problems. The term "social engineers" suggests a role that involves analyzing, questioning, and potentially restructuring social and political institutions to bring about positive change. It signifies a proactive and transformative approach to social work, aligning with the author's call for a deeper study of societal problems, the development of a social philosophy, and the ability to make informed judgments based on facts.

97. (B): The author seems to be addressing social work students, emphasizing the role of a school of social work in understanding and addressing societal problems. The passage encourages individuals to utilize their time in the institution to study the causes of social problems, develop a social philosophy, and acquire the ability to make informed judgments. The call to be "social engineers" aligns with the transformative goals of social work education, suggesting that students should go beyond serving society and actively engage in questioning and potentially restructuring social and political institutions for positive change. The reference to societal problems, social philosophy, and the functions of a school of social work strongly indicate that the audience is likely composed of individuals undergoing social work training.

98. (B):

(*b*) **Undertake a deep study of the problem of society:** The author encourages social workers to engage in a thorough examination and analysis of societal problems. This implies a need for a comprehensive understanding of the root causes and complexities of social issues.

(*c*) **Develop a social philosophy and reflect on the problems of society:** The author emphasizes the importance of social workers developing a philosophical perspective that guides their approach to societal issues. This involves reflecting on the ethical, moral, and value-based considerations in addressing problems within society.

(*d*) **Develop the ability to make judgments based upon facts:** The author stresses the acquisition of critical thinking skills to make informed judgments grounded in facts rather than being swayed by sentimentalism or hearsay. This indicates the need for social workers to base their interventions on evidence and objective analysis.

99. (C):

(*a*) **Explain the cause of social problems:** The author suggests that one of the functions of a school of social work is to seek to explain the causes of social problems. This involves a comprehensive analysis and understanding of the underlying factors contributing to societal issues.

(*b*) **Suggest methods of approach to solve social problems:** The passage indicates that a school of social work should not only identify the causes of social problems but also play a role in suggesting effective methods of approach to address and solve these problems. This implies a practical and solution-oriented approach to social work education.

(*c*) **Believe that our larger problem is the problem of prevention:** The author emphasizes that the larger problem for social workers is the problem of prevention. This suggests that a school of social work should instill in its students a proactive mindset, focusing on preventing social issues rather than merely responding to them.

100. (A): Statement I: "Our knowledge in the social sciences has not kept pace with the advance in technology." This statement suggests a concern that advancements in technology have outpaced the development of knowledge in the social sciences. This is a common observation as technological progress often moves rapidly, and social sciences might lag in keeping up.

Statement II: "The efforts of society seem to be directed towards widening the gap rather than narrowing it." This statement implies that societal efforts may be contributing to the widening gap between technological advancements and social sciences, rather than closing this gap. This observation highlights a potential imbalance in the focus and priorities of societal efforts.

UGC-NET JRF

SOCIAL WORK

PART-A

CHAPTER

1

Evolution of Social Work

Social Service based on humanitarian ground is an age old phenomenon for India and for West. We could see it from the historical perspective throughout the ages. Age old epics like the Vedas, the Bhagawat Gita and the Bible taught the whole world the lessons of life, service to mankind and compassion for the poor and disadvantaged. Since the ancient time the social fabric of the society has changed immensely. The complexity of the society has given the rise to many personal and social problems which in turn made social service activities into organized social work profession.

HISTORY OF SOCIAL WORK IN UNITED KINGDOM AND UNITED STATES OF AMERICA

The discipline of social work has a long history of evolution from charity based tradition to the full-fledged profession of today.

- **1215 :** King John of England signs the Magna Carta, which establishes some human rights (for the privileged class). It is considered a forerunner of modern civil rights.
- **1531 :** The first State regulation of relief is found in a 1531 statue concerning the punishment of beggars and vagabonds.
- **1560 :** Churches provided hospitals, infirmaries and alms houses for the old and the sick in United Kingdom.
- **1601 :** The Elizabethan Poor Law which was collection of laws meant to formalised earlier practices of poor relief was enacted. The law authorized the raising of taxes to pay for services to those who were poor, needy and had no family support.

  It classified the poor into three groups.

  - **The Impotent Poor:** Those who were too old/ill/young to work.
  - **The Able bodied Poor:** Those who would like work but could not.
  - **The Idle Poor:** Those who could work but would not.
- **1624 :** Based on the contribution of disabled soldiers and sailors Virginia colony passed the legislation recognising their problems and needs.
- **1642 :** Based on the Elizabethan Poor Law the Plymouth colony also approved a poor law that directs that relief cases must be discussed at meetings held in towns.
- **1650 :** The "protestant work ethics", emphasizing self discipline, frugality and hardship becomes prominent, justifying those who adopted its views to look down upon people who are unemployed or dependent on others.
- **1657 :** Scots Charitable Society, The first American society founded in Boston. It represents the beginning of voluntary societies to meet the need of poor and disadvantaged.

- **1776 :** The United States declaration of independence is signed promoting freedom for everyone but not for the slaves.
- **1812 :** The First American textbook on psychiatry written by Dr. Benjamin Rugh is published.
- **1813 :** The first labour legislation was enacted to require factory owner to have children in factories taught reading, writing and arithmetic.
- **1834 :** The Poor Law Amendment Act of 1834 divided the poor in England and Wales into two groups : i.e. the deserving poor and the undeserving poor.
- **1837 :** The First State institution for blind people is established in Ohio.
- **1843 :** The New York Association for improving the condition of the poor is established.
- **1844 :** The first Young Men's Christian Association (YMCA) was organized by Drapery Clerk George in London.
- **1848 :** The first Minimum Wages law of United States was established in Pennsylvania.
- **1869 :** Charity Organisation Society was founded in England by Helen Bosanquet and Octavia Hill.
- **1877 :** The first Charity Organisation Society (USA) was founded in Buffalo. The society operates on four principles
  1. Detailed investigation of applicants.
  2. A central system of registration to avoid duplication.
  3. Cooperation between the various relief agencies.
  4. Use of the volunteers in the role of 'Friendly Visitors'.
- **1886 :** The first settlement house in the United States named the Neighbourhood Guild was established with an objective of eliminating the distance between socio economic classes by locating housing for the poor in working class neighbourhood.
- **1898 :** The first Social Work training institute was established by the New York Charity Organisation Society, which in 1904 becomes the New York School of Philanthropy.
- **1900 :** The term 'Social Workers' was coined by Simon Pattern. Abraham Flexner issues his report declaring that social work is not yet a profession because it lacks a written body of knowledge and educationally communicable techniques.
- **1917 :** The first text book on Social Case Work named *Social Diagnosis* written by Marry Richmond known to be the first important contribution in the social work body of knowledge.
- **1933 :** US president Franklin D. Roosevelt proclaims a 'New Deal' for Americans establishing major social development program responding to poverty and unemployment.
- **1950 :** The Social Security Act of 1935 is amended to include children and relatives with whom needy children are living, and to aid permanently and totally disabled people.
- **1952 :** The Council on Social Work Education was established.
- **1955 :** The National Associations of social workers was established.
- **1960 :** The National Associations of social workers adopts its first code of ethics.
- **1964 :** US President Lyndon B. Johnson establishes the "Great Society" programs and made racial discrimination in public places illegal.
- **1965 :** More "Great Society" programs, providing for medical case, the needs of older Americans, and children education are established.
- **1990 :** The American with Disabilities Act makes it illegal to discriminate against disabled people.
- **1990 :** The Ryan white comprehensive AIDS Resource Emergency Act provides

funding for prevention, Intervention, treatment and commends planning in relation the HIV/AIDS.

- **1996 :** US president Clinton signs into law the Personal Responsibility and Work Opportunity Reconciliation Act, restricting or eliminating many entitlement program and replacing them with more temporary aid designed to promote independence.

HISTORY OF SOCIAL WORK IN INDIA

Healthy, ethical and spiritual traditions were part of the Indian tradition since early Vedic period. The seeds of human development were served since the origin of Indian society.

The Vedic Period provides life's highest order, which is found in the Indian scriptures entitled 'Veda' i.e. Rigveda, 'Samaveda', 'Yajurveda', 'Atharvaveda'. It emphasized that the religious hymns and music, sacrifices and knowledge are the soul of human life. The learning of Veda was called 'shruti' which was memorizing through listening. One of the finest skills of case work is listening which was practiced in Pathshala mode of education where the 'Guru' used to recite and disciples practiced the listening and oratory skills and learn the lessons.

Charities in Vedic era were considered as morality. Helping the needy and beggar were praised as moral behaviour.

We have many examples in Indian literature on 'Dana' (charity) we have example of 'Maryadapurshottam' and the 'Ram Rajya' of Rama as an example of 'welfare state'. 'Danveer Karna'. Raja Harishchandra as 'Satyavadi', Raja Bhoj as an advocate whose justice mechanism was based on human values.

During the early vedic era women were enjoying equal positions. There is a reference of 'Rishis', 'Apala', 'Maitreyi'.

The Ashrama systems of ancient times delegated duties associated with relationship to provide discipline in human life.

The Smrat Ashok adopted Buddhism and devoted his life to humanistic values.

The Eight fold Paths of Buddhism finds its relevance in social work principles that is peace, dignity and right to livelihood, acceptance etc.

'Charaka' in the regime of Krishna developed indigenous medical treatment of known as :

Bhaisajyagraha – a medical store and Kautilya mentioned about the veterinary surgeons who were the in charge of cattle's. There was a provision of Samsthudyaska (Controller of establishment who looked after public health).

The ancient books such as Manu Smriti by Manu, Aarthshastra by Kautilya, Mahabharata by Vedvyas and Ramcharit Manas by Tulsidas mentioned the political institutions as examples of scientific governance.

Welfare state was an ideal feature of ancient India as the king was custodian of law and trustee of public property emerged from Dharma.

The concept of welfare state has been beautifully summarized by Apastamba. According to this text the state had to provide food, clothing, shelter and medical treatment to people. No one in the Kingdom shall suffer from hunger, sickness, and cold or heat either through want or otherwise, royal quest house at the capital was to be made open and accessible to all.

The issue of morality and ethics lies in the story of Panchtantra and the issue of animal protection and their dignity finds space in 'Hitopadesha'.

Mughal emperor Akbar acted as social reformer and prohibited child marriage introduced law against slavery and alcoholism. He founded a new cultural order called Din-e-Ilahi (divine faith)—A collection of moral from all religions.

We find reference of high orders practiced by Shivaji, Maharana Pratap, Laxmi Bai who fought for people and nation.

No example of social welfare is found during the early days of British rule in India. Due to the regular occurrence of famine Colonial state appointed famine commission in 1880. Further Famine Code was developed in 1883.

By the Charter Act of 1813 the company administration had accepted the responsibility of education in India.

In 1835 the cleverer general William Bentinck had decided to impart western education in India on the recommendation of Mr. Mcaley.

In 1844 English becomes official language and it was declared that people having the knowledge of English would be preferred for public employment.

The colonial state appointed the sanitation commissioners in 1880 in the five British provinces. The plague commission was also appointed in 1896.

Due to industrial expansion many Acts were passed in India such as the Apprentice Act, 1853, The Fatal Accident Act, 1853, The Merchant Shipping Act, 1859, the Reformatory School Act of 1870, First Factory Act, 1881.

Series of Labour legislations were also passed by government such as Factory Commission was appointed in 1890, Indian Factory Act was passed in 1891. The Factory Act was amended in 1912, 1923 and 1934. The Workmen's Compensation Act of 1923 (Now Employees Compensation Act), Payment of Wages Act, 1936, Bombay Industrial Disputes Act of 1938.

Some social legislations were also enacted like the Apprentice Act of 1850, Children Act in 1920, Control Prevention and Treatment of Beggary Act was passed in 1945, Abolition of Sati in 1829, the Abolition of Slavery in 1843, the Abolition of Female Infanticide and Human Sacrifice in 1802 and Widow Remarriage Act in 1856.

The social reformers like Raja Ram Mohan Roy, Ishwar Chandra Vidyasagar, Mahadev Govind Ranade, Ram Krishan Parmhans, Swami Vivekananda reeled an atmosphere which made British government to pass important social legislation. In the year 1905 Gopal Krishna Gokhle established 'Servants of India Society'. It was first attempt by an Indian in the form of organised social work. In the year 1936 Sir Dorabji Tata Graduate School of Social Work was established —the first of its type in India with the help of Christian missionary named Clifford Manshardt.

Medical social work courses were first started in India in 1946 at the Tata Institute of Social Sciences.

After independence several initiatives has been taken by the Government for the social progress of the weaker society. The Factory Act 1948, Plantation Labour Act 1951, The Mines Act 1952, embodying the Directive Principles of State Policy in the Constitution, Maternity Benefit Act 1961, The Payment of Bonus Act 1965, The Contract Labour (Prohibition and Regular) Act 1970, Payment of Gratuity Act 1972, Equal Remuneration Act 1972, Protection of Civil Rights Act 1955 amended in 1976, Scheduled Castes and Scheduled Tribes (prevention of Atrocities) Act 1989, Nilokhedi projects in 1948 as the refugee rehabilitation project, in 1952 Firka development scheme in Madras province, Etowah Pilot project was launched in 1948 for rural development in the state of Uttar Pradesh. The national extension service was launched in 1953 and the 73rd, 74th Constitutional Amendment in 1992-93.

SOCIAL WORK PHILOSOPHY

Herbert Bison has described the philosophy of social work in detail in his book *The Philosophy of Social Work*. He has narrated the philosophy of social work by following basic thoughts.

Each individual by the very fact of his existence is of worth. Human suffering is undesirable and should be prevented or at least alleviated whenever possible.

All human behaviour is the result of interaction between the biological organization and its environment. Man does not 'naturally' act in rational manner. Man at birth is neither moral or immoral, social or antisocial. He is neutral and the behaviour of individual is result of many forces.

There are both individual and common human needs. In addition to these needs every individual also has other needs and desires which are uniquely his. The social work believes that it is essential for individuals to have an opportunity to express these needs and decries in a satisfying and socially useful manner.

There are important differences between individuals and they must be recognized and allowed. Social work places paramount importance to individualization.

Human Motivator is complex and frequently obscure. It is the result of certain needs which initiates it, thus behaviours is the symptom of these causes. When needs are not fulfilled he feels frustrated and abnormal symptoms appear in his behaviour.

Family relationship is primary importance in the early development of individual. Having experience is an essential aspect of the learning process.

Social work rejects the doctrine of survival of the fittest instead it believes in the survival of the weakest.

The rich powerful are not necessarily 'Fit' while the poor and weak are not necessarily 'Unfits'.

"Socialized individuals" is preferable to "rugged individualism" and social work believe in socialized individualism.

A major responsibility for the welfare of its members rests with the community.

All classes of persons in the community have an equal right to the social services. There is a community responsibility to relieve adequate and without discrimination among the members of the community.

Public assistance should be based on needs. Social work believes that needs should be scientifically examined and after finding their validity assistance should be given.

Organized labour makes positive contribution to community life and should be accepted as constructive rather than destructive force.

Freedom and security are not mutually exclusive security and freedom is part of the same problems.

Social work has functionally dualistic approach. The case work and social action are two district methodologies. Social work operates to assist individuals in adjusting to the institutional framework of society and also attempt to modify institutional framework itself in required areas through social action method.

The social work believes on the development of insight and/or environmental manipulation for the purpose of modifying individual's behaviour.

Social work services should be provided by professionally trained social worker by both public and private agencies.

Social work accepts democracy as an important method and support to the attainment and maintenance of all civil rights.

Evolutionary type 'reform is both possible and desirable in our society'.

There is a need for social planning. Social work believes in the possibility of the intelligent direction of social changes in other works they recognize the need for and feasibility of social planning.

Principles of Social Work

Principles are guiding beliefs and statement of do's and don'ts. Social work principles are guiding assertions of statement that have come from experiences and research. The most commonly discussed principles of social work are as follows:

Principles of Acceptance: Social work accepts the individual as he or she is with all his/her limitations. Social work believes that acceptance is the crux of all help. Social worker does not condemn or feel hostile towards a client because his behaviour differs from the approved one. The principle of acceptance implies that social worker must perceive, acknowledge, receive and establish a relationship with the individual client as he actually is, not as he wishes him to be or think he should be.

Principle of Individualization: The principle of individualization is fundamental to effective social work practice. Social work believes in the uniqueness of individual. Each individual is different from that of every other individual nature. As we know that individual is unique as his thumb print. The social worker views the problem of each client as specific and helps the client move forward finding the most satisfactory means for client to deal with particular problem situation.

Principle of Communications: Communication is a two way process most of the problem that give pain are precisely the problem of communication. When the communication is inadequate or insufficient the problems occurs either automatically or because of misunderstanding. The social worker should have enough skills to grasp the communication. The proper communication is crucial in social work relationship because the background of the client and worker may be different, the mental status of the client and the worker may vary. Therefore the social worker should make all the efforts to see that communication between him and client is proper. The client should be made feel comfortable and at ease to express his thoughts feelings and facts.

Principle of Confidentiality: Social work believes that during the professional help between the client and social worker, client have the right of personal information about themselves in relationship with a social agency. The principle believes that confidential things of the client must be kept confidential and other agencies and individual should be consulted only with the clients consent.

Principle of Self-determination: The principle emphasizes clients right to self-determination. Every individual client has the right to decide what is appropriate for him and decides the ways and means to realize it. In other words, social worker should not force decisions or solutions on the clients because the client has come to him for help. Therefore social worker should support and guide the client to develop insight into his social situations in correct perspective and encourage and involve him to like decisions that are good and acceptable to him.

Principle of Non-judgmental Attitude: Principle of non-judgmental attitude presumes that the social worker should begin the professional relationship without any bias. He should not form opinion about the client, good or bad, worthy or unworthy. He has to treat the client as somebody who has come to him for help and he should be willing to help the client without being influenced by the opinions of other about the client or his situation. This enables the worker and the client feel free to develop understanding of each other.

Principle of Controlled Emotional Involvement: This principle guides social work professional not to indulge too much personally in the client's difficult situation or being too objective. Therefore the social worker should maintain a reasonable emotional distance even while sympathizing with the client social worker should indicate the understanding of the difficult situations of the client without showing pity or appearing to be indifference.

System Approach to Social Work Practice: System approach had been having a successful time in biology, ecology and engineering. System theory encourages practitioner to see their client and problems as part of a whole. The behaviour of each component affected and in its turn was affected by all other part of the whole or system. Thus, to treat one problem entailed understanding the functioning of other related part of the whole or system. So, for example, with the difficult child, the behaviour of his parents, his peers and his school may all have a bearing on his conduct. After a system analysis the practitioner might well conclude that altering the anti-social outlook of the local peer group is in fact the best way to tackle the client's difficult behaviour and not to send him to an educational psychologist.

Role of Social Worker: Social worker plays various types of roles in catering the needs of his clients. As **care giver** he counsel and support people with problems in a therapeutic way to promote change. As a **consultant** he works with individual and groups to assist in their problems and programs. As a **broker** he helps people to reach services they need and make the system more useful. As a **mobilizer** he tries to bring new resources to individual and groups.

As an **evaluator** he evaluates the weakness and strengths of individual and groups, their need and problems. As an **advocate** he works for the improvement of policies and laws in order to make system more effective.

SOCIAL WORK AND HUMAN RIGHTS: COMMON DOMAIN AND CONCERNS

According to Friedlander social work is a professional service based on scientific knowledge and skills in human relation to obtain personal and social satisfaction and to live happily life. The basic thought is to help people so that they can help themselves. On the other hand human rights seeks to ensure the condition that make life humane and enable people to live together in harmony and mutual respect.

Common Domain

Basic premise and foundation of the social work and human rights is equality, freedom, harmony and justice. The foundation problem of our society is disparity, discrimination, alienation and exploitation. Indian society is also affected by class, caste, creed, gender, disparity and inequitable distribution of material resources. Those are the core concern of social work and human rights.

The victims of inequality are poor, the women, the children, the aged and mentally and physically handicapped. The Social work attempts to work with disadvantaged, weaker and vulnerable sections of society who require professional assistance. The paradigm of compassion has changed to rights of the individual and this orientation gave the idea of human rights.

Major Human Rights Concern with Social Work Practice

The foundation of social work in the worth and dignity of individual is also the basic premise of human rights. Article 22, 25, 26, 27 of universal declaration of human rights could be understood to concern directly with social security protection against unemployment. Right of standard of living, special care and protection for motherhood and childhood and right to education, the practice of social work emphasize on this issue. These groups are concerned for special attention as far as social work practice is concerned.

Dilemma

The Social Work profession has yet to make a mark on the vast rural hinterland of the country. It is concentrating in urban areas and known only to the educated mass of the country similarly concern awareness and understanding related to human rights has yet to be understood by illiterate, unaware and ignorant population. Thus unfortunately Social Work profession has failed to make seminal contribution in awareness and understanding of human rights.

SOCIAL WORK EDUCATION

Social Work education in India was started by the House of Tatas under the "Sir Dorabji Tata Graduate School of Social Work" in the year 1936. This was the first institute which started imparting specialized professional training in social work. Now this school of social work is known as "Tata Institute of Social Sciences" (TISS), Mumbai. In the beginning Tata Graduate School of Social Work used to award a post graduate diploma in Social Service Administration. The School got recognition by the University Grants Commission in the year 1964. Consequently the diploma course has converted into Masters Degree course in Social Work in the academic year 1964-65. After 1936 other institutes like Department of Social Work, University of Delhi (1946), Department of Social Work, Mahatma Gandhi Kashi Vidyapeeth University (1947), Faculty of Social Work, MS University of Baroda (1950), Indore School of Social Work, Indore (1952), Madras School of Social Work, Chennai (1952), College of Social Work, Nirmala Niketan, Mumbai (1955), Udaipur School of Social Work, Janardan Rai Nagar Rajasthan Vidyapeeth (1959), Karve Institute of Social Sciences, Pune (1963), Department of Social Work, Loyala College of Social Sciences,

Thiruvanantpuram (1963), Department of Social Work, Jamia Milia Islamia, New Delhi (1967), also begin to impart social work training.

UGC on Social Work Education

To ensure a systematic development of Social Work education in the country's University Grants Commission has appointed review committees. The first such review committee was appointed by the UGC in the year 1960, which submitted its report in June, 1965. UGC Second Review Committee for Social Work education was appointed in 1975, the committee submitted its report in the year 1978.

Goals of Social Work Education

The education of Social Work should address itself towards the following goals: .

1. Organization of teaching and practical experience in order to provide professionally trained manpower in social welfare to ensure better service delivery, and to create support system specially for the underprivileged population groups or area.
2. Development and dissemination of scientific knowledge in regard to welfare and development needs, tasks and services.
3. Deepening of understanding, acquisition of skills and inculcation of a perspective for bringing about improvement in the human environment situation and services through institutional change and organizations of people.
4. Promotion of close collaboration among different disciplines for a better understanding of human problems, services, issues of social development, and also for initiating corresponding action in these areas.
5. Ensure better integration between scientific social theory and practice in the field of social welfare, social policy and social justice.
6. Development of position attitudes, values, professional leadership, social commitment and holistic approach to deal with socio-ecological issues.

Field Work Training in Social Work Education

Field work is considered to be an integral part of the social work education by all school of social work in India. The review committee on social work education has mentioned the following objectives of field work.

1. Development of professional skills through learning.
2. Development of skills among social work trainees in problems solving at the macro and micro level.
3. Integration of class room learning with field practice.
4. Development of skills required for professional practice at the particular level of training.
5. Development of professional attitudes, values and commitments.

SOCIAL WORK EDUCATION—PROBLEMS AND CHALLENGES

After passing 77 years of history of social work in India there is no authority in social work education for the regulations and enforcement of standards. There is no government policy to regulate and control the direction of social work education in India. Social Work profession in India is seems to face many problems and challenges.

(1) Problem of Communication of Knowledge
(2) The Lack of Universality in Social Work Education
(3) The Problem of International Communication in Social Work
(4) Lack of Universally Accepted Professional Body of Knowledge
(5) Mushroom Growth of Institutions Imparting Social Work Training
(6) The Problem of Acceptance
(7) Lack of Employment Opportunities to Trained Social Workers
(8) Problem of Infrastructure and Field Work Practice Institutions.

MULTIPLE CHOICE QUESTIONS

1. Which of the following is NOT an objective of Social Work?
   A. To solve Psycho-Social problems
   B. To promote Voluntary Labour
   C. To develop Self-dependence
   D. To fulfil humanitarian needs

2. In which year the Elizabeth Poor Law was constituted?
   A. 1624 B. 1601
   C. 1602 D. 1632

3. Social Work has originated from:
   A. Charity Organization Society Movement
   B. Settlement House Movement
   C. Reform Movement
   D. Christian Missionaries' Movement

4. The classification of poor into impotent, able bodied and idle poor was done by:
   A. Charity Organization Society
   B. Settlement House Movement
   C. Elizabeth Poor Law
   D. Protestant Work Ethics

5. Human rights are not :
   A. Universal
   B. Alienable
   C. Enforceable
   D. Internationally recognized

6. Which one of the following is NOT a recognized function of field work supervision?
   A. To combine the principle of rapport building with field work
   B. To help in understanding the agency limitations
   C. To provide help to the students/trainee in understanding the client system
   D. To conduct surprise visit to find faults to initiate disciplinary action

7. Integrated Social Work Practice is :
   A. Working simultaneously with individual, family and community
   B. Working in collaboration with bureaucracy
   C. Helping Clients by suing all the accepted methods of social work
   D. Working with exploited sections of society

8. The system referred to in the integrated social work practice model are:
   A. The education, social and health care model
   B. The client and social systems
   C. The client, action and change agents system
   D. The client, action, change agent and environment system

9. Social work profession has evolved from :
   A. Charity Organization Society
   B. Settlement House Movement
   C. Elizabeth Poor Law
   D. Emergency Relief

10. Social work is closest to :
    A. Social Services
    B. Social Welfare Services
    C. Social Reforms
    D. Public Assistance

11. Social Work philosophy is :
    A. Democratic
    B. Humanitarian
    C. Neither democratic nor Humanitarian
    D. Democratic as well as Humanitarian

12. Which of the following is NOT a principle of Social work?
    A. Individualization
    B. Self-development
    C. Acceptance
    D. Self-determination

13. Social work practice is NOT directly concerned with :
    A. Correction
    B. HIV/AIDS
    C. Sexually Transmitted Diseases
    D. Consolidation of Land Holdings

14. System approach to Social work practice is NOT based on which of the following assumptions?
A. There are various sub-system of a system
B. Various sub-systems are interrelated
C. Well-established rules are created to define the patterns of interrelations between system and sub-system as also between sub-system themselves
D. Systems are not integrated

15. Who gave the integrated model for social work practice?
A. Pincus and Minhan
B. Specht and Vickery
C. Howard Goldstein
D. Chris Payne

16. Who among the following social work educator define social work as a professional service based on scientific knowledge ?
A. Clarke B. Boehm
C. Friedlander D. Konopka

17. Which one of the following is NOT the role performed by social workers?
A. Prohibitory B. Remedial
C. Preventive D. Developmental

18. Which is the oldest institute of social work education in India ?
A. Tata Institute of Social Sciences
B. Delhi School of Social Work
C. Kashi Vidyapeeth
D. Indore School of Social Work

19. Which of the following is MOST difficult problems faced by Social worker today?
A. Non-availability of literature
B. Non-recognition of social work by state and societies
C. Non-existence of regulating authority at the apex level
D. Problem of Acceptance

20. Which of the following is the MOST distinctly emerging trend in social work in India?
A. Encroachment by other disciplines in the fields of social work
B. Establishment of sub-standard social work educational school/institutes/ university departments
C. Internationalisation of Social Work
D. Availability of employment opportunities in non-governmental organisation

21. Social Work in India is :
A. Charity B. Social Service
C. A movement D. Semi-profession

22. Objective of social work is :
A. Improve social functioning
B. Increase happiness and satisfaction
C. Develop cordial relationship
D. All the above

23. In social work practice the right to self-determination lies with:
A. Social Worker
B. Social Welfare Agency
C. Client
D. None of the above

24. The practice of social work is based on :
A. Humanitarian Philosophy
B. Scientific Knowledge and Skills
C. Democratic Philosophy
D. All the above

25. The principle of individualisation means:
A. Conducting individual study
B. Discrimination against certain individuals
C. Working according to the needs and aspiration of an individual
D. None of the above

26. Social work provides services to :
A. Weaker and vulnerable sections
B. People with emotional stress
C. People with the maladjustment
D. All the above

27. Social work believes in :
A. Evolutionary Approach
B. Revolutionary Approach
C. Evolutionary as well as Revolutionary Approach
D. Neither Evolutionary nor Revolutionary Approach

28. In India which of the following is different from the pattern of Western training?
A. Social Casework
B. Social Group Work
C. Psychiatric Social Work
D. Labour Welfare

29. Social Work is a profession only because :
A. It has a value base and community sanction
B. It assures jobs to graduating students
C. It is concerned with charity
D. It has a body of knowledge and practice within the framework of values

30. Servants of India Society was established by :
A. Bal Gangadhar Tilak
B. Lala Lajpat Rai
C. Rabindranath Tagore
D. Gopal Krishan Gokhale

31. The American Association of School of Social Work was founded in :
A. 1924 B. 1919
C. 1911 D. 1932

32. Professional Journal titled "Social Work and Development Issues" was started by :
A. Udaipur School of Social Work
B. Indian Society of Professional Social Workers
C. Indian Association of Professionally Trained Social Workers
D. Association of Schools of Social Work in India

33. Professional Journal titled "Contemporary Social Work" was started by :
A. Udaipur School of Social Work
B. Department of Social Work, Lucknow University, Lucknow
C. Indian Association of Professionally Trained Social Workers
D. National Association of Professional Social Workers in India

34. Professional Journal titled "Indian Journal of Social Work" was started by ;
A. Udaipur School of Social Work
B. Department of Social Work, Lucknow University, Lucknow
C. Tata Institute of Social Sciences, Mumbai
D. Association of Schools of Social Work in India

35. Professional Journal titled "Perspectives in Social Work" was started by :
A. Udaipur School of Social Work
B. Department of Social Work, Lucknow University, Lucknow
C. Tata Institute of Social Sciences, Mumbai
D. Nirmla Niketan, Mumbai

36. Council on social work education was established in the year :
A. 1952 B. 1947
C. 1936 D. 1949

37. Identify the correct sequence :
A. Radical social work, Social diagnosis, Unitary approach
B. Social diagnosis, Unitary approach, Radical social work
C. Unitary approach, Radical social work, Social diagnosis
D. Unitary approach, Social diagnosis, Radical social work

38. Which of the following is NOT a professional Social Work journal?
A. Indian Journal of Social Work
B. Contemporary Social Work
C. National Journal of Professional Social Work
D. Social Science Gazetteer

39. The author of the book 'From Charity to Social Work' is :
A. Mary Richmond
C. Friedlander, W
B. Elizabeth. N. Agnew
D. Jane Adams

40. Which one of the following is MOST suitable for bringing about changes in a social system?
A. Social welfare administration
B. Community organisation
C. Social action
D. Social work research

41. Social Work practice with adolescents should maximally focus on:
A. Recreation
B. Recreation and Health
C. Recreation and Self-growth
D. None of the above

42. Match the pairs :

1. The Industrial Disputes Act		(i) 1961
2. The Maternity Benefit Act		(ii) 1948
3. The Contract Labour Act		(iii) 1947
4. The Minimum Wages Act		(iv) 1970

Codes :

	1	2	3	4
(A)	(iii)	(i)	(iv)	(ii)
(B)	(iv)	(ii)	(i)	(iii)
(C)	(i)	(ii)	(iii)	(iv)
(D)	(ii)	(iii)	(iv)	(i)

43. Social work promotes development to :
A. Realize of potentials
B. Promote social justice
C. Increase in Sarva Dharma Sambhav
D. All the above

44. Social Work primarily aims at :
A. Economic Betterment
B. Political Participation
C. Effective social functioning
D. Physical well-being

45. Values of Social Work are :
A. Democratic
B. Humanitarian
C. Democratic as well as humanitarian
D. Sectarian

46. Social work in India is primarily :
A. a social technique
B. a social engineering
C. a social profession
D. None of the above

47. In which year the central Social Welfare board was established to promote voluntarism in Social Welfare?
A. 1951 B. 1952
C. 1953 D. 1954

48. Who was the first chairperson of the central Social Welfare board ?
A. Jawahar Lal Nehru
B. Morarji Desai
C. Durga Bai Deshmukh
D. B.R. Ambedkar

49. Indicate which one of the following is not an assumption of Social case work.
A. Every human being is to be respected
B. Every human being can change
C. Every human being has a right to be heard
D. Every human being is a child of God.

50. Social Work knowledge is :
A. Composite
B. Distinctive
C. Composite as well as distinctive
D. Neither composite nor distinctive

51. The Scots Charitable Society was founded in the year
A. 1657 B. 1660
C. 1663 D. 1647

52. Juvenile Justice (Care and Protection of Children) Act has been enacted in :
A. 1985 B. 1986
C. 1987 D. 2000

53. Who has propounded the "Theory of Trusteeship"?
A. Ravindranath Tagore
B. Vinoba Bhave
C. Mahatama Gandhi
D. Jawahar Lal Nehru

54. "Constructive Programme" was launched by:
A. Jai Prakash Narayan
B. Ram Manohar Lohia
C. Mahatma Gandhi
D. Vinobha Bhave

55. The first school of social work established in India was named as :
A. Tata Institute of Social Sciences
B. Tata Institutes of Social Reforms
C. Tata Institute of Social Work

D. Sir Dorabji Tata Graduate School of Social Work

56. The First School of Social Work in India was established in:
A. Delhi B. Madras
C. Bombay D. Calcutta

57. Social Work is NOT related with:
A. Education
B. Physics
C. Home Science
D. Public Administration

58. Social Work is closely related with :
A. Biology B. Social Psychology
C. Geo-physics D. Bio-chemistry

59. Major tool of Social Work is:
A. Motivations B. Relationship
C. Conscious Ego D. All the above

60. Components of Social Case Work have been propounded by:
A. Aptekar B. Mary Richmond
C. Perlman D. Hamilton

61. Widow Re-marriage was advocated most by:
A. Iswar Chandra Vidhyasagar
B. Vidhan Chandra Rai
C. Ravindra Nath Tagore
D. Raja Ram Mohan Rai

62. Which one of the following factors is primarily responsible for problems of Indian tribes ?
A. Civil and Criminal Laws
B. Restrictive Forest Policy
C. Land Revenue Policies
D. All the above

63. Who established the Depressed Classes Welfare League?
A. Baba Saheb Bhimrao Ambedkar
B. Balkrishna Gokhale
C. Lokmanya Tilak
D. Mahatama Gandhi

64. Which one of the following is NOT an objective of marriage?
A. Satisfaction of individual interests
B. Constitution of family
C. Fulfilment of sexual desires
D. Upbringing of Children

65. Principle of "Panch Sheel" was propounded by:
A. Mahatma Gandhi
B. Jawahar Lal Nehru
C. Vinoba Bhave
D. Jai Prakash Narayan

66. The call for "Sampoorna Kranti" was given by:
A. Lal Bahadur Shastri
B. Jai Prakash Narayan
C. Ram Manohar Lohia
D. Raj Narain

67. "Jai Jawan Jai Kisan" slogan was given by:
A. Ram Manohar Lohia
B. Jawahar Lal Nehru
C. Acharya Narendra Dev
D. Lal Bahadur Shastri

68. "Garibi Hatao" slogan was coined by:
A. Indira Gandhi B. Rajiv Gandhi
C. Sanjay Gandhi D. Sonia Gandhi

69. "Sarva Dharm Sambhav" was propounded by:
A. Mahatma Gandhi
B. Jawahar Lal Nehru
C. Vinoba Bhave
D. Indira Gandhi

70. Chipko Movement is associated with :
A. Save Animal B. Save Trees
C. Save Water D. Save Children

71. Kaka Kalelkar is associated with :
A. Scheduled Caste Commission
B. Scheduled Tribe Commission
C. Backward Classes Commission
D. Women Commission

72. Which one of the following is NOT a research design :
A. Exploratory B. Descriptive
C. Experimental D. Social Survey

73. Who had started the first school of social work in India:
A. G.D. Birla

B. S.P. Godrej
C. Sir Dorabjee Tata
D. M.K. Tata

74. NABARD stands for :
A. National Agricultural Bank for Rural Development
B. National Association of Blind for Rural Development
C. National Association of Banks for Rural Development
D. None of the above

75. Arrange in sequence :
A. Tabulation, Data Entry, Scrutiny
B. Scrutiny, Data Entry, Tabulation
C. Data Entry, Scrutiny, Tabulation
D. Tabulation, Scrutiny, Data Entry

76. Acceptance is a principle of social work which implies:-
A. Accepting client in his/her appearance
B. Extending warm welcome to the client
C. Accepting the client as she/he is
D. Accepting the client's version as it is

77. Friedlander has classified primary values of social work into:
A. 2 categories B. 3 categories
C. 4 categories D. 5 categories

78. The Poor Law enacted in the Elizabethan England is also referred as :
A. Elizabeth 40 B. Elizabeth 41
C. Elizabeth 42 D. Elizabeth 43

79. Sturdy Beggars are also termed as:
A. Able bodies poor
B. Rural Poor
C. Disabled poor
D. Urban Poor

80. The statement "caste is a closed group" has been given by:
A. T.B. Bottomore B. Andre Betelle
C. D.N. Mazumdar D. Mac Iver

81. Who among the following gave the concept of "in-group, out-group"?
A. W.G. Sumner B. C.H. Cooley
C. R.K. Merton D. R. Linton

82. Which of the following tools, a social researcher may use in studying social reality of an illiterate population?
(i) Questionnaire
(ii) Schedule
(iii) Field notes
(iv) Interview
A. (i) only
B. (ii) and (iii) only
C. (ii), (iii) and (iv) only
D. (i), (ii), (iii) and (iv)

83. A marriage in which a women of higher cast marries a man of a lower caste is known as:
A. Exogamy B. Hypergamy
C. Endogamy D. Hypogamy

84. According to the traditional Hindu belief marriage is :
A. A romantic union
B. A religious sacrament
C. A contract
D. None of these

85. Consider the following statements and select your answer according to the codes given below :
Assertion (A) : An essential feature of a healthy family is its cohesiveness.
Reason (R) : Cohesiveness facilitates healthy parenting.
A. Both (A) and (R) are true and (R) is the correct explanation of (A)
B. Both (A) and (R) are true but (R) is not the correct explanation of (A)
C. (A) is true but (R) is not true
D. (A) is not true but (R) is true

86. Mary Richmond is associated with:
A. Social Action
B. Community Organisation
C. Social Group Work
D. Social Case Work

87. The first school to provide Social Work training in India was established in:
A. 1936 AD B. 1946 AD
C. 1926 AD D. 1916 AD

88. Social Work does NOT solve :
A. Psychological Problems
B. Emotional Problems
C. Physical Problems
D. Social Problems

89. Which one of the following is NOT an auxiliary method of Social Work?
A. Community Organization
B. Social Group Work
C. Social Welfare Administration
D. Social Casework

90. Widow remarriage was advocated most by :
A. Raja Ram Mohan Roy
B. Vidhan Chandra Rai
C. Rabindranath Tagore
D. None of the above

91. Professional social work is based on:
A. Humanitarian Philosophy
B. Technical Skills
C. Scientific Knowledge
D. All the above

92. Aim of social work is:
A. To enhance the capacity of individual to adjust
B. To provide happiness and satisfaction to individual
C. To develop capacity for self-help by developing individual on the basis of social justice
D. All the above

93. The ultimate aim of social work research is:
A. To develop theories
B. To give recommendations on social issues
C. To find out solution to social problems
D. To develop all the above

94. Theory of 'Differential Association' was propounded by:
A. Neumeyer B. Merton
C. Sutherland D. Reckless

95. The theory that 'criminals are born' was propounded by:
A. Ferri B. Baccaria
C. Lombroso D. Benthem

96. Panchayati Raj Institution in India have brought about one of the following :
A. Eradication of untouchability
B. Spread of land ownership to the Depressed Classes
C. A formal representation of the weaker sections in village governance
D. Spread of education to the masses

97. The book, Community Welfare Organisation-principles and practice, has been written by :
A. K.D. Gangrade B. Murray G. Ross
C. M.S. Gore D. Arthur Dunham

98. The term Ageism refers to :
A. Provision of welfare services to the aged
B. The negative attitudes towards the aged
C. The positive attitudes towards the aged
D. None of the above

99. Maslow's hierarchy of needs, which need stands at the top is?
A. Self esteem
B. Self actualisation
C. Social acceptance
D. None of the above

100. Provision of drinking water facility fulfils women's :
A. Strategic need B. Practical need
C. Immediate need D. Longterm need

101. Match the items in List-I with items in the List-II select the correct answer using the codes:

List-I	List-II
1. 15th June	(i) World Alzheimer's Day
2. 12th January	(ii) Women's Day
3. 8th March	(iii) National Youth Day
4. 21st September	(iv) World's AIDS Day
	(v) World Elder Abuse Day

Codes :

	1	2	3	4
A.	(v)	(iii)	(ii)	(i)
B.	(iii)	(v)	(ii)	(iv)
C.	(ii)	(iv)	(v)	(iii)
D.	(iii)	(i)	(v)	(ii)

102. 'Operation Black Board' refers to :

A. Improvement of non-formal education in villages

B. Improvement of. basic facilities in primary schools

C. Improvement of Education of girls

D. Improvement of Vocational education

103. Under the Right to information Act, The Chief Appeleate Authority is :

A. Chief Justice of High Court

B. Chief Information Commission

C. Registrar, Information Commission

D. None of the above

104. Which of the following is not a principle of social case work :

A. Confidentiality

B. Non-judgemental attitude

C. Self-determination

D. Specific objectives

105. Family members are :

A. Category

B. Primary group

C. Secondary group

D. Mob

106. Which of the following statement is correct:

A. Caste is based on the individual's position

B. Caste is determined by occupational mobility

C. Caste is created by Lord Brahma

D. Caste is determined by birth

107. Probation of Offenders Act came into being in the year :

A. 1948 B. 1952

C. 1958 D. 1962

108. Which of the following articles in the Directive Principles of State Policy of Indian Constitution Articulates the protection of schedule caste from any form of exploitation:

A. Article 36 B. Article 46

C. Article 30 D. Article 28

109. Who gave the acronym 'POSDCORB' to list the functions of Social Welfare Administration?

A. Amitai Etizioni

B. Luther Gullick

C. H.B. Trecker

D. Awasthi and Maheshwari

110. Bhoodan Movement was started by :

A. Vinoba Bhave

B. Gopal Krishna Gokhale

C. Rama Bai

D. Sardar Patel

111. Which one of the following is not part of group processes ?

A. sub-group

B. group diagnosis

C. clique

D. isolation of a member in the group

112. Recognition of an individuals positive worth as a human being without necessarily condemning the individuals acting is termed as :

A. Recognition B. Acceptance

C. Admission D. Approval

113. Which one of the following is not secondary data in research ?

A. Information collected from Journals

B. Information collected from Reports

C. Information collected from Respondents

D. Information collected from Websites

114. Where is the National Institute for Empowerment of persons with multiple disabilities located ?

A. Chennai B. Mumbai

C. Delhi D. Hyderabad

115. Which one of the following is not the objective of an NGO ?

A. Capacity Building

B. Awareness Building

C. Spread of Literacy

D. Profit Making

116. Who, from the following list, is NOT an environmental activist ?

A. Sundarlal Bahuguna

B. Medha Patkar

C. Dr. Vandana Shiva

D. M.S. Gore

117. Which one of the following is NOT a technique of case work ?
A. Interviewing B. Observation
C. Counselling D. Lobbying

118. While working with an individual client on a one-to-one basis, the relationship is :
A. a friendly association
B. a contract
C. purposeful to meet the psycho-social needs of the client
D. a sympathetic understanding of the client

119. Which one of the following constitutes the main basis of a Welfare State in India ?
A. Fundamental Rights
B. Directive Principles of State Policy
C. Judicial Independence
D. Public Interest Litigation

120. Which one of the following authors has contributed exclusively in the area of social group work ?
A. Hollis B. Murray Ross
C. Trecker D. Perlman

121. Psychoanalytic theory about human personality was proposed by :
A. Carl Jung B. Skinner
C. Sigmund Freud D. Alfred Adler

122. The book 'Social Diagnosis' is authored by:
A. Murray Ross B. Mary Richmond
C. Fried Lander D. Helen Perlman

123. People's needs occur in ascending order. The view was proposed by :
A. Freud B. Watson
C. Maslow D. Jung

124. Mean, Mode and Median are :
A. Measures of Central Tendency
B. Measures of Correlation
C. Measures of Dispersion
D. Measures of Time Series

125. Regulation XVII of 1829 of Lord Bentinck was enacted to :
A. Ban Sati
B. Encourage widow remarriage
C. Ban child marriage
D. None of the above

126. Consider the following statements and select your answer according to the codes given below :

Assertion (A) : The Poor Laws were enacted in England.

Reason (R) : To help the poor to have better working conditions.
A. Both (A) and (R) are true and (R) is the explanation of (A).
B. Both (A) and (R) are not true
C. (A) is true but (R) is false
D. (A) is not true but (R) is true

127. Integrated social work practice takes into account the following :
(a) The client system
(b) The change agent system
(c) Action system
(d) Agency system
Indicate the correct answer
A. (a), (b) and (c) are correct
B. (b), (c) and (d) are correct
C. (a), (c) and (d) are correct
D. (a), (b), (c) and (d) are correct

128. Professional Supervision in Social Work is best described as :
A. Evaluating the performance of the supervisee
B. Making sure that the supervisee does not make a mistake
C. Helping the supervisee acquire social work knowledge, skills and values
D. Reflecting with the supervisee and be a guide
Indicate which is the correct answer
A. (a) and (b) are correct answer
B. (b) and (c) are correct answer
C. (a) and (c) are correct answer
D. (c) and (d) are correct answer

129. Consider the following statements and select your answer according to the codes given below :

Assertion (A) : Professional Social Work has not taken root in India.

Reason (R) : People are too poor to pay for the services.

A. Both (A) and (R) are true and (R) is correct the explanation of (A).
B. Both (A) and (R) are true but (R) is not the correct explanation of (A).
C. (A) is true but (R) is false
D. (A) is not true but (R) is true

130. Society in sociological terms is understood to mean :
A. A group of refined people
B. An organisation to undertake some constructive activities
C. A web of relationships
D. An association to honour scholarship

131. Which one of the following is the correct statement regarding social change as a concept ?
A. Social change has a direction
B. Social change is controlled
C. Social change is structured
D. Social change is value neutral

132. Which one of the following shows the correct evolutionary order in which various types of societies emerged ?
A. Tribal, rural, urban
B. Tribal, urban, rural
C. Urban, rural, tribal
D. Rural, tribal, urban

133. Which one of the following does not feature in the Indian constitution ?
A. Federal structure
B. Unitary government
C. Separation of judiciary
D. Fundamental rights of the citizens

134. New Economic Policy in India is characterised by :
(a) Privatization (b) Globalization
(c) Safety Nets (d) Liberalization

Choose the correct answer using the following code :
A. (a) and (b)
B. (a), (b) and (c)
C. (a), (b) and (d)
D. (a), (b), (c) and (d)

135. Match List-I and List-II and select the correct answer by using the codes given below :

List-I Type of Therapy	**List-II Proponent**
(a) Client Centred Therapy	(1) William Glasser
(b) Behaviour Therapy	(2) Carl Rogers
(c) Transactional Analysis	(3) Joseph Wolpe
(d) Reality Therapy	(4) Eric Betne

Codes :

	(a)	(b)	(c)	(d)
A.	(2)	(3)	(4)	(1)
B.	(3)	(4)	(1)	(2)
C.	(4)	(3)	(2)	(1)
D.	(3)	(1)	(2)	(4)

136. Match List-I and List-II and select the appropriate answer by using the codes given below :

List I Level of Intervention	**List II Action of Social Worker**
(a) Micro Level	(1) With disabled child
(b) Mezzo Level	(2) Working with Panchayat for water harvesting
(c) Macro Level	(3) Working with self-help group of cancer patients

Codes :

	(a)	(b)	(c)
A.	(1)	(2)	(3)
B.	(1)	(3)	(2)
C.	(3)	(2)	(1)
D.	(2)	(1)	(3)

137. Who among the following is associated with the Gestalt system of therapy ?
A. C. R. Rogers
B. Sigmund Freud
C. F.S. Perls and Laura P. Perls
D. B.F. Skinner

138. The Elizabethan Poor Law Act was enacted in the year.
A. 1601
B. 1605
C. 1635
D. None of the Above

139. The 1215 Magna Carta in England establishes human rights for
A. Beggars B. Privileged Class
C. Orphans D. All the Above

140. The book 'Social Diagnosis' was written by
A. Marry Richmond
B. GR Banerji
C. Mirza R Ahmed
D. Murli Desai

141. The First Charity Organization Society was established in the year
A. 1847 B. 1874
C. 1867 D. 1877

142. The First United States Settlement house was established in the year
A. 1886 B. 1887
C. 1902 D. 1874

143. A New Cultural order called 'Din E Ilahi' was founded in India by
A. Akbar
B. Mohd. Bin Tuglak
C. Bahadurshah Jafar
D. None of the Above

144. "Papers on social work-An Indian perspective" was written by
A. G R Banarjee B. G R Madan
C. Sachdev D. None of the Above

145. Who is the author of the book "Social Group Work-A Helping Process"?
A. Wilson G and Ryland
B. Trecker H.B.
C. Philips H.U.
D. Konopka G

146. Who is the author of the book "Social Case Work-A Problem Solving Process"?
A. H.H.Perlman B. M.G. Ross
C. Philips H.U. D. Konopka G

147. Who is the author of the book "Community Organisation-Theory and Practice"?
A. H. H. Perlman
B. M.G.Ross
C. Marry Richmond
D. Konopka G

148. Who is the author of the book "Introduction to Social Work''?
A. Skimod and Thakery
B. M.G.Ross
C. Marry Richmond
D. Konopka G

149. The goal of social work is:
A. To reduce social tension
B. To provide service to all
C. To promote social justice
D. To service the elite

150. Satyashodhak Samaj was founded by:
A. Dr.B.R.Ambedkar
B. Ramesh Bhandari
C. Jyotiba Phule
D. Anna Hazare

151. Which one of the following is not a social legislation?
A. Protection of civil rights act
B. Beggars act
C. Right to information act
D. Forest conservation act

152. The oldest social security legislation in India is
A. Employee Compensation Act
B. Provident Fund Act
C. Maternity Benefit Act
D. Payment of Gratuity Act

153. Which of the following is not an objective of social policy in India?
A. Equality
B. Social Justice
C. Inclusive Growth
D. Population Growth

154. Field Work based approach is classified as:
A. Empirical B. Historical
C. Experimental D. Biographical

155. Who from the following is not a social activist?
A. Arundhati Roy
B. Medha Patkar
C. Dr.P.D.Kulkarni
D. Anna Hazare

156. The toll free number 1098 is related to
- A. Women help line
- B. Child help line
- C. Police help line
- D. None of the above

157. Servants of India society was established by
- A. Gopal Krishna Gokhale
- B. Ram Krishna Paramhans
- C. Swami Dayanand Saraswati
- D. Mahatma Gandhi

ANSWERS

1	**2**	**3**	**4**	**5**	**6**	**7**	**8**	**9**	**10**
B	B	A	C	B	D	C	C	A	A
11	**12**	**13**	**14**	**15**	**16**	**17**	**18**	**19**	**20**
D	B	C	D	A	C	A	A	C	B
21	**22**	**23**	**24**	**25**	**26**	**27**	**28**	**29**	**30**
D	D	C	D	C	D	C	D	C	D
31	**32**	**33**	**34**	**35**	**36**	**37**	**38**	**39**	**40**
B	A	B	C	D	A	B	D	A	C
41	**42**	**43**	**44**	**45**	**46**	**47**	**48**	**49**	**50**
C	A	D	C	C	C	C	C	D	C
51	**52**	**53**	**54**	**55**	**56**	**57**	**58**	**59**	**60**
A	B	C	C	D	C	B	B	D	C
61	**62**	**63**	**64**	**65**	**66**	**67**	**68**	**69**	**70**
A	D	A	A	B	B	D	A	A	B
71	**72**	**73**	**74**	**75**	**76**	**77**	**78**	**79**	**80**
C	D	C	A	B	C	C	D	A	C
81	**82**	**83**	**84**	**85**	**86**	**87**	**88**	**89**	**90**
A	C	B	B	A	D	A	C	C	D
91	**92**	**93**	**94**	**95**	**96**	**97**	**98**	**99**	**100**
D	D	D	C	C	C	D	C	B	C
101	**102**	**103**	**104**	**105**	**106**	**107**	**108**	**109**	**110**
A	B	B	D	B	D	C	B	B	A
111	**112**	**113**	**114**	**115**	**116**	**117**	**118**	**119**	**120**
D	B	C	A	D	D	D	B	B	C
121	**122**	**123**	**124**	**125**	**126**	**127**	**128**	**129**	**130**
C	B	C	A	A	A	D	D	C	C
131	**132**	**133**	**134**	**135**	**136**	**137**	**138**	**139**	**140**
D	A	B	C	A	B	C	A	B	A
141	**142**	**143**	**144**	**145**	**146**	**147**	**148**	**149**	**150**
D	A	A	A	D	A	B	A	C	C
151	**152**	**153**	**154**	**155**	**156**	**157**			
D	A	D	A	C	B	A			

➢➢➢➢➢

CHAPTER

2

Society

SOCIETY

In common language the concept of Society is used to designate the members of specific in-group, persons rather than social relationship of those persons. Thus, we speak of Brahmin society, but in sociology, the term 'society' refers not to a group of people but to the complex pattern of the norms of interaction that arise among them. The important aspect of society is the system of relationships, the pattern of norms of interaction by which the members of the society maintain themselves. Thus, the relations which are not organised in definite associations are excluded from the definition of society. According to Giddings a number of likeminded individuals, who know and enjoy their like mindedness, and are, therefore, able to work together for common ends forms the society.

Some Definitions

MacIver and Page: "Society" is a system of usages and procedures, authority and mutual aid, of many groupings and divisions of controls of human behaviours and of liberties.

Ginsberg: A 'Society' is a collection of individuals united by certain relations or modes of behaviour which mark them off from others who do not enter into these relations or who differs from them in behaviour.

COMMUNITY

MacIver defines community as "an area of social living marked by some degree of social coherence". A man cannot live or exist alone. He is connected in many ways to his fellows who form a group. As the man could not become the member of all the existing groups. He can establish and maintain relations only with the people who inhabit near him in a certain part of the territory. The people who over any duration of time inhabit in a particular locality should develop social likeliness, should have common social idea, common traditions and the sense of belongingness. All these common factors give birth to community.

Some Definitions of Community

Lundberg: "Community is a human population living within a limited geographical area and carrying on a common inter dependent life."

Bogardus: "Community is a social group with some degree of we feeling and living in a given area."

Characteristics of Community

(1) **Group of people:** Community is a group of people.

(2) **Locality:** The group of people forms a community when it begins to reside in a definite locality.

(3) **Sentiments or Belongingness:** The belongingness means feeling of community sentiments that developed among community people while residing together.

(4) **Permanency:** Community is unlike crowd. It basically includes a permanent life in a definite place.

(5) **Not made by act of will:** Communities are not made or created by an act of will but are natural.

(6) **Commonness:** Community shares common language, customs, morals etc.

(7) **Specific Name:** Every community have some specific name.

(8) **Wider ends:** In communities the people associate not for the fulfillment of a particular end. The ends of a community are wider. These are natural and not artificial.

Difference between Community and Society

Community is the group of people who live together in a specific area or locality and share common life. The community people also have community sentiments.

Society includes every relation which is established among the people. Society has no definite boundary, in fact it is universal. Society is the name of our social relationship. On the contrary, community is the group of people living together in a particular locality. Community is the part of society and exists within society and possesses its distinguishable structure which differentiates it from other communities. Society is a web of social relationship which cannot be seen or touched. It is an abstract concept. On the contrary, community is a concrete concept. It is a group of people residing together in a geographical area having a sense of belongingness.

SOCIAL STRUCTURE

Social structure is a basic concept in sociology. Since long several efforts have been made to define 'social structure' but still there is no unanimity of opinion on its definition.

According to S.F. Nadel: Social structure refers to the network of social relationship which is created among the human being when they interact with each other according to their status and according with the patterns of society.

According to Talcott Parsons: Social Structure is a term applied to the particular arrangement of the interrelated institutions agencies and social patterns as well as the status and roles which each person assumes in the groups.

From the above definitions we can understand social structure as :

(1) Social structures is a abstract phenomenon.

(2) It refers to the external aspects of society.

(3) Individual is the unit of social association, social institutions and these social association and institutions are part of social structure.

(4) These institutions and associations are interrelated and created the pattern of social structure.

(5) Social structure is a patternised arrangement of human relationship structures.

SOCIAL INSTITUTION

Institutions have been defined by MacIver as the established forms or conditions of procedures characteristics of group activity. According to Summer, institutions consist of a concept (idea, notion, doctrine or interest) and a structure. The institutions are collective ways of behaviour or a way of doing things and bind the group member together. For example family, school, temple, state and many other are the institutions of society.

SOCIAL GROUPS

A man is social animal, who can't live in isolation; most of the routine activity that a man performs is in group. Therefore a social group is collections of human beings.

According to Bogardus – A social group may be thought of a number of persons, two or more, who have some common objects of attentions who are stimulating to each other, who have common loyalties and participate in similar activities.

Horton and Hunt – Groups are aggregates of categories of people who have consciousness of membership and of interaction.

Characteristics of Social Group

(1) **Mutual relationship:** The groups members are interrelated to each other. A gathering of individuals forms a social group only when they are interrelated.

(2) **Senses of unity:** The members of a group are united by a sense of unity and a feeling of sympathy.

(3) **We feeling:** The members of a groups help each other and defend their interest collectively.

(4) **Common Interests:** The interests of the groups members are common. It is for the realization of the common interest that they meet together.

(5) **Similar Behaviour:** The members of a group behave in a similar way to achieve common interest.

(6) **Group Norms:** Every group has its own rules or norms which the members are supposed to follow.

CLASSIFICATION OF GROUPS

Dwight Sanderson suggested a three fold classification of social groups. He classified them into involuntary, voluntary and delegate groups. Tonnis classified groups 'in communities and associations'. Cooley classified groups on the basis of kind of contact into primary and secondary groups. In a primary group there is a face-to-face and intimate relationship such the family. In Secondary group relationships are indirect, secondary or impersonal such as political party.

F.H. Giddings classified groups into genetic and congregate. The genetic group is the family in which a man born involuntarily. The congregate group is the voluntary group into which he moves or which he joins voluntarily. George Hasen classifies groups on the basis of their relations to other groups into unsocial, psedo-social, antisocial or pro-social. Meller divided social groups into horizontal and vertical groups. Charles A Ellwood distinguished among involuntary and voluntary, institutional and non-institutional, temporary and permanent group.

Summer made distinction between an in-group and out-group. The groups with which the individual identifies himself are his in-groups such as family, friend's religion etc. An out-group consists of those persons, whether formally organized or not, towards whom we feel the sense of indifference, avoidance, disgust, competition or outright conflict. The distinction between in-group and out-group is usually expressed in the contrast between "they" and "we" for example, we are democrats, they are communists. Such attitude that 'these are my people' and 'those are not my people' produce a sense of attachment to the other members of in-group while a sense of indifference with the members of out-group.

Cooley's Classification

Primary Group: A Primary group is a small group in which a small number of persons come into direct contact with one another. They meet face-to-face for mutual help, companionship and discuss on common questions. They live in the presence and thought about one another.

Secondary Group: A secondary group is one which is large in size such as a city, nation or political party. Here, human contacts become superficial and undefined. The relationship of the members are limited in scope and arrived at by much trial and error and in terms of self-interest calculations of the members.

Reference groups: Man is an imitative animal. The desire to imitate others individuals is instinctive in him. When one finds another person progressing in life, he also desire to progress like him. He compares himself with other and begins behaving like them in order to reach their status and positions. Such behaviour after comparisons with other is called reference behaviour. The concept of social reference group behaviour was given by Hayman later, Turner, Merton and Sheriff further elaborated this concept.

SOCIAL STRATIFICATION

The society is heterogeneous in nature; we find rich and poor industrialists and peasantry, the rulers and beggars; everywhere society is divided into various classes—economic, political, social and religious. The process by which individuals and groups are ranked in more or less hierarchy of status is known as stratification.

According to Raymond W. Murray, "Social stratification is a horizontal division of society into "higher", "lower" and "social units". Sorokin pointed out "unstratified society" with real equality of its members is a myth which has never been realized in the history of mankind. According to him social stratification means the differentiation of a given population into hierarchically superposed classes.

THEORIES OF SOCIAL CHANGE

Sociologists, historians and social anthropologists have proposed a number of general theories of social change. These theories may conveniently be grouped into four main categories: Evolutionary, cyclic, conflict theories and functional theories.

1. Evolutionary Theory

Evolutionary theories are based on the assumption that societies gradually change from simple beginning into even more complex forms. Early sociologists beginning with Auguste Comte believed that human societies evolve in a unilinar way—that is one line of development.

According to them social change means "Progress" towards something better. They saw change as positive and beneficial. To them evolutionary process implied that societies would necessarily reach new and higher level of civilization. Morgan, for examples, believed that there were three basic stages in the process savagery, barbarism and civilization. Auguste Comte's ideas relating to the three stages in the development of human thought and also of society are namely the theological, the metaphysical and the political.

2. Cyclical Theory

Cyclical theories of social change focus on the rise and fall of the civilization attempting to discover and account of these patterns of growth and decay. Spangler, Toynbee and Sorokin can be regarded as the champion of this theory. Their ideas may be briefed here.

(a) **Spangler—The Destiny of Civilization:** Spangler in his book "The Decline of the West" 1918, pointed out that the fate of civilization was a matter of destiny. Each civilization is like a biological organism and has a similar life-cycle of birth, maturity, old age and death. He said that modern western society is entering a period of decay as evidenced by wars, conflicts and social breakdown that heralded their doom. The theory is almost out of fashion today.

(b) **Toynbee—Challenge and Response:** Toynbee a British historian with enough sociological insight has offered a somewhat more promising a theory of social change. In his famous book "A study of History" Toynbee explained the key concept of "challenge and response." Every society faces challenges, at first challenges posed by the environment later challenges from internal and external enemies. The nature of response determines the society's fate. The achievement of a civilization consists of its successful responses to challenges if it cannot mount an effective response it dies.

(c) **Sorokin—Sensate and Ideational Culture:** Sorokin in his book "Social and Cultural Dynamics" 1938, has offered his explanation of social change. Instead of viewing civilisation into terms of development and decline he proposed that they alternate or fluctuate between two cultural extremes: The sensate and the ideational culture. The sensate culture stresses those things which can he perceived directly by the senses. It is practical, sensual and materialistic. Ideational culture emphasizes those things which can be perceived only by mind. It is abstract, religious, concerned with faith and ultimate truth. It is opposite of sensate culture.

Functionalists Theories

Talcott Parsons and his followers have been the main advocates of this theory. Parsons stressed on the importance of culture in controlling the stability of a society. According to him society has the ability to absorb disruptive forces while maintaining overall stability. Because it is 'constantly straining for equilibrium or balance' the conservative forces of society such as shared norms and values resist radical changes and serve to hold the society together.

Deterministic Theories of Social Change

The deterministic theory of social change is a widely accepted theory of social change among the scholars. According to this theory there are certain forces, social or natural or both, which bring about social change. It is not reason or intellect but the presence of certain forces and circumstances which determine the course of social change. Summer and Keller insisted that social change is automatically determined by economic factors. Keller maintained that conscientious efforts and rational planning have very little chance to effect change unless and until the folkways and mores ready for it.

Conflict Theory

The most famous and influential of the conflict theories is the one put forward by Karl Marx, a famous German social thinker and philosopher. 'All history is the history of class conflicts' wrote Marx and Angels in the Communist Manifesto. "Violence is the midwife of history", Marx declared. Individuals and groups with opposing interests are bound to be in conflict—Marx asserted. Since the two major social classes, that is the rich and the poor or capitalist and labourers have mutually hostile interests, they are at conflict. History is actually the history of conflict between the exploiting (the rich) and the exploited (the poor) classes. They consider conflict as normal and not an abnormal process. They also believe that "The existing condition of any society contain the seeds of future social changes."

Social Disorganization

Society is dynamic in nature when the various parts of society are properly adjusted, we have a well organised society but when they fail to adjust themselves to the changing conditions the result is social disorganisation leading to social problems.

Emile Durkheim defined social disorganization as a state of disequilibrium and lack of social solidarity or consensus among the members of a society." According to R.E.L. Faris, "Social disorganization is a disturbance in the patterns and mechanism of human relations. According to Elliott and Merrill, "Social disorganization is the process by which the relationships between the members of the groups are broken or dissolved." Thus, Social disorganization can be said as the process by which the relationship between the members of social group, whether a family, a society or a nation are broken down or dissolved.

APPROACH OF SOCIAL DISORGANIZATION

The Social Problem Approach

According to this approach maladjustment delayed the human progress and happiness. Social problems were regarded as 'the disease of society' which threatened the welfare of the groups. This approach also suggests that social problems existed in those societies where individual and collective deviation considered society desirable.

The Bio-Psychological Approach

The theory is given by Gobinean and his followers. According to them the decay of all societies is the result of social admixture of races not equal in capability. The social problem arises out of the lack of capabilities of the members of inferior classes. They were of the opinion that disorganization of the society was the direct outgrowth of deficiencies in the biological make up passed on from generation to generation through heredity.

The Geographical Approach

The geographical approach assumes that the superiority of culture or the backwardness of the peoples is due to geographical factor of which the most important are the land and water resources, climate, soil, minerals, natural flora and fauna temperature, natural change of seasons, phenomena of gravitation, storms, earthquakes, sea current rainfall etc. Geographical factors have brought about crime, illiteracy, suicide, divorce and insanity.

The Cultural Lag Approach

This approach of social disorganization is known as cultural lag approach of Ogburn. According to this approach social problems develop in the area of lag between the adoption of material changes and the formulation of appropriate social institution. The process of social change in which current social institutions do not satisfy human needs and different aspects of culture are not synchronized is thus, called 'disorganization'. We can understand various forms of social disorganisation like unemployment, depression, poverty crime through cultural lag theory. The term cultural lag explained by Ogburn is based upon the distinctions between material and non-material culture. Rapid changes takes place in material culture whereas slow changes in non-material culture. According to this approach the disorganisation of modern family system is the result of lag in the continued functioning of a failure to develop suitable substitute for the old folkways and moral governing family relations.

THE RURAL COMMUNITY

The earliest human communities were perhaps the loosely organised aggregations of a few facilities that carried on mutually interdependent activities in gathering food and defending themselves against their enemies. Gradually man acquired skills and knowledge in agriculture food and begin to live settled life in villages. It is difficult to define villages but generally it is understood as a small area with a small population which follows agriculture not only as an occupation but also as a way of life.

Characteristic Features of Village/ Rural Communities

The rural community marked by several features the important one are the following :

(1) **Community Consciousness:** The dwellers of rural community have a sense of unity. The relation between the people is intimate. They personally know each other customs and traditions.

(2) **Role of Neighbourhood:** In rural community neighbourhood plays an important role. There is not enough individuality and people pay attention to their neighbour in his sorrows and joys in the village. People assist each other and thus they have closest neighbourhood relations.

(3) **Joint Family:** In rural communities we can still see very strong joint family system. People live together in a close tie with their brothers and sisters. The agriculture occupation also requires the cooperation of all the members.

(4) **Faith in Religion:** The rural people have deep faith in religion and deities. Their main occupation is agriculture which largely depends upon the change of nature. The rural people acquire an attitude of fear and respect towards natural forces and start worshipping them.

(5) **Simplicity:** The rural people live a simple life and remain far away from the evils of modern civilization. Generally they are simple people believing in God. Their behaviour is natural not artificial and they live a peaceful life.

Characteristic Features of Urban Community

(1) **Namelessness:** According to the observations of Bogardus urban communities have a reputation for namelessness. By virtue of its size and population there cannot be a primacy group. The members of a city do not come into primary contact with each

other. Usually they met and speak without knowing each others name, basically life of the citizens of a city are mechanical. A citizen may live for several years in a city and may not know the names of one-third of the people who live in the same city area.

(2) **Homelessness:** Homelessness is another distinguish feature of city community. The problem of shelter in a city is very common and many people pass their life homeless in city and are forced to live in slums.

(3) **Class Extremes:** Class extremes characterize urban community. In a city one can find the richest as well as the poorest people, the people rolling in luxury and living in a grand mansion as well as the people living on pavement and hardly getting two meals a day.

(4) **Social Heterogeneity:** The urban areas are more heterogeneous than the rural areas. We can see a cosmopolitan culture and melting pot of races, people and culture and is a most favourable breeding ground of new biological and cultural hybrids.

Social Distance

Social distance in an urban area is mainly focused due to anonymity and heterogeneity. The city dwellers feel lonely. Most routine contracts are impersonal and segmented, formal politeness takes the place of genuine friendliness.

Energy and Speed

Residual of urban area work with tremendous energy and speed, day and night which stimulate other also to work. Similarly in urban areas people indulge in too many activities and inconceivable efforts. Urban life also produces greater emotional tension and insecurity that is unlike rural communities.

Urban Community

Generally by an urban area we mean an area with high density of population which characterized by its size heterogeneity, social differentiation and stratification, mobility, environment and system of interaction. The census of India 2011 defines urban area as follows:

(1) All places with municipality, corporation, cantonment board or notified town area committee etc.

(2) All other places which satisfied the following requirements:

- A minimum population of 5000
- At least 75% of the working population engaged in non-agriculture pursuits and
- A density of population at least 400 persons per square kilometer.

TRIBAL COMMUNITY

According to Oxford dictionary "A tribe is a group of people in a primitive or barbarous stage of development acknowledging the authority of chief and usually regarding themselves as having a common ancestor."

D.N. Majumdar define tribe as a social group with territorial affiliation, endogamous with no specialization of functions ruled by tribe officers hereditary or otherwise united in language or dialect recognizing social distance with other tribes or castes.

The Constitution of India defines scheduled tribes under Article 366(25) as "such tribes or tribal communities or parts of groups within such tribes or tribal communities as are deemed under Article 342 to be scheduled tribe for the purpose of this constitution".

The established criterion followed for specification of a community as scheduled tribe are indication of primitive traits, distinctive culture, geographical isolation, shyness of contact with the community at large and backwardness.

T.B. Naik has given the following features of tribes in Indian context:

(1) A tribe should have least functional interdependence within the community.

(2) It should be economically backward (i.e., primitive means of exploiting natural resources, tribal economy should be at an

underdeveloped stage and it should have multifarious economic pursuits).

(3) There should be a comparative geographical isolation of its people.

(4) They should have a common dialect.

(5) Tribe should be politically organized and community panchayat should be influential.

(6) A tribe should have customary laws.

Weaker Sections

It is difficult to define weaker sections as there is no uniformly accepted definition. There are some sections of society which might be considered as weaker sections due to their social and economical backwardness. Such as Scheduled Castes, which are traditionally regarded as 'untouchables' and socially disadvantaged. The scheduled tribe, which are geographically isolated not in the mainstream of the society living with primitive traits and other backward class, who are educationally and socially backward also considered weaker section of the society. The women, that constitutes almost half of the population but having minimum economic and political power also considered as weaker sections of the society.

Vulnerable Section

It is difficult to distinguish between weaker and vulnerable sections as many people use them interchangeably, some factors are common in weaker and vulnerable section as both sections combined form the disadvantaged group of the society and need special attention of the civil society and the government. We can include certain section under vulnerable section such as – children, aged and physically or mentally challenged people irrespective of their caste or class in the society. Their incapability due to their disability or age can easily exposed in the social, economical and ecological adversity.

MINORITY GROUP

A minority group is a sociological category within a demographic, the term refers to a category that is differentiated and defined by the social majority, that is, those who hold the majority of positions of social power in a society. The differentiation between majority and minority can based on one or more observable human characteristics including for example, ethnicity, race, gender wealth, health or sexual orientation.

Sociologist Louis Wirth defined a minority group as "a group of people, because of their physical or cultural characteristics are singled out from the others in the society in which they live for deferential and unequal treatment, and who therefore, regard themselves as object of collective discrimination". Minority group in a society can be categorized into many category such as:-

(1) **Racial or ethnic minorities:** Every society contains ethnic minorities and linguistic minorities. Their life style, language, culture and origin can differ from the majority. The minority status is conditioned not only by clearly numerical relations but also by question of political power. Such as Blacks in South Africa under apartheid.

(2) **Gender and sexuality minorities:** In most of the societies including India men and women are considered equal still some people perceive status of women as a 'subordinate' group has laid some to equate them with minority. The lesbian, gay, bisexual and transgender people are also considered as sexual minorities.

(3) **Religious Minorities:** Person belonging to religious minorities have a faith which is different from that hold by the majority. Most countries including India have religious minorities, for example, Islam, Christianity, Jainism, Sikhism considered as minority group in India.

POPULATION

The population of the world has grown from a few person to 7.141 billion people. It has been estimated by United Nations Food and Agriculture Organisation that nearly 870 million people are suffering from chronic undernourishment and around 1.29 billion population were living in absolute poverty in 2008 estimated by United Nations and World Bank. One in every five people of the planet is illiterate and 205 million people are unemployed in the world.

The world which fails to support the present population could not support more inhabitants. The science of population sometimes called the demography represents the study of statistics such as births, deaths, income or the incidence of disease, which explain the changing structure of human population.

Theories of Population

Thomas Robert Malthus was the first economist who proposed a systematic theory of population. He articulated his views in his book 'Essay on the Principle of Population' (1978). Malthus proposed the principle that human populations grow exponentially (*i.e.*, doubling with each cycle) while food production grows at an arithmetic rate (*i.e.*, by the repeated addition of a uniform increment in each uniform interval of time). Thus, while food output was likely to increase in a series of twenty five year intervals in the arithmetic progression 1, 2, 3, 4, 5, 6, 7, 8, 9 and so on population was capable of increasing in geometric progression 1, 2, 4, 8, 16, 32, 64, 128, 256 and so forth.

This scenario of arithmetic food growth with simultaneous geometric human population growth predicted a future when humans would have no resources to survive on. To avoid such a situation, Malthus urged control on population growth.

Demographic Transition Theory

Two different interpretations have been given for this theory. One by Frank Notestein and W.S. Thompson which says that every country passed through three stages of population growth.

1. High birth rate and high death rate
2. High birth rate and low death rate (population explosion)
3. Low birth rate and low death rate

The theory says the developed nation approaching a new equilibrium with both birth rates and death rates quite low and little population growth. The other theory is given by C.P. Blacker. There are four phases in this theory.

(1) Early expanding phase marked by high fertility but declining mortality
(2) Late expanding phase with declining fertility but mortality declining more rapidly
(3) Low stationary phase with cow fertility and equally cow mortality
(4) Declining phase with low mortality, low fertility and an excess of deaths over births.

Optimum Theory of Population

The theory has been propounded by Cannan. According to him there is direct relationship between the size of population and available resources in the country. He divided the world into three categories:

(1) **Over populated:** If due to increase in the population per capita income begins to fall, the country is said to be over populated.
(2) **Under populated:** If the number of people are less than the resources of the country and they are unable to make full use of these resources the country is said to be under populated.
(3) **Optimum size of population:** When the size of population is according to the size of natural resources, in this case per capita output will be maximum and country is said to have an ideal size of population or optimum population.

POVERTY

Poverty is not only a challenge for India, as more than one-fifth of the world poor live in India alone, but also for the world, where more than 260 million poor are not been able to meet their basic needs. Poverty has many faces, which have been changing from place-to-place and across time and has been described in many ways. Most often poverty is a situation that people want to escape. In all localities and neighbourhoods, both in rural and urban areas, there are some who are poor and some who are rich. There are many people who belong to this category such as push cart vendors, street cobblers, rag pickers; Vendors, beggars are some examples of poor and vulnerable groups in urban areas. They possess few assets. They reside in Kutcha helmets; the poorest of them do not have even such dwelling. Two scholars, Shaheem Rafi Khan and Damian Killer put the conditions of the poor in a nutshell:

"Poverty is hunger, poverty is being sick and not being able to see a doctor, poverty is not been able to go to school and not knowing how to read, poverty is not having job. Poverty is fear for the future, having food once in a day. Poverty is losing a child to illness, brought about by unclear water, poverty is powerlessness, lack of representation and freedom".

Categorizing Poverty

There are many ways to categories poverty. In one such way people who are always poor and those who are usually poor but who many sometimes have a little more money (example casual workers) and grouped together as the chronic poor. Another group is the churning poor who regularly move in and out of poverty (example—small farmers and seasonal workers) and the occasionally poor who are rich most of the time but may sometimes have a patch of bad luck and then, those who are never poor and they are non-poor.

The Poverty Line

There are many ways of measuring poverty, one way is to determine it by the monetary value (per capita expenditure), of the minimum calorie intake that was estimated at 2,400 calories for a rural person and 2,100 for a person in the urban area. Based on this in 1999-2000, the poverty line was defined for rural areas as consumption worth ₹ 328 per person a month and for urban areas it was ₹ 454.

THE FEATURES OF NEW ECONOMIC POLICY 1991

The New Economic Policy has been adapted by the country in the year 1991 by the then Finance Minister Dr. Manmohan Singh under the regime of Prime Minister Narsimha Rao. It was considered that opening of economy will result in to economic growth, progress and social development.

The main characteristics of new Economic Policy 1991 are:

- **Delicencing:** Only six industries were kept under Licensing scheme.
- **Entry to Private Sector:** The role of public sector was limited only to four industries; rest all the industries were opened for private sector also.
- **Disinvestment:** Disinvestment was carried out in many public sector enterprises.
- **Liberalisation of Foreign Policy:** The limit of foreign equity was raised to 100% in many activities, *i.e.*, NRI and foreign investors were permitted to invest in Indian companies.
- **Liberalisation in Technical Area:** Automatic permission was given to Indian companies for signing technology agreements with foreign companies.
- **Setting up of Foreign Investment Promotion Board (FIPB):** This board was set up to promote and bring foreign investment in India.
- **Setting up of Small Scale Industries:** Various benefits were offered to small scale industries.

Three Major Components or Elements of New Economic Policy

There are three major components or elements of new economic policy-Liberalisation, Privatisation, Globalisation.

1. Liberalisation

Liberalisation refers to end of license, quota and many more restrictions and controls which were put on industries before 1991. Indian companies got liberalisation in the following way:

- Abolition of license except in few.
- No restriction on expansion or contraction of business activities.

- Freedom in fixing prices.
- Liberalisation in import and export.
- Easy and simplifying the procedure to attract foreign capital in India.
- Freedom in movement of goods and services.
- Freedom in fixing the prices of goods and services.

2. Privatisation

Privatisation refers to giving greater role to private sector and reducing the role of public sector. To execute policy of privatisation government took the following steps:

- Disinvestment of public sector, *i.e.*, transfer of public sector enterprise to private sector.
- Setting up of Board of Industrial and Financial Reconstruction (BIFR). This board was set up to revive sick units in public sector enterprises suffering loss.
- Dilution of Stake of the Government. If in the process of disinvestments private sector acquires more than 51% shares then it results in transfer of ownership and management to the private sector.

3. Globalisation

It refers to integration of various economies of world. Till 1991 Indian government was following strict policy in regard to import and foreign investment in regard to licensing of imports, tariff, restrictions, etc. but after new policy government adopted policy of globalisation by taking following measures:

- Import Liberalization. Government removed many restrictions from import of capital goods.
- Foreign Exchange Regulation Act (FERA) was replaced by Foreign Exchange Management Act (FEMA).
- Rationalization of Tariff structure.
- Abolition of Export duty.
- Reduction of Import duty.

As a result of globalization physical boundaries and political boundaries remained no barriers for business enterprise. Whole world becomes a global village. Globalisation involves greater interac ion and interdependence among the various nations of global economy.

THE POSITIVE AND NEGATIVE IMPACTS OF GLOBALIZATION

Globalization has had far reaching consequences to both the people living in India and the economy in general. Defining what is meant by globalization is important in the assessment of its advantages and disadvantages to India. This is particularly crucial since the exclusion of those who clearly support the phenomenon in its present form, that is, those who believe that globalization has many advantages and that these advantages will automatically be felt by the poor, also hold various and divergent views concerning this process. People, who are opposed to globalization or those concerned with its possible detrimental impacts on employment and poverty, constitute a wide political spectrum. It has been opposed from the perspective of economic and cultural nationalism by the extreme Right while liberals on the other hand are concerned about the loss of national sovereignty since globalization minimizes the effectiveness of the government to intervene in the regulation of labour and capital, eradicate poverty, among other things (Hensman 2000).

According to Guy Brainbant, the process of globalization encompasses the opening up of world trade, the establishment of advanced communication methods, financial market internalization, increased importance of multinational companies, the migration of populations, increased mobility of people, goods, ideas, capital, pollution, data, diseases and infections. The term not only refers to the integration of global economies through unrestricted trade and financial flows but also exchanges in knowledge and technology.

Globalization also includes unrestricted movement of labour between countries. Within the context of India, globalization means that the economy is being opened up to direct foreign investment by making facilities available to the foreign companies so that they may invest in various sectors of economic activities in India, clearing of obstacles and constraints to the entry of multinational companies in India, allowing collaboration between Indian and foreign companies and also encouraging the Indian companies to take part in foreign ventures.

Advantages of Globalization

There are numerous implications of globalization on the national economy. The phenomenon has intensified competition and interdependence between economies in the global market.

- In India, the economic reforms have resulted in the overall economic growth.
- The growth in the Gross Domestic Product has improved the global position of India.
- Due to globalization, the service sector is now the main driver of Indian economy.
- The overall rate of growth of India's economy is one of the major advantages of globalization in India owing to the fact that during the 1970s, its rate of growth was as low as 3 per cent.
- Foreign direct investment has also increased due to globalization in India.
- All these have helped the speeding up of growth of Indian economy. Globalization has seen an increase in the number of fortune companies in India.
- The implication is that there are more employment opportunities than before.
- This also means that the standards of living have been raised with more wealthy people being created due to the numerous opportunities that exist within the country.
- The liberalization of trade which consequently led to flexibilities in business policies to allow for equal opportunities for multinational companies has therefore resulted in desirable impacts for the overall Indian economy.
- New technologies and products have been introduced in India and this has created new opportunities.
- The multinational companies have made big investments and set up research and development centers which have brought about positive impacts in the lives of Indian people.
- As a result, India is among the leading countries in information technology, business processing and research and development investments.
- Globalization has also had positive impacts on the social and cultural realm. By opening new opportunities for employment, globalization has improved both economic and social life of individuals.
- The standard of living has been raised and more Indians can now enjoy the luxuries that were not known to them before.
- The perceptions of ordinary Indians have also been changed through increased cultural interaction through mediums. Indian companies are now gaining more recognition in the global arena than before.
- Products from other parts of the world are also finding their way into the Indian market with more people being in a position to purchase them owing to improved economic conditions.
- More Indians can also access goods from other parts of the world owing to reduced prices.
- Generally, globalization has improved the economic life of Indians due to more job opportunities as people are no longer worried about government jobs; there are numerous multinational companies that pay more attractive salaries than the government. As such, Indians have gained more from globalization in ways that are beneficial to both the state and the individuals within the state.

Disadvantages of Globalization

As much as there has been numerous economic gains attached to globalization in India, there are also disadvantages.

- The rapid growth of industries due to globalization has not brought about benefits for everyone.
- There are various sectors that this growth has further aggravated the conditions of particular groups within the Indian society.
- Globalization has brought about rapid growth in the informal sector which has resulted in undesirable impacts on the working population.
- As much as it has led to the creation of jobs for many individuals, globalization is also contributing to the suffering of people within the informal sector.
- The multinational companies mainly investing in the 'zero technology' market and threatening to India's small scale and cottage industries.
- It is important to note that the informal sector is deliberately not included in the labour legislation. For instance, informal workers are not subject to the 1948 Factories Act which covers the general working conditions, working hours, safety and health, prohibition of child labour, basic amenities among other things (Stone 1996). With globalization finding its way into India, it is clear that its consequences have been undesirable for workers in the informal sector.
- Globalization has resulted in poor health, deplorable working conditions and bondage.
- Employers have been able to impose working conditions that are extremely hazardous due to chronic insecurity among worker. For instance, the construction industry which is the second largest employer in India has not taken into consideration the working conditions of its employers. The employers are not concerned about the hazards involved. The proportion of fatal accidents is very high with some of the causes of serious injuries and deaths being crushes under collapsing structures, electrocution, and being buried under mud (Menon 1999).
- The negative impact of globalization is also felt in the Indian agricultural sector. A great number of labourers in this sector come from the 'Scheduled Castes and Tribes'. In other words, they are from communities that are most exploited economically and oppressed socially under the caste system. The plight of this population has been worsened by globalization owing to the need to increase production to meet the growing demand from the global markets.
- As such, globalization has resulted in increased poverty and difficulties among particular populations in the Indian society.
- Human beings have been turned into machines simply because of the need to increase profits and be competitive in the global market.
- Apart from these impacts on particular groups, globalization has also contributed to the destruction of the environment through pollution and clearing of vegetation cover. With the construction of companies, the emissions from manufacturing plants are contributing to environmental pollution which further affects the health of many individuals.

Globalization has had both desirable and undesirable consequences for India. These consequences have been felt from the general economy to more specific conditions of life for the individual. As mentioned, globalization has resulted in the growth of Indian economy which in turn has improved the lives of many people. It has also created many employment opportunities. However, it has also widened the gap between the rich and the poor part from resulting in more oppression for those at the bottom of the social ladder. However, it may be said that globalization is inevitable in the twenty first century despite these disadvantages considering the advances in information technology which has led to more integration between nations. Various ills such as inequality that it has created are also some of its inevitable consequences which results from the competitive environment and the need to increase production so as to meet the growing global demand.

CONSTITUTIONAL HISTORY

- Parliamentary control over East India Company began with the Regulation Act, 1773. Written Constitution prepared first time for the company along with the establishment of a Supreme Court in Calcutta.
- The Amendment Act of 1781 authorized the Calcutta Government to make law for Bengal, Orissa and Bihar, with a directive to lay stress on the respect of socio-religious customs of Indians in the process of law making.
- Fox Ministry resigned due to failure of Fox Indian Bill, 1783 for the first time the resignation of a British Cabinet on an Indian issue.
- The Pitts Indian Act empowered the Governor-General and the Board of Control to superintend direct and control all operations of the Civil and military Govt. of the British Possessions in India.
- Through the Charter Act of 1813 Indian trade was thrown open to all British merchants but trade in tea and trade with China were still exclusive to the company.
- The Charter Act of 1833 cancelled the Company's rights to trade in tea and trade with China. The Governor-General of Bengal was henceforth to be styled as the Governor-General in council.
- The Charter Act of 1853 took a decisive step in separating the legislative machinery from the executive. This was the last Charter Act of British India.
- Indian Council Act of 1861 brought about the beginning of the representative institutions. For the first time Indians were, associated with the work of legislation.
- The Indian Council Act, 1892 introduced the election system partially.
- The introduction of Separate Electorate was the basic fault of the Indian Council Act, 1909 or Morley Minto Reforms.
- The Government of India Act, 1919 introduced a system of Dyarchy in the provinces. The provincial matters were divided into 'reserved' and 'transferred'.
- The Government of India Act, 1935 provided for the establishment of an All India Federation. Under this Act Union Bank and Federal Court were respectively established in 1935 and 1937.
- 16 August, 1946 was declared as the Direct Action Day by the Muslim league.
- The Cabinet Mission of 1946 was consisted of three members A.V. Alexander, Patrice Lawrence and Sir Stafford Cripps.
- The Indian Independence Act was presented in the British parliament on July, 1947 which attained Royal consent on July 18, 1947.

The Preamble

- The preamble makes clear that the source of the constitution is the people of India.
- The preamble helps where the language of the constitution is vague.
- The words 'Socialist', 'Secular' and the 'Unity and integrity' of the nation were added by the 42nd Amendment Act of 1976.
- The Supreme Court expressed the view that 'the Preamble is the key to its makers'.
- Justice Madholkar said in Sajjan Singh *vs.* Rajasthan State case that the Preamble is the sum and substance of the Constitution.
- In the Golaknath *vs.* Punjab State case, Justice Hidaytullah remarked that the Preamble is the synopsis of those principles on which the government has to work upon.
- The objective of the constitution is to secure Justice, Liberty, Equality and Fraternity for every Citizen.

Members of the Drafting Committee

1. Dr. B.R. Ambedkar – Chairperson
2. Alladi Krishna Swami Ayyar
3. K.M. Munshi
4. K.G.S. Ayangar
5. Md. Sadullah
6. N. Madhav Rao (In place of B.L. Mitra)
7. D.P. Khetan (T. Krishnamachari after Khetan's death in 1948)

Making of the Constitution

- Constituent Assembly was formed according to the proposals of the Cabinet Mission.
- The idea of a Constituent Assembly was propounded by M.N. Roy.
- Election was held in November 1946 to form a Constituent Assembly when there were 389 members. The reorganised Constituent Assembly had 299 members.
- The first sitting of the Constituent Assembly was held on 9 December, 1946 with its pro-speaker Dr. Sachchidanand Sinha, Dr. Rajendra Prasad bacame the permanent speaker after two days.
- The process of making the Constitution began on 13 December, 1946 with the introduction of an "Objective proposal" by J.L. Nehru.
- B.N. Rao was appointed the Constitutional Advisor of the Assembly.
- On 29th August, 1947, it set up the Drafting Committee under the chairmanship of Dr. B.R. Ambedkar.
- The draft of the Constitution was conferred to the Assembly on 8th February, 1948.
- The Constituent Assembly next met in November 1948 and the whole work was completed on October 17, 1949.
- The coping stone was placed on 26 November, 1949 when the Preamble was adopted to complete the structure of the Basic Law of the land.
- The President of the Assembly Dr. Rajendra Prasad placed his signatures and declared it as finally passed.
- Some of the provisions as those relating to citizenship, elections, provisional Parliament, temporary and transitional provisions were given immediate effect.
- The Constituent Assembly turned into Interim parliament on 26 January, 1950 with the appointment of Dr. Rajendra Prasád as the president of the Union.
- It took 2 years 11 months and 18 days to finish the whole work.
- There were 395 articles and 8 schedules in the Constitution when it was finally passed.
- At present it consists 448 Articles in 26 parts, 12 schedules, 5 appendices and 98 amendments.
- The Constitution of India is the largest written constitution of the worlds.
- The first sitting of the Constituent Assembly was boycotted by Muslim league.

INDIAN UNION

- Article 1 says: India, that is Bharat, shall be a Union of 'States'. The States and Territories there of shall be specified in the first schedule.
- The Territory of India shall comprise (a) the territories of the states, (b) the Union Territories and (c) such other territories as may be acquired.
- The Fazl Ali or States Reorganization Commission submitted its report in 1955 and the Act came into force in 1956.
- At present there are 29 States and 7 Union Territories in India.
- As per Article merit may by law admit into the union or establish new states on such terms and conditions as it thinks.
- Under Art. 3, the parliament is empowered to form a new state by separation of territory from any state of by merging two or more states or part of states or by uniting any territory to a part of any state.

- The Parliament can increase or diminish the area of any state or to alter the boundaries or names of any state.
- A Bill, giving effect to any or all the changes, can be introduced in either House of the Parliament only on the recommendation of the President.
- The President, before introducing it in the Parliament, shall refer the Bill to the State Legislature concerned for its opinion must be expressed by the State Legislature.
- The President is not bound to accept or act upon the views of the state legislature.
- Any change concerning the name and the boundary of the State Jammu and Kashmir can be created by its state legislature.
- The parliament has the rights only to organise the new states or to create the boundaries or names of existing states.
- Meanwhile the making of the new states and their entrance has been mentioned in the constitution but there is no provision for separation of state areas. So, the ninth amendment of the constitution had been done for mergence of Rubari State area into Pakistan.
- At the time of Independence there were nine British provinces and 542 princely states in India.
- V.B. Patel is known as "Bismark of India" because the integration of the princely states had been done by S.V.B. Patel.
- In 1912, the reorganisation of the States had been done on Linguistic basis, when Bihar, Orissa and Assam were created. On the linguistic basis Andhra Pradesh was the first state in Independent India.
- By the means of 7th amendment of the constitution in 1956 the four categories of the States ended.
- In the year 1956, the states were reorganized by State Reorganisation Act. According to this there were 14 states and 5 union territories, at that time.
- In 1956 the 6th union territory Pondicherry was formed by merging French areas.
- In 1961 Goa, Daman and Diu became 7th union territory.
- In 1987 Goa was converted, into full fledged state.
- At present there are 29 states and 7 union territories in Indian Union.
- There is no freedom for separation of units of Indian Union from the Union.

CITIZENSHIP

There is provision for single citizenship in India. On the other hand, there is provision for double citizenship in America and Switzerland. In these Countries a person can acquire citizenship through birth place, (state) as well as national citizenship. But there is single citizenship in India even for people from different states.

In Indian Constitution, citizenship is mentioned from Article 5 to Article 11 under Section 2. Under Article 11 Indian Parliaments can change citizenship rules whenever it will be necessary. By this power, parliament passed the Citizenship Act 1955. In this Act many amendments have been done in the year 1986 and 1992. There is provision for acquisition and termination of citizenship in this act.

FUNDAMENTAL DUTIES

Originally there was no description of fundamental duties in the constitution. The 42nd Constitution amendment act has inserted Part IV-A with Art. 51A having a set of fundamental duties.

There are 10 fundamental duties which have been mentioned in Indian Constitution. According to which, it shall be the duty of every citizen of India

(i) To obey the rules of the constitution and respect its ideals, institution and the national anthem and the national flag.

(ii) To cherish and follow the noble ideals which inspired our national struggle for freedom.

(iii) To protect the Sovereignty, unity and integrity.

(iv) To defend the country and render national service when called upon to do so.

(v) To boost harmony and the spirit of common brotherhood amongst all the people of India transcending religious linguistic and regional or sectional diversities.

(vi) To value and preserve the rich heritage of our composite culture.

(vii) To protect and improve the natural environment including forests, lakes, rivers and wildlife and to have love for living things.

(viii) To develop the scientific temper, humanism and the spirit of inquiry and reform.

(ix) To safeguard public property and to abjure violence.

(x) To strive for excellence in all spheres of individual and collective activity so that the nation constantly rises to higher levels of endeavour and achievement.

THE DIRECTIVE PRINCIPLES OF STATE POLICY

The directive principles of state policy has been mentioned under Part IV of the constitution. Article 37 says that the directive principles are fundamental in the governance of the country and it will be the duty of the state of apply these principles in making laws.

Art. 38 : The state will strive to promote, the welfare of the People and complete development of the social system.

Art. 39 : The state will, in particular direct its policy toward securing

(i) the men and the women equally have the right to earn their money for life.

(ii) that the ownership in & control of the material resources of the community are so distributed 4s best to subserve the common goods.

(iii) that the operation of the economic system does not result in the concentration of wealth to the common detriment.

(iv) that there is equal pay for equal work for both men and women.

(v) that the health and strength of workers, men and women and, the tender age of children are not abused.

Art. 40 : The state shall take steps to organise village panchayats as a unit of self-government.

Art. 41 : The state will: within the limits of its economic capacity and development, make effective provision for securing the right to work, to education and to public assistance in cases of unemployment, old age, sickness and disablement.

Art. 42 : The state will make provisions for securing just and humane conditions of work and for maternity relief.

Art. 43 : The state will endeavour to secure to all workers, agricultural, industrial or otherwise, work, a living wage and the state will responsible to promote cottage industries.

Art. 44 : The state will try to secure for the citizens a uniform civil code throughout the territory of India.

Art. 45 : The state will endeavour to provide, within a period of 10 years from the Commencement of this constitution free and compulsory education ιor all children until they complete the age of fourteen years.

Art. 46 : The state shall promote with special care for the, educational and economic interests of the weaker sections of the people in particular of the scheduled castes and the scheduled tribes.

Art. 47 : The state will regulate the raising of the level of the nutrition and the standard of living of its people and the state will endeavour to bring about prohibition of drinks and of drugs which are injurious to health.

Art. 48 : The state will endeavour to protect and improve the environment and to safeguard the forests and wildlife of the country.

Art. 49 : State will protect every historical monument or place of object of artistic nature.

Art. 50 : The state will separate the judiciary from the executive in the public services of the state.

Art. 51 : The state will endeavour to

(a) promote international peace and security.

(b) maintain honourable relation in between nations.

(c) respect for international law and people with one another

(c) encourage settlement of international disputes by arbitration.

Directive Principles Added after 42th Amendment (1976)

Art. 39 (B): The children should be educated in fresh and prestigious environment.

Art. 39 (A) : The legal system promotes justice on a basis of equal opportunity and will in particular provide free legal aid by suitable legislation

Art. 43 (A) : To secure the participation of workers in the management of undertaking engaged in any industry.

Art. 48 (A) : To protect the environment and to safeguard the forests and wildlife of the country.

Directive Principles Added after 44th Amendment (1978)

Art. 39 (B) : The state shall, in particular strive to minimise the inequalities in income and endeavour to eliminate inequalities in status facilities and opportunities not only amongst groups of people residing in different areas.

Directive Principles mentioned in other part of the Constitution

Art. 350: It is duty of the officers of concern states to provide primary education in mother tongue to the people of minorities particularly to the children of minorities class.

Art. 351: It will be duty of the union to spread Hindi language amongst the people of India which will develop our cultural and social element.

INDIA'S DEVELOPMENT MODEL

Prior to Indians development planning there was debate and discussion on what model of planned development India should adopt. The choice was between capitalist and socialist model. Market economy or capitalism depends on the market forces of supply and demand, in a capitalist model only those consumer goods will be produced that are in demand, *i.e.*, goods that are in demand. In a capitalist society the goods produced are distributed among people not on the basis of what people need but on the basis of what people can offered and are willing to purchase. This means that a patient will be able to use required medicine only if he/she can afford to purchase it, if he or she cannot afford to purchase it, if he or she will not able to use it even if they need it urgently. In a socialist model the government decides what goods are to be produced in accordance with the need of society. It is assumed that government knows everything about problems needs and aspiration of the country and individual desires are not given due importance. Under socialism model distribution is supposed to be based on what people need and not on what they could afford to purchase.

For example – In a socialist society free health care for its people provided by the state, a socialist society has no private property since everything is owned by the state.

In both the models capitalist and socialist have some drawbacks and limitations. The Indian government adopted a middle path known as mixed economy or democratic socialism. In the mixed economy the government and the market together answer the questions of what and how to produce and how to distribute what is produced. In a mixed economy the market produce whatever they can produce well and government produce and provide essential goods and services which the market fails to do.

- Mahalanobis model is a neo-Marxist model of economic development created independently by society economist G.A. Fedman in 1928 and Indian statistician Prasanta Chandra Mahalanobis in 1953.
- D.D. Dhar was a man who proposed the fifth five years plan (1974-79) having main objectives of poverty removal, self-reliance

high growth rate and domestic scorings. The fifth five year plan was terminated due to change in government in 1978.

- The concept of five years plan is borrowed from the Soviet Union.

WELFARE STATE

The concept of welfare state indicates about a government or state which seeks to ensure the maximum happiness of maximum number of people being with its territory. A welfare state also denotes efficient administration, speedy justice, a state totally free from corruption and inefficiency. Along with this a welfare state expect social welfare legislation, adequate health and medical facilities for the weaker and vulnerable section of the society.

Our constitution seek to establishes India as a welfare state. The Preamble of the Constitution clearly indicates 'general welfare' of the people as one of the objectives of the union of India. The Preamble aims to secure to all its citizen justice—social, economic and political, liberty of thought, expression, belief, faith and worship, equality of status and opportunity.

This concept is further strengthened by the Directive Principle of State Policy which set out the economic, social and political goal of the Indian constitution system. The directive principles of state policy gives directions to the state to achieve and maximize social welfare and basic social values like education, employment, health etc.

UNEMPLOYMENT

The unemployment rate in the country during 2012-13 was estimated to be 13.3 per cent of the age group 15-29, a government report has revealed.

The labour ministry report on youth employment-unemployment scenario 2012-13 further revealed unemployment rate among the person who cannot read and write any language or are considered illiterate was the lowest with 3.7 per cent without work in the 15-29 age group.

It said one out of every three persons in the age group 15 to 29 years who have completed at least their graduation has been found to be unemployed.

Based on the survey the report said that unemployment rate at all India level was 133 person out of 1000 person for the age group 15-29 years.

Although the problem of Youth unemployment and under employment is prevalent around the world because young people lack skills, work expressions, job search ability and financial resources to find employment.

An unemployed person is one who is an active member of labour force and is able to and seek work but is unable to find work during specified period say a week, a month or a year. Unemployment can be classified into following categories.

(1) **Structural Unemployment:** This type of unemployment is associated with economic structure of the country. When demand for labour falls short to supply of labour due to rapidly growing population and their immobility, the problem of unemployment appears in the economy. Besides, due to growing population, rate of capital formation falls down which again limits the employment opportunities. This type of structural unemployment is basically related to this category of unemployment.

(2) **Under-Employment:** Those labourers are under-employment who obtain work but their efficiency and capability are not utilized at their optimum and as a result they contribute in the production upto a limited level. A country having this type of unemployment fails to exploit the efficiency of their labourers.

(3) **Disguised unemployment:** If a person does not contribute any thing in the production process or in other words, if he can be removed from the work without affecting the productivity adversely, he will be treated as disguisedly unemployed. The marginal productivity of such unemployed person is zero. Agriculture sector of underdeveloped/developing economics

posses this type of unemployment at a large scale.

(4) **Open unemployment:** When the labourers live without any work and they don't find any work to do, they come under the category of open unemployment. Educate unemployment and unskilled labour unemployment are included in the open unemployment.

(5) **Educated unemployment:** Even when a person who is educated/trained and skilled, fails to obtain a suitable job suited to his qualifications, he is to be educated unemployed. Presently this type of unemployment has become a problem for developing economies, particularly for India.

(6) **Frictional unemployment:** The unemployment generated due to the change in market conditions is called frictional unemployment. Agriculture is the main occupation in India. The supply condition still depends on weather's mood and similarly demand conditions depend on availability of resources. Any change arising either of any or both creates a diversion from the equilibrium which results in frictional unemployment.

FIVE YEARS PLAN

First Five Years Plan (1951-56)

The basic objectives of our planning were growth, employment, self-reliance and social justice. At the first five years plan (1951-56) Indian was faced with three problems—influx of refugees, severe food shortage and mounting inflation. India has also current disequilibrium in the economy caused by the Second World War and the partition of the country. The objectives of the first five years plan were rehabilitation of refugee and rapid agriculture development. Although program could not make much headway because of the inadequate administrative structure and financial allocation. The establishment of central social welfare board in 1953 was the most significant achievement during this period. The state social welfare board was also set up to supplement the efforts of central social welfare board. At the end of the plan period in 1956 Indian Institute of Technology were started as major technical institute, University Grants Commission was also set up in November 1956 to take care of the higher education system of the country.

Second Five Years Plan (1956-61)

At this stage it was felt that Indian economy had reached a stage where agriculture could be assigned a lower priority and a forward thrust made in the development of heavy and basic industries of the economy for a more rapid advance in future. The basic philosophy of the second plan was thereof to give a big push to the economy so that it enters the take off stage. The government announced its industrial policy in 1956 accepting the establishment of socialistic pattern of society as the goal of economic policy. This necessitated the orientation of economic policy to confirm the national goal of 'socialist economy'.

It emphasized that "social welfare is concerned with the well being of entire community and not only of particular section of the society which may be handicapped in one way or other". Targeting the 25 per cent increase in the national income through rapid industrialization actual achievement was only 20 per cent. Hydroelectric power projects and five steel mills at Bhilai, Durgapur and Rourkela were established. The inputs on modern industrial development towards building a domestic consumptions good sector in India was given by a well known statistician Mr. Prasanta Chandra Mahalanobis also known as 'Mahalanobis Model'.

Third Five Years Plan (1961-66)

By beginning of third five years plan Indian planner felt that the Indian economy had entered in "Take off stage" and that the first two plan had generated an institution structure needed for rapid economic development. Consequently the third plan was set as its goal the establishment of self-reliant and self-generating economy. But the working of second plan had also shown that the rate of growth of agriculture production was the main limiting factor in India's economic development. The third plan accordingly gave top priority to agriculture but it also laid adequate emphasis on the development of the basic industries. However because of the conflict with China in 1962, Nehru's death in 1964, Pakistan War in 1965 and Shastri's death in 1966 the approach to the third plan was later shifted from development to defense. The third five years plan laid special emphasis on women and children welfare. Most significant event was the establishment of department of social welfare in the country in 1964. Providing for the first time a fully fledged administrative set up to sponsor and implement program.

Fourth Five Years Plan (1969-74)

Due to some disaster experience in last five years plan three annual plan (1966-69) described as plan holiday were implemented. The fourth plan set before itself the two principle objectives of "Growth with distributive justice" and "Progressive achievement of self reliance". The plan gave special attention to the need of the destitute children, family planning program and technical training. The Indira Gandhi government nationalized 14 major Indian banks, green revolution in some part of the country also advanced agriculture production.

Fifth Five Years Plan (1974-79)

The fifth plan was introduced at the time when the country reeling under a veritable economic crisis arising out of a runaway inflation and the hike in oil prices. The main objectives were set as removal of poverty and attainment of self-reliance through promotion of higher rate of growth and better distribution of income. Social welfare program such as minimum need program were introduced. Accordingly several new program were launched important among them was Integrated Child Development Scheme launched on 2nd October, 1975 popularly known as ICDS, National Policy on Children, 1974 and setting up of the National Children Board.

Sixth Five Years Plan (1980-85)

This model has criticized the Nehru model of development responsible for growing unemployment. For the concentration of economic power in the hand of few powerful business and industrial family for the widening of inequalities of income and wealth and for mounting of poverty.

The plan sought to reconcile the objectives of higher production with those of greater employment so that millions of people living below poverty line could benefit there from. Poverty alleviation was given priority and Integrated Rural Development Program, National Rural Youth Employment Program and Tribal Rural Youth for Self Employment scheme was launched. The sixth five years plan was a milestone in women development. First time the separate chapter for women and development was included in the plan document.

Seventh Five Years Plan (1985-90)

Country had enjoyed a reasonable rate of growth during the sixth plan. This plan sought to emphasis policies and programs which could accelerate the growth in foodgrain production, increase employment opportunity and raise productivity.

Social services and human resource development, employment guarantee program, National Rural Employment Program, Rural Landless Employment Guarantee Program, Self Employment Program for Urban Poor, Jawahar Rojgar Yojna, National Education Policy, 1986 and National Literacy Mission, 1988 were launched.

Eighth Five Years Plan (1992-97)

There was a series of changes in the government in the center. The fourth version of eighth five year plan was approved when the country was facing series of social and economic crisis. The Narsima Rao government initiated the process of fiscal reforms as also of economic reforms with a view to provide a new dimension to the economy. The eighth five years plan attempted to accelerate economic growth and improve the quality of life of the common man. The plan created facilities for universalization of elementary education, health for all by the year 2000, mid day meal program was also launched in August 1995.

Ninth Five Years Plan (1997-2002)

The focus of the ninth five years plan was "Growth with Social Justice and Equality". This objective was sought to be achieved through a policy of concentration on agriculture and rural development to provide more employment, ensuring food and nutrition security to all, providing basic minimum need, empowerment of women, sustainable development in rural areas and promotion of Panchayat Raj Institutions.

Tenth Five Years Plan (2002-2007)

There was a significant growth during last decade for the tenth five years plan following objectives was identified. Reduction of poverty ratio by 5 per cent points by 2007 and 15 per cent points by 2012, providing gainful high quality employment in the additional labour force over the 10th plan period, all children in school by 2003, all children to complete five years of school by 2007, increase literacy rate to 75 per cent by 2007, reduction of infant mortality rate to 45 per thousand live birth by 2007 and 28 by 2012, reduction of mothers mortality rate to 2 per thousand births by 2007 and 1 by 2012, increase forest and tree cover to 25 per cent by 2007 and 33 per cent by 2012. The tenth five years plan also saw the advent of National Rural Employment Guarantee Act, 2005. Social and economic empowerment of women and gender justice was also focused.

Eleventh Five Years Plan (2007-12)

The target set for the eleventh five years plan were as follows, create 70 million new work opportunities and reduce educated unemployment to below 5 per cent, raise real wage rate of unskilled workers by 20 per cent, reduce dropout rate of children from elementary school from 52.2 per cent in 2003-04 to 20 per cent by 2011-12, increase literacy rate of persons of age 7 years or above to 85 per cent, reduce infant mortality rate to 28 and maternal mortality ratio to 1 per 1000 live births, reduce total fertility rate to 2.1, provide clean drinking water for all by 2009, raise the sex ratio for age group 0-6 to 935 by 2011-12 and to 950 by 2016-17, connect every village by telephone by November 2007 and provide broad band connectivity to all villages by 2012, increase forest and tree cover by 5 percentage point. The National Rural Health Mission and The Right to Children to Free and Compulsory Education Act, 2009 was also enacted and launched during this period.

Twelfth Five Years Plan (2012-17)

The main objective of the twelfth five years plan is "Faster, sustainable and more inclusive growth". The plan aims towards betterment of the infrastructure projects as well as improving the conditions of SC, ST and OBC and minorities, generate at least 50 million employment opportunities for youth, eliminating gender and social gap in education, achieve universal road connectivity and access to power for all villages, access banking service for 90 per cent of households, major welfare facilities and subsidies through Aadhaar, enhance energy efficiency in all sectors with focus on renewable energy, *i.e.*, wind, solar and storage hydro. Overall the current five year plan combines the proper program approach with efforts to get a growth pattern which is faster and inherently more inclusive.

INTRODUCTION TO SOCIAL PROBLEM

Certain adverse situations that may have harmful consequences may affect societies. They may hinder the normal functioning of the society. Such harmful situations are known as social problems. These problems arise because every society has certain norms and values. When these norms and values are violated, they result in social problems. They are problems because such deviation of norms and values are dysfunctional in the society. Some of the examples of social problems are drug addiction, terrorism, youth unrest, juvenile delinquency, corruption, offences against women, environmental degradation, etc.

However, not all violations of social norms and values result in social problems. For example, when a person sports an unusual hairstyle it does not become a social problem. Similarly, social problem may vary with time and over space. Smoking was not considered a social problem earlier. At present with rising health consciousness, smoking is considered a major social problem. Similarly, sati was not considered as a problem in the medieval India. However, in modern India it is seen as a social problem.

A society may consider a certain practice as a social problem where as it may not be a problem in another society. This is because the norms and values are not the same in all the societies. Divorce may be seen as a serious problem in some societies, but it may not be so in other societies. However, there are certain practices that are considered harmful in all societies' viz. murder, terrorism, rape, etc.

Definition

Many scholars have tried to define social problem but it is difficult to arrive at a commonly accepted definition.

According to Fuller and Myers, a social problem is "a condition which is defined by a considerable number of persons as a deviation from some social norms which they cherish".

Merton and Nisbet define social problem as "a way of behaviour that is regarded by a substantial part of society as being in violation of one or more generally accepted or approved norms".

However, these two definitions are applicable for certain social problems like corruption, drug addiction and communalism. It is not applicable to problem like population explosion. Further some problems are caused not by the abnormal and deviant behaviour of the individuals but by the normal and accepted behaviour. For example, the degradation of the soil in certain regions of Punjab and Haryana is being caused by the accepted methods of farming.

Therefore, according to Carr, "a social problem exists whenever we become conscious of a difficulty, a gap between our preference and the reality".

Characteristics of Social Problems

On the basis of the above discussion and definitions, following characteristics of social problems can be deduced:

- All social problems are situations that have harmful consequences for the society.
- All social problems are deviations from the ideal situation.
- Social problems are caused by many factors.
- All these factors are social in origin.
- Social problems are interrelated.
- Social problems affect every individuals of the society.
- Social problems affect different individuals differently.

Social Problems in Indian Context

We have discussed that social problems vary with time. Similarly, social problems in India have changed with different historical phases. The major social problems in each of these phases reflect the then existing social norms and values.

The major social problems in the early phase of the Indian civilization were increasing rigidity of social hierarchy, continuous conflicts between the Aryans and the Dasas, emphasis on the observance of rituals, sacrifice of animals etc. With the advent of the Muslim rule in India, new social problems like *sati, purda,* introduction of caste system among the Muslims, etc. emerged.

In the contemporary phase, India is facing several social problems. We have the problems of terrorism, violence, offences against women, children and minorities, unemployment, poverty, drug addiction, communalism, youth unrest, corruption, migration and displacement, environmental degradation, population explosion, prostitution, HIV/AIDS, etc. These problems are the result of various factors that include economic, political, legal, cultural as well as historical.

Types of Social Problems

Broadly, social problems can be divided into two types:

- Social problems at the individual level
- Social problems at the collective level.

Social problems at the individual level include juvenile delinquency, drug addiction, suicide etc.

Social problems at the collective level emerge when the mechanisms of social control fail to regulate the behaviour of its members or when there is breakdown of effective institutional functioning. For example, poverty, exploitation, population explosion, untouchability, famine, floods etc.

Social problems can also be divided into following types in relation to their causative factors:

- Social problems due to social factors.
- Social problems due to cultural factors.
- Social problems due to economic factors.
- Social problems due to political and legal factors.
- Social problems due to ecological factors.

Social Problems Due to Social Factors

The nature of heterogeneous societies has been the cause of a number of social problems. In heterogeneous societies like India, where there are people of several religions, castes, linguistic groups and tribal groups living together, several types of social problems can be seen.

The conflict among the different religious groups has given rise to the problem of communalism. In India, Hindu-Muslim conflict has been a major problem. Similarly, the caste system in India has divided the society into various groups. It has led to the discrimination of one group by the other. The problem of untouchability in India is due to the caste system. Caste system is also responsible for the educational backwardness of the country.

Traditionally, the caste determined the eligibility of the people for education. In the traditional system, education was considered to be the prerogative of the upper castes. As a result, the masses were deprived of education. This explains the high rate of illiteracy in India. Another social factor that may lead to social problem is language. In a country where several languages are spoken, conflict between different linguistic groups can be seen. In India, we have experienced the conflict between different linguistic groups.

Social Problems Due to Cultural Factors

Several cultural factors have been responsible for a number of social problems. In a traditional society like India, some of the cultural factors that have led to social problems are:

- Male child preference,
- Patriarchal system,
- Lack of regard for public property.

In India the value system is such that a son in the family is considered necessary. It is desirable to have more sons. As a result, the members in the family go on multiplying. This has led to population explosion. The population in India has grown at a phenomenal rate after independence. At present, the population of the country is well beyond one billion that makes India the second most populated country of the world. As elsewhere in the world, Indian society, by and large, has been patriarchal where woman is subjected to man. They are not seen beyond the roles of a wife or a mother. The woman is given an inferior social status to that of a man in almost every walk of life. As a result, almost half of the population has remained deprived. This deprivation is compounded when the woman belongs to the Scheduled Caste or the Scheduled Tribe.

Another trait of the Indian society that has implications for corruption is the disregard for public property. This lack of respect for public property is one of the root causes of corruption, black money, tax evasion, misappropriation of public goods and use of substandard materials in public construction.

Social Problems Due to Economic Factors

Economic factors are also responsible for some of the major social problems being faced by the contemporary society. It is more conspicuous in societies of developing countries like India. Unequal distribution of wealth has led to disparity in the distribution of benefits occurring due to development. As a result there is the problem of poverty. Poverty in turn aggravates other problems like high morbidity and mortality, crime, slum, illiteracy, etc. Further, the process of urbanization and industrialization in India has been very slow.

This has resulted in regional disparity in economic development. There are pockets of development where high level of urban and industrial growth can be seen. However, the other regions are still under-developed. It has attracted large number of people to migrate from the under-developed region to the developed region. This in turn has affected the population structure of both the regions. In addition to it, the regions receiving the migrants are facing the problems of slum, congestion, unemployment, pollution, etc.

Social Problems Due to Political and Legal Factors

Some of the political factors that may cause social problems include electoral politics, political functioning, corruption, etc. In order to win elections and come to power, political parties do not shy away from using communal or parochial modes of mobilization like caste, religion, and language. Even some of the decisions taken by the ruling party may lead to social problem as they may benefit a particular section of the society at the cost of the entire society. It may result in conflict between different sections of the society. Another problem is the increasing political corruption. Leaders are found indulging in nepotism and red-tapism. They are also seen accepting money in return of some favour.

Social Problems Due to Ecological Factors

Earlier, in an attempt to develop rapidly, environment was grossly ignored. The ecological consequence of such an attempt has now emerged as a major social problem. Rapid industrialization has led to increase in environmental pollution that includes air pollution, water pollution, noise pollution, and degradation and desertification of the land. This in turn has led to increase morbidity and mortality, emergence of new types of diseases, global warming, ozone depletion, floods etc.

That has threatened the existence of mankind itself. Further, to feed the increasing population of the world more and more land is being brought under cultivation. This has disturbed the global ecological balance. Application of modern technological inputs in agriculture like the pesticides, weedicides, insecticides, high yielding variety of seeds, genetically modified crops are threatening the biodiversity of the world. It has also increased the probability of the emergence of super weeds and insects that may be beyond the human control.

MULTIPLE CHOICE QUESTIONS

1. The Directive Principle of State Policy is given under which part of the constitution?

A. Part I　　B. Part II
C. Part III　　D. Part IV

2. By which Constitutional amendment the word 'Socialist' and 'Secular' were added in the Preamble?

A. 42nd Amendment Act of 1976
B. 42nd Amendment Act of 1978
C. 43rd Amendment Act of 1976
D. 43rd Amendment Act of 1978

3. From which country 'The Directive Principle of State Policy' is borrowed?

A. USA　　B. Ireland
C. France　　D. Soviet Union

4. The Fundamental Rights of the Constitution is borrowed from?
A. USA B. UK
C. France D. Soviet Union

5. The Fundamental Duties of the Constitution is borrowed from?
A. South Africa B. Germany
C. Japan D. Soviet Union

6. The Federal System is borrowed from
A. Canada B. UK
C. France D. Soviet Union

7. The Parliamentary System is borrowed from
A. Japan B. UK
C. South Africa D. Soviet Union

8. Which country has the biggest written Constitution?
A. Indonesia B. France
C. South Africa D. India

9. What type of Fundamental Right is given to the Indian citizens by Article 21A of the constitution?
A. Right to Information
B. Right to Property
C. Right to Education
D. Right to Equality

10. An Unemployed person is one who
A. is able for employment but unable to get
B. is unable for employment
C. failed in a competitive exam
D. All the above

11. Who gave the Bio-psychological Theory of Social Disorganization?
A. Karl Marx B. Gobinean
C. Sutherland D. Ogburn

12. The Cultural Lag Approach was propounded by
A. Bogardus B. Ogburn
C. Sorokin D. Toynbee

13. Who wrote the book 'Social and Cultural Dynamics'?
A. Karl Marx B. Talcott Parsons
C. Sorokin D. Ogburn

14. Who among the following gave the Functionalist theory of Social Change?
A. Karl Marx B. Talcott Parsons
C. Sorokin D. Ogburn

15. Who among the following gave the Conflict theory of Social Change?
A. Karl Marx B. Talcott Parsons
C. Sorokin D. Ogburn

16. Who asserted that the "All history is the history of Class Conflict"?
A. Emile Durkheim
B. Talcott Parsons
C. Max Weber
D. Karl Marx

17. The Concept of Primary and Secondary Group has been propounded by
A. Bogardus B. Ogburn
C. Sorokin D. C.H. Cooley

18. Globalisation means :
A. Promotion of International Co-operation
B. Tolerance for one another among nation states
C. The opening of economy for all the national states of the world
D. Settlement of disputes between nation states through mediation of the United Nations and its various organisation

19. Welfare state is the creation of:
A. Capitalist Economy
B. Socialist Economy
C. Communist Economy
D. All the above

20. Government of India followed which model of Development :
A. Capitalist Model
B. Socialist Model
C. Democratic Socialism
D. All the above

21. Which of the first and foremost objective of the Constitution of India?
A. Equality B. Liberty
C. Justice D. Fraternity

22. Which among the following is not the objective of the Constitution of India?

A. Equality
B. Liberty
C. Livelihood Security
D. Fraternity

23. Which of the following is NOT a national duty as per the constitution of India?
A. To abide by constitution and respect to ideals and institutions, the National Flag and National Anthem
B. To value and preserve the rich heritage of our composite culture
C. To cast vote in elections to Panchayati Raj Institutions
D. To strive for excellence in all spheres of individual and collective activity

24. Which of the following is NOT related to principles of policy to be followed by the state as per provisions of Article 39 of Directive principles of state policy?
A. Citizen's right to an adequate employment
B. Equal pay of equal work
C. Opportunities to be given to youth to realize their potentials
D. Opportunities and facilities to be given to children to develop in healthy

25. What is the major thrust of the Twelfth Five Years Plan?
A. Faster, sustainable and more inclusive growth
B. Inclusive Growth
C. Growth with Justice
D. Development of Other Backward Classes

26. Under the present policy of Public-Private Partnership which of the following has become more important :
A. Public Sector
B. Private Sector
C. Cooperative Sector
D. All the above

27. What is the role of social workers in social problems ?
A. Conducting scientific social surveys
B. Analysing data logically and statistically
C. Arriving at sound conclusions
D. All the above

28. "Assumed Average Need" is accepted in :
A. Public Assistance
B. Social Assistance
C. Social Insurance
D. Social Service

29. "Moral Requirements" are generally attached in case of :
A. Social Insurance Programmes
B. Public Assistance Programmes
C. Social Service Programmes
D. Social Welfare Service

30. Which of the following commissions has NOT been established in India so far?
A. National Commission for Children
B. National Commission for Women
C. National Commission for Protection of Child Rights
D. National Commission for Youth Rights

31. How many schedules have been added to the Constitution of India?
A. Eleven B. Twelve
C. Ten D. Thirteen

32. What is the goal of social worker research?
A. Conducting scientific social surveys
B. Analysing data logically and statistically
C. Provide solutions to the prevailing Social problems
D. All the above

33. Social Disorganization consists of :
A. Personal disorganization
B. Family disorganization
C. Community disorganization
D. All the above

34. Social disorganization primarily results form:
A. Economic conflicts
B. Political conflicts
C. Value conflicts
D. None of the above

35. What is NOT found in animals?
A. Brain
B. Instincts
C. Social Relationships
D. Memory

36. Which of the following is NOT a stage of Social Evoluation?
A. Witchcraft B. Hunting
C. Agriculture D. Industrialization

37. Which of the following does NOT characterize a primary group?
A. Intimate relationship
B. Formal relationship
C. Face-to-face contact
D. Status-role arrangement

38. Crime is a act which is :
A. Anti-Legal
B. Anti-Social
C. Anti-Organizational
D. All the above

39. Personal Disorganisation means :
A. Personal Faults
B. Personal Vices
C. Attitudinal and Value Conflicts
D. None of the above

40. Under the Juvenile Justice (Case and Protection of Children) act, a girl will be treated as delinquent who has not attained the age of :
A. 14 years B. 16 years
C. 18 years D. 21 years

41. A broken home is one where :
A. One or both the parents are dead
B. There is a serious marital discord
C. Children do not get parental love and affections
D. All the above

42. Family is a :
A. Primary Group
B. Secondary Group
C. Quasi Primary Group
D. None of the above

43. Who classified the Social Group into Primary and Secondary :
A. Robert Marton B. C.H. Cooley
C. F.H. Giddings D. None of the above

44. Husband, wife and their unmarried children constitute :
A. a joint family
B. a nuclear family
C. an extended family
D. None of the above

45. Which one of the following theories of socialisation has been propounded by Durkheim?
A. Looking Glass-Self
B. Id, Ego and Super-Ego
C. Collective Representations
D. I and Me

46. Who propounded the theory "Looking Glass Self"?
A. Emile Durkheim
B. C.H. Cooley
C. Robert Merton
D. None of the above

47. The function of Social control is to:
A. Promote Uniformity
B. Check Deviance
C. Maintain law and order
D. All the above

48. Which among these is not social Process?
A. Competition B. Co-operation
C. Conflict D. Reservation

49. The most important role in socialization is played by:
A. Primary Group
B. Secondary Group
C. Quasi-primary Group
D. Out-groups

50. What of the following is NOT an example of Social Change?
A. Improvement in economic status
B. Change in family
C. Change in marriage
D. Change in caste

51. Culture is not:
A. Acquired B. Learned
C. Shared D. Innate

52. The basic assumption of evolutionary approach is that :
A. Society changes
B. Complex form develop out of simple ones

C. Barbaric forms develop into civilized forms
D. Culture is replaced by civilization

53. Who was the Chairman of Constitution drafting committee?
A. Sardar Vallabh Bhai Patel
B. Dr. Rajendra Prasad
C. B.N. Rao
D. Dr. B.R. Ambedkar

54. Social Security is basically :
A. An income generation device
B. An income maintenance device
C. An income redistribution device
D. All the above

55. Which of the following is NOT the characteristic feature of public assistance?
A. Availability of funds from state exchequer
B. Fulfilment of existing actual needs
C. Contribution by beneficiaries
D. Protection from destitution

56. Social Changes implies :
A. Change in Social structure
B. Change in Social functions
C. Change in Social relationships
D. Change in all the above

57. Poverty eradication programmes could not succeed in India because of:
A. Widely rampant corruption in government machinery
B. Lack of determined political will
C. Lack of people's participation
D. All the above

58. Who gave the concept of 'Culture of Poverty'?
A. George Simmel B. Alfred Weber
C. Oscar Lewis D. None of the above

59. The Optimum Theory of Population was given by?
A. Robert Malthus B. Cannan
C. Frank Notestein D. C.P. Blacker

60. Who wrote the book 'Essay on the Principle of Population'?
A. Robert Malthus
B. Cannan
C. C.P. Blacker
D. W.S. Thompson

61. Who propounded The Demographic Transition Theory of Population ?
A. Robert Malthus
B. Cannan
C. Frank Notestein & W.S. Thompson
D. None of the above

62. The Mahalanobis Model is concerned with which Five Years Plan?
A. I[st] Five Years Plan
B. IInd Five Years Plan
C. IIIrd Five Years Plan
D. IVth Five Years Plan

63. The concept of Five Year Plan is borrowed from?
A. Soviet Union B. UK
C. South Africa D. USA

64. The Delhi Pilot Project was initiated in the Year:
A. 1952 B. 1957
C. 1955 D. 1948

65. The First Charity Organization Society (USA) was established in the Year
A. 1877 B. 1874
C. 1867 D. 1886

66. The term Social Workers was coined by
A. Marry Richmond
B. Simon Paatern
C. Gisela Konopka
D. W.A. Friedlander

67. Which development model Indian Government followed for planned develop-ment?
A. Capitalism
B. Socialism
C. Democratic Socialism
D. None of the Above

68. Drug addiction is caused by:
A. Desire for new experience
B. Frustration in life
C. Peer group pressure
D. All the above

69. A person is unemployed when she/he is not able to get employment although she/he is:
A. able to work
B. willing to work
C. available for work
D. All the above

70. Social control is exercised through :
A. Law B. Customs
C. Traditions D. All the above

71. Provision relating to free and compulsory education for all children up to the age of fourteen years has been made in the constitution of India under:
A. Article 21-A B. Article 44
C. Article 46 D. None of the above

72. "Cultural Lag" means :
A. Unequal cultural development
B. Decay in moral value
C. Non-corresponding change in the material and non-material culture
D. None of the above

73. Which one of the below is not Fundamental Right?
A. Right to Self-destruction
B. Right to Constitutional Remedies
C. Right to Freedom of Religion
D. Right to Equality

74. The basis of Social Stratification is:
A. Social Justice B. Social Inequality
C. Social Injustice D. Social Equality

75. Tribals in a scheduled area demanded special care for the education of their children under their constitutional rights. They demanded such care under:
A. Article 21 B. Article 46
C. Article 52 D. Article 73

76. Which of the following is an example of the social groups?
A. Church B. Labour Union
C. Married People D. Family

77. The caste system is a:
A. Social institution
B. Religious Institution
C. Economic Institution
D. Cultural Institution

78. The Concepts are known as :
A. Steps in Social Research
B. Causal explanation
C. Steps in Operationalization
D. Building blocks of Theory

79. Who from amongst the following propounded the concept of primary group?
A. E.S. Bogardus B. R.M. MacIver
C. Herbert Spencer D. C.H. Cooley

80. Which one of the following is an example of Secondary Group?
A. Family B. Friend Circle
C. Neighbourhood D. Trade Union

81. Which one of the following is the characteristic of primary group?
A. Inclusive Knowledge
B. Formal Relationship
C. Formal Control
D. Large Number

82. Family is :
A. An Institution
B. An Association
C. An institution as well as an association
D. Neither an institution nor an association

83. Who suggested to classify social group into Involuntary, Voluntary and Delegate Social Group?
A. F.H. Giddings B. George Hasen
C. Meller D. Dwight Sanderson

84. Who classified social group into Communities and Associations ?
A. Hayman B. Summer
C. Tonnis D. Dwight Sanderson

85. Who classified social group into Genetic and Congregate ?
A. F.H. Giddings B. Tonnis
C. Meller D. Dwight Sanderson

86. Who gave the concept of Reference Group?
A. F.H. Giddings B. George Hasen
C. Meller D. Hayman

87. Socialisation is the process of:
A. Providing knowledge of Material objects
B. Promote understanding of Science and Technology
C. Internalisation of Values of Society
D. Pursuit of Religion

88. Poverty means:
A. Inadequate income
B. Unwise expenditure
C. Both of the above
D. None of the above

89. Calorie requirement for determining poverty in rural areas is:
A. 2100 Calories B. 2200 Calories
C. 2300 Calories D. 2400 Calories

90. A person is under employed when she/he is not getting:
A. Adequate Wages
B. Suitable Employment
C. Full-time Employment
D. All the above

91. Unemployment leads to :
A. Personality Disorganisation
B. Family Disorganisation
C. Community Disorganisation
D. All the above

92. Main cause of unemployment in India is:
A. Inappropriate technological development
B. Inadequate industrilisation
C. Ineffective implementation of public policies and programmes
D. Rapid rate of population growth

93. Who is the Chairman of Planning Commission?
A. Finance Minister
B. President
C. Prime Minister
D. Minister of Planning

94. Socialisation takes place with :
A. Family B. Peer Group
C. School D. All the Above

95. Which one of the following is a primary Group?
A. Political Party
B. Club
C. Family
D. Cooperative Society

96. What type of relations are found in Secondary Group?
A. Informal Relations
B. Intimate Relations
C. Formal Relations
D. All the above

97. The theory that "Criminals are born" was propounded by
A. Ferri B. Baccaroa
C. Lombraso D. Benthem

98. Main basis of Juvenile Delinquency is :
A. Age of the offender
B. Family background of the offender
C. Religion and Caste of the offender
D. Nature of offence

99. Theory of "Differential Association" was propounded by:
A. Neumeyer B. Merton
C. Sutherland D. Reckless

100. Theory of Class Conflict was propounded by:
A. Sorokin B. Engels
C. Hegal D. Marx

101. The Twenty-Point Programme was started by:
A. Morarji Desai
B. Indira Gandhi
C. Lal Bahadur Shastri
D. Jawahar Lal Nehru

102. Aganwari is concerned with:
A. Development of Children and Youth
B. Development of Women and Youth
C. Development of Children and Women
D. None of the above

103. First Review Committee For Social Work Education was appointed by the UGC in the Year:
A. 1965 B. 1960
C. 1967 D. 1970

104. Which one of the following is NOT a means of Social Change?

A. Propaganda B. State
C. Public Opinion D. Ridicule

105. The Protection of Civil Rights Act is concerned with:

A. Upper Castes
B. Scheduled Castes
C. Other Backward Classes
D. None of the above

106. Which one of the following constitutes the main basis of a Welfare States in India ?

A. Fundamental Rights
B. Directive Principles of State Policy
C. Judicial Independence
D. Public Interest Litigation

107. Who founded Arya Samaj?

A. Dayanand Saraswati
B. Vinoba Bhave
C. M.G. Ranade
D. Swami Vivekanand

108. Who coined Sanskritisation?

A. Radhakamal Mukherjee
B. M.N. Srinivas
C. Vogendra Singh
D. S.C. Dube

109. The practice of untouchabitity has been abolished by the Indian Constitution in Article:

A. 17 B. 19
C. 38 D. 42

110. Match the following :

1. Rabindranath Tagore (i) Sabarmati Ashram
2. Mahatama Gandhi (ii) Bellur Math
3. Vinoba Bhave (iii) Pavnar
4. Ramkrishna Paramhansa (iv) Shanti Niketan

Codes :

	1	2	3	4
A.	(iii)	(i)	(iv)	(ii)
B.	(i)	(ii)	(iii)	(iv)
C.	(iv)	(i)	(iii)	(ii)
D.	(ii)	(iii)	(i)	(iv)

111. Match the following :

1. Sarvodaya (i) Mahatama Gandhi
2. Satyagraha (ii) Vinoba Bhave
3. Sampoorna Kranti (iii) Verghese Kurien
4. White Revolution (iv) Jayprakash Narayan

Codes :

	1	2	3	4
(A)	(iii)	(ii)	(i)	(iv)
(B)	(ii)	(i)	(iv)	(iii)
(C)	(iv)	(ii)	(i)	(ii)
(D)	(i)	(iv)	(iii)	(ii)

112. Socialisation means:

A. Developing friendship with unknown persons
B. Ensuring equity to the society
C. The process of internalization of social norms
D. The establishment of rapport with clients

113. De-notified Tribes are:

A. Ex-criminal tribes
B. Untouchables
C. Wandering communities
D. Artisans

114. Which of the following are the main cause of social change in India?

(1) Independence
(2) Industrialisation
(3) Education
(4) Sanskritisation

Choose the answer from the following:

A. 1, 2 and 3 B. 2, 3 and 4
C. 1, 3 and 4 D. 1, 2 and 4

115. Brahmo Samaj was founded in the year:

A. 1828 B. 1928
C. 1892 D. 1982

116. The National Rural Employment Guarantee Programme seeks to provide employment at the statutory minimum wage for at least:

A. 150 days
B. 365 days
C. 100 days
D. 90 days

117. Match the pairs:

1. Narmada Bachao Aandolan (i) Sunderlal Bahuguna
2. Chipko Movement (ii) Medha Patkar
3. Sarvodaya (iii) Jayprakash Narayan
4. Total Revolution (iv) Vinoba Bhave

Codes :

	1	2	3	4
A.	(ii)	(i)	(iv)	(iii)
B.	(iv)	(i)	(ii)	(iii)
C.	(ii)	(iii)	(i)	(iv)
D.	(ii)	(iii)	(iv)	(i)

118. Which of the following are social institution?

(i) Caste
(ii) Family
(iii) Socialisation
(iv) Education

A. (i), (ii) and (iv)
B. (ii), (iii) and (iv)
C. (i), (ii) and (iii)
D. (i) and (ii)

119. Match the items in List-I with items in List-II :

List-I	List-II
1. My Experiments with truth	(i) Gunnar Myrdal
2. The Radical Social Work	(ii) Joseph Stiglitz
3. Asian Drama	(iii) Saul Alinsky
4. Globalization and its discontents	(iv) M.K. Gandhi
	(v) J.K. Galbraith

Choose correct code for answer :

Codes :

	1	2	3	4
(A)	(iii)	(i)	(ii)	(iv)
(B)	(iv)	(iii)	(i)	(ii)
(C)	(ii)	(i)	(v)	(iii)
(D)	(ii)	(v)	(iv)	(i)

120. Social Class is a :

A. Category
B. Primary Group
C. Secondary Group
D. Mob

121. Which of the following statement is Correct?

A. Caste is based on the individual's position
B. Caste is determined by occupational mobility
C. Caste is created by Lord Brahmas
D. Caste is determined by birth

122. Which of the following article in the Directive Principles of State Policy of Indian Constitution guarantees the protection of schedule caste for any form of exploitation:

A. Article 36 B. Article 46
C. Article 30 D. Article 28

123. Match the items in List-I with the items in List-II and choose the correct answer using the column given below:

List–I	List–II
1. Reference Group	(i) Randall Collins
2. Bureaucracy	(ii) G.H. Mead
3. Symbolic Interactionism	(iii) Max Weber
4. Micro Sociology	(iv) R.K. Merton
	(v) Radcliffe-Brown

Codes :

	1	2	3	4
(A)	(iv)	(ii)	(v)	(i)
(B)	(i)	(iii)	(iv)	(ii)
(C)	(iii)	(v)	(iv)	(ii)
(D)	(iv)	(iii)	(ii)	(i)

124. An organisation formed by individuals to achieve some goals is called:

A. Society B. Association
C. Institution D. Community

125. Which one of the following is known to be Universal Social Institution?

A. Caste B. Religion
C. Family D. Tribe

126. The basic characteristic of cast system is:

A. Equality B. Hierarchy
C. Equal status D. Openness

127. Who among the following authored "Human Society"?

A. T. Parsons B. R.K. Merton
C. K. Davis D. MacIver

128. Social norms are set by;
A. The state B. Religion
C. Society D. Elites

129. The marriage of a man to two or more women is known as:
A. Monogamy
B. Polyandry
C. Fraternal Polyandry
D. Polygamy

130. The marriage of a woman to two or more men is known as:
A. Monogamy
B. Polyandry
C. Fraternal Polyandry
D. Polygamy

131. According to Robert Redfield a community characterized by distinctiveness, smallness, homogeneity and self-sufficiency is known as:
A. Little community
B. Great community
C. Society
D. Social Group

132. Theory of Malthus focus on:
A. Cultural factors of social change
B. Economic factor of social change
C. Demographic factor of social change
D. Technological factor of social change

133. Which one of the following is NOT an indicator of Social Development?
A. Increased Per Capita Income
B. Equality
C. Literacy Rate
D. Foreign Direct Investment

134. Which one of the following is NOT a symptom of social disorganization?
A. Uncertainty in position and functions
B. Lack of control
C. Balance between position and functions
D. Lack of consensus

135. Social disorganization includes:
A. Community disorganization
B. Family disorganization
C. Personal disorganization
D. All the above

ANSWERS

1	2	3	4	5	6	7	8	9	10
D	A	B	A	D	A	B	D	C	A
11	**12**	**13**	**14**	**15**	**16**	**17**	**18**	**19**	**20**
B	B	C	B	A	D	D	C	B	C
21	**22**	**23**	**24**	**25**	**26**	**27**	**28**	**29**	**30**
A	C	C	C	A	D	D	C	B	D
31	**32**	**33**	**34**	**35**	**36**	**37**	**38**	**39**	**40**
B	D	D	C	C	A	B	D	C	C
41	**42**	**43**	**44**	**45**	**46**	**47**	**48**	**49**	**50**
D	A	B	B	C	B	D	D	A	A
51	**52**	**53**	**54**	**55**	**56**	**57**	**58**	**59**	**60**
D	C	D	D	C	D	D	C	B	A
61	**62**	**63**	**64**	**65**	**66**	**67**	**68**	**69**	**70**
C	B	A	C	B	B	C	D	D	D
71	**72**	**73**	**74**	**75**	**76**	**77**	**78**	**79**	**80**
A	C	A	B	B	D	A	D	D	D

81	82	83	84	85	86	87	88	89	90
A	C	D	C	A	D	C	C	D	D
91	92	93	94	95	96	97	98	99	100
D	C	C	C	C	C	C	A	C	D
101	102	103	104	105	106	107	108	109	110
B	C	B	D	B	B	A	B	A	C
111	112	113	114	115	116	117	118	119	120
B	C	A	B	A	C	A	A	B	C
121	122	123	124	125	126	127	128	129	130
D	B	D	B	B	B	C	C	D	B
131	132	133	134	135					
A	C	D	C	D					

➢➢➢➢➢

CHAPTER

3

Human Behaviour

HUMAN BEHAVIOUR

In this world there are millions of species. All are unique in themselves but higher rate of survival and adaptability with the environment makes human being special among all species. The human beings have three important features (1) A bigger and developed brain with increased capacity for cognitive bahaviours like memory, perceptions, reasoning, problem solving and use of language for communication (2) Ability to walk upright on two legs and (3) A free hand with a workable opposing thumb. Apart from these feature human behaviour is highly complex and more developed than any other species.

There are some important factors that determine human behaviour.

1. **Biological basis of Behaviour:** Neurons is the basic unit of our nervous system. Neurons are specialized cells, which possess the unique property of converting various forms of stimuli into electrical impulses. They are also specialized for reception, conduction and transmission of information in the form of electrochemical signals. They receive information from sense organs, carry them to central nervous system (brain and spinal cord) and bring motor information from the central nervous system to the motor organs (muscles and glands). Nearly 12 billions neurons are found in the human nervous system. The normal functioning of all the biological components such as neurons, nerve impulse, nervous system and brain is crucial to the behavioural well being of human beings, their inefficiency of imbalance could change the state of internal equilibrium.
2. **Genes and Behaviour:** Human beings inherent characteristics from their parents in the form of genes. A child at birth possesses a unique combination of genes received from both parents. These inheritances provide distinct biological blue print and determine the physical and psychological characteristics of an individual.
3. **Socio-cultural sapping of human behaviour:** The most effective factor that determine the human behaviour is cultural base. The human behaviour is unlike other creatures because they have a culture to regulate behaviour. For example, the need of hunger has a biological basis, which is common among the animal and human beings, but the way human beings satisfy this needs is different and complex from animals, different in a way that we have set pattern of eating and complex in a way that some of us eat vegetarian food and some non-vegetarian food. The individuals food eating habit or behaviour is determinedly by their culture.

MOTIVATION

The concept of motivation focus on reasons of acting and behaving in a particular way. Our behaviour is governed by our motives that are the general states that enable us to make prediction about beahviour in many different situation. In other word, motivation is one of the determinants of behaviour. Instincts drives, needs, goals and incentives come under the broad cluster of motivation.

The Motivation Cycle

Psychologists use the concept of need to describe the motivational properties of behaviour. A need is lack or deficit of some necessity. The condition of need leads to drive. A drive is a state of tension produced by a need. It energies random activity when one of the random activities leads to a goal. It reduces the drive and the organism stop being active and the organism returns to a balanced state.

Types of Motives

Basically there are two types of motives : biological motives and psycho-social motives.

- **Biological Motives:** Biological motives are directly related to individual's physiological needs. These are also called primary drives, which are deeply rooted in human being, satisfaction of these drives is necessary. Some of our most powerful biological motives are hunger, thirst, sex, sleep etc.
- **Psycho-social Motives:** Psycho-social motives are mostly learned or acquired. Social groups and such as family, neighbourhood, friends' relatives and experiences of life do contribute a lot in acquiring social motives. These are complex form of motives mainly resulting from the individuals interaction with his/her social environment. Such as need for affiliation, need for power, need for achievement, curiosity and exploration etc.

Therefore, motivation is the force that initiates, guides and maintains goal-oriented behaviours. It is what causes us to take action, whether to grab food to reduce hunger or enroll in college to earn a degree. The forces that lie beneath motivation can be biological, social, emotional or cognitive in nature. Researchers have developed a number of different theories to explain motivation. Some of the theories can be understand as:

Instinct Theory of Motivation

According to instinct theories, people are motivated to behave in certain ways because they are evolutionarily programmed to do so. An example of this in the animal world is seasonal migration. These animals do not learn to do this; it is instead an inborn pattern of behaviour. William James created a list of human instincts that included such things as attachment, play, shame, anger, fear, shyness, modesty and love. The main problem with this theory is that it did not really explain behaviour, it just described it. By the 1920s, instinct theories were pushed aside in favour of other motivational theories, but contemporary evolutionary psychologists still study the influence of genetics and heredity on human behaviour.

Incentive Theory of Motivation

The incentive theory suggests that people are motivated to do things because of external rewards. For example, one might be motivated to go to work each day for the monetary reward of being paid. Behavioural learning concepts such as association and reinforcement play an important role in this theory of motivation.

Drive Theory of Motivation

According to the drive theory of motivation, people are motivated to take certain actions in order to reduce the internal tension that is caused by unmet needs. For example, one might be motivated to drink a glass of water in order to reduce the internal state of thirst. This theory is useful in explaining behaviours that have a strong biological component, such as hunger or thirst. The problem with the drive theory of motivation is that these behaviours are not always motivated purely by physiological needs. For example, people often eat even when they are not really hungry.

Arousal Theory of Motivation

The arousal theory of motivation suggests that people take certain actions to either decrease or increase levels of arousal. According to this theory, we are motivated to maintain an optimal level of arousal, although this level can vary based on the individual or the situation.

Humanistic Theory of Motivation: Maslows hierarchy of needs

Humanistic theories of motivation are based on the idea that people also have strong cognitive reasons to perform various actions. This is famously illustrated in Abraham Maslow's hierarchy of needs, which presents different motivations at different levels. First, people are motivated to fulfil basic biological needs for food and shelter, as well as those of safety, love and esteem. Once the lower level needs have been met, the primary motivator becomes the need for self-actualization, or the desire to fulfil one's individual potential.

Abraham Maslow an American psychologist wanted to understand what motivates people. He believed that individual possess a set of motivation system unrelated to rewards or unconscious desires. Maslow (1943) stated that people are motivated to achieve certain need. When one need is fulfilled a person seeks to fulfill the next one and so on.

Maslows model can be conceptualized as a pyramid in which the bottom of this hierarchy represents basic physiological or biological needs which are basic to survival such as hunger, thrust etc. Only when these needs are met, the need to be free from threatened danger arises. This refers to the safety needs of physical and psychological nature. The next is the needs to love and to be loved. After these needs are fulfilled the individual strives for esteem i.e. need to develop a sense of worth, dignity and respect. The last higher need according to Maslow is individual motives towards the full development of potential *i.e.* self actualization. A self actualization person is self aware, socially responsive, and creative, open to novelty and challenges.

COPING MECHANISM

Coping mechanism is basically 'adaptation skill'. They are tactics that people use in order to deal with stresses, pain and natural changes that we experience in life. Coping mechanism are learned behavioural patterns used to cope. There are two type of coping mechanism—positive and negative. A person experiences range of emotions throughout his life *i.e.* good, not so good, bad etc. The behaviour of an individual usually a result of how he handle his emotions. If emotions handled positively the outcome will be positive behaviour if not the behaviour will be considered as negative.

There is variety of coping mechanism positive as well as negative. The positive coping mechanism could be grounding skills (stay focused, use all five senses), manage stress, manage anger, communication, respect other, learn acceptance and forgiveness etc. Negative coping mechanism could be violence and abuse addiction, denial, developing a 'false self' running away, self harm, suicide attempt, depression etc.

DEFENSE MECHANISM

Sigmund Freud describes how the ego uses a range of mechanism to handle the conflict between the id, the ego and the super ego. His daughter Anna Freud introduced the principle of inner mechanism that defends the ego in her book 'The Ego and the mechanism of defense, written in the year 1936.'

Defense Mechanism is a strategy developed by the ego to protect against anxiety. Defense Mechanism are thought that protect or safeguard the mind against Feelings and thoughts that are too difficult for the conscious mind to cope with, for example, if a person is faced with a particularly unpleasant task, his mind may chose to forget the responsibility in order to avoid the unpleasant assignment.

Common Defense Mechanism

- **Denial:** Protecting oneself from unpleasant reality by refusing to perceive or face it.
- **Displacement:** Diverting emotional feelings from their original source to a substitute target.

- **Repression:** Keeping distressing thoughts and feelings buried in the unconscious.
- **Rationalization:** Creating false but credible justifications.
- **Sublimation:** Redirecting 'wrong' urges into socially acceptable action.
- **Reaction Formation:** Behaving in a way that exactly the opposite of one's true feelings.

ERIC ERIKSON STAGES OF PSYCHO SOCIAL DEVELOPMENT

Eric Erikson (1950, 63) does not explain psychosexual stages of development, he discussed psychosocial stages. He was greatly influenced by Freud. However, whereas Freud was an Id psychologist, Erikson was an ego psychologist. He emphasized the role of culture and society and the conflict that can take place within the ego itself, whereas, Freud emphasized the conflict between the Id and superego. According to Erikson, the ego develops as it successfully resolve crisis that are distinctly social in nature. These involve establishing a sense of trust in others, developing a sense of identity in society, and helping the next generation prepare for the future.

Erikson explains 'Eight Stage' through which a healthily developing human should pass begins from infancy. In each stage the person confronts and hopefully master news challenges. Each stage builds a successful completion of earlier stage. The challenges of stages not successfully completed may be expected to reappear as problem in future.

I[st] Stage : Trust vs Mistrust (Infants, Birth to 12-18 months)

- The first stage of Erik Erikson theory centers on the infants basic needs met by the parents.
- The infant depends on the parents especially the mothers for food, substance and comfort.
- The child relative understanding of the world and society come from the parents and their interaction with the child.
- If parents expose the child with warmth regularity and of dependable affection the infant view of the world will be one of truest.
- If the parents fails to provide a secure environment and to meet the Childs basic needs a sense of mistrust will result.

IInd Stage : Autonomy vs Shame & Doubt

- The child gains control over eliminative functions of motor ability, by this stage he/she begin to explore his/her surroundings.
- The parents still provide a base of security.
- The parent's patience and envisagement helps foster autonomy in the child. Children at this age like to explore the world around them.
- Caution must be taken at this age because children may explore things that are dangerous to their health and safety.
- Parents need to encourage the child to becoming more independent whilst at the same time protecting the child so that constant failure is avoided.
- If children in this stage are encouraged and supported in their increased independence, they become more confident and secure in their own ability to survive in the world.
- If children are criticized, overly controlled, or not given the opportunity to assert themselves, they begin to feel inadequate in their ability to survive, and may then become overly dependent upon others, lack self-esteem, and feel a sense of shame or doubt in their own abilities.

IIIrd Stage: Initiative vs. Guilt 3 to 6 yrs

- During this period the primary feature involves the child regularly interacting with other children at school.
- Central to this stage is play, as it provides children with the opportunity to explore their interpersonal skills through initiating activities.
- Children begin to plan activities, make up games, and initiate activities with others.

- If given this opportunity, children develop a sense of initiative, and feel secure in their ability to lead others and make decisions.
- Conversely, if this tendency is squelched, either through criticism or control, children develop a sense of guilt.
- They may feel like a nuisance to others and will therefore remain followers, lacking in self-initiative.
- The child takes initiatives which the parents will often try to stop in order to protect the child. The child will often overstep the mark in his forcefulness and the danger is that the parents will tend to punish the child and restrict his initiatives too much.
- It is at this stage that the child will begin to ask many questions as his thirst for knowledge grows.
- If the parents treat the child's questions as trivial, a nuisance or embarrassing or other aspects of their behaviour as threatening then the child may have feelings of guilt for "being a nuisance".
- Too much guilt can make the child slow to interact with others and may inhibit their creativity. Some guilt is, of course, necessary otherwise the child would not know how to exercise self control or have a conscience.
- A healthy balance between initiative and guilt is important. Success in this stage will lead to the virtue of purpose.

IVth Competence : Industry vs Inferiority (childhood 6 to 12 years)

- Children at this age are becoming aware of themselves as individuals.
- They work hard at being responsible, being good and doing it right.
- In this stage that the child's peer group gain greater significance and become a major source of the child's self esteem.
- The child now feels the need to win approval by demonstrating specific competencies that are valued by society, and begin to develop a sense of pride in their accomplishments.
- If children are encouraged and reinforced for their initiative, they begin to feel industrious and feel confident in their ability to achieve goals.
- If this initiative is not encouraged, if it is restricted by parents or teacher, then the child begins to feel inferior, doubting his own abilities and therefore may not reach his or her potential.

V[th] Identity vs Role confusion (12-18 yrs)

- During adolescence, the transition from childhood to adulthood is most important.
- Children are becoming more independent, and begin to look at the future in terms of career, relationships, families, housing, etc.
- The individual wants to belong to a society and fit in.
- This is a major stage in development where the child has to learn the roles he will occupy as an adult.
- It is during this stage that the adolescent will re-examine his identity and try to find out exactly who he or she is.
- Erikson suggests that two identities are involved: the sexual and the occupational.
- During this stage the body image of the adolescent changes.
- Erikson claims that the adolescent may feel uncomfortable about their body for a while until they can adapt and "grow into" the changes.
- Success in this stage will lead to the virtue of fidelity.
- Fidelity involves being able to commit one's self to others on the basis of accepting other even when there may be ideological differences.
- During this period, they explore possibilities and begin to form their own identity based upon the outcome of their explorations.

- Failure to establish a sense of identity within society ("I don't know what I want to be when I grow up") can lead to role confusion. Role confusing involves the individual not being sure about themselves or their place in society.
- In response to role confusion or identity crisis an adolescent may begin to experiment with different lifestyles (e.g. work, education or political activities). Also pressuring someone into an identity can result in rebellion in the form of establishing a negative identity, and in addition to these feelings of unhappiness.

VIth Intimacy vs Isolation (19 to 40 years)

- The intimacy *vs* isolation conflicts starts around 30 yrs. of age. At this point identify vs role confusion is coming to an end.
- Erikson believes we are isolated due to intimacy we are afraid or refection.
- Once people have established their identities, they are ready to make long term commitments to others.
- They become capable of forming intimate, reciprocal relationship—through close friendship, marriage and willingly make the sacrifices and compromises that such relationship requires.
- Avoiding intimacy, fearing commitment and relationships can lead to isolation, loneliness, and sometimes depression. Success in this stage will lead to the virtue of love.
- Successful completion of this stage can lead to comfortable relationships and a sense of commitment, safety, and care within a relationship.

VIIth Generativity vs Stagnation (40 to 65 years)

- Generativity is concerned with establishing and guiding the next generation. Socially valued work and disciplines are expression of generativity simply having children or wanting children does not in and of itself achieves generality.
- An individual work for the betterment of society that develops a sense of generatively and productivity.
- In contrast if a person is self centered and unable or unwilling to help society more forward develop feeling of stagnation.

VIIIth Ego integrity vs Despair (65 and onwards)

- As individual grow older (65 years and over) and become senior citizens, he tend to slow down productivity, and explore life as a retired person. It is during this time that he contemplate his accomplishments and able to develop integrity if he see himself as leading a successful life.
- Erick Erikson believed if we see our lives as unproductive, feel guilt about our pasts, or feel that we did not accomplish our life goals, we become dissatisfied with life and develop despair, often leading to depression and hopelessness.
- Success in this stage will lead to the virtue of wisdom. Wisdom enables a person to look back on their life with a sense of closure and completeness, and also accept death without fear.

SIGMUND FREUD (1856-1939)

- Freud (1905) proposed that psychological development in childhood takes place in a series of fixed stages.
- These are called psychosexual stages because each stage represents the fixation of libido (roughly translated as sexual drives or instincts) on a different area of the body.
- As a person grows physically certain areas of their body becomes important as sources of potential frustration (erogenous zones), pleasure or both.
- Freud believed that life was built round tension and pleasure.

- Freud also believed that all tension was due to the build up of libido (sexual energy) and that all pleasure came from its discharge.
- In describing human personality development as psychosexual Freud meant to convey that what develops is the way in which sexual energy accumulates and is discharged as we mature biologically.
- Freud used the term 'sexual' in a very general way to mean all pleasurable actions and thoughts.
- Freud stress that the first five years of life are crucial to the formation of adult personality.
- The id must be controlled in order to satisfy social demands; this sets up a conflict between frustrated wishes and social norms.
- The ego and superego develop in order to exercise this control and direct the need for gratification into socially acceptable channels.
- Gratification centers of different areas of the body at different stages of growth, making the conflict at each stage psychosexual.
- Human beings from birth possess an intellectual libido (sexual appetite) that develops in five steps (physical desire). These steps are:
  - ➢ Oral
  - ➢ Anal
  - ➢ Phallic
  - ➢ Latent
  - ➢ Genital
- Sigmund Freud proposed that if the child experience anxiety, thwarting his or her sexual appetite during any psychosexual development stage, said anxiety would persist into adulthood as a neurosis—a functional mental disorder.

Oral Stage: (0 to 1 Year)

- The first stage of personality development where libido is centered in a baby's mouth.
- It gets much satisfaction from putting all sorts of things in its mouth to satisfy libido, and thus its id demands which at this stage in life are oral, or mouth orientated, such as sucking, biting, and breast-feeding.
- Freud said oral stimulation could lead to an oral fixation in later life.
- We can see oral personalities all around us such as smokers, nail-biters, finger-chewers, and thumb suckers.
- Oral personalities engage in such oral behaviours particularly when under stress.

Anal stage (Age range 1 to 3 yrs)

- During the anal stage Freud believe that the primary focus of the libido was on controlling bladder and bowl movements.
- The libido now becomes focused on the anus and the child derives great pleasure from defecating.
- The child is now fully aware that they are a person in their own right and that their wishes can bring them into conflict with the demands of the outside world (*i.e.* their ego has developed).
- Freud believed that this type of conflict tends to come to a head in potty training, in which adults impose restrictions on when and where the child can defecate. The nature of this first conflict with authority can determine the child's future relationship with all forms of authority and could become capable and constructive individual.
- However if parents not provide required support, according to Freud inappropriate parental response can result in negative outcomes. Through which individual could develop wasteful, destructive personality.

The Phallic Stage: Age range (3 to 6 yrs)

- During this stage the primary focus of the libido is on genitals. At this children also begin to discover difference between male and females.

- Freud also believes that boys begin to view their father as a rival for the mother affection.
- According to Freud the boy develops sexual (pleasurable) desires for his mother. He wants to possess his mother exclusively and get rid of his father to enable him to do so. Irrationally, the boy thinks that if his father were to find out about all this, his father would take away what he loves the most. Freud called such behaviour as 'Oedipus complex.'
- The term 'Electra complex' has been used to describe a similar set of feeling experienced by young girls.
- This is resolved through the process of identification which involves the child adopting the characteristics of the same sex parent.

The latent Stage : (Age range 6 Years to Puberty)

- No further psychosexual development takes place during this stage (latent means hidden).
- The libido is dormant.
- Freud thought that most sexual impulses are repressed during the latent stage and sexual energy can be sublimated (re: defense mechanism) towards school work, hobbies and friendships. Much of the child's energies are channeled into developing new skills and acquiring new knowledge and play becomes largely confined to other children of the same gender.
- The latent stage/period is a time of exploration in which the sexual energy is still present, but it is directed into other areas such as intellectual pursuits and social interactions.
- This stage is important in the development of social and communication skill and self development.

The Genital Stage: (Age range- Puberty to Death)

- During the final stage of psycho-sexual development the individual develops a strong sexual interest in the opposite sex.
- The stage begins during puberty but last throughout the rest of person's life.
- It is a time of adolescent sexual experimentation, the successful resolution of which is settling down in a loving one-to-one relationship with another in our 20's or so.
- Sexual instinct is directed to heterosexual pleasure, rather than self pleasure during the phallic stage.
- For Freud, the proper outlet of the sexual instinct in adults was through heterosexual intercourse. Fixation and conflict may prevent this with the consequence that sexual perversions may develop.
- If the other stages have been completed successfully, the individual should now be well balanced, warm and caring. The goal of this stage is to establish a balance between various life areas.

PERSONALITY

Personality is derived from the Latin word *persona* meaning mask. Personality can be defined as the dynamic and organized set of characteristics possessed by a person that uniquely influence his or her *cognitions*, action, motivation and behaviours in various situations.

A brief definition of personality would be that personality is made up of characteristic pattern of thought, feelings and behaviour that makes a person unique. In addition to this personality arises from within the individuals and remain fairly consistent throughout life.

Personality is the sum total of the physical, mental, emotional and social characteristics of an individual. It is the sum total of all the behavioural and mental characteristics by means of which an individual recognized as being unique.

Behavioural Theories of Personality

Behavioural theories suggested that personality is a result of interaction between individual and environment. Behavioural theorist includes B.F. Skinner and Albert Bandura.

Psychodynamic Theories of Personality

Psychodynamic theories of personality heavily influenced by the work of Sigmund Freud and emphasized the influence of the unconscious mind and childhood experience on personality (it includes psychosexual and psychosocial theories).

Humanist Theories of Personality

Humanist theories emphasized the importance of free will and individual experience in the development of personality. Humanist theorist emphasized the concept of self actualization, which is an innate need of personal growth that motivates behaviour. Humanist theorist includes Carl Rogers and Abraham Maslow.

Trait Theories of Personality

The trait theory approach is one of the largest area within personality psychology. According to this theory personality is made up of number of broad traits. A trait is basically a relative stable characteristic that causes an individual to behave in certain ways. Some of the best known trait theory includes Eysenck's three dimension theory and five factor theories.

Factors Influencing Personality

Heredity vs. Environment

You got you green eyes from your mother and your Freckles from your father. But where did you get your thrill seeking personality and talent for singing? Ultimately, the old argument of nature is: nature has never really been won. We do not yet know how much of what we are is determined by our DNA and how much by our life experience. But we do know that both play an important part in our life.

Nature vs. Nurture

Some scientist thinks that people behave as they do according to genetic predisposition. This is known as the nature theory of human behaviour.

Other scientist believe that people think and behave in certain ways because they are taught to do so. This is known as 'nurture' theory of human behaviour.

Recent study made it clear that both sides are partly right. Nature endows us with inborn abilities and traits, Nurture takes these genetic tendencies and molds them as we learn and mature.

The Nature Theory : Heredity

Scientist has known for years that trait such as eye color and fair color are determined by specific genes encoded in each human cell. The nature theory takes thing a step further to say that more abstract trait such as intelligence, personality, aggression and sexual orientation are also encoded in an individual DNA. Criminal act can be explained as an example. An article in life magazine by George House Colt, claimed that 'it mostly in your gene'. If genetics didn't play a part, then fraternal twins reared under the same condition would be alike, regardless of differences in their genes, but while studies show they do more closely resembles each other.

Nurture Theory : The Environment

The nurture theory emphasized on the following points:

- Behavioural aspects originate only from the environmental factors of our upbringing.
- American psychologist John Watson, best known for his controversial experiments, with young orphan named Albert, demonstrated that acquisition of a phobia could be explained by classical conditioning.
- A strong proponent of environmental learning. He said "Give me a dozen healthy infants, well formed, and may own specified world to bring them up in and I will guarantee to take any one at random and train him to become any type of specialist,

I might select regardless of his talents abilities, vocations and race of his ancestors.

- Psychologist B.F. Skinner's early experiments produced pigeons that could dance and play tennis. Today known as the **father of behavioural science**, went on to prove that "Human behaviour could be conditioned."
- A study suggested that sense of humour is a learned trait, influenced by family and cultural environment and not genetically determined.
- If environment didn't play a part, then identical twins should theoretically be exactly the same in all respects.

Impact of Mass Media on Personality

Films, television, radio, newspapers and magazines are the most prominent forms of the mass media and each influence the behaviour pattern of persons in different manners.

Personality Disorganization

Society everywhere demands from its member's conformity to its folkways and mores, to its values and standards. But often the individual fails to meet the requirement of the society in which he lives. As a result he develops personality problems and become disorganized.

He remains socially isolated because in his case there is breakdown of communicative understanding. Personality disorganization therefore means that the individual is out of adjustment with society who has failed to organize the chief goals of his life into an integrated whole so as to achieve unity of the self.

Personality disorganization may take the milder or serious forms of mental disorder in addition to mentally disorganized persons. There are other examples of personality disorganization – alcoholics, criminals, gamblers and drug addicts, who are mentally normal but socially abnormal.

HUMAN DEVELOPMENT

Human development is a process of human becoming biologically mature, in psychology it means scientific study of systematic psychological changes, emotional changes and perception changes that occur in human beings over the course of their life.

Stages of Development

- Pre Natal Development
- Infancy (1 month)
- Babyhood (1 month) to 24 yrs
- Early childhood (2-6 yrs)
- Late childhood (6-12, 13 yrs)
- Adolescence (13-18 yrs)
- Early Adulthood (20-39 yrs)
- Middle Age (40-59 yrs)
- Old Age (60 yrs - till death)

Pre Natal Development

The whole prenatal development involves three main stages:

- Germinal Stage,
- Embryonic Stage and
- Fetal Stage

Germinal stage begins at conception until 2 weeks; embryonic stage means the development from 2 weeks to 8 weeks; fetal stage represents 9 weeks until birth of the baby. The senses develop in the womb itself: a fetus can both see and hear by the second trimester (13 to 24 weeks of age). Sense of touch develops in the embryonic stage (5 to 8 weeks). Most of the brain's billions of neurons also are developed by the second trimester. Babies are hence born with some odour, taste and sound preferences, largely related to the mother's environment.

Infancy

The terms infant derived from Latin word *infans* meaning unable to speak or speechless. An infant is a very young offspring of human. In medical contexts newborn or urgent neonate refers to an infant in the first 28 days after birth. The term newborn includes pre mature infants, post mature infants and full term newborns.

Emotional Development

Attachment theory is primarily an evolutionary and ethological theory whereby infant seeks proximity to a specified attachment figure. The forming of attachments is considered to be the foundation of the infant's capacity to form and conduct relationship throughout the life. Attachment and attachment behaviour tend to develop between the age of six months and 03 three years.

Babyhood

Babyhood occupies the first two years of life following the brief two week period of infancy. Infancy is the extreme helplessness period. Whereas, during the babyhood months there is gradual decrease in helplessness. This does not mean that helplessness disappears but is replaced by independence.

- Babyhood is true foundation age because many behaviour patterns, many attitude, many pattern of emotional expression are being established in this stage of development. Personality maladjustment in adulthood had their origin in unfavourable childhood experiences.
- Feeling of basic trust or distrust, viewing the world as safe reliable and nurturing or as full of threat, unpredictability and treachery depends on the experiences of babyhood.
- Babyhood is an age of Rapid Growth and change—Physically and Psychologically.
- Babyhood is an age of decreasing dependency as child learns to sit, stand, walk.
- Babyhood is the age of increasing individuality.
- Babyhood is the age of Beginning of socialization.
- Babyhood is the age of sex role typing.
- Babyhood is the beginning of creativity.
- Babyhood is hazardous age.
- Common Emotion Pattern in Babyhood are anger, fear, curiosity, joy and affection.

Childhood

Early childhood or childhood begins from two years and extends to the line when the child became sexually mature. Roughly girls sexually mature at 11 years (13 years average) and boys 12 years (14 years average).

- Childhood is time when the individual is relatively helpless and dependent on others.
- Childhood is time when society regard them 'grown ups'.
- Childhood begins when babyhood is over.
- It begins approximately at the age of two years and extend up to the time when the child becomes sexually mature.
- 2 years – 6 years considered early childhood and 6 years – 13 years as late childhood.

Physical development in Early childhood: Height, Weight, Body Proportions (baby look disappear), Body Build, Bones and Muscles, Fat, Teeth.

Common Emotions: Grief, Envy, Joy, Anger, Fear, Jealousy, Curiosity and Affection.

Social Behaviour pattern: Imitation, Rivalry, Cooperation, Sympathy (occasionally), Empathy (few children), Social Approval, Sharing (sharing is social approval).

Common category of concept that develops during early childhood are about: Life (living), Death (associate with any thing that goes away), Space – (short, long distance), Weight, Time, Self (know about sex, name, body, parts), Sex Role, Social Awareness – nice, smart differentiation.

Late Childhood (6 years to 12, 13 years)

- Late childhood is troublesome age.
- Late childhood is the age when children are no longer willing to do what they are told to do.
- Late childhood is the age when they are more influenced by their peer group than their parents.
- Late childhood is the age when children acquire rudiment of knowledge.

- Late childhood is the age when children develops the habit of working up to their capacities in school.
- Late childhood is about learning physical skill necessary for ordinary games.
- In late childhood the child built an attitude towards oneself as a growing organism
- In late childhood the child develop appropriate masculine or feminine social roles.
- In late childhood the child develops fundamental skills in reading, writing and calculating.
- In late childhood the child develops conscience, a sense of morality and scale of values.
- In late childhood the child achieves personal independence, speech improvement and vocabulary building.
- Some ways in which gangs (friends) belonging leads to improve socialism in late childhood. He learns to be cooperative, learns socially acceptable behaviour, learns to compete with others, learns to accept and carryout responsibilities, learns to play games and sports, learns to confirm the groups standards, learns to be loyal to group and learns to be independent of adults.

Some favourite amusement of late childhood: Reading comic books, movies, radio, television, daydreaming or fantasizing, imagine themselves as conquering heroes, sex role playing, increasing in understanding, development of moral codes, development of conscience and guilt. The term conscience means a conditioned anxiety response to certain kind of situations and actions. It is an internalized policeman which motivates children to do what they know is a right and thus avoids punishment. Guilt is a special kind of negative self evaluation that occurs when an individual acknowledges that his behaviour is at variance with a given moral values to which he feels obligated to confirm.

Common misdemeanors of late childhood: Fighting with siblings, breaking possessions of other family members, being rude to other family members, neglecting home responsibilities, lying, spoiling things intentionality.

School Misdemeanors: Stealing, cheating, whispering and fighting with classmates, reading comic books, watching comic serials, annoying other children by teasing them.

Puberty – Puberty is the closing years of childhood and beginning years of adolescence period.

Adclescence period (13-18 years)

- Adolescence period is an important period.
- Adolescence period is a transitional period
- Adolescence period is a period of change emotional, sexual maturing, interest and role behaviour pattern.
- Adolescence is a time of search of identity.
- Adolescence is a age of unrealism.
- Adolescence is a time of physical and mental change.
- Adolescence is transactional period.
- Transactional period means what has happened before will leave its marks on what happen now and in future.
- When children's go from childhood to adolescence they are told to put away "childish things" and to act their age.

Developmental tasks of Adolescence

- Achieving new and more mature relation with age mates of both sex.
- Achieving a masculine or feminine social roles.
- Desiring, accepting and achieving socially responsible behaviour.
- Achieving emotional independence from parents and other adults.
- Preparing for an economic career.
- Preparing for marriage and family life.

- Acquiring a set of values and an ethical system as a guide to behaviour- developing an ideology.

Adulthood

Adulthood is the longest period of the life span usually divided into three periods—

- Early Adulthood (18 years to 39 years)
- Middle Adulthood (39 years to 60 years)
- Late Adulthood (60 years to till death)

Early adulthood is the settling down age and reproductive age, a problem age and one of emotional tension, a time of social isolation, a time of commitments and often a time of dependency, a time of value changes, a time of creativity and adjustment to a new life pattern.

There are certain aid to mastering the developmental task of early adulthood – physical efficiency, motor and mental ability, motivation and good role model. Because many of interests carried over from adolescence are no longer appropriate for the adult role, changes in all areas of interests are inevitable in this stage. The greatest change is in narrowing down the range of interests.

- Personal interest in early adulthood include interest in: Appearance, clothes, personal adornment, status symbol, money and religion.
- Change in recreational activities: Talking, entertaining, cinema, travelling.
- Social activities in early adulthood are often greatly curtailed because of educational and family pressure. As a result many young adults experience what Erickson has called an 'isolation crises'.
- Isolation Crisis is a time of isolation due to isolation from social group.
- Social mobility in men comes mainly through their own efforts which in women, it comes mainly through marriage.
- Most young married women find sex roles adjustment in early adulthood very difficult especially when they are forced into traditional roles.

Development tasks during Early Adulthood

- Getting started in an occupation
- Selecting a mate
- Learning to live with a marriage partner
- Starting a family
- Rearing children
- Managing home
- Taking on civic responsibilities
- Finding a congenial social group
- Adjustment with working, family, sexual partner, children and in law adjustment

Middle Adulthood or Middle Age

Middle age is generally considered to extend from the age 40 to age 60. Middle age is an especially difficult time in the life span. How well individual adjust to it depends on the foundation laid during earlier stages in the life span.

Characteristics age is a dreaded period: The period is recognized as next to old age. Mental and physical deterioration, the cessation of the reproductive life, importance of youth in culture, all such things influence adult attitude unfavourably. Most adults become nostalgic about their younger years and wish they could turn back the hand of the cock.

Middle Age is Time of Transition: Middle age is the time when men and women leave behind the physical and behavioural characteristics of adulthood and enter a period of life when new physical or behavioural characteristics will prevail. It is a time when men undergo change in virility and women a change in fertility. Transition always means adjustment to new interests, new values and new patterns of behaviour.

Middle Age is a Time of Stress: Radical adjustment to changed role pattern of life when accompanied by physical changes always tends to disrupt the individual physical and psychological homeostasis. It is a time when a number of major adjustment must be made in the home, business and social aspect of their lives.

Middle Age is an "Awkward age:" Just as adolescents are neither children nor adults, so middle age men and women are no longer 'young' nor are they yet 'old'. The middle aged person stands between the younger rebel generation and senior citizen generation.

Middle age a Time of Achievement: According Erikson, during middle age people either become more successful or they stand still and accomplish nothing more. Women like men, who have worked throughout the years of early adulthood generally reach their pick during middle age. Middle age should be a time not only for financial and social success but also for authority and prestige.

Middle Age is a Time of Evaluation: It is mainly a time of self evaluation because middle age is when men and women normally reach their peaks of achievement. It is logical that it also would be the time when they would evaluate their accomplishments in light of their earlier aspirations and the expectation of others especially family and friends.

Middle Age is the Time of Empty Nest: It is the time when the children no longer want to live under the parental roof. Middle age is the 'empty nest' stage in marital lives.

Middle age a time of boredom: Men become bored with their daily routine of work and with a family life that offers little excitement. Women, who have spent most of their adulthood caring for the home and raising children, wonder what they will do for next twenty or thirty years.

Development task middle age:

- Achieving adult clinic and social responsibilities.
- Assisting teenage children to become responsible and happy adults.
- Relating oneself to ones spouse as a person.
- Reaching and maintaining satisfactory performance is ones occupational career.
- Adjusting to aging parents.

Old Age

Closing period of life span.

Old Age is a Period of Decline: People constantly changes early part of life changes leads to maturity but in second part of life involving regression to earlier stages. Physical changes, body cells decline and psychologically unfavourable attitude towards oneself is developed and also for other people, work and life.

Old age is judged by different criteria: Meaning of age is vague and undefined some judge age in terms of physical appearance and activities illusion.

Old Age: Development task:

- Adjusting to decreasing physical strength and health.
- Adjusting to retirement and reduce income.
- Adjusting to death of spouse.
- Establishing an explicit affiliation with members of ones age group.
- Adapting to social roles in a flexible way.

LEARNING

Learning is a relatively permanent change in the behaviour or behavioural potential produced by experience or practice. It is an inferred process and differs from performance which is the observed behaviour, response or action.

The main types of learning are: classical and operant conditioning, observational learning, cognitive learning, verbal learning, concept learning and skill learning.

Pavlov Theory of Classical Conditioning

Ivan Pavlov was a Russian Psychologist who developed a procedure for studying behaviour and principle of learning that had profound effects on the field of psychology. Pavlov was involved in the study of gastric secretions in the dogs. As part of his research he placed some food powder inside the mouth of a dog and measured the resulting amount of salvation. Coincidently he noticed that after a number of such trials a dog begin to salivate to certain stimuli before the food was placed in its mouth. This salvation occurred in response to cues such as the sight of the food dish or the approach of a person who generally brought the food. In other words, stimuli which previously did not lead to this response (called natural stimuli) could now elicit the salvation response because of their association with the food powder that automatically caused the dog to salivate. The event has led Pavlov to conduct some very significant research known as classical conditioning.

The essential characteristic of classical conditioning is that a previously neutral stimulus becomes capable of eliciting a response because of its association with a stimulus that automatically produces the same or similar response. In other words, the dog salivates to the first presentation of the food powder. One need not speak of a conditioning or learning process at this point. The food can be considered as unconditioned stimulus (US) and the salvation an unconditioned response (UR). This is because the salivation is automatic, reflex response to the food. A neutral stimulus, such as bell will not lead to salivation. However, if on a number of trials the bell is sounded just before the presentation of the food powder, the sounding of the bell itself without the subsequent appearance of the food may take on the potential for eliciting the salivation response. In this case, conditioning has occurred since the presentation of the bell alone is followed by salivation. At this point the bell may be referred to as conditioned stimulus (CS) and the salivation may be considered as conditioned response (CR).

US (Food)_______________ elicit UR (salivation)

US + CS (Food + Bell)_______elicit UR (salivation)

CS (Bell)_________________elicit CR

Operant Conditioning

The term operant conditioning was coined by Burrhus F. Skinner, who has conducted extensive research on this process. Operant conditioning describes how we develop behaviour that "operates upon the environment "to bring out behavioural consequences in that environment. He explained that one should focus on the external observable causes or behaviour (rather than try to unpack internal thoughts and motivations).

Operant conditioning can be described as a process that attempts to modify behaviour through the use of positive and negative reinforcement. Through operant conditioning an individual makes an association between a particular behaviour and consequence. For example a parent rewarding a child's excellent performance in exams with some prize or an industry recognize its employee's regularity and punctuality by giving him incentives or promotion.

According to operant conditioning reinforcement comes in two forms: Positive and Negative reinforcement.

Positive reinforces are favourable events or outcomes that are given the individual after the desired behaviour. This may come in the form of praise, reward etc.

Negative reinforces typically are characterized by the removal of an undesired or unpleasant outcome after the desired behaviour. A response is strengthened as something considered negative is removed. The goal in both of these cases of reinforcement is for the behaviour to increase.

SOCIALIZATION

The human infant comes into the world as biological organism with animal needs. He is gradually molded into a social being and he learns social ways of acting and feeling. Without this process of molding, the society could not continue, itself nor could culture exist, nor could the individual become a person. This process of molding is called socialization.

Definition of Socialization

According to Bogardus, it is the process of working together of developing group, responsibility of being guided by the welfare needs of the other. According to Ogburn, "socialization is the process by which how individual learns to conform to the norms of the group."

Socialism and Socialization

Socialism is a theory not a quality or process. It is a theory of the future structure of society. Every person and brand project themselves as socialist. Joad had compared socialism to a hat which has lost his shape because every person wears it. Actually socialism is a theory that the means of production exchange and distribution should be owned and controlled either by the state or by other association directly responsible to community. Such ownership will result in more equitable distribution of wealth and give sense of social security as well.

Factors of the Process of Socialization

Socialization is the process of learning group norms, habit and ideals. There are four factors of this process of learning. These are imitation, suggestions, identification and language.

Imitation: Imitation is copying by an individual the action of another. Mead defines it as "self-conscious assumption of another acts or roles". Thus when the child attempts to walk impressively like his father, swinging a stick and wearing a spectacles, he is imitating. Imitation may be conscious or unconscious, deliberately, perceptual or ideational. In imitation person imitating performs exactly the same activity as the one being performed before him.

Suggestion: Suggestion is the process of communicating information which has no logical or self evident basis. It may be conveyed through language, pictures or some similar medium. Suggestion influence the behaviour, actually propaganda and advertising are based on the fundamental psychological principle of suggestion.

Identification: In his early age, the child can't make any distinction between his organism and environment. Most of his actions are random. They are natural reaction of which he is not conscious. As he grows in age he comes to know of the nature of things which satisfied his needs. Such things become the object of his identification. Thus, the toys which he plays or looking at the mother who feeds him become the object of his identification. Through identification he became sociable.

Language: Language is the medium of social intercourse. It is the means of cultural transmission. At first the child utters some random syllabus which has no meaning but gradually he comes to learn his mother toung. So, language plays a vital role in shaping the personality of an individual.

Role of socialization: The role of socialization in the development of human mentality and behaviour may be shown by citing the two cases of Anna and Isabelle. Anna, an intelligent child was caused to be kept all alone in upstairs room. When removed from the age of nearly six years, Anna could not talk, walk or do anything that showed intelligence. She was expressionless and indifferent to everything. She could not make any move in her own behalf. This show that in the absence of socialization the purely biological resource is too poor to contribute to the development of a complete personality. Communicative contact is the core of socializations.

Isabelle was found at the age of six and a half year like Anna. She was an intelligent child and had been kept in isolation for that reason. When found she was apparently unaware of relationship of any kind. Her behaviour was comparable to that of a child of six months. Later attempts were made to teach her to speak. At first the task seemed hopeless but lately she responded and ultimately reached the normal level of development by the time she was eight and a half years old.

Both these cases show the role of socialization in personality development. In short socialization is said to be the most important factor in development of personality.

MULTIPLE CHOICE QUESTIONS

1. Which one of the following is related to community organisation? Choose the answer by selecting the correct code.
1. Locality development model
2. Social planning model
3. Social action model

Code :

A. 1 & 2 B. 1 only
C. 2 & 3 D. All

2. 'What a person thinks, feels and assumes he/ she is which is often reinforced by the comments and behaviour from those around' — is termed as :

A. Perception B. Maturation
C. Growth D. Self-Concept

3. Match the concept with the author who has developed the same :

List-I (Concept)	**List-II (Author)**
(a) Hierarchy of Needs	(i) Abraham Maslow
(b) Transaction Analysis	(ii) Ivan Pavlov
(c) Behaviour Modification	(iii) Eric Berne
(d) Psycho Analysis	(iv) Sigmund Freud
	(v) H.B. Trecker

Codes :

	(a)	(b)	(c)	(d)
A.	(v)	(iv)	(iii)	(ii)
B.	(i)	(iii)	(ii)	(iv)
C.	(iii)	(ii)	(i)	(iv)
D.	(v)	(iii)	(ii)	(i)

4. Which of the following is a correct matching?

A. Juvenile Justice Act – 1985
B. Untouchability Offences Act – 1954
C. Dowry Prohibition Act – 1962
D. Factories Act – 1948

5. Panchayati Raj Institutions in India have brought about one of the following:

A. Eradication of untouchability
B. Land ownership to depressed classes
C. A formal representation of weaker sections in village governance
D. Spread of education

6. Who is the author of the book "Social Group Work – A Helping Process"?

A. Wilson G and Ryland
B. Trecker H.B.
C. Philips H.U.
D. Konopka G.

7. The objective of Social Legislation is

A. To solve social problems.
B. To bridge the gap between current needs and existing laws.
C. To make new laws.
D. To review the laws and problems.

8. Manifestation of repressed ideas in the form of finer things is

A. Sublimation B. Ambivalence
C. Compensation D. Fixation

9. Who gave the concept of 'Looking glass self'?

A. Karl Marx B. G.H. Mead
C. C.H. Cooley D. M.K. Gandhi

10. 'Operationalization of Variables' in social work research means

A. Making the variables simple enough to understand
B. Making the variables measurable
C. Arranging the variables in a logical order
D. Making the variables fit for research.

11. Which one of the following is not a correct matching?

A. Arya Samaj – Swami Dayanand Saraswati
B. Bhrahma Samaj – Raja Ram Mohan Roy
C. Prarthana Samaj – Ramabai Ranade
D. Satysodhak Samaj – Jyothiba Phule

12. The book 'Social Diagnosis' was written by

A. Mary Richmond
B. Joseph Luft
C. Perelman
D. Ross

13. **Assertion (A) :** Panchayati Raj Institutions have provided women's representation in local self government institutions in Rural India.

Reason (R) : Panchayati Raj Institutions facilitates capacity building and empowerment of women.

Choose your answer from the codes given below :

A. Both (A) and (R) are not correct
B. (A) is correct and (R) is the correct explanation of A
C. (A) is correct but (R) is not the correct explanation of (A)
D. (R) is correct but (A) is wrong

14. The formula used to determine 'Intelligence Quotient' is

A. $I.Q. = \frac{PA}{CA} \times 100$

B. $I.Q. = \frac{CA}{MA} \times 100$

C. $I.Q. = \frac{CA}{MA} \times 200$

D. $I.Q. = \frac{MA}{CA} \times 100$

15. ________ refers to the protection of society against crime.

A. Social Welfare
B. Social Defence
C. Social Security
D. Social Development

16. Conscience is identified with :

A. Id B. Ego
C. Super Ego D. All the above

17. ________ was associated with conscientization model.

A. Murray G. Ross
B. Paulo Friere
C. H.B. Trecker
D. None of the above

18. ________ Theory propounds that childhood experiences influence the adult behaviour.

A. Person Centered Theory
B. Psycho-analytical Theory
C. Behaviour Modification Theory
D. Existential Theory

19. Gandhiji was associated with

I. Trusteeship
II. Non-Violence
III. Imperialism
IV. Truth

Codes :

A. I and II are correct
B. I, II and III are correct
C. I, II and IV are correct
D. II, III and IV are correct

20. Practice of untouchability is abolished by the Indian Constitution under the Article :

A. 17 B. 19
C. 38 D. 42

21. Which is not the principle of experimental design?

A. Principle of Replication
B. Principle of Universalization
C. Principle of Randomization
D. Principle of Local control

22. Which of the following is not the part of ESI benefits?

A. Sickness benefit
B. Maternity benefit
C. Fringe benefit
D. Medical benefit

23. The best known expert of the problem solving model is

A. Gladstein
B. Perlman
C. Mary Richmond
D. Garret

24. Balwant Rai Mehta was associated with

A. Community Participation
B. Community Welfare
C. Community Development
D. Community Organization

25. Who is the author of the book "Integrated Social Work Practice"?
A. A.S. Desai B. S.B. Desai
C. Murli Desai D. S.K. Khinduka

26. Which of the following is not the function of a hospital social worker?
A. Fund-raising for financial support to deserving patients.
B. Counselling the patient and his/her family reluctant to undergo surgery.
C. Registering new patients and issuing OPD cards.
D. Facilitating communication between the doctor and the patient.

27. The book on "Social Work : An Integrated Approach" was authored by
A. Sanjay Bhatt
B. Sanjay Bhattacharya
C. Surendra Singh
D. Sanjay Pandey

28. The organized non-profit activity for public purpose outside of both market and state is called
A. Corporate sector
B. Civil society sector
C. Government sector
D. All the above

29. Balika Divas in India is being observed on
A. 9th October B. 9th November
C. 9th December D. 9th September

30. Life satisfaction is/an
A. Concrete concept B. Abstract concept
C. Hypothesis D. None of the above

31. Identify the correct term/s
The tools of social casework are :
(i) Home visit (ii) Summarization
(iii) Recording (iv) Interviewing
A. (i), (iii), (iv) B. (i), (ii), (iii)
C. (ii), (iii), (iv) D. (i), (ii), (iii), (iv)

32. Identify the correct response
The Magsaysay award was given to :
(i) Manibhai Desai
(ii) Banoo Coyaji
(iii) Medha Patkar
(iv) Kiran Bedi
A. (i), (ii), (iii) B. (i), (ii), (iv)
C. (i), (ii), (iii), (iv) D. (i), (iii), (iv)

33. Identify the social process from the following:
(i) Actualisation
(ii) Acculturation
(iii) Adoption
(iv) Socialisation
A. (i), (iii) B. (ii), (iii)
C. (ii), (iv) D. (i), (iv)

34. Which of the following are social institutions?
(i) Caste (ii) Family
(iii) Socialisation (iv) Education
A. (i), (ii), (iv) B. (ii), (iii), (iv)
C. (i), (ii), (iii) D. (i), (ii)

35. Who had started the first school of social work in India ?
A. G.D. Birla
B. S.P. Godrej
C. Sir Dorabjee Tata
D. M.K. Tata

36. Field work in social work helps to acquire :
A. Knowledge
B. Skills
C. Attitudinal change
D. All the above

37. Which of the following is **not** part of the U.N. ?
A. FAO B. ILO
C. WHO D. Ford Foundation

38. Adoption of children in India is regulated by :
(a) Special Adoption Act
(b) Hindu Adoption Act
(c) Guardianship and Wards Act
(d) Uniform Adoption Act
A. (a) and (b) B. (a) and (c)
C. (b) and (c) D. (a) and (d)

39. In HIV Counselling VCTC refers to :
A. Voluntary Condom use Training Centre
B. Voluntary Counselling and Testing Centre
C. Voluntary Centre for Training and Care
D. Voluntary Care and Treatment Centre

40. Match the items in List-I with items in List-II :

List-I	List-II
(a) My Experiments with Truth	(i) Gunnar Myrdal
(b) The Radical Social Work	(ii) Joseph Stiglitz
(c) Asian Drama	(iii) Saul Alinsky
(d) Globalisation and its discontents	(iv) M.K. Gandhi
	(v) J.K. Galbraith

Choose correct code for answer :

	(a)	(b)	(c)	(d)
A.	(iii)	(i)	(ii)	(iv)
B.	(iv)	(iii)	(i)	(ii)
C.	(ii)	(i)	(v)	(iii)
D.	(ii)	(v)	(iv)	(i)

41. The term Ageism refers to :
A. Provision of welfare services to the aged
B. The negative attitudes towards the aged
C. The positive attitudes towards the aged
D. None of the above

42. Mention the year in which Government of India appointed the Rural-Urban Relations Committee :
A. 1963 B. 1973
C. 1953 D. 1983

43. Maslow's hierarchy of needs, which need stands at the top, is ?
A. Self esteem
B. Self actualisation
C. Social acceptance
D. None of the above

44. A closely related technique to role reversal is :
A. the expression of empathy
B. the expression of sympathy
C. the expression of apathy
D. the expression of antipathy

45. The report of the National Commission on self employed women and women in the unorganised sector is titled as :
A. Towards equality
B. Daughters of India
C. Shram Shakti
D. Invisible women

46. Who has propounded the theory of 'Class struggle' :
A. Frederic Engles B. Karl Pearson
C. Karl Marx D. Max Weber

47. An educated guess about the nature of the relationship between two or more variables is termed as :
A. Antithesis B. Hypothesis
C. Generalisation D. Prognosis

48. Mary Richmond's 'Social Diagnosis' can be considered as the first book of :
A. Social Group Work
B. Social and Preventive Medicine
C. Social Case Work
D. Social Action

49. Match the following pairs :

(a) Lewis Coser	(i) Field Theory
(b) Malinowski	(ii) Conflict Theory
(c) Kurt Lewin	(iii) Rational Choice Theory
(d) James Coleman	(iv) Exchange Theory

Codes :

	(a)	(b)	(c)	(d)
A.	(ii)	(iv)	(i)	(iii)
B.	(i)	(ii)	(iii)	(iv)
C.	(ii)	(iii)	(iv)	(i)
D.	(iii)	(ii)	(i)	(iv)

50. Which conference has brought in the concept of sustainable development?
A. Montreal Conference
B. The Doha Conference
C. The Rio Conference
D. The World Social Forum 2005

51. The Human Development Index (HDI) as an index of measurement of development is developed by :
A. UNDP B. World Bank
C. WTO D. IMF

52. **Assertion (A):** Economic growth created opportunites for people and post-reform period showed slow performance on macro-economic variables.

Reason (R): There is complementarity between economic growth and equity.

Which of the following is correct ?

A. Both (A) and (R) are correct but (R) is not the correct explanation of (A)

B. Both (A) and (R) are correct and (R) is a correct explanation of (A)

C. Both (A) and (R) are wrong

D. (R) is correct but (A) is wrong

53. Assertion (A) : Indian Constitution authorises the Indian State to make special provisions for weaker sections of society.

Reason (R) : People belonging to weaker sections require special attention of the State.

Codes :

A. Both (A) and (R) are correct but (R) is not the correct explanation of (A).

B. Both (A) and (R) are correct and (R) is the correct explanation of (A).

C. (A) is correct and (R) is wrong.

D. (A) is wrong and (R) is correct.

54. Arrange in order the steps in Research.

A. Problem Formulation, Hypothesis, Research Design, Data Collection, Data Analysis and Report Writings.

B. Hypothesis, Research Design, Data Collection, Data Analysis and Report Writing, Problem Formulation

C. Data Collection, Problem Formulation, Hypothesis, Research Design, Data Analysis and Report Writing

D. Data Collection, Data Analysis and Report writing, Research Design, Hypothesis, Problem Formulation

55. Assertion (A) : Continuous increase in the population of elderly is a concern of modern society.

Reason (R) : Active participation of elderly should be ensured for the development of the society.

Codes :

A. Both (A) and (R) are correct.

B. (A) is wrong but (R) is correct.

C. (A) is correct but (R) is wrong.

D. Both (A) and (R) are wrong.

56. Assertion (A) : Multinational corporations ignore the needs of millions of people by controlling innovations.

Reason (R) : For poor people the technological progress remains out of reach.

Codes :

A. Both (A) and (R) true but (R) is not the correct explanation of (A).

B. (A) is correct and (R) is wrong.

C. (A) is wrong (R) is correct.

D. Both (A) and (R) are correct and (R) is the correct explanation of (A).

57. What is the sequence of action in a Disaster Management strategy?

A. Alarming, Preparedness, Relief, Rescue, Rehabilitation.

B. Preparedness, Alarming, Rescue, Relief, Rehabilitation.

C. Preparedness, Alarming, Relief, Rescue, Rehabilitation.

D. Alarming, Preparedness, Rescue, Relief, Rehabilitation.

58. Arrange the process of communication in sequence.

A. Coding, Decoding, Recipient, Channel

B. Channel, Encoding, Recipient, Decoding

C. Channel, Decoding, Recipient, Encoding

D. Encoding, Channel, Recipient, Decoding

59. Match the following :

List-I (Author)	**List-II (Books)**
(a) Gisela Konopka	(i) Social Group Work
(b) H.B. Trecker	(ii) Introduction to Social Case Work
(c) Grace Mathew	(iii) Theory and Practice of Social Case Work

(d) Gordon Hamilton (iv) Group Work in the Institution

Codes :

	(a)	(b)	(c)	(d)
A.	(i)	(ii)	(iii)	(iv)
B.	(ii)	(i)	(iv)	(iii)
C.	(iii)	(ii)	(iv)	(i)
D.	(iv)	(i)	(ii)	(iii)

60. Match the following :

List – I (Act)	List – I (Year of Passing)
(a) The Juvenile Justice Act	(i) 1986
(b) The Right to Education Act	(ii) 1998
(c) The Child Labour (Prohibition and Regulation) Act.	(iii) 2009
(d) Child Trafficking and Pornography Act.	(iv) 2000

Codes :

	(a)	(b)	(c)	(d)
A.	(iv)	(iii)	(ii)	(i)
B.	(i)	(ii)	(iii)	(iv)
C.	(i)	(iii)	(iv)	(ii)
D.	(iv)	(iii)	(i)	(ii)

61. Match the List-I with List-II :

List-I (International Days)	List-II (Date)
(a) International Day of Elders	(i) 4th Feb.
(b) World Environment Day	(ii) 1st October
(c) World Blood Donor Day	(iii) 14th June
(d) World Cancer Day	(iv) 5th June

Codes :

	(a)	(b)	(c)	(d)
A.	(i)	(ii)	(iii)	(iv)
B.	(ii)	(iv)	(iii)	(i)
C.	(i)	(iii)	(ii)	(iv)
D.	(iii)	(i)	(ii)	(iv)

62. Match items in List-I with List-II and choose correct code given below :

List-I	List-II
(a) Social Case Work	(i) Social Planning Model
(b) Social Group Work	(ii) Behaviour Modification Model
(c) Community Orga-nization	(iii) Reciprocal Model
(d) Social Action	(iv) Conscienti-zation Model

Codes :

	(a)	(b)	(c)	(d)
A.	(i)	(iii)	(ii)	(iv)
B.	(ii)	(iv)	(iii)	(i)
C.	(iii)	(i)	(ii)	(iv)
D.	(ii)	(iii)	(i)	(iv)

63. Match items in List-I with List-II and choose correct code given below :

List-I	List-II
(a) National Youth Day	1. 5th October
(b) International Women's Day	2. 5th June
(c) International Teachers Day	3. 12th January
(d) World Environment Day	4. 8th March

Codes :

	(a)	(b)	(c)	(d)
A.	1	2	3	4
B.	2	3	4	1
C.	3	4	1	2
D.	4	1	2	3

64. Match the following Labour Legislation given in List-I with the year of enactment given in List-II.

List-I	List-II
(a) The Trade Union Act	1. 1972
(b) The Mines Act	2. 1948
(c) The Payment of Gratuity Act	3. 1952
(d) The Minimum Wages Act	4. 1926

Codes :

	(a)	(b)	(c)	(d)
A.	4	3	1	2
B.	3	2	1	4

C. 2 4 1 3
D. 2 1 4 3

65. Match the following process given in List-I with the items given in List-II.

List-I	**List-II**
(a) Listening	1. Directing
(b) Reassurance	2. Free association
(c) Inertia	3. Resistence
(d) Non-editing	4. Facilitation

Codes :

	(a)	(b)	(c)	(d)
A.	4	2	3	1
B.	4	1	3	2
C.	3	4	1	2
D.	4	3	2	1

66. Match the following fears with their technical names.

List-I	**List-II**
(a) Hydrophobia	1. Fear of heights
(b) Nictophobia	2. Fear of darkness
(c) Acrophobia	3. Fear of water
(d) Pyrophobia	4. Fear of fire

Codes :

	(a)	(b)	(c)	(d)
A.	3	2	4	1
B.	2	3	1	4
C.	2	3	4	1
D.	3	2	1	4

67. Match the following items given in List-I with the items given in List-II.

List-I	**List-II**
(a) Right to equality	1. Article 51 A
(b) Right to free legal aid	2. Article 46
(c) Fundamental duties	3. Article 14
(d) Welfare of weaker sections	4. Article 21

Codes :

	(a)	(b)	(c)	(d)
A.	3	4	1	2
B.	1	4	2	3
C.	4	1	3	2
D.	3	4	2	1

68. What is Catharsis?

A. The reduction of tension by telling one's problems to someone else.
B. The reduction of tension by talking, one's problem to everyone.
C. Not making any attempt to tell problems to anyone else.
D. The reduction of tension by telling one's problems to professionals only.

69. Assertion (A) : Women's participation in Natural Resource Management is essential for its success.

Reason (R) : Awareness and empowerment of women will enhance their participation.

Codes :

A. Both (A) and (R) are correct and (R) is the correct explanation of (A).
B. Both (A) and (R) are wrong.
C. (A) is correct, but (R) is wrong.
D. (A) is correct, but (R) is not the correct explanation of A.

70. Which one of the following is not an objective of social policy in India?

A. Equality
B. Social Justice
C. Inclusive Growth
D. Population Growth

71. Which of the following is not a social legislation ?

A. Protection of Civil Rights Act
B. Beggars Act
C. Right to Information Act
D. Forest Conservation Act

72. What is the theme of Prime Minister's High Level Committee popularly known as Sachar Committee?

A. Social, Economic and Educational status of Muslim Community in India.
B. Imbalances in development of different regions in the country.
C. Impact of double taxation on domestic economy.
D. Social, Economic and Educational status of the Rajput Community of India.

73. Social Audit refers to

A. Security and analysis of the working of any public utility vis-à-vis its social relevance.

B. Audit of all the work done by the social sector.
C. Auditing of all the accounts of NGOs.
D. None of the above

74. Which one of the following is not a Fundamental Right ?
A. Right to Work
B. Right to Constitutional Remedies
C. Right to Freedom of Religion
D. Right to Equality

75. The oldest social security legislation in India is
A. The Workmen's Compensation Act
B. Provident Fund Act
C. Maternity Benefit Act
D. Payment of Gratuity Act

76. Which organisation among the following publishes the records of accidental deaths and suicides in India ?
A. National Commission of Women
B. Ministry of Social Justice and Empowerment
C. National Crime Records Bureau
D. Census of India

77. Classical conditioning technique used to eliminate phobias, is used in
A. Generalization
B. Operant conditioning
C. Spontaneous recovery
D. Systematic desensitization

78. Put the following events in the order of their occurrence :
i. Charity organisation society (London)
ii. Publication of a book on social case work
iii. Charity organisation society (USA)
iv. Emergence of Freudian theory

Codes :

A.	i	iii	ii	iv
B.	iv	ii	i	iii
C.	i	iv	ii	iii
D.	iii	iv	ii	i

79. Arrange the following steps in the process of establishment of NGOs in a sequence :
i. Mission
ii. Vision
iii. Strategies
iv. Objectives

Codes :

A.	i	ii	iv	iii
B.	i	ii	iii	iv
C.	ii	i	iii	iv
D.	ii	i	iv	iii

80. What is the proper sequence of the following?
i. Members of similar age-group available with interest in recreational activities.
ii. Group becomes cohesive and goals achieved.
iii. Group goals are identified and clearly stated.
iv. Programme planned and carried out.

Codes :

A.	iii	iv	ii	i
B.	i	iii	iv	ii
C.	i	ii	iii	iv
D.	ii	i	iv	iii

81. Match items given in List-I with those in List-II by selecting the correct code given below :

List-I (Author)	**List-II (Book)**
(a) Caplan, G. (1961)	i. A Theory of Human Motivation
(b) Douglas, T. (1993)	ii. Common Human Needs
(c) Maslow, A. (1943)	iii. A Community Approach to Mental Health
(d) Towle, Charlotte (1945)	iv. A Theory of Group Work Practice

Codes :

	(a)	(b)	(c)	(d)
A.	ii	i	iv	iii
B.	iii	ii	i	iv
C.	iv	iii	ii	i
D.	iii	iv	i	ii

82. Without warmth the professional social worker may be 'technically correct but therapeutically impotent' has been said by
A. Mary Richmond

B. Florance Hollis
C. Goldstein
D. Gordon Hamilton

83. Who gave the three dimensional model of personality – the child, the adult, the parent?
A. Sigmund Freud B. Otto Rank
C. Eric Berne D. Joseph Wolpe

84. Behavioural modification involves
A. solving problems through insight.
B. bringing behaviour under stimulus control.
C. demonstrating learning in the absence of reinforcement.
D. application of learning principles to change behaviour.

85. One of the following techniques contribute a lot for the skewed sex ratio.
A. Pre-natal diagnostic techniques
B. Post-natal diagnostic techniques
C. Peri-natal diagnostic techniques
D. None of the above

86. In which year the National policy for women empowerment was announced?
A. 1981 B. 1991
C. 2001 D. 2011

87. CEDAW stands for
A. Customary elimination of discrimination against adult women.
B. Conference on elimination of all forms of discrimination against women.
C. Convention on empowerment and development of adult women.
D. Convention on elimination of all forms of discrimination against women.

88. What Act deals with 'Intimate Violence'?
A. Domestic Violence Act
B. Violence against Women Act
C. Indian Dowry Prohibition Act
D. Indian Penal Code

89. Marginalization of targeted individuals, excluding them from community life and denying access to resources is called
A. Prejudice B. Discrimination
C. Isolation D. Stigma

90. The practice of untouchability is abolished by the Indian Constitution in Article :
A. 17 B. 19
C. 38 D. 42

91. Consider the following statements and select your answer according to the codes given below :
Assertion (A) : Joint Family is disintegrating fast in Modern India.
Reason (R) : Transition from agrarian to Industrial economy is responsible for this disintegration.
Code :
A. Both (A) and (R) are true and (R) is the correct explanation of (A)
B. Both (A) and (R) are true, but (R) is not the correct explanation of (A)
C. (A) is true, but (R) is false
D. (A) is false, but (R) is true

92. Consider the following statements and select your answer according to the codes given below :
Assertion (A) : People's participation is essential for the success of developmental program.
Reason (R) : Education and Awareness lead to participation.
Code :
A. Both (A) and (R) are true and (R) is the correct explanation of A
B. Both (A) and (R) are true and (R) is the not correct explanation of A
C. (A) is true, but (R) is false
D. (A) is false, but (R) is true

93. **Assertion (A) :** The phase and complexity of any group will be the same.
Reason (R) : Social group work supports people to make use of leisure time.
Codes :
A. Both (A) and (R) are correct.
B. Both (A) and (R) are wrong.
C. (A) is correct and (R) is wrong.
D. (A) is wrong, but (R) is correct.

94. **Assertion (A) :** The criminal justice system is designed to punish and reform the criminal.

Reason (R) : The law in India is not victim-oriented.

Codes :

A. Both (A) and (R) are true and (R) is the correct explanation of (A).

B. Both (A) and (R) are not correct.

C. Both (A) and (R) are true, but (R) is not the correct explanation of (A).

D. (A) is not correct, but (R) is correct.

95. Following are the steps of social research. Arrange the steps to prepare a plan of research study :

(1) Data collection

(2) Hypothesis

(3) Problem formulation

(4) Objectives

(5) Processing and analysis of data

(6) Report writing

Codes :

A. (1) (3) (2) (4) (5) (6)

B. (2) (3) (1) (4) (5) (6)

C. (4) (3) (2) (1) (5) (6)

D. (3) (4) (2) (1) (5) (6)

96. Identify the correct sequence among the following :

A. Selection, recruitment, induction, placement

B. Induction, selection, placement, recruitment

C. Recruitment, selection, induction, placement

D. Recruitment, induction, selection, placement

97. Arrange the different phases of disaster management in correct sequence :

(i) Warning messages on the impending disaster

(ii) Evacuation

(iii) Community based preparedness

(iv) Rescue

(v) Resettlement

(vi) Rehabilitation

Codes :

A. (i), (ii), (iii), (iv), (v), (vi)

B. (i), (ii), (iv), (iii), (v), (vi)

C. (i), (ii), (v), (iii), (iv), (vi)

D. (iii), (i), (ii), (iv), (v), (vi)

98. Arrange the following steps in the proper sequence :

1. Attending the call on child helpline.
2. Producing the child before the Juvenile Justice Competent Authority with case details.
3. Picking up the child and seeking permission to provide shelter.
4. Assessing the child's needs and providing suitable services.
5. Sending the child to after care home.

A. 2, 3, 4, 5, 1 B. 1, 3, 2, 4, 5

C. 4, 2, 5, 1, 3 D. 5, 1, 2, 3, 4

99. List the following days of international observance in the order of their occurrence in the calendar month of October.

i. World Mental Health Day.

ii. International Day of Older Persons.

iii. World Food Day.

iv. International Day of Girl Child

A. i, ii, iii, iv

B. ii, i, iii, iv

C. ii, iii, iv, i

D. ii, i, iv, iii

100. The sensing of skin through touch or pressure is

A. Visual perception

B. Olfactory perception

C. Kinesthetic perception

D. Auditory perception

101. 12th August is celebrated as

A. International Day of Rural Women

B. World Humanitarian Day

C. World Habitat Day

D. International Youth Day

102. What does a population pyramid signify?

A. Maternal mortality rate

B. Fertility rate

C. Death rate

D. Age-sex distribution at a given time

103. The phrase 'Human Rights' was first used in

A. League of Nations Covenant

B. French Declaration of the Rights
C. Charter of the United Nations
D. American Declaration of Independence

104. The International Covenant for Economic, Social and Cultural Rights was adopted in the year

A. 1926 B. 1948
C. 1956 D. 1966

105. According to whom groups must accomplish the four functional tasks, *i.e.*, integration, adaptation, pattern maintainance and goal attainment to remain in equilibrium?

A. Talcott Parsons B. Ghurye
C. Cooley D. Durkheim

106. In Second Five Year Plan, the primary emphasis shifted to

A. Rural Development
B. Industrial Development
C. Agricultural Development
D. Urban Development

107. The 'Problem Solving Approach' emerged from the work of

A. Florence Hollis
B. Mary Richmond
C. H.H. Perlman
D. B. Swift

108. A theory of deviant behaviour which holds that deviant behaviour results when there is a lack of socially approved means to achieve a socially approved goals :

A. Anomie theory
B. Personality theory
C. Differential association
D. Containment theory

109. Defining the relevant variables to remove the ambiguity in measurement is called

A. problem formulation
B. operationalisation of variables
C. statistical inference
D. selection of scales

110. Match the pairs :

(a) Sepoy Mutiny (i) 1975
(b) National Emergency (ii) 1953
(c) Central Social Welfare Board (iii) 1857
(d) Prevention of Immoral Traffic in Women and Girls Act (iv) 1978

Codes :

	(a)	(b)	(c)	(d)
A.	(iv)	(i)	(iii)	(ii)
B.	(iii)	(i)	(ii)	(iv)
C.	(ii)	(iv)	(i)	(iii)
D.	(i)	(iii)	(ii)	(iv)

111. Match the pairs :

(a) National Policy on Education (i) 1956
(b) National Policy on Health (ii) 1952
(c) Prevention of Bigamy Act (iii) 1983
(d) Special Marriage Act (iv) 1986

Codes :

	(a)	(b)	(c)	(d)
A.	(iv)	(iii)	(ii)	(i)
B.	(ii)	(iv)	(iii)	(i)
C.	(i)	(iii)	(ii)	(iv)
D.	(iii)	(i)	(iv)	(ii)

112. Consider the following statements and answer according to the codes given below:

Assertion (A) : There is no substantial difference between Social Work Research and Social Science Research.

Reason (R) : Social Science Research and Social Work Research deal with the same social realities.

A. Both (A) and (R) are true and (R) is a correct explanation of (A)
B. Both (A) and (R) are not true
C. (A) is true but (R) is not true
D. (A) is not true but (R) is true

113. Operationalisation of variables in social work means :

A. Making the variables measurable
B. Making the variables simple to understand
C. Arranging the variables in a logical order
D. Making the variables fit for research

114. Consider the following statements and select your answer according to the codes given below :

Assertion (A) : In quantitative research, the appropriate method of sampling is random sampling.

Reason (R) : One can use statistical methods and generalisation is possible.

A. Both (A) and (R) are true.
B. Both (A) and (R) are not true
C. (A) is true but (R) is false
D. (A) is not true but (R) is true

115. The most important central tendency is :

A. Mode
B. Mean
C. Median
D. Standard Deviation

116. Primary data means :

A. Data collected for the specific research
B. Data collected by the researcher
C. Data that is very important
D. Data collected with great care

117. Sociometry is a technique widely used for study of :

A. Group structure
B. Status of members in the group
C. Leadership
D. All the above

118. Societies Registration Act was passed in the year :

A. 1861 B. 1947
C. 1960 D. 1860

119. The Nobel Laureate Prof. Amartya Sen's most significant contribution is in the field of :

A. Econometrics
B. Micro-credit
C. Environmental Economics
D. Welfare Economics

120. The act of perceiving, understanding and responding to emotional state and ideas of another person is known as :

A. Sympathy
B. Empathy
C. Transference
D. Displacement

121. Match the authors List-I with the subjects given in List-II by using the code given below:

List-I	**List-II**
(a) Specht H and Kramer R M	(i) Social case work
(b) Grace Mathew	(ii) Social movements
(c) M S Gore	(iii) Social development
(d) M S A Rao	(iv) Community work

Codes :

	(a)	(b)	(c)	(d)
A.	i	ii	iii	iv
B.	iv	i	iii	ii
C.	ii	iv	ii	iii
D.	iii	ii	iv	i

ANSWERS

1	2	3	4	5	6	7	8	9	10
D	D	B	D	C	D	B	A	C	B
11	**12**	**13**	**14**	**15**	**16**	**17**	**18**	**19**	**20**
C	A	B	D	B	C	B	B	C	A
21	**22**	**23**	**24**	**25**	**26**	**27**	**28**	**29**	**30**
B	C	B	C	B	C	B	B	C	B
31	**32**	**33**	**34**	**35**	**36**	**37**	**38**	**39**	**40**
A	C	B	A	C	D	D	C	B	B
41	**42**	**43**	**44**	**45**	**46**	**47**	**48**	**49**	**50**
B	A	B	A	C	C	B	C	A	C

51	52	53	54	55	56	57	58	59	60
A	B	A	A	A	C	B	D	D	D
61	**62**	**63**	**64**	**65**	**66**	**67**	**68**	**69**	**70**
B	D	C	A	B	D	A	D	A	D
71	**72**	**73**	**74**	**75**	**76**	**77**	**78**	**79**	**80**
D	A	A	A	A	C	D	A	D	B
81	**82**	**83**	**84**	**85**	**86**	**87**	**88**	**89**	**90**
D	C	C	D	A	C	D	A	D	A
91	**92**	**93**	**94**	**95**	**96**	**97**	**98**	**99**	**100**
A	A	D	C	D	C	D	B	D	C
101	**102**	**103**	**104**	**105**	**106**	**107**	**108**	**109**	**110**
D	D	C	D	A	B	C	A	B	B
111	**112**	**113**	**114**	**115**	**116**	**117**	**118**	**119**	**120**
A	A	A	B	B	B	D	D	D	B
121									
B									

➤➤➤➤➤

CHAPTER

4

Case Work

CASE WORK

Concept of Social Case Work

Social case work is one of the important method and technique of professional social work. It aims to find individual solutions to individual's problems. The focus of social case work is on an individual. People often faced with difficulties due to personal or environmental factors, leading to their malfunctioning and consequent maladjustment in society. The case worker thoroughly understands the person and problems and helps him to balance himself to strengthen out his difficulties. Social case work is an art of helping individual to work out better social relationship and adjustment, it is a method of helping people individual by individual, to tackle effectively the various problems confronting them and that it is a way of helping individual to use their own resources both material and psychological for the treatment and prevention of personal and social problems.

Objectives of Social Case Work

1. To understand and solve the internal problems of the individual.
2. To strengthen his ego power.
3. Remediation of problems in social functioning.
4. Prevention of problems in social functioning.
5. Development of resources to enhance social functioning.

Principles of Social Case Work

Principles are certain statements and guiding beliefs, which directs our professional action. In social case work practice, the principles are as discussed under:

(1) Principle of Acceptance: Acceptance in social case work meaning accepting the client irrespective of his negative behaviour and qualities. It is about expressing warmth, and positive attitude. The social worker perceive, acknowledge, receive and establish a relationship with the client as he actually is not as he wish him to be or think he should be.

(2) Principle of Confidentiality: Confidentiality in social case work implies keeping the confidential things confidential. As everyone prefers to keep his things to himself and leak out only when its disclosure is more beneficial to the person. The person has the right of personal information about themselves in their relationship with the social worker during and following the process of obtaining service, this right may be superseded only in exceptional situations. Confidentiality is fundamental to case work and relationship with the client and base for having therapeutic relationship with the client. Once the client loses confidence on worker he will not believe the worker and the whole process of communication will break down.

Principle of Relationship

According to this principle relationship is the crux of helping process. There should be positive relationship between the client and the worker. Relationship is an emotional bond between the client and the worker if negative or no relations there will be no communication.

Principle of Resource Utilization

This principle believes that being a member of the society, society provides facilities to the individual and takes care of those who needs help or assistance e.g. orphans, destitute, physically or mentally challenged, etc. Therefore all the resources whether personal, community or government should be utilized in the best interest of the client.

Principle of Right to Self-Determination

This principle is based on the value that every individual has the right to determine the destiny of his life. In social case work the worker have to give this right to the client so that he can decide and take best possible action in his self interest. Case worker works as an enabler or facilitator who helps client through his professional knowledge and skills to take the best possible decision and action in the given situations.

Principle of Self Awareness

The principle suggest that social worker should not substitute or apply their personal values or norms in social case work process, the principle guides the case worker to use only professional values and norms and help the client in such a way that he is able to relive comfortably when he goes back to his own society. The principle based on the value that social worker should be objective and non-judgmental in his approach and attitude.

Principle of Purposiveness of Behaviour

The principle suggest that all behaviour is functional and serves useful purpose. Behaviour includes all expression of our body, whether verbal or non-verbal. Therefore all the relevant behaviours expressed during the case work process should be analyzed and assessed to plan a realistic approach to help the client to replace his inappropriate behaviour with an appropriate one and to critically examine the purpose behind his problem behaviour.

Principle of Individualisation

As social work profession believes that every individual is unique in himself. This uniqueness come to him because of different background of every individual and because of different attitude, beliefs and experiences. Thus, case worker should identify special ways for the client and should help every client as an individual who is unique and whose problems needs and aspirations all special to him.

SOCIAL CASE WORK PROCESS

There are three phases of social case work process: Intake and psycho-social study, social diagnosis treatment and termination.

Intake

Intake is an administrative procedure and not a process of social case work to take in the person with problem, for example, admit him or enroll him as a client of the agency. After this phase the case worker is able to assess the needs and problems of applicant person and how and where his needs can be best met.

Psycho-Social Study

Social investigation is a psycho-social process. It is the initial phase in which the worker gains his first understanding of the kind of help his clients needs. The worker must understand what the client sees his problem as, what he think can be cone about it, what he himself/herself tried to do about it, and what are the reasons the client has identified for his present difficulty.

Perlman has given the following contents of the case work study in the beginning phase:

1. The nature of the problem

2. The significance of this problem
3. The causes of the problem.
4. The efforts made to cope with problem solving
5. The nature of the solutions or ends sought from the case work agency.
6. The actual nature of the agency and its problem solving means in relation the client and his problems.

Method

Perlman has suggested four methods for operating in the beginning phase:-

1. Relating to the client
2. Helping the client to talk about his troubles
3. Focusing and partializing
4. Helping the client to engage with the agency

Tools and Techniques in the beginning phase

1. Interview
2. Objective observation
3. Examination of records and documents
4. Collection of information for collateral and family sources
5. Special examination of test

Social Diagnosis (Assessment)

On the basis of the study of the problem in its past, present and future setting and the clients positive and negative reactions and interactions, the internal pressure and environmental factors the case worker assess or diagnose the clients problematic situation. Diagnosis is an explanation formulated in the light of known fact.

Content of the Social Diagnosis

The content of the case work diagnosis fall into the triangular pattern. It consist of

1. The nature of the problem brought and the goals set by the client, in their relationship to;
2. The nature of the person who bears the problem (his social and psychological situation and functioning) and who seek (or needs) help with his problem, in relation to;
3. The nature and purpose of the agency and the kind of help it can offer and/or make available.

Types of Diagnosis

Perlman has described three types of diagnosis that is carried on in social case work process.

These are :

Dynamic diagnosis;

Clinical diagnosis;

Etiological diagnosis

Dynamic Diagnosis: Gives on understanding of the current problem of the client and forces currently operating within the client, within social environment and between him/his environment. It is a cross sectional view of the forces currently operating in the clients problem. The dynamic diagnosis seeks to establish what the trouble is, what role psychological, biological, social and environmental factors are playing in the causation of the problems, what effect it has on the individuals well being. What solution is sought and what means exist within the client his situation and the organised services and resources by which the problem may be affected. In dynamic diagnosis there is no attempt to dig the life history of the problem, rather reasons for the problem are traced in the current situation.

Clinical diagnosis: Under clinical diagnosis, the case worker attempts to classify the client by the nature of his problem. He identifies certain forms and qualities of clients personality maladaptation and malfunctioning in his behaviour.

Etiological diagnosis: Etiological diagnosis is concerned with the explanation of the beginning of the life history of problems of the client, basically that problem that lies in the clients personality make up or functioning. The history of his development or a problem encountering, problem solving human being may provide the case worker with an understanding of what his clients suffers from and what the extent of his coping ability is likely to be.

Steps in Diagnosis

The following steps are taken while diagnosing a problem :

1. The worker begins with focusing on problematic bahaviours. He investigate both functional and dysfunctional behaviours in his social milieu. He clarifies various complaints and problems in terms of excesses and deficits. He evaluates the client's personal strengths and his surrounding environment.
2. He targets the specified behaviour and break down complex behaviour into their component parts.
3. Baseline data are collected to specify those events that appear to be currently controlling the problematic behaviours.
4. An analysis and interpretation is done from collected information and objectives for intervention established.
5. Selecting priorities for intervention is the final step of the diagnosis.

Intervention (Treatment)

Intervention or treatment is the next step and it's based on the study and diagnosis which indicates whether the problem is the result of personal or environmental factors and whether the remedy lies in the form of material or psychological assistance. The course of action undertaken by case worker after studying and understanding the problem has been described as treatment.

The objectives of social case work treatment:

1. To prevent social breakdown;
2. To conserve clients strength;
3. To restore social functioning;
4. To provide happy experiences to the client;
5. To create opportunities for growth and development;
6. To compensate psychological damage;
7. To increase capacity for self direction;
8. To increase his social contribution.

Social Case Work Treatment Process

The process of intervention or treatment begins with initial contact with the client. The process of treatment passes through many phases, *i.e.*, (1) Initial phase (2) Motivation and role induction (3) Primary contract (4) Diagnosis and assessment (5) Establishing treatment goals (6) Developing treatment plan (7) Preparation for actual treatment (8) Treatment in practice (9) Monitoring and evaluating the effects of treatment and (10) Planning of follow up termination of therapeutic relationship.

Application of Intervention Methods

In order to active goals set by the worker, conventionally the following methods of social intervention have been mentioned

(1) Direct Method

(2) Environment Modification

(3) Administration of Practical Service

(1) Direct Method: Direct method of intervention is used to promote specific behaviour on the part of the client. According to Perlman it is a systematic intervention through which client can work over his problems and possible solutions. Here, the case worker applies his influence directly on the client. The techniques of direct intervention used where the clients needs direction because of his/her ignorance, anxiety and weakness of his/her strength. Direct intervention is given through counseling, therapeutic interviewing, clarification and interpretation, leading to an insight. Supportive intervention is provided through guidance, externalization of interests, re-assurance, suggestion, persuasion and advice.

Counselling: It is direct intervention towards the solution of a problem in which a person find that he cannot solve the problem himself, therefore seeks the help of a skilled person whose knowledge, experience and expertise could be used to solve the problem. It is a psychological technique in which information and clarification are used for making the client aware of the problem.

Therapeutic Interviewing: Therapeutic interview is used where intra-psychic conflict is present in the environment. The purpose of such interview is that of psychotherapy which aims at personality, competence and self actualizations. For the analysis of the unconscious, social case worker applies the techniques of free association, dream interpretation, analysis of resistance and transference. For behaviour modification, social case worker makes use of the techniques of positive enforcement, negative enforcement, positive punishment, negative punishment, systematic desensitization and covert desensitization.

It is the process through which clarification about the client himself, his environment and the public with whom he is associated is made. Clarification may consist of information given to the client so that he becomes capable of understanding himself, his environment and his social network, which he does not posses and without which he cannot see clearly what step he ought to take.

Psychological support: Psychological support is useful in decreasing tension and guilt, increasing self confidence, encouraging healthy functioning that maintains the client's equilibrium and in helping him to build up compensatory strength and satisfaction. The case worker accepts him and his feeling and shows keep interest in him. He clarifies the problem and encourages him to take his own decision. The social case worker helps him to strengthen client's ego through the techniques of guidance, reassurance, persuation and psychological support.

(2) Environmental Modification: Means to bring change in the social as well as physical conditions of the client so that he may be relieved from excessive stresses and strains. The case worker suggest positive steps to client to cope better with his problems. He plans with him emotional, professional and recreational activities. He gives appropriate advice to be the member of his environment and modifies their attitude favorably.

(3) Administration of Practical Service: According to Hamilton administration of practical service is the oldest and best known case work method of intervention. Porter Lee was the first social worker who emphasized and classified such resource. Administration of practical services means to help the client in such a way that he could select and use the resources available in the community in this process social case worker helps the client for adequate knowledge of available resource through the techniques of discussion information, classification and direction.

Termination and follow up

Here termination means ending the process of social case work intervention process. The termination process in decided mutually by client and worker. Termination is the stage when the worker has the confidence in the client ability to cope with the present and future situation.

Evaluation

In social case work evaluation is the process in which worker tries to find out the effectiveness and success of the process. It is an activity which shows whether the social case work process has activated the desired goals or not. Social case worker evaluates the content of the program and its effectiveness inner strength gained by the client and the success of himself in helping the client.

THEORIES AND APPROACHES IN SOCIAL CASE WORK

Psychoanalytical Theory

The theory propounded by Sigmund Freud. The theory believes that unconscious process plays important role in determining behaviour and the behaviour is the out come of the interaction of three subsystems of personality that is 'id', 'ego' and 'super ego'. The 'id' consists of primitive biological drives and immediate gratification of needs. 'Ego' mediates between the demands of the 'id' and the realities of the external world. The third sub system 'super ego' develops by learning the taboos and moral values of the society.

It controls the 'id' and directs the 'ego' to hold back desires that are considered wrong or immoral. The interrelationship between these sub systems of personality are of crucial significance in determining behaviour. There is regular conflict between the natural urge and drives of the 'id' with the demand of external world (ego and super ego). The adequate resolution of such conflicts by the 'Ego' is considered essential for personality development. According to the psychoanalytical theory every moment of human life is determinable by the conscious, preconscious and unconscious psychological processes.

Psycho-Social Theory

Gordon Hamilton an article on "The underlying philosophy of social case work" in 1941 in which the word 'diagnosis' was used to express psycho-social problems. According to this theory the client is seen in the context of his interactions and transactions with the outer world. The history of the problem and impact on social function of the client is given due importance. It is considered that for proper diagnosis and treatment client's social environment must be understood and mobilized. Treatment must be differentiated according to the need of the client.

Functional Theory

The theory was developed by the school of social work of the university of Pensylvania in 1930. The theory believes that center for change is located in the client. The theorists used the world 'helping' instead of 'treatment'. According to them social case work is not a form of social treatment but a method of administering some specific social service and creating such a psychological understanding in the client so that he may become skilful in utilizing the agency services.

Behaviour Modification theory

The theory is based upon the principle of learning and conditioning propounded by Pavlov and Thorndike. In essence, behavioural modification is about decreasing undesired behaviour and increasing desired behaviours with the systematic application of established principles of learning. The behaviorist theory views problems as essentially the result of a failure to learn necessary adaptive behaviours. The theory views maladjusted person as an individual who has learned faulty copping patterns and has failed to learn required competencies for coping with the problem he is facing.

The Eclectic approach

It has been observed that no theoretical approach explains human behaviour in a conclusive manner. Therefore, it is important to develop an electic approach, an approach that is characterized by a solid knowledge of many systems of theories and a skill for selecting useful concepts and techniques with reference to clients. Eclecticism approach does not believes in social worker choosing casually a methodology for client rather means electing a methodology purposefully with explainable reasons and with reference to particular client or clients. As every school of thought has its own strengths and limitation. The approach believes that skill of social worker lies in taking advantage of strengths of every school of thought in the best interest of the client.

SKILLS IN SOCIAL CASE WORK

Skill is the ability of an individual to apply his knowledge in a given satiation. The development of skill depends upon training, practice, experience and knowledge of human behaviour. Skills required for effective case work practice are:-

(1) **Skill in Relationship:** In social case work relationship between client and case worker is essential for helping process skill lies in showing respect and genuine interest in the client and his problems, respecting his opinions and values and involving him in every stage of finding solution of his problems.

(2) **Skill in exploring problems in depth:** The case worker has to undergo psycho-social study and thorough investigation of client's problems. This requires capacity to listen,

to express interest and show respect to the behaviour and human problems.

(3) **Skill in use of resources:** Various physical and human resources are used to help the client in social case work. Case worker needs capacity to use all such resources to help the client.

The case workers skill lies in locating and using these resources for helping the client in such a way that it does not damage his self image.

Skill in Finding out Alternative Solutions

After having established a good relationship, explored his problems and used the available resources, next important step is to discuss the possible approach to solve the problem in effectively and efficiently. Skill required in helping the client to understand each alternative with its all implications and to decide for the best possible course of action in the situation.

Interviews

The interview is the most frequently used social work skill by the social case worker. It is the structured interaction between a worker and client. In the interview process the case worker and the client have face to face purposeful and professional conversation. The objective of an interview in social case work may be as informational (to make a social study), diagnostic (to arrive at an appraisal) and therapeutic (to effect change).

Social Study Interviews: Information regarding life history is collected through the interviews. The information enables the worker to understand the client in relation to the social situation.

Diagnostic decision Making Interviews: This type of interviews geared towards appraisal and determination of the eligibility for a service. These interviews help in making administrative decisions. For example the child welfare worker interviews the faster case or adoptive applicant to determine it the agency should place the child with them.

Therapeutic Interview: The interview aims at bringing change in the client, in social situation or personality or both. The goal is more effective social functioning on the part of the client as consequence of the therapeutic changes.

Skills to be used by the case worker during interview

Five groups of skills that should be used during an interview: observation skills, listening skills, questioning skills, focusing, guiding and interpretation skills and climate setting skills.

Observation Skills: It includes the workers ability to use understand non verbal behaviour of the client. It includes understanding the body language, opening and closing sentences, shifts in conversation, recurrent references, inconsistencies or gaps in information shared and points of stress and conflict indicated by the client.

Listing skills: It involves understanding what the client is attempting to communicate. Listening includes an attitude of acceptance, openness and focus on what being said by the client.

Questioning Skills: This skill refers to knowing and asking the various types of questions. Questioning is an art and an important skill. Various type of questions such as open ended and close ended should be asked while interview. Open ended question allows expression of feeling and give the workers an opportunity to understand the client's perception of the situation.

Focusing, guiding and interpretation skills: It includes capacity to paraphrase and summarize, confront and to be silent. Paraphrasing and summarizing clarity what has been said. Confrontation is bringing out into the open feelings, issues and discontents. It involves looking at these elements and attempting to find ways to deal with them. Silence may indicate resistance, frustration, or anger but it also can provide a time for worker and client to be reflective. It is the workers responsibility to direct the interview but not to control it. The worker by focusing, guiding and directing enables the process of case work to proceed towards the desired out come.

Climate setting skills: This skill refers to enabling or facilitating work. The three characteristics that enable the case work process are empathy, genuineness and non possessive warmth. Empathy is the capacity to communicate to the client that the worker accepts and care for the client. Genuineness is the capacity of the worker to communicate to the client that the worker is trust worthy and non possessive warmth is the capacity to communicate to the client both concern and desire for an intimacy.

Recording

In social work practice recording has been given paramount importance. In social case work detail investigation of an individuals personality performed through interviews. Recording is a tool to organize scientifically and systematically all the relevant information related to the client.

Records serves various purpose such as, recorded information is useful for learning purposes, it gives an opportunity to reflect back upon our interactions and to identify the wrong committed by us.

Recording helps in organizing the information and observation. It helps in developing knowledge and literature. It helps in administrative and research purpose. It is useful for teaching purpose, recording is useful for evolution and recording offers constructive criticism for the writer and the reader both.

Types of Recording

Process Recording: It is a detailed form of recording. Everything that takes place during a client in contact, including the workers feelings and thinking is noted down. It is extremely useful to the social workers striving to further develop understanding and skills in difficult situation in which the worker is developing new skills.

Summary Recording: Summary records are short and easy way to use, it includes entry data, social history, a plan of action, periodic summaries of significant information, action taken by the worker and a statement of what was accomplished as the case gets closed. Summary records are important in situations where long term, ongoing contact with the client and a series of worker may be involved and provide a picture of what happened with the client.

Problem Oriented Recording: It is a contemporary kind of recording used in interdisciplinary setting. Problem oriented records contain four parts. First there is a data base that contains information pertinent to client and work with the client. This includes such things as age, sex, marital status etc.

Second is a problem list that includes a statement of initial complaints and assessment of the concerned staff. Third are plans and goals related to each identified problem. Further are follow-up notes about what was done and outcome of the activity.

Home Visit

Home visit is an important tool used by the case worker for gathering information about client. The foundation for providing home based care by trained home visitor was laid by Florence Nightingale. Three terms are frequently used to describe the rationale for home visits : empowerment, enablement and enhancement. Empowerment can be described as facilitating or maintaining the client or families abilities to define its goal and make its own decisions. Enhancement indicates the concept of building upon strengths that already exists, and enablement suggests helping families locate resources that can facilitate the families own decision. According to Cameron (1961)-"In a few minutes at home, an experienced observer can gain more pertinent information about the client and his environment than can be gained during hours of probing in an office."

Referral

In social case work sometimes when a different type of worker or therapy is required to achieve the final goals of treatment or when the worker and the client find it difficult to move or assume new responsibility. The case may be referred to some other agency, case worker or therapist.

In referral the helping process continues but the contact with a particular case worker terminates.

Before, referral case worker should make preparation. This involves (i) explaining the reasons for referral (ii) tackling of the positive and negative feeling involved in referral process (iii) tackling separation anxiety in one or more the sessions (iv) handling the questions factually and (v) Preparing the client for a new contact.

Communication

Commutation is exchange of ideas and meaning between tow persons or groups. According to Dr. McFarland "communication is the process of meaningful interactions among human being. It is a process by which, meaning are perceived and understanding are reached among human beings."

Communication, therefore can be through words, the way we stand the tone of our voice, the way we look at another i.e. any behaviour that we use to express what we are experiencing. There is a message in communication, which may be expressed verbally, non verbally or through postures or body language.

Basic elements involved in the process of communication can be described as given below:

1. The intention, ideas, feeling of the sender lead to his sending a message which conveys some content.
2. The sender encoding his message by translating his ideas, feeling and intentions into a message appropriate for transmission.
3. The transmission of the message to the receiver.
4. The channel through which the message is transmitted.
5. The receiver decoding the message by taking the stimuli received and interpreting its meaning. The interpretation of the meaning of a message depends upon the receiver's comprehension of the content of the message and of the intention of the sender.
6. The receiver responding internally or externally to the interpretation of the message.

Means of Communication: The effectiveness and completeness of communication takes place when the receiver receives exactly the same message which is being sent to him or intended by the sender. One can communicate through variety of ways such as verbal non verbal etc.

Communication Through Touch: Communication of caring and openness can occur through touching. Physical contact conveys a sense of reassuring, sharing closeness, understanding, pleasure or anger. Touch shows warmth and sympathy and conveys feelings for another which cannot be expressed through word alone.

Body Language

Body language refers to any movement of all or part of our body which express an intention to those concerned. It can be the way we sit, stand, hold our head, our eyes and lips movement etc. Often the feeling we expressed through our body do not get expressed verbally and may even in conflict with our verbal statements. Therefore, it is extremely important that what message we are sending to other through our body.

Use of Symbols

Words are symbols for communication, the meaning is not in the word but in the person who uses it. Words are self selected symbols chosen to represent a particular experience. They have little meaning in themselves. Forgetting the abstract nature of works (i.e. the word in themselves have no meaning) is an important cause of failure to communicate properly and adequately.

Feedback

Feedback is used to know how we are affecting others and if we are sending any contradictory message. Feedback refers to conscious communication, giving information as to how we are affecting others or in other words, how others in the situation feel or think of the action of the person.

Receiving message

Sending a message is only the beginning of the process of communication. Valid communication does not complete until the receiver has received the intended message of the sender. This is accomplished by the recipient interpreting the message and checking this interpretation with the sender.

Active Listening

The concept of 'Active listening' was developed by Rogers (1966) in his client centered therapy . In active listening we listen to what the person is saying, both the contents and feelings expressed and we verbally acknowledge that we are hearing him.

OTHER IMPORTANT INFORMATION

- Miss Virginia Robinson in her book 'A changing psychology in social case work' in 1939 discussed about the importance of relationship in social case work.
- Hollis in his book – Case work: A psycho social theory 'distinguished two type of relationship the basic and the special or professional relationship.'
- Marry Richmond was the first person to define social case work in her book Social diagnosis' written in 1917.
- W.R. Friedlander in his book 'concepts and methods of social work', 1958 mentioned about the generic and differential principles of social case work.
- H.H. Perlman in her book 'Social case work- A problem solving process' in 1957 discussed about the psycho social study diagnosis and treatment process of social case work.
- The diagnostic school of social case work is founded on the Frication theory of psycho-analysis.
- The Functional school of social case work practice was developed by the family members of the school of social work of the University of Pennsylvania. Jessie Traft and Virginia Robinson.
- The Functional approach is based on the personality theory of Otto Rank.
- Transference in social case work is the tendency of human beings to relate their emotions and attitude with people in his immediate environment.
- Counter transference in social case work indicates an unconscious tendency to transfer his positive and negative feeling and attitude on the client.
- Counseling in social case work was started by Bertha Reynolds in 1932.
- Counselling in social case work aims at enabling individuals to solve present problems to propose themselves for future task, to attain higher standards of efficiency and well being and develop personal resources for growth.
- Psycho analytical therapy was developed by Freud.
- The client centered therapy is also known as humanistic psychotherapy was developed by Carl Rogers.
- Eric Berne in 1964 developed an innovative technique of interpersonal therapy known as 'Transactional Analysis'.
- Transactional analysis is based on the notion that there are three 'ego slates' in human personality – child ego Adult ego and parent ego.
- 'The Ego and the Mechanism of defense' book was written by Anna Freud.
- Aversion therapy is a technique used for the modification of undesirable behaviour was first used by Kantorvich in 1930
- Social Case work is considered on offspring of charity organization societies movement which was introduced in the 1969 (London) and 1877 (USA).
- The concept of Friendly Visitors is derived from charity organization society of USA.

- The four basic components of social case work viz., person, problem, place and process is described by Perlman in 1957.
- Problem solving model of social case work is identified with the work of Perl Mon (1957).
- Task centered model developed by William Reid at Chicago University.
- Goldstein (1973) presented the unitary or integrated model of practice.

MULTIPLE CHOICE QUESTIONS

1. Which one of the following is not a part of social case work process ?
A. Treatment
B. Assessment
C. Study
D. Content Analysis

2. In order to find the degree of relationships, we have to use a statistical test called
A. t-test
B. Anova
C. Chi-square test
D. Pearson's correlation

3. "Papers on Social Work – An Indian Perspective" was written by
A. G.R. Banerjee
B. G.R. Madan
C. Sachdev
D. Marula Siddaiah

4. World Summit on Social Development was held in the year
A. 1994 B. 1995
C. 1996 D. 1963

5. The Theory of Demographic transition includes
A. High birth rate and high death rate
B. Rapidly falling death rate and high birth rate
C. Low birth rate and low death rate
D. All the above

6. Pilot study refers to
A. Preliminary testing of the tools used for the research.
B. Follow up study done within a year after the original study.
C. Preliminary study conducted on a limited scale before the original study.
D. Macro level study undertaken to test the hypothesis.

7. What Rights are Human Rights ?
A. Rights which are provided by Constitution of India.
B. Rights which are Fundamental.
C. Rights provided to all human beings by nature.
D. Rights desired by human beings.

8. Diagnostic School of Social Case Work was developed by
A. Ross B. Jung
C. Rank D. Mead

9. Public Interest Litigation refers to
A. Mechanism to provide justice out of the Court.
B. To provide speedy justice.
C. To provide justice to poor, needy and weaker sections of society with the help of the NGOs' and media.
D. None of the above.

10. Paulo Friere's approach could be briefly stated as
A. Organization of services for people.
B. Mobilization of community leaders.
C. Action-reflection process with people.
D. Identification of target systems for work.

11. Which of the following is not a social process?
A. Accommodation B. Acculturation
C. Annihilation D. Assimilation

12. **Assertion (A):** Sigmund Freud claims that sex instinct is the source of all human endeavours.

Reason (R) : Social psychologists have tried to explain human behaviour in terms of instincts.

Codes :

A. Both (A) and (R) are true.
B. Both (A) and (R) are not true.
C. (A) is true, but (R) is not true.
D. (A) is not true, but (R) is true.

13. Assertion (A): Social work profession recognises the family as an important system in its own right.

Reason (R) : The family as a unit is worthy of study and intervention.

Codes :

A. Both (A) and (R) are true but (R) is not the correct explanation of A..
B. Both (A) and (R) are true and (R) is the correct explanation of (A).
C. Both (A) and (R) are false.
D. (A) is true but (R) is false.

14. Match the following :

List-I	**List-II**
(a) Payment of Bonus Act	i. 1936
(b) Payment of Gratuity Act	ii. 1948
(c) Payment of Wages Act	iii. 1965
(d) Minimum Wages Act	iv. 1947
	v. 1972

Codes :

	(a)	(b)	(c)	(d)
A.	iii	v	i	ii
B.	iv	v	ii	i
C.	v	ii	iv	iii
D.	ii	iii	v	i

15. Mandatory testing for HIV/AIDS can be done when

(i) Government wants it.
(ii) One wants to know about HIV/AIDS patients in the population.
(iii) Regular medical checkups are held.
(iv) During blood donation

Codes :

A. (i) and (ii) are correct.
B. (ii) and (iii) are correct.
C. (iii) and (iv) are correct.
D. Only (iv) is correct.

16. Which of the following does not threaten internal validity ?

A. Maturation of passage of time
B. History
C. Instrumentation
D. Randomization

17. The hypothesis by which the researcher not only asserts that the variables will be found to be related, but also predicts the direction of their relationship is called

A. one tailed
B. two tailed
C. null hypothesis
D. none of the above

18. Match the following :

List-I (Event)	**List-II (Date of Observance)**
a. World Anti Tobacco Day	i. Jan 12
b. National Youth Day	ii. May 31
c. International Youth Day	iii. Oct 12
d. World Girl Child Day	iv. Aug 12

Codes :

	(a)	(b)	(c)	(d)
A.	ii	i	iii	iv
B.	ii	i	iv	iii
C.	i	iii	ii	iv
D.	iii	ii	i	iv

19. According to H.H. Perlman, the four basic components of social case work are :

A. Person, place, problem and process
B. Person, problem, purpose and process
C. Purpose, problem, process and programme
D. Process, purpose, planning and principles

20. Differential association theory was profounded by ....

A. Aristotle B. Sutherland
C. Durkheim D. Reckless

21. Perceiving something which is not physically present is called :

A. Colour blindness
B. Hallucination
C. Faulty perception
D. None of the above

22. ESI stands for :
A. Employees Service Insurance
B. Employers Service Insurance
C. Employees State Insurance
D. None of the above

23. The 'operation flood' is known for :
A. watershed management
B. production of edible oil
C. production of milk
D. flood control

24. **Assertion (A):** The protection of women by Domestic Violence Act, 2006 has increased the responsibility of the family.
Reason (R) : The protection of women by Domestic Violence Act will further weaken the already weak institution of family.

Choose your answer from the codes given below :
A. Both (A) and (R) are correct, but (R) is not the correct interpretation of (A).
B. Both (A) and (R) are correct and (R) is the correct interpretation of (A).
C. (A) is correct and (R) is wrong.
D. Both (A) and (R) are wrong.

25. **Assertion (A):** Professional prejudice is thwarting the growth of medical social work in India.
Reason (R) : Lack of conviction on the part of the medical social workers is the reason.

Choose your answer from the codes given below :
A. Both (A) and (R) are correct.
B. Both (A) and (R) are not correct.
C. (A) is correct but (R) is not correct.
D. (A) is not correct but (R) is correct.

26. **Assertion (A):** Most of the development programmes have failed in benefiting the target groups.
Reason (R) : Developmental administrators lack the right approach and commitment.

Choose your answer from the codes given below :
A. Both (A) and (R) are correct and (R) is the correct explanation of (A).
B. Both (A) and (R) are not correct.
C. Both (A) and (R) are correct, but (R) is not the correct explanation of (A).
D. (A) is correct, but (R) is not the correct explanation of (A).

27. **Assertion (A): 'All Human Rights for All'** cannot be realised without Right to Development
Reason (R) : Right to development ensures the realization of human rights.

Choose your answer from the codes given below :
A. Both (A) and (R) are correct and (R) is the correct explanation of (A).
B. Both (A) and (R) are not correct.
C. (A) is correct, but (R) is not the correct explanation of (A).
D. Both (A) and (R) are correct, but (R) is not correct explanation of (A).

28. **Assertion (A):** Reformation of crime convicts is possible with the appointment of professional social worker in prisons.
Reason (R) : Professional social workers are equipped with knowledge and skills to deal with such issues.

Choose your answer from the following codes :
A. (A) is correct, but (R) is not correct explanation to (A).
B. Both (A) and (R) are correct and (R) is not the correct explanation of (A).
C. Both (A) and (R) are not correct.
D. Both (A) and (R) are correct and (R) is the correct explanation to (A).

29. **Assertion (A):** Gordon Allport was awarded Nobel prize.
Reason (R) : Allport classified human traits into (1) Cardinal traits (2) Central traits and (3) Secondary traits.
A. Both (A) and (R) are true and (R) is the correct explanation of (A).

B. (A) and (R) are true but (R) is not the correct explanation of (A).
C. (A) is true but (R) is false
D. (A) is false but (R) is true

30. Mode is defined as :
A. The middle measure in a series in which all measures have been arranged in the order of size
B. The arithmetic average of a series of measures
C. The item which occurs most frequently in the series
D. The square root of the mean

31. The period of Zygote is :
A. From fertilization to 7 days
B. From fertilization to 7 lunar months
C. From fertilization to the end of two weeks
D. From fertilization to the end of two lunar months

32. Oedipus Complex is associated with :
A. Oral Stage
B. Anal Stage
C. Phallic stage
D. Latency period

33. Hypogamy is :
A. Where a lower caste man marries a higher caste woman
B. Where a higher caste man marries a lower caste woman
C. Where a man marries more than one woman
D. Where a woman is married to more than one man

34. Match the List I with II and choose the correct answers from the codes given below:

List-I	List-II
(I) Quota sampling	(1) Probability sampling
(II) Causal research	(2) Nonprobability sampling
(III) Cluster sampling	(3) Conclusive research
(IV) Qualitative research	(4) Unstructured

Codes :

	(I)	(II)	(III)	(IV)
A.	(4)	(2)	(1)	(3)
B.	(2)	(3)	(1)	(4)
C.	(3)	(2)	(4)	(1)
D.	(4)	(1)	(3)	(2)

35. Match the following items given in List-I with the items given in List-II :

List-I	List-II
(I) Prohibition of discrimination	(1) Article 14
(II) Equality before law	(2) Article 16
(III) Abolition of untouchability	(3) Article 17
(IV) Equality of opportunity	(4) Article 15

Codes :

	(I)	(II)	(III)	(IV)
A.	(4)	(3)	(2)	(1)
B.	(4)	(1)	(3)	(2)
C.	(2)	(3)	(4)	(1)
D.	(2)	(1)	(4)	(3)

36. Assertion (A): Self decision making is an important aspect in growth and development of the client.

Reason (R) : Case workers are not involved in making use of community resources.

Choose your answer from codes given below:
A. Both (A) and (R) are correct, and (R) is the correct explanation of (A).
B. Both (A) and (R) are not correct.
C. Both (A) and (R) are correct, but (R) is not the correct explanation of (A).
D. (A) is correct, but (R) is not the correct explanation of (A).

37. Assertion (A): Intelligence is an ability to learn.

Reason (R) : The ability to deal with abstraction is intelligence.

Codes :
A. Both (A) and (R) are correct.
B. Both (A) and (R) are not correct.
C. (A) is correct, but (R) is not correct.
D. (A) is not correct, but (R) is correct.

38. **Assertion (A):** A census is the procedure of systematically acquiring and recording information about the members of a given population.

Reason (R) : It is regularly occurring and official count of a particular population.

Codes :

A. (A) is correct and (R) is wrong.
B. Both (A) and (R) are correct and (R) is the correct explanation of (A).
C. Both (A) and (R) are wrong.
D. Both (A) and (R) are correct, but (R) is not correct explanation of (A).

39. The gas responsible for the depletion of the ozone layer in the atmosphere is :

A. Carbon dioxide
B. Sulphur dioxide
C. Chloro fluoro carbon
D. Methane

40. The most advanced method of test used by modern forensic science is :

A. Enzymology B. Ultra sound
C. DNA D. Finger print

41. Match the following pairs :

(a) Erich Fromm	(i) Das Kapital
(b) Jane Austen	(ii) The Sane Society
(c) Karl Marx	(iii) Pride and Prejudice
(d) J. Coleman	(iv) Psychology and effective behaviour

Codes :

	(a)	(b)	(c)	(d)
A.	(i)	(iii)	(ii)	(iv)
B.	(iv)	(ii)	(iii)	(i)
C.	(ii)	(iii)	(i)	(iv)
D.	(iii)	(i)	(iv)	(ii)

42. Which of the following is a principle of social group work ?

A. Acceptance
B. Identification of the felt needs
C. Specific objectives
D. Non-judgemental attitude

43. Brahmo Samaj was founded in the year :

A. 1829 B. 1928
C. 1892 D. 1982

44. Gender is a :

A. Biological construct
B. Social construct
C. Economic construct
D. Psychological construct

45. The National rural employment guarantee programme seeks to provide guaranteed employment at the statutory minimum wage for atleast :

A. 150 days B. 365 days
C. 100 days D. 90 days

46. Human Development Report is published by:

A. World Bank B. CIVICUS
C. UNDP D. UNICEF

47. Consider the following statements and answer according to the codes given below:

Assertion (A): Social Workers should make eye contact with clients during interview process.

Reason (R) : Eye contact results in effective non-verbal communication.

Codes :

A. Both (A) and (R) are true but (R) is a partial explanation of (A)
B. Both (A) and (R) are not true
C. (A) is true but (R) is not true
D. (A) is not true but (R) is true

48. 'Cliques' are made up of

A. group of close friends
B. group of people
C. football team
D. crowd

49. UGC Second Review Committee for Social Work Education submitted its report in the year

A. 1964 B. 1972
C. 1978 D. 1981

50. Match the following pairs :

(a) Progressive Programme Experiences	(i) Social Welfare Administration
(b) Confidentiality	(ii) Community Organization
(c) Need identification	(iii) Social Case Work

(d) Authority and Obedience — (iv) Social Group Work

Codes :

	(a)	(b)	(c)	(d)
A.	(iii)	(iv)	(i)	(ii)
B.	(ii)	(i)	(iv)	(iii)
C.	(i)	(ii)	(iii)	(iv)
D.	(iv)	(iii)	(ii)	(i)

51. Which one of the Articles of Indian Constitution made the provision for free and compulsory education for all the children up to the age of 14 ?

A. Article – 42 B. Article – 43
C. Article – 44 D. Article – 45

52. Which of the following is not a form of intervention ?

A. Enhancement B. Competence
C. Prevention D. Control

53. Who of the following acted as Constitutional Advisor to the Constituent Assembly ?

A. B.R. Ambedkar
B. Rajendra Prasad
C. B.N. Rao
D. Sachidananda Sinha

54. The year 1999 – 2000 was observed as the year of

A. Gram Sabha
B. Municipal Governance
C. Child Rights
D. Human Rights

55. Labour court is a :

A. Adjudicating authority
B. Settlement authority
C. Voluntary authority
D. Social authority

56. According to the payment of wages Act 1936, the employer is authorised to deduct from the wages of employee upto the maximum of:

A. 25% B. 50%
C. 75% D. 90%

57. Council on social work education was established in the year :

A. 1952 B. 1947
C. 1936 D. 1949

58. The Medical termination of pregnancy Act came into force in the year :

A. 1971 B. 1972
C. 1973 D. 1974

59. Arrange the following in correct sequence :

(i) Specific protection
(ii) Early diagnosis
(iii) Primary prevention
(iv) Prompt and accurate treatment
(v) Rehabilitation

A. (i) (ii) (iii) (iv) (v)
B. (iii) (i) (ii) (iv) (v)
C. (v) (iii) (ii) (i) (iv)
D. (iv) (v) (iii) (ii) (i)

60. Which one of the following is not an indicator of job satisfaction ?

A. High rate of Labour Turnover
B. High Morale
C. High Motivation
D. High Productivity

61. Assertion (A): Non-violence is the core of Buddhist doctrine.

Reason (R) : Buddhist's philosophy can be followed for maintaining peace and harmony.

Codes :

A. Both (A) and (R) are wrong.
B. (A) is correct but (R) is wrong.
C. (A) is wrong but (R) is correct.
D. Both (A) and (R) are correct.

62. Match the following legislations with the year of enactment :

List-I	List-II
(I) The Child Marriage Restraint Act	(1) 1929
(II) The Juvenile Justice Act	(2) 1904
(III) The Factories Act	(3) 1986
(IV) The Cooperative Societies Act	(4) 1948

Codes :

	(I)	(II)	(III)	(IV)
A.	(4)	(3)	(2)	(1)
B.	(3)	(2)	(1)	(4)
C.	(1)	(3)	(4)	(2)
D.	(3)	(4)	(1)	(2)

63. A variable is an empirical property that takes
A. One value
B. Two or more values
C. Quantitative value
D. Qualitative value

64. Which one of the following is the basis of membership of caste ?
A. By Name
B. By Religion
C. By Economic Status
D. By Birth

65. Arrange in correct sequence the stages of human growth.
A. Oral stage, Phallic stage, Latency stage, Anal stage, Genital stage
B. Oral stage, Genital stage, Latency stage, Phallic stage, Anal stage
C. Oral stage, Anal stage, Phallic stage, Latency stage, Genital stage
D. Oral stage, Anal stage, Genital Stage, Phallic stage, Latency stage

66. When there is an equal chance for each unit in the universe to be included in the sample, that type of sampling is called
A. Purposive sampling
B. Non probability sampling
C. Systematic sampling
D. Probability sampling

67. Functional approach in case work was developed by
A. Jessy Taft
B. Gordon Hamilton
C. Otto Rank
D. Gisele Konopka

68. Arrange Maslow's Needs Hierarchy in order.
A. Physical needs, Safety needs, Social needs, Esteem and Selfactualization
B. Social needs, Safety needs, Physical needs, Esteem and Self-actualization
C. Esteem, Social needs, Safety needs, Physical needs and Selfactualization
D. Physical needs, Selfactualization, Esteem, Safety needs and Social needs

69. Almoners (outside visitors) were related to which country ?
A. U.S.A. B. England
C. India D. France

70. 'The individual in society in which one lives are interdependent is
A. An assumption of Social Work
B. An objective of Social Work
C. A principle of Social Work
D. A value of Social Work

71. Integrated Social Work method means :
A. simultaneous use of all social work methods.
B. using social work techniques in a reasonably responsible manner.
C. trying out alternative solutions to deal with the problem.
D. seek the advice of experts and develop the solutions.

72. The social institution is
A. an established procedure that regulates human behaviour.
B. a place where social functions are organised.
C. an organisation where social positions are formally defined.
D. an organisation that administers social service.

73. The division of society into upper and lower order is known as
A. Class B. Caste
C. Stratification D. Differentiation

74. Who used the concept of 'Persona' related to the theory of personality.
A. Carl Jung B. Freud
C. Erikson D. Adler

75. Change or stability in mental abilities such as learning, attention, memory, language, thinking, reasoning and creativity is known as
A. Human development
B. Cognitive development
C. Social development
D. Political development

76. The principles of Social Case work are
(a) Joint decision making
(b) Acceptance
(c) Non-judgemental attitude
(d) Individualization
A. (a), (b), (c) B. (a), (b), (d)
C. (c), (d) D. (b), (c), (d)

77. Treatment in Social case work involves
A. Counselling
B. Environmental Modification
C. Administration of Social Services
D. Counselling, Environmental Modification and Administration of social services.

78. Principle of Social group work is
A. Planned group formation
B. Group dynamics
C. Democratic decision making
D. Specific programme

79. The 'Group' in the Social Group work is
A. Spontaneous
B. Disunited
C. Formed in a planned manner
D. Disorganised

80. Sequence the following steps in social research :
(i) Collection and analysis of data
(ii) Conclusions and areas for further research
(iii) Objectives of the study
(iv) Review of literature

Codes :
A. (iv) (ii) (i) (iii)
B. (ii) (iii) (iv) (i)
C. (iii) (iv) (i) (ii)
D. (ii) (i) (iii) (iv)

81. Which of the following is not a principle of Group Work ?
A. Appropriate modification of the group process.
B. Indifferent attitude towards members.
C. Enabling group members to involve themselves in the process of problem solving.
D. Recognition of unique differences of each individual.

82. National Institute for the Visually Handicapped (NIVH) is based in
A. Hyderabad B. Mumbai
C. Kolkata D. Dehradun

83. "Each for all and all for each" is a slogan associated with
A. Panchayati Raj B. Co-operation
C. Democratic Sprit D. NGOs

84. Gandhiji's Concept of Trusteeship is based on
A. The property should be privately owned.
B. The faith that human beings are not selfish.
C. The faith that human nature is very selfish.
D. The use of wealth should be through legislative regulation.

85. Assertion (A): Working with minorities requires that social worker has an indepth understanding of the effect of oppression on the minority groups.
Reason (R) : Oppression of minority change the mindset of oppressed which requires the attention of social workers.
Choose your answer from the following codes:
A. Both (A) and (R) are correct and (R) is the correct explanation of (A).
B. Both (A) and (R) are correct, but (R) is not the correct explanation of (A).
C. (A) is correct, but (R) is not correct.
D. Both (A) and (R) are not correct.

86. Assertion (A): Persons with low selfesteem tend to find fault with others.
Reason (R) : Improper socialization is not the root cause of low selfesteem.
Choose your answer from the following codes :
A. Both (A) and (R) are correct.
B. Both (A) and (R) are not correct.
C. (A) is correct, but (R) is not correct.
D. (A) is not correct, but (R) is correct.

87. Who pointed out that 'development implies qualitative change'?

A. La BanVie B. Vauden daele
C. Siegel D. Piaget

88. The correlation co-efficient tends to lie between.....
A. 0 to + 1 B. +1 to +2
C. 0 to −1 D. +1 to −1

89. Human Development Report is published by
A. World Bank B. ADB
C. UNDP D. UNICEF

90. Match the enactment of the following Acts with the years.
(a) Mental Health Act (1) 1983
(b) The Environment Protection Act (2) 1984
(c) Developmental Disabilities Act (3) 1986
(d) Job Training and Partnership Act (4) 1987

Codes :

	(a)	(b)	(c)	(d)
A.	(2)	(4)	(1)	(3)
B.	(1)	(2)	(3)	(4)
C.	(3)	(4)	(2)	(1)
D.	(4)	(3)	(2)	(1)

91. Sequence the following steps of Community Organization process :
(i) Identifying needs
(ii) Exploring the resources
(iii) Prioritising the needs
(iv) Developing Programmes

Codes :

A.	(i)	(ii)	(iii)	(iv)
B.	(i)	(iii)	(ii)	(iv)
C.	(ii)	(i)	(iii)	(iv)
D.	(ii)	(i)	(iv)	(iii)

92. The sequencing in research process is :
(i) Studying existing literature in a field.
(ii) Generating new theories
(iii) Analysis of the findings
(iv) Synthesing ideas

Codes :

A.	(i)	(ii)	(iii)	(iv)
B.	(i)	(iv)	(iii)	(ii)
C.	(i)	(ii)	(iv)	(iii)
D.	(i)	(iv)	(ii)	(iii)

93. Put the following events in the order of their occurrence in a calender year :
(i) World Food Day
(ii) World AIDS Day
(iii) International Day for Elderly
(iv) World Disabled Day

Codes :

A.	(iii)	(i)	(ii)	(iv)
B.	(iii)	(i)	(iv)	(ii)
C.	(i)	(iii)	(ii)	(iv)
D.	(i)	(iii)	(iv)	(ii)

94. People's needs occur in ascending order. The view was proposed by :
A. Freud B. Watson
C. Maslow D. Jung

95. Mean, Mode and Median are :
A. Measures of Central Tendency
B. Measures of Correlation
C. Measures of Dispersion
D. Measures of Time Series

95. Intervention by a professional social worker with a group of family members who are considered to be a single unit of attention, is termed as :
A. Group therapy
B. Play therapy
C. Individual therapy
D. Family therapy

96. Match items in List-I with List-II and choose the correct answer from the codes given below :

List-I (Method)	List-II (Technique)
(a) Social case work	i. Funnelling
(b) Social group work	ii. Gherao
(c) Community organisation	iii. Person situation configuration
(d) Social action	iv. Norming and storming

Codes :

	(a)	(b)	(c)	(d)
A.	ii	iv	iii	i
B.	iii	iv	i	ii
C.	i	iii	iv	ii
D.	iv	ii	iii	i

98. Which one of the following is not a treatment group ?
A. Growth group
B. Socialisation group
C. Educational group
D. Study team

99. Indecent Representation of Women (Prohibition) Act was enacted in year
A. 1976 B. 1986
C. 1996 D. 2006

100. Which of the following governance mechanism is the highest body for policy formulation in NGOs ?
A. General body
B. Managing Committee
C. Sub Committee
D. Chairperson

101. Match the items in List-I with items in List-II and choose the correct answer from the codes given below :

List-I (Author)	**List-II (Method/approach)**
(a) Octavia Hill	i. Problem solving approach
(b) Murry G. Ross	ii. Social group work
(c) H.H. Perlman	iii. Community organisation
(d) Gisela Konopka	iv. Housing reforms

Codes :

	(a)	(b)	(c)	(d)
A.	ii	iii	iv	i
B.	iii	iv	i	ii
C.	iv	iii	i	ii
D.	i	ii	iii	iv

102. Objectively in research means the willingness and ability to examine evidence dispassionately is called
A. espirit de corps of the scientific method
B. cours de philosophic of the scientific method
C. la carriere of the scientific method
D. sine qua non of the scientific method

103. In participatory development, people's participation is
A. an end, not just a means to development
B. only a means to development
C. neither an end nor a means to development
D. only a means not an end to development

104. If the client persists in verbal attacks, the technique used is
A. Confrontation B. Scanning
C. Fogging D. Explaining

105. ________ helps in reclassification of variables and causal inferences.
A. Research design
B. Analysis of data
C. Sampling procedure
D. Sampling frame

106. The influence of one variable on the other can be analysed by using
A. Correlation B. t-test
C. Chi-square test D. Regression

107. Which among the following does not come under probability sampling ?
A. Simple Random Sampling
B. Stratified Sampling
C. Purposive Sampling
D. Cluster Sampling

108. Which one of these are techniques of social case work?
A. Universalization
B. Encouraging
C. Both A and B
D. None of A and B

109. To carry out Broker's role the social worker:
A. thoroughly understand the client's situation, his motivation, capacities and opportunities for change.
B. identifies client needs, assess their motivation and capacity to use various resources and helps them gain access to the most appropriate resources.
C. teach clients to adopt necessary skills required to change behaviour.
D. Uses his capacities to develop activities, implementing and monitoring a social service plan.

110. Which of the following is the most important task of an effective group leader ?
A. Enforce group discipline

B. Assert group to achieve the desired goal
C. Exert decisions unilaterally
D. Punish a social group behaviour

111. Latent learning is an example of
A. Avoidance learning
B. Cognitive learning
C. Escape learning
D. None of the above

112. The book entitled 'The Mentality of Apes' by Wolfgang Kohler, is about
A. Latent learning
B. Insight learning
C. Escape learning
D. Avoidance learning

113. Who amongst the following scholars has described tribal population as 'submerged humanity'?
A. Dr. Ghurye
B. A.V. Thakkar
C. Dr. Das and others
D. K.D. Gangrade

114. Correlation is a statistical tool for
A. Discovering and measuring the relationship and expressing it in a brief formula.
B. Measuring dispersion.
C. Calculation of variation.
D. Locating the point around which variables cluster.

115. Match the pairs :
(a) Behaviour is meaningful — (i) Group work
(b) Specific objectives — (ii) Public Administration
(c) Principle of responsibility — (iii) Casework
(d) External agent approach — (iv) Community organization

Codes :

	(a)	(b)	(c)	(d)
A.	(ii)	(iii)	(iv)	(i)
B.	(iii)	(i)	(ii)	(iv)
C.	(iv)	(iii)	(ii)	(i)
D.	(ii)	(i)	(iv)	(iii)

116. Match the pairs :
(a) B.R. Ambedkar — (i) Graduate School of Social Work
(b) Sir Dorab Tata — (ii) Stree Zarathostri Mandal
(c) Ratan Tata — (iii) Women's University
(d) SNDT — (iv) Peoples' Education Society

Codes :

	(a)	(b)	(c)	(d)
A.	(iv)	(i)	(ii)	(iii)
B.	(iii)	(iv)	(ii)	(i)
C.	(iii)	(iv)	(i)	(ii)
D.	(iv)	(iii)	(i)	(ii)

116. Match the pairs :
(a) Community organisation — (i) Programme media
(b) Casework — (ii) Coordination
(c) Group work — (iii) Conscientisation
(d) Social welfare administration — (iv) Interview

Codes :

	(a)	(b)	(c)	(d)
A.	(iii)	(iv)	(i)	(ii)
B.	(iv)	(iii)	(i)	(ii)
C.	(ii)	(i)	(iv)	(iii)
D.	(i)	(ii)	(iv)	(iii)

117. Identify the correct sequence :
A. Families as launching centres, families with schooling centres, families with adolescent children, families in middle years
B. Families with schooling children, families with adolescent children, family as launching centre, families in middle years
C. Families with adolescent children, families with schooling children, families as launching centres
D. Families as launching centres, family with adolescent children, families with school going children

37. Choose according to chronological order :
A. Indian Penal Code, Hindu Marriage and Divorce Act, Societies Registration Act, Child Marriage Restraint Act

B. Societies Registration Act, Indian Penal Code, Hindu Marriage and Divorce Act, Child Marriage Restraint Act
C. Societies Registration Act, Indian Penal Code, Child Marriage Restraint Act, Hindu Marriage and Divorce Act
D. Child Marriage Restraint Act, Hindu Marriage and Divorce Act, Indian Penal Code, Societies Registration Act

120. Identify the correct sequence :
A. Child Marriage Restraint Act, Bombay Children Act, Hindu Adoption and Maintenance Act, Juvenile Justice Act
B. Juvenile Justice Act, Child Marriage Restraint Act, Bombay Children Act, Hindu Adoption and Maintenance Act
C. Bombay Children Act, Hindu Adoption and Maintenance Act, Child Marriage Restraint Act, Juvenile Justice Act
D. Hindu Adoption and Maintenance Act, Child Marriage and Restraint Act, Bombay Children Act, Juvenile Justice Act

121. Identify the correct sequence :
A. Factories Act, Law of Family Courts, Societies Registration Act, Persons with Disability Act
B. Societies Registration Act, Factories Act, Law and Family Courts, Persons with Disabilities Act
C. Law of Family Courts, Factories Act, Societies Registration Act, Persons with Disability Act
D. Persons with Disability Act, Societies Registration Act, Factories Act, Law of Family Courts

122. Who among the following is associated with the Gestalt system of therapy ?
A. C.R. Rogers
B. Sigmund Freud
C. F.S. Perls and Laura P. Perls
D. B.F. Skinner

123. The National Association of Social Workers was established in which year
A. 1954 B. 1952
C. 1955 D. 1964

124. Consider the following statements and select your answer according to the codes given below :

Assertion (A): An essential feature of a healthy family is its cohesiveness.

Reason (R) : Cohesiveness facilitates healthy parenting.

A. Both (A) and (R) are true and (R) is the correct explanation of A.
B. Both (A) and (R) are true but (R) is not the correct explanation of A.
C. (A) is true but (R) is not true
D. (A) is not true but (R) is true

125. Indicate which one of the following is not an assumption of Social case work.
A. Every human being is to be respected
B. Every human being can change
C. Every human being has a right to be heard
D. Every human being is a child of God.

126. Match List I with List II in relation to the milestones in case wor

List I	List II
(a) Psychoanalysis	(1) 1930s
(b) Economic Factors	(2) 1940s
(c) Ego psychology	(3) 1920s
(d) Shift from self to continuous interaction	(4) 1980s

Choose the correct code:

	(a)	(b)	(c)	(d)
A.	(4)	(2)	(3)	(1)
B.	(3)	(1)	(2)	(4)
C.	(3)	(1)	(4)	(2)
D.	(1)	(2)	(3)	(4)

127. The main purpose of group work is :
A. To provide experience and growth opportunities
B. To promote social relationships
C. To train for citizenship
D. All of the above

128. The National Commission for women was established in the year :

A. 1957 B. 1986
C. 2001 D. 1990

129. Qualitative variables comprise of categories which are :

A. Concrete B. Continuous
C. Discrete D. Numerical

130. The new economic policy in India was Introduced in the year :

A. 1980 B. 1991
C. 1990 D. 1992

131. WTO is concerned with :

A. Borrowing and lending at the international level
B. Management of the rules of trade between nations
C. The violation of human rights at the international level
D. The policies pertaining to climate change at international level

ANSWERS

1	2	3	4	5	6	7	8	9	10
D	D	A	B	D	C	C	D	C	C
11	12	13	14	15	16	17	18	19	20
C	A	B	A	D	D	A	B	A	B
21	22	23	24	25	26	27	28	29	30
B	C	C	C	C	A	A	D	D	C
31	32	33	34	35	36	37	38	39	40
C	C	B	B	B	D	A	B	C	C
41	42	43	44	45	46	47	48	49	50
C	C	A	B	C	C	A	A	C	D
51	52	53	54	55	56	57	58	59	60
D	B	C	A	A	C	A	B	B	A
61	62	63	64	65	66	67	68	69	70
D	C	C	D	C	D	C	A	B	D
71	72	73	74	75	76	77	78	79	80
A	A	C		B	D	D	A	C	C
81	82	83	84	85	86	87	88	89	90
B	D	B	B	A	C	B	D	C	D
91	92	93	94	95	96	97	98	99	100
B	B	A	C	A	D	B	D	B	A
101	102	103	104	105	106	107	108	109	110
C	D	D	C	B	A	C	C	B	B
111	112	113	114	115	116	117	118	119	120
B	B	C	A	B	A	A	B	C	A
121	122	123	124	125	126	127	128	129	130
B	A	B	A	D		A	D	A	B
131									
B									

➤➤➤➤➤

CHAPTER

5

Group Work

SOCIAL GROUP WORK

Social group work is a method of social work which helps individuals to enhance their social functioning through purposeful group experiences, and to cope more effectively with their personal, group or community problems.

Konopka has outlined the essential parts of the social group work methods as follows:

(1) The function of social group worker is a helping or enabling function. This means that his goal is to help the members of the group and the group as a whole to move towards greater independence.

(2) In determining his way of helping the group worker uses the scientific methods, fact finding (observation) analyzing, diagnosis, in relation to individual the group and the social environment.

(3) The group work method includes the worker forming purposeful relationship to group members and group.

(4) One of the main tools in achieving such a relationship is the conscious use of self. This includes self knowledge and discipline in relationship without the loss of warmth and spontaneity.

(5) There should be acceptance of people without accepting all their behaviour. This involves the capacity for empathy as well as incorporation of societal demands.

(6) Starting where the group is, the involves the capacity to let the group develop from their own point of departure of capacity without immediately imposing outside demands.

(7) The constructive use of limitations, it means limitation must be used judiciously in relation to individual and group needs and agency function. The group worker will mainly use himself, program material, interaction of the group and awakening of insight in the group members.

(8) Individualization, in group work method the individual should not be lost in the whole, but he should be helped considering a unique person who can contribute to the whole.

(9) Use of interacting process, it involves the capacity to help, balance the group to allow for inflict when necessary and to prevent it when harmful.

(10) The understanding and conscious use of non-verbal as well as verbal materials.

ASSUMPTIONS

In general social group work is based on the following basic assumptions:-

(a) Man is a group animal,

(b) Social interaction is the result of the group life

(c) Man's achievements can be increased, changed and developed through group experiences.

(d) The capacity to solve problems may be increased through group experience.

(e) Group experience change the level of individuals aspirations and desires.

(f) Group recreational activities are beneficial to both individual and society.

(g) Group experiences have permanent impact on individual.

(h) Group work always focuses its attention on two types of activities—program and social relationship in group.

(i) Social group work believes in the principles of 'whole man'.

(j) Evaluation of program activities is done on the basis of its effects on group members.

(k) Individual member may fully understood and helped in group activities.

(l) Knowledge of social science is essential for working with the group.

(m) Professional knowledge and skills are essential for working with the group.

BASIC SKILLS OF SOCIAL GROUP WORK

Social group work requires variety of skills to accomplish its objectives. Some of the skills are described below:

(1) **Skill in establishing purposeful relationship :** The group worker must be skilful in gaining the acceptance of the group and in relating himself to the group on a positive professional basis. The group worker must be skilful in helping individuals in group to accept one another.

(2) **Skill in analyzing the group situation :** The group worker must be skilful in judging the developmental level of the group to determine what the level is, what the group needs and how quickly the group can be expected to move. The group worker must be skilful in helping the group to expose idea, workout objectives, clarify immediate goals and see both its potentialities and limitations as a group.

(3) **Skill in participation with the group :** The group worker must be skilful in determining interpritating, assuming and modifying his own role with the group. The group worker must be skilful in helping group members to participate, to locate leadership among themselves and to take responsibility for their own activities.

(4) **Skill in dealing with the group feeling:** The group worker must be skilful in controlling his own feelings about the group and must study each new situation with high degree of objectivity. The group worker must be skilful in helping group to realise their own feelings, both positive and negative.

(5) **Skill in program development :** The group worker must be skilful in guiding group thinking so that interests and needs will be revealed and understood. The group worker must be skilful in helping groups to develop programs which they want as a means through which their needs may be met.

(6) **Skill in using agency and community recourses:** The group worker must be skilful to locating and then acquitting the group with various helpful resources which can be utilized by them for program purposes.

The group worker must be skilful in helping certain individual members to make use of specialized services by means of referral when they have needs which cannot be met within group.

(7) **Skills in Evaluation:** The group worker must have skill in recording the development processes that are going on as he works with the group.

The group worker must be skilful in using his records and in helping the group to review its experiences as means of improvement.

Tracker has explained the following principles of social group work:

(1) The principle of planned group formation: In social group work, group is the basic unit through which service is provided to the individual consequently, the agency and worker responsible for formation of groups or the acceptance into the agency of already framed groups must be aware of the factors inherent in the group situation that make the given group a positive potential for individual growth and for meeting recognizable needs.

(2) The principle of specific objectives: In social group work, specific objectives of individual and group development must be consciously formulated by the worker on the basis of the needs of the individual and group.

(3) The principle of purposeful worker group relationship: In social group work, a consciously purposeful relationship must be established between the worker and the group members based on the workers acceptance of the group members as they are and upon the groups willingness to accept help from the worker because of the confidence the members have in him and in the agency.

(4) The principle of continuous individualization: In social group work it is recognized that groups are different and that individuals utilize group experience in a variety of ways to meet their different needs, consequently continuous individualization must be practiced by the worker. Groups and the individuals in the groups must be understood as developing and changing.

(5) The Principle of Guided group interaction: In social group work the primary source of energy which propels the group and influences the individual to change are the interaction or reciprocal responses of the member. The group worker influences this interaction by the type and quality of his participation.

(6) The principle of democratic group self determination: In social group work, the group must be helped to make its own decisions and determine its own activities taking the maximum amount of responsibility in line with its capacity and ability the primary source of control over the group is the group itself.

(7) The principle of Flexible functional organization: In social group work the process through which the worker guides the group in setting up formal organisation is just as important as the actual structure details of that organization. Formal organisation should be flexible and should be encouraged only as it meet a felt need, is understood by the members and can function accordingly the formal organisation should be adaptive and should change as the group changes.

(8) The principle of progressive program experiences: In social group work, the program experiences in which the group engages should begin at the level of member interest, needs, experience, and competence and should progress in relation to the developing capacity of the group.

(9) The principle of resource utilization: In social group work the total environment of agency and community possesses resources which should be utilized to enrich the content of the group experience for individual and the group as a whole.

(10) The principle of evaluation: In social group work continuous evaluation of process and programs in terms of outcome is essential worker group and agency share in this procedure as a means of guaranteeing this greatest possible self fulfillment for all.

ROLES OF A SOCIAL WORKER WORKING WITH GROUPS

Roles refer to the behaviours through which the client – an individual, a family, a group or a community – expects the worker to help accomplish goals, agreed upon mutually by the client and the worker. The roles conceptualized by the authors include the following:

(a) **Social broker:** Connecting the client system with the community resources based on broad knowledge of community resources and the operating procedures of the agencies; the worker may bring the specialized resources to the group; referral is a basic part of enactment of the broker's role.

(b) **Enabler:** Assisting clients to find coping strengths and resources within themselves to produce changes necessary for accomplishing the stated objectives with the supporting and enabling function for the client, whether individual or group.

(c) **Teacher:** Providing groups with new information necessary for coping with difficult situations, assisting group members in practicing new behaviour or skills. It is different from broker's role as it implies providing additional resources to members' environment.

(d) **Mediator:** Efforts to resolve conflicts that may exist between the client system and external systems like other persons or organizations by finding a common ground on which they might reach a resolution of the conflict.

(e) **Advocate:** Speaking for the client (individual, family, group or community) by presenting and arguing the clients' cause. It becomes essential when working with client-systems who belong to disadvantaged and marginalized groups in society, are oppressed due to structural social inequalities, or are invisible and voiceless. Advocacy is becoming increasingly popular role of social workers in the context of focus on social justice concerns and human rights. Unlike other roles, advocacy can be used without direct involvement of the client-system.

CONCEPT OF PROGRAM PLANNING

Groups achieve their objectives through programs that are split into achievable targets, tasks and activities. Therefore, deciding on appropriate programs becomes very important for the progress and development of group and its members.

Principles of Program Planning

Providing a program of activities is one of the main tasks of a group. Planning the group's activities in advance helps a group run smoothly because:

- Members understand and accept their responsibilities Optimum utilization of resources
- Better coordination between group members, agency and the worker in accomplishment of objectives

Programs in group work have to be effective since the groups' effectiveness is largely dependent on its programs. Program planning is an instrument in the hands of the group and the worker and its efficient use results in feasible, well thought out programs. Program planning in social group work has to follow certain principles, termed by Trecker (1955) as the 'criteria of effectiveness':

- Program should grow out of the needs and interests of the individuals who compose the group.
- Program should take into account such factors as age of group members, cultural backgrounds, and economic differences.
- Program should provide individuals with experiences and opportunities which they voluntarily choose to pursue because of their inherent values.
- Program should be flexible and varied to satisfy a variety of needs and interests and

to afford a maximum number of opportunities for participation.

- Program should evolve from the simple to the more complex with movement coming as a result of group growth in ability and readiness. Movement from initially "personal" to "social" or "community" concerns should be an ultimate objective if our programs are to have a greater social significance.

STAGES OF GROUP DEVELOPMENT

The achievement of the goals is the objective of any professional encounter; the tasks are done with a purpose. The Social Group Work process is conceived of as one that is systematic and proceeds through stages also referred to as phases. A group can pass through various stages of development; from the initial stage where it may appear as a mere assembly of individuals, it can go on to become a group with a strong 'we feeling'. The stages and the activities associated with it provide structure and direction to the process. The different stages are but a reflection of the process of maturity of the group. Theoretically, we may segregate different stages of group development for conceptual clarity but in reality they are intertwined. Throughout the stages there are two concerted concerns of the Social group worker, namely, building and sustaining a collaborative relationship and working on the tasks directed at achieving goals. The tasks and activities chosen reflect the Social Group Worker's ideas about what is necessary at different points in time to bring about change.

First Stage: Planning and Forming the Group (Beginning)

This phase marks the beginning of the process of group development and is also called the pre-group or pre-affiliation stage by some experts. In India the groups have to be formed by the group worker in most cases. She/he may form the group from among the existing clientele of the social welfare agencies/NGO's or from among the open community settings. Before forming a group, the group worker must study the target population along the following points such as geographical location, age, gender, socio-economic background, needs/problems, interests and any other relevant detail.

This information helps the group worker to form the group on some common grounds and accordingly determine the group goals. Careful planning should precede the formation of the group which includes decision about the target population, needs and goals, the resources available etc.

The members may have to be convinced to join the group as they may be ignorant of the usefulness of being a part of a group and may not have had any such experience in the past. "Groups in India are initially conceived by an organization or welfare agency, as people themselves generally do not take such initiatives. Both the voluntary and the government organizations have found working with

The other details that have to be focussed while planning and forming the group are:

(1) The size of the group: The decision about the size of the group is dependant on various factors such as the needs of members, purpose of group, nature of group membership etc. for instance self help groups may be large in size but therapeutic groups work best when they are small. Though there is no ideal size, a group size ranging from eight to fifteen members may be a good size.

(2) Composition of the group: Planning about the composition of the group has to be in keeping with its purpose. Whether it is a self-help group, task group or treatment oriented group, it may be either homogenous or heterogeneous. Before deciding the nature of membership, the group worker should familiarize herself with the client group along the points already mentioned above such as their socio-economic background etc.

(3) **Frequency of the sessions and their duration:** Though there is no hard and fast rule, frequency of the sessions may be decided in accordance with the needs and purpose of the group. There should not be too long gaps between the sessions, lest the group gets disintegrated. Recreation groups, therapeutic groups, task groups should meet at least once or twice a week.

(4) **Time and place of meetings:** The place where the group is to meet at the designated time has to be decided in consultation with the members. The guiding factors are the convenience of the members, availability and adequacy of space and resources.

(5) **Duration of the group:** Whether the group will exist for a long or short term may again have to be in keeping with the needs and goals of the group. The group can be terminated after achieving its objectives and a tentative time may be earmarked for it. There should however be an element of flexibility in deciding the time-frame.

Second Stage: Explorations (Initial Sessions)

Exploration: In the initial sessions the group may appear more as a collection of different individuals than an organized entity. This stage is usually characterized by a low group consciousness. There may be shyness, hesitation, indecision and lack of participation. Some members maybe hyper active, and some may be insecure and nervous, not having had such an experience in the past. However, this phase marks the beginning of the development of a feeling of belonging and oneness among the members. Tuckman has used the term 'storming' to explain this process of exploration. In the initial meetings a semblance of order has to be restored so as to ensure a free flow of ideas and actions.

This stage involves the following steps:

Orientation and Induction: The initial stage is important as it lays the foundation of the success or failure of the group work program. The worker should introduce the members to the group by outlining his role and the purposes for which the group has been formed, the members should be encouraged to speak about themselves, their hopes and aspirations. In the initial sessions the members have to be inducted into the group with a certain sensitivity so as to raise their level of comfort and sense of ease. The members may be unfamiliar with each other and may be interested in finding out about the agency, the worker, other members and the purpose of the group.

Preparation of the Profile of the Members: Just as there is a need for the members to know each other, the worker too should study and observe the members closely. The worker should prepare a profile of each member giving his age, family background, physical characteristics, habits, interests, level of confidence, any peculiar habits or traits etc. It would help if this is based on the facts gathered and his/her observations in the initial sessions. This would not only help him understand the group relationship levels and interaction patterns better but also begin from where the group is. Further this may help him map the development over a period of time, especially at the stage of evaluation.

Setting Specific Objectives: While there may be larger goals which a group may strive to ultimately achieve, specific interim goals also need to be explored, which can form the basis of program planning. Here the worker has to help the group determine the desired level of behaviour or social change. Although in the first stage the group has been formed keeping in mind some purpose, It is at this stage that goals have to be specifically delineated. Here the group worker encourages the active participation of the group members and helps the group assume the responsibility to determine the level of change they desire to achieve in their behaviour or social situation. e.g. kicking up the habit of smoking/ chewing tobacco, giving up using abusive language. Objectives are nothing but statements of what the group worker is trying to achieve through the group work process. They give meaning to the process. "Objectives serve the same purpose as a compass; they guide the agency and the worker to a determined destination". (Trecker, 1955, 57).

Developing a Structure: As the group is now ready to settle down, it can be structured at this stage. The members must now be prepared and encouraged to assume roles and responsibilities. They are to be told about the expectations of the group from them in terms of tasks, on the basis of their capabilities and talents. In the Indian context the members may have to be closely assisted till they learn to assume responsibilities on their own. Some may need constant help of the group worker to carry out their roles. The worker at this stage must constantly encourage the members to use their latent talents and capacities.

Third Stage: Performing (Action Phase)

Action Phase: After some sessions, the signs of group development start emerging as the group progresses into its active phase. The focus of this stage is on the provision of program experiences designed to offer opportunities for adjustment and growth. The programs may be of a long or short term depending on the immediate and long term objectives.

Program Planning and Execution: Program is a series of activities based on the discovery of interests and needs of the members and an important component of Social Group Work process; the way it is planned even more important. It may range from art and craft to music, dance, social events to picnics excursions. At this stage the program interests are likely to emerge from within the group. The members who may be initially be at a loss from where to begin must now be encouraged to take over. The members are stimulated to discover and use their own resources. The program planning and development process by itself is an important tool in helping the group to realize its potential

"Program should evolve from simple to more complex, with movement coming as a result of group growth in ability and readiness. Movement from initially 'personal' to 'social' or 'community concerns' should be an ultimate objective if our programs are to have greater social significance" (Trecker, 1955, 162)

Task accomplishment: "When the group begins to show signs of readiness to move ahead, the worker should help the members realize their wishes for different and more demanding experiences. When group members begin to express desires to correct inadequacies and improve their work, they have reached an advanced point in their development. Programs that may have been self-centered shift in emphasis to the larger agency and community concerns. Specialized interests may be revealed, and there may be an interest in a variety of small group activities within the larger group. Here the worker is called upon to use his knowledge of agency and community resources. His role becomes that of an interpreter to the group, especially in regard to future possibilities. Evaluation occupies a larger share of time as the group becomes confident of its capacities" (Trecker, 1955)

Monitoring Progress: The group worker at this stage steps down and allows the group to take over. However he needs to constantly monitor and keep a track of the ways the program is being conducted. As work towards the group goals gathers momentum it is important to monitor the progress on a regular basis. The program can be monitored on the basis of specific indicators such as interaction patterns, self improvement, emotional integration with the group, leadership and communication skills etc.

Fourth Stage: Assessment (Evaluation)

Evaluation: After the action phase is over, the group should be ready to evaluate the outcome of its efforts in a free, frank and objective manner. "Evaluation is that part of Social Group Work in which the worker attempts to measure the quality of a group's experience in relation to the objectives and functions of the agency. Evaluation may centre upon individual growth, program content or worker performance because all these aspects tend to influence the general achievement of the group."(Trecker, 1955) Evaluation is continuously done during the group work process, but, after the group activities are over, before the termination phase; a comprehensive assessment of the entire experience is a must. This helps in improving subsequent group work experiences on the basis of the lessons learnt; a guide to future.

GROUP DYNAMICS

The behaviour of individual in a group is determined not only by his inner forces but also by the people around him. Thus apart from the individual dynamics, a social group worker must understand group dynamics or various concepts of the group process. The concepts like acceptance or refection, isolation (neglected and reflected) sub groups, group bonding, group hostility and group contagion, group support and group conflict are studied under group dynamics.

Acceptance or Refection

A group worker must know every individual group member's relationship with other group members or how much power each one has over others *i.e.*, whether he is accepted by other or isolated

Sub Groups

The sub groups in a group is very natural as people tend is divide in groups based on their affinity or interests. The group worker should observe whether these sub groups are functional, dysfunctional groups. If they are threatening the unity of the group the group worker should act accordingly.

Group Bond

It refers to 'group cohesiveness' or 'sense of belonging'. It is the force bringing group member together. Group bond may be emotional or task related. Group bond is a powerful aspect of the group dynamics.

Group Hostility and Group Contagion

Hostility means aggression or resentment or unfriendliness group contagion is the tendency to catch and feel emotions that are similar to influenced by other in the group. In this regard, Barsade (2002) comments : "it is a process in which a person or group influences the emotion or behaviour of another person or group through the conscious or unconscious induction of emotion states and behavioural attitudes. Group contagion may occur in examination or when two children are upset in a camp or when some external threat comes.

Group Support

Any work become easy in group when support and courage come from other member. It is a positive attitude and moral support shared by group members for helping each other. The group worker must observe this dynamics to get better knowledge about group members.

Group conflict

Conflict among human is inevitable and every group exist with some kind of conflict. Maturity of a group can be understood by observing how a group resolves conflict. Normally conflict is resolved through withdrawal, subjugation, majority rule minority consent, compromise and integration, integration is considered to be the best way to resolve conflict.

- **Team Evaluation and Maturation** (TEAM) model of social group work identified by Morgan, Salas and Glickman has seven main stapes of group development such as first meeting (forming) unstable situation (storming), accommodation (norming), inefficient patterns of performance (performing-I), re-evaluation and transition (reforming), effective performance (performing-II), and completion of assignments (conforming).
- Acquisition and Behavioral change (ABC) model of social group work was developed by Tom Caplan.

MULTIPLE CHOICE QUESTIONS

1. Duncan's Socio-Economic Index (SEI) measures one of the following :
   A. occupational goals
   B. occupational Hazards
   C. occupational differences
   D. occupational advantages

2. Who suggested 28 principles of community organisation :
   A. Dunham B. Murray Ross
   C. Alzoni D. Scanzorci

3. Robert Redfield's famous book is
   A. The little community
   B. The small community
   C. The large community
   D. The big community

4. Kibbutzim means :
   A. common good
   B. community participation
   C. cooperative living
   D. crisis intervention

5. Ross suggested three approaches for Community Organization. Specific content approach and the general content approaches are the two approaches. What is the third approach?
   A. Problem Approach
   B. Process Approach
   C. Propaganda Approach
   D. Planning Approach

6. National Youth Policy was introduced in :
   A. 1986 B. 1987
   C. 1988 D. 1989

7. **Assertion (A):** A Crisis is a turning point hence immediate inputs of brief therapy must be provided.

   Reason (R) : Field work training facilitates skills of early accurate diagnosis, hence human resource management must include sensitivity training and information update.
   A. (A) is correct and (R) is wrong
   B. (R) is correct and (A) is wrong
   C. Both (A) and (R) are wrong
   D. Both (A) and (R) are correct

8. **Assertion (A):** Residential Social Welfare Institutions are termed as the "safety valves of a society".

   Reason (R) : Delinquency cannot be controlled in Open Institutions because behaviour needs to be structured.
   A. (A) is correct but (R) is not the correct explanation of (A).
   B. (R) is correct but (A) is wrong
   C. Both (A) and (R) are correct but (R) is not related to (A)
   D. Both (A) and (R) are wrong

9. **Assertion (A):** The Protection of Women from Domestic Violence Act 2006 has increased the responsibility of the family.

   Reason (R) : The Protection of Women from Domestic Violence Act will further weaken the already weak institution of family.
   A. Both (A) and (R) are correct but (R) is not the correct interpretation of (A).
   B. Both (A) and (R) are correct and (R) is the correct interpretation of (A).
   C. (A) is correct and (R) is wrong
   D. Both (A) and (R) are wrong

10. Regulation XVII of 1829 of Lord Bentinck was enacted to :
    A. Ban Sati
    B. Encourage widow remarriage
    C. Ban child marriage
    D. None of the above

11. Consider the following statements and select your answer according to the codes given below :

    Assertion (A) : The Poor Laws were enacted in England.

    Reason (R) : To help the poor to have better working conditions.
    A. Both (A) and (R) are true and (R) is the explanation of (A).
    B. Both (A) and (R) are not true

C. (A) is true but (R) is false
D. (A) is not true but (R) is true

12. Integrated social work practice takes into account the following :
(a) The client system
(b) The change agent system
(c) Action system
(d) Agency system Indicate the correct answer
A. (a), (b) and (c) are correct
B. (b), (c) and (d) are correct
C. (a), (c) and (d) are correct
D. (a), (b), (c) and (d) are correct

13. Professional Supervision in Social Work is best described as :
(a) Evaluating the performance of the supervisee
(b) Making sure that the supervisee does not make a mistake
(c) Helping the supervisee acquire social work knowledge, skills and values
(d) Reflecting with the supervisee and be a guide Indicate which is the correct answer
A. (a) and (b) are correct answer
B. (b) and (c) are correct answer
C. (a) and (c) are correct answer
D. (c) and (d) are correct answer

14. Social group work as a method does not help
A. individuals to enhance social functioning through purposeful group experience.
B. community to solve problems of groups in a community.
C. provide a context in which individuals help each other.
D. individuals and groups to influence and change social situations.

15. Who propounded that social action is mass betterment through propaganda and social legislation, a method of bringing about a change in the social environment of the clients?
A. M.V. Murthy B. Peter Lee
C. Philip Kohler D. Mary Richmond

16. Which Article of Constitution of India suggests for the protection from social injustice and all forms of exploitation and promotion of economic and educational interests of the weaker sections of the people?
A. Article 44 B. Article 45
C. Article 46 D. Article 47

17. Example of Personality Test includes
A. Minnesota Multiphasic Personality Inventory.
B. Rorschach Inkblot test
C. Thematic Apperception test
D. All the above

18. The largest professional social work association in the United States is :
A. International Federation of Social Workers
B. National Association of Social Workers
C. American Association of Social Workers
D. None of the above

19. The Central Government Scheme to prevent trafficking of women and children for commercial sexual exploitation is
A. Ambedkar Hastshilp Vikas Yojana
B. Swadhar Yojana Scheme
C. Ujjawala Scheme
D. Rashtriya Swasthya Bima Yojana

20. Conscientization model is associated with
A. Mary Richmond B. Paul Chowdhary
C. Paul Friere D. Perlman

21. Which among the following is not an award instituted by the Ministry of Labour and Employment ?
A. Shram Awards
B. National Safety Awards
C. Viswakarma Awards
D. Arjuna Awards

22. The flexibility in handling change is termed as
A. Altruism B. Innovation
C. Adaptability D. Aggressiveness

23. The two main forms of social stratification are
A. Class and Estate

B. Society and Community
C. Caste and Class
D. Family and Kinship

24. The book 'Social Diagnosis' was written by
A. H.H. Perlman B. Mary Richmond
C. Trecker D. Herbert Bisno

25. The word 'set-on' and 'set-off' is related to
A. The Payment of Bonus Act
B. The Payment of Wages Act
C. The Minimum Wages Act
D. The Factories' Act

26. **Assertion (A):** Ozone layer protects living beings from being exposed to excessive ultra-violet rays.
Reason (R) : Ozone hole in the atmospheric layer is over Antarctic ocean.
A. Both (A) and (R) are true, but (R) is not the correct explanation of (A).
B. Both (A) and (R) are true and (R) is the correct explanation of (A).
C. (A) is false, but (R) is true.
D. (A) is true, but (R) is false.

27. **Assertion (A):** The Directive Principles of State Policy are predominantly based on the principle of Distributive Justice.
Reason (R) : Unequal opportunities slow down the achievement of distributive justice.
A. Both (A) and (R) are correct and (R) is the correct explanation of (A).
B. Both (A) and (R) are correct, but (R) is not the correct explanation of (A).
C. (A) is correct, but (R) is wrong.
D. Both (A) and (R) are wrong.

28. Match the following pairs :
(a) Complex Organizations (i) Margaret Mead
(b) Symbolic Interaction (ii) Talcott Parsons
(c) Bureaucracy (iii) Amitai Etzioni
(d) Functionalism (iv) Max Weber

	(a)	(b)	(c)	(d)
A.	(ii)	(iv)	(iii)	(i)
B.	(iii)	(i)	(iv)	(ii)
C.	(iv)	(iii)	(ii)	(i)
D.	(i)	(ii)	(iii)	(iv)

29. The likelihood of a measure producing same result under various conditions is called
A. Reliability B. Outcome
C. Validity D. Replicability

30. Match the following pairs and choose your answer from the codes given below :
(a) Psychoanalytic Theory (i) Began
(b) Ego-Psychology (ii) Anna Freud
(c) Psycho-Social Therapy (iii) Hamilton
(d) Problem Solving Therapy (iv) Sigmund Freud

Codes :

	(a)	(b)	(c)	(d)
A.	(i)	(ii)	(iii)	(iv)
B.	(iv)	(ii)	(i)	(iii)
C.	(ii)	(i)	(iv)	(iii)
D.	(iii)	(ii)	(i)	(iv)

31. Which one of the following is **not** a technique of case work?
A. Interviewing B. Observation
C. Counselling D. Lobbying

32. While working with an individual client on a one-to-one basis, the relationship is :
A. a friendly association
B. a contract
C. purposeful to meet the psycho-social needs of the client
D. a sympathetic understanding of the client

33. Which one of the following constitutes the main basis of a Welfare State in India ?
A. Fundamental Rights
B. Directive Principles of State Policy
C. Judicial Independence
D. Public Interest Litigation

34. Which one of the following authors has contributed exclusively in the area of social group work ?
A. Hollis B. Murray Ross
C. Trecker D. Perlman

35. Psychoanalytic theory about human personality was proposed by :
A. Carl Jung B. Skinner
C. Sigmund Freud D. Alfred Adler

36. The book Social Diagnosis is authored by :
A. Murray Ross B. Mary Richmond
C. Fried Lander D. Helen Perlman

37. One of the following is not a true experimental research design :
A. Solomon Four — group design
B. Post test — only control group design
C. Pretest — Post test control group design
D. One shot case study

38. Accepting the null hypothesis as tenable when it should be rejected is a :
A. Type I error B. Type II error
C. Standard error D. Type V error

39. Variable is a ________
A. Concept B. Method
C. Tool D. None of the above

40. Gerontology is the study of
A. Disability B. Genome
C. Childhood D. Ageing

41. Who is the Editor of the book 'Field Work in Social Work Education':
A. Surendra Singh
B. A.N. Singh
C. Shankar Pathak
D. R.R. Singh

42. Which of the following is not a principle of social case work :
A. Confidentiality
B. Non-judgemental attitude
C. Self-determination
D. Specific objectives

43. Mental Health Act for case and rehabilitation of Mentally ill was passed in :
A. 1987 B. 1982
C. 2000 D. 1986

44. To identify developmental tasks and changes occuring in various stages in the life of a family is :
A. Family tree
B. Family life cycle
C. Life skill approach
D. None of the above

45. Social Class is a :
A. Category
B. Primary group
C. Secondary group
D. Mob

46. Which of the following statement is correct:
A. Caste is based on the individual's position
B. Caste is determined by occupational mobility
C. Caste is created by Lord Brahma
D. Caste is determined by birth

47. Understanding approach and manipulating approaches are used in :
A. Community participation
B. Collective bargaining
C. Counselling
D. Cooperative living

48. ICDS was launched on which birth anniversary of Mahatma Gandhi :
A. 105 B. 106
C. 107 D. 108

49. Which article of Indian Constitution lays down the provision of free and compulsory education for children ?
A. 45 B. 46
C. 47 D. 48

50. Who described 8 principles of social work ?
A. Konopaka B. Khinduka
C. Hamilton D. Trecker

51. Juvenile Justice (Care and Protection) Act was introduced in :
A. 2001 B. 2002
C. 2003 D. 2004

52. Friedlander classified primary values of social work into :
A. 2 B. 3
C. 4 D. 5

53. The first committee on social work Education was commissioned in the year :
A. 1956 B. 1958
C. 1960 D. 1962

54. Who was the first Director of the Dorobji Tata Graduate School of Social Work ?
A. Kinduka
B. Kumarappa
C. Clifford Manshardt
D. Bilmoria

55. Mangroth village is associated with :
A. Bhoodan Movement
B. Sarvodaya Movement
C. Gramadan Movement
D. Peasant Movement

56. Match the following concepts of List-I with their meaning listed in List-II :

List-I	List-II
(I) Polygamy	(1) One husband and more than one wife
(II) Polyandry	(2) Residing at wife's place
(III) Patrilocal	(3) Residing at husband's place
(IV) Matrilocal	(4) One wife and more than one husband

Codes :

	(I)	(II)	(III)	(IV)
A.	(4)	(1)	(3)	(2)
B.	(3)	(2)	(1)	(4)
C.	(1)	(4)	(3)	(2)
D.	(2)	(3)	(1)	(4)

57. Match the design of research study given in List-I with its nature/quality given in List-II:

List-I	List-II
(I) Descriptive study	(1) Study of a unit in its totality
(II) Case study	(2) Detailed description
(III) Exploratory study	(3) Experimental controlled groups
(IV) Experimental study	(4) Identifying new perspectives

Codes :

	(I)	(II)	(III)	(IV)
A.	(2)	(1)	(3)	(4)
B.	(2)	(1)	(4)	(3)
C.	(1)	(2)	(3)	(4)
D.	(4)	(3)	(2)	(1)

58. Match the following international days given in List-I with List-II.

List-I	List-II
(I) International Day for the Elderly	(1) 8th March
(II) World AIDS Day	(2) 16th October
(III) World Food Day	(3) 1st October
(IV) International Women's Day	(4) 1st December

Codes :

	(I)	(II)	(III)	(IV)
A.	(3)	(4)	(2)	(1)
B.	(4)	(3)	(1)	(2)
C.	(1)	(2)	(3)	(4)
D.	(2)	(1)	(3)	(4)

59. The ultimate goal of a women's self help group is :
A. Savings
B. Loans
C. Insurance
D. Empowerment

60. The agency that estimates the National Income of India is :
A. Reserve Bank of India
B. Planning Commission
C. Finance Ministry
D. Central Statistical organisation

61. The study team on Social Welfare and welfare of Backward Classes was constituted in the year ________.
A. 1948
B. 1950
C. 1958
D. 1960

62. Which among the following is associated with 'Token Economics' ?
A. Transactional Analysis
B. Behaviour Therapy
C. Client Centered Therapy
D. Short term case work

63. Match the following pairs :

(a) Theory of culture lag	(i) E.M. Sutherland
(b) Theory of differential association	(ii) Karl Marx
(c) Routinisation of Charisma	(iii) William Ogburn
(d) Conflict theory of change	(iv) Max Weber

Codes :

	(a)	(b)	(c)	(d)
A.	(iii)	(i)	(iv)	(ii)
B.	(iv)	(iii)	(i)	(ii)
C.	(iii)	(ii)	(iv)	(i)
D.	(ii)	(iii)	(iv)	(i)

64. Millennium development goals consist of :
A. 8 goals, 18 targets and 48 indicators
B. 8 goals, 20 targets and 31 indicators
C. 18 goals, 28 targets and 38 indicators
D. 28 goals, 28 targets and 28 indicators

65. The Child Labour Prohibition and abolition in Domestic and Hospitality services, Act is passed in the year :
A. 2005 B. 1986
C. 2006 D. 2007

66. The successor of General Agreement on Tariffs and Trade (GATT) is :
A. WTO B. IMF
C. ADB D. World Bank

67. The Civil society Index is proposed by :
A. UNDP
B. IMF
C. CIVICUS
D. Transparency International

68. Social case work aims at
A. Giving charity to client
B. Controlling the client
C. Solving the problems of the client
D. Enabling the client

69. Match the following persons with the organizations they associated :

List-I	List-II
(I) Jyotibha Phule	(1) Bharatiya Adimajati Sevak Sangh
(II) Thakarbappa	(2) Servants of India Society
(III) Gopal Krishna Gokhale	(3) Harijan Sevak Sangh
(IV) M.K. Gandhi	(4) Satya Sodhak Samaj

Codes :

	(I)	(II)	(III)	(IV)
A.	(1)	(2)	(3)	(4)
B.	(4)	(1)	(2)	(3)
C.	(2)	(4)	(3)	(1)
D.	(1)	(3)	(4)	(2)

70. Empathy means
A. Showing sympathy
B. Entering into the feelings and experiences
C. Patronising
D. Being critical of others

71. Community Chest is related to
A. Community Participation
B. Community Problems
C. Community Awareness
D. Community Resources

72. The proponent of 'Need for achievement theory' is
A. McClelland
B. Maslow
C. Herzberg
D. McGregor

73. Manifestation of repressed ideas in the form of finer things (Poetry and Art) is known as
A. Sublimation
B. Ambivalence
C. Catharsis
D. Fixation

74. Rejection of a null hypothesis when it is known as
A. Absolute error
B. Standard error
C. Non-sampling error
D. Type-I error

75. The objective of Action Research is
A. to provide knowledge about what intervention or treatment really help in resolving social problems.
B. to provide action plan.
C. to provide tool for statistical analysis.
D. to provide technique for data collection.

76. Which of the following is in correct sequence?
A. Forming, Norming, Storming, Performing
B. Storming, Forming, Norming, Performing
C. Forming, Storming, Norming, Performing
D. Forming, Performing, Storming, Norming

77. Match items in List-I with List-II by choosing the correct code given below :

List-I (Scholar)	List-II (Model)
(a) William Reid	(i) Problem solving model.
(b) F. Hollis	(ii) Locality Development Model
(c) Jack Rothman	(iii) Task centred model
(d) H.H. Perlman	(iv) Psycho-social model.

Codes :

	(a)	(b)	(c)	(d)
A.	(ii)	(iv)	(i)	(iii)
B.	(i)	(iii)	(ii)	(iv)
C.	(iii)	(iv)	(ii)	(i)
D.	(iii)	(ii)	(i)	(iv)

78. Match items in List-I with List-II by choosing the correct code given below :

List-I (Movement)	List-II (Propounder)
(a) Arya Samaj	(i) Jotiba Rao Phule
(b) Brahma Samaj	(ii) Swami Dayanand Saraswati
(c) Satya Sodhak Samaj	(iii) Mrs. Annie Besant
(d) Theosophical society	(iv) Raja Ram Mohan Roy

Codes :

	(a)	(b)	(c)	(d)
A.	(iii)	(iv)	(ii)	(i)
B.	(ii)	(iv)	(i)	(iii)
C.	(iv)	(iii)	(ii)	(i)
D.	(i)	(ii)	(iv)	(iii)

79. Match items in List-I with List-II.

List-I	List-II
(a) Null hypothesis	(i) Karl Pearson
(b) Alternative hypothesis	(ii) Assumption that two variables are equal
(c) Chi-square	(iii) Assumption that one variable is supporter to other
(d) Correlation	(iv) Test of hypothesis

Codes :

	(a)	(b)	(c)	(d)
A.	(i)	(ii)	(iii)	(iv)
B.	(iv)	(iii)	(ii)	(i)
C.	(ii)	(iii)	(iv)	(i)
D.	(iii)	(iv)	(ii)	(i)

80. Match the following items of List-I with the correct items of List-II.

List-I	List-II
(I) Charity organisation society	1. 1601
(II) The Beveridge Report	2. 1905
(III) Elizabethen Poor Law	3. 1941
(IV) Poor Law Commission	4. 1869

Codes :

	(I)	(II)	(III)	(IV)
A.	4	3	1	2
B.	4	3	2	1
C.	3	4	2	1
D.	3	4	1	2

81. Match the following :

List-I	List-II
(a) Anna Hazare	(i) Narmada Bachao Andolan
(b) Baba Amte	(ii) 'Raleganssiddhi'
(c) Medha Patkar	(iii) 'CHIPKO'
(d) Chandi Prasad Bhatt	(iv) 'Anandwan'

Codes :

	(a)	(b)	(c)	(d)
A.	(i)	(ii)	(iv)	(iii)
B.	(i)	(ii)	(iii)	(iv)
C.	(ii)	(i)	(iv)	(iii)
D.	(ii)	(iv)	(i)	(iii)

82. Developmental Social Work aims at

A. Maximum utilization of resources
B. Minimum utilization of resources
C. Optimum utilization of resources
D. Liberal utilization of resources

83. Social Pathology means

A. Study of origin, nature and causes of social ills.
B. Study of history of society.
C. Study of psychopaths.
D. Study of social taboos.

84. Match the following theories with their proponents :

Theories	Proponents
(a) Phenomenological	1. Skinner
(b) Psycho-Analytical	2. Maslow
(c) Motivational	3. Karl Rogers
(d) Learning	4. Sigmund Freud

Codes :

	(a)	(b)	(c)	(d)
A.	2	1	3	4
B.	3	4	2	1
C.	3	4	1	2
D.	1	2	3	4

85. Arrange the following international years in the chronology of their observance by UN (ascending order) :

I. International Year of Child.
II. International Women's Year.
III. International year of Elderly Persons.
IV. International Year of Family.

A. IV, III, II, I B. II, III, IV, I
C. II, I, IV, III D. II, I, III, IV

86. Family Counselling is
A. Macro social work practice
B. Meso social work practice
C. Micro social work practice
D. All of the above

87. **Assertion (A):** The function of professional social worker is empowering and capacity building of the oppressed sections of society.
Reason (R) : Professional social workers have the requisite skills and sensitivity to deal with problems of oppressed section of society.

Codes :
A. Both (A) and (R) are correct.
B. Both (A) and (R) are wrong.
C. (A) is correct, but (R) is wrong.
D. (R) is correct, but (A) is wrong.

88. **Assertion (A):** The joint family system is disintegrating in modern India.
Reason (R) : Transition from Agrarian to Industrial economy is responsible for its disintegration.

Codes :
A. Both (A) and (R) are wrong.
B. Both (A) and (R) are correct and (R) is the correct explanation of (A).
C. (A) is correct, but (R) is not the correct explanation of (A).
D. (R) is correct, but (A) is wrong.

89. What percentage of seats in educational institutions are reserved for Scheduled Castes in India?
A. 22 per cent B. 17 per cent
C. 15 per cent D. 19 per cent

90. Juvenile Justice (Care and Protection) Act was introduced in
A. 2001 B. 2002
C. 2003 D. 2004

91. Which of the following is not a mechanism for settlement of Industrial Disputes in India?
A. Indian Labour Conference
B. Conciliation Officers
C. Labour Courts
D. National Tribunals

92. National Institute of Empowerment of Persons with Multiple Disabilities is located in
A. Chennai B. Delhi
C. Mumbai D. Hyderabad

93. **Assertion (A):** Supervision in social work practicum, to be effective, should not be mere policing.
Reason (R) : Supervision in social work is essentially an enabling process.
A. Both (A) and (R) are true and (R) is not the correct explanation of (A).
B. Both (A) and (R) are true and (R) is the correct explanation of (A).
C. (A) is true and (R) is not true.
D. (A) is not true and (R) is true.

94. Field work based approach is classified as
A. Empirical B. Historical
C. Experimental D. Biographical

95. Match the following :

List-I	List-II
(a) Health Survey and Planning Committee	(i) 2007

(b) Mental Health Act (ii) 1959
(c) Atrocities against Women Act (iii) 1952
(d) Hindu Code Bill (iv) 1987

Codes :

	(a)	(b)	(c)	(d)
A.	(ii)	(iv)	(i)	(iii)
B.	(i)	(ii)	(iii)	(iv)
C.	(iii)	(i)	(iv)	(ii)
D.	(iv)	(iii)	(ii)	(i)

96. The concept of Management by objectives was introduced by

A. Mary Parket Foilet
B. Keith Davis
C. Peter Drucker
D. F.W. Taylor

97. Job security would fall under which of the following needs ?

A. Ego B. Social
C. Safety D. Self Actualization

98. Following are the steps of social research. Arrange the steps to prepare a plan of research study :

(a) Data collection
(b) Hypothesis
(c) Problem formulation
(d) Objectives
(e) Processing and analysis of data
(f) Report writing

Codes :

A. (a) (c) (b) (d) (e) (f)
B. (b) (c) (a) (d) (e) (f)
C. (d) (c) (b) (a) (e) (f)
D. (c) (d) (b) (a) (e) (f)

99. Match the items of List-I with items of List-II :

List-I	List-II
(a) Monogamy	(i) More than one wife
(b) Polygamy	(ii) Perfect relationship and living together
(c) Consensual union	(iii) Some earlier wives have got re-married
(d) Serial monogamy	(iv) One and only wife

Codes :

	(a)	(b)	(c)	(d)
A.	(iv)	(i)	(ii)	(iii)
B.	(i)	(ii)	(iv)	(iii)
C.	(iv)	(iii)	(i)	(ii)
D.	(iv)	(i)	(iii)	(ii)

100. Match items in List-I with List-II and choose the correct answer from the codes given below :

List-I	List-II
(a) Transference	(i) Law
(b) Parole	(ii) Sociology
(c) Cultural lag	(iii) Psychiatry
(d) Award	(iv) Criminology

Codes :

	(a)	(b)	(c)	(d)
A.	(iii)	(i)	(iv)	(ii)
B.	(ii)	(iii)	(i)	(iv)
C.	(iii)	(iv)	(ii)	(i)
D.	(i)	(ii)	(iii)	(iv)

101. Match the following :

List-I	List-II
(a) Jane Adams	(i) Methods of social work
(b) Johari Window	(ii) Problem-solving model
(c) H.H. Perlman	(iii) Social Diagnosis
(d) Mary Richmond	(iv) Known to others: unknown to self

Codes :

	(a)	(b)	(c)	(d)
A.	(i)	(iv)	(ii)	(iii)
B.	(i)	(iv)	(iii)	(ii)
C.	(ii)	(i)	(iii)	(iv)
D.	(iv)	(iii)	(ii)	(i)

102. Match the following:

List-I	List-II
(a) Probation Department	(i) Rehabilitation of offender
(b) Parole	(ii) Juvenile Justice
(c) Vocational Training	(iii) District Court
(d) Child Welfare Committee	(iv) Reward for good conduct

Codes :

	(a)	(b)	(c)	(d)
A.	(i)	(ii)	(iii)	(iv)
B.	(iii)	(iv)	(i)	(ii)
C.	(iv)	(i)	(ii)	(iii)
D.	(ii)	(iii)	(iv)	(i)

103. International Day for the disabled is celebrated every year in the month of
A. October B. September
C. November D. December

104. Rehabilitation Council of India was established in the year
A. 1986 B. 1992
C. 1993 D. 1994

105. The first World Assembly on Aging was held in
A. Austria B. Vietnam
C. Australia D. Zambia

106. The Chairperson of National Human Rights Commission holds office for a period of
A. 5 years B. 6 years
C. 7 years D. 4 years

107. Provisions relating to economic and social justice are incorporated in which part of Indian Constitution ?
A. Part III B. Part IV
C. Schedules D. None of the above

108. Perceiving something which is not physically present is called
A. Colour blindness
B. Hallucination
C. Faulty perception
D. None of the above

109. Old Age, Survivors, Disability and Health Insurance (OASDHI) a social insurance programme was created by
A. The 1935 Social Security Act
B. The Poor Law of 1601
C. The Statute of 1572
D. The Laws of Settlement 1662

110. The salient features of National Policy for persons with disability are
A. Physical rehabilitation.
B. Educational and vocational rehabilitation.
C. Economic rehabilitation.
D. All the above.

111. The law of three stages of Social Development is originally propounded by
A. Karl Marx
B. Talcott Persons
C. Auguste Compte
D. Herbert Spencer

112. 'Sanatorium' means
A. Institution for open air treatment of tuberculosis.
B. Institution for help of elderly people.
C. Institution for the treatment of mentally sick.
D. Institution for the treatment of lepers.

113. ICD-10 means
A. International certification of diseases.
B. The 10th revision of the International Classification of diseases.
C. Indian classification of 10 deadly diseases.
D. International classification to determine burden of diseases

114. Match the correct author with the book that he/she has written and select the correct answer by seeing the code given below :

Author	**Books**
(a) Arthur Fink	(i) Social group work—A helping process
(b) Gisela Konopka	(ii) Social care work—A problem solving process
(c) Murray G. Ross	(iii) Community Organization
(d) Helen Perlman	(iv) The Field of social work
	(v) Integrated social work practice

Codes :

	(a)	(b)	(c)	(d)
A.	(iv)	(i)	(iii)	(ii)
B.	(v)	(iii)	(ii)	(i)
C.	(i)	(v)	(ii)	(iv)
D.	(iii)	(ii)	(iv)	(v)

115. Which of the following is not a principle of social case work ?
A. Principle of Confidentiality
B. Principle of Acceptance
C. Principle of Assimilation
D. Principle of Self-determination

116. Which of the following is a Reference Group?
A. Occupational group
B. Group taken to evaluate one's own aspect of life
C. A relatively larger group
D. A group which allows for social mobility

117. The principle element/elements in program planning include :
A. Group member's participation
B. Group member's interests
C. The program content
D. All the above

118. Which Indian state has lowest child sex ratio, from among the following ?
A. Kerala B. Karnataka
C. Tamil Nadu D. Punjab

119. Which one of the following is not the professional view of social work ?
A. Client as object
B. Client as citizen
C. Client as recipient
D. Client as resource

120. The tendency to commit crime repeatedly without any sense of repentance is called
A. De facto action B. Terrorism
C. Return-back D. Recidivism

121. Which of the following is recognised as decade for Natural Disaster Reduction ?
A. 1980s B. 1990s
C. 1970s D. 1960s

122. The National Rural Employment Guarantee Act came into force in the year
A. 1999 B. 2001
C. 2005 D. 2009

123. Written or visual materials read or viewed primarily for the purpose of sexual pleasure is called
A. Sexual photography
B. Pornography
C. Papers on sex
D. Blue film

124. Who introduced the concept of 'Role Playing' ?
A. E. Durkheim
B. G.H. Mead
C. W.I. Thomas
D. Sigmond Freud

125. Negative reinforcement leads to
A. Extinguish a behaviour
B. Increase in desired responses
C. Eliminate desirable responses
D. Learned helplessness

126. 12 years old Ashad need not be told that he had failed in his exams, on returning home he could guess by the looks on his father's face and his posture, what his result was? This is an example of
A. Involvement of visual modality
B. Non-verbal communication
C. Extra-sensory perception
D. Facial cues

127. When monotony in work is reduced by giving a wider variety of duties to employees; it is known as
A. Job enlargement
B. Job rotation
C. Job redesign
D. Job enrichment

128. NICP means
A. National initiative for child protection.
B. National integrative for child program.
C. National integrative for child policy.
D. National initiative for child planning.

129. The curved line type relationship is referred by
A. Linear Correlation
B. Non-Linear Correlation
C. Simple Correlation
D. Multiple Correlation

130. Social Forestry scheme was initiated in India –

1. to increase fuel availability in rural areas
2. to prevent soil erosion
3. to compensate deforestation activities
4. to maintain the biodiversity of the nation

Codes :

A. 1 and 2 are correct
B. 3 and 4 are correct
C. 1, 2 and 3 are correct
D. 1, 2 and 4 are correct

131. In the principle of 'Right to self determination' social worker
A. recognises the right and need of clients to freedom in making their own choices and decisions.
B. recognises the right to privacy of the client.
C. examines the situations of clients without bias.
D. recognises the client's genuine concern, points of view and help in taking decision.

132. Emotional disorders in which an individual remains oriented to reality but suffers from chronic anxiety is
A. Schizophrenia
B. Depression
C. Paranoid states
D. Neuroses

133. Individualization as both goal and process of social work practice was suggested by :
A. H.H. Perlman
B. Florance Hollis
C. G. Konopka
D. Carol Mayer

134. Scheme for analysing group interactions called as 'Interaction process' is developed by
A. Robert Bales
B. Charles D. Garvin
C. Maeda J. Galinsky
D. Alex Gitterman

135. The Indian Journal of Social Work was started in the year
A. 1938 B. 1940
C. 1948 D. 1952

136. An Achieved Status is based on
A. Birth
B. Caste
C. Abilities
D. Financial position of family

137. Marriage is a _____ among Hindus.
A. contract
B. measure to exchange property
C. sacrament
D. legal need

ANSWERS

1	2	3	4	5	6	7	8	9	10
D	B	A	C	B	C	D	A	C	A
11	**12**	**13**	**14**	**15**	**16**	**17**	**18**	**19**	**20**
A	D	D	B	D	C	D	B	C	C
21	**22**	**23**	**24**	**25**	**26**	**27**	**28**	**29**	**30**
D	C	C	B	A	A	A	B	A	B
31	**32**	**33**	**34**	**35**	**36**	**37**	**38**	**39**	**40**
D	C	B	C	C	B	D	B	D	D
41	**42**	**43**	**44**	**45**	**46**	**47**	**48**	**49**	**50**
D	D	A	B	A	D	B	B	A	A
51	**52**	**53**	**54**	**55**	**56**	**57**	**58**	**59**	**60**
A	C	C	C	C	C	B	A	D	D

61	62	63	64	65	66	67	68	69	70
C	B	A	A	C	A	C	D	B	B
71	**72**	**73**	**74**	**75**	**76**	**77**	**78**	**79**	**80**
D	A	C	D	A	C	B	B	C	A
81	**82**	**83**	**84**	**85**	**86**	**87**	**88**	**89**	**90**
D	C	A	B	C	C	A	B	C	A
91	**92**	**93**	**94**	**95**	**96**	**97**	**98**	**99**	**100**
A	A	B	A	A	C	C	D	A	C
101	**102**	**103**	**104**	**105**	**106**	**107**	**108**	**109**	**110**
A	B	D	A	A	A	B	B	A	D
111	**112**	**113**	**114**	**115**	**116**	**117**	**118**	**119**	**120**
C	A	B	A	C	A	D	D	B	D
121	**122**	**123**	**124**	**125**	**126**	**127**	**128**	**129**	**130**
B	C	B	B	B	B	B	A	B	A
131	**132**	**133**	**134**	**135**	**136**	**137**			
A	D	D	A	B	C	C			

➤➤➤➤➤

CHAPTER

6

Community Organisation

HISTORY OF COMMUNITY ORGANISATION

Community organisation is as old as our community life because wherever people live together, some organisation becomes necessary. But when life became more complicated, some formal organisations were set up for the community welfare. Historically Elizabethan Poor Law in England was one of the first efforts to provide services for the needy. But charity organisations societies were forerunners of modern community organisation planning. They were first organised in London in 1869 to eliminate discriminate alms giving by the relief agencies at that time. In America the first charity organisation society was organised in Buffalo in 1877. Later on it spread to the other cities of USA. The charity organisation movement is an influential factor for emergence of community organisation.

Concept of Community Organization

Young Husband defined community organisation as primary aimed at helping people with in a local community to identify social needs, to consider the most effective ways of meeting them and to set about doing so, in so for as their available resources permits.

Approaches of Community Organization

Ross (1955) identified three approaches of community organisation

(1) **The 'specific content' approach**, where by a worker or an agency or organisation identifies problem and launches a program to meet them.

(2) **The 'general content' approach** whereby a group, association or council, such state social welfare board, attempts a coordinated and orderly development of service in a particular area.

(3) **The 'process approach'** where the objective is not the content *i.e.*, facilities or services of some kind.

Definition of community organisation by M.G. Ross 'Community organisation is a process by which a community identifies its needs or objectives, develops the confidence and will to work for these needs or objectives, finds the resources (internal and/or external) to deal with these needs or objectives takes action in respect them, and in doing so extends and develops cooperative and collaborative attitudes and practices in the community.'

Objectives of Community Organization

Community organisation is essentially concerned with influencing the course of social change through a process of analysing social situation and forming relationship with different groups to bring about desirable change, it has three main objectives:

(1) To involve the people democratically in thinking deciding, planning and playing an active part in the development and operation of services that affect their daily lives.

(2) Value for personal fulfilment of belonging to a community.

(3) Concerned with the need in community planning to think of actual people in relation to other people and meeting their needs as persons, instead off, on a series of separate needs and problems.

Steps in Community Organisation

Lindeman has suggested ten steps in community organisation

(1) Some person, either within or without the community, expresses the need which is later represented by the definite project.

(2) A leader, within some institution or group within community convinces the group about the reality of the need.

(3) The interested group attempts to project the consciousness of need upon the leadership of community; the consciousness of need becomes more general.

(4) Some influential assistance is enlisted in an attempt to arrive at quick means of meeting the needs.

(5) Other means of meeting the need are presented.

(6) Various groups provide their support to one or the other of the various solutions presented.

(7) It appears to be increasingly customary to pause at this point and to investigate of the project with an expert assistance.

(8) A public mass meeting is held at which the project is presented and the groups with most influence attempts to secure adoption of their plans.

Principles of Community Organisation

M.G. Ross in his book 'community organisation theory, principles and practice' has identified the following principles of community organisation.

1. Discontent with existing conditions in the community must initiate and/or nourish the development of the association.
2. Discontent must be focused and channeled into organiation, planning and action in respect to specific problems.
3. The discontent which initiates or sustains community organisation must be widely shared in the community
4. The organisation must involve leaders (both formal and informal) identified with and accepted by major subgroups in the community.
5. The organisation must have goals and methods of procedure of high acceptability.
6. The program of organisation should include some activities with emotional content.
7. The organistion should seek to utilise the manifest and latent good will which exists in the community.
8. The organisation must develop active and effective lines of communication both within the organization and between the organization and the community.
9. The organization should seek to support and strengthen the groups which it brings together in cooperative work.
10. The organization should be flexible in its organizational procedures without disrupting its regular decision making routines.
11. The organization should develop a pace for its work relative to existing conditions in the community.
12. The organization should seek to develop effective leaders.
13. The organization must develop strength, salability and prestige in the community.

MODELS OF COMMUNITY ORGANISATION

Rothman (1979) suggested three models for community organisation i.e. locality development model, social planning model and social action model.

- **The locality development model** refers to the popular notion of community organisation practice whereby a worker or an agency attempts to develop various services or program to meet the need of target population in a defined area. This may also include the coordination of various agencies providing services in the area and the generation of new program and services as well.
- **The social planning model** refers to community work where a worker or an agency undertakes an exercise evaluating the welfare needs and existing services in a town, village or municipal area or may be in a state and suggest a possible blueprint for more efficient delivery of social services. Generally such attempts are confined to a particular field such as housing, education, health, child care or women's development.
- **The social action model** refers to community work which is issue oriented and attempts to generate a social movement. The worker or agency attempts to moblilise public opinion on a particular issue by educating people. The issue may range reorganizing relief during natural calamity, or combating problems like dowry or wife battering to a more radical change in society or in social institution.

SOCIAL MOVEMENT

In a society a large number of changes have been brought about by efforts exerted by people individually and collectively. Such efforts have been called social movement. Therefore we can define social movement as a voluntary association of people engaged in a concerted effort to change, attitudes, behaviour and social relationships in a larger society. Social movements may be of numerous kind, such as religious movements, reform movements or revolutionary movements.

The following features of the social movement may be marked out:

(1) It is an effort by a group.

(2) Its aim is to bring change in society.

(3) It may be organised or unorganised.

(4) It may be peaceful or violent.

(5) Its life is not certain. It may continue for a long period of time or it may end soon.

Causes of Social Movement

- The values, behaviour and attitude or people is changing every time, people develop new ideas to bring change in the exhibiting system and organize a movement.
- When a section of society feels isolated from the rest of the society and community leaders. Develops insecurity confusion and frustration. This confusion, frustration and discontent produces social movement.
- When a group of people feel that injustice has been done with them, they become frustrated and alienated. Such feeling of injustice provides fertile soil for social movement.

Kinds of Social Movement

(1) Migratory Movement: Migratory movement take place when a large number of people leave one country and settle at some other places. The reason for mass migration may be discontent with present circumstances or the attraction of a bright future.

(2) Expressive Movements: When people are faced with a social system form which they cannot come out and they feel powerless to change, the result is an expressive social movement.

(3) Utopian Movement: A utopian movement is one which seek to create an ideal social system which can be found only in men's imagination and not in reality. The Sarvodaya Movement can be called utopian movement.

(4) Reform Movement: The reform movement is an attempt to modify some part of society without completely transforming it. The movement to abolish untouchability can be considered reform movement.

(5) **Revolutionary Movement:** The revolutionary movement seek to overthrow the existing social system and replace it with greatly different one. The revolutionary movement wants to root out the system itself. The communist movements in Soviet Russia and China were revolutionary movement.

(6) **Resistance Movement:** The resistance movement is an effort to block a proposed change. Generally resistance movement arises because people consider social change too fast. The D.M.K. social movement in Tamilnadu against Hindi can be considered resistance social movement.

SOCIAL ACTION

Social action as a method of social work can be defined as efforts to bring about change or prevent change in current social practices or situations, through education, propaganda, persuasion, or pressure on behalf of objectives believed by the actionists to be socially desirable. Generally social action involves organised efforts to influence public opinion or official policy or executive action with the support of groups or individuals.

Characteristics of Social Action

- Social action is concerned with change in current social practices.
- Social action involves a goal accepted as desirable and worthwhile by the social actionists.
- Social action always involves an attempt to bring about action by people other than the social actionist.
- Social action may include methods such as education, propaganda, persuasion or pressure but it does not recommend physical coercion or compulsion.
- Social action to be identified with certain method and procedures rather than certain social values.

Forms of Social Action

Brito has identified two type of social action:

(1) Action initiated and conducted by the elites for the benefits of the masses.

(2) Popular social action.

He identified three sub-models of each type of social action. In the first model he has mentioned the following types.

(1) **Legislative action model:** In this model elites try to modify the social policy by creating public opinion against the problems.

(2) **Sanction model:** The elites by gaining control over some economic, social, political or religious weapons to obtain benefits for the society.

(3) **Direct physical model:** Elites take action and punish those responsible for the cause of injustice

The popular social action model has the following three sup-models:

(1) **Conscientization model** based on Paulo Friere's concept of creating awareness among masses through education.

(2) **Dialectical model** promoting conflict to exploit the contradictions in a system with the belief that a better system will emerge as a result.

(3) **Direct mobilization model** where by specific issues are takes up by the actionists and masses are mobilized to protest and strike to active the objectives.

Principles of Social Action

Britto has described the following principles of social action.

Principle of Credibility Building: The principle suggest to create a public image of the leadership of the concerned organization and the followers of the movement as promoter and supporter of justice equity and truth.

Principle of Legitimization: Legitimization is the process of convincing the public that the movement objectives are legal and morally right.

Principle of Dramatization: Dramatization is the principle of mass mobilization by which the leaders of a movement motivates the population by emotional appeal of heroism, sensational news, powerful slogans and other techniques.

Principle of Multiple Strategies: Achieving the goals and objective of social action requires the application of multiple strategies. Four strategies have been identified by Zeltman and Duncan. These are: (1) educational strategy (2) Persuasive strategy (3) Facilitative strategy and (4) Power strategy .

Principle of Dual Approach: The principle suggests that social actionist should build counter system. Which is believed to be beneficial to the needs of the mobilized public on self help basis without involving opponents. Counter system must be built up and traditional systems inputs be transformed in any developmental operation.

Principle of Manifold Programs: The principle recommends three categories of program such as social program, economic programs and political programs.

Strategies of Social Action: Desai (1984) has classified the strategies for social action into three categories.

Bargaining, Negotiating and Advocacy: These strategies could include technique of bargaining, negotiation, publicity which leads to discomfort for the target of change. Advocacy through the media, 'Satyagrah', 'March' method could also be used to persuade and change the target group.

Conflictual/confrontational: This strategy assumes that strong pressure tactics become necessary in some critical circumstances such as demonstration, civil disobedience or direct action.

Techniques of Social Action: Social action involves variety of tactics, often a combination of there depending on the philosophy and ideological beliefs of the sponsors. Some of the techniques have been explicitly identified and are listed below:

- Fact finding
- Publicity, advocacy, using both formal and informal media.
- Education, awareness building, concretization.
- Mobilizing support and favorable opinion through establishing institutional system and political process.
- Expressing anger, warmth, and hatred in dramatic and innovative ways.
- Cooperation and collaboration.
- Using slogans
- Negotiation, bargaining and arbitration
- Disruption (interrupt thee progress of) and mild coercion (mild resistance, protest, marches, morcha, dharna, strikes, boycotts, fasts, gharaos etc.)
- Strong coercive tactics (extra legal measures and direct action)

Steps

(1) Identifying the problems (in this case injustice), diagnosing it, gathering information about it, about whom the principle actor are, and what roles they play, what interest they have and what benefit they derive.

(2) Determining the position to be taken.

(3) Identifying the social action goals, *i.e.*, expected outcome.

(4) Mobilizing support using both non formal and formal methods and locating the network of influence and power.

(5) Setting up the machinery to carry out the struggle canvas action, provides leadership.

(6) Laying down the strategy. A well drawn out plan indicating the series of action and their networking among leaders.

(7) Laying down the communication channels and the decision making loci of the social action movement.

(8) Carrying out the action

(9) Reviewing the implementation of the strategy, weighing alternative approaches and working out alternative plans.

(10) Sustaining the pressure.

Some writers have suggested the stages as:

- Awareness Building (step 1 & 2 of the above stages)
- Organising people (step 3,4, & 5 of the above stages)
- Developing the strategy (step 6 & 7 of the above stages)
- Action (step 8,9 & 10 of the above stages)

CONCEPT OF VOLUNTARY ORGANISATION

A voluntary organisation is an organisation which whether its worker are paid or unpaid, is initiated and governed by its won members without external control (Sundagram, I.S., 1986)

A voluntary organisation is an agency (organized or unorganised structured or unstructured) which work for the welfare of a community in any given area of its own preference. It may be just an individual or collection of individual or it may have a more formal subculture. It is basically a group of professionally trained, socially sensetised and committed persons living in area of activity and dealing and interacting with the community people.

A voluntary organisation has special qualities in its style of functioning such as innovation, flexibility in operation and sensitivity to changing needs and high level of motivation of the functionaries. A voluntary organisation aims at helping the people to help themselves by mobilizing their own resources, taping their potential, identifying problems, finding solution to them to achieve their goals.

ROLE OF VOLUNTARY ORGANISATION IN DEVELOPMENT

The role of voluntary organisation in rural development has been recognised and considered vital because of the following reasons.

1. Government alone cannot mobilise resources needed for meeting peoples need;
2. The quality and efficiency of government sponsored program increase when people are involved in progrm planning and implementation.
3. Voluntary organisation can complement very well with the development efforts of government in terms of geographic and program needs;
4. They have firsthand experience and knowledge of local needs, problems and resources at local level;
5. They are closer to the minds and hearts of the people.
6. Commitment and zeal of voluntary action;
7. Voluntary sector is more responsive and can operate with greater flexibility.

The Background, aims, motivation, ideology, legal status, dedication, and level of operation, program, personnel, funding sources and limited external control are the distinguished factures of non government organisation or voluntary organisation.

Voluntary organisation can play the following constructive roles in the field or social development

(1) Helping in identification of potential beneficiaries of different schemes of development, their proper selection and getting service of public institution.

(2) Securing peoples participation which is very important for the success of any development program as it increases acceptability and utilization of services.

(3) Implementing different social development programs.

(4) Ensuring that benefit of different development programs reach to the target beneficiary.

(5) Acting as a link between the administration and the people to bring about changes in their attitude through education, persuasion, motivation and building up of awareness.

(6) Supplementing government programs in rural areas by providing wide range of choices and alternatives to the people.

(7) Educating, mobilising and organising the society and economically backward population at the grass root level and

making them aware of their rights and responsibilities.

(8) Functioning as watchdogs of the people to prevent the administration from slackening and reporting irregularities, checking misuse of funds and avoiding delays.

(9) Disseminating information, education and communication by using demonstration and technology.

(10) Assisting in monitoring and evaluation and periodical verification of the utilization of a assets by the beneficiaries.

(11) Assisting government machinary in the formulation of block plan based on household survey.

(12) Demonstrating as to how local initiatives and local resources can be better utilised.

(13) Activating delivery system and streamlining its functioning.

(14) Giving proper guidance to the illiterate and ignorant beneficiaries in the use of new technology and innovations in the field of agriculture and rural development.

(15) Providing direct services to the beneficiaries at individual level.

(16) Training and motivating grass root level worker and organising seminar, conferences and workshops for their professional growth.

(17) Mobbilising financial and human resources from within the community and promoting self reliance.

(18) Improving the condition of poor, empowering the women, preventing environmental degradation and promoting literacy and good health.

(19) Studying the problems of rural and urban areas and monitoring and evaluating different development programs and documenting information of voluntary efforts.

(20) Imparting professional skill to the functionaries and upgrading their competence in different areas of their responsibilities.

CONCEPT OF COMMUNITY DEVELOPMENT

Community development has been used especially in the decade from 1950 to 1960 to describe a comprehensive method of raising standard of living in which the emphasis is on the participation of people themselves albeit with the assistance of both governmental and non governmental organisation work carried out under this approach has covered an immensely wide scope, for building of roads and dams to the running of community centers and literacy classes (Kuenstler, 1961)

- In India, the term community development refers governmental efforts to bring about social and economic development, particularly in rural areas.
- Community development refers to creation of social services, human development, community education program and other welfare programs.
- Community development in fact was seen as a movement designed promote better living for the whole community, with active participation if possible at the community initiatives, but if this initiatives is not forthcoming spontaneously, then by making use of techniques to arouse and stimulate it, in order to secure its active and enthusiastic response to the movement (Mukerji, 1961)
- The term 'community development' used to describe a goal of bringing about social and economic development in areas which are underdeveloped. It was coined to refer to governmental projects undertaken during the 1950's in most of the developing countries which has just acquired on independent status after years of colonial rule.
- Sunders (1958) describes community development as the process of 'change from a condition where one or two people or a small elite within or without the local community make decision for the rest of the people, to a condition where people

themselves make decisions about matters of common concern, form a state of minimum to one of maximum cooperation, form a condition where all resources and specialists come from outside to one where local people make the most of their resources.'

- Community development can be considered as a goal and community organisation as the process or the method by which community development can be achieved.

Difference between Community Organisation and Community Development

(1) Community development programs are made available by the government to its people basically for their economic development and progress. The main emphasis is on improving the condition of people with the help of government services. Community organization is a process which strives to make adjustment between communities felt needs and community resources.

(2) Community development aims to provide services to the people mainly for their economic improvement in community organization, community services are organised and planned by themselves under the guidance of a community organizer.

(3) Community development programs are practiced mainly in underdeveloped or developing communities for economic enlistment of the people. The basic aim of community organisation is to develop cooperative and collaborative attitude among people in the community.

(4) Community organisation worker is not necessarily a government functionary. He is skilled in community planning but the functionaries of community are expert in removing economic back wardens.

MULTIPLE CHOICE QUESTIONS

1. Concepts are known as :

A. Steps in Social Research
B. Causal explanation
C. Steps in Operationalization
D. Building blocks of Theory

2. Independent variables are generally shown on :

A. Y axis B. X axis
C. Column D. Row

3. Match the pairs :

(a) The Industrial Disputes Act (i) 1961
(b) The Maternity Benefit Act (ii) 1948
(c) The Contract Labour Act (iii) 1947
(d) The Minimum wages Act (iv) 1970

Codes :

	(a)	(b)	(c)	(d)
A.	(iii)	(i)	(iv)	(ii)
B.	(iv)	(ii)	(i)	(iii)
C.	(i)	(ii)	(iii)	(iv)
D.	(ii)	(iii)	(iv)	(i)

4. Which of the following is not a nominal variable ?

A. Buddhist B. Indian
C. Catholic D. I Q Score

5. Select the correct sequence :

A. Block placement, Orientation visits, Concurrent field work
B. Orientation visits, Block placement, Concurrent field work
C. Orientation visits, Concurrent field work, Block placement
D. Concurrent field work, Block placement, Orientation visits

6. Select which is in proper sequence :

A. Receiving, explaining agency objective, filling intake sheet, listening
B. Listening, explaining agency objective, receiving, filling intake sheet

C. Filling intake sheet, receiving, listening, explaining agency objective
D. Explaining agency objective, filling intake sheet, listening, receiving

7. Select which is in correct sequence :
A. Study, diagnosis, treatment, termination
B. Termination, treatment, diagnosis, study
C. Diagnosis, treatment, study, termination
D. Study, termination, diagnosis, treatment

8. Identify the correct sequence :
A. Title of study, data analysis, data collection
B. Data collection, data analysis, title of study
C. Title of study, data collection, data analysis
D. Data analysis, title of study, data collection

9. Identify the correct sequence :
A. Data collection, Scrutiny, Tabulation
B. Scrutiny, Tabulation, Data collection
C. Data collection, Tabulation, Scrutiny
D. Tabulation, Scrutiny, Data collection

10. The National Commission for Women was established in the year
A. 1957 B. 1986
C. 2001 D. 1992

11. Kaka Kalelkar was associated with
A. Scheduled Caste Commission
B. Scheduled Tribe Commission
C. Backward Classes Commission
D. Minorities Commission

12. The method by which the relative worth of Jobs in an organisation is determined is called as
A. Job Description
B. Job Evaluation
C. Job Specification
D. Job Analysis

13. Arrange the following Acts in order in which they were enacted. Use the code given below:
(i) The ESI Act
(ii) The Provident Fund Act
(iii) The Maternity Benefit Act
(iv) Workmen's Compensation Act

Codes :
A. (ii) (i) (iv) (iii) B. (i) (iv) (ii) (iii)
C. (iv) (i) (ii) (iii) D. (iv) (i) (iii) (ii)

14. 'Cognitive needs' of human beings are the needs
A. to develop abilities
B. for symmetry, order and beauty
C. for security and freedom from attack
D. to know, to understand and to explore

15. 'Learned helplessness' is a concept based on
A. Unconditional positive learning
B. Social learning theory
C. Hypothetical constructs
D. Psychoanalytic approach

16. Match the following :

List-I	List-II
(a) Social investigation report	i. Medical social work
(b) Discharge planning	ii. Child guidance centre
(c) Workmen's compensation	iii. Probation
(d) Behavioural problems	iv. Social security

Codes :

	(a)	(b)	(c)	(d)
A.	iii	i	iv	ii
B.	i	iv	ii	iii
C.	iv	iii	ii	i
D.	i	ii	iii	iv

17. Which one of the following is not necessary for project formulation?
A. Setting objectives and targets
B. Design of strategies
C. Identification of potential obstacles
D. Documentation

18. FCRA stands for
A. Foreign Contribution (Rules) Act
B. Foreign Contribution (Regulation) Act
C. Federal Contribution (Regulation) Act.
D. None of the above

19. Match List-I and List-II and select the correct answer by using the code given below :

List-I	List-II
(a) Argumentative Indian	(i) Thomas Harris
(b) I am OK, you are OK	(ii) Chetan Bhagat
(c) One night at the call center	(iii) A.P.J. Abdul Kalam
(d) Wings of Fire	(iv) Amartya Sen
	(v) Eric Berne

Codes :

	(a)	(b)	(c)	(d)
A.	(ii)	(iv)	(i)	(iv)
B.	(iv)	(i)	(ii)	(iii)
C.	(iii)	(i)	(iv)	(ii)
D.	(i)	(iii)	(ii)	(iv)

20. Arrange the following steps in Research process in a logical sequence :

(i) Objectives
(ii) Data reduction
(iii) Code Book preparation
(iv) Data collection instrument
(v) Data Analysis
(vi) Report writing

A. (iii) (i) (iv) (ii) (v) (vi)
B. (iv) (i) (iii) (ii) (v) (vi)
C. (i) (iv) (ii) (iii) (v) (vi)
D. (i) (ii) (iii) (iv) (v) (vi)

21. One of the following is not in the list of Eight MDGs :

A. Achieving Universal Primary Education
B. Opposing Racial Discrimination
C. Improving maternal health
D. Ensuring Environmental Sustainability

22. Match the following:

List-I	List-II
(a) Hepatitis-B	(i) Respiratory system
(b) Asthma	(ii) Thyroid gland
(c) Diabetes	(iii) Eye
(d) Trachoma	(iv) Pancreas
	(v) Liver

Codes :

	(a)	(b)	(c)	(d)
A.	(i)	(ii)	(iv)	(iii)
B.	(iv)	(i)	(iii)	(ii)
C.	(iii)	(i)	(iv)	(ii)
D.	(iv)	(i)	(iv)	(iii)

23. The World Development report is brought out by :

A. WTO B. UNDP
C. UNRISD D. World Bank

24. The maintenance and welfare of parents and senior citizens bill was passed in the year :

A. 2007 B. 1950
C. 1986 D. 2005

25. Lobbying's in Social Action stands for :

A. Winning support
B. Winning confidence
C. Winning gains
D. Win over crisis

26. Embourgeoisement :

A. Rich becomes Poor
B. Poor becomes Rich
C. Rich becomes much richer
D. Poor becomes much poorer

27. Gemeinschaft and Gesellschaft refers to:

A. Community and Groups
B. Community and Caste
C. Community and Society
D. Community and Neighbourhood

28. Muta Marriage is performed in :

A. Jains B. Sikhs
C. Muslims D. Buddhists

29. Which Part of the Indian Constitution promotes the welfare?

A. Part I B. Part II
C. Part III D. Part IV

30. The Child Marriage Restraint Act came into force on :

A. April 1, 1928 B. April 1, 1929
C. April 1, 1930 D. April 1, 1931

31. Crime is a learned behaviour. Who propounded it?

A. Cohen B. Sutherland
C. Vold D. Bentham

32. Probation means :

A. Release on Licence
B. Release on bail

C. Conditional suspension of Punishment
D. Suspension of Punishment

33. The first Juvenile Court was established in :
A. Madras B. Lucknow
C. Bombay D. Calcutta

34. Poverty is related to :
A. Relative Theory
B. Cultural Theory
C. System Theory
D. Anomie Theory

35. Locality Development, Social Planning and Social Action as models of community organisation were given by
A. Murray Ross B. Jack Rothman
C. Perlman D. Sanders

36. The concept of Conscientization is given by
A. Paulo Frierie
B. Martin Luther King
C. GAA Britto
D. Saul Alinsky

37. The value of middle item of series when arranged in ascending or descending order of magnitude is known as
A. Mean B. Median
C. Mode D. Standard Deviation

38. In social research, the design used to search for 'what' of the problem is
A. Exploratory design
B. Experimental design
C. Comparative study design
D. Descriptive design

39. Which one of the following is the source of social policy?
A. Ministry of Human Resource Development
B. Indian Constitution
C. Non-Government Organisation
D. None of the above

40. Ramification is
A. Name of a technique to work with the tribal people
B. An evaluation technique
C. A criteria to decide the kind of policies to be pursued for allocation of resources
D. A selection method for community workers

41. Which one of the following homes is not the part of the Juvenile Justice (Care & Protection of Children) Act of 2000 ?
A. Observation Home
B. Shelter Home
C. Protective Home
D. Special Home

42. Which of the following explains the concept of 'Right' ?
A. Which is morally or socially correct or just
B. A justification or fair claim
C. A thing which may be claimed legally or morally
D. All the above

43. Which of the following is not a goal of the Millennium Development Goals ?
A. Achieving universal primary education
B. Reducing child mortality
C. Ensuring environmental sustainability
D. Improving mental health

44. Assertion (A): Authorisation, approval or permission needed to perform certain professional tasks and activities is known as sanction.
Reason (B): Person with problem can take help from professional social worker.
Choose your answer from the following :
A. Both (A) and (R) are wrong.
B. (A) is correct and (R) is the correct explanation of (A).
C. (A) is correct and (R) is not the correct explanation of (A).
D. (A) is wrong, but (R) is correct.

45. Human Poverty Index (HPI) is developed by:
A. WHO B. WTO
C. FAO D. UNDP

46. "The integration of all functions and processes within an organization in order to achieve continuous improvement of quality of goods and services". Which among the following terms is described by above definition given by Omachonu and Ross :

A. TQM B. HRM

C. Theory Z D. Collegial Model

47. The number of classes to which the values can be assigned arbitrarily or at will without violating restrictions or limitations placed, is :

A. Mean value

B. Chi-square

C. Degree of Freedom

D. Type I Error

48. Arrange the sequence of following in context of social work profession :

(i) charity

(ii) empowerment

(iii) welfare

(iv) religious reform and

(v) development

A. (i) (ii) (iii) (v) (iv)

B. (iv) (i) (iii) (v) (ii)

C. (i) (iv) (iii) (ii) (v)

D. (i) (iv) (iii) (v) (ii)

49. Whose approach in case work is considered an eclectic approach ?

A. Florence Hollis B. Jessy Taft

C. H. H. Perlman D. Mary Richmond

50. 'Role' is :

A. a social group position

B. a part in a play

C. a move in some direction

D. an undulating motion

51. Assertion (A): People who are poor in mathematics join social sciences.

Reason (R) : Social sciences do not require high mathematical abilities. Identify correct statements from below.

A. Both (A) and (R) are wrong

B. Both (A) and (R) are correct and (R) is the correct explanation of (A).

C. Both (A) and (R) are correct

D. (A) is correct and (R) is wrong

52. The National Rural Employment Guarantee Act was passed in the year :

A. 2003 B. 2005

C. 2004 D. 2000

53. Assertion (A): Social Justice does not lead to equity.

Reason (R) : Social Justice demands reverse discrimination in favour of the worst off. Identify the correct statement from the statement below :

A. (A) is correct but (R) is wrong

B. Both (A) and (R) are wrong

C. (A) is wrong but (R) is correct

D. (A) and (R) are correct but (R) is not the correct explanation of (A)

54. Dispersion refers to the

A. variability in the value of items

B. frequency

C. distribution

D. central tendency

55. A declarative statement of relationship between or among variables is called

A. Concept B. Value

C. Hypothesis D. None of the above

56. Assertion (A): The profession of social work is concerned with oppressed and marginalised sections of society.

Reason (R) : Social worker must collect all information regarding different sections of society for the empowerment of oppressed and marginalised people.

Codes :

A. Both (A) and (R) are correct.

B. Both (A) and (R) are correct and (R) is the correct explanation of (A).

C. Both (A) and (R) are correct but (R) is not the correct explanation of (A).

D. (A) is correct but (R) is wrong.

57. Select which one of the given is correctly sequenced as system approach.

A. Change-agent system, Target system, Client system, Action system.

B. Change-agent system, Client system, Target system, Action system.

C. Change-agent system, Client system, Action system, Target system.
D. Change-agent system, Action system, Target system, Client system.

58. Psycho-social approach in social case work is dependent on
A. Behavioural thought
B. Freudian thought
C. Client centred therapy
D. Transactional analysis

59. The term "Personality" derived from
A. Spanish word
B. Latin word
C. Greek word
D. German word

60. Wilson & Ryland wrote the book
A. Social Groupwork
B. Social Work with Groups
C. Groupwork Practice
D. Social Groupwork Practice

61. Who said that "religion is the opium of masses"?
A. K. Davis B. Karl Marx
C. Durkheim D. Max Weber

62. The objective of social reform is
A. to help a minority group
B. to assist the marginalised group
C. to bring about social change
D. None of the above

63. Right to Free Legal Aid is included in
A. Article 14 B. Article 15
C. Article 16 D. Article 21

64. Elizabethan Poor Law, 1601 was based on
A. Concept of Rehabilitation
B. Concept of Determining the Needs of Clients
C. Concept of Charity
D. Concept of Empowerment

65. Friendly visitors are related to
A. Charity Organisation Society, USA
B. Elizabethan Poor Law, 1601
C. Charity Organisation Society, London
D. None of these

66. The classification of social system as (i) Mechanical Social System and (ii) Organic Social System is given by
A. E. Durkheim B. P. Sorokin
C. MacIver D. T. Parsons

67. Prohibition of discrimination on grounds of religion etc. is a Fundamental Right classified under
A. The Right to Freedom of Religion
B. The Right Against Exploitation
C. The Right to Equality
D. The Cultural and Educational Rights

68. Social stratification means
A. Socialisation
B. Social Change
C. Division of Labour
D. Division of People on the basis of birth and social status

69. "Electra complex" is a situation found in
A. Oral Stage B. Anal Stage
C. Phalic Stage D. Latency Stage

70. In Freudian Psychoanalytic Theory, death or aggressive instinct is referred as
A. Triebe B. Libido
C. Thanotos D. None of these

71. The capacity of a person to put oneself in somebody's else situation and understand the feelings and emotions is known as
A. Sympathy B. Empathy
C. Telepathy D. None of these

72. 'Principle of Confidentiality' was given by
A. Perlman B. Hamilton
C. Biestek D. Beker

73. The principle of 'Continuous Individualisation' is related to
A. Social Case Work
B. Social Group Work
C. Community Organisation
D. All the above

74. In social group work the principal instrument of change is
A. Organisation of Programme
B. Leadership Development

C. Guided Group Interactions
D. None of the above

75. What is not a function of a Welfare State ?
A. To meet the needs of the disadvantaged population.
B. To bridge the gap between the poor and the rich.
C. To cater to the materialistic needs of the population.
D. To provide specific services on subsidised basis in the area of health and education.

76. Which is not a developmental characteristic of adulthood?
A. Enuresis.
B. Adjustment to the role of the head of the family.
C. Earning for aging parents.
D. Saving for future.

77. Make correct pairs by matching the code given below :

(a) Early childhood	1. Adjusting to loss of partner
(b) Declining age	2. Walking
(c) Late childhood	3. Competence at work
(d) Adulthood	4. Getting used to living away from parents

Codes :

	(a)	(b)	(c)	(d)
A.	2	1	4	3
B.	3	4	1	2
C.	1	2	3	4
D.	4	3	2	1

78. Arrange the following in correct sequence and select the given answer code :
(i) Diagnostic summary
(ii) Home visit
(iii) Intake interview
(iv) Referral

Codes :
A. (iv), (iii), (ii), (i)
B. (i), (ii), (iii), (iv)
C. (iii), (i), (iv), (ii)
D. (ii), (iv), (i), (iii)

79. Who made the following statement ? "Problems are unmet needs"
A. Felix Biestek
B. G.R. Bannerjee
C. G. Mathew
D. H.H. Perlman

80. Which of the following is not a principle of case work ?
A. Specific objectives
B. Confidentiality
C. Individualization
D. Evaluation

81. Which of the following is not a principle of group work?
A. Recognition of unique differences of each individual.
B. Appropriate modification of group process.
C. Enabling group members to involve themselves in the process of problem solving.
D. Principle of indifferent attitudes towards members.

82. Which one of the following is a reference group ?
A. Occupational group.
B. Group taken to evaluate one's own aspect of life.
C. A relative longer group.
D. A group which allows for social mobility.

83. Which one of the following is not a defense mechanism ?
A. Sublimation
B. Rationalisation
C. Projection
D. Confrontation

84. 360 degree feed-back is associated with
A. Recruitment
B. Selection
C. Performance Appraisal
D. Lay off

85. Medical and public health social workers do not provide

A. psychosocial support to individual and families
B. help to care givers
C. medical aid and diagnostic services
D. support discharged patients in their rehabilitation

86. Shareholders, employees, customers, suppliers, vendors and society constitute
A. Community B. Organisation
C. Stakeholders D. Society

87. Match the items in List-I with List-II :

List-I	List-II
(a) Manic depressive psychoses	(i) Bizarre behaviour
(b) Anorexia Nervosa	(ii) Speech deficit
(c) Schizophrenia	(iii) Bipolar mood disorder
(d) Aphasia	(iv) Fantasy of oral impregnation

Codes :

	(a)	(b)	(c)	(d)
A.	(iv)	(iii)	(i)	(ii)
B.	(ii)	(iv)	(iii)	(i)
C.	(iii)	(iv)	(i)	(ii)
D.	(i)	(ii)	(iii)	(iv)

88. Assertion (A): Clients in metro cities demand problem resolution in a rational and effective manner in limited time.

Reason (R) : Education creates more expectation and counsellors must become sensitive to result-oriented intervention.

Select your answer from the following :
A. Both (A) and (R) are true and (R) is the correct explanation of (A).
B. (A) is correct, but (R) is not the correct explanation of (A).
C. (A) is correct, but (R) is wrong.
D. Both (A) and (R) are wrong.

89. Urban Local bodies need to be strengthened by
A. defining clear functions
B. providing independent financial resources
C. providing autonomy to take decisions
D. All mentioned above

90. Match items given in List-I with those in List-II by selecting the correct code given below :

List-I (Social Reform)	List-II (Social Reformers)
(a) Widow Remarriage	(i) Raja Ram Mohan Roy
(b) Sarvodaya	(ii) K.C. Sen
(c) Abolition of Child Marriage	(iii) Ishwar Chandra Vidya Sagar
(d) Sati	(iv) M.K. Gandhi
	(v) Dayanand Saraswati

Codes :

	(a)	(b)	(c)	(d)
A.	(i)	(ii)	(iii)	(iv)
B.	(v)	(iii)	(ii)	(i)
C.	(v)	(iv)	(iii)	(i)
D.	(iv)	(iii)	(ii)	(i)

91. Match the following :

List-I (Events)	List-II (Date of Observance)
(a) World Day of Water	(i) June 5th
(b) World Earth Day	(ii) July 11th
(c) World Environment Day	(iii) March 22nd
(d) World Population Day	(iv) April 22nd

Codes :

	(a)	(b)	(c)	(d)
A.	(ii)	(iii)	(i)	(iv)
B.	(iii)	(i)	(ii)	(iv)
C.	(iv)	(ii)	(i)	(iii)
D.	(iii)	(iv)	(i)	(ii)

92. Match the following :

List-I (Item)	List-II (Act)
(a) Works Committee	i. Payment of Gratuity Act

(b) Set on and Set off	ii. Industrial Disputes Act
(c) Continuous service	iii. Standing orders
(d) Subsistence allowance	iv. Payment of Bonus Act
	v. Factories Act

Codes :

	(a)	(b)	(c)	(d)
A.	ii	iv	iii	v
B.	ii	iv	i	iii
C.	iii	ii	v	i
D.	v	iii	iv	ii

93. Match the items of List-I with items of List-II :

List-I	List-II
(a) Dissolution of Muslim Marriage Act	i. 1939
(b) Child Marriage Restraint Act	ii. 1955
(c) Dowry Prohibition Act	iii. 1961
(d) Hindu Marriage Act	iv. 1929

Codes :

	(a)	(b)	(c)	(d)
A.	i	iv	iii	ii
B.	i	iii	iv	ii
C.	iii	iv	ii	i
D.	i	ii	iii	iv

94. Assertion (A): Socialization is a life long process.

Reason (R) : Socialization process ends with one's death.

Codes :

A. Both (A) and (R) are true.
B. (A) is true and (R) is not true.
C. (A) is not true and (R) is not the correct explanation of (A).
D. Both (A) and (R) are not true.

95. Assertion (A): Position of labour welfare officer is only ornamental but not practical.

Reason (R) : Right person for right job is a prerequisite.

Codes :

A. (A) is true, but (R) is not true.
B. (A) is not true, but (R) is true.
C. (A) is true, but (R) is not the correct explanation of (A).
D. (A) and (R) are not true.

96. Ethical dilemmas in social work include instances where practitioners face

A. Conflicting duties or obligations
B. Conflicting values
C. Conflicting beliefs
D. Conflicting approaches

97. In which part of the Indian Constitution social policy is outlined?

A. Part I B. Part II
C. Part III D. Part IV

98. Match the following :

List-I (Event)	List-II (Date of observance)
(a) Alzheimer Day	(i) March 16th
(b) World TB Day	(ii) April 7th
(c) World Health Day	(iii) September 21st
(d) National Vaccination Day	(iv) March 24th

Codes :

	(a)	(b)	(c)	(d)
A.	(iv)	(iii)	(ii)	(i)
B.	(iii)	(iv)	(i)	(ii)
C.	(iii)	(iv)	(ii)	(i)
D.	(ii)	(iv)	(i)	(iii)

99. Match items in List-I with List-II and choose the correct code given below :

List-I (Scholar)	List-II (Model)
(a) William Reid	(i) Problem solving model
(b) F. Hollis	(ii) Locality development model
(c) Jack Rothman	(iii) Task centred model
(d) H.H. Perlman	(iv) Psycho-social model

Codes :

	(a)	(b)	(c)	(d)
A.	(ii)	(iv)	(i)	(iii)
B.	(i)	(iii)	(ii)	(iv)
C.	(iii)	(iv)	(ii)	(i)
D.	(iii)	(ii)	(i)	(iv)

100. Match the following persons List-I with the area that they are associated with List-II.

List-I	List-II
(a) Sigmund Freud	(i) Social Case Work
(b) Yogendra Singh	(ii) Environmental movement
(c) G.R. Banerjee	(iii) Psycho analysis
(d) Sunderlal Bahuguna	(iv) Modernistion of Indian tradiation

Codes :

	(a)	(b)	(c)	(d)
A.	(i)	(ii)	(iii)	(iv)
B.	(iii)	(iv)	(ii)	(i)
C.	(iii)	(iv)	(i)	(ii)
D.	(iv)	(ii)	(iii)	(i)

101. Which is the World Consumer Rights Day?
A. March 15 B. October 1
C. September 8 D. June 14

102. Which one of the below is not a Fundamental Right ?
A. Right to self destruction
B. Right to constitutional remedies
C. Right to freedom of religion
D. Right to equality

103. Which of these is not a tool of data collection in Social Work Research?
A. Interview Schedule
B. Interview Guide
C. Case Records
D. Questionnaire

104. Pilot study Refers to a :
A. Preliminary study conducted on a limited scale before the original study.
B. Preliminary testing of the tools used for the Research.
C. Follow up study done within a year after the original study.
D. Macro-level study undertaken to test the hypotheses.

105. 'Operation Flood' is known for :
A. Watershed Management
B. Production of edible oil
C. Production of milk
D. Flood control

106. One of the following is not a technique that come under paraphrase.
A. Restatement
B. Reflection
C. Summary
D. Open ended question

107. The study of the distribution and determinants of health related status or events in specified populations and the application of this study to the control of health problems is called
A. Entomology
B. Biology
C. Epidemiology
D. Geology

108. "Felt difficulty in fulfilling role obligation" is known as
A. Inter role B. Role variation
C. Role strain D. Role ambiguity

109. The model of Social Policy called 'residual welfare' has been advanced by
A. Norman Ginsburg
B. Richard Titmus
C. Lewis
D. David Danison

110. The activity that inter-relates various parts of the welfare agency so that it functions as a whole is
A. planning
B. programming
C. co-ordination
D. policy determination

111. Which of the following statement is correct?
A. Reliability ensures validity.
B. Validity ensures reliability.
C. Reliability does not depend on objectivity.
D. Reliability and validity are independent of each other.

112. Who has divided Family into 'Family of orientation' and 'Family of procreation' ?
A. Murdock B. Kapadia
C. Robertson D. Warner

113. Probation of Offenders Act came into being in the year
A. 1948 B. 1952
C. 1958 D. 1962

114. The strength of association between two variables is called
A. Correlation B. Inference
C. Hypothesis D. None of the above

115. The independent variable is also called
A. Predictor variable
B. Criterion variable
C. Construct
D. None of the above

116. The Research design in which identification of relationship between variables is attempted, is called
A. Experimental design
B. Case Study
C. Descriptive design
D. None of the above

117. What would be mean of 1, 0, 2, 3, 0, 2, 3, 4, 0, 2, and 5.
A. 0 B. 2
C. 4 D. 2.5

118. Institutional Re-distributive model is linked with
A. Totalitarian state
B. Welfare state
C. Capitalist state
D. Communist state

119. The process of generalizing sample results to the population results is called
A. Generalization
B. Normal distribution
C. Level of significance
D. Statistical inference

120. _____ is/are the process of catharsis.
A. Helping to reduce eating
B. Ventilation of feelings
C. Supporting for better sleep
D. All the above

121. The tripartite body which was set in pre-independence period to deal with industrial relations problems in India is
A. Indian Labour Committee
B. Indian Labour Congress
C. Indian Labour Conference
D. Indian Labour Bureau

122. Alcohol is in the category of
A. Stimulants B. Hallucinogens
C. Solvents D. Depressants

123. Which among the following Acts is correctly matched with its year of Enactment ?
A. Juvenile Justice Act-2000
B. National Trust Act-1987
C. Mental Health Act-1997
D. Factories Act-1946

124. Match the List-I with List-II and choose the correct answers from the codes given below:

List-I	List-II
(I) National Environment Policy	(1) 1986
(II) Environment Protection Act	(2) 2005
(III) Sarva Shiksha Abhiyan	(3) 2006
(IV) National Rural Health Mission	(4) 2001

Codes :

	(I)	(II)	(III)	(IV)
A.	(4)	(2)	(1)	(3)
B.	(2)	(3)	(4)	(1)
C.	(3)	(1)	(4)	(2)
D.	(4)	(1)	(3)	(2)

125. Owenite socialist experiment in community organisation believes in :
A. New Direction B. New Philosophy
C. New Culture D. New Harmony

126. Self-culture is also known as :
A. Cultural conflict
B. Cultural crisis
C. Cultural lag
D. Cultural co-existence

127. SOS Means :
A. Save Our Right B. Save Our Soul
C. Save Our Spirit D. Save Our System

128. The Poor Law of 1601 also referred as :
A. 40 Elizabeth B. 41 Elizabeth
C. 42 Elizabeth D. 43 Elizabeth

129. Sturdy Beggars also termed as :
A. Able bodied poor
B. Rural poor
C. Disabled poor
D. Urban poor

130. Community chart refers to :
A. Community resources
B. Community cooperation
C. Community needs
D. Community conflicts

131. Who studied the effectiveness of social casework ?
A. Fisher Joel B. Epstein Irwin
C. Goyder John D. Cohen Jacob

132. Arrange the following in correct sequence:
(i) Specific protection
(ii) Early diagnosis
(iii) Primary prevention
(iv) Prompt and accurate treatment
(v) Rehabilitation
A. (i) (ii) (ii) (iv) (v)
B. (iii) (i) (ii) (iv) (v)
C. (v) (iii) (ii) (i) (iv)
D. (iv) (v) (iii) (ii) (i)

133. What is Anuloma Marriage ?
A. High caste man marrying lower caste woman
B. Higher caste woman marrying lower caste man
C. Lower caste man marrying higher caste woman
D. Lower caste woman marrying higher caste man

134. Euphoria explains :
A. State of Equilibrium
B. State of Jealousy
C. State of Conflict
D. State of well-being

135. Who founded Arya Samaj ?
A. Dayanand Saraswathi
B. Vinoba Bhave
C. Ranade
D. Vivekananda

136. Who coined Sanskritisation ?
A. Radhakamal Mukherjee
B. M.N. Srinivas
C. Yogendra Singh
D. S.C. Dube

137. Widow remarriage was promoted by :
A. Dr. Irawathi Karve
B. Dr. D.K. Karve
C. Mr. B.D. Karve
D. Dr. A.D. Karve

138. Garibi Hatao popularised by :
A. Jawaharlal Nehru
B. Indira Gandhi
C. Rajiv Gandhi
D. Morarji Desai

139. The oldest social security legislation in India is :
A. The Workmen's Compensation Act
B. Provident Fund and Bonus Act
C. Maternity Benefit Act
D. Payment of Gratuity Act

140. Kaka Kalelkar is associated with :
A. Scheduled Caste Commission
B. Scheduled Tribe Commission
C. Backward Classes Commission
D. Women Commission

141. One of the following articles in the Directive Principles of State Policy states that the state shall take steps to organize village panchayats and endow them with such power and authority as may be necessary to enable them to function as units of self governance is :
A. Article 31 B. Article 40
C. Article 39 D. Article 36

142. Which of the following is NOT a part of social case work process ?
A. Content analysis
B. Treatment

C. Assessment
D. Evaluation

143. Which of the following is NOT a primary group ?
A. Gang B. Crowd
C. Family D. Peer group

144. Social control refers to :
A. Constraints on freedom
B. Support to antisocial behaviour
C. Social mechanisms for encouraging conformity and reducing deviance
D. Treatment of deviants

ANSWERS

1	2	3	4	5	6	7	8	9	10
D	B	A	D	C	C	A	C	A	D
11	12	13	14	15	16	17	18	19	20
C	D	C	D	B	A	D	B	B	C
21	22	23	24	25	26	27	28	29	30
B	D	D	A	A	B	C	C	D	B
31	32	33	34	35	36	37	38	39	40
B	C	C	A	B	A	B	D	D	C
41	42	43	44	45	46	47	48	49	50
C	D	D	D	D	A	C	D	A	A
51	52	53	54	55	56	57	58	59	60
B	B	B	A	C	B	C	B	C	B
61	62	63	64	65	66	67	68	69	70
B	C	D	B	A	A	C	D	C	C
71	72	73	74	75	76	77	78	79	80
B	C	B	A	C	A	A	A	D	A
81	82	83	84	85	86	87	88	89	90
D	B	D	C	C	C	C	A	D	C
91	92	93	94	95	96	97	98	99	100
D	B	A	A	B	A	D	C	C	C
101	102	103	104	105	106	107	108	109	110
A	A	B	A	C	C	C	C	B	C
111	112	113	114	115	116	117	118	119	120
D	C	C	A	A	A	B	B	D	B
121	122	123	124	125	126	127	128	129	130
C	D	A	C	D	D	B	D	A	A
131	132	133	134	135	136	137	138	139	140
A	B	A	D	A	B	B	B	A	C
141	142	143	144						
B	A	B	C						

➤➤➤➤➤

CHAPTER

7

Social Research

Social research is a scientific study of analyzing and conceptualizing social life and social relationship. It is a process to investigate facts about social life and of verifying old facts related to society. The social research process includes:-

- Formulation of a problem
- Formulation of hypothesis
- Formulation of research design
- Collection of data
- Analysis and interpretation of data
- Generalization

SOCIAL WORK RESEARCH

Social work research is the application of research method to the production of knowledge that social workers needs to solve problems they confront in the practice of social work. Social work research provides information that can be taken into consideration by social workers prior to making decisions, that affect their clients, programs or agencies such as use of alternative intervention techniques or change or modification of programs and so forth.

Goals of Social Work Research

Social Work is a pragmatic subject. The major objective of social work research is to search for answer regarding the following questions- How to make intervention and treatment effective in social work practice, How to deal with the problems faced by the social work practioners in practicing their profession and how to develop the theory, Knowledge and social work practice.

Social Work Research Process

Social work research begins with identification of problem and setting up of goals, followed by the process of need assessment of the clients problems, the next step is to set up goals to be achieved.

The goals should be specific, precisely defined and measurable. The next step is to have pre-intervention measurement, that is, measurement prior to intervention. It is used as base through which clients' condition has been compared after intervention. Next step is the introduction of intervention. In the last stage, research assesses the effects of intervention by comparing the two measurements that is pre-intervention measurement and post intervention measurement.

Nature of Social Work Research

Social work research primarily deals with problems, faced by professional social workers, social work agencies and community in its concern with social work functions. In other words in social work research the problems to be investigated are always found in the course of doing social work or planning to do it. (Dasgupta, 1968)

Scope of Social Work Research

Social work research is conducted to know the effectiveness of different methods of social work and to search for alternative treatment and intervention. Social work research also organised to identify social work needs and resources, evaluate the programs and services of social work agencies are the areas in which social work research are conducted.

Social work research may be conducted to know the problem faced by social work professionals and the concerned community. Overall, social work research covers entire social work profession concept, theories, methods, program, services and the problems faced by social workers in their practice. As social work is diverse profession, other possible broad research area could be : community health, community mental health, child welfare, women welfare, youth welfare, aged welfare, substance abuse, poverty alleviation, mental retardation, juvenile delinquency crime and correctional administration etc.

RESEARCH DESIGN

The term design means "drawing an outline" or planning or arranging details. It is a process of making decision before the situation arises in which the decision has to be carried out. Research design is planning a strategy of conducting research. It plans as to: what is to be observed, how it is to be observed, how to record observations, how to analyze/interpret the observation and how to generalize. Research design is, thus a detailed plan of how the goals of research will be achieved.

Descriptive Research Design

Descriptive research studies are designed to obtain information concerning the current status of a given phenomenon. Descriptive research is concerning with the existing conditions or relationship, prevailing practices, attitude process and their effects. The aim of descriptive research is to describe "what exists" with respect to variables or conditions in a given situation.

Evaluation Research Design

Evaluation or evaluatory research is basically carried out to know the outcome or effect of a particular efforts, it evaluates the programs and services and determine how effectively they are achieving their goals. Evaluation research often used for testing of cause effect relationship. As such experimental designs are more appropriate for the purpose of evaluation research.

The after – only evaluation design without a control group: In this type of design the measurements are limited in the target group and taken only at the time after completion of the project activities. As no evaluation done before project implemented so it is difficult to assess through this design the degree to which changes occurred.

The After only Evaluation design with a control (comparison) group: In this design a control group or comparison group similar to the experimental group for which project activates have been implemented, is selected and both the groups (experimental, control) are evaluated with respect to dependent variable only after completion of project activities.

The 'Before' – 'After' Evaluation Design without Control Group: This design involves two measurements of the target group, one before the implementation of the project and another after the completion of the project. The difference in target groups' position after the project implementation is measured to know the effect of the program.

The 'Before' 'After' Evaluation design with control group: In this study design one or more control groups similar in characteristics where the program is not being implemented are involved. In this design of study, both the target group and control group are measured at the beginning and also at the end of the project.

Action Research Design

Action research is conducted for problem solving. It is also known as applied research; it is the combination of research and practice. Therefore, while we undertake action research we have to keep in mind the action plan to resolve the problem of study. The involvement of people for whom the action research is conducted is the key to action research, accordingly some authors use to call it 'Participatory action research'. This type of action research always contains the following:-

(1) The investigator

(2) Participation of people who are fundamental to the issue being researched; and

(3) Focus on action to bring social change.

Action research intends to solve problems through research and planned action. In this research, the focus is on solving problems through adoption of alternative practices suggested by research study. Two important objectives of action research are (1) to find out the cause of the problem (2) to suggest action to resolve the problem.

Diagnostic Research Design

The diagnostic research is concerned with finding and analysing the cause of a problem. It examines variables leading to diagnose the cause of the problems. For example: Why girls obtain more marks in higher education than boys? Another example could be study to find out why people from low income group seem to be better adjusted and satisfied to their life than those from higher income group? This means the focus of a diagnostic study is on the nature and causes of problem. The course of action used in diagnostic studies must be cautiously planned since the objective here is to diagnose the problem. The research design for these studies must make a much greater provisions for protection against bias.

Exploratory Research Studies

The purpose of exploratory studies is to formulate a problem for a more precise or specific research or to develop hypothesis. Although, an exploratory study can also be conducted to enhance the familiarity of researcher with the phenomena he wishes to study later some time in a more specific and accurate way. For example If a researcher wanted to study social interaction patterns of HIV infected patients but knew little or nothing about the phenomenon; an exploratory research would be appropriate. A preliminary interview with the relative of HIV infected patients would enable researcher to develop a specific study design. Exploratory studies, thus, help researchers to acquaint themselves with the characteristics of their research problem.

Steps in scientific Research

According to Theodorson and Theodorson (1969) scientific methods involves the following steps: **First** the problem is defined, **second** the problem is stated in terms of particular theoretical framework and related to relevant finding of previous research. **Third,** a hypothesis relating to the problem is developed. **Forth**, the procedure to be used in gathering data is gathered. **Fifth**, the data are analysed to determine if the hypothesis is accepted or rejected. **Finally** the conclusion of the study is related to the original body of theory which is modified in accordance with the new finding. Earl Babbie in the book 'Practice of Social Research' has proposed the following six elements of a research proposal.

- **Problem or objective** *i.e.*, stating what is to be studied, its worth and practical significance and its contribution to the construction of social theories.
- **Literature review**, *i.e.*, what other have said about this topic, what theories have been addressed to it and what are the flaws in the existing research that can be remedied.
- **Subject for study**, *i.e.* from whom is the data to be collected, how to reach persons who are available for study whether selecting sample will be appropriate and if yes, how to select this sample and how to insure that research that is being conducted will not harm the respondents.
- **Measurement,** *i.e.*, determining key variables for the study and how these variables will be defined and measured.
- **Data collection method,** *i.e.*, determining methods to be used for collecting data survey or experiment etc., statistics to be used or not.
- **Analysis,** *i.e.*, spell out the logic of analysis whether variations in some quality are to

be accounted or not and the possible explanatory variable to be analyzed.

Horton and Hunt (1984) have pointed out eight steps in scientific research

- Define the problem which is worth studying through the methods of science.
- Review of literature, so that errors of other scholars may not be repeated.
- Formulation of hypothesis, *i.e.* propositions which can be tested.
- Plan the research design *i.e.* outlining the process as to how, what and where the data is to be collected, processed and analyzed.
- Collection of data, *i.e.* actual collection of facts and information in accordance with research design.
- Analysis of data, *i.e.* classify tabulate and compare the data making whatever tests are necessary to get the results.
- Draw conclusion, *i.e.* whether the original hypothesis is found true or false and is confirmed or rejected or are the results inconclusive? What has the research added to our knowledge and what new question have been posed for further research.
- Replicate the study. Although the above mentioned seven steps complete a single research study but research finding are confirmed by replication.

Formulation of a Research Problem

Formulation of research problem is the real starting point in preparation of research. The researcher must have clearly formulated research questions at the time of taking up the research, otherwise he may have some loosely connected ideas about what should be researched and he might be confused in further course of action.

The research questions have to be related to three aspects: what, why and how? 'what' questions seek description, 'why' questions seek explanations and understanding and 'how' question seek interventions to bring about change.

Zikmund (1988) has said that formulation of the problem of research is to be linked with the following : what is the purpose of the study? How much is already known? Is additional information necessary? What is to be measured, how it is to be measured? Can the required data be collected, *i.e.* whether the respondents give correct information? Is the present time appropriate for undertaking research? Is time/money adequate for the research?

The important points to be borne in mind while selecting a right problem are:

- The problem should focuses on assessing relationship between two or more concepts.
- It should be stated clearly without any confusion.
- General problem should be broken down in to sub concept or several research questions.
- It should be possible to collect the information relating to research problem.
- Research problem should represent moral and ethical position.

OPERATIONALISATION OF VARIABLE

For any inquiry accurate definition of concepts and variables is considered very essential. Operationalization is the process of converting concepts in their empirical measurement or of quantifying variables for the purpose of measuring their frequency. For example regular students of a college may be operationally defined as "students who attended more than 75 percent of the total lectures" or in measuring level of intelligence a persons having a IQ of less than 75 is identified as 'feeble-minded' of 100 as an average person and more than 130 as a genius person.

SAMPLING

A sample as the name suggests is a smaller representation of a larger whole. The investigation of a phenomenon in complete detail would involve such a mass of data that analysis would be slow and tedious. Therefore, spending many hours over the analysis of mass material form one point of view, researcher may use that time to examine

of the research report because any decision takes on the basis of research will be based upon the recommendations, suggestions and conclusions.

Summary: The summary helps to present the research briefly and presents al the information about research in a capsule form.

(C) End matter—Appendices: All technical data such as questionnaire, sample information, mathematical derivation etc. should form a part of the appendix. It should be numbered alphabetically or numerically.

Bibliography and references: The source consulted must be given. Bibliography forms all the relevant subject matter studied by the research for conducting the research while references is specific or particular subject matter or text that not only researcher studied but used for his investigation.

Glossary:This includes a list of special terms used in the research along with their definitions.

Subject Index: Sometimes a subject index given alphabetically works as a guide to the reader for the contents of the report. **Points to remember while writing a research report:**

(1) The report should be lengthy enough to cover all the points but short and crisp enough to hold the interests of the reader.

(2) The report should provide relevant and important information leaving out undesirable, extra information.

(3) Technical terms used in the report should be explained in the glossary.

(4) Charts, graphs, statistical table and figures should be used for readability, interest and quick grasp of the research.

(5) The layout of the report should be as per the format discussed earlier or as per the outline of the institution.

(6) The report should be free of grammatical mistake and should contain sound sentence construction. Use of quotation, footnotes, etc. should be done in the correct manner and context.

(7) The research report should be on original work.

(8) The analysis of data must be done in a logical manner.

(9) Appendices must be numbered and attached if needed.

(10) The index should be clear and the pagation should be done correctly.

(11) A detailed bibliography and references must be given.

(12) The report must be neat and attractive in appearance.

(13) The summary must be given in the end.

(14) The objective of the study, nature and scope of the study must be mentioned in the beginning of the study and the conclusions, suggestions and recommendations must justify it in the end.

ROLES AND RESPONSIBILITIES OF THE RESEARCHER

As someone defined Social Research is as a systematic and original contribution to the knowledge. The researcher has to play many roles. The following might be roles and responsibilities of a researcher.

- He must make original contribution and should avoid manipulation of data.
- He must not have prejudice on the research subject, objectivity should be ensured at every level of research.
- He must follow the scientific approach of investigation and fact finding.
- Researcher must be well acquainted with the subject matter and trained in doing research.
- He must have a quest for new knowledge.
- He must have a neutral attitude towards the subject without any prejudice.

STATISTICS

In our daily language the word 'statistics' is used in two distinct senses: Singular and Plural. In plural sense Prof. Horace Secrist defined statistics as follows "By statistics we mean aggregates of facts affected to a marked extent by multiplicity of causes, numerically expressed, enumerated or estimated according to reasonable standards of accuracy collected in a systematic manner for a predetermined person and place in relation to each other". The above definition covers the following main points about the statistics as numerical presentation of facts (Plural Sense)

Statistics are aggregates of facts

A single observation is not statistics it is a group of observation, e.g., if we stated that income of Mr. X. is Rs. 10,000 per month, this would not constitute statistics although it is a numerical statement of facts. But monthly income of Mr. X, Y and Z are Rs. 10,000, 9,000 and 8,000 respectively are statistics'.

Statistics are affected to a marked extent by multiplicity of causes: Statistics are generally not isolated facts, they are dependent on, or influenced by number of phenomenon for example statistics of production of wheat are affected by the rainfall, quality of soil, seeds, manure and method of cultivation.

Statistics are numerically expressed – Qualitative statements are not statistics unless they are supported by numbers. For example if we say that the student of a class are very good in studies, it is not a statistical statement. But when a statement reads as 40 students got first division, 30 got second division, 20 third divisions and 10 failed out of 100 students. It is a statistical statement expressed numerically.

Statistics are estimated accordingly to reasonable standard of accuracy: We can derive facts and figure about any phenomenon in two ways, viz., by actual counting and measurement or by estimates. Estimates cannot be accurate as actual counts. For example, an estimate that 1 lakh people witnessed a rally held by a political party does not mean exactly 1 lakh; it may be few hundred or thousand more or less. On the other hand, If we count the number of students in a class and say there are 65 students, this figure would be 100 per cent accurate.

Statistics are collected in a systematic manner: Statistics collected without any order and system is unreliable and inaccurate. They must be collected in a systematic manner.

Statistics are collected for a pre determined purpose: Unless statistics are collected for a specific purpose they would be more or less useless. For example, if we want to collect statistics of agriculture production, we must decide before hand the regions, commodities and period for which they are required.

Statistics are placed in relation to each other: Statistics data are often required for comparison. Therefore, they should be comparable period wise, region wise, commodity wise etc.

Statistics defined in Singular Sense: Statistics in its singular sense refer to the methods adopted for scientific empirical studies. According to Croxton and Cowdon, "Statistics may be defined as a science of collection, presentation, analysis and interpretation of numerical data".

The above definition covers the following statistical tools:

Collection of data: This is the first step in a statistical study and is the foundation of statistical analysis. Therefore, the data should be collected by the investigator himself or obtained from reliable published or unpublished sources.

Organization of data: Data that are collected by an investigator need to be organized by editing, coding, classifying and tabulating.

Presentation of data: Data collected and organized are presented in some systematic manner to make statistical analysis easier. The organized data could be presented with the help of table, graphs and diagrams etc.

Analysis of Data: The next stage is the analysis of presented data. There are large numbers of methods used for analysis the data such as averages, dispersion, correlation etc.

Interpretation of Data: Interpretation of data implies the drawing of conclusions on the basic of data analyzed in the earlier stage. On the basis of conclusion certain decisions can be taken.

Functions of Social Statistics

Statistics simplifies complex data: With the help of statistical methods a mass of data ban be presented in such a manner that they become easy to understand.

Statistics Presents the facts in a definite form: The definiteness is achieved by stating conclusions in a numerical or quantitative form.

Statistics provides a technique of comparison: Comparison is an important function of statistics for example comparison of data of different class, categories etc., are helpful for drawing conclusion about social and economic change.

Statistics studies relationship: Correlation analysis is used to discover relationship between different phenomenon's. For example relationship between supply and demand, cost and benefit, illiteracy and unemployment etc.

Statistics helps in formulating policies: Social policies such as health, education, population, rehabilitation policy etc. are formed on the basis of statistically collected data. Some laws such or Malthus theory of population and Engel's law of family expenditure is also based on statistics.

Statistics helps in forecasting: Statistics also helps to predict the further behaviour of phenomenon such as population stabilization of India by 2035 is predicted on the basis of available statistics of past and present.

Statistics helps in testing and formulating theories: When some theory is to be tested, statistical data and techniques are useful. For example, whether cigarette smoking causes cancer, whether demand increase affects the price, can be tested by collecting and composing the relevant data.

Limitations of Statistic

Statistics are widely used in all science and social work profession but it is not without limitations. The following are the limitations of statistics:

It does not study qualitative aspect of a problem: The most important condition of statistical inquiry is that subject of investigation and inquiry should be capable of being quantitatively measured. Qualitative phenomenon cannot be studied in statistics unless these attributes are expressed in terms of numerical.

It does not study individuals: Individual values of observation have no importance in statistics because statistics is the study of mass data and deals with aggregates of facts. For example, the income of a family is say Rs. 10,000 does not convey statistical meaning while the average income of 100 families say Rs. 4,00 is statistical statement.

Statistical laws are true only on an average: Laws of statistics are not universally applicable like the laws of physics and mathematics. They are true on an average because the results are affected by a large number of causes. The ultimate results obtained by statistical analysis are true under certain circumstances only.

Statistics can be misused: Statistics liable to be misused. The result obtained can be manipulated according to ones own criteria and such manipulated results can mislead the community.

Statistics simply is one of the methods of studying a phenomenon: statistical calculations are simple expression which should be supplemented by other methods for a complete comprehension of the results. Thus, statistics is the only means and not the end.

Statistical results lack mathematical accuracy: The results drawn from statistical analysis are normally in approximate. As the statistical analysis is based on observation of mass data, number of inaccuracies may be present and it is difficult to rectify them. Therefore, these results are estimates rather than exact statements. Statistical studies are a failure in the field where one hundred percent accuracy is desired.

MULTIPLE CHOICE QUESTIONS

1. Abortive runaway means :
A. Habituated to runaway
B. Runaway in different short-term intervals
C. Attempt to runaway but does not succeed
D. Runaway in different long-term intervals

2. What is Catharsis ?
A. The reduction of tension by telling one's problems to someone else
B. The reduction of tension by talking, one's problems to every one
C. Not making any attempt to tell problems to any one else
D. The reduction of tension by telling one's problems to professionals only

3. Epistemology stands for :
A. Knowing B. Sharing
C. Listening D. Participating

4. Paradigm stands for :
A. Model B. Role
C. Skill D. Quality

5. Dramatization is the principle of :
A. Social Case Work
B. Social Group Work
C. Community Organization
D. Socialization

6. Chipko Movement is associated with :
A. Save Animals B. Save Trees
C. Save Water D. Save Children

7. Which among the following is not the developmental task during adolescence ?
A. Accepting one's physique and adjusting to body changes
B. Achieving a masculine or feminine social role
C. Achieving emotional independence from parents and adults
D. Adjusting to empty nest syndrome

8. From the options given below, one of the following matches best with Quantitative study in social science research :
A. Historical Reports
B. Statistical Tests
C. Case Study
D. Group Intervention

9. Assertion (A): India's population has crossed the billion mark at the turn of the century
Reason (R) : The available birth control measures have not been accepted by the people.
Code :
A. Both (A) and (R) are true and (R) is the correct reason for (A)
B. (A) and R are true but (R) is not the correct answer for (A)
C. (A) is correct but (R) is false
D. (A) and (R) both are false

10. In which year the Dowry Prohibition Act was passed ?
A. 1960 B. 1971
C. 1961 D. 1984

11. Assertion (A): The worker in a therapeutic setting is a facilitator to small groups.
Reason (R) : The technique of confrontation can be safely used in large groups because the larger the group, the weaker it is.
A. (A) is correct but (R) is not a correct explanation of (A)
B. Both (A) and (R) are wrong
C. (A) is correct but (R) is wrong
D. Both (A) and (R) are correct but (R) is not the correct explanation of (A)

12. Assertion (A): The Social Reform Movements in the nineteenth century made an effort to improve the status of women in society.
Reason (R) : The situation of women in India remained unchanged because their literacy level remained low.
Identify the correct statement from the statements below :
A. Both (A) and (R) are correct and (R) is the correct interpretation of (A)
B. Both (A) and (R) are wrong

C. (A) and (R) are correct but (R) is not the correct explanation of (A)
D. (R) is correct but (A) is wrong

13. Which of the following are not principles of group work ?
(i) Orientation
(ii) Self-actualisation
(iii) Progressive Programme Experiences
(iv) Guided Group Interaction
A. (i), (iv) B. (ii), (iii)
C. (iii), (iv) D. (i), (ii)

14. Identify the correct statements : Field work in social work includes :
(i) Efforts made by the learner to develop practice skills
(ii) Outcome of Learner's efforts and quality of work as well as supervisor's ability to put ideas across
(iii) Learning by doing, evaluative records weekly conferences and trainer's sensitivity to encourage learner motivation.
(iv) Conditioned responses of trainee social worker and supervisor
A. (i), (iv) B. (i), (ii), (iii)
C. (iii), (iv) D. (ii), (iv), (i)

15. Match the following pairs :

List-I	List-II
(a) The Social Division of Labour	(i) E. Durkheim
(b) Social Process	(ii) C.H. Cooley
(c) Social Change	(iii) T.H. Marshall
(d) Social Class	(iv) W.F. Ogburn

Codes :

	(a)	(b)	(c)	(d)
A.	(i)	(ii)	(iii)	(iv)
B.	(i)	(ii)	(iv)	(iii)
C.	(iii)	(ii)	(iv)	(i)
D.	(iv)	(i)	(iii)	(ii)

16. Match the items in List-I with List-II and choose the correct code given below:

List-I (Stages)	List-II (Tasks)
(a) Oral stage	(i) Trust v/s Mistrust
(b) Anal stage	(ii) Industry v/s Inferiority
(c) Genital stage	(iii) Autonomy v/s Shame & doubt
(d) Latency	(iv) Initiative v/s Guilt

Codes :

	(a)	(b)	(c)	(d)
A.	(ii)	(iv)	(i)	(iii)
B.	(iii)	(ii)	(iv)	(i)
C.	(i)	(iv)	(ii)	(iii)
D.	(i)	(iii)	(iv)	(ii)

17. Match items in List-I with List-II and choose the correct code given below :

List-I	List-II
(a) Transference	(i) Law
(b) Parole	(ii) Sociology
(c) Cultural lag	(iii) Psychiatry
(d) Decree	(iv) Criminology

Codes :

	(a)	(b)	(c)	(d)
A.	(iii)	(i)	(iv)	(ii)
B.	(ii)	(iii)	(i)	(iv)
C.	(iii)	(iv)	(ii)	(i)
D.	(i)	(ii)	(iii)	(iv)

18. Match the List-I with List-II :

List-I	List-II
(I) Psycho-Social Model	1. Edwin J. Thomas
(II) Functional Model	2. Virginia Robinson
(III) Behaviour modification Model	3. Gordon Hamilton
(IV) Task-centred Model	4. Willium Read

Codes :

	(I)	(II)	(III)	(IV)
A.	2	3	1	4
B.	3	2	1	4
C.	1	2	3	4
D.	4	1	3	2

19. Match the List-I with List-II :

List-I	List-II
(I) Measures of Central Tendency	1. Quartile

(II) Measures of Dispersion 2. Range
(III) Measures of Skewness and Kurtosis 3. Median
(IV) Measures of Relationship 4. Regression

Codes :

	(I)	(II)	(III)	(IV)
A.	2	3	4	1
B.	1	2	3	4
C.	3	2	1	4
D.	4	3	2	1

20. The specific characteristic of a subject that assumes one or more different values is called as

A. Data B. Variable
C. Hypothesis D. Scale

21. International Women's Year was

A. 1979 B. 1978
C. 1975 D. 1976

22. The chronic condition present from birth with impaired adaptation towards daily demands is

A. Mental illness
B. Mental retardation
C. Both of the above
D. None of the above

23. Repression is also known as

A. Roaming in the past
B. Isolation
C. Rationalization
D. Inhibition of threatening impulse

24. The base of age pyramid in India is broad due to

A. High death rate
B. High morbidity
C. High birth rate
D. High maternal mortality

25. Difficulty in falling asleep is called

A. Hyposomnia B. Anorexia nervosa
C. Insomnia D. Bulimia nervosa

26. Public Interest Litigation as a concept originated in ________

A. USA B. UK
C. Australia D. India

27. The book 'Social Work Philosophy' is written by

A. Herbert Bisno B. Lindomen
C. Thorndike D. Trecker

28. Who amongst the following is a leading contributor to our understanding of groups as a system ?

A. Bogardus B. Davis
C. Talcott Parsons D. Garvin

29. Which one of the following is not a correctional programme/service ?

A. Anti-beggary programme
B. Prison welfare services
C. Community based youth club
D. Special school for juvenile offenders

30. Psycho social theory was propagated by

A. Sigmund Freud B. Skinner
C. Hamilton D. Erick Erikson

31. 'Apartheid' refers to

A. Social discrimination
B. Political discrimination
C. Racial discrimination
D. Spatial discrimination

32. Match the following :

(a) Papers in Social Work (i) Murli Desai
(b) Some aspects of Social Development (ii) G. R. Banerjee
(c) Towards a Philosophy of Social Work in India (iii) M.S. Gore
(d) Ideologies in Social Work (iv) Sujata Dasgupta

Codes :

	(a)	(b)	(c)	(d)
A.	(i)	(ii)	(iii)	(iv)
B.	(iv)	(iii)	(ii)	(i)
C.	(ii)	(iii)	(iv)	(i)
D.	(iii)	(iv)	(i)	(ii)

33. The failure to recognize that the concept is not the phenomenon itself is called

A. Ecological Fallacy
B. Delimitation
C. Fallacy of reification
D. Induction

34. Assertion (A): Civil Society Organizations contribute towards participative democracy.
Reason (R) : Rich associational network is one of the characteristics of participative democracy.

Identify the correct statement from below :
A. Both (A) and (R) are correct.
B. (A) is correct, but (R) is wrong.
C. Both (A) and (R) are correct and (R) is the adequate explanation of (A).
D. Both (A) and (R) are correct, but (R) is not an adequate explanation of (A).

35. Match the pairs :

(a) States' re-organization	(i) Morarji Desai
(b) States' Merger	(ii) Roman Empire
(c) Bilingual State	(iii) K.M. Panikkar
(d) City States	(iv) Vallabh Bhai Patel

Codes :

	(a)	(b)	(c)	(d)
A.	(iv)	(iii)	(ii)	(i)
B.	(iii)	(iv)	(i)	(ii)
C.	(i)	(ii)	(iii)	(iv)
D.	(ii)	(i)	(iv)	(iii)

36. The process of translating social policy into social service is
A. Social Welfare
B. Social Action
C. Social Service Administration
D. Public Administration

37. Marital Status is
A. Internal variable
B. Nominal variable
C. Ordinal variable
D. Ratio variable

38. Assertion (A): The emphasis on 'person-in-situation' is to understand and help the individual Client better.

Reason (R): The person-in-situation configuration is subjective.
A. Both (A) and (R) are wrong.
B. Both (A) and (R) are correct, but (R) is not correct explanation of (A).
C. Both (A) and (R) are correct, but (R) is the correct explanation of (A).
D. (A) is correct, but (R) is wrong.

39. Identify the correct chronological sequence.
A. Nagappa Neighbourhood House, Nilokheri Project, Etawa Pilot Project, Delhi Pilot Project.
B. Nagappa Neighbourhood House, Etawa Pilot Project, Nilokheri Project, Delhi Pilot Project.
C. Nilokheri Project, Nagappa Neighbourhood House, Delhi Pilot Project, Etawa Pilot Project.
D. Etawa Pilot Project, Nilokheri Project, Nagappa Neighbourhood House, Delhi Pilot Project.

40. The Employees State Insurance Act was passed in the year :
A. 1978 B. 1928
C. 1860 D. 1948

41. Which one is a feature of community chest?
A. To develop leadership in the community
B. To distribute funds to various agencies
C. Abolish discrimination between different castes
D. To develop religious harmony in the community

42. National Human Rights Commission was created in the year :
A. 1963 B. 1973
C. 1983 D. 1993

43. According to Erik Erikson's theory of personality the crisis during the period of young adulthood is :
A. Generativity versus stagnation
B. Identity versus role confusion
C. Industry versus inferiority
D. Intimacy versus isolation

44. Octavia Hill and Samuel Barnett are connected with which of the following ?
A. Charity Organisation
B. Beveridge Report
C. Children's Aid Society
D. Poor Law Report

45. Assertion (A): The practice of social group work is important for social action.

Reason (R) : Social action is essentially a group activity.

Codes :

A. Both (A) and (R) are true and (R) is correct explanation of (A).

B. Both (A) and (R) are true and (R) is not the complete explanation of (A).

C. (R) is true and (A) is not true.

D. (A) is true, but (R) is not true.

46. Programme planning in group work practice includes

A. Group members participates

B. Group members interests

C. The programme content

D. All the above

47. The model of community organization propounded by Rothman is

A. Locality Development

B. Social Development

C. Sustainable Development

D. Community Development

48. Bottom-up concept related to

A. Mega planning B. Macro planning

C. Meso planning D. Micro planning

49. Venn diagram is one of the commonly used method in

A. Institutional appraisal

B. Governmental appraisal

C. Non-Governmental appraisal

D. Participatory Rural appraisal

50. Assertion (A): The efforts of initiating community chests at the level of local communities are quite few in India at present.

Reason (R) : Had there been better efforts at the level of community to pool together the social resources, the community life in India would have been much better.

Codes :

A. (A) is true and (R) is not true.

B. (A) is not true and (R) is true.

C. Both (A) and (R) are true.

D. Both (A) and (R) are not true.

51. Match the following international initiatives with the origin of their nationality.

International Initiative	National Origin
(a) DFID	1. USA
(b) USAID	2. Canada
(c) CIDA	3. UK
(d) DANIDA	4. Denmark

Codes :

	(a)	(b)	(c)	(d)
A.	3	1	2	4
B.	3	1	4	2
C.	4	1	2	3
D.	4	1	3	2

52. The research design that explains the relationship between variables is

A. Experimental Design

B. Caste Study Design

C. Descriptive Design

D. None of the above

53. Semi-inter quartile range is also known as

A. Range B. Mean

C. Mode D. Quartile Deviation

54. 'Home visiting' can most appropriately be called :

A. Tool B. Skill

C. Method D. None of these

55. Which among the following is not an approach to prevent burnout?

A. Relaxation Techniques

B. Positive Thinking

C. Exercise

D. Ethnocentricism

56. Acceptance is a principle of social work which implies :

A. Accepting client in his/her appearance

B. Extending warm welcome to the client

C. Accepting the client as she/he is

D. Accepting the client's version as it is

57. Which organization among the following publishes the records of Accidental Death and Suicides in India?

A. National Crime Records Bureau

B. National Commission for Women

C. Ministry of Social Justice and Empowerment

D. Census of India

58. Handicapism refers to :

A. Prejudice and discrimination directed against disabled person

B. Favoured attitude towards disabled persons

C. Social movement for handicap welfare

D. None of the above

59. Consider the following statements and select your answer according to the codes below :

Assertion (A): Gender Aware social work means provision of services with sensitivity to the impact of gender.

Reason (R) : Gender is a social construct which places men and women in different position in terms of power, privileges and resources.

A. Both (A) and (R) are true and (R) is the correct explanation of (A)

B. Both (A) and (R) are not true

C. (A) is true but (R) is false

D. (A) is not true but (R) is true

60. The technique of Dream Analysis is associated with :

A. Sigmund Freud B. Eric Berne

C. Pavlov D. William Glasser

61. Which country among the following has not ratified the 'Convention on Elimination of All Forms of Discrimination Against Women' (CEDAW) :

A. Germany B. India

C. United States D. Pakistan

62. Match the items in List-I with items in List-II :

List-I	List-II
(a) Sampling	(i) Wealth matrix
(b) Experimental Research Design	(ii) Logical Frame-work Analysis
(c) Participatory Research	(iii) Control variable
(d) SPSS	(iv) Confidence interval
	(v) Variable view

Codes :

	(a)	(b)	(c)	(d)
A.	(iv)	(v)	(ii)	(i)
B.	(ii)	(v)	(iii)	(i)
C.	(iii)	(ii)	(i)	(iv)
D.	(iv)	(iii)	(i)	(v)

63. Match the following pairs :

(a) Rembrandt	(i) Extremist
(b) Tagore	(ii) Moderate
(c) B.G. Tilak	(iii) Art
(d) G.K. Gokhale	(iv) Poetry

Codes :

	(a)	(b)	(c)	(d)
A.	(ii)	(iii)	(i)	(iv)
B.	(iv)	(i)	(ii)	(iii)
C.	(iii)	(i)	(iv)	(ii)
D.	(i)	(iv)	(iii)	(ii)

64. The Universal Immunization programme was started in India in the year :

A. 1975 B. 1995

C. 1955 D. 1985

65. The test for identifying HIV antibodies is :

A. CDM COUNT B. ELISA

C. CULTURE Test D. HDL Test

66. Arrange steps in order in testing hypothesis.

A. Research Hypothesis, Null Hypothesis, Statistical Test, Significance Level

B. Null Hypothesis, Research Hypothesis, Statistical Test, Significance Level

C. Statistical Test, Research Hypothesis, Null Hypothesis, Significance Level

D. Null Hypothesis, Research Hypothesis, Significance level, Statistical Test

67. Match the following :

List-I	List-II
(I) The Employment Exchange Act	(1) 1986
(II) The Payment of Bonus Act	(2) 1961
(III) Juvenile Justice Act	(3) 1959
(IV) The Maternity Benefit Act	(4) 1965

Codes :

	(I)	(II)	(III)	(IV)
A.	(4)	(1)	(2)	(3)
B.	(3)	(4)	(1)	(2)
C.	(2)	(4)	(1)	(3)
D.	(1)	(2)	(3)	(4)

68. Select the correctly arranged case work components in order.
A. Problem, Person, Place, Process
B. Process, Person, Problem, Place
C. Place, Person, Problem, Process
D. Person, Problem, Place, Process

69. **Assertion (A):** The person educated through foreign language is unpatriotic.
Reason (R) : Foreign language breeds unpatriotism.

Codes :
A. Both (A) and (R) are correct.
B. (A) is correct and (R) is wrong.
C. (A) is wrong and (R) is correct.
D. Both (A) and (R) are wrong.

70. The National Rural Employment Guarantee Act was passed in the year
A. 2005 B. 2003
C. 2004 D. 2000

71. Gender-related Development Index is used in
A. World Development Report
B. Human Development Index
C. UNDP Report
D. UN Report

72. Social legislation attempts to
A. provide justice as well as security
B. anticipates social needs
C. provide for change in the social order
D. All the above

73. Which Article of Indian Constitution declares untouchability as an offence ?
A. Article 26 B. Article 23
C. Article 25 D. Article 17

74. According to Maslow, which one of the following is not the need in his hierarchy model?
A. Physiological needs
B. Safety needs
C. Esteem needs
D. Hygiene needs

75. **Assertion (A):** Due to the strong family ties women in India are sacrificing for their family.
Reason (R) : Because it is a product of social conditioning.

Choose your answer from the following :
A. Both (A) and (R) are true and (R) is correct explanation of (A).
B. Both (A) and (R) are true, but (R) is not the correct explanation of (A).
C. (A) is true, but (R) is false.
D. (R) is true, but (A) is false.

76. **Assertion (A):** Socialization is a significant process of human groups.
Reason (R) : Long period of dependency allows children to learn things they need to know.

Choose your answer from the following :
A. Both (A) and (R) are true and (R) is the correct explanation of (A).
B. Both (A) and (R) are true, but (R) is not the correct explanation of (A).
C. (A) is true, but (R) is false.
D. Both (A) and (R) are false.

77. **Assertion (A):** Relationship is the basis of all help in social case work.
Reason (R) : Personal relations can help in solving all the problems.
Choose your answer from the following :
A. Both (A) and (R) are true and (R) is the correct explanation of (A).
B. Both (A) and (R) are true, but (R) is not the correct explanation of (A).
C. (A) is true, but (R) is false.
D. Both (A) and (R) are false.

78. **Assertion (A):** The basic theme of self-help, group is 'you are not alone'.
Reason (R) : Being member of selfhelp group Rekha, a widow is alone.

Choose your answer from the following :
A. Both (A) and (R) are wrong.
B. (A) is wrong but (R) is correct.

C. (A) is correct, but (R) is wrong.
D. Both (A) and (R) are correct.

79. Assertion (A): Panchayat Raj Institutions have been in existence for a long time, however, these institutions have not been able to acquire the status and dignity of viable and responsive people's bodies.

Reason (R) : Due to absence of inadequate devolution of powers and lack of financial resources.

Choose your answer from the following :
A. Both (A) and (R) are true and (R) is the correct explanation of (A).
B. Both (A) and (R) are true and (R) is not the correct explanation of (A).
C. (A) is true, but (R) is false.
D. (A) is false, but (R) is true.

80. Assertion (A): Quantitative research approach involves generation of data in quantitative form which can be subjected to rigorous quantitative analysis in formal and rigid passion.

Reason (R) : Because it deals with subjective assessment of attitudes, opinions and behaviour.

Choose your answer from the following :
A. Both (A) and (R) are true and (R) is the correct explanation of (A).
B. Both (A) and (R) are true and (R) is not the correct explanation of (A).
C. (A) is true, but (R) is false.
D. (A) is false, but (R) is true.

81. The degree to which an instrument really measures what it intends to measure is called?
A. Construct B. Reliability
C. Validity D. All the above

82. The sequential steps in research process are
A. selection of topic, review of literature, collection of data, analysis, report writing and interpretation.
B. selection of topic, review of literature, collection of data, analysis, interpretation and report writing.
C. selection of topic, collection of data, review of literature, analysis, interpretation and report writing.
D. selection of topic, collection of data, review of literature, analysis, report writing and interpretation.

83. Assertion (A): To improve the visibility of professional social work, much of its research should be action oriented.

Reason (R) : Lack of action research is not the only reason for limited visibility to professional social work.

Choose your answer from the following :

Codes :
A. (A) is true, but (R) is false.
B. (A) is false, but (R) is true.
C. Both (A) and (R) are true and (R) is the correct explanation of (A).
D. Both (A) and (R) are true and (R) is not the correct explanation of (A).

84. Match List-I with List-II.

List-I	**List-II**
(a) Chipko Movement	1. Medha Patkar
(b) Narmada Bachao Andolan	2. Sundarlal Bahuguna
(c) Lokpal Andolan	3. Madhav Gadgil
(d) Western Ghat Bachao	4. Anna Hazare

Codes :

	(a)	(b)	(c)	(d)
A.	1	2	3	4
B.	2	1	4	3
C.	4	3	1	2
D.	2	3	4	1

85. Arrange the various stages of Program Management in logical sequence :
(i) Monitoring and Evaluation
(ii) Project Formulation
(iii) Identification of Felt Needs
(iv) Recording

Codes :
A. (i), (ii), (iv), (iii)
B. (iii), (ii), (i), (iv)
C. (ii), (i), (iii), (iv)
D. (iv), (ii), (iii), (i)

86. Who from the following is not Social Activist?

A. Arundhati Roy
B. Medha Patkar
C. Dr. P.D. Kulkarni
D. Anna Hazare

87. Welfare programmes based on Social Policy in India are not provided in one of the sectors mentioned below :

A. Health B. Education
C. Employment D. Entertainment

88. Match the following :

List-I	List-II
(a) Enuresis	(i) Low achievements
(b) School drop out	(ii) Threatening reality
(c) Aversion to food	(iii) Poor mother-child relationship
(d) Day dreaming	(iv) Insecurity

Codes :

	(a)	(b)	(c)	(d)
A.	(iii)	(ii)	(iv)	(i)
B.	(iv)	(i)	(iii)	(ii)
C.	(ii)	(iii)	(i)	(iv)
D.	(i)	(iv)	(ii)	(iii)

89. Match the following :

List-I	List-II
(a) Home visit	(i) Tool of learning and teaching
(b) Face sheet	(ii) Evaluation
(c) Process Record	(iii) Holistic assessment
(d) Evaluative summary	(iv) Intake

Codes :

	(a)	(b)	(c)	(d)
A.	(iv)	(iii)	(ii)	(i)
B.	(i)	(ii)	(iii)	(iv)
C.	(ii)	(i)	(iv)	(iii)
D.	(iii)	(iv)	(i)	(ii)

90. Match the following :

List-I	List-II
(a) Parole	(i) Dependence on court
(b) Ticketless travel	(ii) Rehabilitation
(c) Securing bail	(iii) Attending a family function
(d) Vocational training	(iv) Petty offence
	(v) Institutional services

Codes :

	(a)	(b)	(c)	(d)
A.	(iii)	(iv)	(i)	(ii)
B.	(i)	(ii)	(v)	(iv)
C.	(iv)	(iii)	(ii)	(v)
D.	(v)	(i)	(iii)	(i)

91. What is the name of the market driven device under the UNFC that allows developing countries to get funds/incentives from the developed countries to adopt better technologies that reduce greenhouse gas emissions?

A. Carbon Footprint
B. Carbon Credit Rating
C. Clean Development Mechanism
D. Emission Reduction Norms

92. Mental health team approach is essential for effective therapeutic process in

A. Day-boarding schools
B. Maternity nursing homes
C. Child guidance centres
D. Recreational youth club

93. Assertion (A): Social action is a systematic and conscious effort to influence the basic social conditions for social progress.

Reason (R) : It involves improving social legislative and social policies.

Codes :

A. Both (A) and (R) are true.
B. (A) is true and (R) is the correct explanation of (A).
C. (A) is not true and (R) is true.
D. (A) is true and (R) is not the correct explanation of (R).

94. Assertion (A): Psychologists generally agree that Intelligence Quotient (I.Q.) gets affected by environment.

Reason (R) : Intelligence Quotient (I.Q.) is a biological trait and it cannot be changed.

Codes :
A. Both (A) and (R) are true.
B. Both (A) and (R) are not true.
C. (A) is true and (R) is not true.
D. (A) is true and (R) is the correct explanation of (A).

95. Assertion (A): Jan Shikshan Sansthan provides vocational training courses to the marginalized.
Reason (R) : Vocational training empowers the beneficiaries who become entrepreneurs.

Codes :
A. Both (A) and (R) are not true.
B. Both (A) and (R) are true and (R) is the correct explanation of (A).
C. (A) is true and (R) is not the correct explanation of (A).
D. (A) is not true and (R) is true.

96. Assertion (A): Crime rate in India is increasing day-by-day.
Reason (R) : Crime rate is increasing because people lack skills and use illegitimate means to achieve their goals.

Codes :
A. Both (A) and (R) are true.
B. (A) is not true and (R) is the explanation of (A).
C. Both (A) and (R) are not true.
D. (A) is true and (R) is not the correct explanation of (A).

97. Assertion (A): For effective management of a children's residential home, the staff should be affectionate and friendly.
Reason (R) : Regular funding is essential to proper functioning of a residential home for children.

Codes :
A. Both (A) and (R) are true.
B. (A) is true and (R) is not true.
C. Both (A) and (R) are not true.
D. (A) is true and (R) is the correct explanation of (A).

98. Arrange the following Acts in order in which they were enacted. And select the correct answer using the codes given below :
i. Payment of Wages Act
ii. Payment of Gratuity Act
iii. Minimum Wages Act
iv. Payment of Bonus Act

Codes :

	(a)	(b)	(c)	(d)
A.	iii	i	iv	ii
B.	i	iv	ii	iii
C.	ii	iv	iii	i
D.	i	iii	iv	ii

99. Assertion (A): Code of ethics is a pre-requisite for a professional social worker.
Reason (R): Social work values and principles are important for the practice of Social work.

Codes :
A. (A) is not true, but (R) is a correct explanation of (A).
B. (A) is true, but (R) is not the correct explanation of (A).
C. Both (A) and (R) are not true.
D. (A) is true and (R) is the true explanation of (A).

100. Assertion (A): Developmental programs meant for tribals have not produced desired results.
Reason (R): Lack of political will and administrative commitment are held as the major reason for tardy progress of tribes in India.

Codes :
A. Both (A) and (R) are true.
B. Both (A) and (R) are not true.
C. (A) is true, but (R) is not true.
D. (A) is not true, but (R) is true.

101. Assertion (A): Criminals are not born but made.
Reason (R): Social environment play a dominant role in committing crime.

Codes :
A. (A) is correct, but (R) is wrong.

B. (A) is wrong, but (R) is correct.
C. (A) is correct, but (R) is not the correct explanation of (A).
D. (A) is correct and (R) is the correct explanation of (A).

102. Assertion (A): Social legislations are effective means of ushering social change in given society.

Reason (R) : When social legislations are with limitations and loop holes, they fail in bringing the expected social change in given society.

Codes :

A. Both (A) and (R) are not true.
B. (A) is true, but (R) is not true.
C. (A) is not true, but (R) is true.
D. Both (A) and (R) are true.

103. Identify the First step of social research from the following steps:

A. Data collection
B. Hypothesis
C. Problem formulation
D. Objectives

104. Arrange the following Acts in order in which they were enacted. Use the codes given below:

(i) The Factories Act
(ii) Shops and Establishment Act
(iii) The Indian Mines Act
(iv) The plantation Labour Act

Codes :

A. (i), (iv), (iii), (ii)
B. (iv), (i), (ii), (iii)
C. (iii), (ii), (iv), (i)
D. (ii), (iii), (i), (iv)

105. Social advocacy is **not** :

A. Lobbying with the government
B. Mobilizing grass root organisations
C. Working with media
D. Organising Welfare Programs

106. The Mental Health Act was enacted in the year :

A. 1985 B. 1987
C. 1989 D. 1990

107. The Equal Remuneration Act, 1976 provides for :

A. Equal pay for equal work of similar nature.
B. Equal pay for equal work irrespective of nature of work.
C. Equal pay for equal work in selected categories of work.
D. Equal pay for equal work in organised sector only.

108. Following are the steps of social research. Arrange the steps to prepare a plan of research study.

(a) Data collection
(b) Hypothesis
(c) Problem formulation
(d) Objectives
(e) Processing and analysis of data
(f) Report writing

A.	(a)	(c)	(b)	(d)	(e)	(f)
B.	(b)	(c)	(a)	(d)	(e)	(f)
C.	(d)	(c)	(b)	(a)	(e)	(f)
D.	(c)	(d)	(b)	(a)	(e)	(f)

109. Match the items in List-I with List-II.

List-I	List-II
(a) Reproductive Child Health	(i) Police Research
(b) The National Rural Employment Guarantee Act	(ii) Trauma
(c) Post Traumatic Stress Disorder	(iii) Mother and Child
(d) Bureau of Police Research and Development	(iv) Employment at village level

Codes :

	(a)	(b)	(c)	(d)
A.	(ii)	(i)	(iii)	(iv)
B.	(iii)	(iv)	(ii)	(i)
C.	(iv)	(iii)	(ii)	(i)
D.	(i)	(ii)	(iii)	(iv)

110. Arrange the following Acts in order in which they were enacted. Use the codes given below:

(i) The Industrial Employment (Standing orders) Act.
(ii) The Indian Trade Unions Act.
(iii) The Industrial Disputes Act.
(iv) The Employment Exchange (Compulsory Notification) Act.

Codes :
A. (ii), (i), (iii), (iv)
B. (iii), (iv), (i), (ii)
C. (i), (ii), (iv), (iii)
D. (iv), (iii), (ii), (i)

111. Put the following steps in the process of Participating Rural Appraisal in a sequence.
I. Use of tools
II. Report generation
III. Rapport building
IV. Initial contact
V. Sharing the learnings
VI. Participating Action Planning

Codes :
A. IV, III, I, II, V, VI
B. IV, II, III, I, V, VI
C. II, IV, III, I, V, VI
D. IV, I, III, II, V, VI

112. Arrange the following Acts in order in which they were enacted. Use the codes given below:
(i) Child Marriage Restraint Act.
(ii) Medical Termination of Pregnancy Act
(iii) Hindu Marriage Act
(iv) Dowry Prohibition Act

Codes :
A. (ii), (i), (iii), (iv)
B. (i), (iii), (iv), (ii)
C. (iii), (ii), (i), (iv)
D. (iv), (iii), (ii), (i)

113. Assertion (A): Prison is a correctional institution that aims at reforming the criminals.
Reason (R) : Prison segregates the criminals to protect the society.

Codes :
A. Both (A) & (R) are correct.
B. Both (A) & (R) are not correct.
C. (A) is correct and (R) is not correct.
D. Both (A) & (R) are correct, but (R) is not correct explanation of (A).

114. Match the items of List-I with those of List-II.

List-I (Event)	List-II (Year)
(a) International Youth Year	(i) 2005
(b) International Micro credit Year	(ii) 1950
(c) Mental Health Act	(iii) 1947
(d) Establishment of Planning Commission	(iv) 1987
	(v) 1985

Codes :

	(a)	(b)	(c)	(d)
A.	(i)	(ii)	(iv)	(iii)
B.	(v)	(i)	(iv)	(ii)
C.	(iii)	(i)	(ii)	(v)
D.	(v)	(i)	(iii)	(iv)

115. Assertion (A): All the problems in case work practice are not treated alike.
Reason (R) : The impact of a problem is same for all individuals.

Codes :
A. Both (A) and (R) are correct.
B. Both (A) and (R) are not correct.
C. (A) is correct and (R) is the correct explanation of (A).
D. (A) is correct and (R) is not the correct explanation of (A).

116. Find the chronological sequence of the Enactment of the following Acts :
1. Trade Unions Act
2. Payment of Wages Act
3. Factories Act
4. Employees Provident Fund Act

Codes :

A.	1	2	3	4
B.	1	3	2	4
C.	2	3	1	4
D.	2	4	3	1

117. Which among the following is in correct sequence ?

A. Study, intake, treatment, diagnosis, termination, follow up

B. Intake, study, diagnosis, treatment, termination, follow up

C. Diagnosis, intake, treatment, study, termination, follow up

D. Treatment, intake, diagnosis, study, termination, follow up

118. Arrange the following Non-Govt. Experiments in order in which they appeared. Use the code given below :

(i) Firka
(ii) Marthandam
(iii) Sevagram
(iv) Gurgaon

Codes :

A.	(i)	(iv)	(ii)	(iii)
B.	(iv)	(ii)	(iii)	(i)
C.	(ii)	(iv)	(iii)	(i)
D.	(iii)	(iv)	(i)	(ii)

119. Capacity and equity enhances :

A. Women Empowerment

B. Community Empowerment

C. Disabled Empowerment

D. Children Empowerment

120. Social action method was recognized by :

A. Hamilton

B. Richmond

C. Firk

D. Friedlander

121. Who coined Elitist Social Action and Popular Social Action?

A. Augustus B. Britto

C. Campbell D. Dunham

122. **Assertion (A):** Ogburn's theory of culture lag appears even more relevant in the context of Social development.

Reason (R) : The conflict theory of social change remains stable at any time in society.

A. Both (A) and (R) are correct but (R) is not the correct explanation of (A)

B. (A) is correct but (R) is wrong

C. (R) is correct but (A) is wrong

D. Both (A) and (R) are correct

123. **Assertion (A):** Leadership is classified as autocratic, democratic and charismatic.

Reason (R) : Autocratic leadership is effective in weak groups, while charismatic leadership is effective among the masses.

A. (A) is correct but (R) is wrong

B. Both (A) and (R) are correct and (R) is the correct explanation of (A)

C. Both (A) and (R) are wrong

D. Both (A) and (R) are correct but (R) is not an explanation of (A)

ANSWERS

1	2	3	4	5	6	7	8	9	10
C	A	A	A	C	B	A	B	A	C
11	**12**	**13**	**14**	**15**	**16**	**17**	**18**	**19**	**20**
A	A	D	B	B	D	C	B	C	B
21	**22**	**23**	**24**	**25**	**26**	**27**	**28**	**29**	**30**
C	B	D	C	A	A	A	C	C	C
31	**32**	**33**	**34**	**35**	**36**	**37**	**38**	**39**	**40**
C	C	C	C	A	C	B	C	A	D
41	**42**	**43**	**44**	**45**	**46**	**47**	**48**	**49**	**50**
B	D	B	A	A	D	A	D	D	C

51	52	53	54	55	56	57	58	59	60
A	A	D	A	D	C	A	A	A	A
61	**62**	**63**	**64**	**65**	**66**	**67**	**68**	**69**	**70**
C	D	D	D	B	D	B	D	D	A
71	**72**	**73**	**74**	**75**	**76**	**77**	**78**	**79**	**80**
C	D	D	D	A	B	B	C	A	A
81	**82**	**83**	**84**	**85**	**86**	**87**	**88**	**89**	**90**
C	B	C	B	B	C	D	B	D	A
91	**92**	**93**	**94**	**95**	**96**	**97**	**98**	**99**	**100**
C	C	B	C	C	A	A	D	D	A
101	**102**	**103**	**104**	**105**	**106**	**107**	**108**	**109**	**110**
D	D	D	A	D	B	A	D	B	A
111	**112**	**113**	**114**	**115**	**116**	**117**	**118**	**119**	**120**
A	B	D	B	B	A	B	B	A	B
121	**122**	**123**							
B	A	A							

➤➤➤➤➤

CHAPTER

8

Social Policy

MEANING OF SOCIAL POLICY

According to concise oxford dictionary policy is a settled course of action adopted and followed by a Government. The term 'policy' is sometimes also used as a paraphrase of the concept of strategy as adopted from the defense science. There is a specific goal to be achieved or reached and the strategist is expected to assess the resources at he has command.

According to professor Titmus, "Social policy represents a summation of facts of Government deliberately designed to improve the welfare of the people".

According to Kulkarni, "Social policy is the strategy of action indicating the means and methods to be followed in successive phases to achieve the declared objectives."

Marshall states that "The term social policy refers to the policy of Government with regards to action having a direct impact on the welfare of the citizen by providing them with services of income."

From the above definitions Social policies could be understood as principles or course of action designed to influence:

- The overall quality of life of the society;
- the circumstances of living of individual and groups in the society; and
- The nature of intra-societal relationships among individuals, groups, and society as a whole.

Characteristics of Social Policy

- Social policy refers to the general guidelines or principles which give direction to a particular course of action by the Government or by the organization.
- The main trait of social policy is its distributive or redistributive character.
- Social policy is the unilateral transfer of resources from one section of the society to another section.

Objectives of Social Policy

- Social policy aims to bring social change
- Social policy aims social integration
- Social policy aims to improve quality of life
- Social policy aims to promote equality and social justice by redistributing resources
- Social policy aims to alleviate the harsh consequences of poverty and control the conditions that are responsible for creating the problem of mass poverty in the long run.

SOCIAL POLICY AND ECONOMIC POLICY

- Titmus stated that social policy operates in the social market unlike the economic policy which is concerned with the economic market, which is characterized by exchange.

- Barker says that social policy tends to concerned with collective provisions and organization and economies with market.
- Economic policy designed in terms of economic objectives like raising the national income, per capita income and sophistication and diversification of science and technology in order to make the economy modern and prosperous.
- Economic policies are considered in purely material terms relying on the input output equations of material resources.
- Both economic and social policy aims to bring social change in the society. Economic policy can bring economic progress, equality of opportunities and narrowing the difference of wealth and income, both could supplementary and complimentary to each other. To bring development any society needs economic growth with social change.

SCOPE OF SOCIAL POLICY AND SOCIAL WELFARE

It is important to distinguish between social policy and social welfare policy. The scope of social policy covers at least four elements as follows:

- Social objectives of national development plans;
- Social service programs in successive five year plans;
- Concerned for the promotion and protection of the interests of the weaker sections of the population; and
- People's own involvement in the formulation and implementation of policies and plans at various levels.

Social welfare policy covers those purposeful and organized interventions that are necessary to protect and rehabilitate such segments of population which are unable to with the demands of life on their own. They are the people who need purposefully well organized interventions by the state to provide need based care. Thus, the underlying principle of social policy is social justice while the principle behind social welfare policy is to provide enabling measures for those who are unable on account of social disability.

Constitutional base of Social Policy

The broad areas of social policy have been expressed in the constitution under the Directive Principles of State Policy. This part forth of the Constitution is usually cited as the main source of the Indian social policy. Specifically Article 38 and 46 are often considered as relevant source of social policy.

The Weaker Section and Social Policy

The most important single element of social policy relates to the specific constitutional safeguards and provisions made for the protection and promotion of the interests of those segments of the population which are traditionally suffered from discrimination, isolation and alienation.

EVOLUTION OF SOCIAL POLICY AS A FIELD OF STUDY

The emergence of social policy as a field of study and an academic department in universities is essentially a British product. In Britain, social policy was originally taught in the department of Social Administration in the London School of Economics, at the London University and later it began to be taught in the other British universities. Social policy in India has come a long way during the last 67 years since the attainment of political independence. The Directive Principles of State Policy are cited as the fountain spring of all national policies; more particularly of the social policy of the country.

EDUCATION POLICIES OF INDIA

National Policy on Education 1968—In the post independence period a major concern of the Government of India and of the States have been to give increasing attention to education a factor vital to national progress and security. In the First National Policy on Education, 1968 the

Government of India laid down the following principles:

- Efforts should be made for free and compulsory education to fulfil the directive principle under Article 45 of the constitution.
- To improve the status, emoluments and education of teachers
- Development of language
- Equalization of education opportunities
- Identification of talent
- Science education and research
- Education for agriculture and industry
- Production of qualitative books
- Reform in education
- Improvement in secondary and University education
- Part time education and correspondence courses
- Spread of literacy and adult education
- Education for minority

National Policy on Education 1986

National policy on education was adopted by the parliament in May 1986. A committee was set up under the chairmanship of Acharya Rammurthi to review national policy on education and to make recommendation for its modification. The national policy on education recommend following goals:

Universalize Elementary Education

- To prevent possibilities of adult illiteracy by reducing drop outs in schools.
- To accelerate non formal education and make education reaches the remotest corner of the country.
- To make provisions of elementary and adult education

Scientific and Technological Education

- Strengthen educational television and radio program capabilities and provide wider access to them.
- To improve scientific education in schools
- Promote rural technology and appropriate technology to achieve economic development
- To develop scientific temper among youth

Social and Cultural Development

- To create awareness regarding our cultural heritage to develop appreciation of diverse culture of our country
- To promote values of national integration and secularism
- To provide equal opportunities to all communities for education
- To provide development of Indian languages

Human Resource Development

- To create awareness about increasing levels of population and the hazards of environment.
- To develop healthy individuals capable of contributing to the social and economic development of the country.
- To develop social and vocational skills.

Equalization of Opportunities

- To provide equal opportunities to the scheduled caste, scheduled tribes, backward class and minority students.
- To provide educational facilities to physically challenged by setting up special institutions.
- To make special provisions for women's education.

School Facilities

To enlarge the scope of operation **Black Board** scheme by providing three reasonably large rooms that are usable in all weather and black boards, maps, charts, toys other necessary learning aids and school library.

Higher Education

- Consolidation and expansion of higher education institutions

- Development of autonomous college and departments
- Redesigning courses
- Training of teachers
- Strengthening research
- Improvement in efficiency
- Rural universities
- Open University and distance education
- Delinking degree from jobs
- Innovation research and development

MAJOR GOVERNMENT PROGRAMS RELATED TO EDUCATION

Sarva Siksha Abhiyan

Launched in 2001 Sarva Siksha Abhiyan is one of India's major flagship program for universalization of education.

Sarva Siksha Abhiyan Goals are:

- Enrolment of all children in school, education guarantee centers, alternative schools
- Retention of all children till the upper primary stage
- Bridging the gender and social category gaps in enrolment, retention and learning
- Ensuring that there is significant enhancement in the learning achievement levels of children at the primary and upper primary stage

Kasturba Gandhi Balika Vidyalaya Scheme

This scheme provides for setting up of residential upper primary schools for girls of SC, ST, OBC and minority communities. This scheme targets areas of scattered habitations.

Mid Day Meal Scheme

With a view to enhancing enrolment, retention and attendance and simultaneously improving nutritional levels among children the mid day meal scheme was launched in 15 August 1995.

Mahila Samakhya Scheme

The scheme was started in 1989 to translate the goals enshrined in the national policy on education into a concrete program for the education and empowerment of women in rural areas particularly those from socially and economically marginalized groups. The mahila sanghs or women forums at the village level provide the women a space to meet, reflect, ask questions and articulate their thoughts and needs and make informed choices

National Council for Teachers Education

The National Council for Teachers Education (NCTE) was established on 1959 with a view to achieve planned and coordinated development of teacher education system throughout the country and for regulations and proper maintenance of norms and standards of teacher education

Right to Education

By 86th amendment of the constitution in 2002, Article 21 A was inserted in the constitution which provides free and compulsory education for all children in the age group of six to fourteen years as a fundamental right.

University Grants Commission

The University Grants Commission (UGC) which came into existence on 28th December 1953 became a statutory organization by an act of parliament in 1956. It is a national body for the coordination, determination and maintenance of standards of university education.

NATIONAL HEALTH POLICY 2002

The main aim of national health policy is to achieve an acceptable standard of good health amongst the general population of the country through an increased access to the decentralized public health system. The objective is planned to be achieved by establishing new infrastructure in existing institutions. Equitable access to health service will receive focus and emphasis will be given to increasing the aggregate public health investment through a substantially increased contribution by the central government. The target is to increase the contribution of private sector in providing health services to all. It has been emphasized that the national health program should be progressively carried out through the state Government, decentralized public health machinery and through autonomous bodies at state/district level.

In addition to the above thrust area, various other issues have also been dealt upon in the national health policy 2002 this includes the expected roles of different participating groups in the health sector –Government, private sector, Non government organization and other members of civil society, disease surveillance, health personnel their norms and education, nursing personnel, medical research and ethics, urban health, mental health, women's health and impact of globalization on the health sector.

MAJOR GOVERNMENT PROGRAMS RELATED TO HEALTH

National Rural Health Mission

The national rural health mission (NRHM) was launched on 12th April 2005 to provide accessible, affordable, accountable and qualitative health services to the poorest households in the remotest rural regions. The thrust of the mission is on establishing a fully functional, community owned, decentralized healthy delivery system with inter sectorial convergence at all levels.

National Urban Health Mission

The proposed urban health mission (NUHM) aims to address the public health care needs of urban population.

Family Welfare

IN 1952, India launched the world's first national program emphasizing family planning to the extent necessary for reducing birth rates and to establish the population at a level consistent with the requirement of national economy.

Census 2011

India's population as per 2011 census was 1.21 billion second only to China in the world. India accounts for 2.4 per cent of the world's area yet it supports more than 17.5 per cent of the world's population.

Total Fertility Rate

Total fertility rate in India has declined 2.5 from 2.6 in 2009.

Maternal Mortality Rate (MMR)

Maternal mortality rate is defined as the number of maternal death per 1000, 00 live birth due to causes related to pregnancy or within 42 days of termination of pregnancy, regardless of the site or duration of pregnancy. The national average of maternal mortality rate is 212 per 1000 live births.

Janani Surksha Yojana (JSY)

The scheme was launched on 1st June 2011. The initiative entitles all pregnant women delivering in public health institutions to absolutely free and expense delivery including caesarean section.

Infant Mortality Rate (IMR)

Infant mortality is defined as the probability of dying before the first birthday. As per the sample registration system 2010 the infant mortality rate for the country was 47 per 1000 live births.

Pre-Conception and Pre-Natal Diagnostic Techniques (Prohibition of Sex selection) Act, 1994

The child sex ratio for the age group 0-6 years as per census 2011 (provisional) has dipped further to 914 girls as against 927 per thousand boys recorded in 2001 census. This is worst dip since 1947. In order to check the female feticide, the Pre-Conception and Pre-Natal Diagnostic Techniques (Prohibition of Sex selection) Act, 1994 was brought in to operation from 1st January 1996.

Universal Immunization Program

Immunization program is one of the key interventions for protection of children from life threatening conditions which are preventable. Immunization program was introduced in India in the year 1978 as expanded program of immunization.

Pulse Polio Immunization

In pursuance of the world health assembly resolution of 1988, the pulse polio immunization program was started nation wise from 1995 to eradicate polio from India covering children in the age group of 0 to 3 years. As a result only 1 polio case was reported in 2011 in the month of January 2011.

National Mental Health Program

National mental health program was started in 1982 with the objectives to ensure availability and accessibility of minimum mental health care for all, to encourage mental health knowledge and skills and to promote community participation in mental health service development and to stimulate self help in the community.

National AIDS Control Program

The first national AIDS control program (NACP) was launched in 1992 for prevention and control of HIV/AIDS in India. This was followed by NACP IInd in 1999, NACP IIIrd in 2007 and NACP IVth in 2007-12.

National Policy on Shelter 1998

Housing is a state subject. A comprehensive housing and habitat policy 1998 had been formulated to address the issue of sustainable development, infrastructure and for strong public and private partnership for shelter delivery.

The objectives of the policy are to create surplus in housing stock by creating a conducive environment and facilitate construction of two million additional dwelling unit each year. It also seeks to ensure that housing along with supportive services is treated as priority sector as per with the infrastructure problem.

MAJOR GOVERNMENT PROGRAMS RELATED TO SHELTER

National Building Organization

The national building organization has been functioning as an apex organization in the country for collection, tabulation and dissemination of statistical information on housing and building construction activities since 1954

Housing and Urban Development Cooperation (HUDCO)

HUDCO is the premier techno financing institution in the field of housing and urban development sector in India. It was established on April 25, 1970 as wholly owned government company with the objective of providing long term finance and undertaking housing and urban infrastructures development program.

Jawahar Lal Nehru Urban Renewal Mission (JLNURM)

The Jawahar Lal Nehru urban renewal mission was launched on 3rd December 2005. The mission comprises two sub mission one for basic services to the urban poor and other for urban infrastructure and governance.

Rajiv Awas Yojana (RAY)

In pursuance of government's vision of creating slum free India, a new scheme Rajiv Awas Yojana has been launched on 2nd June 2011. The scheme is expected to cover about 250 cities, across the entire country by the end of the 12th plan (2017). This centrally sponsored scheme will provide financial assistance to states that are willing to assign the property rights to slum dwellers for provisions of decent shelter and basic civic and social services for slum redevelopment and for creation of affordable housing stock.

NATIONAL ENVIRONMENT POLICY 2006

The policy evolved from the recognition that only such development is sustainable, which respects ecological constraints and the imperatives of justice. The objectives stated in the policy are to be realized through various strategic interventions by different public authorities at central, state and local government level. The principles followed in the policy are:

- Human beings are at the center of sustainable development concerns.
- Right to development must be fulfilled so as to equitably meet developmental and environmental needs of present and future generations.
- In order to achieve sustainable development environmental protection shall constitute an integral part of the development process and cannot be considered in isolation from it.
- Where there are credible threats of serious or irreversible damage to key environmental resources, lack of full scientific certainty shall not be used as a reason for postponing cost effective measures to prevent environmental degradation.
- In various public actions for environmental conservation, economic efficiency would be sought to be realized.

Objectives of the Policy

- Conservation of critical environmental resources.
- Intra-generational equity: livelihood security for the poor.
- Inter-generational equity.
- Integration of environmental concerns in economic and social development.
- Efficiency in environmental resource use.
- Environmental governance.
- Enhancement of resources for environmental conservations.

MAJOR GOVERNMENT PROGRAMS RELATED TO ENVIRONMENT PROTECTION

Forest Policy 1988

The forest policy in India was launched in 1988. The basic objectives of the national forest policy 1988 were:

- Maintenance of environment stability through preservation and restoration of ecological balance that has been adversely disturbed by serious depletion of the forest of the country.
- Conserving natural heritage of the country by preserving the remaining natural forest with the vast variety of flora and fauna which represents the remarkable biodiversity and genetic resources of the country.
- Checking soil erosion and denudation in the catchment areas of rivers, lakes, reservoirs in the interest of soil and water conservation for mitigating floods and droughts.
- Checking the extension of sand dunes in the desert areas of Rajasthan.
- Increasing the forest cover in the country through a forestation and social forestry.
- Meeting the requirements of fuel wood, fodder, minor forest produce and small timber for the rural and tribal population.

Project Tiger (National Tiger Conservation Authority)

The 'Project Tiger' was launched in April 1973 with the objective to ensure maintenance of viable population of tiger in the country. A tiger census published in 2011 estimated that there are 1,706 tigers roaming free in the country.

Project Elephant

The project elephant was launched by the government in 1991-92. The objectives were to protect elephant their habitat corridors, to address issues of man animal conflict and welfare of domesticated elephants.

Central Pollution Control Board

The central pollution control board performs functions as laid down under the water (Prevention and Control of Pollution) Act, 1974, and the Air

(Prevention and Control of Pollution) Act, 1981. It is responsible for planning and executing comprehensive nationwide programs for prevention and control of water and air pollution.

Climate Change

Climate change is a global environmental phenomenon caused primarily by the building up of greenhouse gases in the atmosphere such as carbon dioxide, methane, nitrous oxide etc. The forth assessment report of the inter governmental panel on climate change brought out in 2007 has projected that human induced climate change if not addressed may result in rising temperature, changed rainfall patterns and increased severity and frequency of floods, droughts and cyclones which can severely impact livelihood, especially of the poor in the developing countries. Therefore, India is committed to control its green house gas emission and ozone layer protection by all means. A national carbon aerosol program is also envisaged under Indian network of climate change assessment.

National Policy on Skill Development

The objectives of national policy on skill development are to:

- Create opportunity for all to acquire skill throughout life and especially for the youth, women and disadvantaged group
- Promote commitment by all stakeholders to own skill development initiatives
- Develop a high quality skilled workforce relevant to current and emerging market needs
- Enable the establishment of flexible delivery mechanism that respond to the characteristics of a wide range of needs of stakeholders.

National Employment Service

The national employment service provides employment assistance to the job seekers with a network of employment exchanges. The employment exchange assists all employment seekers including special groups like handicapped, ex service man, scheduled castes and scheduled tribes etc.

SOCIAL SECURITY

Social security can be understood as security that furnishes through appropriate organizations against certain risk to which its members are exposed. It is a program of protection provided by society against the contingencies of modern life like sickness, unemployment, old age dependency, industrial accidents against which the individual cannot be expected to protect himself and his family by his own ability.

The Employees Compensation Act, 1923

A beginning was made in social security with the passing of the Workman's Compensation Act, 1923. The Act provides for payment of compensation to the employees and their dependents in case of injury and accident among railway servant and person employed in any such capacity as specified in the schedule IInd of the Act. It includes person employed in factories, mines, plantation, machinery propelled vehicles, construction works and certain other hazardous occupations.

The Maternity Benefit Act, 1961

The Act enacted to promote the welfare of working women. The Act prohibits the working of pregnant women for a specific period before and after delivery. It also provides for maternity leave for a specific period before and after delivery. It also provides for maternity leave and payment of certain monetary benefits to women workers. The services of women workers cannot be terminated during the period of their absence on account of pregnancy except for the gross misconduct. Maximum period to which women can get maternity benefits is twelve weeks. Of this six weeks must be taken prior to the date of delivery of the child and six weeks immediately following that date.

The Employee's State Insurance Act, 1948

The employee state insurance act, 1948 is applicable to non seasonal factories using power and employing 10 or more person and non power using factories employing 20 or more persons. It covers employees drawing wages not exceeding Rs. 15000/- per month with effect from 1st May 2010. The act provides for medical care in kind and cash benefits payments in contingency and sickness, maternity and employment inquiry and pension for dependents in the event of death of a worker because of employment injury.

The Employee Provident Funds and Miscellaneous Provision Act, 1952

The Act seeks to provide the financial security to the employees in the form of provident fund, pension and deposit linked insurance. It extends the whole of India except the state of Jammu & Kashmir. It applies to every establishment specified in the schedule and in which twenty or more persons are employed.

The Employees Provident Fund Scheme, 1952

The employee provident fund scheme, 1952 provides financial security to the employees in an establishment by providing a system of compulsory savings. The scheme covers the employees getting wages not exceeding Rs. 6500/- per month from 1st November 1990 onwards the employees becomes the member of fund from the date of joining the factory/establishment.

The Employee Pension Scheme, 1995

The employee pension scheme, 1995 came into effect from 16th November 1995 aims at providing for economic support during old age and survivorship coverage. The employee pension scheme, 1995 provides the following benefits to member and their families:

- Monthly member pension
- Permanent total disablement pension
- Widow/widower pension
- Children pension
- Orphan Pension
- Disabled children
- Nominee pension
- Pension to dependent father/mother

The scheme is financed by diversion of 8.33 per cent of wages from employers' share of provident fund contribution and central government contribution at the rate 1.16 per cent of the wage of the employee. The upper wage limit is raised to Rs. 6500 with effect from 1st June 2001.

The Payment of Gratuity Act, 1972

The payment of gratuity act, 1972 is applicable to factories, mines, oil fields, plantation, ports, railways, motor transport undertakings, companies, shops and other establishments. The act provides payment of gratuity at the rate of 15 days wages of each completed year of service or part thereof in excess of six months subject the maximum of Rs. 10 Lakh.

NATIONAL POLICY FOR CHILDREN

The national policy on children was adopted on 22nd August 1974. The policy lay down that the state shall provide adequate services for children, both before and after birth and during the growing stages of their full physical, mental and social development. The measures suggested in the policy includes amongst others, a comprehensive health program, supplementary nutrition for mothers and children, free and compulsory education for all children up to the age of 14 years, promotion of physical education and recreational activities, especial consideration for weaker section prevention of exploitation of children etc.

National Charter for Children

The government of India adopted the National Charter of Children on 9th February 2004. The document emphasizes government of India's commitment to children's rights to survive, health and nutrition, standards of living, play and leisure, early childhood care, education, protection of the girl child, empowering adolescents, equality of life and liberty, freedom of expression, freedom of association and peaceful assembly, the right to a family and the right to be protected from economic exploitation and all forms of abuse.

Integrated Child Development Scheme (ICDS)

The scheme was launched in 1975 with the following objectives:

- To improve the nutrition and health status of children below the age of six years and pregnant and lactating mothers.
- To lay the foundation for the proper psychological, physical and social development of the child.
- To reduce the incidents of mortality, morbidity, malnutrition and school drop outs.
- To achieve effective coordination of policy and implementation among various departments to promote child development.
- To enhance the capabilities of mothers to look after the health and nutritional needs of the child through proper health and nutrition education.

Scheme provides for a package of services to children below 6 years and pregnant women and lactating mothers, comprising:

- Supplementary Nutrition
- Nutrition and Health Education
- Pre School and Non Formal Education
- Immunization
- Health Check ups
- Referrals

Integrated Child Protection Scheme (ICPS)

The scheme was launched in the year 2009-10. The objectives of the scheme are to contribute to the wellbeing of children in difficult circumstances as well as reduction of vulnerabilities to situation and action that lead to abuse, neglect, exploitation, abandonment, separation of children from parents.

Childline Services

Childline is 24 hour toll free emergency outreach telephone service (1098) for children in need of care and protection. At present childline is functioning in 174 cities/districts.

National Commission for Protection of Child Rights (NCPCR)

National commission for protection of child rights was set up on 5th March 2007 in accordance with the provision of the protection of Child Rights Act, 2007. Its mission is to protect, promote and defend child rights in India.

National Institute of Public Cooperation and Child Development (NIPCCD)

Popularly known as NIPCCD, an autonomous organization under the Ministry of Women and Child Development is the premier organization devoted to promotion of voluntary action research, training and development in the overall domain of women and child development.

Central Adoption Resource Authority (CARA)

The central adoption and research authority is a autonomous body under the Ministry of Women and Child Development. It functions as the nodal body of adoption of Indian children and is mandated to monitor and regulate in—country adoptions.

POLICY AND PROGRAMS FOR YOUTH

Youth represents the most vibrant part of the society. They play a pivotal role in the socio-economic changes and development in the society. In our country youth forms nearly 40 per cent of the total population. Government of India has been implementing several programs for them.

National Youth Policy

Formulated in 1988, the main objective of the policy are to instill in youth respect for the principles and values enshrined in constitution, to promote an awareness of historical heritage, to help develop scientific temper and the quality of discipline, self reliance, justice and fair play, and to provide them access to education in addition to developing their personality. It also aims making the youth conscious of implementing issues and involving them in promoting world peace and just international economic order.

National Youth Policy, 2003

The national youth policy, 2003 recognizes training and employment, health and family welfare and education as key sectors of concerns for youth. The national youth policy, 2003 also envisages youth empowerment as one of the thrust area.

Draft National Youth Policy, 2012

The draft national youth policy, 2012 is first of its kind as it recognizes that youth is not a homogeneous group and has numerous differentials based on habitate, environment, socio-economic status of their families and their own life styles. In addition the draft policy proposes to change the target age group from the existing 13-35 years to 16-30 years.

The target groups identified under the draft policy are (1) Student youth, (2) Migrant youth, (3) Rural youth, (4) Tribal youth, (5) Youth at risk, (6) Youth in violent conflict, (7) Dropouts, (8) Youth with social, moral stigma, (9) Youth in institutional care, youth women, youth belonging to social and economically disadvantaged communities and differently able youth.

The draft national youth policy, 2012 has observable indicators under five domains. Accordingly, youth development index will include the indices viz. youth health index, youth education index, youth work index, youth amenities index, youth participation index.

National Service Scheme (NSS)

National service scheme has the objective to develop character and personality of student youth in school and college. The scheme was launched during the birth anniversary of Mahatma Gandhi in 1969.

National Commission for Youth

Set up on 15th March, 2002, the commission comprises of chairman and five members and the member secretary will study the areas of concerns for the youth in the country with particularly focus on the problems of youth such as unemployment etc.

Nehru Yuva Kendra Sanghatan

It is a autonomous organization of government of India with its office in more than 500 district of the country. Rural youth enrolled in this club through youth club. These youth club working in the area of education and training, awareness generation, skill development and self employment, entrepreneurial development etc.

Youth Festivals

Every year beginning from 12th January which is the birth anniversary of Swami Vivekananda, a five days long youth festival is held at selected place.

National Youth Awards

National youth awards are given every year to 25 young people and voluntary organization for their excellent work in the field of social development.

NATIONAL POLICY ON EMPOWERMENT OF WOMEN

The national policy for women empowerment was formulated in 2001 as a blueprint for the future, with the goals of bringing about the advancement, development and empowerment of women. The policy laid down detail prescription to address discrimination against women, strengthening existing institutions which includes the legal system, provide better access to health care and other services, equal opportunities for women's participation in decision-making and main-streaming gender concerns in the development process, to name a few. The policies programs of the government are all directed towards achieving inclusive growth with special focus on women in line with the objective of the national policy for empowerment of women.

Swadhar

The swadhar scheme was launched by the ministry of women and child development during the year 2001-02 as a scheme for providing holistic and integrated service to women in difficult circumstances. Such as destitute, widow, women survivors of natural disaster, runaway from brothels, mentally challenged women etc.

Short Stay Home

The scheme was launched in the year 1969 to provide temporary accommodation, maintenance and rehabilitation services through voluntary organization to women and girls rendered homeless due to family discord of crime. The shelter is provided for six months to three years.

Rajiv Gandhi Scheme for Empowerment of Adolescent Girls (RGSEAG)-*SABLA*

The scheme introduced in the year 2010 on a pilot basis in 200 districts across the country. The scheme focuses on all out of school adolescent girls in the age group of 11 to 18 years under all ICDS projects in selected districts. It also covers school going girls in the same age group.

Gender Budgeting Initiatives

Gender budgeting is a powerful tool for achieving gender mainstreaming so as to ensure the benefits of development reach to women as much as men. To institutionalize gender budgeting in India, the setting up of gender budgeting cell in all ministries was mandated by the Ministry of Finance in 2005.

WELFARE OF SCHEDULED CASTES

The ministry of social justice & empowerment is the nodal ministry to oversee the interests of the scheduled castes. Constitutional safeguards as well as program for the protection and development of scheduled castes have been implemented by the government.

National commission for Scheduled Castes

The national commission for scheduled castes is a constitutional body monitors the safeguards for scheduled castes and also reviews issues concerning their welfare. The commission has been constituted on 25 may 2007.

Protection of Civil Rights Act, 1955 and Scheduled Castes and Scheduled Tribes (Prevention of Atrocities) Act, 1989

The following two acts specially aims at curbing untouchability and atrocities against Scheduled Caste and Scheduled Tribe and therefore very important legislation.

Other important schemes are:

- Post metric scholarship
- Free coaching
- Babu Jagjivan Chhatrawas Yojana
- Dr. Ambedkar foundation

Development of Scheduled Tribes

Scheduled areas and Tribal areas: Scheduled tribes live in contiguous areas unlike other communities. It is therefore, much simpler to have an areas approach for developments activities and also regulatory provision to protect their interests.

In order to protect the interests of scheduled tribes provisions of Fifth Schedule and Sixth Schedule have been enshrined in the constitution. The Fifth schedule under article 244 (1) of constitution defines Scheduled areas or such areas as president may by order declare to be scheduled areas after consultation with the governor of the state.

The sixth schedule under article 244 (2) of the constitution related to those areas in the states of Assam, Meghalaya, Tripura and Mizoram which are declared as tribal areas and provides for district council and /or regional councils for such areas. There councils have been conferred with wide ranging, legislative, judicial and exclusive power.

Welfare of Persons with Disabilities

As per census 2001, there are 2.19 crore persons with disabilities and they constitute 2.13 percent of the total population of the country. These include persons with visuals, hearing, speech, locomotor and mental disabilities.

Person with Disabilities Act, 1995

A comprehensive law, namely the person with disabilities (Equal Opportunities, Protection of Rights and Full Participation) Act, 1995 have been enacted and enforced in 1996. The law deals with both promotional and prevention aspects for the persons with disabilities.

Rehabilitation Council of India

The Rehabilitation council of India is a statutory body set up under the Rehabilitation Council of India Act, 1992. Its functions include:

- Standardization and regulation of training courses.
- Recognition of Institutions running training courses in the area of the rehabilitation of the disabled within and outside the country on a reciprocal basis.
- Promotion of research and rehabilitation and special education.
- Maintenance of a central rehabilitation register.
- Encouragement of continuing rehabilitation education program in collaboration with organizations working in the area of disability.

National Institutions

In order to effectively deal with the multi dimensional problem of the disabled population, the following national institutions/ apex level institutions have been set up in each major area of disability.

- National Institute of Visually Handicapped, Deharadun.
- National Institute of Orthopedically Handicapped, Kolkata.
- Ali Yavar Jung National Institute of Hearing Handicapped, Mumbai.
- National Institute of Mentally Handicapped, Secundarabad.
- National Institute of Rehabilitation, Training and Research, Cuttack.
- Institute of the Physically Handicapped, New Delhi.
- National Institute for Empowerment of Persons with Multiple Disabilities, Chennai.

WELFARE OF AGED PERSON

National Policy for Older Person

The national policy for the older person was announced in January, 1999, with the primary objective to encourage individuals to make provisions for their own as well as their spouses' old age; to encourage families to take care of their older family members; to enable and support non government organization to supplement care provided by the family; to provide care and protection to the vulnerable elderly people; to provide health care facility to the elderly; to promote research and training facilities; to train geriatric care givers and organizers of service for the elderly; and to create awareness regarding elderly persons to develop them into fully independent citizens.

National Council for Older Persons

The government has constituted the national council for older persons to advise the government on developing policies and programs for older persons. It provides feedback to the government on the implementation of the national policy on older persons.

Integrated Program Older Persons

Under this scheme financial assistance upto 90 per cent of the project cost is provided to non government organizations for establishing and maintaining old age homes, day care centers, mobile medical units and to provide non-institutional service to older persons.

Meaning of a Project

A project is a plan with specified objectives to be achieved within a specified time frame and with specified resources. With reference to non governmental organization a project is means to bring certain desirable changes in the conditions of a group within a specified time period and cost.

Project Formulation

The process of project formulation involves—

- Project planning keeping in view the project 'idea'.
- Comparative appraisal for determining priority of the project and allocation of resources within the financial constraints.

- The exercise of project formulation is necessary to ensure that the project is technically sound, economically and socially viable and fits within the overall economic objectives of the donor or sponsoring agency.

Following steps should be followed in project formulation process:

Step One—Conceptualization

Identifying the Problem: Conceptualization of a problem is first step for project formulation. Program activities have direct relationship with the conceptualization of problem. Program activities are the conscious efforts to reduce the problem.

The problem can be something that is hampering or disturbing the economical, social, psychological, environmental or educational development of the persons or group of people. Different methods can be used to get the real understanding of the problem such as observation, individual contacts, group meetings, focused group interaction, surveys, secondary data, research studies, record available with different groups, organization or departments, etc. are the most common ways of data collection.

Finding Solutions of the Problem: After identifying and understanding the problem, possible solutions of the problem find out through the program activities. The problem may be dealt in two ways—

Remedial approach provides an immediate solution and generally of short term in nature.

Developmental approach relies on providing a permanent solution to the problem and has generally a long term effect.

The solutions can be evolved through team work by involving other likeminded people, staff and outside experts in the field.

Listing the Activities: Possible activities to achieve the desired objectives should be enlisted. Program activities should not only reduce the negative factors but also take care of the promotive activities.

Building Consensus opinion: A project is not an aloof activity rather it is a team effort. Therefore, community people, stake holders, volunteers and staff must be included in all the steps of project and all aspects of the problem, possible solutions and plan of action should be thoroughly discussed with them. Various components of the project, their relevance to the people, requirement of resources, implementing strategy, etc. should be discussed in detail.

Step Two—Planning

Planning is fundamentally an intellectual process, a mental predisposition to do things in an orderly way, to think before action, and to act in the light of facts rather than the guesses. Planning is the provision to implement guaranteed minimum of resources, both physical and social according to needs and necessities for better life conditions and adjustment.

The basic principles of planning are:

Participation at all level: Planning involves discussions with all concerned peoples, departments and individuals. It should not just come from the top. Planning ensures participation of all levels instead of one man at the top deciding everything on his own thinking.

Continuity: Planning is a continuous process. Regular monitoring, review and introspection are required in the planning so that constraints in the plan are removed if the plan is not achieving the targets. Planning thus has to be done on a continuous basis.

Objectivity: In order to make a plan effective, its objectives must be stated in advance, in clear and unambiguous terms.

Evaluation: Effective methods of evaluation should be used to ensure the effectiveness of planning.

Step Three—Objectives

Objectives are statements of what an organization intends to achieve. The general purpose of not for profit organization is to render service to humanity. For example, to provide education to poor children, to provide vocational training to school dropouts, to provide health education to college students, etc. The objectives should always be stated in positive terms. The objective of a project should be SMART, meaning specific, measurable, achievable, relevant and time based.

Step Four—Organizing

Organizing means systematic arrangement and allocation of resources including human, physical and financial resources with a view to achieve the predetermined goals in most effective manner.

Organizing involves:

- Drawing an activity plan based on the target set;
- Seeking volunteers for delivering the services;
- Staffing of paid employees;
- Arranging necessary supplies by way of donations in kind or by procuring from the market;
- Arranging finance for the activities.

Once the resources have been acquired, they need to be coordinated and controlled in such a manner that they do not work in conflict to the other and they achieve the desired goals in most cost effective manner.

Step Five—Budgeting

Once the resource necessary in achieving the organizations objectives have been identified, these are then translated into monetary terms. The various sources from which the necessary funds can be tapped are also identified. This process is known as budgeting which involves stating the various sources from which money is to be raised during a particular period and the activities on which the money will be utilized.

The budget is thus, an important document for assessing the financial requirements of a project. A budget should normally be prepared for a period of 12 months, which may a financial year or a calendar year.

The income (sources of funds) and expenditure (application of funds) sides should always be balanced showing deficit or surplus. If there is deficit then the sources from which it shall be met or the measures to reduce the expenditure should be indicated.

A budget should be prepared well in advance. It should be realistic and accurate, while also providing for unforeseen or abnormal expenditure.

Step Six—Raising Funds

Donors play an important role in translating a project into reality. Donors have to be influenced to consider a project, convinced about the projects validity and persuaded to extend their cooperation.

Raising funds for a project involves:

Identifying the donors: Potential donors for a project may be individuals, corporate bodies, industrial houses, other trust/organization, funding agencies, government etc. Donors should be identified with respect to availability of funds with them and their conviction to a particular social cause.

Communicating with the Donors: The most common means of communicating with the donors are through post, personal visits, giving advertisements/pamphlets in newspaper/magazines etc. The initial communication should be brief but convincing and persuasive. Interested donors may be sent detailed proposal either by post or personally.

Preparing for Project Proposal: Usually a large funding agency requires information about the project in a specific format known as project proposal. A project proposal should carry sufficient information about the problem and why it is necessary to find solution, feasibility of program, resources required etc.

An outline for preparing a project proposal is given hereunder:

SPECIMEN PROJECT PROPOSAL FORMAT

Section A: General Information

1. Title of the project
2. Organization—name, address, contact person, legal status, present activities, etc.

3. Project-problem, size of the problem, project area, existing facilities in the project area.
4. Budget—Resource requirements and availability of funds

Section B: Organization

5. Organizational background
6. Organizational structure
7. Area covered
8. Activities in the previous three years
9. Participants
10. Beneficiaries

Section C: Proposed project

11. Target area
12. Objectives (General and Specific)
13. Activities/Plan
14. Implementation strategy at the central, intermediate and grassroot level
15. Staffing
16. Training and development
17. Monitoring and evaluation
18. Project coordination and management

Section D: Budget

19. Resource requirements (Equipments and furniture, transport, staff, finance)
20. Source of funds
21. Sustainability of the project without outside support

    Internal generation of funds;

    Making maximum utilization of volunteers and voluntary donation in kind;

    Sale of project services /products for generating funds

    Investment of surplus

Section E: Project Evaluation

22. Procedure for monitoring the project activities
23. Indicators
24. Expected impact of the project on the target beneficiaries, community and society at large
25. Conclusion

Checklist for preparing a project proposal

- The proposal should contain all details which may be required by a donor agency.
- The document should be comprehensive but brief and not bulky.
- Heavy charts and tables should be avoided or given as appendix.
- Avoid use of uncommon abbreviations and unexplained short terms.
- Figures and data given in the document should be accurate.
- Copy of registration certificate, memorandum, rules and regulations, audited balance sheet and final accounts, latest annual report and list of beneficiaries should be attached to the document.

REGISTRATION OF A SOCIETY

The main advantage of the registration of the society is that it will give legal authority and identity to the organization. It is also necessary because community will be able to know the legally authorized person of the organization and instead of meeting individually with all the members of the board individually they can meet a single person. It also prevents duplication and makes effective and specialized services possible. An organization can cope with intricacy and variety of modern problems as the lone individual cannot. The humanitarian organization with its board of directors, its paid staff, and its constituency can develop the benefits of group thinking and collective action. It can work out division of responsibility among these groups collectively and individually, so that each interested individual may serve as according to his ability. It can develop specialized functions, establish permanent and steadily improving standards of service and follow a continuous progressive policy independent of the life or death of any individual. It can secure public support and funds impossible for the individual to obtain and can conserve them through the years.

Advantages of Registration as Society

Registration gives continuity and permanency to the work of the agency.

It has the advantage of group thinking.

It ensures collective action with division of responsibility.

An agency can sue or be sued as one person. It gives the benefit to the members of the organization of being relieved from unlimited personal financial responsibility for the organization.

It gives the organization recognition inside and outside the community.

Every country has the law for registration. In India registration of a society can be made through Societies Registration Act, Indian Trusts Act, Cooperative Societies Act or any other similar legislation. Most of the organizations are registered under Societies Registration Act of 1860.

The Societies Registration Act of 1860

The following associations may be registered under the Act, Charitable societies, the military orphan funds, societies established for the promotion of science, literature or fine arts, for instructions, the diffusion of useful knowledge, the foundation or maintenance of libraries or reading rooms for general use among the members or to open the public museum and galleries of painting and other works of art, collection of natural history, mechanical and philosophical inventions, instruments, or designs.

Memorandum of Association

Any seven or more person associated for any scientific or charitable purpose or for any such purpose indicates above, may by subscribing their names to a memorandum of association and feeling the same with the Registrar of Joint Stock Companies or any other officer appointed under the Act by the State government form a society.

The memorandum of association should contain the following particulars.

(A) Name and Address of the Association: The selection of the name for the agency is very important. The following points may be kept in mind while selecting a name for an agency.

The name should be simples.

It should be short so that it can be readily used.

It should be comprehensible.

It should indicate the broad purpose for which the organization is set up

(B) Purpose: The broad purpose for which the agency has been set up should be clearly stated.

(C) Membership Requirement: The constitution should also indicate the qualifications for becoming members of the agency. These may be:

1. Financial provision that is paying a certain amount to the organization regularly. (There may be different type of membership depends upon the amount of money they contributed to the agency. There may be life members, active members, contributing members etc.)
2. Minimum age limit for membership of (1) the general body, (2) the board.
3. Special interest of a member in the agency's programs

(D) Other particulars: The constitution should also deal with the following aspects: Board of Directors, Office Bearers, Elections, Sub-Committees, Meetings, Official Year, Amendments to the constitution, Finances: maintenance and operation of the bank account

Constitution and Bye laws

The objects of an organization are to be broadly indicated in the constitution which also indicates the duties, powers and functions of the various limbs of the organization. Apart from the constitution, the agency also prepares bye laws or detailed rules and regulations governing the day to day working of an organization. A constitution is a brief statement setting forth the general organization of an agency without giving the details of procedures to be followed which are contained in the bye laws. Every staff member in the organization and the members of the board must have copies of constitution and the bye laws for ready reference.

Procedure for Registration

The registering society has to file with the Registrar a memorandum showing the name of the society, its object, names and address and occupation of the members of the governing body together with the rules and regulations of the society and a copy of the proceedings of the general meeting at which it was resolved to get the society registered.

The memorandum of association prepared in the manner indicated above signed by seven or more persons sponsoring the organization should be submitted along with the prescribed fees, to the Registrar who will record the name of the Society in the register to keep under the Act and issue a certificate of registration to the agency. Thereafter, the registered agency has to submit to the Registrar an annual list of the managing body and any other information required under the Act.

Any person interested in the affairs of the society can inspect any document or obtain a copy thereof from the office of the Registrar on payment of necessary fees.

Upon such registration, all the property, movable and immovable, will become the property of the society, and all suits by or against the society will be commenced or defended in the registered name of the society. In case of the dissolution of the society, the court has to decide the steps to be taken for disposal of the property, for recovering its claims and for discharging its liabilities according to the rules of the society. Any modification in the constitution can be made only subject to the approval of the Registrar.

Registration of a Trust

Welfare programs are also rum by charitable trusts. In order to give a legal personality to an organization formed in the fulfilment of the objectives of a trust, registration under the Indian Trusts Act is very essential.

What is a Trust

Section 3 of the Indian Trusts Act, defines the term 'trust' in the following words:

"A trust is an obligation annexed to the ownership of property and arising out of a confidence reposed in and accepted by the owner, or declared and accepted by him, for the benefit of another, or of another and the owner."

The person who reposes or declares the confidence is called the 'author of the trust'; the person who accept the confidence is called the 'trustee'; the person whose benefit the confidence is accepted is called the 'beneficiary'.

Section 6 of the Indian Trusts Act lays down that a trust is created when the author of the trust indicates with reasonable certainty by words or act: (1) an intention to create a trust; (2) the purpose of the trust; (3) the beneficiaries; (4) the trust property. Unless the trust is declared by will or the author of the trust himself is trustee, or transfers the trust property to the trustee.

The public or charitable trust is a trust for the benefit of the public at large or a considerable and indeterminate section of the public.

Objects of a Charitable Trust

The following may be the objectives of a charitable trust:

(1)Trusts for the relief of poverty; (2) trusts for the advancement of education; (3) trusts for the advancement of religion and (4) trusts for the other purposes beneficial to the community, not falling under any of the above three heads.

Section 18 of The Transfer of the Property Act also classifies charity under the following heads: (1) Advancement of religion, (2) Knowledge, (3) Commerce, health and safety, or (4) Any other object beneficial to mankind.

The following are the duties of a trustee:

1. Trustee is to execute the trust
2. He must inform the state of trust property
3. He must protect title to trust property
4. He must not allow or aid any title to the trust property adverse to the interest of the beneficiary
5. He must exercise reasonable care in regard to the trust property
6. Trustee must be impartial to all the beneficiaries
7. He must prevent waste by the beneficiary in possession of trust property
8. A trustee is bound to keep clear and accurate accounts of thé trust property, and furnish at all reasonable times full and accurate information as the amount and state of the trust.

MONITORING & EVALUATION

Monitoring is the periodic oversight of the implementation of an activity which seeks to establish the extent to which input deliveries, work schedules, other required actions and targeted outputs are proceeding according to plan, so that timely action can be taken to correct deficiencies detected. "Monitoring" is also useful for the systematic checking on a condition or set of conditions, such as following the situation of women and children.

Evaluation is a process which attempts to determine as systematically and objectively as possible the relevance, effectiveness, efficiency and impact of activities in the light of specified objectives. It is a learning and action-oriented management tool and organizational process for improving current activities and future planning, programming and decision-making.

Importance of Monitoring and Evaluation

To evaluate means "to ascertain the value or worth of," according to its Latin root. Knowing what difference programmes are making motivates workers and their supporters to renewed effort. Although evaluations may be retrospective, they are essentially forward looking with regard to their purpose. Evaluation applies the lessons of experience to decisions about current and future programmes. Good evaluation presents alternatives for decision-makers to consider. Evaluation can be an excellent learning tool as well as a means to improve programme performance and demonstrate accountability. Too often evaluation is perceived as threatening; it should be constructive. For example, an evaluation can be tapped for developing human resources and improving management and planning capabilities. Evaluation results can be used in advocacy and fund raising efforts to obtain greater support from governments, private organizations, and the general public.

The relationship between monitoring and evaluation

Both monitoring and evaluation are management tools. In the case of monitoring, information for tracking progress according to previously agreed on plans and schedules is *routinely* gathered.

Discrepancies between actual and planned implementation are identified and corrective actions taken. When findings are used to monitor the development results (effects, impacts) it is sometimes referred to as *ongoing evaluation.*

Evaluation is more episodic than monitoring. It is facilitated by monitoring but utilizes additional sources of information. Many such sources are identified during project reviews when there is a need to understand why inputs did not lead to planned outputs. Evaluation focuses on specific questions related to effectiveness and impact in order to influence future programmes or services.

Impact assessment is often difficult because causality is difficult to determine, in addition to being costly and time-consuming. However, managers need to know the effects of project activities on the intended beneficiaries during implementation. Community monitoring programmes can record impacts locally and use results to modify project activities. Impacts may be assessed informally, through conversations with beneficiaries, women's groups, village elders. This allows

1710 (SW) [II & III (A)]–25-II

managers to adjust strategies, if necessary, during implementation, rather than continue less than effective activities.

The objectives of monitoring and evaluation are:

(a) To improve management of programmes, projects and supporting activities and to ensure optimum use of funds and other resources;

(b) To learn from experience so as to improve the relevance, methods and outcomes of cooperative programmes;

(c) To strengthen the capacity of co-operating government agencies, non-governmental organizations (NGOs) and local communities to monitor and evaluate;

(d) To meet the requirements of donors to see whether their resources are being used effectively, efficiently and for agreed upon objectives; and

(e) To provide information to enhance advocacy for policies, programmes and resources, that improves the condition of women and children.

MULTIPLE CHOICE QUESTIONS

1. 'What is Social Case Work' is written by
A. G.R. Banerjee
B. Mary Richmond
C. H.H. Perlman
D. F. Biestek

2. Match the following pairs :

(a) S. Freud — (i) Hierarchy of needs
(b) Erich Fromm — (ii) Child Development
(c) Abraham Maslow — (iii) The Unconscious
(d) Elizabeth Harlock — (iv) Freedom

Codes :

	(a)	(b)	(c)	(d)
A.	(ii)	(iii)	(iv)	(i)
B.	(iii)	(iv)	(i)	(ii)
C.	(i)	(ii)	(iii)	(iv)
D.	(iv)	(iii)	(ii)	(i)

3. The Quota Sampling is called
A. Opportunistic sampling
C. Probability sampling
B. Poor man's stratified sampling
D. Dense sampling

4. Who defined Statistics as the science of estimates and probabilities ?
A. Bodington B. Bowley
C. Fisher D. Agrawal

5. The point where two axes intersect is known as
A. X axis B. Y axis
C. Origin D. Table

6. Quartile deviation is also known as
A. Range
B. Mode
C. Semi-Inter Quartile Range
D. Dispersion

7. The first country in the world to launch a nation wide family planning programme is
A. China B. Russia
C. America D. India

8. Identify the correct chronological sequence.
A. Association for improving the conditions of the poor, Ram Krishna Mission, Charity Organizations Society, Sriniketan Institute of Rural Reconstruction.
B. Association for improving the conditions of poor, Charity organisation society, Ram Krishna Mission, Sriniketan Institute of Rural Reconstruction.
C. Charity organisation society, Association for improving the conditions of poor, Ram Krishna Mission, Sriniketan Institute of Rural Reconstruction.

D. Sriniketan Institute of Rural Reconstruction, Charity Organisation Society, Ramkrishna Mission, Association for improving the conditions of poor.

9. The value that is repeated most of the times in data set is known as
A. Median B. Mode
C. Frequency D. Variance

10. The main opportunistic infection among AIDS cases in India is
A. Cancer B. Tumour
C. Ulcer D. Tuberculosis (TB)

11. The book 'The poor and their money' is written by
A. Rutherford B. Amartya Sen
C. Yunis Khan D. Davis

12. What is the sex-ratio of women as per 2001 census ?
A. 927 per thousand
B. 923 per thousand
C. 933 per thousand
D. 930 per thousand

13. Match the scientific words given in List-I with the nature of their focus of study given in List-II.

List-I	List-II
(I) Ecology	(1) Study of Crime
(II) Gerontology	(2) Study of Diseases
(III) Criminology	(3) Study of Environment
(IV) Epidemiology	(4) Study of Older People

Codes :

	(I)	(II)	(III)	(IV)
A.	(3)	(4)	(2)	(1)
B.	(1)	(2)	(3)	(4)
C.	(1)	(2)	(4)	(3)
D.	(3)	(4)	(1)	(2)

14. Assertion (A): Certain children need special care and support.
Reason (R) : State offers services to orphaned and destitute children.

A. Both (A) and (R) are correct and (R) is the correct explanation of (A).
B. Both (A) and (R) are correct but (R) is not the correct explanation of (A).
C. Both (A) and (R) are wrong.
D. (A) is correct but (R) is wrong.

15. Assertion (A): Tribals are yet to be integrated into mainstream of the society.
Reason (R) : Tribals want to maintain their identity and culture.

Codes :
A. Both (A) and (R) are wrong.
B. Both (A) and (R) are correct and (R) is the correct explanation of (A).
C. Both (A) and (R) are correct and (R) is not the correct explanation of (A).
D. (A) is wrong and (R) is correct.

16. Match the following organizations given in List-I with the professional Journals they are publishing given in List-II.

List-I	List-II
(I) NIRD	(1) Perspectives in Social Work
(II) TISS	(2) Contemporary Social Work
(III) University of Lucknow	(3) Indian Journal of Social Work
(IV) Nirmala Niketan (Mumbai)	(4) Journal of Rural Development

Codes :

	(a)	(b)	(c)	(d)
A.	(2)	(3)	(1)	(4)
B.	(4)	(3)	(2)	(1)
C.	(1)	(2)	(4)	(3)
D.	(3)	(1)	(4)	(2)

17. Assertion (A): Indian Government has initiated adequate measures for protection against trafficking of women and girls.
Reason (R) : Trafficking in India is increasing and moving towards legalisation.

Choose your answer from the following :
A. Both (A) and (R) are wrong.
B. (A) is correct and (R) is wrong.

C. (A) is wrong and (R) is correct.
D. Both (A) and (R) are correct.

18. Assertion (A): Right to Education ensures to access and quality of education.

Reason (R) : No legislation can ensure quality education in India.

Choose your answer from the following :
A. Both (A) and (R) are true and (R) is the correct explanation of (A).
B. Both (A) and (R) are true and (R) is not the correct explanation of (A).
C. (A) is true, but (R) is false.
D. (A) is false, but (R) is true.

19. Assertion (A): Sustainable development is a pattern of using resources that aims to meet human needs while preserving the environment.

Reason (R) : So that these needs can be met not only in the present, but also for future generations.

Choose your answer from the following :
A. Both (A) and (R) are true and (R) is the correct explanation of (A).
B. Both (A) and (R) are true and (R) is not the correct explanation of (A).
C. (A) is true, but (R) is false.
D. (A) is false, but (R) is true.

20. Identify the correct sequence :
A. Case Study, Prognosis, Diagnosis, Treatment
B. Case Study, Diagnosis, Prognosis, Treatment
C. Prognosis, Case Study, Diagnosis, Treatment
D. Diagnosis, Prognosis, Case Study, Treatment

21. Identify the correct sequence regarding process of communication :
A. Medium, Sender, Recipient, Feedback
B. Sender, Medium, Feedback, Recipient
C. Sender, Medium, Recipient, Feedback
D. Sender, Feedback, Medium, Recipient

22. Identify the correct sequence of stages of learning during childhood development :
A. Innate abilities, Sensory and Motor Skills, Cognitive, Instructions
B. Cognitive, Instructions, Innate abilities, Sensory and Motor Skills
C. Innate abilities, Cognitive, Instructions, Sensory and Motor Skills
D. Cognitive, Innate abilities, Sensory and Motor Skills, Instructions

23. In research the data is processed in order of
A. Classification, Editing, Coding, Master-sheet
B. Coding, Editing, Classification, Master-sheet
C. Editing, Master-sheet, Coding, Classification
D. Editing, Coding, Classification, Master-sheet

24. Identify right sequence of declarations made in the Indian Constitution :
A. Sovereign, Socialist, Secular, Democratic, Republic
B. Sovereign, Secular, Socialist, Democratic, Republic
C. Sovereign, Socialist, Secular, Republic, Democratic
D. Sovereign, Democratic, Socialist, Secular, Republic

25. Which one of the following programmes are not based on Affirmative Action Policies?
A. Programmes to meet economic needs of poor.
B. Specific programmes for the development of Scheduled Castes.
C. Programmes for Industrial Growth.
D. Programmes for the Welfare of Women.

26. Assertion (A): The role of professional social worker is empowering and capacity building of the oppressed and marginalized sections of society.

Reason (R) : Professional social workers have requisite skill and sensitivity to deal with the problems of such sections of society.

Codes :
A. Both (A) and (R) are correct and (R) is the explanation of (A).
B. Both (A) and (R) are not correct.
C. (A) is correct, but (R) is wrong.
D. (A) is not correct, but (R) is correct.

27. Accountability in governance refers to
A. the ability of citizens to hold leaders, government and public organisations to account.
B. the ability of citizens to open accounts in the bank.
C. the national income account that show profit and loss of the government.
D. the behaviour of chartered accountants in corporate banks.

28. Panchayati Raj institutes in India have brought about which one of the following ?
A. Eradication of untouchability.
B. Spread of land ownership to depressed classes.
C. Formal representation of the weaker sections in village governance.
D. Spread of education to the masses.

29. Which article of Indian Constitution lays down the provision of free and compulsory education for children?
A. 45 B. 46
C. 47 D. 48

30. Probation means :
A. Release on licence
B. Release on bail
C. Conditional suspension of punishment
D. Suspension of punishment

31. Consider the following statements and select your answer according to codes given below:
Assertion (A): Social Workers working with minorities requires the knowledge and indepth understanding of the effects of oppression on minority groups.
Reason (R) : Social Workers are duty bound to serve the oppressed and marginalized.

Codes :
A. Both (A) and (R) are true and (R) is the correct explanation of (A).
B. Both (A) and (R) are true and (R) is not the correct explanation of (A).
C. (A) is true, but (R) is not true.
D. (A) is not true, but (R) is true.

32. Report on Correctional Administration 1951 (Government of India) was prepared by
A. Justice A.N. Mullah
B. Bureau of Police Research and Development
C. Sir Alexander Cardew
D. Dr. W.C. Reckless

33. The First Model Prism Manual was prepared in the year
A. 1919 B. 1959
C. 1943 D. 2001

34. Social work intervention with Elderly does not include
A. Providing psychosocial support
B. Arranging for treatment of health problems
C. Guiding group interaction
D. Distribution of clothes and sweets

35. Match the following :

List-I	List-II
(a) Adjusting to marriage partner	(i) Young adulthood
(b) Maintaining stable job	(ii) Mental deficiency
(c) Genetic disorder	(iii) Middle years
(d) Consistent career achievement	(iv) Late adulthood

Codes :

	(a)	(b)	(c)	(d)
A.	(iv)	(iii)	(ii)	(i)
B.	(i)	(ii)	(iii)	(iv)
C.	(ii)	(i)	(iv)	(iii)
D.	(iii)	(iv)	(i)	(ii)

36. The major principles of social group work are
A. progressive programme experience, guiding group interaction, specific objectives, evaluation

B. Programme planning, development sequence, systematic study, frequency distribution
C. Group enhancement, specific learning, rejection study, development
D. Planning, organising, facilitation, evaluation

37. Parenting has become challenging because of
A. Disintegration of joint family system
B. Migration of rural population to urban areas
C. Women getting into gainful employment
D. All of the above

38. Consider the following statements and select your answer according to codes below :
Assertion (A): Jan Shikshan Sansthan provides vocational training courses to the marginalized for their empowerment.
Reason (R) : Inclusion of SC and ST is emphasized as beneficiaries in Jan Shikshan Sansthan due to their disadvantaged position.
A. Both (A) and (R) are true.
B. Both (A) and (R) are not true.
C. (A) is true and (R) is false.
D. (A) is false and (R) is true.

39. Behaviour that is contrary to the standards of conduct or social expectations of a group or society, is defined by
A. Elliot and Merill
B. Fuller and Myers
C. Louise Weston
D. Ogburne

40. One of the following theories propounds childhood experiences influence the adult behaviour:
A. Person-Centred theory
B. Behaviour modification theory
C. Psychoanalytic theory
D. Existential theory

41. A declarative statement of relationship between or among variables is called
A. Concept B. Value
C. Hypothesis D. None of the above

42. The extent of difference between population parameters and the sample statistic is called
A. Sampling error B. Statistic
C. Sampling bias D. None of the above

43. Quartile deviation is also known as
A. Range
B. Mode
C. Semi-inter quartile range
D. None of these

44. The time interval between invasion by an infectious agent and appearance of first sign or symptom of the disease in question is called
A. Quarantine
B. Inoculation
C. Incubation period
D. None of the above

45. Find the mode of following marks obtained by 10 students : 10, 6, 11, 8, 9, 11, 7, 11, 12 and 10.
A. 12 B. 8.5
C. 11 D. None of the above

46. Quota sampling is the method of
A. Non-probability sampling
B. Area sampling
C. Simple random sampling
D. The lottery method

47. Emotional insulation is
A. covering himself from physical threats.
B. involves the justification for inappropriate behaviour.
C. a maneuver aimed at withholding an emotional investment in a desired but unlikely outcome.
D. involves the use of abstractions as a way of avoiding feelings and distancing one's self from emotional pain.

48. Cone of the layers protecting environment from ultraviolet rays is
(i) Ozone (ii) Ionosphere
(iii) Stratosphere (iv) Troposphere

Codes :
A. Only (i) is correct.
B. (ii) and (iii) are correct.

C. (iii) and (iv) are correct
D. None of them is correct.

49. Gender is defined as
I. A social construct
II. A biological difference
III. An achieved status
IV. An ascribed status

Codes :
A. I is correct.
B. I and II are correct.
C. I, II and III are correct.
D. All are correct.

50. The various types of measurement are
A. Nominal, Ordinal, Interval and Ratio.
B. Nominal, Interval, Likert and Ratio.
C. Thurstone, TAT, Likert and Social Distance Scale.
D. Ratio, Proportions, Statistics and Data.

51. Epistemology refers to
A. a software package
B. acceptable knowledge in a field of study
C. a statistical test
D. a form of inter viewing

52. What is the proper sequence of the following?
(i) Rehabilitation
(ii) Immunization and awareness generation
(iii) Early detection and treatment
(iv) Disability limitation

Codes :
A. (iv), (iii), (ii), (i)
B. (i), (ii), (iii), (iv)
C. (ii), (iii), (iv), (i)
D. (iii), (ii), (i), (iv)

53. The statement that 'As variable A changes, there will be corresponding change in variable B', demonstrates what kind of relationship among variables ?
A. Linear B. Curvilinear
C. Causal D. Power

54. Who among the following is associated with Gestalt therapy ?
A. C.R. Rogers B. Sigmund Freud
C. B.F. Skinner D. F. Perl

55. One of the following is not a part of Memorandum of Association.
I. Name of the society
II. Address of the registered office
III. Objects of the society
IV. Logo of the society

Codes :
A. I, II and III B. II, III and IV
C. III, IV and I D. IV, I and II

56. What types of evidence can only be given to a court by an expert ?
A. The oath B. Opinion
C. Photographs D. Hearsay

57. The values of Mean, Median and Mode are equal :
A. in a normal distribution
B. in a skewed distribution
C. in a binominal distribution
D. in a abnormal distribution

58. Which *one* of the following is **not** a research design?
A. Exploratory B. Descriptive
C. Experimental D. Social Survey

59. The sampling plan which more accurately reflects the characteristics of the population from which the sample is chosen ?
A. Snowball Sampling
B. Stratified Random Sampling
C. Accidental Sampling
D. Convenient Sampling

60. The mental Health Program was adopted in India in the year :
A. 1987 B. 1980
C. 1982 D. 1990

61. Juvenile Justice (Care and Protection) Act was enacted in the year :
A. 1990 B. 1996
C. 1998 D. 2000

62. Which is the International Voluntary Organizing Promoting the Pulse Polio Program?
A. Oxfam International
B. Action Aid International

C. Rotary International
D. Care International

63. Match the following :

List-I (Event)	List-II (Date of observance)
(a) World Consumer Day	(i) Oct 24th
(b) International Literacy Day	(ii) Sept. 8th
(c) World Mental Health Day	(iii) Oct 10th
(d) UN Day	(iv) March 15th

Codes :

	(a)	(b)	(c)	(d)
A.	(iv)	(ii)	(iii)	(i)
B.	(iii)	(iv)	(ii)	(i)
C.	(i)	(iii)	(iv)	(ii)
D.	(i)	(iv)	(iii)	(ii)

65. Match the items in List-I with List-II and choose the correct code given below :

List-I	List-II
(a) Oral stage	(i) Trust *V/s* Mistrust
(b) Anal stage	(ii) Industry *V/s* Inferiority
(c) Genital stage	(iii) Autonomy *V/s* Shame & Doubt
(d) Latency	(iv) Initiative *V/s* Guilt

Codes :

	(a)	(b)	(c)	(d)
A.	(ii)	(iv)	(i)	(iii)
B.	(iii)	(ii)	(iv)	(i)
C.	(i)	(iv)	(iii)	(ii)
D.	(i)	(iii)	(iv)	(ii)

65. Assertion (A): Inspite of best efforts Sarva Shiksha Abhiyan failed to achieve desirable literacy rate.

Reason (R) : Results can be achieved without political will.

Codes :

A. Both (A) and (R) are correct.
B. Both (A) and (R) are not correct.
C. (A) is correct and (R) is correct explanation of (A).
D. (A) is correct but (R) is not the correct explanation of (A).

66. Assertion (A): Goitre is a common disease in mountainous regions.

Reason (R) : The diet of the people in mountainous regions lack iodine content.

Codes :

A. Both (A) and (R) are true, but (R) is not the correct explanation of (A).
B. (A) is true, but (R) is false.
C. Both (A) and (R) are true and (R) is the correct explanation of (A).
D. Both (A) and (R) are false.

68. Assertion (A): Due to strong family ties, women in India sacrifice for their family.

Reason (R) : It is a product of social conditioning.

Codes :

A. Both (A) and (R) are true and (R) is correct explanation of (A).
B. Both (A) and (R) are true but (R) is not the correct explanation of (A).
C. (A) is true but (R) is false.
D. (R) is true, but (A) is false.

69. Assertion (A): Disaster affected population can take care of their emotional and psychological needs with their own resources.

Reason (R) : The strong sociocultural traditions are powerful support in such situation.

Codes :

A. Both (A) and (R) are true, but (R) is not the correct explanation of (A).
B. (A) is true, but (R) is false.
C. Both (A) and (R) are true and (R) is the correct explanation of (A).
D. Both (A) and (R) are false.

69. Assertion (A): The goal of Social Work Education is to train manpower to tackle the intricate realities of threatening, situations and enable victims of undeserved want to recover to normalcy with their own effort.

Reason (R) : While social work professionals develop their expertise in professional intervention from training, they appear to work in isolation hence cannot standardise the techniques of intervention.

A. (A) is correct and (R) is wrong
B. (A) is correct but (R) is not the correct explanation of (A)
C. Both (A) and (R) are wrong
D. Both (A) and (R) are correct

70. Assertion (A) : A Clique is a nuisance to organisational environment.

Reason (R) : A Cliche' leads to stagnation of group interests.

A. Both (A) and (R) are correct but (R) is not an the correct interpretation of (A)
B. (A) is correct but (R) is wrong
C. Both (A) and (R) are correct and (R) is a correct interpretation of (A)
D. (A) is wrong and (R) is correct

71. Assertion (A) : As per principle of human growth and development "Earlier development is conducive to later development".

Reason (R) : An unresolved Oedipus Complex is an outcome of emotional deprivation in early childhood.

A. Both (A) and (R) are correct but (R) is not the correct interpretation of (A)
B. Both (A) and (R) are correct and (R) is the correct interpretation of (A)
C. (A) is correct but (R) is wrong
D. Both (A) and (R) are wrong

72. Social development has failed to make appreciable headway in India. The most common reason is :

A. Corruption
B. Absence of trained manpower
C. Unwilling beneficiaries
D. Absence of resources

73. Strategies for achieving social development objectives include :

A. Growth with equity
B. Minimum Needs Programme
C. Neither of the above
D. Both of the above

74. Medical Termination of Pregnancy Act was passed in the year:

A. 1971 B. 1961
C. 1978 D. 1981

75. The tenth Five Year Plan period is :

A. 2000-2005
B. 2002-2007
C. 2003-2008
D. 2004-2009

76. Which among the following is not a characteristic of culture ?

A. Culture is social
B. Culture is adaptive
C. Culture is inborn
D. Culture is a complex whole

77. Assertion (A) : Gandhiji formulated 'Constructive Programme' for the upliftment of the rural poor.

Reason (R) : To lead India to political independence.

A. Both (A) and (R) are correct and (R) is the correct explanation of (A)
B. Both (A) and (R) are correct. (R) is not the correct explanation of (A)
C. (A) is false but (R) is correct
D. (A) is correct but (R) is false

78. International year of the Disabled Persons was in the year :

A. 1971 B. 1981
C. 1991 D. 2001

79. Point out the option not associated with Sarvodaya:

A. The well being of all in all phases of life
B. Social Reconstruction
C. Swarajya and Lokniti
D. Political and administrative consolidation of a country

80. Provision of drinking water facility fulfills women's :

A. Strategic need
B. Practical need

C. Immediate need
D. Longterm need

81. Match the items in List-I with items in the List-II select the correct answer using the codes:

List-I	List-II
(a) 15th June	(i) World Alzhemier's Day
(b) 12th January	(ii) Women's Day
(c) 8th March	(iii) National Youth Day
(d) 21st September	(iv) World's AIDS Day
	(v) World Elder Abuse Day

Codes :

	(a)	(b)	(c)	(d)
A.	(v)	(iii)	(ii)	(i)
B.	(iii)	(v)	(ii)	(iv)
C.	(ii)	(iv)	(v)	(iii)
D.	(iii)	(i)	(v)	(ii)

82. 'Operation Black Board' refers to :
A. Improvement of non-formal education in villages
B. Improvement of basic facilities in primary schools
C. Improvement of Education of girls
D. Improvement of Vocational education

83. Approach where social worker serves clients and situations using variety of technique and levels of interventions is :
A. Generalist perspective
B. Ecosystem perspective
C. General systems perspective
D. Strengths perspective

84. Arrange the following parts of a Table in sequence :
(i) Stub
(ii) Caption
(iii) Title of the table
(iv) Table number and
(v) Body of the table

A.	(i)	(ii)	(iii)	(iv)	(v)
B.	(iv)	(iii)	(ii)	(i)	(v)
C.	(v)	(iv)	(iii)	(ii)	(i)
D.	(ii)	(iii)	(iv)	(i)	(v)

85. Putting oneself in the shoes of another person and understanding his/her perceptual world is :
A. Empathy
B. Positive Regard
C. Genuiness
D. None of the above

86. To link a client with an agency, programme or professional person that can provide the service needed by the client is called :
A. Referral
B. Consent for release
C. Problem Checklist
D. Person-in-environment configuration

87. Right to Information Act was passed in the year :
A. 2006 B. 2004
C. 2005 D. 2003

88. What among the following best describes 'Projection' ?
A. Seeing others as responsible for one's own shortcomings or unacceptable behaviour
B. Excluding threatening and painful experiences from one's consciousness
C. Denying realities by refusing to acknowledge them
D. None of the above

89. Consider the following statements and select your answer according to the codes given below :

Assertion (A): Professional Social Work has not taken root in India.

Reason (R) : People are too poor to pay for the services.

A. Both (A) and (R) are true and (R) is the explanation of (A).
B. Both (A) and (R) are not true
C. (A) is true but (R) is false
D. (A) is not true but (R) is true

90. Society in sociological terms is understood to mean :
A. A group of refined people
B. An organisation to undertake some constructive activities
C. A web of relationships
D. An association to honour scholarship

91. Which one of the following is the correct statement regarding social change as a concept ?
A. Social change has a direction
B. Social change is controlled
C. Social change is structured
D. Social change is value neutral

92. Which one of the following shows the correct evolutionary order in which various types of societies emerged ?
A. Tribal, rural, urban
B. Tribal, urban, rural
C. Urban, rural, tribal
D. Rural, tribal, urban

93. Which one of the following does not feature of the Indian constitution ?
A. Federal structure
B. Unitary government
C. Separation of judiciary
D. Fundamental rights of the citizens

94. Who among the following is associated with Gestalt therapy?
A. C.R. Rogers B. Sigmund Freud
C. Perls and Perls D. B.F. Skinner

95. Trickle down theory of development holds that :
A. Global prosperity spreads to domestic economy.
B. Development spreads downwards through greater demand for labour.
C. Rate of growth of economy is inversely proportional to the rates of taxation.
D. None of the above.

96. UN principles for older persons come into force in the year
A. 1990 B. 1999
C. 1981 D. 1991

97. Decision-making means
A. Choosing among alterations
B. Choosing among alternatives
C. Choosing for allocations
D. All the above

98. Which of the following is not a principle of group work ?
A. Progressive programme experience
B. Specific objectives
C. Group experiment planning
D. Continuous evaluation

99. Team building involves
A. Recognizing active members of the team.
B. Recognizing those members who contribute for the growth of the team.
C. Recognizing all the members of the team.
D. Recognizing knowledgeable members of the team.

100. The ultimate goal of Women's Self Help Group is
A. Saving money
B. Taking loans
C. Getting revolving fund
D. Empowerment

101. The full form of MDP is
A. Mean Democratic Participation
B. Major Development Project
C. Methods Development Plan
D. Manic Depressive Psychosis

102. Main source of India's Social Policy is
A. Social Legislation
B. Five Year Plans
C. Directive Principles of State Policy
D. None of the above

103. Grape-wine communication relates to
A. Formal communication
B. Informal communication
C. Upward communication
D. Downward communication

104. Arrange in right sequence :
A. Tabulation, Data entry, Scrutiny
B. Scrutiny, Data entry, Tabulation

C. Data entry, Scrutiny, Tabulation
D. Tabulation, Scrutiny, Data entry

105. Match the pairs :

(a) Jane Addams	(i) Social Development
B. Harleigh Trecker	(ii) Problem-solving model
C. M.S. Gore	(iii) Methods of social work
D. H.H. Perlman	(iv) Social group work

Codes :

	(a)	(b)	(c)	(d)
A.	(i)	(ii)	(iv)	(iii)
B.	(iv)	(iii)	(i)	(ii)
C.	(iii)	(iv)	(i)	(ii)
D.	(ii)	(iii)	(iv)	(i)

106. Match the pairs :

(a) "Jo Hari window"	(i) Mechanism of defense
B. Regression	(ii) Insecurity
C. Atoning for reality	(iii) Threatening reality
D. Thumb sucking	(iv) "Known to others : unknown to self"

Codes :

	(a)	(b)	(c)	(d)
A.	(ii)	(i)	(iv)	(iii)
B.	(i)	(iii)	(iv)	(ii)
C.	(iii)	(ii)	(i)	(iv)
D.	(iv)	(iii)	(i)	(ii)

107. The author of the book 'Why Survive ? Being old in America' is :
A. Amartya Sen
B. Phillipson, C
C. Butler, R. N
D. Margaret Mead

108. The data generated by using observation methods is :
A. Secondary data
B. Primary data
C. Meta analysis
D. Text analysis

109. Identify the correct sequence :
A. Radical social work, Social diagnosis, Unitary approach
B. Social diagnosis, Unitary approach, Radical social work
C. Unitary approach, Radical social work, Social diagnosis
D. Unitary approach, Social diagnosis, Radical social work

110. The degree to which an instrument really measures what it claims to measure is called:
A. Construct B. Delimitation
C. Validity D. Reliability

111. When was the All India Trade Union Congress formed ?
A. 1919 B. 1920
C. 1921 D. 1922

112. The Law of three stages of social development was originally propounded by :
A. Karl marx B. Talcott Parsons
C. Auguste Compte D. Herbert Spencer

113. **Assertion (A):** Conflicts arise due to misperceived messages.

Reason (R) : Communication always creates conflicts.

Codes :
A. (A) is correct but (R) is wrong.
B. Both (A) and (R) are correct.
C. (A) is wrong but (R) is correct.
D. Both (A) and (R) are wrong.

114. **Assertion (A):** Urbanization leads to the conglomeration of population.

Reason (R) : Urbanization makes people 'nomadic'.

Codes :
A. Both (A) and (R) are correct.
B. Both (A) and (R) are wrong.
C. (A) is wrong but (R) is correct.
D. (A) is correct but (R) is wrong.

115. Match the following persons (List-I) with the movements they headed (List-II).

List-I (Person)	List-II (Movement)
(I) Medha Patkar	(1) Right to Information
(II) Sundarlal Bahuguna	(2) Bhrashtrachar Nirmulan Andolan
(III) Arundathi Roy	(3) Chipco Movement
(IV) Anna Hazare	(4) Narmada Bachao Andolan

Codes :

	(I)	(II)	(III)	(III)
A.	(4)	(3)	(1)	(2)
B.	(4)	(3)	(2)	(1)
C.	(3)	(4)	(2)	(1)
D.	(2)	(3)	(1)	(4)

116. **Assertion (A):** Indian Constitution provides equity and social justice.

Reason (R) : Protection is available against discrimination and exploitation.

Codes :

A. Both (A) and (R) are wrong.
B. (A) is correct and (R) is wrong.
C. (A) is wrong and (R) is correct.
D. Both (A) and (R) are correct.

117. Match the following with their proponents :

List-I	List-II
(I) Psychoanalytical theory	(1) Skinner
(II) Insight Learning theory	(2) Thorndike
(III) Operant Learning theory	(3) Kohler
(IV) Trial and Error Learning theory	(4) Sigmund Freud

Codes :

	(I)	(II)	(III)	(IV)
A.	(3)	(1)	(4)	(2)
B.	(4)	(3)	(1)	(2)
C.	(1)	(2)	(3)	(4)
D.	(2)	(3)	(4)	(1)

118. Social Policy does **not** aim to achieve :

A. Equality
B. Social Justice
C. Eradication of disparity
D. Population growth in India

119. The Employees State Insurance Act was enacted in the year :

A. 1942 B. 1944
C. 1947 D. 1948

120. Which of the following is **not** a social legislation?

A. The Protection of Civil Rights Act
B. The Beggars Act
C. The Hindu Marriage Act
D. The Forest Conservation Act

121. Match List-I with List-II :

List-I	List-II
A. Free Association	(i) Carl Rogers
B. Transactional Analysis	(ii) Jacobson
C. Relaxation Therapy	(iii) Freud
D. Client Centered Therapy	(iv) Eric Berne

Codes :

	(a)	(b)	(c)	(d)
A.	(iii)	(iv)	(ii)	(i)
B.	(ii)	(iii)	(i)	(iv)
C.	(i)	(ii)	(iv)	(iii)
D.	(iv)	(i)	(iii)	(ii)

122. Who coined the term conjugal family?

A. William J. Goode
B. Murdock
C. Cooper
D. Talkot Parsons

123. Match the items of List-I with items of List-II :

List-I	List-II
(a) Patrilocal	(i) Living at brides residence
(b) Matrilocal	(ii) Having own set up
(c) Avanchulocal	(iii) Living at bride-groom's residence
(d) Neolocal	(iv) Living at brides maternal uncle's residence

Codes :

	(a)	(b)	(c)	(d)
A.	(iii)	(i)	(iv)	(ii)
B.	(iii)	(ii)	(iv)	(i)
C.	(iii)	(i)	(ii)	(iv)
D.	(iv)	(iii)	(ii)	(i)

124. One of the following is not the reason for single parent families :

A. Death B. Divorce
C. Desertion D. Transfer

125. Probation services entail –

A. Leniency in correctional services
B. Institutional services
C. Community based treatment of offenders
D. Letting off of offender

126. Which of the following is not an intervention method in the correctional setting?

A. Group work and group therapy
B. Social case work
C. Entertaining guests
D. Family-centred counselling

127. Consider the following statements and select your answer according to codes below :

Assertion (A): Social defence is a broad concept that aims at defending society against crime by re-integrating the offenders back into the society.

Reason (R) : Social defence attempts to prevent the emergence of criminogenic situations through preventive programmes.

A. Both (A) and (R) are true.
B. Both (A) and (R) are not true.
C. (A) is true and (R) is false.
D. (A) is false and (R) is true.

128. Which one of the following is not a challenge of managing urbanization?

A. Sustaining the momentum of economic growth.
B. Addressing urban poverty.
C. Energizing cities to become engines of national development.
D. Separating rural from urban areas.

ANSWERS

1	2	3	4	5	6	7	8	9	10
B	B	B	A	C	C	D	B	B	D
11	**12**	**13**	**14**	**15**	**16**	**17**	**18**	**19**	**20**
A	C	D	A	B	B	B	C	A	B
21	**22**	**23**	**24**	**25**	**26**	**27**	**28**	**29**	**30**
C	A	A	A	C	A	A	C	A	C
31	**32**	**33**	**34**	**35**	**36**	**37**	**38**	**39**	**40**
A	D	B	D	A	A	D	A	C	C
41	**42**	**43**	**44**	**45**	**46**	**47**	**48**	**49**	**50**
C	A	C	C	C	A	C	A	A	A
51	**52**	**53**	**54**	**55**	**56**	**57**	**58**	**59**	**60**
B	C	B	D	A	B	A	D	B	C
61	**62**	**63**	**64**	**65**	**66**	**67**	**68**	**69**	**70**
D	C	A	D	D	C	A	C	B	B
71	**72**	**73**	**74**	**75**	**76**	**77**	**78**	**79**	**80**
B	A	D	A	B	C	A	B	D	B
81	**82**	**83**	**84**	**85**	**86**	**87**	**88**	**89**	**90**
A	B	A	B	A	A	C	A	A	C

91	92	93	94	95	96	97	98	99	100
D	A	B	C	B	D	B	C	C	D
101	**102**	**103**	**104**	**105**	**106**	**107**	**108**	**109**	**110**
D	C	B	B	C	D	C	B	B	C
111	**112**	**113**	**114**	**115**	**116**	**117**	**118**	**119**	**120**
B	C	A	A	A	D	B	D	D	D
121	**122**	**123**	**124**	**125**	**126**	**127**	**128**		
A	A	A	D	C	C	A	D		

➤➤➤➤➤

CHAPTER

9

Social Justice

CONCEPT OF SOCIAL JUSTICE

Justice is the hallmark of any civilized society. The term justice is too broad having no precise definition (Dias; 1985). The nature, form, methods and systems of justice vary depending upon the values and norms of a society. These systems of justice broadly have two approaches:

- Protective—safeguarding people against abuse and exploitation
- Promotive—creating such conditions in society as may spontaneously ensure equality, freedom, fraternity and provide special opportunities to those who for some reason lag behind and are out of the mainstream.

The term 'justice' is used in two senses:

- The abstract—referring to a code of conduct, legal as well as moral, which promotes people's welfare,
- The concrete—denoting the faithful implementation of existing laws Justice gives rise to a sense of duty and concern for others, as well as creates and sustains trust and confidence among people. Not only does it generate an atmosphere of peace and calmness, but it also sustains law and order thereby optimizing the personal and social functioning.

Social Justice impels to establish a just social order by favouring the removal of structural and systemic inequalities in order to ensure equalization of opportunities to weaker and vulnerable sections of society, who either because of being subjected to social suppression and oppression or being the victims of varied kinds of disabilities and handicaps, are prone to be misused and even abused and exploited. Thus, social justice, in its narrowest sense, means rectification of injustice in personal relations of people and in broader terms refer to the removal of imbalances in the political, economic and social life of people.

Social justice, according to Justice Krishna Iyer (1980), is a generous concept assuring every member of society a fair deal—remedial of injury, injustice, inadequacy or disability suffered by a member for which he is not directly responsible.

Our country is characterized by fairly widespread and serious problems of unemployment, poverty, illiteracy, ill-health and insanitation and ignorance. Our country is committed to promote welfare and justice to its people; Article 38 of the Constitution of India proclaims our commitment to promote the welfare of people by securing and protecting as effectively, a social order in which justice—social, economic and political—are preserved.

The specific objectives of social justice are to:

- Ensure the 'rule of law'
- Guarantee 'equality of opportunity'
- Ensure special opportunities to weaker and vulnerable sections

- Ensure equality of outcome
- Prevent abuse and exploitation of weaker and vulnerable sections
- Preserve the religion and culture of minorities, providing them the necessary freedom to pursue and propagate them without endangering public order and peace.

Wherever discrimination, abuse and exploitation existed in the name of color, caste or creed, some kind of arrangement for social justice spontaneously evolved; e.g. in India, where social stratification and discrimination in the form of caste prevails, the Constitution of India assigned special privileges to Scheduled Castes and Scheduled Tribes as well as the 'Other Backward Classes' in the form of fundamental rights and other Constitutional safeguards.

LAW

A law in general is a regime of adjusting relations and ordering human behaviour through the force of a socially organized group.

Characteristics of Law

- Law is an attribute of human beings and is found only when groups of such beings have associated and organized themselves into a political society.
- It is concerned with what a man should or must do in particular circumstances and with what is to happen if he deviates beyond the permitted limits of conduct.
- It is concerned with regulating human relations defining permissible and non permissible conduct.

SOCIAL LEGISLATION

Society is a union of individual units existing together for the fulfilment of the multiple needs. This implies the existence of mutual dependence. Yet society forms itself into various groups with power to exploit the less powerful group. As society became more and more complex it is necessary for state to intervene in between these groups to ensure justice and equality. Therefore, social legislations are introduced to protect the social groups from one another. Thus, Social legislation especially in a democratic society should be living force, an adjustable instrument satisfying a requirement of ever-changing society.

Social legislations may be defined as laws designed to retain and strengthen positive human institutions and to reduce the occurrence of socially harmful behaviour.

According to Oliver Wendell "Legislation of today serves the need of yesterday". Legislations calculated to bridge the gulf between the existing laws and the current needs of the society may be called social legislation.

Objectives of Social Legislation

- To establish order and provide justice as well as security
- To anticipate social needs and provides for changes in social order
- To help in creating a new/just social order

CIVIL RIGHTS

Civil rights are the rights acquired by an individual by being a citizen or automatic entitlement to certain freedoms conferred by law or customs. The civil rights are provided to us by the Constitutions as fundamental rights.

Right to Equality

- **Article 14 :** Equality before law and equal protection of law
- **Article 15 :** Discrimination will not take place against religion, race, caste, sex, place of birth or any of them
- **Article 16 :** Equality of opportunity in matter of public employment
- **Article 17 :** Abolition of untouchability
- **Article 18 :** Abolition of titles

Right to Freedom

- **Article 19 :** Freedom of speech and expression

- **Article 20 :** Protection in respect of conviction for offences
- **Article 21 :** Protection of life and personal liberty
- **Article 21A :** Right to education
- **Article 22 :** Protection against certain arrest and detention in some cases

Right against Exploitation

- **Article 23 :** Prohibits discrimination against traffic in human beings and beggar
- **Article 24 :** Prohibits the employment of child labour in factories, mines and other hazardous job

Right to Freedom of Religion

- **Article 25 :** All persons are equally entitled to freedom of conscience and the right to freely propagate religion
- **Article 26 :** Freedom to manage religious programs
- **Article 27 :** Prohibits taxes on religious ground and freedom to spread any religion
- **Article 28 :** Freedom to attend religious instructions in educational institutes

Cultural and Educational Rights

- **Article 29 :** Protection of needs of minorities
- **Article 30 :** Clears the minority rights to establish their own educational institutions

Right to Constitutional Remedies

- **Article 32:** The right to move the supreme court in case of their violation. At the time of framing the constitution, Dr. B.R. Ambedkar had described the provision under article 32 as the very soul and heart of the Constitution.

HUMAN RIGHTS

Man has been waging an eternal war for the recognition of his rights from very early times. But his fight for the increasing recognition of rights became intense only after the eighteenth century. **The French Revolution** (1789) was based on the abstract rights of man whereas **The Glorious Revolution** in England (1688) was based on the customary rights of the people of that country. The French Revolution itself was the result of the conditions which were prevailing in that country at that time, but its slogan was liberty, equality and fraternity, the three abstract principles of universal application. The glorious revolution was on the other hand, simply a reassertion of the historic liberties of the Englishman.

While the Glorious Revolution in the England and French Revolution stirred the minds of man in regard to their social and political rights, **The Russian Revolution** made an important contribution in the matter of economic rights. The Soviet Declaration aimed eradicating the canker of economic inequality which makes a mockery of social and political rights. The Declaration seeks to achieve economic equality by abolishing the institution of private property by nationalizing all the means of production and conducting them in conformity with national economic plan. These three revolutions in the different part of the world have laid the foundation of Universal Declaration of the Human Rights.

Universal Declaration of the Rights of Man

An event of epoch-making importance is the universal declaration of the rights of man passed by the Paris session of the General Assembly of the UNO on December 10, 1948.

The Economic and Social council appointed an eighteen member commission of human rights with **Mrs. Eleanor Roosevelt** as its chairman in January 1947. After thorough discussion, the Declaration, in its final form was presented to the General Assembly of the UNO in the autumn of 1948 for approval. On the night of December 10, 1948 it was finally adopted. It contains a preamble and thirty articles.

The Rights of Man

The following are some of the Rights embedded in the Declaration:

- **The Right to Life**: The most fundamental of all rights is the right to life on which the superstructure of other rights can be built. A state which does not safeguard this minimum right is not worth its name.
- **The Right to Personal Safety**: It implies the right against cruel treatment or inhuman punishment.
- **The Right to Fair Trial and Freedom from Arbitrary Arrest**: It would mean that no individual shall be assaulted, wounded or imprisoned except by due process of law. The law of the country should treat everybody alike.
- **The Right to Freedom of Movement**: It would mean the power of locomotion, of changing one's situation or removing one's person to whatever place one's own inclination may direct, without imprisonment or restraint, except by due process of law.
- **The Right To Nationality**
- **The Right of Asylum from Political Persecution**: As in the case of the Tibetanes, to seek asylum in a foreign country to escape persecution by the Chinese.
- **The Right to Own Property**
- **The Right to Freedom of Thought, Conscience and Religion**: It would imply that subject to public order, morality and health, every person is equally entitled to freedom of conscience and the right freely to profess, practice and propagate religion.
- **The Right to Freedom of Opinion and Expression**: This means the right to say or write what one chooses provided it is not intend to harm or defame of another's reputation.
- **The Right to Freedom Assembly and Association**
- **The Right to take part in the Government of Ones Country**: That is, every individual has the right to participate in the governing of his country through such rights as the right to vote. The right to stand as a candidate for elections etc.
- **The Right to Social Security**: This would imply the right to protection against unemployment, sickness, accident, etc.
- **The Right to Work, To Free Choice of Employment and to Equal Pay for Equal Work**
- **The Right to Rest and Leisure**
- **The Right to Adequate Standards of Living**
- **The Right to Education**
- **The Right to Marriage and the Right to Family**
- **The Right to Participate in the Cultural Life of the Country in which the Individual Lives.**

ISSUES OF SOCIAL JUSTICE IN INDIA : HUMAN RIGHTS WATCH REPORT 2012

- **Arbitrary and Unlawful deprivation of Life:** There are reports that government committed arbitrary or unlawful killings, including extra judicial killings of suspected criminals and insurgents, fake encounters by police and security forces in the conflicting area.
- **Disappearance:** There were reports that police throughout the country failed to file required arrest report for detained persons, resulting in hundreds of unresolved and unreported disappearance.
- **Physical Condition in the Prison:** Prison conditions were frequently did not meet international standards. Prisons are found to be severely overcrowded and food, medical care, sanitation and environmental conditions were often inadequate.
- **Arbitrary Arrest or detention:** Although law prohibits arbitrary arrest and detention but it used to happen quiet often in the country. Police also used special security laws to delay judicial review arrests. Pretrial detention was arbitrary, lengthy and

sometimes exceeded in duration of the sentence given to those convicted.

- **Denial of Fair Public Trial:** The law provides for an independent judiciary, and the government generally respected judicial independence in practice, although judicial corruption is wide spread. The judicial system was seriously over burdened and lacked modern care management system, often delaying or denying justice.
- **Use of Excessive Forces and other abuses in Internal Conflict:** During the year the countries armed forces, individual state security forces, and paramilitary forces continue to engage in armed conflict with insurgent groups in Jammu & Kashmir, in several north eastern states and with Naxalites insurgent in the central eastern part of the country.
- **Other Issues:** The other issues of human rights violation are: Use of child soldiers by insurgents, Child labour, child marriage and abuse, Political prisoners and detainees, physical abuse, punishment and torture, violence and harassment, internally displaced persons, protection of refugees, corruption and lack of transparency in government, discrimination, societal abuse and trafficking in persons.

SOCIAL DEFENCE

In an age where it is strongly advocated that criminals are not born but are created by adverse and oppressive social conditions, a concern for the protection of society, as also for promoting the interests of offender as a human person belonging to a civilized society, social defense is gaining wide currency. In its narrowest sense social defense, confines to the treatment and welfare of persons coming in conflict with law. In the broader context, it includes within its ambit the entire gamut of preventive, therapeutic and rehabilitative services to control deviance in general, and crime that may lead to social disorganization. Thus, social defense is a deliberate and organized effort made by society to defend itself against the onslaught of disruptive forces which endanger its law and order, impeding it's socio economic development. The magnitude of violation of the prevalent laws has made it essential to formulate policies and plans and organize programs to prevent illegal activities, as well as and treat and rehabilitate the offenders in order to help them contribute their best towards effective functioning of society.

Social defense includes measures to prevention and control of juvenile delinquency and crime, welfare services in prisons, aftercare services for discharged prisoners, probation services, suppression of immoral traffic, prevention of beggary and rehabilitation of beggars, prevention and control of drug abuse and alcoholism and treatment and rehabilitation of the affected. Correctional services which are part of social defense programs employ social workers as care workers, probation officers, managers of juvenile cadres, etc.

Legislations Pertaining to Social Defense

- Juvenile Justice (Care and Protection of Children) Act, 2000
- Children Act, 1960
- Suppression of Immoral Traffic in women Act, 1956
- Prevention of Begging Act, 1959

SOCIAL SECURITY

Every person wants protection against any kind of unforeseen event which may endanger his safety and threaten the continuity of his income. This security has been guaranteed to people through varied kinds of institutions. Initially, this was provided through the joint family and caste system which in the course of time is disintegrating. Especially due to rapid urbanization people are becoming highly individualistic and insecure that they don't want or not capable to provide security to fellowman by their own efforts.

Realizing that some deliberate efforts were required to ensure security, for the first time in

1935 in England, William Beveridge came forward with the idea of 'social security' as means of protection against five great giants:

- want
- disease
- ignorance
- idleness and
- squalor

The International Labour Organization (1942) defined social security "as the security that society furnishes through appropriate organization, against certain risks to which its members are exposed."

Friedlander (1963) thought social security as a program of protection provided by society against those contingencies of modern life sickness, unemployment, old age, dependence, industrial accidents and invalidism against which the individual by his own ability or foresight cannot protect him or his family.

Thus, the major characteristic features of social security are:

- It is a security deliberately provided as a matter of right, by collective efforts of people in society
- It protects people against different types of contingencies—biological, economic or even bio-economic that confront people from their birth to decay
- Such contingencies imperil the working capacity of people and disrupt the continuity of income and impair their ability to lead a decent and dignified life
- Contingencies are such that it is impossible for common people to effectively face the challenges posed by them, utilizing their own as well as their dependants' private resources.
- Such collective endeavours made may or may not require the beneficiaries to contribute nominally, for the benefits which they may avail of in case of occurrence of certain specified kinds of contingencies
- Social security benefits may be in the form of cash, kind or both
- Social security provides the necessary confidence that, benefits adequate in quality and quantity will be available whenever required.

There are three major forms of social security:

- Social insurance
- Public/social assistance, and
- Public or social services.

In **social insurance**, prospective beneficiaries are required to make some very nominal contribution for the benefits which they are given in case of occurrence of contingencies. These benefits are so decided that they may be able to cater their needs.

Public/social assistance may be given in cash and / or kind to enable people to meet the existing actual need and to lead a minimum desirable standard of living.

There is a sharp difference between public and social assistance

Public assistance is provided through the State exchequer after assessing the existing actual need and ensuring that prospective beneficiaries fulfill certain prescribed eligibility requirements—family responsibility and morality.

Social assistance is provided to indigent people considered to be eligible based on specified criteria, by some civil society organizations to enable them to satisfy their basic minimum needs.

Public/social services are made available by the state/ society to promote human/social development. Sometimes a very fine distinction is made between public and social services, the former organized and provided by the state and the latter by society through some civil society initiative.

Legislation Pertaining to Social Security

- Workman's Compensation Act, 1923
- The Employee State Insurance Act, 1948
- Employee's Family Pension Scheme, 1971
- The Employee's Deposit Linked Insurance Scheme, 1976

- Employee's Provident Funds and Miscellaneous Provision Act, 1952
- Maternity Benefit Act, 1961
- Payment of Gratuity Act, 1972

LEGISLATION PERTAINING TO WOMEN AND CHILDREN

The government of India has enacted following important legislations for women and children:

- The Immoral Traffic (Prevention) Act, 1956 (as amended in 1986)
- The Indecent Representation of Women (Prevention) Act, 1986
- The Dowry Prohibition Act, 1961 as amended in 1986
- The Commission of Sati (Prevention) Act, 1987
- The Prohibition of Child Marriage Act, 2006
- Protection of Women from Domestic Violence Act, 2005
- National Commission for Women Act, 1990
- Infant Milk substitutes, Feeding Bottles and Infant Food (Regulation of Production, Supply and Distribution) Act, 1992
- Commission for Protection of Child Rights Act, 2005
- Juvenile Justice (Care and Protection of Children) Act, 2000
- Hindu Marriage Act, 1955
- Child marriage Restraints Act, 1929
- Hindu Succession Act, 1956
- Hindu Adoption and Maintenance Act, 1956
- The Equal Remuneration Act, 1976
- Apprentice Act, 1850
- Pre Natal Diagnostic and Techniques Act, 1994

LEGISLATIONS PERTAINING TO WEAKER SECTIONS OF THE SOCIETY

- Protection of Civil Rights Act, 1955
- Bonded labour System (abolition) Act, 1976
- Representation of the Peoples Act,.1951
- Scheduled Castes and Scheduled Tribes (Prevention of atrocities) Act, 1989
- Article 338 & 338A make provision for the National Commission for Scheduled Castes and Scheduled Tribes (By virtue of 89th Constitutional amendment)
- Article 330, 332 & 334 provides special reservations for Scheduled Castes and Scheduled Tribes in the Lok Sabha and Vidhan Sabha
- Article 335 provides claim of Scheduled Castes and Scheduled Tribes to services and posts
- Article 340 provides provision for appointment of a commission to investigate the conditions of backward classes
- Three parliamentary committee have been set up to look after the conditions of Scheduled Castes and Scheduled Tribes in the year 1966, 1971 & 1973.

ACTION & LEGISLATION PERTAINING TO PEOPLE WITH DISABILITY

As per census 2001, there are 2.19 crore persons with disabilities and they constitute 2.13 per cent of the total population of the country. This includes person with visual, hearing, speech, locomotors and mental disabilities.

The Constitution of India ensures equality, freedom, justice and dignity of all individuals and implicitly mandates an inclusive society for all including the person with disabilities.

India is a signatory to the Declaration on the full participation and equality of people with disabilities in the Asia Pacific region. India is also a signatory to the Biwako Millennium Framework for action towards an inclusive and right based society. India signed the UN convention on protection and promotion of the rights and dignity of persons with disabilities on 30th March 2007.

For the marginalized section of the society, National Policy on Person with Disabilities has been finalized in 2005. The policy focuses on the prevention of disabilities, the physical and economic rehabilitation measures for disabled persons.

Persons with Disabilities Act, 1995

A comprehensive law, namely, the Person with Disabilities (Equal Opportunities, Protection of Rights and Full Participation) Act 1995 has been enacted and enforced in February 1996. The law deals with both prevention and promotion aspects of the rehabilitation such as education, employment and vocational training, creation of barrier free environment, provision of rehabilitation services for persons with disabilities, institutional services and supportive social security measures like unemployment allowance and grievance redressal machinery both at the central and state level.

ROLE OF SOCIAL WORKER IN PROMOTING SOCIAL LEGISLATION AND SOCIAL JUSTICE

There are three areas in which the professional social worker could play an effective role in implementing social legislation and bringing social justice

- Because of the grassroot level approach that they have social worker can most effectively identify prevailing social injustice in the society. He/she can bring such phenomenon in to the notice of government.
- Because of their expertise in the field and knowledge they can mobilize people to act as pressure groups and could help not only in designing and developing legislations but in the proper enforcement and implementation as well.
- Because of their deeper root in the public and professional knowledge they can assist to the government by helping the government staff as well as undertake investigation on behalf of the government.
- Social worker can undertake research studies to know the causes and consequences of the phenomenon and could recommend the possible solution of the problem.
- Social worker can also play an effective role by making public aware about the social legislations designed for them by organizing general meeting, seminars, workshops, training programs etc.

HEALTH RELATED LEGISLATIONS

- **Article 47:** The state shall regard the raising of the level of nutrition and the standard of livings of its peoplé and the improvement of public health as among its primary duties and, in particular, the state shall endeavour to bring about prohibition of drinks and of drugs which are injurious to health.
- The Prevention of Food Adulteration Act, 1954
- Drugs and Cosmetics Act, 1940
- Mental Health Act, 1987
- The Cigarette and other Tobacco (Prohibition of Advertisement and Regulation of Trade and Commerce, Production, Supply and Distribution) Act, 2003
- The Narcotic Drugs and Psychotropic Substances Act, 1985
- Maternity Benefit Act, 1961
- The Prenatal Diagnostic and Techniques (Regulation and Prevention of Misuse) Act,1994
- The Infant Milk Substitutes, Feeding Bottlers and Infant Foods (Regulation of Production, Supply and Distribution) Act, 1992
- The Child Marriage Restraints Act, 1929
- The Medical Termination of Pregnancy Act,1971
- National Health Policy, 1983, 2002
- National Population Policy, 2000
- National Blood Policy, 2003
- National Nutrition Policy, 1993

MULTIPLE CHOICE QUESTIONS

1. Field work in social work aims at
I. Development of professional skills.
II. Integration of classroom learning with field practice.
III. Development of service mentality.
IV. Development of career orientation.

Code :
A. I, II B. I, II, III
C. I, II, III, IV D. III, IV

2. The goal of social work is
A. to reduce social tensions
B. to provide services to all
C. to promote social justice
D. to service the elite

3. Arrange the following international years in the chronology of their observance (ascending order) :
I. International year of cooperatives
II. International year of forests
III. International year of youth
IV. International year of Human Rights Learning
A. I, II, III, IV B. IV, III, II, I
C. IV, III, I, II D. I, II, IV, III

4. Service rendered voluntarily by an individual or group to another individual or a group is called as
A. Professional Social Work
B. Social Development Services
C. Social Service
D. Social Reform

5. Satyasodhak Samaj was founded by
A. Dr. B.R. Ambedkar
B. Ramesh Bandari
C. Jyotiba Phule
D. Anna Hazare

6. Denotified tribes are
A. Untouchables
B. Ex-criminal tribes
C. Wandering communities
D. Artisans

7. Which of the following is not an agent of social change in India?
A. Industrialization
B. Population Growth
C. Spread of literacy
D. Sanskritization

8. Which one of the following is **not** part of group processes?
A. sub-group
B. group diagnosis
C. clique
D. isolation of a member in the group

9. Recognition of an individuals positive worth as a human being without necessarily condemning the individuals acting is termed as :
A. Recognition B. Acceptance
C. Admission D. Approval

10. Which one of the following is **not** secondary data in research?
A. Information collected from Journals
B. Information collected from Reports
C. Information collected from Respondents
D. Information collected from Websites

11. Where is the National Institute for Empowerment of persons with multiple disabilities located?
A. Chennai B. Mumbai
C. Delhi D. Hyderabad

12. Which one of the following is **not** the objective of an NGO?
A. Capacity Building
B. Awareness Building
C. Spread of Literacy
D. Profit Making

13. Who, from the following list, is **not** an environmental activist?
A. Sundarlal Bahuguna
B. Medha Patkar
C. Dr. Vandana Shiva
D. M.S. Gore

14. The statement 'caste is a closed group' is made by :
A. T.B. Bottomore
B. Andre Betelle
C. D.N. Mazumdar
D. MacIver

15. Probation of Offenders Act came into being in the year :
A. 1948 B. 1952
C. 1958 D. 1962

16. Which of the following articles in the Directive Principles of State Policy of Indian Constitution Articulates the protection of schedule caste from any form of exploitation:
A. Article 36 B. Article 46
C. Article 30 D. Article 28

17. Who gave the acronym 'POSDCORB' to list the functions of Social Welfare Administration ?
A. Amitai Etizioni
B. Luther Gullick
C. H.B. Trecker
D. Awasthi and Maheshwari

18. Bhoodan Movement started at :
A. Sabarmati Ashram
B. Vardha Ashram
C. Jaipur
D. Pochampalli

19. Who has divided Family into 'Family of Orientation' and 'Family of Procreation'?
A. Murdock B. Kapadia
C. Morgan D. Warner

20. Catharsis means
A. Ventilation
B. Psycho analysis
C. Behavioural modification
D. Problem solving

21. Which of the following is not a mechanism for settlement of Industrial Disputes in India?
A. Labour Court
B. Tribunal
C. National Tribunal
D. Standing Labour Committee

22. Deterioration of mental functions caused by the loss of nerve cells in brain is called
A. Mental retardation
B. Delirium
C. Dementia
D. Depressive neurosis

23. The Token economy is a procedure in which
A. the patients are helped to understand their home economics.
B. the patients are given understanding of economic gains.
C. the patients are given generalized conditioned reinforcer in exchange for performing certain target behaviour.
D. the patients are helped to come out of the loss they suffered due to economic crisis.

24. Cost-benefit analysis relates to
A. Analysis of profit and loss
B. Program returns
C. Analysis of income and expenditure
D. Comparison between program costs with program effects.

25. Human Poverty Index is developed by
A. World Bank B. WHO
C. UNDP D. UNICEF

26. 'Electra Complex' is a situation found in
A. Oral stage B. Annal stage
C. Phalic stage D. Latency stage

27. The first social work text that used the word 'supervision', is
A. The New Practice of Supervision and Staff Development by Abels Paul A
B. 'Group Methods in Supervision and Staff Development', by Abrahamson Arthur C
C. 'Supervision and Education in Charity', by Jeffrey R. Brackett
D. 'The MSW Supervisor : Problems of Role Transition', by Abramczyk, Lois W

28. Who among the following suggested two tier system for Panchayati Raj?
A. Balwantrai Mehta
B. Ashok Mehta

C. Vasantrao Naik
D. None of the above

29. Which of the following is not an ascribed status?
A. Age B. Caste
C. Sex D. Knowledge

30. Skewness tells us about
A. The direction of the variation or departure from symmetry
B. Amount of variation in the data
C. Estimates of the values of variables
D. The measurement of the scattered values

31. Variance is
A. Range
B. Quartile Deviation
C. Measure of Skewness
D. The average of the squared differences from the mean

32. World Elder's day observed on
A. 1st October B. 1st November
C. 1st April D. 1st May

33. Personification is
A. a method of identifying persons as a resource.
B. a technique whereby the group worker gives instructions.
C. a method of working with groups in which the group worker is presented as a model.
D. a procedure to select working participation.

34. 'Acrophobia' is the fear of
A. Water B. Place
C. Blood D. Height

35. A Researcher is generally expected to
A. study the existing literature in a field.
B. generate new principles and theories.
C. synthesize the ideas given by others.
D. All the above

36. Arrange the following Acts in order in which they were enacted :
i. The Workmen's Compensation Act
ii. The Indian Trade Unions Act
iii. The Payment of Wages Act
iv. The Industrial Employment (Standing Orders) Act Codes :

A.	i	iii	iv	ii
B.	ii	i	iii	iv
C.	i	ii	iii	iv
D.	iii	iv	ii	i

37. One of the sections of Income Tax Act that gives tax exemption to nonprofit organizations on their income is
A. 12 A B. 17 B
C. 80 G D. All the above

38. Case study is the form of
A. Subjective analysis
B. Qualitative analysis
C. Quantitative analysis
D. Objective analysis

39. An NGO is registered under :
A. Indian Penal Code
B. Society's Registration Act
C. Industrial Tribunal Act
D. ESI Act

40. The social security measures, first of all was adopted in ancient India by :
A. Kautilya B. Shukracharya
C. King Ashoka D. Harshvardhan

41. Central Social Welfare Board does not fund:
A. Holiday Homes Programmes
B. Family Counselling Centres
C. Women Hostels
D. I.C.D.S.

42. The national education policy was adopted in the year:
A. 1970 B. 1986
C. 1995 D. 2001

43. Welfare activities in rural areas are not hampered by:
A. Lack of finance
B. Lack of data on population needs
C. Absence of leadership
D. Poverty

44. Which one of the following does not directly refer to social development?
A. Process of change
B. Quality of life

C. International trade
D. Growth with justice

45. Global Human Development Index reports are brought out by :
A. UNICEF B. UNESCO
C. UNDP D. UNHCR

46. Sustainable Development's main concern centres around :
A. Poverty alleviation
B. Well being of incoming generations
C. Removal of illiteracy
D. Reduction of infant mortality rate (I.M.R.)

47. Who developed the Physical Quality of Life Index? (PQLI)
A. Richard Estes
B. D.M. Morris
C. Md. Yunus
D. Amartya Sen

48. Gender related Development Index is used in
A. Millenium Development Goals
B. World Development Report
C. Human Development Report
D. None of the above

49. Which of the following is not correct? 'A belief' becomes a 'scientific truth' when it
A. is established experimentally.
B. is arrived logically.
C. is accepted by many people.
D. can be replicated.

50. The hypothetical statements denying what are explicitly indicated in working hypothesis are known as
A. Relational hypothesis
B. Complex hypothesis
C. Statistical hypothesis
D. Null hypothesis

51. The acronym "BIMARU" represents states
A. Bihar, Madhya Pradesh, Rajasthan and U.P.
B. Bihar, Maharashtra, Ranchi and U.P.
C. Bihar, Mizoram, Rajasthan and U.P.
D. None of the above

52. Accountability in governance refers to
A. The ability of citizens to hold leaders, government and public organisations to account.
B. The ability of citizens to open accounts in banks.
C. The National income account that show profit and loss of government.
D. The behaviour of chartered accountants in the corporate world.

53. 'Glass Ceiling' is
A. A transparent surface of a building where plants are kept.
B. A transparent barrier which women face as they attempt to achieve promotion to the higher levels of organisation.
C. A place with clear surface where reptiles breed.
D. A biological problem with women during pregnancy.

54. 'Yellow revolution' is
A. A tribal custom of North-Eastern States.
B. A symbol of criticism of political decisions adopted by opposition parties.
C. The growth, development and adoption of new varieties of oil seeds and technologies to increase oil seed production.
D. A revolution to bring changes in the mind of masses for environmental concerns.

55. Biomagnification is a process
A. Where some compounds remain in the eco-system in virtually unchanged form as they are passed from one organism to another by predation.
B. When some compounds change their properties and become part of other organism.
C. Magnification of compounds with one step after the other.
D. Bio-degradation of environmental system in which some compounds continuously change their characteristics.

56. Tata Institute of Social Work was established in the year:

A. 1937 B. 1946
C. 1936 D. 1947

57. The Ecological framework for understanding person-environment relations operate with the person in centre and systems around Persons. These systems are :

(i) micro system
(ii) macro system
(iii) exo system
(iv) meso system

Arrange these system in ascending order :

A. (i) (ii) (iii) (iv)
B. (ii) (i) (iii) (iv)
C. (i) (iv) (iii) (ii)
D. (iii) (ii) (iv) (i)

58. An irrational fear and negative emotional reaction to homosexuality, their life style and identity is called :

A. Homophobia
B. Homo Sexphobia
C. Both (A) and (B)
D. None of the above

59. NABARD stands for :

A. National Agricultural Bank for Rural Development
B. National Association of Blind for Rural Development
C. National Association of Banks for Rural Development
D. None of the above

60. The 189 member states of United Nations adopted the Millenium Development Goals (MDGs) in the year :

A. 2000 B. 2001
C. 2002 D. 2003

61. Which of the following is not a means of social control?

A. Religion
B. Polity
C. Criminal Justice
D. Physical Education

62. Field work in social work training aims :

A. To practice what is being learnt
B. To know problems
C. To understand society
D. To understand theories

63. Match List-I with List-II in relation to the author and the theoretical perspective :

List-I	List-II
(a) Psychoanalysis	(i) Sigmond Freud
(b) Client Centered Therapy	(ii) Eric Berne
(c) Rational Therapy	(iii) Albert Ellis
(d) Transactional Analysis	(iv) Carl Rogers

Codes :

	(a)	(b)	(c)	(d)
A.	(iv)	(ii)	(i)	(iii)
B.	(i)	(iv)	(iii)	(ii)
C.	(ii)	(iii)	(i)	(iv)
D.	(iii)	(i)	(ii)	(iv)

64. Crisis intervention is

A. Psychological first aid
B. An event that alters the total life situation
C. A modifying form of intervention
D. Gratification of a variety of personal needs

65. The word 'grapevine' in Management refers to a type of

A. Incentives
B. Motivation technique
C. Communication technique
D. Training programme

66. Match the pairs and choose your answer from the codes given below:

List-I	List-II
(a) Cognitive Social Work	(i) Soren Kierkeygaard
(b) Existential Social Work	(ii) Robert Sunley
(c) Radical Social Work	(iii) Baily
(d) Medical Social Work	(iv) Goldstein

Codes :

	(a)	(b)	(c)	(d)
A.	(i)	(ii)	(iii)	(iv)
B.	(i)	(iii)	(ii)	(iv)
C.	(ii)	(i)	(iii)	(iv)
D.	(ii)	(iii)	(iv)	(i)

67. Who made the following statement? "Problems are unmet needs"
A. Mary Richmond
B. H.H. Perlman
C. Murray Ross
D. Yohan Galtung

68. The independent variable is also called as
A. Criterion variable
B. Predictor variable
C. Construct
D. Extraneous variable

69. In which year the publication entitled as 'Social Diagnosis' was done?
A. 1922 B. 1915
C. 1917 D. 1921

70. One of the following does not figure in the Millennium Development Goals (MDGs).
A. Eradication of extreme poverty and hunger
B. Improvement of maternal health
C. Combating HIV/AIDS, malaria and other diseases
D. Promoting good governance

71. "The Maintenance and Welfare of Parents and Senior Citizens Act" was passed in
A. 1997 B. 2006
C. 2007 D. 2004

72. One of the criticisms against Narco analysis is that :
A. It is a tentative method
B. It is not a reliable method
C. It exploits the helplessness of the subject
D. It is a risk to life

73. Casework methods are classified as :
(i) Sustaining procedures
(ii) Procedures of direct influence
(iii) Catharsis and
(iv) Reflective procedures; by :
A. Helen Harris Perlman
B. Mary Richmond
C. Florence Hollis
D. Gordon Hamilton

74. Mark the correct explanation : PORK, SOAP, SAP and STRAP are :
A. Types of casework records
B. Methods of treatment for juvenile delinquents
C. Articles of utility
D. Known shortforms

75. The author of the book 'From charity to social work' is :
A. Mary Richmond
B. Friedlander, W
C. Elizabeth. N. Agnew
D. Jane Adams

76. Programme planning in social group work should grow out of
A. Needs and interests of group members.
B. Needs of community.
C. Consultation with leaders
D. None of the above

77. Assertion (A): Right to education makes provision that every child has right to get education.

Reason (R): Private schools are also responsible for giving education to poor children.

Codes :
A. Both (A) and (R) are correct, but (R) is not the correct explanation of (A).
B. (A) is wrong but (R) is correct.
C. (A) is correct but (R) is wrong.
D. Both (A) and (R) are correct, (R) is the correct explanation of (A).

78. Assertion (A): Health, education and income are the indicators used for measuring Human Development Index.

Reason (R): Unemployment may vitiate the human development.

Codes :
A. Both (A) and (R) are wrong.
B. Both (A) and (R) are correct.

C. (A) is correct but (R) is wrong.
D. (A) is wrong but (R) is correct.

79. The continuous scrutiny of the factors that determine the occurrence and distribution of disease and other conditions of ill-health is called
A. Survey
B. Evaluation
C. Surveillance
D. Sentinel surveillance

80. "Turning aside from the right way is"
A. Culture B. Normative system
C. Social deviance D. All the above

81. National Policy for Empowerment of Women was adopted in the year
A. 2002 B. 2001
C. 1999 D. 1986

82. **Assertion (A):** Affirmative action leads to the participation of weaker sections in decision making.

Reason (R): Women need affirmative action to take part in decision-making.

Codes :
A. (A) is wrong and (R) is correct.
B. (A) is correct and (R) is wrong.
C. Both (A) and (R) are correct, and (R) is the correct explanation of (A).
D. Both (A) and (R) are wrong but (R) is not the correct explanation of (A).

83. The zero point is absolute in this type of level of measurement :
A. Interval level
B. Nominal level
C. Ratio level
D. Ordinal level

84. Match the following for their association :

List-I	**List-II**
(I) Variable	(1) Qualitative data
(II) Attribute	(2) Secondary Data
(III) Empirical Evidence	(3) Numerical Data
(IV) Documentary Evidence	(4) Primary Data

Codes :

	(I)	(II)	(III)	(IV)
A.	(3)	(1)	(2)	(4)
B.	(3)	(1)	(4)	(2)
C.	(3)	(4)	(1)	(2)
D.	(3)	(4)	(2)	(1)

85. The specific objectives of the group in group work are formed:
A. In Consultation with other workers.
B. In Consultation with the agency.
C. By the worker in consultation with the members.
D. By the worker in Consultation with the members of the community.

86. Movements that are deeply dissatisfied with the social order and work for radical change are called
A. Reform Movements
B. Revolutionary Movements
C. Revivalist Movements
D. Resistance Movements

87. What is not regarded as Social Action?
A. A group effort to solve mass social problems.
B. The members of the society ready for violent attack.
C. To spell out issues for their necessary implementation.
D. The organised effort with the aim of solving mass social problems.

88. Which is not a parametric test for testing hypotheses?
A. z-test B. t-test
C. f-test D. q-test

89. Usually an introduction of element of randomness into sampling by using random numbers to pick up the unit with which we start is known as
A. Systematic random sampling
B. Simple random sampling
C. Quota sampling
D. Area sampling

90. National policy for Women Empowerment was released in the year

A. 2002 B. 2001
C. 2004 D. 2000

91. Maintenance and welfare of parents and Senior Citizens Act was passed in
A. 2005 B. 2008
C. 2007 D. 2004

92. As per the Right of Children to Free and Compulsory Education Act, 2009 every child shall be provided free and compulsory education in the age-group of
A. 3-14 years B. 2.5-16 years
C. 6-14 years D. 1-14 years

93. The Human Development Index (HDI) is a comparative measures of
(a) Life expectancy
(b) Literacy
(c) Standard of living
(d) Income
A. (a), (b), (c) B. (a), (b), (d)
C. (a), (c), (d) D. (b), (c)

94. Assertion (A): Social Diagnosis is the important part of social care work process.
Reason (R): It is a reflective thinking that gives direction to problem solving process.
Choose your answer from the following :
A. Both (A) and (R) are true and (R) is the correct explanation of (A).
B. Both (A) and (R) are true, but (R) is not the correct explanation of (A).
C. (A) is true, but (R) is false.
D. Both (A) and (R) are false.

95. Sequential phases in the process of community organisation are :
(i) Organisational phase
(ii) Action phase
(iii) Exploratory phase
(iv) Discussional phase

Codes :

A.	(iii)	(i)	(ii)	(iv)
B.	(iii)	(i)	(iv)	(ii)
C.	(iv)	(i)	(ii)	(iii)
D.	(iv)	(ii)	(iii)	(i)

96. The right sequence of the different phases in a post-disaster situation are
i. Relief
ii. Rehabilitaiton
iii. Resettlement
iv. Rescue

Codes :

A.	iv	i	iii	ii
B.	i	ii	iii	iv
C.	i	ii	iv	iii
D.	i	iii	iv	ii

97. Arrange the following steps in Research Process in a logical sequence
i. Data collection
ii. Setting of objectives
iii. Report writing
iv. Data analysis

Codes :

A.	ii	i	iv	iii
B.	i	ii	iii	iv
C.	iii	iv	i	ii
D.	iv	iii	ii	i

98. Program formulation involves :
i. Identifying the indicators.
ii. Developing activities.
iii. Specifying the objectives.
iv. Setting the goal.

Codes :

A.	i	ii	iii	iv
B.	iv	iii	ii	i
C.	iv	iii	i	ii
D.	ii	i	iii	iv

99. Put the data analysis process in sequential order.
i. Classification ii. Tabulation
iii. Coding iv. Editing

Codes :

A.	i	iv	iii	ii
B.	ii	iii	i	iv
C.	iv	iii	i	ii
D.	iii	ii	i	iv

100. Assertion (A): Interpersonal relationship is the enabling factor to solve the problems of individuals through case work process.

Reason (R): Establishing professional relationship can help in solving the problems of individuals.

Codes :

A. (A) is correct but (R) is not correct.
B. (A) is not correct but (R) is correct.
C. Both (A) and (R) are correct and (R) is the correct explanation of (A).
D. Both (A) and (R) are correct but (R) is not the correct explanation of (A).

101. Assertion (A): Sustainable development is a pattern of resource use that aims to meet the human needs while preserving the environment.

Reason (R): It serves the needs of present as well as future generations.

Codes :

A. (A) and (R) are not correct.
B. (A) is correct but (R) is not the correct explanation of (A).
C. (A) is correct and (R) is the correct explanation of (A).
D. (R) is correct but (A) is not correct.

102. What is the sequence of PRA process ?

(i) Sensitizing the team.
(ii) Rapport building with target group.
(iii) Sharing the observations with target group.
(iv) Conducting the PRA.

Codes :

A. (i) (ii) (iii) (iv)
B. (i) (ii) (iv) (iii)
C. (i) (iv) (ii) (iii)
D. (i) (iv) (iii) (ii)

104. Match the following persons with the area of their association

List-I	List-II
(i) Balwant Rai Mehta	(1) Marthandam Project
(ii) Spencer Hatch	(2) 3 tier P.R. System
(iii) S.K. Dey	(3) Shantiniketan
(iv) Ravindranath Tagore	(4) Power to People

Codes :

	(i)	(ii)	(iii)	(iv)
A.	(1)	(2)	(3)	(4)
B.	(2)	(4)	(1)	(3)
C.	(2)	(1)	(4)	(3)
D.	(2)	(1)	(3)	(4)

104. Match the items of List-I with List-II.

List-I	List-II
(i) Mode	(1) Association of Attributes
(ii) Mean Deviation	(2) Dispersion
(iii) Chi-square	(3) Correlation
(iv) Karl Pearson Method	(4) Central tendency

Codes :

	(i)	(ii)	(iii)	(iv)
A.	(2)	(4)	(3)	(1)
B.	(2)	(4)	(1)	(3)
C.	(4)	(2)	(1)	(3)
D.	(4)	(2)	(3)	(1)

105. Match the name of the activists given in List-I with the name of movements given in List-II.

List-I	List-II
(i) M.K. Gandhi	(1) Chipko Movement
(ii) Vinoba Bhave	(2) Narmada Bachao Andolan
(iii) Arundati Roy	(3) Bhudan Movement
(iv) Sundarlal Bahuguna	(4) Constructive Programme

Codes :

	(i)	(ii)	(iii)	(iv)
A.	(4)	(2)	(3)	(1)
B.	(4)	(3)	(2)	(1)
C.	(1)	(2)	(4)	(3)
D.	(2)	(3)	(1)	(4)

106. Match the following names of the journals given in List-I with the institutions given in List-II.

List-I	List-II
(i) Indian Journal of Social Work	(1) Nirmala Niketan Mumbai
(ii) Social Work Perspectives	(2) N.I.R.D. Hyderabad

(iii) Contemporary Social Work	(3) Tata Institute of Social Sciences Mumbai
(iv) Journal of Rural Development	(4) Department of Social Work Lucknow University

Codes :

	(i)	(ii)	(iii)	(iv)
A.	(1)	(3)	(4)	(2)
B.	(4)	(2)	(1)	(3)
C.	(3)	(1)	(4)	(2)
D.	(2)	(1)	(3)	(4)

107. Robert Redfield's famous book
A. The Little Community
B. The Small Community
C. The Large Community
D. The Big Community

108. Emotional disorders in which an individual remains oriented to reality but suffers from chronic anxiety is
A. Schizophrenia B. Depression
C. Paranoid states D. Neuroses

109. One of the following theories is known as growth oriented theory
A. Psycho analytic theory
B. Client-Centred theory
C. Existential theory
D. Cognitive learning theory

110. A concept made measurable is called
A. Attribute B. Variable
C. Theory D. None of the above

111. Intervening variables can be controlled by
A. Randomization
B. Conceptualisation
C. Description
D. None of the above

112. Which government body promotes measures for care and protection of persons with disability in the event of death of their parents or guardians ?
A. Child Welfare Committee
B. Central Social Welfare Board
C. National Trust
D. National Handicapped Finance and Development Corporation

113. The author of the book, 'Practice of Social Research-Social Work perspectives' is
A. D.K. Lal Das
B. H.B. Trecker
C. J. Galtung
D. Nan Lin

114. Detachment from work, inability to accomplish goals and emotional discharge is known as
A. Blockade B. Burnout
C. Ambiguity D. Lockout

115. Which conference has brought in the concept of sustainable development?
A. The Rio Conference
B. The Doha Conference
C. The Montreal Conference
D. None of the above

116. 'Power' is gained whereas 'authority' is
A. acquired B. possessed
C. imposed D. nested

117. The point where two axes intersect is known as
A. X axis B. Y axis
C. Origin D. Table

118. The value that is repeated most often in data set is known as
A. Median B. Mode
C. Frequency D. Variance

119. Who among the following said that justice is crucial to understand human rights?
A. Peterson B. John Rawl
C. Smith D. Stephenson

120. The Universal Declaration of Human Rights was adopted in
A. 1944 B. 1945
C. 1947 D. 1948

121. Assertion (A): Maintaining case files is an important duty of a psychiatric social worker.

Reason (R): Case files are important sources of data collection in mental health research.

Codes :
A. Both (A) and (R) are true.
B. (A) is true and (R) is not the correct explanation of (A).
C. Both (A) and (R) are not true.
D. Both (A) and (R) are true and (R) is the correct explanation of (A).

122. **Assertion (A):** Human Resource Manager have to be a good human being.
Reason (R): Human values and ethics should be essential part of management education.
Codes :
A. (A) is correct and (R) is not the correct explanation of (A).
B. (A) is correct and (R) is the correct explanation of (A).
C. (A) is not correct but (R) is the correct explanation of (A).
D. Both (A) and (R) are not correct.

123. **Assertion (A):** When professional social work ingrains itself, in a practice modes, it can reduce the enormity of social problems in a given society.
Reason (R): Unless professional social workers develop competencies and convictions, they cannot address complex social problems.
Codes :
A. (A) is true but (R) is not true.
B. (A) is not true but (R) is true.
C. Both (A) and (R) are true.
D. Both (A) and (R) are not true.

124. A set of guidelines that give direction to action by an organization or government is called
A. Social policy
B. Social planning
C. Social principles
D. Strategic planning

125. Marriage is defined as
A. An approved social pattern for establishing a family.
B. A socially sanctioned union of male and female.
C. A contract for production and maintenance of children.
D. All the above

126. The part of mind that lies on reality is
A. Id
B. Ego
C. Super Ego
D. None of the above

127. Which among the following is not the purpose of Human Resource Planning ?
A. Configuring fixed skill setup for the departments in a same manner.
B. Analyze people market environment.
C. Forecasting future skill requirement.
D. Optimum use of currently employed human resources.

128. Article 41 of Indian Constitution states
A. Free compulsory education for all children up to 14 years of age.
B. Right to Education and work.
C. Educational and cultural relations with foreign countries.
D. Educational grants for the benefit of Anglo-Indian communities.

129. Classical conditioning was propagated by
A. Ivan Pavlov B. Sigmund Freud
C. Maslow D. Thorndike

130. Golden Triangle is
A. known as three areas of a continent where drug supply is common.
B. known as a set of three countries producing heroin.
C. a combination of three countries with sound economic position.
D. a combination of three countries with poor economic position.

131. Match List-I with List-II and select the correct answers from the codes given below :

List-I	List-II
(I) Social work Tool	(1) Interview
(II) Social work Technique	(2) Labour welfare
(III) Social work Method	(3) Social Action
(IV) Social work Field	(4) Interaction

Codes :

	(I)	(II)	(III)	(IV)
A.	(3)	(1)	(2)	(4)
B.	(2)	(3)	(4)	(1)
C.	(3)	(2)	(4)	(1)
D.	(4)	(1)	(3)	(2)

132. Match List-I with List-II and select the correct answers from the codes given below :

List-I	List-II
(I) Human Rights Day	(1) 7th April
(II) World Day of Social Justice	(2) 10th December
(III) World Humanitarian Day	(3) 20th February
(IV) World Health Day	(4) 19th August

Codes :

	(I)	(II)	(III)	(IV)
A.	(3)	(4)	(1)	(2)
B.	(2)	(3)	(4)	(1)
C.	(2)	(1)	(3)	(4)
D.	(1)	(2)	(4)	(3)

133. Match the pairs :

(a) Casework Technique	(i) Authority
(b) Group work Technique	(ii) Conscientisation
(c) Technique of C.O.	(iii) Individualisation
(d) Principle of Public Administration	(iv) Confrontation

Codes :

	(a)	(b)	(c)	(d)
A.	(ii)	(iv)	(i)	(iii)
B.	(iv)	(iii)	(ii)	(i)
C.	(i)	(iii)	(iv)	(ii)
D.	(iii)	(iv)	(i)	(ii)

134. Match the pairs :

(a) Social Reforms	(i) Voluntary action
(b) Social Service	(ii) Correctional work
(c) Probation	(iii) Change in social structure
(d) Coordination	(iv) Welfare Administration

Codes :

	(a)	(b)	(c)	(d)
A.	(iv)	(iii)	(i)	(ii)
B.	(iii)	(i)	(ii)	(iv)
C.	(ii)	(i)	(iv)	(iii)
D.	(ii)	(iv)	(i)	(iii)

135. Match the pairs :

(a) Narmada Bhachao Bahuguna	(i) Sunderlal
(b) Chipko Movement	(ii) Medha Patkar
(c) Sarvodaya Movement	(iii) Jay Prakash Narayan
(d) Total Revolution	(iv) Vinoba Bhave

Codes :

	(a)	(b)	(c)	(d)
A.	(ii)	(i)	(iv)	(iii)
B.	(iv)	(i)	(ii)	(iii)
C.	(ii)	(iii)	(i)	(iv)
D.	(ii)	(iii)	(iv)	(i)

136. Identify the correct sequence :

A. Hindu Widow Remarriage Act, Payment of Gratuity Act, Juvenile Justice Act, Bombay Children Act

B. Juvenile Justice Act, Payment of Gratuity Act, Hindu Widow Remarriage Act, Bombay Children Act

C. Hindu Widow Remarriage Act, Payment of Gratuity Act, Bombay Children Act, Juvenile Justice Act

D. Hindu Widow Remarriage Act, Bombay Children Act, Payment of Gratuity Act, Juvenile Justice Act

137. Match the pairs :

(a) Human Groups	(i) J.J. Anjaria and C. Nanawaty
(b) Interaction Process Analysis	(ii) Yogesh Atal
(c) Group Prejudice and Social Distance	(iii) G.C. Homaas
(d) Indian Society fromwhere to where	(iv) R.F. Bales

Codes :

	(a)	(b)	(c)	(d)
A.	(iv)	(iii)	(ii)	(i)
B.	(i)	(iv)	(iii)	(ii)
C.	(iii)	(iv)	(i)	(ii)
D.	(ii)	(iii)	(iv)	(i)

138. Match the pairs :

(a) C.S.W.B. — (i) Banu Coyaji
(b) Family Planning — (ii) Leelabai Mulgaonkar
(c) Child Marriage Restraint Act — (iii) Lord Bentinck
(d) Abolition of Sati Act — (iv) Harbilas Sarda

Codes :

	(a)	(b)	(c)	(d)
A.	(ii)	(i)	(iv)	(iii)
B.	(iv)	(ii)	(i)	(iii)
C.	(iii)	(ii)	(iv)	(i)
D.	(i)	(iii)	(iv)	(ii)

139. Match List I with List II in relation to Social Case Work :

List-I	List-II
(a) Principles of case work	(1) Self worth
(b) Tools of case work	(2) Clarification
(c) Assumptions of case work	(3) Assessment
(d) Process of case work	(4) Self-determination

Choose the correct code

Codes :

	(a)	(b)	(c)	(d)
A.	(1)	(2)	(4)	(3)
B.	(4)	(2)	(1)	(3)
C.	(2)	(4)	(1)	(3)
D.	(3)	(4)	(2)	(1)

140. In Social Case Work, the "Friendly Visitors" were :

A. Community workers identified by American Charity Organisation
B. Early voluntary case workers
C. Paid agents of case work
D. None of the above

141. In Social Case Work, interview is an important :

A. Tool
B. Method
C. Technique
D. All the above

142. Who is the Author of the book titled "Social Group Work : A helping process" ?

A. Wilson G. and Ryland G.
B. Trecker H.B.
C. Phillips H.U.
D. Konopka G.

143. The Indian journal of social work is published by:

A. Jamia Millia Islamia, New Delhi
B. Delhi School of Social Work, Delhi
C. Tata Institute of Social Sciences, Mumbai
D. Nirmala Niketan, Mumbai

144. The Convention on Child Rights was ratified by India in:

A. 1991
B. 1992
C. 1995
D. 1986

145. Match the items of List-I with those of List-II:

List-I (Event)	List-II (Year)
(a) The International Youth Year	(i) 2005
(b) The International Micro Credit Year	(ii) 1950
(c) The Mental Health Act	(iii) 1947
(d) Setting up of Planning Commission, Govt. of India	(iv) 1987
	(v) 1985

Codes :

	(a)	(b)	(c)	(d)
A.	(i)	(ii)	(iv)	(iii)
B.	(v)	(i)	(iv)	(ii)
C.	(iii)	(i)	(ii)	(v)
D.	(v)	(i)	(iii)	(iv)

ANSWERS

1	**2**	**3**	**4**	**5**	**6**	**7**	**8**	**9**	**10**
A	C	B	C	C	B	B	B	B	C
11	**12**	**13**	**14**	**15**	**16**	**17**	**18**	**19**	**20**
A	D	D	C	C	B	B	D	A	A
21	**22**	**23**	**24**	**25**	**26**	**27**	**28**	**29**	**30**
D	C	C	D	C	C	C	B	C	A
31	**32**	**33**	**34**	**35**	**36**	**37**	**38**	**39**	**40**
D	A	C	D	D	C	A	B	B	A
41	**42**	**43**	**44**	**45**	**46**	**47**	**48**	**49**	**50**
D	B	D	C	C	B	B	C	A	D
51	**52**	**53**	**54**	**55**	**56**	**57**	**58**	**59**	**60**
A	A	B	C	A	B	C	A	D	A
61	**62**	**63**	**64**	**65**	**66**	**67**	**68**	**69**	**70**
D	A	B	A	C	C	A	B	C	D
71	**72**	**73**	**74**	**75**	**76**	**77**	**78**	**79**	**80**
C	B	C	A	A	A	D	B	D	C
81	**82**	**83**	**84**	**85**	**86**	**87**	**88**	**89**	**90**
B	C	C	B	C	B	B	D	A	B
91	**92**	**93**	**94**	**95**	**96**	**97**	**98**	**99**	**100**
C	C	B	A	B	A	A	B	C	C
101	**102**	**103**	**104**	**105**	**106**	**107**	**108**	**109**	**110**
C	B	C	C	B	C	A	D	B	B
111	**112**	**113**	**114**	**115**	**116**	**117**	**118**	**119**	**120**
A	C	A	B	A	D	C	B	B	D
121	**122**	**123**	**124**	**125**	**126**	**127**	**128**	**129**	**130**
B	B	C	A	D	B	A	B	A	B
131	**132**	**133**	**134**	**135**	**136**	**137**	**138**	**139**	**140**
D	B	B	B	A	D	C	A	B	A
141	**142**	**143**	**144**	**145**					
A	D	C	B	B					

➤➤➤➤➤

CHAPTER 10

Social Development

GROWTH, CHANGE AND DEVELOPMENT

Growth

Growth is used in an economic sense, synonymously with 'economic growth'. It means generally speaking an increase in the amount of economic goods (commodities and services) that are produced in a society and a concomitant increase in the inhabitants' ability to acquire economic goods.

Development

Development is a broader and more diverse concept denoting improvements in the quality of life of the people existing much beyond direct gains from increased production of commodities and services. The dominant view has been that economic growth in a society if sustained over sufficient long period would ensure gradual improvement in the quality of life of the people. This would occur through:

- Transfer of growth from some core production unit and economic sectors to other units and sectors.
- Transformation of economic surplus from increased production into increased income for the people who incorporated into the growth process.
- Transformation of the increased income into broader economic and social welfare.

Social change, growth and development are interrelated concept and frequently they have been treated as inter-changeable terms. **Social change** is capable of value free objective description of certain societal process; the **social development** is a value laden term which refers to a subjective statement of the desired direction of social change and also the constituent element of the end products.

Shankar Pathak has explained this in detail, he says that "Social development includes programs for universal literacy or primary education, comprehensive preventive health, measure and control of contagious diseases, housing, family planning and preservation of ecological balance. Moreover, social development philosophy assumes that a substantial investment is required for social services for which economic development is essential."

Thus, social development is a comprehensive concept which implies major structural changes political, economic, cultural and its goal is to create a new society in place of the present where living condition of the people are improved so that they do not suffer from hunger and they are not denied the basic necessities of life.

Some other definitions of social development is described below:

M.S. Gore—"The concept of social development is inclusive of economic development but differ from it in the sense that it emphasis the development of totality of society in its economic, political, social and cultural aspects. In this sense social development planning is not concerned with planning exclusively for social services, any more than it is with the exclusive planning of economic growth. There are many areas, apart from social or welfare services, wherein the "social" perspective has relevance. Prominent among these are areas relating to population policy, policy relating to urbanization, industrial location and environmental pollution, policies relating to regional development, policies of income growth, income distribution and land reform, policies governing administration and peoples' participation in planning and the implementation of plans".

M.S. Rao—"Social development consists largely of efforts to improve the social situation in regard to social development, housing, health and nutrition, education and training, employment and working conditions, social security, social stability and social welfare".

P.N. Sharma and C. Shashtri—"Social development has been defined as a micro strategy of planned interventions to improve the capacity of existing social system to cope with demands of change and growth."

ASSWI (Association of School of Social Work in India)—"Social development is a process of systematic change (values, attitudes, institutions and practices) purposefully initiated through the instruments of social policy and planning for enhancement of the levels of living and quality of life of the mass of people especially the weaker sections in an eco friendly, socially just and participator environment".

Declarations in World Summit on Social Development

The world summit on social development has made some declarations and commitments. Major of them are listed below:

- Leveling the incomes of rich and poor in order to promote social justice
- Alleviating poverty and generating employment
- Working for global compact plan for social development
- Fighting against global problems like drug mafia and terrorism.
- Fighting against the discrimination on the basis of gender, race, religion, age or disability
- Protecting the disadvantaged group and sections
- Providing especial assistance for social development programs and working to promote public and private assistance
- Integrating poverty reduction and gender equity objectives into the program of structural adjustment by using social impact assessment and other relevant methods to ensure a greater upon issues of social development and basic human needs
- Improving the international economic environment to improve international financial assistance for helping under-developed countries.

CHARACTERISTICS OF SOCIAL DEVELOPMENT

By the analysis of various definitions, we find the following characteristics of social development:

- Social development is a program as well as a movement, approach and method of treating any broad based issue. Campaigning and mass mobilization are required much more in social development in comparison to social welfare.
- Social development may not provide direct type of readymade services with immediate solution of the problems. It means long term planning which is based on investing in people, environment and social system.
- Social development consist largely of efforts to improve the social situation in regard to developing, housing, health and nutrition, education and training, employment and working conditions, social security, social stability and social welfare.
- Social development is a process of systematic change purposefully initiated

through the instrument of social policy and planning for the enhancement of the level of living and quality of life of the mass of people.

- Providing special assistance for social development programs and working to promote public and private assistance
- Integrating poverty reduction and gender equity objectives into the program of structural adjustment.

SOCIAL WORK AND SOCIAL DEVELOPMENT

Professional social workers have felt that their expertise in developing country should be used not only for providing ameliorative services for handicapped groups but also for generating development efforts among people.

When community development programs were introduced in rural areas, it was felt that professional social work had a significant contribution to make. However, a few professional social workers were employed in community development programs, especially as social education organizer, the contribution of professional social work was more indirect than direct. Professional social work educators contributed to the development of training program for the village level workers, social education organizers and block development officers.

Community development programs when they were started in the sixties were similar in nature though it was more substantial. The training of urban community organizers included many elements from professional social work and few school of social work was closely associated with the urban community development projects.

Family and child welfare programs and substantially the integrated child development services introduced by the central government provided yet another area of involvement although indirect in social development. Some of the schools of social work were involved in the training of the personnel of this project. The evaluation of these projects too was undertaken through these institutions. Similarly, schools of social work have been involved in the implementation of national service scheme which seeks to draw university student into development and welfare work on a voluntary basis.

In recent years professional social work has shown special interest in family planning programs, AIDS awareness program. It was in the mid sixties that the family planning in India was given new orientation emphasizing community education as its major instrument.

Many seminars and conferences of professional social workers have emphasized the need for major involvement in the area, interest in which undoubtedly been stimulated by the action taken by UN and other international agencies in providing funds for manpower development and research project.

The international association of school of social work set up a special project involving several schools in Asia for preparing social workers to take up responsibilities connected with the implementation of family planning programs. However, the direct involvement of the profession in the family planning has been marginal.

The professional social workers are also actively involved in the implementation of the programs like Mahatma Gandhi National Rural Employment Guarantee Scheme (MNAREGA) and National Rural Health Mission (NRHM) and other programs of national importance. However, their number throughout the country is less than the expectations.

The glimpse of professional social work has been observed recently during the movements for anticorruption and related to good governance. The indirect involvement of social workers by using social action method is widely admired.

The non-involvement of professional social work at the direct service level in most welfare and developmental program is directly related to the organization of professional education at the graduate level. The jobs at the direct service level do not have salary scales which can attractive to those who graduate from school of social work.

Some of this opts out of the social work profession many go in the field of labour management and the few who stay in the welfare field operate more as social administrator then as social worker. However, professional have been involved in formulation and administration of training courses for field level workers and many of these courses show the unmistakable imprint of professional approach. If training of workers at direct service level has gained some acceptance. It is no small measure due to effort of the professionals.

Thus, the impact of professional social work on the welfare scheme in India is more pervasive than the small number of professionals employed in the development and welfare field would seem to suggest.

INDICATORS OF SOCIAL DEVELOPMENT

Social development is a vague concept and involves many things; therefore it is imperative to assess the development process to know the direction and process of development. By developing Indicators we can assess the status of development. Following indicators might be used for social development:

- Literacy Rate
- Adult Literacy Rate
- Gross Domestic Product
- Gross National Product
- Per Capita Income
- Per Capita Income and Expenditure
- Maternal Mortality Rate
- Infant Mortality Rate
- Birth Rate
- Sex Ratio
- Life Expectancy at birth

Some other Indicators and Index

- **Human Development Index**, which based on three criterion such as
  - access to resources
  - longevity
  - education
- **Public Spending on Development:** That is percentage of national income going into public expenditure (25 per cent is approved)
- **Social allocation Ratio:** That is percentage of public expenditure allocated on social service items such as health and education (40 per cent is approved)
- **Social Priority Ratio:** That is percentage of social allocation allocated for priority needs (50 per cent is suggested) such as primary education, primary health etc.
- **Human Expenditure Ratio:** This should be 5 per cent of the national income
- **U5MR:** The indicator is suggested by UNICEF which means mortality rate less than 5 years of age in a particular year for every thousand birth
- **Human Poverty Index**
- **Quality of Life Index**
- **Happiness Index**
- **Gender Related Development Index**

Characteristics of Social Development

- The process of social development is deeply linked to economic development. It is this aspect which gives social development a unique character when compared to other institutionalized approaches for enhancing peoples' welfare.
- Social development has an interdisciplinary focus which draws on the insight or various social sciences. Social development is particularly inspired by political economy offers on interdisciplinary basis for analysing and dealing with current social problem and promoting social welfare.
- Social development is a dynamic concept in which the notion of growth change is explicit.
- The proponent of social development reject the idea of that social improvement occurs naturally as a result of the working of the economic market, instead, they believe that organized efforts are needed to bring about improvement in social welfare.

- Social development is concerned with the population as a whole and it is, therefore, inclusive or universalistic in scope.
- The goal of social development is the promotion of social welfare, meaning, a condition of social well being which occurs when social problems are satisfactory managed, social needs are met and social opportunities are created.
- **Distributive Justice:** The growth should not be measured exclusively in terms of GDP; GNP, Per Capita Income. Rather economic growth and progress should be measured in terms of an economic progress in which fruits of people are not distributed among the other class especially the lower class, cannot yield positive results in the success of the nation. Therefore, economic growth should be regulated in such a manner that reduces economic disparity's and disparities can be between persons, groups or regions. In an unequal society, a poor is tend to become poorer because he/she is already in disadvantaged position and a rich person grow richer because he/she is already in advantaged position, better motivated, equipped with resources, they have better education and technical skills, they are more familiar with the rules and procedures of government and know how to manipulate them for their advantages. As a result the benefit of public supported programs of social and economic development often go to the better off sections in the community, creates social inequality and disparity between poor and rich. Therefore, the concept of distributive justice suggests equal distribution of resources and equal distribution of benefits and development.

SUSTAINABLE DEVELOPMENT

The World Commission on Environment and Development was set up by the General Assembly of the United Nations headed by Norway prime minister Mr. Gro Harlem Brundtland. The commission was asked to formulate 'A global agenda for Change' and accordingly the commission has submitted its report in March, 1987. The report also known as *Brundtland report* or *our common future*.

The report, focused on the sustainable development says that "Humanity has the ability to make development sustainable—to ensure that it meets the need of present without compromising the ability of future generations to meet their own needs". The concept of sustainable development does imply limits-not absolute limits but limitations imposed by the present state of technology and social organization on environmental resources and by the ability of the biosphere to absorb the effects of human activities. But technology and social organization can be both managed and improved to make way for new era of economic growth. The commission believes that widespread poverty is no longer inevitable. Poverty is not only an evil in itself, but sustainable development requires meeting the basic needs of all and extending to all the opportunity to fulfil their aspirations for a better life. A world in which poverty is endemic will always be prone to ecological and other catastrophes.

Meeting essential needs requires not only a new era of economic growth of nations in which the majority are poor, but an assurance that those poor get their fair share of the resources required to sustain that growth. Such equity would be aided by political system that secure effective citizen partnership in decision making and by greater democracy in international decision making.

Sustainable development requires that those who are more affluent adopt life styles within the planets ecological means—in their use of energy, for example. Further, rapidly growing populations can increase the pressure on resources and slow any rise in living standards; thus sustainable development can only be pursued if population size and growth are in harmony with the changing productive potential of the ecosystem".

Capra (1996) promoted the ideology that the world is not a collection of isolated objects, but a network of phenomenon that are fundamentally interconnected and interdependent. In nature there is no 'above' or 'below' and there are hierarchies, there are only networks nesting within other networks.

According to him the principle of planets ecosystem organize them to maximize sustainability through interdependence, recycling, partnership, flexibility and diversity. The same principles can be used as a guideline to build sustainable human communities. As Haq (1998) stated that "sustainable development is a process in which economic, fiscal, trade, energy, agriculture, industrial and other policies are designed to bring about development that is economically, socially and ecologically sustainable." It means that natural resources must be used in ways that do not create ecological debt by overexploiting the earth's carrying and productive capacity.

Features of Sustainable Development

Economic Security: A sustainable community possesses a healthy and diverse economy that adapts to change, provides long term security to residents, and recognizes social and ecological limits. Prosperity of a community's economy is based upon preservation of its assets and natural resource by maximizing income generation while also maintaining or increasing the diversity of assets that yields these benefits and are key to its productivity. A sustainable community has a variety of business, industries and institutions which are environmentally sound and financially viable, while retaining residents' money within the community.

Ecological Integrity: In sustainable communities environment and ecosystem are maintained both for their own essential natural functions, their beauty, their livability as a landscape, and their ability to provide sustainable supplies of natural resources and waste assimilation. Sustainable communities emphasize the importance of healthy, diverse ecological system that continually provides life sustaining function and other resources for humans and all other spices. A sustainable community is in harmony with natural system and reducing and converting waste into non-harmful and beneficial purposes, and by utilizing the natural ability of environmental resources for human needs without undermining their function and longevity.

Social Equity and Well-Being: A sustainable community recognizes and supports people's evolving sense of well being which includes a sense of belonging, a sense of place, a sense of self worth, a sense of safety, a sense of connection with nature, and provision of goods and services which meet their needs, both as they define them and as can be accommodated within the ecological integrity of natural systems. A community that is truly sustainable provides for the health of all community members, respect cultural diversity, is equitable in its action, and considers the need of future generations.

Bare Facts

- More than 1 billion people in the world live below the poverty line; 2 billion lack access to safe water; 3.1 billion have no sanitation.
- Developed countries have 20 per cent of the global population but are responsible for 85 per cent of world consumption of aluminium and synthetic chemical; 80 percent of paper, iron and steel; 80 per cent of commercial energy; 75 per cent of timber; 65 per cent of meat, fertilizers and cement; half the world's fish and grain; and 40 per cent of its fresh water. Developed countries also generate most of the world's hazardous chemical waste and 96 per cent of radio-active waste and 90 per cent of all ozone-depleting chlorofluorocarbons (CFCs).
- If consumption in developing countries were to grow as fast as in the developed countries known cooper reserves would last only 96 more years, lead reserves 3.4 years, aluminium reserves 341 more years; and 16 million hectors of arable land would lost every year.

- One billion people around the world suffer from micronutrient deficiency and eight hundred million people sleep hungry every day.
- It is predicted that by 2050 as much as 42 per cent of the world's population will live in nations which will not have sufficient fresh water stock to meet their combined needs of agriculture industry and domestic use.
- There has been 0.6 degree Centigrade rise in the earth's average temperature since the Industrial Revolution, caused by human activities—mainly the burning of coal, oil and gas pouring 850 billion tons of carbon dioxide into the atmosphere.
- 75 per cent of carbon dioxide emissions are caused by industrialized world.
- There has been a 40 per cent of reduction in the thickness of Western Arctic ice over the 40 years, the area is warming three times faster than the global average.
- 600 million tons of carbon dioxide is emitted annually by U.S.A., which is 25 per cent of the world's total emission. A similar level of emission is made by the entire developing world.
- There has been a 1 degree centigrade increase in tropical sea temperature over the past 100 years, damaging coral reefs and the fishing industries.
- 1 billion tons of carbons as oil, gas and coal is held in existing industrial reserves in the world.
- Ageing is accelerated by five years as a result of exposure to lead, according to a study of former workers at a chemical company in USA.

GLOBAL EFFORTS FOR HUMAN DEVELOPMENT: MILLENNIUM DEVELOPMENT GOALS (MDG)

The disappointing balance of development in the 1980s led to the calling, in the early 1990s, of a number of international conferences in the UN framework that dealt with various aspects of social and ecological development one such conference was the 1995 Copenhagen World Summit for Social Development. Among other things, the conference adopted a 10-point Declaration on Social Development that later formed the basis of the MDGs. At the end of the decade, there was a large measure of consensus on numerous development related issues and it was this that paved the way for the adoption of the Millennium Declaration. In particular, the conferences served to establish a broad consensus on a common goal system as well as on strategic approaches for translating it into practice.

In September 2000, the Millennium Declaration was adopted at the Millennium Summit, held in the framework of the 55th General Assembly of the United Nations (UN). The summit was attended by the heads of state or government of nearly all UN member states. In the wake of the Millennium Summit, a joint working group was constituted with representatives from the UN, the World Bank, the Organisation for Economic Co-operation and Development (OECD) and other international organisations. It extracted 08 Goals, 18 targets and 48 indicators. Most of the goals are set to be implemented by 2015. In September 2001, the MDGs were approved by the 56th UN General Assembly. The international community was thus in possession of a common goal system that has been agreed upon by all relevant actors and that is both measurable and set to be implemented by a fixed date.

The Millennium Development Goals (MDGs) and targets come from the Millennium Declaration, signed by 189 countries, including 147 heads of State and Government, in Setember 2000. The eight (8) Goals are as under:

- ***Goal 1: Eradicate Extreme Poverty and Hunger***
- ***Goal 2: Achieve Universal Primary Education***
- ***Goal 3: Promote Gender Equality and Empower Women***
- ***Goal 4: Reduce Child Mortality***

- ***Goal 5: Improve Maternal Health***
- ***Goal 6: Combat HIV/AIDS, Malaria and TB***
- ***Goal 7: Ensure Environmental Sustainability***
- ***Goal 8: Develop Global Partnership for Development***

Eighteen (18) targets were set as quantitative benchmarks for attaining the goals. The United Nations Development Group (UNDG) in its 2nd Guidance note (endorsed in 2003) on 'Country Reporting on the Millennium Development Goals' provided a framework of 53 indicators (48 basic + 5 alternative) which are categorized according to targets, for measuring the progress towards individual targets.

Subsequently the targets and indicators under the 8 goals have been increased to 21 and 60 respectively. The objectives are specified in many different ways. Some objectives are set out in proportional terms: reducing the proportion of people who live in poverty or hunger by one-half; reducing child mortality rates by two-thirds; reducing maternal mortality rates by three-fourths; or reducing the proportion of people without access to safe drinking water and basic sanitation facilities by one-half. Other objectives loss in bio-diversity or improve the lives of slum-dwellers are set out in terms of completion: universal primary education; gender equality in school education; productive employment with decent work for all; or universal access to reproductive health. Yet other objectives are set out as statements of intentions: reduce loss in bio-diversity or improve the lives of slum-dwellers.

World MDG Report 2012

The World Report on progress towards MDGs highlights several milestones. Three important targets on poverty, slums and water have been met three years ahead of 2015. Some of the developments highlighted in the Report are :

Extreme poverty is falling in every region for the first time since poverty trends began to be monitored, the number of people living in extreme poverty and poverty rates fell in every developing region—including in sub Saharan Africa, where rates are highest. The proportion of people living on less than $1.25 a day fell from 47 per cent in 1990 to 24 per cent in 2008—a reduction from over 2 billion to less than 1.4 billion.

The poverty reduction target was met Preliminary estimates indicate that the global poverty rate at $1.25 a day fell in 2010 to less than half the 1990 rate. If these results are confirmed, the first target of the MDGs— cutting the extreme poverty rate to half its 1990 level—will have been achieved at the global level well ahead of 2015.

The world has met the target of halving the proportion of people without access to improved sources of water. The target of halving the proportion of people without sustainable access to safe drinking water was also met by 2010, with the proportion of people using an improved water source rising from 76 per cent in 1990 to 89 per cent in 2010. Between 1990 and 2010, over two billion people gained access to improved drinking water sources, such as piped supplies and protected wells.

Improvements in the lives of 200 million slum dwellers exceeded the slum target. The share of urban residents in the developing world living in slums declined from 39 per cent in 2000 to 33 per cent in 2012. More than 200 million gained access to either improved water sources, improved sanitation facilities, or durable or less crowded housing. This achievement exceeds the target of significantly improving the lives of at least 100 million slum dwellers, well ahead of the 2020 deadline.

The world has achieved parity in primary education between girls and boys Driven by national and international efforts and the MDG campaign, many more of the world's children are enrolled in school at the primary level, especially since 2000. Girls have benefited the most. The ratio between the enrolment rate of girls and that of boys grew from 91 in 1999 to 97 in 2010 for all developing regions. The gender parity index value of 97 falls within the plus-or-minus 3-point margin of 100 per cent, the accepted measure for parity.

Many countries facing the greatest challenges have made significant progress towards universal primary education. Enrolment rates of children of primary school age increased markedly in sub-Saharan Africa, from 58 to 76 per cent between 1999 and 2010. Many countries in that region succeeded in reducing their relatively high out-of-school rates even• as their primary school age populations were growing.

Child survival progress is gaining momentum. Despite population growth, the number of under-five deaths worldwide fell from more than 12.0 million in 1990 to 7.6 million in 2010. And progress in the developing world as a whole has accelerated. Sub-Saharan Africa—the region with the highest level of under-five mortality—has doubled its average rate of reduction, from 1.2 per cent a year over1990-2000 to 2.4 per cent during 2000-2010.

Access to treatment for people living with HIV increased in all regions. At the end of 2010, 6.5 million people were receiving antiretroviral therapy for HIV or AIDS in developing regions. This total constitutes an increase of over 1.4 million people from December 2009, and the largest one-year increase ever. The 2010 target of universal access, however, was not reached.

The world is on track to achieve the target of halting and beginning to reverse the spread of tuberculosis. Globally, tuberculosis incidence rates have been falling since 2002, and current projections suggest that the 1990 death rate from the disease will be halved by 2015.

Global malaria deaths have declined. The estimated incidence of malaria has decreased globally, by 17 per cent since 2000. Over the same period, malaria-specific mortality rates have decreased by 25 per cent. Reported malaria cases fell by more than 50 per cent between 2000 and 2010 in 43 of the 99 countries with ongoing malaria transmission.

Vulnerable employment has decreased only marginally over twenty years. Vulnerable employment—defined as the share of unpaid family workers and own-account workers in total employment—accounted for an estimated 58 per cent of all employment in developing regions in 2011, down only moderately from 67 per cent two decades earlier. Women and youth are more likely to find themselves in such insecure and poorly remunerated positions than the rest of the employed population.

Decreases in maternal mortality are far from the 2015 target. There have been important improvements in maternal health and reduction in maternal deaths, but progress is still slow. Reductions in adolescent childbearing and expansion of contraceptive use have continued, but at a slower pace since 2000 than over the decade before.

Use of improved sources of water remains lower in rural areas. While 19 per cent of the rural population used unimproved sources of water in 2010; the rate in urban areas was only 4 per cent. And since dimensions of safety, reliability and sustainability are not reflected in the proxy indicator used to track progress towards the MDG target, it is likely that these figures overestimate the actual number of people using safe water supplies. Worse, nearly half of the population in developing regions—2.5 billion—still lacks access to improved sanitation facilities. By 2015, the world will have reached only 67 per cent coverage, well short of the 75 per cent needed to achieve the MDG target.

Hunger remains a global challenge. The most recent FAO estimates of undernourishment set the mark at 850 million living in hunger in the world in the 2006/2008 period—15.5 per cent of the world population. This continuing high level reflects the lack of progress on hunger in several regions, even as income poverty has decreased. Progress has also been slow in reducing child under nutrition. Close to one third of children in Southern Asia were underweight in 2010.

The number of people living in slums continues to grow. Despite a reduction in the share of urban populations living in slums, the absolute number has continued to grow from a 1990 baseline of 650 million. An estimated 863 million people now live in slum conditions.

MDG- India Country Report 2011

India's MDG framework recognizes all the 48 indicators that were included in UNDG's 2003 framework for monitoring of the 8 MDGs. However, India has found 35 of the indicators as relevant to India. India's MDG framework has been contextualized through a concordance with the existing official indicators of corresponding dimensions in the national statistical system. Some of the goal wise achievements highlighted in the recent Country Report are given below.

Goal 1: Eradicate Extreme Poverty and Hunger

Target 1: Halve, between 1990 and 2015, the percentage of population below the national poverty line

The Planning Commission data reveals decline in poverty headcount ratio. However, to achieve the target under MDG, the pace of decline in poverty needs to be accelerated.

Target 2: Halve, between 1990 & 2015 , the proportion of people who suffer from hunger

Malnutrition continues to be a major hurdle. All India trend of the proportion of underweight (severe & moderate) children below three years of age shows India is going slow in eliminating the effect of malnourishment. From estimated 52 % in 1990, the proportion of underweight children below three years is required to be reduced to 26% by 2015. According to the official estimates the proportion of underweight children has declined by 3 percentage points from about 43% during 1998- 99 to about 40% in 2005-06. At the historical rate of decline, the proportion is expected to come down to only about 33% by 2015 vis-a-vis the target value of 26%.

Goal 2: Achieve Universal Primary Education

Target 3: Ensure that by 2015 children everywhere, boys and girls alike, will be able to complete a full course of primary education

A trend based on DISE (District Information System on Education) data shows that the country is now well set to achieve cent per cent primary education for children in the primary schooling age of 6-10 years ahead of 2015. In the years 2008-09 and 2009-10, India's NER for primary education by the DISE statistics were 98.6% and 98.3% respectively.

Goal 3: Promote Gender Equality and Empower Women

Target 4 : Eliminate gender disparity in primary and secondary education, preferably by 2005, and in all levels of education, no later than 2015.

Gender Parity has already been achieved in primary education (in 2007-08 itself) and the disparity in secondary education is set to disappear by 2015.

Goal 4: Reduce Child Mortality

Target 5 : Reduce by two-thirds, between 1990 and 2015, the Under-Five Mortality Ratio

As per MDG targets under 5 mortality rate was to be reduced to 42 per thousand live births by 2015. India, however, is likely to attain the mortality rate of about 52 (per 1000 live births) by 2015 as per the trend shown below, missing the target by ten percentage points.

As per historical trend IMR is likely to miss the 2015 target. However, the faster decline in recent years indicates that the gap between target and likely achievement by 2015 is narrowing down.

Goal 5: Improve Maternal Health

Target 6 : Reduce by three quarters, between 1990 & 2015, the Maternal Mortality Ratio

Data reveals that more efforts are required for safer motherhood. At the historical pace of decrease, India would reach MMR of 139 per 1 lakh live births by 2015, against the target of 109.

Goal 6: Combat HIV/AIDS, Malaria and T.B.

Target 7 : *Have halted by 2015 and begun to reverse the spread of HIV/AIDS*

As per the data base maintained by HIV Sentinel Surveillance, trend reversal in prevalence of HIV/AIDS continues since 2005 even though the reduction in prevalence has become less noticeable after 2007.

Target 8 : *Have halted by 2015 and begun to reverse the incidence of Malaria and other major diseases.*

The data reveals that the stability in reversing the trends in prevalence of Malaria & TB is still to be achieved. Prevalence of TB shows an increase since 2009.

Goal 7: Ensure Environmental Sustainability

Target 9: Integrate the principles of sustainable development into country policies and programs and reverse the loss of environmental resources

Past measures regarding conservation of environment have shown some results. There is an increase in forest cover by about 1128 sq. km between 2007 and 2011 and the consumption of CFCs (Ozone depleting products) has gone down.

Target 10 : Halve, by 2015, the proportion of people without sustainable access to safe drinking water and basic sanitation.

Target of halving the proportion of households without access to safe drinking water by 2015, from its 1990 level of about 34%, has already been attained by 2007-08. The prevailing trend over time suggests attainability of almost cent per cent coverage of safe drinking water by 2015, including both rural and urban sectors. Improved sanitation facility still eludes half the households. In 1990, about 76% households in India had no sanitation facility. The target, presently, is to reduce the proportion of households having no access to improved sanitation to 38%, by 2015. However likely reduction by 2015 seems to be only about 43%, a 5% points deviation from the target.

Target 11: By 2020, to have achieved a significant improvement in the lives of at least 100 million slum dwellers.

As per Census 2001, 640 towns spread over 26 States/UTs reported existence of slums, with 42.6 million people, consisting of 8.2 million households, residing in slums of these towns . The share of slum population as percentage of urban population in respect of these town/cities was about 23.1% in 2001. The condition of slum dwellers in India's urban areas, as revealed from NSS results 2008-09 compared with corresponding results of 2002, shows signs of marginal improvement in terms of roads, water supply, electricity connection, sanitation, sewerage, garbage disposal, education and medical facilities.

Goal 8: Develop Global Partnership for Development

Target 18 : In co-operation with the private sector, make available the benefits of new technologies, especially information and communication. Indian Telecom market is one of the fastest growing markets in the world. Information provided by TRAI shows that connectivity in terms of teledensity has increased significantly. However, Rural Urban gap in telephone connectivity continues to rise despite faster growth in rural subscriber base. Number of internet subscribers has also increased significantly to about 13.54 million subscribers in 2009.

MULTIPLE CHOICE QUESTIONS

1. The 'Structure of Social Action' was propounded by :
A. Max Weber B. Robert Milton
C. Talcott Parsons D. Radcliffe Brown

2. Who propounded the concept 'Conjugal Family'?
A. Talcott Parsons
B. Murdock
C. William J. Goode
D. None of the above

3. The Government of India adopted the National Policy for children in the year
A. 1975 B. 1974
C. 1963 D. 1985

4. Who proposed 'Client Centered Therapy'?
A. Carl Rogers B. Anna Freud
C. Paul Goodman D. Addler

5. The essential characteristics of research :
A. Description
B. Exploration
C. Experimentation
D. All the above

6. Child Labour (Prohibition and Regulation) Act came into being in the year :
A. 1947 B. 1952
C. 1986 D. 1991

7. Lok Adalat refers to :
A. Out of court settlement.
B. Decreasing the case load of courts for speedy justice.
C. Summary trial.
D. People deciding about their problems.

8. Charity Organisation Society (COS) in USA was established in the year :
A. 1870 B. 1877
C. 1818 D. 1900

9. Medial Social Work courses were First started in India in the year?
A. 1946 B. 1949
C. 1959 D. 1956

10. Who is the author of 'Pattern of Culture' ?
A. Ruth Benedict B. G.W. Allport
C. Kimball Young D. M.N. Srinivas

11. The values of mean, median and mode are same in the case of :
A. Normal distribution
B. Skewed distribution
C. Binomial distribution
D. Abnormal distribution

12. The 73rd Constitutional Amendment relating to Panchayati Raj came into force in the year :
A. 1992 B. 1993
C. 1994 D. 1995

13. Identify the correct answers :
Recording in social casework can be classified as :
(i) Narrative recording, Process recording, Evaluative recording and Summary recording
(ii) Problem oriented, Field oriented, Process oriented and individual centered
(iii) Referral summaries, diagnostic summaries, narrative records and problem oriented records
(iv) Process oriented, narrative, situational and analytical
A. (i), (iii), (iv) B. (iii), (iv)
C. (i), (iv) D. (i), (ii), (iii)

14. Identify the procedures classified by Florence Hollis :
(i) Sustaining Procedures
(ii) Procedures of Direct Influence
(iii) Amputation
(iv) Reflective Procedures
A. (i), (iv) B. (i), (iii), (iv)
C. (i), (ii), (iii) D. (i), (ii), (iv)

15. Identify the correct sequence :
A. Newly married couple, Child bearing families, families with pre-school children

B. Child bearing families, Newly married couple
C. Pre-school children, Child bearing families
D. Pre-school children, Newly married couple, Child bearing families

16. The Book 'History, Philosophy and Fields of Social Work in India' is written by
A. M.S. Gore
B. S.K. Khinduka
C. A.R. Wadia
D. R.R. Singh

17. Integrated approach in social work means
A. Synthesis of social work methods
B. Integration of techniques of social work
C. Application of social work approaches
D. Practice of all the theories

18. Classification of primary group and secondary group is given by
A. Cooley B. MacIver
C. Sumner D. Giddings

19. The millennium development goals are adopted by UN countries in the year
A. 2004 B. 2007
C. 2000 D. 2001

20. Social stratification is a horizontal division of society into higher and lower social units – defined by
A. Lundberg B. Cooley
C. Williams D. Murray

21. According to structural theory, personality consists of
A. Id and Ego
B. Conscious, unconscious and subconscious
C. Id, Ego and Super ego
D. Ego and Super ego

22. Encoding is essential for
A. Sender B. Receiver
C. Message D. None

23. Inductive statistics refers to
A. Summarizing of information
B. Application of research methods
C. Application of x^2 test
D. Making generalization about some population on the basis of sample

24. The variable that is the effect of another variable is
A. Nominal variable
B. Intervening variable
C. Independent variable
D. Dependent variable

25. Which of the following is a correct matching?
A. V.T. Krishanamachary – Social work research
B. P.L. Brayne – Women welfare
C. Rabindranath Tagore – Community Development programmes in India
D. S.K. Dey – Child welfare

26. Match the following with the year of commencement :

List-I	List-II
(I) Human Rights	(1) 1950
(II) Indian Constitution	(2) 1948
(III) Convention on Child Rights	(3) 1974
(IV) National Policy for Children	(4) 1989

Codes :

	(I)	(II)	(III)	(IV)
A.	(3)	(1)	(2)	(4)
B.	(2)	(1)	(3)	(4)
C.	(2)	(1)	(4)	(3)
D.	(1)	(2)	(3)	(4)

27. Identify the correct sequence of stages of Group Development :
A. Intimacy, Negotiation, Orientation, Resistance, Termination
B. Orientation, Resistance, Negotiation, Intimacy, Termination
C. Negotiation, Intimacy, Resistance, Termination
D. Orientation, Intimacy, Resistance, Negotiation, Termination

28. Identify the correct sequence :

A. Need Identification, Resource Mobilisation, Rapport Building, Programme planning, Programme management, Evaluation.

B. Need Identification, Rapport Building, Resource Mobilisation, Programme Planning, Programme Management, Evaluation

C. Rapport Building, Need Identification, Resource Mobilisation, Programme Planning, Programme Management, Evaluation

D. Rapport Building, Need Identification, Programme Planning, Resource Mobilisation, Programme Management, Evaluation

29. Match the items in List-I with List-II :

List-I	List-II
(a) Thorstein Veblen	(i) Right to Constitutional Remedies
(b) Dr. B.R. Ambedkar	(ii) Unsocial groups
(c) George Hasen	(iii) Theory of leisure class
(d) In Group	(iv) Ethnocentrism

Codes :

	(a)	(b)	(c)	(d)
A.	iii	i	ii	iv
B.	ii	i	iii	iv
C.	iii	ii	i	iv
D.	iv	iii	ii	i

30. Match the following :

List-I (Author)	List-II (Books)
(a) Dandekar V.M.	(i) Social Work in India
(b) Gangrade K.D.	(ii) Dimensions of Social Work in India
(c) Gore M.S.	(iii) Poverty in India
(d) Kinduka S.K.	(iv) Some Aspects of Social Development in India

Codes :

	(a)	(b)	(c)	(d)
A.	i	ii	iii	iv
B.	ii	i	iv	iii
C.	iii	ii	iv	i
D.	iv	i	ii	iii

31. Which one of the following is not an indicator of social development of a country?

A. Infant mortality rate

B. Average life span

C. Incidence of litigation in the courts

D. Literacy rate

32. The Child Marriage Restrain Act was enacted in the year

A. 1929 B. 1930

C. 1931 D. 1932

33. The best example of verbal communication skill is

A. Good vocabulary

B. Competence in oral presentations

C. Fluent speech

D. Participate in training and research

34. Acceptance is a principle of social work which implies

A. Accepting client in his/her appearance.

B. Extending warm welcome to the client.

C. Accepting the client as he/she is.

D. Accepting the client's version as it is.

35. 'Mongolism' is the type of

A. Geographical division of land

B. Topographical structure

C. Mental retardation

D. A religious sect

36. What is Anuloma marriage ?

A. Higher caste man marrying lower caste woman

B. Higher caste woman marrying lower caste man

C. Lower caste man marrying higher caste woman

D. Lower caste woman marrying higher caste man

37. Identity V/S role confusion is the task of

A. Adulthood

B. Oral stage
C. Old age
D. Adolescence

38. The Rio Earth Summit of 1992 dealt with the theme

A. Sustainable development
B. Climate change
C. Poverty reduction
D. Agricultural development

39. Match the following names of the books given in List-I with the authors given in List-II and select answer from the codes given below :

List-I (Book)	**List-II (Author)**
a. Social Work Education and Social Work Practice in India	i. B. Kuppuswamy
b. An Introduction to Social Psychology	ii. T.K. Nair
c. Social Group Work Practice	iii. Polansky
d. Social Work Research Methods for the Helping Professions	iv. Wilson and Ryland

Codes :

	(a)	(b)	(c)	(d)
A.	iii	iv	i	ii
B.	ii	i	iv	iii
C.	iv	ii	i	iii
D.	iii	iv	ii	i

40. Assertion (A) : Participation in SHGs leads to women's empowerment.

Reason (R) : Through participation in SHGs women improve their self-image, make better choices and enhance their financial status.

Codes :

A. Both (A) and (R) are true.
B. Both (A) and (R) are false.
C. (A) is true, but (R) is not the correct explanation of (A).
D. (A) is true and (R) is the correct explanation of (A).

41. Assertion (A) : Workers participation in industry result in industrial democracy.

Reason (R) : Workers education program does not encourage the participation of workers.

Codes :

A. Both (A) and (R) are true.
B. Both (A) and (R) are not true.
C. (A) is true and (R) is not the true explanation of (A).
D. (A) is true and (R) is the true explanation of (A).

42. Assertion (A) : Right to self determination is a principle of social work.

Reason (R) : In social work practice the client is given free hand to decide about his/her future.

Codes :

A. Both (A) and (R) are true and (R) is correct explanation of (A).
B. Both (A) and (R) are true, but (R) is not the correct explanation of (A).
C. (A) is true, but (R) is false.
D. (R) is true, but (A) is false.

43. Assertion (A) : Females have higher life expectancy than males.

Reason (R) : Females receive a better diet.

Codes :

A. Both (A) and (R) are true and (R) is the correct explanation of (A).
B. Both (A) and (R) are true, but (R) is not the correct explanation of (A).
C. (A) is true, but (R) is false.
D. Both (A) and (R) are false.

44. Consider the following statements and select your answer according to the codes given below :

Assertion (A) : Peoples participation is essential for the success of development programme.

Reason (R) : Education and Awareness lead to participation.

Codes :

A. Both (A) and (R) are true and (R) is the correct explanation of (A).
B. Both (A) and (R) are true and (R) is not correct explanation of (A).
C. (A) is true, but (R) is false.
D. (A) is false, but (R) is true.

45. Assertion (A) : The connection between industrialization and breakdown of joint family system needs to be studied.

Reason (R) : This calls for variety of researches to be carried out in rural areas alone.

Codes :

A. Both (A) and (R) are true.
B. Both (A) and (R) are not true.
C. (A) is true and (R) is not the correct explanation of (A).
D. (A) is not true and (R) is true.

46. According to Evelin Burns, who is a social work educator, 'an examination of how well the target population was reached, to what degree the goals were achieved, the cost-effectiveness of the endeavour and the consequences ensuing from the policy" refers to :

A. Policy formation B. Policy analysis
C. Monitoring D. Policy design

47. Questions that push or pull the client towards a certain response are called :

A. Stacking Questions
B. Leading Questions
C. Open-ended Questions
D. None of the above

48. Person's most intimate relationships such as those with parents, siblings, spouse, friends are :

A. Meso system B. Micro systems
C. Exo systems D. Macro systems

49. The book 'The Decline of the West' has been written by:

A. Toynbee B. Auguste Comte
C. Spangler D. Sorokin

50. Which Article of the Constitution of India states that no child below 14 years shall be employed to work in any factory or mine?

A. Article 22 B. Article 14
C. Article 45 D. Article 24

51. The failure to recognise that the concept is not the phenomenon itself is called :

A. Delimitation
B. Ecological Fallacy
C. Fallacy of reification
D. Induction

52. Match List-I with List-II in relation to models of social work :

List-I	List-II
(a) Problem solving model	(i) Perlman
(b) Functional model	(ii) Pinkus and Minnhan
(c) Love model	(iii) Smalley, Taft and Robinson
(d) Four system model	(iv) Holmos

Choose the correct codes :

	(a)	(b)	(c)	(d)
A.	(i)	(ii)	(iv)	(iii)
B.	(i)	(iii)	(iv)	(ii)
C.	(ii)	(iii)	(iv)	(i)
D.	(iii)	(iv)	(ii)	(i)

53. Which among the following is a prominant symptom of depression :

A. Irrational fear of an object
B. Delusions and Hallucinations
C. Loss of interest and pleasure
D. A vague feeling of apprehension

54. Which one of the following most adequately defines the nature of social work?

A. Social propaganda
B. Administering psychological testing
C. Enforcing Social Legislations
D. Problem solving by applying specific techniques

55. Family is a :

A. Reference group
B. Primary group
C. Secondary group
D. Recreational group

56. Concept made measurable is :
A. Definition
B. Variable
C. Symbol
D. None of the above

57. The father of Indian renaissance is :
A. Devendranath Tagore
B. Dayanand Saraswati
C. Vivekananda
D. Raja Ram Mohan Roy

58. Directive Principle of State policies can not be enforced :
A. by public
B. by NGO
C. by bureaucrat
D. None of the above

59. Arrange the following stages in correct order:
(i) Identification of problem
(ii) Data collection instrument
(iii) Code book preparation
(iv) Research Questions
(v) Objectives of the study
(vi) Data reduction
(vii) Data analysis

Codes :
A. (v) (iv) (iii) (ii) (i) (vi) and (vii)
B. (i) (ii) (iii) (v) (iv) (vii) and (vi)
C. (i) (iv) (v) (ii) (iii) (vi) and (vii)
D. (iv) (v) (i) (ii) (iii) (vi) and (vii)

60. The difference between population parameter and sample statistic is called :
A. Sampling error B. Statistic
C. Sampling bias D. Variance

61. Intervening variables can be controlled by :
A. Randomization
B. Conceptualization
C. Description
D. Operationalization

62. A concept made measurable is called :
A. Attribute
B. Variable
C. Theory
D. Value

63. Arrange case work process in order.
A. Study, Diagnosis, Intake, Treatment, Follow-up
B. Intake, Study, Diagnosis, Treatment, Follow-up
C. Study, Intake, Follow-up, Diagnosis, Treatment
D. Intake, Diagnosis, Treatment, Study, Follow-up

64. CEDAW stands for
A. Convention on elimination of all forms of discrimination against women
B. Convention on empowerment, development of adult women
C. Conference on elimination of all forms of discrimination against women
D. Customary elimination of discrimination against adult women

65. Match the statistical methods with their application.

List-I	List-II
(I) Standard Deviation	(1) Explains relationship between variables
(II) Correlation	(2) Explains association of attributes
(III) Chi-square	(3) Explains dispersion within a distribution
(IV) t-test	(4) Explains significance of difference between two samples

Codes :

	(I)	(II)	(III)	(IV)
A.	(3)	(1)	(4)	(2)
B.	(1)	(3)	(4)	(2)
C.	(4)	(1)	(3)	(2)
D.	(3)	(1)	(2)	(4)

66. Match the following :

(I) The Industrial Employment (S.O) Act	(1) 1986
(II) The Trade Union Act	(2) 1936
(III) The Payment of Wages Act	(3) 1926
(IV) The Mental Health Act	(4) 1946

Codes :

	(I)	(II)	(III)	(IV)
A.	(4)	(3)	(2)	(1)
B.	(3)	(2)	(1)	(4)
C.	(2)	(3)	(1)	(4)
D.	(1)	(4)	(3)	(2)

67. Match the following :

List-I	List-II
(I) Gesela Konapka	(1) Social Case work
(II) Murray G. Ross	(2) Social Group work
(III) N.A. Polansky	(3) Community organization
(IV) H.H. Perlman	(4) Social Work Research

Codes :

	(I)	(II)	(III)	(IV)
A.	(3)	(4)	(2)	(1)
B.	(4)	(3)	(1)	(2)
C.	(1)	(2)	(3)	(4)
D.	(2)	(3)	(4)	(1)

68. Match the following international years with the year of their declaration.

List-I	List-II
(I) International Year of Disabled	(1) 2007
(II) International Year of Older Person	(2) 1994
(III) International Year of the Family	(3) 1975
(IV) International Year of Women	(4) 1981

Codes :

	(I)	(II)	(III)	(IV)
A.	(4)	(1)	(2)	(3)
B.	(4)	(1)	(3)	(2)
C.	(2)	(3)	(4)	(1)
D.	(3)	(2)	(4)	(1)

69. Assertion (A) : The Human Development Index (HDI) is a comparative measures of life expectancy, literacy, education and standard of living for countries worldwide.

Reason (R) : HDI is not used to distinguish whether the country is developed, a developing or an underdeveloped.

Choose your answer from the following :

A. (A) is false, but (R) is true.
B. (A) is true, but (R) is false.
C. Both (A) and (R) are wrong.
D. Both (A) and (R) are true, and (R) is the correct explanation of (A).

70. The society has been passed through three stages according to Auguste Comte. Identify the correct order of the stages

A. Positive, Theological, Metaphysical
B. Theological, Metaphysical, Positive
C. Metaphysical, Positive, Theological
D. Positive, Metaphysical, Theological

71. Identify the right sequence among the following stages given by Frued

A. Anal, Oral, Phallic, Genital, Latency
B. Oral, Anal, Phallic, Latency, Genital
C. Oral, Anal, Phallic, Genital, Latency
D. Oral, Anal, Genital, Phallic, Latency

72. Find out the correct sequence.

A. Microsystem, Macrosystem, Mesosystem, Exosystem
B. Macrosystem, Microsystem, Mesosystem, Exosystem
C. Microsystem, Mesosystem, Exosystem, Macrosystem
D. Mesosystem, Microsystem, Exosystem, Macrosystem

73. Identify an answer on the Acts on marriages in the order of their enactment.

A. The Parsi Marriage and Divorce Act, The Hindu Marriage Act, The Muslim Marriage Act, The Special Marriage Act.
B. The Special Marriage Act, The Parsi Marriage and Divorce Act, The Hindu Marriage Act, The Muslim Marriage Act.
C. The Muslim Marriage Act, The Hindu Marriage Act, The Special Marriage Act, The Parsi Marriage and Divorce Act.
D. The Parsi Marriage and Divorce Act, The Muslim Marriage Act, the Special Marriage Act, The Hindu Marriage Act.

74. One of the following explains the sequence of the research process. Identify the right sequence from the following :

A. Objectives, Hypothesis, Problem Formulation, Data Analysis, Data Collection

B. Objectives, Hypothesis, Data Collection, Data Analysis, Problem Formulation.

C. Problem Formulation, Objectives, Hypothesis, Data Collection, Data Analysis.

D. Problem Formulation, Hypothesis, Objectives, Data Collection, Data Analysis.

75. Identify the correct sequence regarding stages in social case work.

A. Study, Intake, Social Diagnosis, Treatment, Termination, Evaluation.

B. Intake, Study, Social Diagnosis, Treatment, Evaluation, Termination.

C. Intake, Study, Social Diagnosis, Treatment, Termination, Evaluation.

D. Study, Social Diagnosis, Intake, Treatment, Termination, Evaluation.

76. Match the models of development given in List-I with the area of focus given in List-II.

List-I	List-II
(a) Institutional Redistribution model	1. Welfare services
(b) Residual welfare model	2. Optimal use of resources
(c) Achievement-Performance model	3. Progressive taxation
(d) Sustainable development model	4. Perks and Benefits

Codes :

	(a)	(b)	(c)	(d)
A.	3	2	1	4
B.	3	1	4	2
C.	3	1	2	4
D.	1	3	4	2

77. Match the following legislations with the year of enactment.

List-I	List-II
(a) Juvenile Justice Act	1. 1955
(b) Untouchability Offences Act	2. 1948
(c) Dowry Prohibition Act	3. 1961
(d) Factories Act	4. 1986

Codes :

	(a)	(b)	(c)	(d)
A.	4	1	2	3
B.	4	1	3	2
C.	1	4	3	2
D.	4	3	2	1

78. Match the following movements given in List-I with their proponents given in List-II.

List-I	List-II
(a) Anti corruption Movement	1. Arundhati Roy
(b) Narmada Bachao Movement	2. Sundar Lal Bahuguna
(c) Chipco Movement	3. Anna Hazare
(d) Right to Information	4. Medha Patkar

Codes :

	(a)	(b)	(c)	(d)
A.	3	4	2	1
B.	4	3	2	1
C.	3	4	1	2
D.	4	3	1	2

79. Match the following concepts given in List-I with their meanings given in List-II.

List-I	List-II
(a) Pathos	1. Detachment from work
(b) Logos	2. Emotional Appeals
(c) Burnouts	3. Reaction to frustration
(d) Defuse mechanism	4. Logic of speakers argument

Codes :

	(a)	(b)	(c)	(d)
A.	2	4	3	1
B.	2	4	1	3
C.	4	2	1	3
D.	4	2	3	1

80. Match the items of List-I with List-II :

List-I	List-II
I. Averages	1. Correlation
II. Averages of averages	2. Measures of dispersion
III. Variables	3. Chi-square
IV. Attributes	4. Measures of central tendency

Codes :

	I	II	III	IV
A.	4	2	1	3
B.	4	2	3	1
C.	4	3	2	1
D.	2	4	1	3

81. Arrange the following steps in a sequence :

I. Designing the tool
II. Review of literature
III. Pretesting
IV. Validation
V. Application of the tool

A. I, II, III, V, IV
B. I, IV, II, III, V
C. I, V, II, III, IV
D. II, I, III, IV, V

82. Assertion (A) : Setting a hypothesis on a logical framework results in good research output.

Reason (R) : Setting a rational hypothesis is a pre-requisite for fruitful research.

Choose your answer from the following :

A. Both (A) and (R) are true and (R) is not the correct explanation of (A).
B. Both (A) and (R) are true and (R) is the correct explanation of (A).
C. (A) is true and (R) is not true.
D. (A) is not true, but (R) is true.

83. Arrange the following types of data in the order of their complexity :

I. Interval　　II. Ratio
III. Ordinal　　IV. Nominal

A. II, I, III, IV　　B. I, II, III, IV
C. IV, III, I, II　　D. IV, III, II, I

84. Which one of the following is not an ecological movement ?

A. Pani Panchayat
B. Chipko
C. Bhoodan
D. Pluck and Plant

85. Match the name of the programmes/ initiatives given in List-I with the year of inception given in List-II.

List-I	List-II
(i) Swarnjayanti Gram Swarojgar Yojna	(1) 1992
(ii) National Rural Employment Guarantee scheme	(2) 1995
(iii) World Trade Organisation	(3) 2000
(iv) Millennium Development – Goals	(4) 2005

Codes :

	(i)	(ii)	(iii)	(iv)
A.	(1)	(4)	(2)	(3)
B.	(4)	(1)	(2)	(3)
C.	(4)	(2)	(1)	(3)
D.	(2)	(4)	(1)	(3)

86. Select the correct sequence of organizational growth

A. Consolidation, initiation, expansion and termination.
B. Initiation, consolidation, expansion and termination.
C. Initiation, expansion, consolidation and termination.
D. Initiation, expansion, termination and consolidation.

87. Encoding is essential for

A. Sender　　B. Receiver
C. Message　　D. None

88. World No Tobacco day is observed on

A. 31st January　　B. 31st May
C. 31st July　　D. 31st August

89. In classical conditioning, what happens to a neutral stimulus after it is associated with the unconditioned stimulus ? It becomes

A. a conditioned stimulus.
B. conditioned response.

C. unconditioned response.
D. a phobia.

90. Emotionally intellectual person can
A. accurately perceive emotions.
B. think without emotions.
C. disregards emotional meaning.
D. has difficulty in managing own emotions.

91. Murry G. Ross suggested 3 approaches for community organization *i.e.*, specific content approach and generic content approach. The third approach is
A. Problem approach
B. Process approach
C. Propaganda approach
D. Planning approach

92. The defence mechanism
A. emerges randomly.
B. helps individuals cope with their internal and external state of anxiety and distress.
C. cannot be brought under conscious control to ward of anxiety.
D. operate to maintain a sense of serenity.

93. Social structures are
A. those aspects of a culture that are held in high regard, are desirable and therefore worthy of emulation.
B. principles of right and wrong actions and the rules & laws that govern the acceptable & unacceptable behaviour.
C. made up of a set of expectations about low people should behave in certain circumstances.
D. methods of placing people in social strata.

94. Panchayati Raj Institution in India have brought about one of the following :
A. Eradication of untouchability.
B. Spread of land ownership to the Depressed Classes.
C. A formal representation of the weaker sections in village governance.
D. Spread of education to the masses.

95. Socialisation means :
A. Developing friendship with unknown persons
B. Ensuring equity in the society
C. The process of internalisation of social norms
D. The establishment of rapport with clients

96. In which year English become the official language of India?
A. 1844 B. 1829
C. 1835 D. 1947

97. Which of the following are the main causes of social change in India?
(1) Independence
(2) Industrialisation
(3) Education
(4) Sanskritisation

Choose the correct answer from the following:
A. 1, 2 and 3 B. 2, 3 and 4
C. 1, 3 and 4 D. 1, 2 and 4

98. Assertion (A) : Every human being has to be regarded as a person with dignity and worth.
Reason (R) : Human beings are inter-dependent.
Choose your answer from the codes given below :
Codes :
A. Both (A) and (R) are correct.
B. Both (A) and (R) are not correct.
C. (A) is correct, but (R) is not correct.
D. (A) is not correct, but (R) is correct.

99. Which one of the following is not an objective of fieldwork ?
A. To relate class-room instructions into the real life situations.
B. To develop skills in working with target groups.
C. To work as a member of staff at the agency.
D. To attain professional growth and development.

100. Assertion (A) : Human beings are not subservient to State.
Reason (R) : All human beings are born free and equal in dignity and rights.

Choose your answer from the codes given below :

Codes :

A. Both (A) and (R) are correct and (R) is not the correct explanation of (A).
B. Both (A) and (R) are not correct.
C. (A) is correct, but (R) is not correct.
D. (A) is correct and (R) is the correct explanation of (A).

101. Assertion (A) : Research Studies overlapping one another are undertaken quite often for want of adequate information.

Reason (R) : Duplication of research studies result in plagiarism.

Codes :

A. Both (A) and (R) are correct and (R) is the correct explanation of (A).
B. Both (A) and (R) are not correct.
C. Both (A) and (R) are correct, but (R) is not the correct explanation of (A).
D. (A) is correct, but (R) is not correct.

102. Assertion (A) : In a simple random sample of a given size, all such subsets of the frame are given an equal probability.

Reason (R) : Any given pair of elements has the same chance of selection as any other such pair.

Codes :

A. (A) is correct and (R) is wrong.
B. Both (A) and (R) are correct and (R) is the correct explanation of (A).
C. Both (A) and (R) are wrong.
D. Both (A) and (R) are correct, but (R) is not an explanation of (A).

103. Assertion (A) : Personality is the particular combination of emotional, attitudinal, and behavioural response patterns of an individual.

Reason (R) : Personality refers to enduring personal characteristics that are revealed in a particular pattern of behaviour in a variety of situation.

Codes :

A. (A) is correct and (R) is wrong.
B. Both (A) and (R) are correct and (R) is the correct explanation of (A).
C. Both (A) and (R) are wrong.
D. Both (A) and (R) are correct, but (R) is not a correct explanation of (A).

104. Which of the following are the salient features of Mahatma Gandhi National Rural Employment Guarantee Scheme?

1. Rights based frame work.
2. Labour intensive work.
3. Decentralised Planning.
4. Women Empowerment.

Codes :

A. 1, 2 and 3 are correct
B. 1, 2 and 4 are correct
C. 1, 3 and 4 are correct
D. All are correct

105. 'Reassurance' is one of the techniques that come under the broad category of

A. Directives
B. Information seeking
C. Minimal responses
D. Complex responses

106. 'Normative System' refers to

A. system of rules and norms of the society.
B. culture of the society.
C. conventional behaviour of the society.
D. All of the above

107. The presence of which of the following will indicate the diversity of population?

A. Secondary association
B. Social tolerance
C. Secondary control
D. Social mobility

108. In which among the following States in India, Community Development Programme was first initiated in 1952?

A. Tamil Nadu
B. Punjab and Haryana
C. Uttar Pradesh
D. Rajasthan

109. Which is/are the approaches to community organization?

A. Community driven development

B. Social capital formation
C. Ecological sustainable development
D. All of the above

110. Which of the following is used to indicate the reliability of an estimate ?
A. Universe
B. Statistical significance
C. Sampling method
D. Confidence interval

111. Which among the following is the department created under the Ministry of Social Justice and Empowerment from May 2012?
A. Department of Higher Education
B. Department of Disability Affairs
C. Department of Health Research
D. Department of Rural Development

112. The author of the book "From Charity to Social Work" is
A. Mary Richmond
B. Friedlander
C. Jane Adams
D. Elizabeth N. Agnew

113. Match the following :

(a) Rabindra Nath Tagore	(i) Sabarmati Ashram
(b) Mahatma Gandhi	(ii) Belur Math
(c) Vinoba Bhave	(iii) Pavnar
(d) Ramakrishna Paramahamsa	(iv) Shanti Niketan

Codes :

	(a)	(b)	(c)	(d)
A.	(iii)	(ii)	(iv)	(ii)
B.	(i)	(ii)	(iii)	(iv)
C.	(iv)	(i)	(iii)	(ii)
D.	(ii)	(iii)	(i)	(iv)

114. Match the following :

(a) Sarvodaya	(i) Mahatma Gandhi
(b) Satyagraha	(ii) Vinoba Bhave
(c) Sampoorna Kranti	(iii) Verghese Kurien
(d) White Revolution	(iv) Jayprakash Narayan

Codes :

	(a)	(b)	(c)	(d)
A.	(iii)	(ii)	(i)	(iv)
B.	(ii)	(i)	(iv)	(iii)
C.	(iv)	(ii)	(i)	(iii)
D.	(i)	(iv)	(iii)	(ii)

115. Match the following pairs :

(a) Mohammad Yunus	(i) Welfare Economics
(b) Amartya Sen	(ii) Grameen Bank
(c) Mother Teresa	(iii) National Anthem
(d) Ravindranath Tagore	(iv) Nobel Peace Prize

Codes :

	(a)	(b)	(c)	(d)
A.	(iv)	(ii)	(iii)	(i)
B.	(iii)	(i)	(ii)	(iv)
C.	(ii)	(i)	(iv)	(iii)
D.	(i)	(iv)	(ii)	(iii)

116. Which of the following is not a principle of Social Group Work ?
A. Recognition of unique differences of each Individual
B. Appropriate modification of the group process
C. Enabling group members to involve themselves in the process of problem solving
D. Principle of indifferent attitude towards members

117. Which one of the following is not part of community as a system ?
A. Population
B. Shared institutions and values
C. Social interaction between the individual and institutions
D. The ability to locate information and resources

118. Which one of the communities is not able to fulfill their functions and peoples needs :
A. the one wherein some primary relationship exists
B. the one which are comparatively autonomous

C. the one which have the capacity to face problems and work to solve them
D. the one which are very large

119. The book, Community Welfare Organisation—Principles and Practice, has been written by:
A. K.D. Gangrade B. Murray G. Ross
C. M.S. Gore D. Arthur Dunham

120. Urban Community Development Services Project in India was started by :
A. American Friends Service Committee
B. Govt. of India
C. UNICEF
D. FORD Foundation

121. Which one of the following was the earliest project of community development in India?
A. Sevagram project
B. Sriniketan project
C. Gurgaon project
D. Itawah project

122. Match the items in the List-I with the items in the List-II :

List-I	List-II
(a) Women's day	(i) 12th January
(b) Youth day	(ii) 8th March
(c) Teacher's day	(iii) 1st December
(d) AIDS day	(iv) 5th September
	(v) 10th October

Codes :

	(a)	(b)	(c)	(d)
A.	(v)	(iii)	(ii)	(i)
B.	(i)	(v)	(iii)	(iv)
C.	(ii)	(i)	(iv)	(iii)
D.	(i)	(ii)	(iv)	(v)

123. Which among these is not the type of diagnosis in social case work?
A. Dynamic B. Logical
C. Clinical D. Etiological

124. Social Security Legislation in India was based on the report of :
A. Lord Baveridge
B. Prof Aradkar
C. V.V. Giri
D. Guljarilal Nanda

125. Social welfare traditionally includes :
A. Relief
B. Curative services
C. Rehabilitative services
D. All the above

ANSWERS

1	2	3	4	5	6	7	8	9	10
C	C	B	A	D	C	B	B	A	A
11	**12**	**13**	**14**	**15**	**16**	**17**	**18**	**19**	**20**
A	B	D	D	A	C	B	A	C	D
21	**22**	**23**	**24**	**25**	**26**	**27**	**28**	**29**	**30**
C	A	D	C	C	C	B	B	A	C
31	**32**	**33**	**34**	**35**	**36**	**37**	**38**	**39**	**40**
C	A	B	C	C	A	D	A	B	D
41	**42**	**43**	**44**	**45**	**46**	**47**	**48**	**49**	**50**
D	C	B	C	C	C	B	B	B	C
51	**52**	**53**	**54**	**55**	**56**	**57**	**58**	**59**	**60**
C	B	C	D	B	D	D	D	C	A
61	**62**	**63**	**64**	**65**	**66**	**67**	**68**	**69**	**70**
B	B	B	D	D	A	D	A	C	B

71	72	73	74	75	76	77	78	79	80
B	C	D	D	C	B	B	A	B	A
81	82	83	84	85	86	87	88	89	90
D	B	C	C	A	C	A	B	A	A
91	92	93	94	95	96	97	98	99	100
B	B	D	C	C	A	A	A	C	D
101	102	103	104	105	106	107	108	109	110
C	B	B	D	A	D	A	D	D	D
111	112	113	114	115	116	117	118	119	120
B	A	C	B	C	D	D	D	D	B
121	122	123	124	125					
C	C	C	A	D					

UGC-NET JRF

SOCIAL WORK

PART-B

CHAPTER

1

Labour Welfare & Human Resource Management

CONCEPT OF LABOUR WELFARE

The term 'Welfare" meaning the state of well being, health, happiness, prosperity and the development of human resources. The word 'labour' means any productive activity. In a broader sense, the phrase labour welfare means the adoption of measures to promote the physical, social, psychological and general well being of the working population.

DEFINITION OF LABOUR WELFARE

Labour welfare has been defined in various ways, The Oxford Dictionary defines. Labour Welfare as "Efforts to make life worth living for worker".

- "Anything done for the comfort and improvement, intellectual and social of the employees over and above the wages paid, which is not necessity of the industry is labour welfare".
- It is also felt that labour welfare covers all the efforts which employers make for the benefits of standards of working conditions fixed by the Factory Act and over and above the provision of social legislation providing against accident, old age, unemployment and sickness.
- Another definition includes in labour welfare such services, facilities and amenities as adequate canteens, rest and recreation facilities, sanitary and medical facilities, arrangements for travel to and from work and for the accommodation of the workers employed at a distance from their homes and such other services, amenities and facilities, including social security measures, as contribute to an improvement in the conditions under which workers are employed.

PRINCIPLES OF LABOUR WELFARE

Labour welfare is dependent on certain basic principles, which are as follows:

- **Principles of Adequacy of Wages** : Labour welfare measures cannot be substitute for wages. Workers have a right to adequate wages. But high wage rate alone cannot create a healthy atmosphere nor bring about a sense of commitment on the part of workers. A combination of social welfare, emotional welfare and economic welfare together would achieve good results.
- **Principle of social responsibility of industry**: The industry has an obligation or duty towards its employees to look after their welfare. The constitution of India, in its Directive Principles of State Policy also emphasis this aspect of labour welfare.
- **Principle of efficiency**: According to this principle the employer should accept the

responsibility for implementing labour welfare measures because it would increase the efficiency of the labour.

- **Principle of Re-Personalization:** The development of the human personality is given here as the goal of industrial welfare which, according to this principle should counteract the baneful effects of the industrial systems.

  Therefore, it is necessary to implement labour welfare services, both inside and outside the factory that is provide intra mural and extra mural labour welfare services.
- **Principle of Totality of Welfare:** This principles emphasises that the concept of labour welfare must spread throughout the hierarchy of an organisation. Employee at all level must accept this total concept of labour welfare because without this acceptance, labour welfare program will never really get off the ground.
- **Principle of Association or Democratic Values:** This principle is based on the assumption that the worker is a mature and rational individual. He must be consulted in the formulation and implementation of labour welfare services.
- **Principles of Responsibility:** The principles is based on the assumption that when responsibility is shared by different groups, labour welfare work becomes simple and easier, it recognizes that both employers and workers are responsible for labour welfare.
- **Principle of Accountability:** It is also known as principle of evaluation, one responsible person gives an assessment of existing welfare services on a periodical basis to a higher authority. This is necessary to judge and evaluate the success of labour welfare programs.
- **Principle of Timeliness:** The timeliness of any service helps in its success. To indentify the labour problem and to discover what kind of help is necessary to solve it and when to provide this help are all very necessary in planning labour welfare programs.
- **Principle of Self Help:** The principle suggest that labour welfare must aim at helping workers to help themselves. In the long run, this helps them to become more responsible and more efficient.

Labour Welfare services should :

- Enable workers to live a richer and more satisfactory life.
- Contribute to the productivity of labour and efficiency of the enterprise.
- Raise the standards of living of workers by indirectly reducing the burden on their purse.
- Be in tune and harmony with similar services obtaining in a neighboring community where an enterprise is situated.
- Be administratively viable and essentially developmental in out look.

DEFINITION OF HUMAN RESOURCE MANAGEMENT

Human Resource Management (HRM) is a Management Function that helps managers plan, recruit, select, train, develop, remunerate and maintain or retain members. For an organisation, HRM is the latest nomenclature used to denote. Personnel Management (PM)

CONCEPT OF ABSENTEEISM

Absenteeism is the term generally used to refer to unscheduled employee absences from the workplace. Many causes of absenteeism are legitimate, for example personal illness or family issues, but absenteeism also can often be traced to other factors such as a poor work environment or workers who are not committed to their jobs. If such absences become excessive, they can have a seriously adverse impact on a business's operations and, ultimately, its profitability.

The Labour Department in India defined the absenteeism rate as the total man-shifts lost because of absences as a percentage of the total number of man-shifts scheduled. So for calculation of the rate of the absenteeism we require the number of persons scheduled to work and the number actually present.

Authorized and Unauthorized Absences

Authorized absences are those about which the employer has advance knowledge and can therefore plan his production during the absence of the worker. Unauthorized absence is those about which the employer has no advance knowledge and therefore cannot plan his production during the period of unauthorized absence. Authorized absences generally include permitted vacations, sickness, accident privilege, casual leave. Ex post facto regularized overstays and any other absence condoned by the management prior to after the occurrence are also regarded as authorized absence. Unauthorized absences includes all those cases where work is available, the worker knows about it, he fails to report himself for the duty and the employer has no prior information of the workers failure.

Measurement of Absenteeism

When absenteeism is considered as the sum total of time loss due to all authorized and unauthorized leaves, it can be measured as under:

$$\frac{\text{No. of authorised absences} + \text{No. of unauthorised absences}}{\text{Total days of scheduled to work}} \times 100$$

(This is known as absent rate)

When absenteeism comprises only unauthorized absence it can be measured as:

$$\frac{\text{No. of authorised absenses}}{\text{Total days scheduled work}} \times 100$$

(This is known as absenteeism rate)

Causes of the Absenteeism

The rate of the absenteeism in Indian industries is very high and cannot be dismissed. It is observed that the basic cause of absenteeism in India is that industrial worker is still part-time peasant. Thus the workers go to find jobs at cities after the harvesting their crops. It means that when the transplanting season. These workers consider to the modern industrialism is insecure. Thus, cause to high rate of the absenteeism in the industrial sector.

According to the Labour Investigation Committee (1946), there were many reasons that caused the absenteeism of the industrial workers. The Commission pointed out many factors which caused the absenteeism in Indian industries. These factors are:

- **Sickness and low vitality:** The committee pointed out that sickness is most important responsible for absenteeism in most of the Industrial sector. Epidemics like cholera, small-pox and malaria always break out in severe from in most industrial areas. The low vitality of the Indian workers makes them vulnerable to such epidemics and bad housing and unsanitary conditions of living aggravate the trouble. However, the Commission has been noticed that the rate of absenteeism among the female workers is higher than their male counterparts.
- **Means of Transport**: The Commission also stated that the transport facilities also play very important role to contribute the absenteeism of the worker in the industries. It has been pointed out that, the rate of absenteeism is higher in those factories where transport facilities are not easily available as compared to those where such facilities are easily available or provided by the factory itself.
- **Hours of work:** The long hours of work also affect the workers' efficiency and consequently their sickness rate and absenteeism rate are increased.
- **Nightshift:** It has also been pointed out that there is a greater percentage of absenteeism during the nightshifts than in the dayshifts, owing to the greater discomforts of work during the night-time.
- **Rural exodus:** The committee also pointed out that probably the most predominant cause of absenteeism is the frequent urge

of rural exodus. It has been noticed that the workers go back to their villages at the time of harvesting and sowing the crops. It increases the rate of absenteeism in factories.

- **Accident:** Industrial accident depends upon the nature of work to be performed by the worker and his ability for doing that work. In case of hazardous nature of job, the accidents occur more frequently which lead to higher rate of absenteeism.
- **Social and religious Function:** It has been noticed that workers become absent form their duty on occasions of social and religious functions. Since the workers like to join their families on such occasions, they go back to their villages for like to join short periods.
- **Drinking and amusement:** The Labour Investigation committee pointed out that drinking and amusements are also responsible for absenteeism. Since drinking and amusements in the late hours of night make it difficult for the workers to reach in time on their duties. They like to become absent rather than late since they know that *badli* workers will be substituted for them, if they are late.
- **After Pay-Day:** The Labour Investigation committee also noted the level of absenteeism is comparatively high immediately after the pay-day because they get their wages, they feel like having a good time or return to their villages to make purchases for the family and to meet them, so the absenteeism is high after they got paid.
- **Nature of work**: The absenteeism rate is also affected by the nature of work. Prof. William pointed out that absenteeism prevails because workers are not accustomed to the factory life and factory discipline. In other words, absenteeism prevails because the nature of work in factories is different from that for which the worker is accustomed. So when they come to work in the factory, they feel strange, this new situation make them uncomfortable, so lead to high rate of absenteeism of the industrial workers.
- **Other causes :** The other factors which caused the absenteeism in the Industrial sector are pointed out briefly by the Labour Commission.

However, there can be two other factors which caused the absenteeism in industrial sector. These factors are: (a) personal factors and (b) workplace factors.

Personal factor

The personal factor also divided into other sub-factors, these are:

- ***Personal Attitude***: There are different attitude of employees. The Employees with strong workplace ethics will respect their work and appreciate the contribution they make to their companies. Such employees will not engage themselves in taking unscheduled off. On the other hand, employees with very low or no work ethics are indiscipline and have lot of integrity and behavioural issues. Since, they feel no obligation towards the company, absenteeism comes easily to them.
- ***Age***: The younger employees are often restless. They want to spend time with their friends and have fun, rather than being tied down with work responsibility. This lack of ownership often leads them to take unauthorized time off. With age, people gain experience and maturity, which makes them focused and responsible. Their approach is rather professional and they prefer to stick to their chairs to get the work done. If ever they are found absent, then it could be due to sickness.
- ***Seniority***: Employees, who have been with the company for a long time are well-adjusted with the working culture and the job, therefore, they find no reason to be absent without permission. On the other hand, new hires are more prone to taking ad hoc breaks to unwind ther lves.

- ***Gender***: Women generally do a balancing act by shuffling their time between home and work. Family, being their foremost priority, they don't think twice before taking a step towards absenteeism.

Workplace Factors

- ***Stress***: The pressure at work sometimes takes a toll on the employees. This results in increased levels of stress. The employees then resort to excuses that can help them stay away from work.
- ***Work Routine***: Doing the same job over a period of time can get monotonous. The employees find the job functions boring. They rather choose time off to do something interesting than come to work.
- ***Job Satisfaction***: If employees do not find their job challenging, dissatisfaction creeps in. That leads to more absenteeism in the workplace.

Effect of Absenteeism

The effects of the absenteeism of the workers in the factories adversely effect to the employers, the cost of production of the factory is increased because of the absent of the workers, by employing extra temporary staffs in order to replace the absentee.

The effects of absenteeism in the workplace are directly proportionate to decreased productivity. The company, eventually, is trying to cover up the direct and indirect cost involved to hire temporary staff, and pay employees for overtime. So the cost of the production of the company is increased as the result they increase the price of the commodity, so the consumers have to pay high price for the commodities. However, the workers themselves also effect of the absenteeism because their income is reduced according to the principle of "no work no pay", as the result their standard of live decreased. Thus, absenteeism adversely affects the employers and the workers, and consumers and ultimately, it can be adverse affect to the growth of the economy in the country. So all these give rises to many industrial labour and social problems.

Method to Remedy the Absenteeism

On the basis of the above analysis, it can safely be concluded that the rate of absenteeism can be reduced by making provisions for:

- Improving the working condition in the factory
- Providing adequate wages,
- Protection from accident and sickness
- Providing facilities for obtaining leave for rest
- Suitable housing facilities
- Creating a sense of responsibility in workers towards industry
- Workers participation in the management of industry,
- Introducing incentive wage scheme and linking wages and bonus with production and adequate transport facilities
- Besides, an affectionate and mild behaviour of the employer will be helpful in reducing the rate of absenteeism.

If the above provisions are provided to employees, the absenteeism of the workers will be decreased and in return the standard of living of the workers is increased and in return the productivity efficiency of the workers also increase, in contrast the cost of the production is decreased. So the employers can earn maximum profits and the industrial peace and industrial harmony take place in the industry.

COLLECTIVE BARGAINING

Industrial harmony is essential for economic growth and progress. The concept of industrial harmony suggests a sense of cooperation between employer and employee. Sometimes, the interests of both the parties may clash but there is always scope for cooperation. Cooperation suggests that while safeguarding / protecting the rights and interests, they must also take into account the interests of the community. Excessive strikes and lockouts work against the interests of community. Therefore, industrial peace can be better maintained, if both the bargaining parties are strong and develop the habit of planned collective bargaining.

Definition of Collective Bargaining

Dale Yoder—"Collective bargaining is essentially a process in which employees act as a group in seeking to shape conditions and relationship in their employment."

"Collective Bargaining is method by which trade unions protect and improve the conditions of their members working lives", the definition given by Sydney and Beatrice who coined the phrase, collective bargaining.

Characteristics of Collective Bargaining

The important features of collective bargaining are as under:

- Flexible and mobile and not fixed or static: Collective bargaining is based on mutual compromise with give and take approach prior to reaching an agreement or arriving at the final settlement.
- It is a Group Action: It is not an individual action, may be initiated by individuals but when bargains are to be made the workers are represented by the trade union and delegates represent management.
- Divergent interests at commencement: The unique feature of collective bargaining is that where negotiation commence, normally both the parties have completely divergent interests, but ultimately come to a half way solution to which both the parties willingly agree.

FACTORIES ACT, 1948

- 'Manufacturing process' means process for-making, altering, ornamenting, finishing, packing, oiling, washing, cleaning, breaking up, demolishing, or otherwise treating or adapting any article or substance with a view to its use, sale, transport, delivery, disposal, or generating, trans-forming or transmitting power; or constructing, reconstructing, repairing, refitting, finishing or breaking up ships or vessels.
- 'Worker' means a person in any manufacturing process or in cleaning any part of the machinery or premises used for manufacturing process, or in any other kind of work incidental to, or connected with the manufacturing process, or the subject of the manufacturing process.
- 'Factory' means any premises including the precincts thereof—whereon ten or more workers are working, or were working on any day of the preceding twelve months, and in any part of which manufacturing process is being carried on with the aid of power or whereon twenty or more workers are working, or were working on any day of the preceding twelve months, and in any part of which manufacturing process is being carried on without the aid of power.
- 'Occupier' of a factory means the person who has the ultimate control over the affairs of the factory.
- Approval, licensing and registration of factories is required for the purposes of this act, for this purpose the state government may make rules, accordingly an occupier of a factory has to obtain it.
- Under section 7 of the Act the occupier shall at least 15 days before he begins to occupy or use any premises as a factory sent to the chief inspector a detailed notice.
- General duties of occupier and of manufacturer are specified in section 7A and 7B respectively.
- The state government may appoint prescribed qualification such persons fit to be appointed as inspector and there powers have been specified in section 9.
- Appointment of certifying surgeon and his duties are provided in section 10 of the Act.

- Health of the worker is very important aspect of working conditions therefore the Act provides under chapter 3 detailed provision regarding various health aspect such as cleanliness, disposal of waste and effluents, ventilation and temperature, dust and fume, artificial humidification, overcrowding, lighting, drinking water, sanitation facilities and providing spittoons in the factories.
- Safety is a very important aspect of working condition and the Act provides detailed provision regarding safety from section 21 to 41 in chapter IV and special provision relating to hazardous processes from section 41A to section 41H in Chapter IVA.
- Welfare of workers is also a very important dimension of working conditions and under Chapter V of the Act various statutory welfare provisions have been provided from Section 42 to 50.
- Such as washing facilities for storing and drying and clothing and for sitting, provision of first aid appliances and establishment of canteen, providing shelters, rest rooms and lunch rooms, creches and appointment of welfare officers in the factory.
- Chapter VI of the Act provides working hours of the Adult workers.
- Daily and weekly hours, compensatory holidays, interval for rest, spread hour, night shift etc, have been provided.
- Employment of young person's is governed by provisions from section 67 to section 77 provided in Chapter VII of the Act.
- Under Chapter VIII provision regarding annual leave with wages has been provided.
- Any worker who has completed not less than 240 days of work in a calendar year will earn annual leave with wages @ one day for 20 actual days of work which he can avail of in the subsequent calendar year.
- Special provisions and penalties and procedures have provided in Chapter IX and X of the Act.

PAYMENT OF GRATUITY ACT, 1972

- An Act to provide for a scheme for payment of Gratuity for employees engaged in factories, mines, oil fields, plantation, ports, railways companies, shop or other establishments and matter connected with.
- Apply to the establishment where ten or more employees are employed on any day of the preceding twelve months.
- Completed year of service means continuous service for one year.
- Continuous service means continuous service for a period, if he has for that period, been uninterrupted service, including service which may be interrupted on account of sickness, accident, leave, absence from duty without leave, lay off, strike, or a lock out or cessation of work not due to the fault of employees or uninterrupted service before or after the commencement of this Act.
- An employee shall be deemed to be in continuous service under the employer if the employee during the period of twelve calendar months has actually worked under the employer for not less than one hundred and ninety days (below the ground) two hundred forty days in any other case.
- For seasonal establishment employee will be deemed to be in continuous service if he has actually worked for not less than seventy five per cent of the working days.
- 'Superannuation' in relation to an employee means the attainment by the employee of such age as is fixed in the contract or condition of service as the age on attainment of which employee should vacate the employment.
- Wages means all emoluments which are earned by an employee while on duty or

leave in accordance with the terms and conditions of his employment includes dearness allowance but does not include any bonus, commission, house rent allowance, overtime wages and any other allowance.

- Payment of Gratuity shall be payable if employee has rendered not less than five years of continuous service.
  - ➢ On his superannuation
  - ➢ On his retirement or resignation
  - ➢ On his death, disablement due to accident or disease
- Completion of continuous service of five years shall not be necessary where the termination of the employment is due to death or disablement.
- For every completed year of service, the employer shall pay gratuity to an employee at the rate of fifteen days wages based on the rate of wages last drawn by the employee concerned.
- In the case of a monthly rated employee, the fifteen days wages shall be calculated by dividing the monthly rate of wages last drawn by him by twenty six and multiplying the quotient by fifteen.
- The amount of gratuity payable to an employee shall not exceed ten lakh rupees.
- For employees working in seasonal establishment the rate of gratuity is seven days per completed year of service.
- The gratuity should be paid within 30 days from the date of retirement etc.

PAYMENT OF WAGES ACT, 1936

- Payment of Wages Act applied for employed persons whose wages do not exceed Rs. 18,000/- per month.
- Employer is responsible for payment of all wages otherwise – manager, controller, supervisor, contractor.
- No wage period shall exceed one month.
- Any establishment where less than 1000 person are employed shall be paid salary / wage on or before expiry of the seventh day from the last day of wage period.
- Any establishment where more than 1000 person are employed shall be paid salary/ wage on or before the expiry of tenth working day from the last day of wage period.
- If the employee is terminated he shall be paid all due wages before the expiry of 2nd working day from the date of termination.
- All payment of wages should be made on working days.
- All wages should be paid in current coin/ currency.
- Every payment made by the employed person to the employer is considered as deduction from wages.
- Any loss of wages due to sufficient cause shall not be considered deduction from wages like stoppage of increment, reduction to a lower post, suspension as a punishment.
- The total amount of deduction shall not exceed 75% of wages in case of cooperative societies recovery and any other case more than 50% of such wages.
- Procedure to impose fine:
  - (A) Fine can be imposed only on acts and omissions for which approval has been obtained from the appropriate government.
  - (B) These acts and omissions should be notified to the employed persons.
  - (C) Before imposing fine the employed person should be issued show cause notice.
  - (D) The maximum amount of fine should not exceed 3 per cent of the wage and salary.
  - (E) No fine can be imposed on a person who is below 15 years of age.
  - (F) Fine cannot be recovered in instalments and beyond 90 days period

from the date of commitment of such acts or omissions.

(G) All fines recovered by the employer shall be entered into a register kept for the above purpose.

THE PAYMENT OF BONUS ACT, 1965

- Tripartite Commission (Meher Commission) was set up in 1961 by the Government for the question of payment of bonus.
- It is an Act to provide for the payment of bonus to person employed in certain establishment on the basis of profit or on the basis of production and productivity and for matters connected therewith.
- The Act will be applicable to all factories of establishments where twenty or more persons are employed.
- Allocable Surplus means in relation to an employer which has not made arrangements of the payment of the dividends payable out of its profits, sixty seven per cent of the available surplus in an accounting year, any other case sixty per cent of such available surplus.
- Available surplus is the amount which is available after the deductions from the gross profits calculated as per section 4 of the Act, (depreciation, direct tax and other deductions according to third schedule) made according to section 6 of the Act.
- Employee will get bonus in an accounting year only when he has worked in the establishment for not less than thirty working days in that year.
- The employee shall be disqualified from receiving bonus under this Act, if he is dismissed from service for—Fraud, riots or violent behaviour on the premises of the establishment; or theft, misappropriation or sabotage of any property of the establishment.
- Minimum bonus (after 1979) 8.33 per cent of wages earned by the employee during the accounting year or hundred rupees which ever is higher.
- Maximum bonus which is payable under the Act should not exceed 20 per cent of the wages earned by an employee in an accounting year.
- Where the salary or wage of an employee exceeds three thousand and five hundred rupees per men sum. The bonus payable to such employee shall be calculated as if the salary or wage were three thousand five hundred rupees per men sum.
- After the disbursement of 20 per cent bonus to all the eligible employees, excess allocable surplus subject to 20 per cent will be carried forward as set on and if there is no allocable surplus or fall short, such deficiency will be carried forward as is set off.
- The amount of set on or set off carried forward shall be utilized for four financial years.
- **Type of Bonus:** Minimum bonus/ statutory bonus, which is also known as deferred wage (8.33 per cent) profit sharing (maximum 20 per cent) and ex gratia (more than 20 per cent).
- The bonus should be paid, if there is a dispute, within one month from the date of operation of award or settlement. In any other case it should be paid within 8 months from the last day of financial year. With the permission of the appropriate government this time limit may extend up to two years.

TRADE UNIONS ACT, 1926

- The objective of the Act is to provide for registration of trade unions and related matters.
- Trade disputes means any disputes between employers and workman, or between employers and employers or between workman and workman, which is connected with employment or non employment or the terms of employment or the condition of labour of any person.

- Workmen means all persons employed in trade or industry. Whether or not in the employment of the employer with whom the trade disputes arises.
- Trade union means any combination whether temporary or permanent, formed primarily for the purpose of regulating the relations between workmen and employers for imposing restrictive conditions on the conduct of any trade or business and includes any federation of two or more trade union.
- Any seven or more members can register trade union. Provided that no trade union of workman shall be registered unless at least ten per cent or one hundred of the workman whichever is less engaged or employed in the industry are the members of such Trade Union.
- The payment of minimum subscription one rupee per annum for rural workers, three rupee per annum for workers in other unorganized sector, twelve rupees per annum for workers in any other case.
- Office bearers of trade union cannot be elected for more than three years.
- No member can be compelled to contribute to the fund constituted for political purpose.
- Any person who has attained the age of fifteen years may become member of registered trade union.
- Not less than one half of the total number of the office bearers of every registered trade union shall be persons actually engaged or employed in an industry with which the trade union is connected.
- Provided that the appropriate government may, by special or general order, declares that the provisions of this section shall not apply to any trade union or class of trade union specified in the order.
- By amending the Act in the year 2001 a new provision has been incorporated that all office bearers of a registered trade union, except not more than one third of the total number of the office bearers or five, whichever is less, shall be persons actually engaged or employed in the establishment or industry with which the trade union is connected.
- Where a registered trade union is dissolved, notice of the dissolution signed by seven members and by the secretary of the trade union should within fourteen days of the dissolution, be sent to the registrar.
- Registered trade unions have been granted immunity from the charges of criminal conspiracy and civil liability for the furtherance of legitimate objectives of the trade union, under section 17 and 18 of the Act.
- The funds of the registered trade union shall be spent on the objectives specified in the section 15 of the Act.
- The process of registration of trade union is provided in sections 4, 5, 6, 7 and 8 of the Act.

THE MINIMUM WAGE ACT, 1942

- An Act to provide for fixing and revision of minimum rates of wages in scheduled employment.
- Adolescent means a person who has completed his fourteen years of age but has not completed 18 years.
- Child means a person who has not completed his fourteen years age.
- Different minimum rates of wage may be fixed for different scheduled employment, different classes of work, adult, adolescent, children and apprentices, different localities.
- Minimum rates of wages may be fixed by any one or more of the following:

  By the hour

  By the day

  By the month

  By other larger wage period as may be prescribed but no wage period should exceed.

- **Minimum rate of wages:** A basic rate of wages with or without the cost of living allowance plus the cash value of any items provided at concessional rate.

  An all inclusive rate allowing for the basic rate the cost of living allowance and the cash value of any concession, if any
- Fixing and revising Minimum rate of wages can be done by either two procedure:
- Committee or committees may be constituted by the appropriate government and as per recommendations Minimum rate of wages may be fixed or revised.
- Appropriate government may publish proposals in the official gazette for fixing and revising Minimum rate of wages.
- Objections, if any, may be raised by the aggrieved parties within two months from the date of publication of proposal.
- The government after hearing both the parties finally decides Minimum rate of wages. If this process is adopted the government should consult advisory board.
- Minimum wages payable under this Act shall be paid in cash.
- **Overtime:** In case of agriculture worker one and half times the ordinary rate of wages and in any other case of twice the ordinary rate of wages.
- Where an employee is employed on piece work for which minimum piece rate has not been fixed under this Act, the employer shall pay to such employee wages at not less than the minimum time rate.
- If wages given is less than the minimum rates of wages, ten times of the remaining amount has to be paid by the employer to the employee.
- If in any scheduled employment if the number of employees exceeds 1000 the appropriate government is under legal obligation to fix the Minimum rate of wages.
- Minimum rate of wages so fixed shall be revised at least once in a period of five years.

THE INDUSTRIAL DISPUTES ACT, 1947

- The Act makes provisions for the investigation and settlement of industrial disputes, it also provides for prevention of illegal strikes and lockouts and providing relief in case of lay off and retrenchment.
- Industrial disputes means any disputes or differences between employer and employer, employers and workmen and between workmen and workmen, which is connected with the employment or non employment or the terms of employment or with the condition of labour of any person.
- Lay off means the failure, refusal or inability of an employer on account of shortage of coal, power or raw materials or the accumulation of stock or the break down of machinery or natural calamity or for any connected reason to give employment to a workmen, whose name is borne on the muster rolls of his industrial establishment and who has not been retrenched.
- Lock out means the temporary closing of a place of employment or the suspension of work or the refusal by an employer to continue to employ any number of persons employed by him.
- Retrenchment means termination by the employer of the service of a workman for any reason what so ever, otherwise than as a punishment inflicted by a way of disciplinary action but does not includes. – VRS , Retirement of workman on reaching the age of superannuation, termination of the service of workmen as a result of non renewal of contract, termination on the grounds of continuous ill health.
- Settlement means a settlement arrived at otherwise than in the course of conciliation proceedings and includes a written agreement between employer and workmen.
- Strike means cessation of work by a body of persons employed in any industry acting in combination or a concerted refusal or a refusal under a common understanding, of

any number of persons who are or have been so employed to continue to work or accept employment.

- Workman means any person (including an apprentice) employed in any industry to do any manual, unskilled, skilled, technical, operational, clerical or supervisory work for hire or reward, whether the terms of employment be expressed or implied, and for the purposes of any proceeding under this act in relation to an industrial dispute, include any such person who has been dismissed, discharged or retrenched in connection with, or as a consequence of that dispute, or whose dismissal, discharge or retrenchment has led to that dispute, but does not include any such person – who is subject to Army, Navy or Air Force Acts or who is employed in the police service or who is employed in managerial or administrative capacity or who being employed in a supervisory capacity draws wages exceeding ten thousand rupees per month.
- Discharge, dismissal, retrenchment or termination of a workman is deemed to be an industrial dispute.
- Machinery for Settlement and prevention of Industrial Disputes:
- **Works committee:** Any establishment where one hundred or more workmen are employed the employer has to constitute a works committee consisting of representatives of employers and workman engaged in the establishment.
- Conciliation Officer is a person appointed by the appropriate government, who mediates for the settlement of industrial disputes.
- Every industrial establishment in which twenty or more workmen are employed has to make a Grievance Settlement Authority for the settlement of industrial disputes.
- Under section 5 Board of Conciliation may be constituted for settlement of industrial disputes.
- For investigation purposes court of inquiry may be constituted under section 6 of the Act.
- For Adjudication of industrial disputed labour court, industrial tribunal and national industrial tribunal may be constituted by the appropriate government under section 7, 7A and 7B of the Act respectively.
- Voluntary arbitration of the industrial disputes may take place under section 10 A of the Act.
- Appropriate government may refer the industrial dispute matter to Board of Conciliation, or to court of inquiry or to labour court or tribunals or national tribunal.
- If appropriate government refers the matter to labour court, tribunal or national tribunal the authority has to deliver the judgment normally within three months from the date of reference.
- Conciliation Officer shall send report within fourteen days of the commencement of the conciliation proceeding.
- The board shall submit its report within two months from the date of reference made to it under section 10 of the Act.
- Court of inquiry is required to submit its report to the appropriate government within a period of six months from the date of reference.
- Every report of a board, labour court, tribunal or National tribunal shall be published within a period of thirty days from the date of receipt by the appropriate government under section 17 of the Act.
- Award shall be enforceable after the expiry of thirty days from the date of its publication under section 17 of the Act.
- No person employed in a public utility service shall go on strike in breach of contract, without giving to the employer a notice of strike, six week before striking;

or within fourteen days of giving such notice; or before the expiry of the date of strike specified in any such notice as aforesaid; or during the pendency of any conciliation proceeding before a conciliation officer and seven days after the conclusion of such proceedings.

- No employer carrying on any public utility service shall lock-out any of his workmen.

  Without giving them notice of lock-out within six weeks before locking out; or within fourteen days of giving such notice; or before the expiry of the date of lock-out specified in any such notice ; or during the pendency of conciliation proceeding before a conciliation officer and seven days after the conclusion of such proceedings.
- Chapter VA of the Act is applicable to industrial establishment employing 50 to 99 workmen in the preceding month and chapter VB is applicable on industrial establishments employing 100 or more workmen during the preceding 12 months.
- These chapters are not applicable on such industrial establishments which are seasonal in character and where work is performed intermittently.
- Any workmen who has completed not less than 1 years continuous service (other than casual or Badli workmen) and whose name is borne on the muster rolls of the establishment is laid off compensation at the rate of 50 per cent of basic wages and dearness allowance for the duration of laid off period.
- Workmen are not entitled to claim lay off compensation if they refuse alternative employment offered by the employer or fail to present themselves at appointed hour to the gate of the establishment and make an entry in a register provided for the purpose or such lay off arises due to strike or go slow by fellow workmen in the establishment.
- If Chapter VB is applicable to the industrial establishment than the employer has to obtain express prior permission from the appropriate government to lay off workmen and follow the other conditions prescribed under section 25 M of the Act.
- No workmen who has completed 1 year continuous service may be retrenched unless; a one-month notice stating reasons thereof is given or in lieu of notice period one month wages has to be paid. At the same time the workmen must be offered retrenchment compensation at the rate of 15 days average wages for every completed continuous service rendered by him and information to the authorities of the government in prescribed manner.
- Workmen are entitled for retrenchment compensation also in case of closure and transfer of the establishment. The procedure for retrenchment of the workmen and for their reemployment is given in section 25 G and 25 H of the Act.
- If chapter 5 B of the Act is applicable on the establishment than an employer has to obtain express prior permission from the authorities of the appropriate government as per the provisions of section 25 N of the Act.
- If any industrial establishment has to be close down than the employer must follow the provision of section 25 FFA and section 25 O of the Act respectively.
- In the year 1982 with the introduction of Chapter 5 C and schedule 5 to the Act unfair labour practices have been prohibited and specified respectively.

MINES ACT, 1952

- Every mine shall be under a sole manager with prescribed qualification.
- The owner, agent and manager of every mine shall each be responsible to see that all operations are conducted in accordance with the provisions of this Act and of the

regulations, rules, bye laws and orders made there under.

- Drinking water in every mine should be provided and maintained at suitable points with sufficient supply of cool and wholesome drinking water.
- Provision of readily accessible first aid box or cupboards with prescribed contents during all working hours.
- Notice of the occurrence / accidents to such authority in such form and within such time as may be prescribed.
- Sending notice of notified diseases to the chief inspector and to such other authorities in such form and within such time as may be prescribed.
- If any medical practitioner who attends on a person with notified disease shall without delay send a report in writing to the chief inspector.
- No work for more than forty eight hours in any week or for more than nine hours in any day and for underground employed persons not more than 8 hours a day.
- The period of work with interval or rest shall not in any day spread over more than twelve hours, and that he shall not work for more than five hours continuously before half an hour rest interval.
- The Act does not allow working in the mine for more than ten hours on any day inclusive of overtime in normal condition.
- Health, welfare, safety and leave with wages provisions are also provided in the Act.

PLANTATION LABOUR ACT, 1951

- It extends to the whole of India except the state of Jammu & Kashmir.
- Every employer of plantation has to make an application to the registering officer for registration of such plantation.
- Certifying surgeons should be appointed by State Government to carryout duties as prescribed in connection with examination and certification of young persons and workers.
- Provision as to health, drinking water and other medical facilities as prescribed by the appropriate government.
- Canteen facility for 150 or more workers.
- Crèches for 50 or more women worker employed or 20 children below 6 years brought to the workplace. This includes worker on contract also.
- Recreational facilities as prescribed by the State Government.
- Educational facilities where the children between six and twelve exceeds 12 in number.
- It is the duty of the employer to provide housing facilities to every employee including his family.
- Liability of employer in respect of accident resulting from collapse of house provided by him.
- Where there are 300 or more workers, the employer should make provision for appointing welfare officer/s.
- Weekly hours for adult workers 48 hours in a week where as for adolescent worker 24 hours.
- Provision for weekly holidays, daily intervals (working up to 5 hours).
- Night work for women and children only with the special permission of State Government.
- Certificate of fitness shall be issued by certifying surgeons and shall be valid for 12 months.
- Provision of leave with wages to an adult for every 20 days working, a young person one day for every 15 days of working.
- Notice of accident.
- Register of accident.
- Penalties and procedure: Obstructing inspector fine up to Rs. 500/- or imprisonment up to 3 months or both.

- Willful refusal to produce documents, fine up to Rs. 500/- or up to 3 months imprisonment or both.

WORKERS PARTICIPATION IN MANAGEMENT

It is a mechanism to facilitate participation of workers in the process of decision-making. It is a power balancing process which recognizes the interest of the two parties' conflict, but that this can be resolved through negotiations. Workers participation is directed towards the identification of common interests between the two parties and their pursuit through cooperation. This definition has put forth certain points in regards to workers participation. These are:

- The participation has to be at different level of management: At the shop floor level; at the department level; and at the top level.
- Participation ensures the willing acceptance of responsibilities by the body of workers. As they become party to decision-making, they have to commit themselves to ensuring implementation.
- Participation is conducted through the mechanism of different forums and practices which provide for the association of workers representatives.

GOALS OF PARTICIPATION

The goals or aims of participation have to be viewed in the context of the aspirations and expectations of the workers, management and the government.

Economic Goals

The primary purpose of an industrial organization is the enhancement of profit. The economic goal of the workers is increased wages and improved working and living conditions in achieving this goal. Participation ensures improvements in working efficiency that ultimately results in the profit of the industrial organization.

Socio-Psychological Goals

Workers participation helps in satisfying socio-psychological needs of workers by way of self expression and improving their self image by association with decision-making. Therefore, participation brings qualitative change in the attitude of both the parties. It develops sense of belonging, mutual trust, respect and understanding between each other and ensures industrial peace. Besides these economic, socio-psychological and attitudinal goals, workers participation also bring change in the organizational set up of production by transferring the management functions entirely to the workers so that the management becomes "Self Management".

FORMS OF WORKERS PARTICIPATION

Participation may take several forms, the different forms of participation are information sharing; consultation, association, and joint decision-making and implementation.

Information Sharing

At this level, employees do not exercise any influence over managerial decision-making, but have an access to information about the industrial organisation in which they are employed.

Consultation

In this form, workers are consulted by the management on certain matters before decisions are taken. There matters may relate to the introduction of, or modification in, certain amenities and facilities to be provided to the workers, or even to the method or system of work and the changes that might be introduced in it. The management may seek advice through consultation, but the ultimate decision rest with the management.

Association of Workers

In consultation, the management seeks advice and invites suggestions, in association the representatives of workers could share in the decision-making process with management by participation in joint committees etc. There are number of committees, such as the safety committee, the canteen committee and the works committee, in which the representatives of workers share responsibility with the management in taking decisions.

Joint Decision-Making

The highest order of participation reached when two parties involved take decision together and administer them joint. At this level of participation, the items on which the decisions are taken are not only of close interest to workers alone, but are matters of common interest, covering improvement in efficiency and cost reduction.

HRD SUB-SYSTEM

Any systematic or formal way of developing the competencies and motivation of individuals in an organisation and building the organisation's climate can be called an HRD method. As such there can be many HRD methods available for organisations. However, the most frequently used methods are as follows:

1. Manpower planning
2. Performance Appraisal and Feedback
3. Training, Education and Development
4. Potential Appraisal and Promotion
5. Career Development and Career Planning
6. Compensation and Reward
7. O.D. Techniques
8. Role Analysis and Role Development
9. Quality of Work Life and Employee Welfare
10. Participative Devices
11. Communication
12. Counselling
13. Grievance Redressal
14. Data Storage and Research
15. Industrial Relations.

Following is a brief description of these methods:

(1) **Manpower planning:** Manpower planning is the sheet anchor of all HRD efforts. It is concerned with the following:

(i) Assessment of manpower needs, including forecasting such needs based on the analysis of the policies of the company, trends of its development, plans for diversification, etc.

(ii) Manpower audit, *i.e.*, examining whether manpower strength for various jobs is inadequate or more than what should be employed. Both under-staffing and overstaffing may be highly demotivating in the company. Thus, manpower planning is linked with corporate plans and strategies on the one hand and the job analysis on the other.

(2) **Performance appraisal and feedback:** It is a very critical HRD mechanism under which the performance of an employee is periodically appraised by the employee himself in collaboration with his boss. In the light of the difficulties faced by the employee he redefines his future goals. The mechanism emphasises the development of the employees (by identifying their growth needs) rather than their evaluation. Open, objective and participative appraisal and feedback develop better superior subordinate relations. During the appraisal interview, the superior shares the concerns of the subordinate and even guides him to achieve his targets.

(3) **Training, education and development:** These are 3 different HRD mechanisms with different focus and purpose as shown in the following table: Three broad areas in which training may be imparted are technical, behavioural and conceptual. It is commonly believed that the rank and file workers need training in the technical area only. Training in the other two areas is not very useful for them. But recent experiences of many

Indian companies, behavioural training to workers produces several useful results such as the following:

(i) Improvement in workers' behaviour with their superior and peers.

(ii) Development of 'we' feeling instead of 'I'.

(iii) Decrease in the habit of hiding one's own mistakes and highlighting others mistakes.

(iv) Increased interest in suggestion scheme.

(v) Increased awareness of family needs and more interest in family affairs.

(4) Potential appraisal and promotion : It is another important HRD sub-system which is concerned with identifying the potential of an employee for future development and promotion in the company. This focuses on finding out periodically the extent to which a given individual possesses the critical attributes required to handle higher level responsibilities. Thus, it is linked with Job and role analysis. In HRD, promotion is not considered to be a reward. This is because it is not based on performance but it is based on the potential of an employee.

(5) Career development and career planning: It may be useful to help new employees become aware of the various phases of development in the company, and plan with senior employee their specific career path. Necessary help may also be given to employees with limited potential to cope with reality. In the HRD system, corporate growth plans are not kept secret. They are made known to the employees to plan their career.

(6) Compensation and reward: These are common positive reinforces. They should be clearly related to the performance and behaviour of employees. Failure to reward employees properly or over rewarding undeserving employees reduces the reinforcing effect of rewards. Under HRD while salary structure is based on job analysis, salary increase is linked with performance.

(7) O.D. techniques: Many organisations make use of several O.D. techniques for the development of their human resource. These include team-building, organizational mirroring, T-group etc. In team-building people learn how to work in collaboration with each others. Under organisational mirroring; the host group gets feedback from representatives from several other organisational groups about how it is perceived and regarded. The intervention is designed to improve the relationship between groups and increase the inter-group effectiveness. In T-group participant learn to be more competent in inter-personal relationship. They learn about themselves, how other react to their behaviour and about the dynamics of group formation, group norms and group growth.

(8) Role analysis and role development : This is an extremely important technique of HRD. Under it the job of an individual in the organisation is analysed and enriched in terms of his role and not in terms of his job. His immediate superior and subordinates sit together to discuss their expectations, about the job from each other. They then arrive at a consensus about the individual's role and prepare his role description. It is always ensured that a role is sufficiently challenging for the individual provides him adequate autonomy for taking initiative and is linked with other organisational roles to avoid a feeling of isolation.

Whereas role analysis, role development and role description are usually, related managerial jobs, job analysis, job enrichment and job description are, related to worker's jobs. Job analysis of a worker's job is done to know its critical attributes which ultimately determine all those, job qualities or attributes which a job-holder should possess. Job descriptions describe these qualities. Job enrichment signifies efforts to make a job more motivating.

(9) Quality of work life: For ensuring a congenial atmospheres in an organisation for implementation of HRD methods, only good wages are, not enough. They also need to be provided with good physical conditions and motivation work. The presence of these factors may not help the success of HRD initiatives but their absence definitely produce adverse effect.

(10) Participative devices : Following are some important participative devices:

- **Bi-partite meetings:** (between management and workers):
  (a) To arrive a settlements concerning worker's wages and service conditions.
  (b) To review the working of existing settlements and examine their impact on workplace discipline, Work ethics, customer service, etc.
- **Information sharing**: To share information about the business profitability, performance of the company competition, marketing etc.
- **Joint surveys**: Management and union to undertake joint surveys on the state of morale, motivation, grievances of workers, etc., and to jointly plan ways of dealing with these problems.
- **Task forces:** To undertake study of problems like 'Absenteeism', 'Indiscipline', etc., and suggests ways to solve the problem.
- **Collaborative projects**: To undertake jointly certain projects e.g. project on employee welfare or workers education.
- **Quality Circles**: To involve workers at the grass root level for periodically discussing work related problems. Quality circles are small groups of employees which are formed voluntarily. They work on the simple premise that the people who do a job every day know more about it than any one else particularly when quality or productivity is involved.

(11) Communication: This process is fundamental to all aspects of life and is vital to the function of integration. Real communication takes place when the listener truly hears and understands the position and intent of the speaker. This requires a type listening which is called 'projective'. While hearing the remarks of the speaker the listener must project himself into the mind of speaker in order to understand the speakers view point.

(12) Counselling and Mentoring : It is an important HRD mechanism to provide timely guidance to workers on problems relating to hand and heart Many Indian companies trained counsellors for this purpose.

(13) Grievance redressal : A grievance redressal procedure vital to all organisation. The mere fact that an employee has access to judicial type of justice is sat even though he never has an occasion to use it.

(14) Data storage and Research : This also is a very important HRD mechanism. It essential to preserve systematic information about every individual, employee on topics such as the employee's personal characteristic performance—potential, salary etc. so that this may be used for counselling, career planning, training, promotion.

(15) Industrial relations : Last though not the least important subsystem of HRD is industrial relations. It is a catalytic force which plays a vital role in facilitating the impact of all other methods. Good industrial relations based on mutual trust and goodwill make the execution of HRD programmes easy. Poor industrial relations based on distrust and fear makes execution difficult.

MULTIPLE CHOICE QUESTIONS

1. Who is not a workman of the following?
A. A clerk
B. A person doing manual labour
C. An unskilled labour
D. A supervisor whose monthly wages exceed Rs. 10,000 per month

2. In which industrial establishment the employer has to constitute a works committee?
A. Employing 50 workmen
B. Employing 75 workmen
C. Employing 100 workmen
D. Employing 25 workmen

3. Which is not the machinery of Adjudication?
A. Labour Court
B. Industrial Tribunal
C. National Industrial Tribunal
D. Court of Inquiry

4. What is the rate layoff compensation?
A. 50% of the basic wages
B. 50% of the basic wages and dearness allowance
C. 100% of the basic wages
D. 75% of the basic wages

5. What is the rate of retrenchment
A. 15 days average pay for every completed year of continuous service
B. 25 days average pay for every completed year of continuous service
C. 45 days average pay for every completed year of continuous services
D. 60 days average pay for every completed year of continuous service

6. In which schedule the unfair labour practices have been specified?
A. Schedule I B. Schedule II
C. Schedule IV D. Schedule V

7. What is the minimum amount of compensation given to an employee in case of death due to an accident?
A. Rs. 80,000 B. Rs. 1,10,000
C. Rs. 1,20,000 D. Rs 1,40,000

8. In which year the title of the Workmen's Compensation Act, 1923 has been changed to the Employee's Compensation Act, 1923?
A. 2009 C. 2011
C. 2010 D. 2007

9. By which manner the rate of compensation for permanent total disablement is calculated?
A. 60% of the wages last drawn x factor.
B. 50% of the wages last drawn x factor.
C. 40% of the wages last drawn x factor.
D. 70% of the wages last drawn x factor.

10. Notice of claim for compensation be given within.
A. One years of the occurrence of the accident
B. Two years of the occurrence of the accident
C. Three years of the occurrence of the accident
D. Six months of the occurrence of the accident

11. What is the minimum number of members required to apply for registration of a trade union?
A. 10 or more members
B. 15 or more members
C. 7 or more members
D. 9 or more members

12. Who can appoint registrar of trade union?
A. An Employer
B. A Trade Union
C. Workman
D. Appropriate Government

13. Which act is not applicable to a registered trade union?
A. The Societies Registration Act, 1860.
B. The Co-operative Societies Act, 1912.
C. The Companies Act, 1956.
D. Above all

14. Which person is qualified to become office bearer of a trade union?
A. He has attained the age of 18 years.
B. He has attained the age of 15 years.
C. He has attained the age of 14 years.
D. He has attained the age of 17 years.

15. Which is not a right of registered trade union?
A. It can acquire property
B. It can sue any person
C. It can enter into an agreement
D. Agreement to commit an offence

16. Under which section of the payment of Bonus Act, 1965, gross profit is calculated?
A. Section 5 B. Section 4
C. Section 6 D. Section 7

17. What is the rate of minimum bonus?
A. 4% of the wage
B. 8% of the wage
C. 8.33% of the wage
D. 10% of the wage

18. What is the monthly wage limit to claim bonus?
A. Rs. 7,500 B. Rs. 3,500
C. Rs. 10,000 D. Rs. 15,000

19. Under which section available surplus is calculated?
A. Section 8 B. Section 10
C. Section 4 D. Section 5

20. What is the time limit for payment of bonus?
A. In case of dispute within one month from the enforcement of award or settlement.
B. Within a period of eight months from the closing of accounting year.
C. Within two years upon application to the appropriate government.
D. Above all

21. Who is responsible to pay wages?
A. Employer
B. Manager appointed under the Factories Act, 1948.
C. A person responsible to the employer for the supervision and control of the industrial establishment.
D. Above all

22. No wage period shall exceed
A. One month B. Two months
C. A year D. Six months

23. When the wages shall be paid in a factory employing less than 1000 employed persons?
A. Before the expiry of 10th day, after the last day of the wage period.
B. Before the expiry of 7th day, after the last day of the wage period.
C. Within one year, after the last day of the wage period.
D. No such time limit.

24. Which item is not deduction from wages?
A. Fine
B. For absence from duty
C. With holding of annual increment
D. Income Tax

25. No fine shall be imposed on any employed person who is:
A. 18 years of age
B. 21 years of age
C. 25 years of age
D. 14 years of age

26. What is the monthly wage limit to become a member of Employees Provident Fund?
A. Rs. 7,500 B. Rs. 10,000
C. Rs. 6,500 D. Rs. 15,000

27. What is the rate of contribution to the Employees Provident Fund?
A. 12% of the wage
B. 12% of the basic wage and DA
C. 13% of the wage
D. 8.33% of the wage

28. In which year the Employees Pension Scheme was implemented?
A. 1996 B. 1993
C. 1997 D. 1995

29. What is the monthly wage limit to calculate employee's pension?
A. Rs. 10,000 B. Rs. 6,500
C. Rs. 15,000 D. Rs. 7,500

30. How many funds are constituted under the Employees Provident Funds Act?
A. Two B. Three
C. Four D. One

31. Initially on which industrial establishment the Industrial Employment (standing orders) Act, 1946 is applicable?
A. Employing 100 workmen
B. Employing 25 workmen
C. Employing 35 workmen
D. Employing 50 workmen

32. What is the meaning of standing orders?
A. Work rules
B. Service conditions
C. Rules framed on items specified in schedule I of the Act.
D. Rules framed and certified on items specified in schedule II of the Act.

33. How many copies of the draft standing orders be submitted to the Certifying Officer?
A. Six B. Five
C. Seven D. One

34. In the absence of any agreement, when certified standing orders can be modified?
A. After one month of its implementation.
B. After three month of its implementation.
C. After five month of its implementation.
D. After six month of its implementation.

35. Which authority shall hear appeal against the order of certifying Officer?
A. Appropriate Government
B. District Court
C. Appellate Authority
D. High Court

36. Which person can be appointed as an apprentice?
A. He is not less than 14 years of age.
B. He satisfies the standard of educational qualifications.
C. He is physically fit person.
D. Above all

37. Every contract of apprenticeship be registered with:
A. Apprentice Adviser
B. Appropriate Government
C. Apprenticeship Council
D. Above all

38. Apprentice means a person who is
A. undergoing any training
B. undergoing training in pursuance of a contract of apprenticeship
C. training in a designated trade
D. Above all

39. Designated trade means
A. Any trade
B. Any occupation
C. Subject field in engineering
D. Above all

40. Apprentices are:
A. Workers B. Not workers
C. Workmen D. Employees

41. What is the wage limit per month to become an insured person under the ESI Act, 1948?
A. Rs. 10,000 B. Rs. 7,500
C. Rs. 6,500 D. Rs. 15,000

42. What is the rate of Employee's contribution to the ESI scheme per month?
A. 1.75% of wages
B. 1.85% of wages
C. 1.95% of wages
D. Above all

43. Which benefit an insured person is entitled to claim?
A. Medical Benefit
B. Sickness Benefit
C. Disablement Benefit
D. Above all

44. In which year unemployment insurance scheme was introduced in the Act?
A. 2006 B. 2005
C. 2007 D. 2010

45. What is the rate of employer's monthly contribution to the ESI scheme?
A. 5.75% of wages
B. 3.75% of wages
C. 4.75% of wages
D. 8.33% of wages

46. The number of benefits period under this scheme in a year are:
A. Three B. Four
C. Two D. Six

47. The Maternity Benefit Act, 1961 applies:
A. on a Factory B. on a Mine
C. on a Plantation D. All of the above

48. When a woman employee is entitled to claim under the maternity benefit:
A. Worked not less than 180 days in a year
B. Worked not less than 80 days in a year
C. Worked not less than 70 days in a year
D. Worked not less than 90 days in a year

49. How many nursing breaks a woman delivered a child will get in addition to the interval of rest?
A. Four B. Three
C. One D. Two

50. Child is defined under the Maternity benefit Act as :
A. Includes a still born-child
B. Born-child
C. Six months child
D. Six weeks child

51. Who is regarded as the father of Scientific Management?
A. Albert Bandura
B. Louis D. Brandies
C. Frederick Winslow Taylor
D. Elton Mayo

52. The Principle of Equifinality operates
A. within the internal environment
B. within the external environment
C. without environment
D. hostile environment

53. Max Weber developed a theory of
A. Autocratic Management
B. Democratic Management
C. Bureaucratic Management
D. Free Style Management

54. Grapevine is a type of
A. Formal Communication
B. Written Communication
C. Lateral Communication
D. Informal Communication

55. Decision-making process is guided by
A. Policy B. Procedure
C. Programme D. Strategy

56. Ten 'C' model of HRM architect was advanced by
A. Katz and Kahn
B. Alan Price
C. Chester I. Bernard
D. Max Weber

57. Recruitment means
A. Total number of inquiries made
B. Total number of applications received
C. Total number of persons short listed
D. Total number of selections made

58. Arrange the following steps of Job analysis in proper sequence :
(a) Prepare the job description report.
(b) Select the job.
(c) Find out the requirements for each part of the job.
(d) Break the job into various parts.

Codes :
A. (b), (a), (d), (c) B. (b), (c), (d), (a)
C. (b), (d), (c), (a) D. (d), (c), (b), (a)

59. Which of the following is not a factor for wage determination?
A. Cost of living
B. Prevailing wages
C. Purchasing power of people
D. Productivity

60. Which of the following is not a part of disciplinary action?
A. Warning B. Suspension
C. Transfer D. Discharge

61. The goal of HRD system is to develop
A. the capabilities of each employee as an individual.
B. the capabilities of each individual in relation to his or her present role.
C. the capabilities of each employee in relation to his or her expected future roles.
D. All the above

62. Which one is not a part of HRD system?
A. Career Planning
B. Manpower Planning
C. Training
D. Organizational Development

63. The other name of Sensitivity Training is
A. T-Group Training
B. Brainstorming
C. In-basket Exercise
D. Managerial Grid Training

64. A small voluntary group of employees doing similar or related work who meet regularly to identify, analyse and solve product quality problems and to improve general operations is known as
A. Task Group B. Kaizen Groups
C. Quality Circles D. Informal Groups

65. Which of the following is not an OD technique?
A. Sensitivity Training
B. Delphi Technique
C. Survey Feedback
D. Grid Training

66. Which of the following statements about Organizational Behaviour is wrong?
A. It is an inter-disciplinary subject.
B. It believes that individual, group and organization are subsystems of OB.
C. Its explanation find roots in systems as well as contingency theories.
D. It deals only with prediction of human behaviour at work.

67. Match the following concepts of OB with their proponents :

Concept of OB	Proponents
a. Classical Conditioning	i. Albert Bandura
b. Operant Conditioning	ii. Ivan Pavlov
c. Social Learning Theory	iii. Sigmund Freud
d. Psycho Analytical Theory	iv. B.F. Skinner

Codes :

	a	b	c	d
A.	ii	i	iii	iv
B.	iii	iv	ii	i
C.	ii	iv	i	iii
D.	iv	iii	i	ii

68. Cultural Diversity explained by Greet Hofstede has four components. Which of the following is not a part of it?
A. Individualism *vs* Collectivism
B. Power Distance
C. Uncertainty Avoidance
D. Quality *vs* Quantity of Life

69. Arrange the following phases of group formation in their right sequence :
(a) forming (b) norming
(c) performing (d) storming
(e) adjourning

Codes :
A. (a), (d), (c), (b), (e)
B. (a), (d), (b), (c), (e)
C. (a), (b), (d), (c), (e)
D. (a), (c), (d), (b), (e)

70. **Assertion (A) :** Psychological contract is an unwritten agreement that exists between employees and employers setting out mutual expectations.

Reason (R) : Role expectations are influenced by role perception of one's own self and others and cannot always be formally defined excepting in setting out role identity.

Codes :
A. (A) is right and (R) logically explains the (A).
B. (A) is wrong and (R) does not explain the (A).
C. (A) is right and (R) attributed is wrong.
D. Both (A) and (R) are wrong.

71. Which of the following is not a field of industrial relations?
A. Study of workers and their trade unions
B. Study of consumers and their associations
C. Management and their associations
D. State and their institutions

72. Which of the following is not a determinant factor of industrial relations?
A. Institutional factors
B. Economic factors
C. Technological factors
D. Social stratification factors

73. Which of the following cannot be said to be an effect of industrial disputes?
A. High Productivity, Peace and Profit
B. High Labour Turnover
C. Higher rate of Absenteeism
D. Higher rate of Man-days lost

74. Which of the following has not been provided under the Code of Discipline?
A. Unfair Labour Practices
B. Recognition of Trade Unions
C. Grievance Procedure
D. Multinational Companies

75. Who among the following propounded the theory of industrial democracy?
A. Allan Flanders
B. Neil W. Chamberlain
C. Sydney & Beatrice Webbs
D. John T. Dunlop

76. Which of the following was the first trade union organised in India?
A. Madras Labour Union
B. Textile Labour Association
C. Bombay Millhands Association
D. Kamgar Hitvardhak Sabha

77. Functional types of trade unions were advocated by
A. Selig Perlman B. Robert F. Hoxie
C. G.D.H. Cole D. S.H. Slitcher

78. The Inter-Union Code of Conduct was evolved in the year
A. 1956 B. 1957
C. 1958 D. 1959

79. Match the following :

	Type of the Union		**Characteristics**
a.	Craft Union	i.	Union of Unions
b.	General Union	ii.	Wage earners in a particular enterprise
c.	Industrial Union	iii.	Any wage earner
d.	Federation	iv.	Workers engaged in similar nature of work

Codes :

	a	b	c	d
A.	iv	iii	ii	i
B.	iv	ii	iii	i
C.	iii	iv	ii	i
D.	ii	iii	i	iv

80. Match the following :

	National Labour Federations		**Year of Formation**
a.	All India Trade Union Congress	i.	1948
b.	Indian National Trade Union Congress	ii.	1970
c.	Hind Mazdoor Sabha	iii.	1920
d.	Centre of Indian Trade Unions	iv.	1947

Codes :

	a	b	c	d
A.	iii	ii	iv	i
B.	iii	i	iv	ii
C.	iii	iv	i	ii
D.	ii	i	iii	iv

81. Which of the following is not a type of Labour Legislation?
A. Regulative Legislation
B. Protective Legislation
C. Uniformity Legislation
D. Social Security Legislation

82. The first Factory Legislation in India was enacted in
A. 1860 B. 1881
C. 1882 D. 1891

83. Which of the following benefits have not been provided under the Employee's State Insurance Act, 1948?
A. Sickness Benefit
B. Unemployment Allowance
C. Childrens' Allowance
D. Disablement Benefit

84. Before the enactment of Employees' Compensation Act, 1923, workers suffering a personal injury in course of employment claimed damages under
A. Economic Law B. Social Law
C. Common Law D. None of the above

85. The Royal Commission on Labour examined which of the two States' Maternity Benefit

Acts and recommended enactment of similar laws all over the country?

A. Bombay and Madhya Pradesh
B. Madras and Mysore
C. Bihar and Bengal
D. Punjab and Assam

86. What will be the minimum number of workers required for organizing a trade union for registration according to the latest amendment under the Trade Unions' Act, 1926?

A. 7 workers B. 10 %
C. 100 D. 10% or 100 or 7

87. The minimum subscription rate for members of trade unions of rural workers shall not be less than

A. Rs. 12 per annum
B. Rs. 3 per annum
C. Rs. 1 per annum
D. No such provision

88. Which of the following statements about the definition of industry as given in the Industrial Disputes Act, 1947 is not right?

A. It means any business, trade, undertaking, manufacture or calling of employers.
B. It includes any calling, service, employment, handicraft or industrial occupation or avocation of workmen.
C. This definition has been revised in 1982 in a leading case of 1978.
D. The revised definition has been implemented after due notification.

89. 'First come last go and last come first go' is the principle of

A. Lay-off B. Closure
C. Retrenchment D. Dismissal

90. Which of the following statements is not true regarding Industrial Employment (Standing Orders) Act, 1946?

A. Within 6 months from the date of application of the Act, the employer shall submit to the Certifying Officer 5 copies of the draft standing orders.
B. There is a schedule which sets out the matters to be incorporated in the standing orders.
C. There is no provision to refer the draft standing orders to the Unions/Workmen by the Certifying Officer.
D. Certifying Officers and appellate authorities shall have powers of Civil Courts.

91. Which of the following statements with regard to labour welfare is not correct?

A. Welfare is a social concept.
B. Welfare is a relative concept.
C. Welfare is a positive concept.
D. Welfare is an absolute concept.

92. Which of the following is not an intramural welfare facility?

A. Canteen
B. Workmen safety measures
C. Housing facility
D. Drinking water facility

93. Match the following :

Principles of Welfare Work	**Theme**
a. Principle of Coordination or Integration	i. When welfare is given for a felt need at the opportune moment.
b. Principle of Association	ii. When welfare is treated as a total concept and not a piece-meal programme.
c. Principle of Accountability	iii. Work with individual is motto of this principle.
d. Principle of Timeliness	iv. Welfare is to be satisfactorily utilized is the motto of this principle.

Codes :

	a	b	c	d
A.	ii	iv	iii	i
B.	ii	iii	iv	i
C.	iii	iv	ii	i
D.	iv	ii	i	iii

94. "The factory and industrial workplaces provide ample opportunities for owners and managers of capital to exploit workers in an unfair manner. This, cannot be allowed to continue" is the philosophy of which theory of Labour Welfare?

A. Placating Theory
B. Functional Theory
C. Policing Theory
D. Religious Theory

95. "A place for everything and everything in its place" is the principle that governs

A. Placement
B. Housekeeping
C. Officekeeping
D. Floor Management

96. Which of the following is not a peculiarity of labour market?

A. Labour market is normally local in nature.
B. The number of buyers is less than the number of sellers.
C. Labour is less mobile.
D. Worker can sell not only his own labour but also the labour of his fellow workers.

97. Which one of the following is not a characteristic feature of Indian labour force?

A. High rate of absenteeism and labour turnover
B. Low degree of unionization rate
C. Lack of mobility
D. Homogeneous in nature

98. Which of the following is not a type of wage differentials?

A. Occupational B. Geographical
C. Industrial D. Social

99. The Concepts of Wages like Minimum Wage, Fair Wage and Living Wages were given by

A. Royal Commission on Labour
B. First National Commission on Labour
C. Committee on Fair Wages
D. Adarkar Committee

100. Which of the following theories of wages was propounded by Karl Marx?

A. Subsistence Theory
B. Surplus Value Theory
C. Wage Fund Theory
D. Residual Claimant Theory

101. Match the following :

Thinker	**Management Principle**
a. F.W. Taylor	i. Authority and Responsibility
b. Henri Fayol	ii. Hierarchy
c. Weber	iii. Separation of planning from doing
d. Elton Mayo	iv. Human Relations Approach

Codes :

	a	b	c	d
A.	iii	i	iv	ii
B.	iii	iv	i	ii
C.	iii	i	ii	iv
D.	iii	ii	i	iv

102. Which of the following is the major element of planning process?

A. Developing leadership abilities
B. Selecting right people
C. Perception of opportunities
D. Motivating people

103. Which principle of management is violated by matrix organisation structure?

A. Division of Labour
B. Unity of Direction
C. Unity of Command
D. None of the above

104. Which of the following involves careful analysis of inputs and corrective actions before operation is completed?

A. Feed forward control
B. Concurrent control
C. Feedback control
D. All the above

105. Which of the following is not a semantic barrier of communication?

A. Faulty translation
B. Ambiguous words

C. Specialist's language
D. Inattention

106. People should be regarded as assets rather than variable costs was emphasised in
A. Personnel Management
B. Human Resource Management
C. Personnel Administration
D. Public Administration

107. The classical theorists favoured organisation based on
A. Civilian model B. Strategic model
C. Military model D. None of the above

108. Job analysis includes:
A. Job description and job enlargement
B. Job enlargement and job enrichment
C. Job description and job specification
D. All of the above

109. A test which measures, what it is intended to measure is
A. Reliable test B. Standardised test
C. Objective test D. Valid test

110. An enquiry that is conducted afresh because of the objections raised by alleged employee is called
A. Domestic enquiry
B. De-novo enquiry
C. Ex-parte enquiry
D. None of the above

111. The concept of HRD score card was introduced in India by
A. Udai Pareek B. Rao and Pareek
C. T.V. Rao D. Arun Honappa

112. Performance appraisal by all the following parties is called 360° performance appraisal:
A. Supervisors and Peers
B. Subordinates and Employees themselves
C. Users of Service and Consultants
D. All the above

113. The following is the right process of training:
A. Instructional design, validation, need analysis, implementation and evaluation
B. Need analysis, instructional design, validation, implementation and evaluation
C. Need analysis, validation, instructional design, implementation and evaluation
D. Instructional design, need analysis, implementation, validation and evaluation

114. Fish bone analysis as a tool of quality circle was advanced by
A. Edward Deming
B. Joseph Juran
C. Kouru Ishi Kawa
D. Phillip Crosby

115. Match the following :

	Books and Concepts		**Authors**
a.	Games People Play	i.	Eric Bernie
b.	I am OK you are OK	ii.	Kurt Lewin
c.	Johari Window	iii.	Thomas A. Harris
d.	Force Field Analysis	iv.	Joseph Lufth & Harry Inghams

Codes :

	a	b	c	d
A.	ii	i	iv	iii
B.	i	iii	iv	ii
C.	iv	ii	iii	i
D.	iii	i	ii	iv

116. Which of the following decreases group cohesiveness?
A. Agreement on group goals
B. Frequency of interaction
C. Large group size
D. All the above

117. Managers subscribing to ______ assumptions attempt to structure, control and closely supervise their employees.
A. Theory 'X'
B. Theory 'Y'
C. Both Theory 'X' and Theory 'Y'
D. Neither Theory 'X' nor Theory 'Y'

118. According to Fiedler's Contingency Model of Leadership, which one of the following is a situational variable?

A. Leader – Member relationship
B. Organisational System
C. Degree of task structure
D. Leader's position power

119. The right sequence of steps in Kurt Lewin's change procedure is
A. Unfreezing – Moving – Freezing
B. Moving – Unfreezing – Freezing
C. Unfreezing – Freezing – Moving
D. Freezing – Moving – Unfreezing

120. Which of the following is not a traditional method of organisational development?
A. Survey feedback
B. Sensitivity training
C. Process consultation
D. Managerial grid

121. Characteristics of Industrial Relations do not include :
A. Industrial Relations are outcome of employment relationship in an industrial enterprise.
B. Industrial Relations promote the skills and methods of adjustment and co-operation with each other.
C. Industrial Relations create complex rules and regulations to maintain cordial relations.
D. Industrial Relations system creates an environment of distrust and conflict.

122. Who are not the Actors of Industrial Relations?
A. Workers and their organisations
B. Employers and their organisations
C. Community and cultural associations
D. Government and the role of the State

123. Which of the following is a machinery for settlement of industrial disputes?
A. Indian Labour Conference
B. Joint Management Council
C. Industrial Tribunal
D. Standing Labour Committees

124. Match List-I with List-II :

List-I	List-II
(a) Joint Management Council consisting of representatives of workers and management was considered by the Indian Labour Conference (ILC) in its 15th Session in the year	i. 1958
(b) Works Committees were set-up under the Industrial Disputes Act in the year	ii. 1947
(c) ILO established in the year	iii. 1919
(d) First National Commission on Labour submitted its report in the year	iv. 1969

Codes :

	(a)	(b)	(c)	(d)
A.	i	ii	iii	iv
B.	iv	i	iii	ii
C.	iii	i	ii	iv
D.	ii	iv	i	iii

125. A Trade Union means
"An association of workers in one or more professions carried on mainly for the purpose of protecting and advancing the members' economic interest in connection with their daily work".
Identify the author :
A. Sidney and Beatrice Webb
B. J. Cunnison
C. G.D.H. Cole
D. Clyde E. Dankert

126. A union may claim recognition for an industry in a local area, if it has membership of
A. 10% of the workers in that industry.
B. 15% of the workers in that area.
C. 25% of the workers of that industry in that area.
D. 30% of the workers in similar industry.

128. Who among the following advocated the Trusteeship Theory of Trade Union?
A. N.M. Lokhande
B. B.P. Wadia

C. G.L. Nanda
D. M.K. Gandhi

128. Inter and intra-union rivalry in Trade Unions is reduced by
A. The provisions of the Industrial Disputes Act 1947
B. By voluntary tripartite code of inter-union rivalry – 1957
C. By bipartite mutual agreement at the industry level
D. Above all

129. Match the following trade unions according to the year of formation :

List-I	List-II
a. AITUC	i. 1947
b. CITU	ii. 1948
c. INTUC	iii. 1920
d. HMS	iv. 1970

Codes :

	a	b	c	d
A.	iii	iv	i	ii
B.	ii	iii	iv	i
C.	iii	i	ii	iv
D.	i	ii	iii	iv

130. 'Employment Injury' means personal injury to an employee caused by accident or occupational disease arising out of and in the course of employment being an insurable employment if the accident occurs or occupational disease is contracted only within territorial limits of India and not outside India.

The above statement is
A. correct.
B. incorrect.
C. true only in case of occupational injury.
D. true only in case of accident.

131. Under ESI Act, 1948 a member of the Corporation, Standing Committee or the Medical Council shall cease to be a member of the body if he fails to attend
A. two consecutive meetings
B. three meetings intermittently
C. three consecutive meetings
D. four consecutive meetings

132. Under Workmen's Compensation Act, 1923
A. individual manager subordinate to an employer cannot act as managing agent.
B. managing agent includes an individual manager subordinate to an employer.
C. only employer can act as managing agent.
D. the appropriate government shall appoint managing agent.

133. The Workmen's Compensation Act, 1923, the Maternity Benefit Act, 1965 and the Employees State Insurance Act, 1948
A. together can be applicable.
B. the Maternity Benefit Act and the Employees State Insurance Act can be applicable at a time.
C. the Workmen's Compensation Act and the Employees State Insurance Act can be applicable at a time.
D. if the Workmen's Compensation Act and the Maternity Benefit Act are applicable, the Employees State Insurance Act is not applicable.

134. What is the content of the Schedule I of the ESI Act, 1948?
A. List of injuries deemed to result in permanent total disablement.
B. List of injuries deemed to result in permanent partial disablement.
C. List of occupational diseases.
D. None of the above

135. A person is qualified to be chosen as a member of the executive or any other office bearer of the registered trade union if he attained the age of
A. Fifteen years
B. Eighteen years
C. Twenty one years
D. Twenty five years

136. The registered trade union can collect political fund from its members as a
A. general fund
B. cannot collect political fund
C. separate fund from the interested members
D. only from political parties

137. 'Award' under Industrial Disputes Act, 1947 is

(a) not interim determination of labour court
(b) not arbitration award under Section 10A
(c) not final determination of labour court
(d) not final determination of arbitration award under section 10A

A. All statements are true.
B. (a) and (d) are true.
C. (b) is true.
D. All statements are wrong.

138. The dispute of individual workman is deemed to be industrial dispute if the dispute or difference is connected with or arising out of the following where no other workman nor any union of workman is a party to the dispute.

A. Grievance of an individual workman.
B. Discharge of an individual workman.
C. Dismissal of an individual workman.
D. Discharge, dismissal, retrenchment or otherwise termination of services of an individual workman.

139. The ceiling on wage or salary for calculation of Bonus under the Payment of Bonus Act 1965 is

A. Rs. 2,500 B. Rs. 3,500
C. Rs. 4,500 D. Rs. 6,500

140. "A desirable state of existence comprehending physical, mental, moral and emotional health or well being" is the theme of which concept of Labour Welfare?

A. Social Concept
B. Total Concept
C. Relative Concept
D. Positive Concept

141. **Assertion (A) :** Labour Welfare is relative to time and space.

Reason (R) : It shall be universal and perpetual.

A. Assertion and Reason are right.
B. Assertion is wrong and Reason is right.
C. Both Assertion and Reason are wrong.
D. Assertion is right but its explanation given in Reason is wrong.

142. Minimum conditions of welfare is explained by

A. Dr. Aykroid's formula
B. Subsistence Theory
C. Both A and B
D. None of the above

143. Which of the following is not a principle of Labour Welfare?

A. The Principle of Uniformity
B. The Principle of Co-ordination and Integration
C. The Principle of Association
D. The Principle of Timeliness

144. Match the following :

List-I (Theme)	**List-II (Theory)**
a. The labour welfare philosophy is meant for guarding the interests of labour against the exploitation of employers.	i. Trusteeship Theory
b. The labour welfare philosophy exposes the cause of empathic considerations by the employer of employee well being	ii. Placating Theory
c. The employer has to set out a portion of the profits for the benefit of the employees	iii. Policing Theory
d. Labour Welfare is provided for pacifying the agitating working class	iv. Philanthropic Theory

Codes :

	a	b	c	d
A.	ii	iv	iii	i
B.	iii	iv	i	ii
C.	iii	i	ii	iv
D.	iv	ii	iii	i

145. "Labour is not a commodity" – is the assertion made by

A. the Declaration of Philadelphia adopted by 26th session of ILO
B. the Magna Carta
C. the Constitution of India
D. the International Labour Conference

146. Match the following :

	Concept		Propagators
a.	Industrial Democracy	i.	Karl Marx
b.	Industrial Citizenship	ii.	Robert Owen
c.	Class Conflict	iii.	Peter F. Drucker
d.	Welfare Movement	iv.	Sydney & Beatrize Webbs

Codes :

	a	b	c	d
A.	iii	i	ii	iv
B.	iv	iii	i	ii
C.	ii	i	iv	iii
D.	ii	iv	i	iii

147. Assertion (A) : Industrial Labour in India has been migratory.

Reason (R) : Driving force in migration comes almost entirely from one end of the channel, that is the village end.

A. Both (A) and (R) are wrong.
B. (A) is wrong and (R) is right.
C. (A) is right and (R) also is right.
D. (A) is right and (R) is wrong.

148. Match the following :

	Theory of wages		Propagators
a.	Wage Fund Theory	i.	John Bates Clark
b.	Marginal Productivity Theory	ii.	John Davidson
c.	Bargaining Theory	iii.	John Stuart Mill
d.	Investment Theory	iv.	Gilelman

Codes :

	a	b	c	d
A.	ii	iv	i	iii
B.	iii	i	ii	iv
C.	iv	ii	iii	i
D.	i	iii	ii	iv

149. The "Marginal Discounted Product of Labour" as a modified version of Marginal Productivity Theory was advanced by
A. Taussig
B. Kalecki
C. Ricardo
D. Adam Smith

150. The Employees State Insurance Act was enacted in the year :
A. 1942 B. 1944
C. 1947 D. 1948

151. The Mental Health Act was enacted in the year :
A. 1985 B. 1987
C. 1989 D. 1990

152. The Equal Remuneration Act, 1976 provides for :
A. Equal pay for equal work of similar nature
B. Equal pay for equal work irrespective of nature of work
C. Equal pay for equal work in selected categories of work
D. Equal pay for equal work in organised sector only

153. The mental Health Policy was adopted in India in the year :
A. 1987 B. 1980
C. 1982 D. 1990

154. Juvenile Justice (Care and Protection) Act was enacted in the year :
A. 1990 B. 1996
C. 1998 D. 2000

155. Labour court is a :
A. Adjudicating authority
B. Settlement authority
C. Voluntary authority
D. Social authority

156. According to the payment of wages Act 1936, the employer is authorised to deduct from the wages of employee upto the maximum of :
A. 25% B. 50%
C. 75% D. 90%

ANSWERS

1	2	3	4	5	6	7	8	9	10
D	C	D	B	A	D	C	B	A	B
11	**12**	**13**	**14**	**15**	**16**	**17**	**18**	**19**	**20**
C	D	D	A	D	B	C	C	D	D
21	**22**	**23**	**24**	**25**	**26**	**27**	**28**	**29**	**30**
D	A	B	C	D	C	B	D	B	B
31	**32**	**33**	**34**	**35**	**36**	**37**	**38**	**39**	**40**
A	C	B	D	C	D	A	D	D	B
41	**42**	**43**	**44**	**45**	**46**	**47**	**48**	**49**	**50**
D	D	D	B	C	C	D	B	D	A
51	**52**	**53**	**54**	**55**	**56**	**57**	**58**	**59**	**60**
C	B	C	D	A	B	B	C	C	C
61	**62**	**63**	**64**	**65**	**66**	**67**	**68**	**69**	**70**
D	B	A	C	B	D	C	D	B	A
71	**72**	**73**	**74**	**75**	**76**	**77**	**78**	**79**	**80**
B	D	A	D	C	A	B	C	A	C
81	**82**	**83**	**84**	**85**	**86**	**87**	**88**	**89**	**90**
C	B	C	C	A	D	C	D	C	C
91	**92**	**93**	**94**	**95**	**96**	**97**	**98**	**99**	**100**
D	C	B	C	B	D	D	D	C	B
101	**102**	**103**	**104**	**105**	**106**	**107**	**108**	**109**	**110**
C	C	C	A	D	B	C	C	D	B
111	**112**	**113**	**114**	**115**	**116**	**117**	**118**	**119**	**120**
C	D	B	C	B	C	A	B	A	C
121	**122**	**123**	**124**	**125**	**126**	**127**	**128**	**129**	**130**
D	C	C	A	A	C	D	B	A	B
131	**132**	**133**	**134**	**135**	**136**	**137**	**138**	**139**	**140**
C	D	D	D	B	C	D	D	B	B
141	**142**	**143**	**144**	**145**	**146**	**147**	**148**	**149**	**150**
D	C	A	B	A	B	C	B	A	D
151	**152**	**153**	**154**	**155**	**156**				
B	A	C	D	A	B				

➤➤➤➤➤

CHAPTER 2

Medical and Psychiatric Social Work

EVOLUTION OF MEDICAL AND PSYCHIATRIC SOCIAL WORK IN INDIA

Introduction

Mental Health by virtue of its ability to deal with human thoughts and emotions and to provide a way for healthy minds is a vital resource for our development, and its absence represents a great burden to the economic, political, and social functioning of human beings, society and nation. The scope of mental health is not only confined to the treatment of some seriously ill persons admitted to mental health centers, rather it is related to the whole range of health activities. India has developed an endogenous, alternative body of knowledge which is more suited to Indian conditions.

PSYCHIATRY IN ANCIENT AND VEDIC INDIA

The descriptions of various mental illnesses in ancient Indian texts are probably the oldest such accounts. Two well-known Ayurvedic manuscripts, the Charaka Samhita by Charaka, and the Sushruta Samhita by Sushruta, have established the roots of modern Indian medicine. The ancient Indian scripture, Atharvaveda, mentions that mental illness may result from divine curses. Descriptions of conditions similar to schizophrenia and bipolar disorder appear in the Vedic texts. A vivid description of schizophrenia is also found in Atharvaveda. Other traditional medical systems such as Siddha, which recognize various types of mental disorders, flourished in southern India. Great epics such as the Ramayana and the Mahabharata made several references to disordered states of mind and means of coping with them. The Bhagavad Gita is a classical example of crisis intervention psychotherapy. Another interesting contribution of the Ayurveda is its knowledge regarding the diet-disease relationship and the association of a disease with a specific physical constitution. Diagnosis was entertained by the five senses and supplemented by interrogation. According to the ancient system, diagnosis was based on cause (nidana), premonitory indications (purva- rupa), symptoms (rupa), therapeutic tests (upashaya) and natural history of the development of the disease (samprapti). According to Sushruta, the physician (chikitshak), the drug (dravya), the attendants or the nursing personnel (upasthata), and the patient (rogi) are the four pillars on which rests the success of the therapy. The highest patronage to the science of Ayurveda was given by the Buddhist kings (400-200 BC).

PSYCHIATRY IN PRE-COLONIAL INDIA

During the reigns of King Asoka, many hospitals were established for patients with mental illness. According to the scribes of Asoka Samhita, hospitals were built with separate enclosures for various practices including keeping the patients and dispensing treatments prevailing during those times. A temple of Lord Venkateswara at

Tirumukkudal, Chingleput, Tamil Nadu, contains inscriptions on the walls belonging to the Chola period. There are some ancient evidences of propagation of alienation of mentally ill patients in Shahdaula's Chauhas in Gujarat and Punjab. Though there is not much evidence for development of psychiatry in the Moghul period, there are references to some asylums in the period of Mohammad Khilji (1436-1469). There is also some evidence of the presence of a mental hospital at Dhar near Mandu, Madhya Pradesh, whose physician was Maulana Fazulur Hakim. There are some historical evidences from the pre-colonial literature that modern medicine and modern hospitals were first brought to India by Portuguese during the seventeenth century in Goa, though documentary evidences are not in good shape to substantiate the claims.

The political instability prevailing in the 1700s saw development of lunatic asylums in Calcutta, Madras and Bombay. It is interesting to observe that these three cities grew up in the beginning largely with British enterprise which conceptualized the segregation of mentally ill patients in mental asylums and their supervision by trained people more in sync with the western conceptualization. The need to establish hospitals became more acute first to treat and manage Englishmen and Indian 'sepoyees' employed by the British East India Company. Waren Hastings, the first Governor General, during his regime in 1784 introduced the 'Pitts India Bill' according to which the activities of the Government of the East India Company came under the direction of a "Board of Control" and systematic reforms and welfare actions were taken during Mr. Cornwallis (1786-93) rule. It was during his rule that there is a reference of the first mental hospital in this part of India at Calcutta recorded in the proceedings of Calcutta Medical Board on April 3, 1787, which became the reference point of inception of colonial influence on development of psychiatric care in India.

PSYCHIATRY IN COLONIAL INDIA

Ernst (1987) described the growth of mental asylums in British India as a 'less conspicuous form of social control'. Mental hospitals (or asylums as they were called) in India were greatly influenced by British psychiatry and catered mostly to European soldiers posted in India at that time. Their function was more custodial and less curative.

Development of lunatic asylums was apparent in the early colonial period from 1745 to 1857 till the first revolution for Indian Independence was started. The earliest mental hospital in India was established at Bombay in 1745, which was made to accommodate around 30 mentally ill patients. Surgeon Kenderline started one of the first asylums in India in Calcutta in 1787. Later, a private lunatic asylum was constructed, recognized by the Medical Board under the charge of Surgeon William Dick and rented out to the East India Company. The first government run lunatic asylum was opened on 17 April 1795 at Monghyr in Bihar, especially for insane soldiers. The first mental hospital in South India started at Kilpauk, Madras in 1794 by Surgeon Vallentine Conolly. During this period, excited patients were treated with opium, given hot baths and sometimes, leeches were applied to suck their blood. Music was also used as a mode of therapy to calm down patients in some hospitals. The mentally ill from the general population were taken care of by the local communities and by traditional Indian medicine doctors, qualified in Ayurveda and Unani medicine.

Under the Indian Lunacy Act 1912, a European Lunatic Asylum was established in Bhowanipore for European patients, which later closed down after the establishment of the European Hospital at Ranchi in 1918. It was the far-sightedness, hard work and the persistence of the then superintendent of the European Hospital (now known as the Central Institute of Psychiatry), Col Owen A R Berkeley-Hill, that made the institution at Ranchi a unique centre in India at that time which attracted many European patients for treatment. Berkeley-Hill was deeply concerned about the improvement of mental hospitals in those days.

The years after 1914 were characterized by gradual expansion rather than building projects and the most significant of these of the period were hangovers from the pre-1914 period. Mental Asylum at Ranchi first opened in 1918 as a hospital for European patients. The sustained efforts of Berkeley-Hill not only helped to raise the standard of treatment and care, but also persuaded the government to change the term 'asylum' to 'hospital' in 1920. The Parsees during that period were keen to spend large amounts of money to guarantee care in modern psychiatric institutions for those who were considered insane in their own community, often guided by financial rather than therapeutic reasoning. The origins of psychiatric rehabilitation in India can be traced to innovative service programs, which were initiated at the Central Institute of Psychiatry (CIP) in 1922 when Occupational Therapy Unit started at this place. Hydrotherapy started in 1923 and during the same time the hospital started to raise interest of public in mental hygiene and prophylaxis, taking initiatives in preventive aspects of psychiatry. Techniques similar to token-economy were first started in 1920 and called by the name "Habit Formation Chart".

Girindra Shekhar Bose first founded the Indian Psychoanalytical Association in 1922 in Calcutta and Berkeley-Hill started the Indian Association for Mental Hygiene at Ranchi. He was one of the earliest practitioners of psychoanalysis in India who used this technique to help British patients to adjust to their lives after the ravages of World War I. CIP was one of the first centers outside Europe to start Cardiazol-induced seizure treatment in 1938, Electroconvulsive Therapy (ECT) in 1943 and Psychosurgery in 1947. Rauwolfia extracts in the form of Santina, Serpasil and Meralfen were also used for treating psychotic conditions in late 1940s.

In the year 1922, CIP got affiliation from the University of London to start Diploma in Psychological Medicine. Grant Medical College, Bombay (now Mumbai) had a Professor of Psychiatry, significantly an Indian, by the year 1936. A library on mental health started in 1918 at CIP with 300 books and journals which dated back to 1910. Child guidance clinic was first established in 1937 at Sir Dorabji Tata Graduate School of Social Work in Bombay. The establishment of Mental Health organization under the Directorate of Health Services was first recommended in 1946 by the health survey and development committee of the Indian Government. The first psychiatric outpatient service, precursor to the present-day general hospital psychiatric units (GHPU), was set up at the R.G. Kar Medical College, Calcutta in 1933 by Ghirinder Shekhar Bose.

In 1946, a health survey and development committee, popularly known as the "Bhore Committee," surveyed mental hospitals. The Health Survey and Development Committee report submitted by Col. Moore Taylor in 1946 reported numerical and professional inadequacy and suggested a focus on training of personnel and students in psychiatry, promotion of occupational and diversionary therapies, and separate child psychiatry units. The committee suggested improvisation and modernization of most hospitals, attachment to medical colleges, and establishment of proper mental health. The World War II saw a separation of military psychiatry from psychiatry in general in India in which the history of modern psychiatry in India seemed to have returned to its origins.

PSYCHIATRY IN INDEPENDENT INDIA: THE FORMATIVE YEARS

A new phase of development of mental hospitals started after India's independence in 1947. The government of India focused upon the creation of GHPUs rather than building more mental hospitals. Emphasis was placed upon improving conditions in existing hospitals, while at the same time encouraging outpatient care through these units. A few new mental hospitals, notably at Delhi, Jaipur, Kottayam and Bengal, were added. Mid-1950 witnessed rapid development in the spread to GHPUs in India. In 1957, Dutta Ray started a psychiatric out-patient service at Irwin Hospital (now G.B. Pant Hospital), in New Delhi. In 1958, N.N. Wig started the first GHPU at Medical College, Lucknow, with both in-patient and out-patient psychiatric services and a teaching program as part of the Department of Medicine. Neki started a similar unit at Medical College, Amritsar a few months later. In the next 25 years most of the teaching hospitals and major general hospitals in the private or government sector had GHPUs which were managed by emerging mental health professionals joining services after completing their post graduation in psychiatry.

By the 1960s, traditional institutions like CIP (Ranchi) and Madras Mental Hospital/Asylum offered a range of specialized services, including child and adolescent clinics. Geriatric, epileptic and neuropsychiatric services were added to complete the range of comprehensive OPDs. Another important innovation in the 1960s was the concept of a day hospital. Slowly, alternative accommodations were explored for patients who had recovered, but could not return to their families. CIP started the Department of Clinical Psychology in 1949 which happens to have the first clinical psychology laboratory in the country. CIP also took initiatives in community mental health services as one of the earliest rural mental health clinic was started at Mandar near Ranchi in 1967.

An industrial psychiatric unit was started at Heavy Engineering Corporation (HEC) at Hatia, Ranchi in 1973. Opening of psychiatry units in general hospitals gave psychiatrists an opportunity to demonstrate their knowledge and skills in the management of neurotic and psychosomatic disorders.

On the recommendation of the Bhore committee, All India Institute of Mental Health was set up in 1954, which became the National Institute of Mental Health and Neurosciences (NIMHANS) in 1974 at Bangalore. The first training program for Primary Health Care was started in 1978-79. During 1978-1984 Indian Council of Medical Research funded and conducted a multicentre collaborative project on 'severe mental morbidity' in Bangalore, Baroda, Calcutta and Patiala. Various training programmes for psychiatrists, Clinical Psychologists, Psychiatric Social Workers, Psychiatric nurses and Primary Care doctors were conducted at Sakalwara unit during 1981-82.

PSYCHIATRY IN INDEPENDENT INDIA: ERA OF CONSOLIDATION

The first draft of Mental Health Act that subsequently became the Mental Health Act of India (1987) was written at Ranchi in 1949 by R.B. Davis, then Medical Superintendent of CIP, S.A. Hasib, from Indian Mental Hospital, Ranchi and J Roy, from Mental Hospital, Nagpur. Initial attempts by the Indian Psychiatric Society to bring about change were unsuccessful. In 1959-60, reforms were considered but no consensus was reached. In the 1980s, there was a resurgence of activity resulting in the passage of the Mental Health Act in 1987.

MEDICAL SOCIAL WORK

Medical social work as a specialized method of social work is of recent origin. It involves the practice of social case work, and sometimes group work in a hospital, a clinic or other medical settings in order to make it possible for the patient to use the available health services most effectively. Medical social work is characterized by emphasis on health in the social and emotional problem which affects the patient in his illness and his cure.

The development of medical social work is based on four main sources. The first was the recognition in England in the 1880's that discharged patient of mental hospitals needed "after care" in their homes in order to avoid recurrence of their illness. "Visitors" went to the patient's home and advised family and friends about the necessary care of the patient after his discharge. A second source of medical social work was the "lady almoners" in English hospitals; they organized, upon the initiatives of Sir Charles S. Loch in London, 1890's and served as volunteer receptionist made social investigation and decided whether the applicant should be admitted as a free patient to the hospital and what charity organization might be asked to assume the patients support. Visiting nurses were the third precursors of medical social work. In 1893 Lillian Wald and Mary Brewster of the Henry Street Settlement House in New York begin to visit the homes of sick people in neighbourhood who were too poor to pay for medical and nursing care. They found many social and personal problems which were caused by the illness of the patient. Some hospital in New York learned from the experiences of the Henary Street Settlement House that visits in the home might greatly improve the effect of medical treatment; they sent nurses from the hospital staff for "after care" and supervision of discharged patient. The forth source of medical social work was medical students trained in social agencies. Dr. Charles Emersion of John Hopkins University at Baltimore in 1902 wanted to include the study of social and emotional problems into medical education and requested that his students serve as volunteers with charity agencies in order to gain an understanding of the influence of social economic and living conditions on the illness of patient. On the basis of these experiences, medical social work was established in 1905 in four different places of America.

Characteristics of Medical Social Work

- The medical social worker acquires an intimate knowledge of the personal and social situation of the patient and he/she assist in using the resources in the community which will help him most effectively to regain his/her health.
- Medical social work does not attempt to solve all the patients problems, but deals with those factors which are directly related to the case and nature of the patients illness and its treatment are called the "social component of illness".
- Medical social work has shifted its emphasis from attention to the disease to the personality of the patients—his anxieties, attitudes and feelings.
- The Medical social worker interprets to the patients and his family requested to recommendation of the physician. He helps the patients understand his disease and to make the best use of the medical treatment and the doctors prescriptions. He thus extends the medical service of the hospital into the patients home and into the community.
- The medical setting in which social work is practiced are private and public hospitals and clinics; voluntary health agencies; local, state and Federal health services; other public and private social welfare agencies; schools of social work, schools of nursing and medical schools.
- The medical social worker in a public welfare department is responsible for the authorization of requests for medical care of an applicant, and for the full utilization of other medical facilities in the community.
- Medical social work is concerned with social and economic conditions of the patient and his family, and with the interrelation of the physical and the emotional factors in illness.
- Finally, medical social work is recognized in such community health planning bodies as municipal or regional welfare council and local health boards, and in coordinated programs of the medical, health, and welfare projects. This also applies to the expanding area of health education in connection with schools and adult civic group and to the use of medical social workers as teachers in the medical schools and schools of public health.

OBJECTIVES OF MENTAL HEALTH SERVICES

Mental health is:

(1) A public health movement which has the aim of preventing mental disorders through mental health education and freeing patients from external and internal conflicts, anxiety and emotional strain;

(2) A science based upon psychiatry and psychology, applied to help people

overcome inner conflicts and maintain or regain mental health, through psychiatric, psychological, and social treatment;

(3) A medical and psychiatric treatment in mental hospitals to aid severely disturbed mental patients;

(4) A special orientation in education based upon recent developments in psychiatry and the social sciences; and

(5) a philosophy of life and a concept of ethics that pursues the goal of healthy living in a democratic society.

National Mental Health Program (NMHP)

National mental health program was started in 1982 with the following three objectives:

- To ensure availability and accessibility of minimum mental health care for all in the near foreseeable future, particularly to the most vulnerable sections of the population.
- To encourage mental health knowledge and skills in general health care and social development.
- To promote community participation in mental health service development and to stimulate self-help in the community.

Legislation Related To Mental Health

Some of the changes mentioned above have been supported by legislation for mental healthcare, namely, the Narcotic Drugs and Psychotropic Substances (NDPS) Act 1985, the Mental Health Act 1987 and Persons with Disability Act 1995. All these legislations have changed the penal approach to mental healthcare to an approach centering around promotion, prevention and rights. The Persons with Disability Act 1995 is important because for the first time, mental illness has been included as one of the disabilities. The United Nations Convention on Rights of Persons with Disabilities (UNCRPD) 2006 adds a new dimension to the rights of the mentally ill. It is expected that some of the other existing laws will be changed to bring them in harmony with the current thinking and approach towards the mentally ill in India.

Major Health Concerns for Disadvantaged Groups

- The economic and political structures which sustain poverty and discrimination need to be transformed in order for poverty and poor health to be tackled.
- Marginalized groups and vulnerable individuals are often worst affected, deprived of the information, money or access to health services that would help them prevent and treat disease.
- Very poor and vulnerable people may have to make harsh choices – knowingly putting their health at risk because they cannot see their children go hungry, for example.
- The cultural and social barriers faced by marginalised groups – including indigenous communities – can mean they use health services less, with serious consequences for their health. This perpetuates their disproportionate levels of poverty.
- The cost of doctors' fees, a course of drugs and transport to reach a health centre can be devastating, both for an individual and their relatives who need to care for them or help them reach and pay for treatment. In the worst cases, the burden of illness may mean that families sell their property, take children out of school to earn a living or even start begging.
- The burden of caring is often taken on by a female relative, who may have to give up her education as a result, or take on waged work to help meet the household's costs. Missing out on education has long-term implications for a woman's opportunities later in life and for her own health.
- Overcrowded and poor living conditions can contribute to the spread of airborne diseases such as tuberculosis and respiratory infections such as pneumonia. Reliance on open fires or traditional stoves can lead to deadly indoor air pollution. A lack of food, clean water and sanitation can also be fatal.

ROLE OF MEDICAL SOCIAL WORKER

Medical social workers work in hospitals, nursing homes, mental health facilities, clinics, drug rehabilitation centers and community health agencies. A medical social worker takes on many roles. They are patients advocate and counselors, perform psychological assessments, refer patients and families to medical resources and provide patient and family assistance in obtaining financial and legal assistance. Most importantly, a medical social worker works to assure that the best interest of the patient are being met.

Counselling

Medical social worker advise and counsel patients and their families. They explain the nature of an illness and advise the patient and family on how to effectively deal with symptoms and treatment. A medical social worker also serves a grief counselor to help patient and families deal with the trauma of experiencing a chronic or acute illness.

Care Planning

Families and patients often do not know where to turn to get medical care. A medical social worker assists patients and families in finding and arranging services such as in home care, nursing home care and counseling.

Financial Assistance

Acute and chronic illness is expensive. Sometimes, families may not be able to arrange the necessary financial resources for the care of an ill family member. If the ill person is a parent, financial support for the care of dependents must also be dealt with. Medical social workers refer and assist patients in obtaining financial assistance, food assistance and health care through voluntary and government programs.

Assessment

When doctors or nurses suspect that a patient is severely mentally ill, is a drug addict or is a victim of abuse, they enlist the services of a medical social worker. The experienced opinion of a medical social worker is highly regarded by hospital staff. The medical social worker evaluates the patient and reports back to the hospital staff. Together, hospital staff and the medical social worker collaborate to find the best approach to helping mentally ill, mentally incompetent, drug-addicted or abused patients.

Advocacy

At times, a medical social worker serves as a patients advocate. The medical social worker acts as an intermediary between patients and the medical community. They are the voice for people who have communication barriers or cultural differences that make effective communication challenging. Without the medical social worker, these types of patients often fall between the cracks, their health and emotional needs are unknown.

Legal Assistance

There are situations where a medical social worker must take legal action to protect a patient. When a medical social worker encounters situations where parents are unable or unwilling to care for their sick child or encounter cases of abuse, legal action must be taken. In these cases, a conservator, a power of attorney or a public guardian may need to be appointed.

CRISIS COUNSELLING

In mental health terms, a crisis refers not to a traumatic event or experience, but to how an individual responds to the situation. The events that trigger this crisis can run the gamut of life experience, from developmental hurdles (such as going through puberty) to natural disasters to the death of a loved one. Crisis counselling can help individuals deal with the crisis by offering assistance and support.

The roots of modern day crisis counselling date back to World War I and World War II. Prior to this time, soldiers who exhibited significant psychological reactions to the experiences they had at war were frequently seen as weak or even disloyal. However, it soon became apparent those soldiers who were immediately offered treatment fared much better than their untreated counterparts.

Elements of Crisis Counselling

Crisis counselling is intended to be quite brief, generally lasting for a period of no longer than a few weeks. It is important to note that crisis counselling is not psychotherapy. Crisis intervention is focused on minimizing the stress of the event, providing emotional support and improving the individual's coping strategies in the here and now.

Like psychotherapy, crisis counselling involves assessment, planning and treatment, but the scope of is generally much more specific. While psychotherapy focuses on a wide range of information and history, crisis assessment and treatment focuses on the client's immediate situation including factors such as safety and immediate needs.

While there are a number of different treatment models, there are a number of common elements consistent among the various theories of crisis counselling.

Assessing the Situation

The first element of crisis counselling involves assessing the client's current situation. This involves listening to the client, asking questions and determining what the individual needs to effectively cope with the crisis. During this time, the crisis counselling provider needs to define the problem while at the same time acting as a source of empathy, acceptance and support. It is also essential to ensure client safety, both physically and psychologically.

Education

People who are experiencing a crisis need information about their current condition and the steps they can take to minimize the damage. During crisis counselling, mental health workers often help the client understand that their reactions are normal, but temporary. While the situation may seem both dire and endless to the person experiencing the crisis, the goal is to help the client see that he or she will eventually return to normal functioning.

Offering Support

One of the most important elements of crisis counselling involves offering support, stabilization and resources. Active listening is critical, as well as offering unconditional acceptance and reassurance. Offering this kind of nonjudgmental support during a crisis can help reduce stress improve coping. During the crisis, it can be very beneficial for individuals to develop a brief dependency on supportive people. Unlike unhealthy dependencies, these relationships help the individual become stronger and more independent.

Developing Coping Skills

In addition to providing support, crisis counsellors also help clients develop coping skills to deal with the immediate crisis. This might involve helping the client explore different solutions to the problem, practicing stress reduction techniques and encouraging positive thinking. This process is not just about teaching these skills to the client, it is also about encouraging the client to make a commitment to continue utilizing these skills in the future.

The Problem of Mental Health Care in India

As per the Economic Review 2012, the major problems affecting the mental health sector in the country has been identified as:

- the lack of a standardized form of care, lack of rehabilitation services
- lack of properly qualified and trained persons
- lack of proper guidelines for care of mentally ill patients
- shortage of the mental health care staff
- There is no properly designed epidemiological and evaluative research in the sector
- The absence of orientation of private sector initiatives and lack of proper regulatory mechanism and accreditation of rehabilitation services by voluntary organizations

- Lack of integration of services of different mental health personnel such as psychiatrists, psychologists and psychiatric social workers.

CHILD GUIDANCE CLINIC

- Child Guidance Clinics were started in 1922, as a part of program sponsored by a private organisation 'Common Wealths Fund Program' for the prevention of Juvenile delinquency. The first child guidance clinic was started in Social Sciences, Mumbai.

- Child guidance clinics are specialised clinics that deal with children on normal of behaviour and psychological problems which are summed up as maladjustment. A child guidance clinic is one of the medico-social amenities for the organised and scientific study and treatment of maladjustment in children. For the overall development of a child the child's physical and physiological functioning and the environment to which he is exposed at home and school, is taken care off, through interaction with and counselling of the child and his family by a health care team.

Objectives of Child Guidance Center

- Providing help for children with behaviour problem like bed wetting, sleep walking, speech defects etc.
- Providing care and guidance for children with mental retardation.
- Providing care for children with learning difficulties.
- Providing counselling, guidance and information to parents regarding care and upbringing of children.

Besides, these objectives child guidance clinics also manage social legal issues development problems, adjustment problems, emotional problem, learning difficulties and behavioural problems of a child.

MULTIPLE CHOICE QUESTIONS

1. Substantially higher performance scores than verbal scores on the subtests of Wechsler Adult Intelligence Scale (WAIS) indicates

A. Gender differences
B. Learning difficulties
C. Genetic influences
D. Cultural biases

2. Ruchi remembers that when she was eight year old she was whimsical. This memory of Ruchi is called

A. Episodic memory
B. Semantic memory
C. Sensory memory
D. Amnesic memory

3. Which is the most basic and common obstacle to problem solving?

A. Confirmation bias
B. Fixation
C. Functional fixedness
D. Mental set

4. The child who says "Milk gone" is engaging in ________. This type of utterance demonstrates that children are actively experimenting with rules of _______.

A. Babbling; syntax
B. Telegraphic speech; syntax
C. Babbling ; semantics
D. Telegraphic speech; semantics

5. Problem solving comprises of four stages. Choose the correct sequence of stages

A. Incubation, preparation, verification, illumination
B. Preparation, incubation, illumination, verification
C. Incubation, preparation, illumination, verification

D. Preparation, illumination, incubation, verification

6. Match the following lists :

List-I (Author)	List-II (Focus/ Emphasis)
a. Kagan & Haveman, 1979	1. Mental manipulation
b. Silverman, 1978	2. Solution of problem
c. Whittaker, 1970	3. Mediating process
d. Humphrey, 1963	4. Goal directed process

Codes :

	a	b	c	d
A.	1	2	4	3
B.	1	2	3	4
C.	1	3	2	4
D.	1	4	3	2

7. Given below are two statements, one labelled as Assertion (A) and the other labelled as Reason (R).

Assertion (A) : Thinking about objects brings change in attitudes.

Reason (R) : Attitudes toward complex issues and objects are typically a mixture of positive and negative feelings.

Codes :

A. Both (A) and (R) are true and (R) is the correct explanation of (A).
B. Both (A) and (R) are true, but (R) is not the correct explanation of (A).
C. (A) is true, but (R) is false.
D. (A) is false, but (R) is true.

8. Match List-I with List-II and indicate your answer using the codes given below :

List-I (Memory Phenomena)	List-II (Brief Description)
a. Semantic memory	1. Memory for events that occur in a particular time, place or context.
b. Priming	2. Memory for skills and habits.
c. Episodic memory	3. Memory for general knowledge and facts about the world.
d. Procedural memory	4. Information that people already have in storage is activated to help them remember new information better and faster.

Codes :

	a	b	c	d
A.	3	2	4	1
B.	4	3	2	1
C.	3	4	1	2
D.	2	4	3	1

9. A subject is presented four non-sense syllabus one by one each for two seconds. After presentation of the four items, the subject is asked to count backward aloud by three from some number for fifteen seconds and after that he/she is asked to recall the non-sense syllabus. What memory storage is being measured in this experiment?

A. Sensory memory storage
B. Working memory storage
C. Short-term memory storage
D. Long-term memory storage

10. When the previously learned task affects the retention of task being currently acquired, the phenomenon is referred to as :

A. Retroactive interference-
B. Proactive interference
C. Retroactive effect
D. Proactive effect

11. **Assertion (A) :** Positive psychology draws its strength from humanistic psychology.

Reason (R) : Both humanistic and positive psychology believe in positive human qualities.

Codes :

A. Both (A) and (R) are true and (R) is the correct explanation of (A).

B. Both (A) and (R) are true, but (R) is not the explanation of (A).
C. (A) is true, but (R) is false.
D. (A) is false, but (R) is true.

12. The basic difference between classical conditioning and instrumental learning is of
A. Presentation of stimulus
B. Emitting of response
C. Temporal contiguity
D. Mechanism

13. Major criticisms of Thurston's theory of intelligence are based on
I. Use of subjective measures
II. Restricted heterogeneity in sample
III. Method of factor analysis
A. I and II are correct.
B. I and III are correct.
C. II and III are correct.
D. I, II and III are correct.

14. Given below are two statements, one labelled as Assertion (A) and the other labelled as Reason (R). Indicate your answer using the codes given below :

Assertion (A) : Heritability of intelligence explains variations due to genetics for individuals within a given population.

Reason (R) : Earlier the children from deprived families were adopted, the higher their intelligence score will be.

Codes :
A. Both (A) and (R) are true and (R) is the correct explanation of (A).
B. Both (A) and (R) are true, but (R) is not the correct explanation of (A).
C. (A) is true, but (R) is false.
D. (A) is false, but (R) is true.

15. Read each of the following two statements Assertion (A) and Reason (R) and indicate your answer using the codes given below :

Assertion (A) : Psychoactive drugs affects the nervous systems to cause change in perception or mood.

Reason (R) : Reticular activating system is related to perception and mood.

Codes :
A. Both (A) and (R) are true and (R) is the correct explanation of (A).
B. Both (A) and (R) are true, but (R) is not the correct explanation of (A).
C. (A) is true, but (R) is false.
D. (A) is false, but (R) is true.

16. Match List-I with List-II and indicate your answer using the codes given below :

List-I (Glands)	List-II (Hormons)
a. Pituitary	1. Melatonin
b. Adrenal Cortex	2. Adrenaline
c. Pineal	3. Prolactin
d. Adrenal Medulla	4. Corticosteroids

Codes :

	a	b	c	d
A.	2	1	3	4
B.	1	3	2	4
C.	4	3	1	2
D.	3	4	1	2

17. What is the correct sequence of ear parts given below?
A. Eardrum – Hammer – Anvil – Stirrup – Oval window
B. Oval window – Hammer – Eardrum – Anvil – Stirrup
C. Eardrum – Anvil – Stirrup – Hammer – Oval window
D. Oval window – Anvil – Hammer – Stirrup – Eardrum

18. We can cope with stress by becoming aware of our irrational, upsetting thoughts and replacing them with rational, calming thoughts. This view represents.
A. Cognitive behavioural approach
B. Psychoanalytical approach
C. Socio-cultural approach
D. Bio-social approach

19. An instrumental response is conditioned only when organism interprets the reinforcement as being controlled by its response. This view is supported by
A. Tolman B. Skinner
C. Seligman D. Beck

20. When a child gets two chocolates once every week for its performance in the class it is an instance of

A. Fixed ratio, variable interval
B. Fixed ratio, fixed interval
C. Variable ratio, fixed interval
D. Variable ratio, variable interval

21. Match List-I with List-II and indicate your answer using the codes given below :

List-I (Learning term)	**List-II (Brief explanation)**
a. Positive reinforcement	1. Removal of a pleasant or appetitive stimulus after a behavioural response.
b. Classical conditioning	2. Delivery of a pleasant or appetitive stimulus that follows a behavioural response.
c. Punishment	3. Presenting a neutral stimulus after a stimulus that usually elicits a specific response.
d. Omission training	4. Presentation of an unpleasant or aversive stimulus after a behavioural response.

Codes :

	a	b	c	d
A.	2	3	4	1
B.	4	1	3	2
C.	1	4	2	3
D.	3	4	1	2

22. Match List-I (Psychologist) with List-II (Test):

List-I (Name of Psychologist)	**List-II (Name of Test)**
a. J.B. Rotter	1. NEO-Personality inventory
b. C. Robert Cloninger	2. Hardy Personality
c. Suzanne Kobasa	3. Locus of control
d. P.T. Costa	4. Temperament and character inventory

Codes :

	a	b	c	d
A.	1	2	3	4
B.	3	4	2	1
C.	3	4	1	2
D.	3	2	4	1

23. In a study on 'Career Aspirations of Students', the respondents were required to state their career aspirations in about sixty words. This would be an example of

A. Fixed-alternative item
B. Scale item
C. Open-end item
D. Checklist item

24. Read each of the following two statements-Assertion (A) and Reason (R) and indicate your answer using the codes given below :

Assertion (A) : In Ponzo illusion and Muller-Lyer illusion, linear perspective is misapplied to the display.

Reason (R) : According to Gregory perception is only a function of stimulus characteristics.

Codes :

A. (A) is true and (R) is false.
B. Both (A) and (R) are true, but (R) is not the correct explanation of (A).
C. (A) is false and (R) is true.
D. Both (A) and (R) are true and (R) is the correct explanation of (A).

25. Match each of the following organizational laws with its meaning. Select the correct answer using the code given below :

List-I (Law)	**List-II (Meaning)**
a. Closure	1. Elements close together are grouped together.
b. Proximity	2. Patterns are perceived in the most basic, direct manner possible.
c. Similarity	3. Groupings are made in terms of complete figures.

d. Simplicity 4. Elements similar in appearance are grouped together.

Codes :

	a	b	c	d
A.	1	4	2	3
B.	2	3	1	4
C.	4	2	3	1
D.	3	1	4	2

26. Which of the following is not one of the Big Five personality factors?

A. Submissiveness
B. Agreeableness
C. Extroversion
D. Openness to experience

27. Read the following two statements Assertion (A) and Reason (R) and indicate your answer using the codes given below :

Assertion (A) : The level of arousal for optimal performance varies for different tasks.

Reason (R) : Too little arousal can be non-motivating, too high arousal can be disruptive.

Codes :

A. Both (A) and (R) are true and (R) is the correct explanation of (A).
B. Both (A) and (R) are true and (R) is not the correct explanation of (A).
C. (A) is true, but (R) is false.
D. (A) is false, but (R) is true.

28. Match List-I with List-II and indicate your answer using the codes given below :

List-I (Behaviour)	**List-II (Expression mode)**
(a) Tone	1. Facial
(b) Crying	2. Glanduar
(c) Laugh	3. Verbal
(d) Eyebrow	4. Muscular

Codes :

	(a)	(b)	(c)	(d)
A.	3	2	4	1
B.	1	4	3	2
C.	2	4	3	1
D.	2	1	3	4

29. A slow graded electrical potential produced by a receptor cell in response to a physical stimulus is

A. Receptor potential
B. Generator potential
C. Transduction
D. Arousal

30. This area contains 'Somoto Sensory Cortex'

A. Parietal lobe B. Frontal lobe
C. Temporal lobe D. Occipital lobe

31. Give the correct sequence of the location of following glands in human body from top to bottom

A. Thyroid – Adrenal – Pancreas – Pituitary
B. Thyroid – Pancreas – Pituitary – Adrenal
C. Pituitary – Adrenal – Thyroid – Pancreas
D. Pituitary – Thyroid – Adrenal – Pancreas

32. A complex behaviour that is rigidly patterned throughout a species and is unlearned is called

A. Imprinting B. Instinct
C. Emotion D. Feeling

33. Our tendency to perceive objects as unchanging despite changes in sensory input is an illustration of

A. Figure-Ground relationship
B. Perceptual constancy
C. Binocular cues
D. Linear perspective

34. Given below are two statements, one labelled as Assertion (A) and the other labelled as Reason (R) :

Assertion (A) : As compared to other methods of psychological research, experimental method is usually considered to be best suited for studying cause and effect relationship.

Reason (R) : Secondary variance is more efficiently controlled in experimental method.

In the context of the above two statements, which one of the following conclusion is correct?

A. Both (A) and (R) are true and (R) is the correct explanation of (A).

B. Both (A) and (R) are true, but (R) is not the explanation of (A).
C. (A) is true, but (R) is false.
D. (A) is false, but (R) is true.

35. Consider the following three types of psychological researches :
1. Field experiment
2. Laboratory experiment
3. Ex post facto study

Arrange these typical investigations in descending order in terms of the researcher's ability to control secondary variance.

A. 3, 1, 2 B. 2, 1, 3
C. 3, 2, 1 D. 1, 2, 3

36. What is the correct sequence of development of the following personality tests :
1. Maudsley Personality Inventory
2. Minnesota Multiphasic Personality Inventory-2
3. Millon Clinical Multiaxial Inventory
4. NEO PI-3

Codes :
A. 1, 2, 3, 4 B. 4, 3, 2, 1
C. 2, 4, 1, 3 D. 1, 3, 2, 4

37. Perceiving one thing in relation to another when both are presented simultaneously is called
A. Simultaneous perception
B. Figure-Ground perception
C. Consecutive perception
D. Successive perception

38. Verbal behaviour that is reinforced when someone else's verbal response is repeated verbation is called
A. Autoclitic behaviour
B. Echoic behaviour
C. Reinforced behaviour
D. Operant behaviour

39. Which of the following are essential to Spearman's methodology of theory development?
I. Tetral equation
II. Tetral difference
III. Specific factor
IV. Neurological basis of intelligence

Codes :
A. I, II and III B. I, III and IV
C. II, III and IV D. I, II and IV

40. Dissociable sub-systems operate simultaneously in each hemisphere and help us recognize similarity at one level and differences at another level in the perceived pattern. This system consists of
1. Top-down processing system
2. Abstract category sub-system
3. Bottom-up processing system
4. Specific-exemplar sub-system

Codes :
A. 1 and 2 only B. 3 and 4 only
C. 2 and 4 only D. 1 and 4 only

41. Based on Eysenkian theory of personality, what is the correct sequence levels of personality from bottom to top?
1. Habit level 2. Trait level
3. Type level 4. S.R. level

Codes :
A. 1, 2, 3, 4 B. 4, 3, 2, 1
C. 4, 1, 2, 3 D. 2, 4, 1, 3

42. Speed and power tests cannot be differentiated on the basis of
I. Time limit
II. Verbal content
III. Non-verbal content
IV. Difficulty level

Codes :
A. I and IV B. II and IV
C. II and III D. I, III and IV

43. According to two factors of Retroactive Interference, RI is caused by two factors : One is unlearning of the first task during the time one is engaged in the second task. What is the second factor?
A. Unlearning of the responses of second task.
B. Competition of the first task responses with the second task responses that inhibits the recall responses of the first task at the time of recall.
C. Inability to recall responses from first task.

D. Decaying of memory-traces of responses of first task.

44. One of the difficulty with the survey method is

A. inability to examine changes overtime.

B. that subjects may give dishonest or inaccurate responses.

C. the relatively small number of subjects used.

D. the impossibility of getting a representative sample.

45. A cell in a contingency table had an obtained frequency of 16 and an expected frequency of 25. What would be the contribution of this cell to the total chi-square value?

A. 3.24 B. 5.06
C. 9.00 D. 81.00

46. In an experiment the stimuli were presented to the subjects in certain order and after the presentation of stimuli their order was disturbed. In the test phase the subjects were needed to set them in the presented order.

Which of the following methods was used in this experiment?

A. Recognition B. Relearning
C. Reconstruction D. Recall

47. Given below are two statements, one labelled as Assertion (A) and the other labelled as Reason (R). Indicate your answer using the codes given below :

Assertion (A) : If your teacher embarrasses you for asking a question in class, it is less likely that you would ask questions in class in future.

Reason (R) : Negative reinforcement reduces the occurrence of a behaviour.

Codes :

A. Both (A) and (R) are true and (R) is the correct explanation of (A).

B. Both (A) and (R) are true but (R) is not the correct explanation of (A).

C. (A) is true, but (R) is false.

D. (A) is false, but (R) is true.

48. What is the correct sequence of sympathetic and parasympathetic division given below?

A. Thoracic – Sacral – Cranial – Cervical – Lumbar

B. Cranial – Lumbar – Thoracic – Cervical – Sacral

C. Sacral – Cervical – Thoracic – Cranial – Lumbar

D. Sacral – Cranial – Cervical – Thoracic – Lumbar

49. The human ear can generally hear sounds ranging from

A. 20 – 1000 Hz B. 10 – 2000 Hz
C. 20 – 2000 Hz D. 1000 – 5000 Hz

50. Match List-I with List-II and indicate your answer using codes given below :

List-I (Personality Theories)	List-II (Focus)
a. Behaviourists	1. Self-concepts
b. Psychodynamic	2. Habits
c. Biological	3. Childhood fixations
d. Humanistic	4. Inheritance of genes

Codes :

	a	b	c	d
A.	1	3	4	2
B.	2	4	3	1
C.	2	3	4	1
D.	1	4	2	3

51. The chronological age that most typically corresponds to a given level of performance is called

A. Intelligence Quotient

B. Maturation

C. Mental age

D. None of the above

52. The role of unconscious in creative thinking is known as the process of

A. Verification B. Illumination
C. Inoculation D. Incubation

53. Which factor is not much related to happiness?

A. High self-esteem

B. Educational level
C. Close friendship or satisfactory marriage
D. Meaningful religious faith

54. Which is the correct order of 'Products' given by Guilford?
A. Units, Relations, Classes, Systems, Implications, Transformations
B. Units, Classes, Systems, Relations, Implications, Transformations
C. Units, Classes, Relations, Systems, Transformations, Implications
D. Units, Classes, Systems, Relations, Transformations, Implications

55. Which is not the obstacle to problem solving?
A. Confirmation bias
B. Fixation
C. Mental Set
D. Heuristics

56. Given below are two statements, one labelled as Assertion (A), and the other labelled as Reason (R). Indicate your answer using the codes given below :

Assertion (A) : Algorithm is a logical rule that guarantees solving a particular problem.

Reason (R) : One can find the solution even to complex problems by following step by step procedure.

Codes :
A. Both (A) and (R) are true, but (R) is not the correct explanation of (A).
B. Both (A) and (R) are true and (R) is the correct explanation of (A).
C. (A) is true, but (R) is false.
D. (A) is false, but (R) is true.

57. Which of the following statements concerning reinforcement is correct?
A. Learning is most rapid with partial reinforcement, but continuous reinforcement produces the greatest resistance to extinction.
B. Learning is most rapid with continuous reinforcement but partial reinforcement produces the greatest resistance to extinction.
C. Learning is the fastest and resistance to extinction is the greatest after continuous reinforcement.
D. Learning is the fastest and resistance to extinction is the greatest following partial reinforcement.

58. The sentence "Blue Jeans wear false smiles" has correct ______ but incorrect ______.
A. Morphemes; phonemes
B. Phonemes; morphemes
C. Semantics; syntax
D. Syntax; semantics

59. Match the following lists according to the types and characteristics of thinking :

List-I (Types of Thinking)	List-II (Characteristics)
a. Autistic thinking	1. Reasoning
b. Realistic thinking	2. Drawing facts
c. Convergent thinking	3. Unusual uses
c. Creative thinking	4. Fantasy

Codes :

	(a)	(b)	(c)	(d)
A.	1	3	4	2
B.	3	1	2	4
C.	2	1	3	4
D.	4	1	2	3

60. The main function of autoclitic behaviour is to
1. Qualify responses
2. Express relations
3. Providing a grammatical framework for verbal behaviour

Codes :
A. 1 only B. 2 and 3 only
C. 1 and 3 only D. 1, 2 and 3

61. The phi-phenomenon, stroboscopic motion, induced motion and autokinetic motion are all
A. Pictorial cues
B. Apparent motion
C. Double images
D. Non-verbal cues

62. Which one of the following is the most important feature of the defense mechanism of Rationalization?

A. Going back to an earlier stage of development.
B. Justifying one's actions.
C. Magically atoning for certain acts that give rise to guilt.
D. Attributing one's emotions to other persons.

63. "People control basic anxiety by moving toward, away from, and against others."

Which group of personality psychologists theorized this statement?

A. Psychoanalytic B. Neo-Freudian
C. Social learning D. Cognitive

64. A psychotic person would probably score the highest on which MMPI-2 scale?

A. Depression B. Hysteria
C. Schizophrenia D. Mania

65. Match List-I with List-II and indicate your answer by using the codes given below the lists :

List-I (Part of eye)	List-II (Function)
a. Pupil	1. Focus images on the retina.
b. Iris	2. Begin the processing of visual information.
c. Lens	3. Allows light to enter.
d. Retina	4. Controls the size of the pupil.

Codes :

	(a)	(b)	(c)	(d)
A.	1	2	3	4
B.	3	4	1	2
C.	1	3	4	2
D.	4	2	1	3

66. Learning by imitating others' behaviour is called ______ learning. The researcher best known for studying this type of learning is

A. Observational : Bandura
B. Secondary : Pavlov
C. Observational : Watson
D. Secondary : Skinner

67. As we enter a movie theatre from bright light the visual sensitivity increases and within 5-10 minutes we are able to see under low levels of illumination. This is due to

A. Visual acuity B. Dark adaptation
C. Saturation D. Transduction

68. Which of the following internal conditions determine perceptual process?

1. Intelligence 2. Emotion
3. Motivation 4. Information

A. 1 and 2 only B. 2 and 3 only
C. 2 and 4 only D. 1 and 4 only

69. Wechsler Adult Intelligence Scale has eleven subtests out of which

A. five are verbal and six are performance.
B. six are verbal and five are performance.
C. seven are verbal and four are performance.
D. four are verbal and seven are performance.

70. What is the correct sequence of memory processes? Indicate your answer using the codes given below :

1. Encoding 2. Storage
3. Attention 4. Retrieval

Codes :

A. 3, 1, 2, 4 B. 2, 3, 1, 4
C. 1, 3, 2, 4 D. 3, 2, 1, 4

71. Match the monocular cues with their explanations and select the correct answer using the codes given below :

List-I (Cues)	List-II (Explanation)
a. Relative size	1. Straight lines seem to join together as they become more distant.
b. Linear perspective	2. An object changes position on the retina as the head moves.
c. Motion Parallax	3. If two objects are of same size, the one producing the smaller retinal image is farther away.

d. Texture gradient	4. The texture of a surface appears smoother as distance increases.

Codes :

	(a)	(b)	(c)	(d)
A.	3	1	2	4
B.	1	3	4	2
C.	4	2	3	1
D.	2	4	1	3

72. Read the following two statements, Assertion (A) and Reason (R) and indicate your answer using the codes given below :

Assertion (A) : Biderman's 'recognition by components' theory states that objects can be thought of as being composed of basic building blocks called Geons.

Reason (R) : The relationship between features and geons does not exist. Geons are not composed of features such as edges, corners etc.

Codes :

A. (A) and (R) are false.
B. (A) is false, but (R) is true.
C. Both (A) and (R) are true, but (R) is not the correct explanation of (A).
D. (A) is true, but (R) is false.

73. Read each of the following two statements – Assertion (A) and Reason (R) and indicate your answer using the codes given below :

Assertion (A) : People just coldly store and retrieve bits of data.

Reason (R) : Psychologists recognize that people reconstruct their own version of the past.

Codes :

A. Both (A) and (R) are correct and (R) is the correct explanation of (A).
B. Both (A) and (R) are correct, but (R) is not the correct explanation of (A).
C. (A) is false, but (R) is true.
D. (A) is true, but (R) is false.

74. Ventromedial nucleus, a central area on the underside of the hypothalamus, lead to

A. Excessive eating
B. Stop-eating
C. Stop sex
D. Excessive obesity

75. Read each of the following two statements : Assertion (A) and Reason (R) and indicate your answer using the codes below :

Assertion (A) : According to interference theory of forgetting, forgetting is caused due to the intervening task which occurs between original task and its recall.

Reason (R) : The intervening task weaken the memory trace.

Codes :

A. Both (A) and (R) are true and (R) is the correct explanation of (A).
B. Both (A) and (R) are true, but (R) is not the correct explanation of (A).
C. (A) is true, but (R) is false.
D. (A) is false, but (R) is true.

76. Match List-I with List-II and indicate your answer using the codes given below :

List-I (Emotion)	List-II (Nerves Activity)
(a) Fear	1. Parasympathetic arousal
(b) Anger	2. Sympathetic arousal
(c) Depression	3. Sympathetic and parasympathetic arousal

Codes :

	(a)	(b)	(c)
A.	2	3	1
B.	1	2	3
C.	2	1	3
D.	3	2	1

77. Read the following two statements, Assertion (A) and Reason (R) and indicate your answer using the codes given below :

Assertion (A) : The high achievement motivation displayed by children has emotional roots.

Reason (R) : Highly motivated children often have parents who encourage their independence from an early age and praise and reward them for their successes.

Codes :

A. Both (A) and (R) are true and (R) is the correct explanation of (A).
B. Both (A) and (R) are true and (R) is not the correct explanation of (A).
C. (A) is true, but (R) is false.
D. (A) is false, but (R) is true.

78. A person, otherwise lnnited in mental ability, has amazing specific skills. This is because of

A. Academic under-achievement
B. Practical Intelligence
C. Academic over-achievement
D. Savant Syndrome

79. A man borrows money and forgets to pay it back because paying back is painful. This is an example of

A. Repression B. Reaction Formation
C. Regressia D. Rationalization

80. Whenever daughter performs well in her studies she receives a chocolate from parents but her brother is given a chocolate only when he gets the highest marks in the class. This is a paradigm of

A. Positive and negative reinforcement.
B. Primary and secondary reinforcement.
C. Continuous and secondary reinforcement.
D. Continuous and partial reinforcement.

81. The location of the optic nerve exit point from the retina of the eye is called as

A. Bipolar cell B. Fovea
C. Blind spot D. Cone

82. For an intelligence test, while computing item-remainder correlations for item analysis, we compute

A. Phi-coefficient
B. Spearman rho
C. Tetrachoric correlation
D. Point-biserial correlation

83. Which of the following personality psychologist does not fall in the group of humanistic approaches of personality?

A. Carl Rogers
B. Rollo May
C. Martin Saligman
D. Abraham Maslow

84. A subject has a T score (Mean = 50; SD = 10) of 40 on an abstract reasoning test. The corresponding percentile rank would be

A. 16 B. 34
C. 40 D. 84

85. Which of the following tests are considered to be culture-fair tests of intelligence?

1. Cattell's Culture-Fair Test of Intelligence
2. Raven's Progressive Matrices
3. Wechsler's Intelligence Scale for Children
4. Goodenough-Harris Test

Codes :

A. 1 only
B. 1 and 2 only
C. 1, 2 and 3 only
D. 1, 2 and 4 only

86. The information in terms of sound is maintained in

A. Semantic code B. Acoustic code
C. Iconic code D. Information code

87. Which of the following personality tests are considered to be the projective in nature?

1. Thematic Apperception Test
2. Kent-Rosenoff Word Association Test
3. NEO Five-Factor Inventory
4. Rotter's Incomplete Sentence Blank

A. 1 only
B. 1 and 2 only
C. 1, 2 and 4 only
D. 2, 3 and 4 only

88. Read each of the following two statements Assertion (A) and Reason (R) and indicate your answer using the codes below :

Assertion (A) : Thalamus and Hypothalamus play an important role in emotions.

Reason (R) : Thalamus and Hypothalamus anatomically lie close each other.

Codes :
A. Both (A) and (R) are true and (R) is the correct explanation of (A).
B. Both (A) and (R) are true, but (R) is not the correct explanation of (A).
C. (A) is true, (R) is false.
D. (A) is false, (R) is true.

89. Taylor conceptualized anxiety as a drive and hypothesized that subjects scoring higher on her anxiety scale would be conditioned faster than the low-scoring subjects. The experimental studies confirmed this hypothesis for eyelid conditioning. The results provide evidence for the
A. predictive validity of the anxiety scale.
B. construct validity of the anxiety scale.
C. concurrent validity of the anxiety scale.
D. content validity of the anxiety scale.

90. Given below are two statements, one labelled as Assertion (A) and the other labelled as Reason (R). Indicate your answer using the codes given below :

Assertion (A) : According to Flynn, performance on IQ tests has substantially increased around the world at all age levels.

Reason (R) : Performance on IQ tests is because of the interaction between genetics and environment.

Codes :
A. Both (A) and (R) are true and (R) is the correct explanation of (A).
B. Both (A) and (R) are true, but (R) is not the correct explanation of (A).
C. (A) is true, but (R) is false.
D. (A) is false, but (R) is true.

ANSWERS

1	2	3	4	5	6	7	8	9	10
B	A	B	B	B	A	A	C	C	D
11	**12**	**13**	**14**	**15**	**16**	**17**	**18**	**19**	**20**
B	D	C	B	C	D	A	A	C	B
21	**22**	**23**	**24**	**25**	**26**	**27**	**28**	**29**	**30**
A	B	C	A	D	A	B	A	A	A
31	**32**	**33**	**34**	**35**	**36**	**37**	**38**	**39**	**40**
D	B	B	A	B	D	B	B	A	C
41	**42**	**43**	**44**	**45**	**46**	**47**	**48**	**49**	**50**
C	C	B	B	A	C	C	A	C	C
51	**52**	**53**	**54**	**55**	**56**	**57**	**58**	**59**	**60**
C	D	B	C	D	B	B	D	D	D
61	**62**	**63**	**64**	**65**	**66**	**67**	**68**	**69**	**70**
B	B	B	C	B	A	B	B	B	A
71	**72**	**73**	**74**	**75**	**76**	**77**	**78**	**79**	**80**
A	D	C	B	B	A	A	D	A	D
81	**82**	**83**	**84**	**85**	**86**	**87**	**88**	**89**	**90**
C	D	C	A	D	B	C	B	B	B

➤➤➤➤➤

CHAPTER

3

Community Development

COMMUNITY DEVELOPMENT

The term community development was first officially used in 1948 at British Colonial Office Cambridge Conference on Development of African Initiative (Hold Craft,1984). The then community development program aimed at helping British colonies in Africa prepare for independence by improving local government and developing their economies. After attaining independence the Indian government also experimented with the community development model. In India it was initiated on 2nd October 1952 with the aim of promoting better living for the whole community in the rural areas. The community development program was also as a result of the conclusion drawn from the 'Grow more food' enquiry report.

MODELS OF COMMUNITY DEVELOPMENT

Neighbourhood development Model

The model assumes that people living in a community have the capacity to meet a number of problem through their own initiatives and resources. Here, the social worker or community worker is expected to induce a process which will make community to realize this capacity and consequently make efforts to achieve a greater degree of satisfaction for all of its members, individually and collectively. The model assumes the role of a worker as catalyst rather than a service provider. The focus is on making community self sustaining rather than depending on outside help.

The Specific Steps in the model are:

- Identification, location and demarcation of the physical area.
- Entry into the community
- Identifying the need of different sections
- Program planning
- Resource planning
- Developing an organizational network in the community
- Partial withdrawal within a time frame.

System Change Model

The basic assumption in this model is that system can become dysfunctional due to variety of factors such as population growth, poverty, unemployment etc. If the system has become dysfunctional due to population means demand for consumption may increase. Similarly, a change in technology may signify a change in methodology of production. The cumulative impact of these factors may generate a host of strain and pressure on any system. The system may become dysfunctional either because what it is producing is not relevant for people, or because not many people have access to what is being produced. At times it may produce various categories of products for different sections of the population rather than serving as an empowering mechanism. Realizing this, social worker may decide to collect more facts to develop a strategy of either restructuring or modifying the system. This term is known as 'system change 'approach to community work.

Some of the specific tasks identified with this model are:

- Collecting relevant facts about the specific deficiency in the system
- Sharing the findings with the community
- Selecting an appropriate strategy to influence decision-making bodies or to focus attention on the issue
- Mobilizing community and outside support to put the plan into action
- Developing an organization in the community and linking it to similar organization in other communities, and other voluntary organization which can help them in demanding change.

Structural Change Model

The structural change model of community work assumes that various small communities constitute a big community, society, state or nation. The major assumption in this model is that the manner in which the relationship between different section of the population is structured formally (By constitution, law or state policy) and informally (By customs, public opinion) largely determines the social rights of the individual.

The social structure in some societies is such that the state regulates individuals to control the production and consumption of economic resources in order to ensure a certain level of need fulfilment for all or for the more needy section of the society. Therefore, in the structural change model, the worker analyzes the link between the macro structuring of social relationship and the micro realities of the society prevailing at the grass root level. The social worker tries to mobilize public opinion to alter and modify the macro structure of the society. This requires skills in understanding human society, the micro-macro realities and its various dimensions.

The specific tasks involved in this model are:

- To develop understanding of the link between micro and macro social realities
- To make conscious decision about an alternative political ideology
- To share this understanding with the community to enable it to make its own decisions
- To help the community in identifying a plan of action to achieve its goals
- To help community to sustain its interest to meet the strain that is likely to arise out of an unavoidable conflict with the existing power structure

L.C. jain (1985) identified the following objectives of the community development program

- Transformation of the outlook of the people;
- Inculcation of the spirit of self reliance;
- Generation of the habit of cooperative action through popular bodies

L.C. jain identified the tasks and duties to be persuade as follows:

- Every family should be assisted in the efforts for increasing employment and production by the practice of scientific agriculture and subsidiary occupations
- The efforts of the families should be organized through panchayat and cooperatives at different levels
- The obligations of the families benefiting from the program should be defined and enforced. Such families were expected to help in building up assets within the community
- Programs of production should be linked up with programs of amenities for villagers
- In all activities, the entire rural community should take participation
- Scientific agriculture should be the core of the entire program.

COMMUNITY DEVELOPMENT PROGRAM

S. No.	Name of the Community Development Program	Started By	Year
1	Sriniketan Project	Shri Rabindranath Tagore	1914
2	Gurgaon Experiment	F.L.Brayne	1920
3	Marthandam Project	Dr. Spencer Hatch	1921
4	Firka Development Scheme	Madras Government	1946
5	Etawah Pilot Project	Albert Mayor	1948
6	Nilokheri Experiment	S.K. Dey	1948
7	Sarvodaya Movement	Shri Vinoba Bhave	1948-49
8	Community Development Program	Government of India	1952
9	National Extension Service	Government of India	1953

Sriniketan: During 1914 Shri Rabindra Nath Tagore established a rural reconstruction institute of Sriniketan involving youth from a group of 8 village. Sriniketan was formally established on 6th February 1922. The main aim of the project was "Rural Reconstruction".

Gurgaon Project : The Gurgaon project of rural welfare was conceived and worked out by Mr. F.L. Brayne in 1920. The objectives of the project were increasing agriculture production, stoppage of wastage on social functions of the society, improvement of health etc.

Marthandam Project : This projects can be regarded as joint venture of YMCA and Christian Churches. The objectives of the project were to develop education, health and economic aspect of life, upliftment of moral and spiritual aspect, social development etc.

Gandhian Constructive Program at Sevagram – The project was started in first at Sevagram in 1920 and later Wardha in 1938. The objectives were to be conceived through self helps, dignity of labour, self respect, simple and honored living etc.

Rural Development Program: This was a Government program initiated in 1935-36 with the announcement of grant of Rs. 1 crore by the Government of India. The program aims at encouragement of village industries improvement of village communication, rural sanitation and a recreation, medical aid, agriculture etc.

Etawah Pilot Project: After the Second World War, a project for rural development and welfare was started in Etawah (U.P.) in September 1948 with the active assistance of Mr. Albert Myor and Mr. Horace Holmes. The objectives of the project were to measure the extent of agriculture development in terms of production and social improvement, initiatives, confidence and cooperation of the people were also evaluated.

Firka Development Scheme: The intensive Rural Reconstruction Scheme popularly known as the Firka development scheme was launched by the Government of Madras towards the end of 1946. It was to improve the living conditions in the area and create in me villagers an active interest in their problems to make them self sufficient and self reliant.

Sarvodaya Scheme: The Sarvodaya scheme is also based on the Gandhian principles. The state of Bombay has been taking active interest in the scheme since 1948-49. The scheme emphasise on the cooperative principles and methods and tries to inculcate the habits of self help, mutual aid and habit of saving among the people.

MAJOR PROGRAMS FOR RURAL COMMUNITY DEVELOPMENT

S. No.	Year	Short Name	Name of the Program
1	1948	GMFC	Grow More Food Campaign
2	1950	JMPC	Japanese Method of Paddy Cultivation
3	1952	CDP	Community Development Programme
4	1953	NES	National Extension Service
5	1961	IADP	Intensive Agriculture District Programme
6	1963	ANP	Applied Nutrition Programme
7	1964-65	IAAP	Integrated Agricultural Area Programme
8	1964	ICDP	Integrated Cattle Development Programme
9	1965	NDP	National Demonstration Project
10	1966	ODP	Oilseed Development Programme
11	1966-67	HYVP	High Yielding Varieties Programme
12	1966	FTEP	Farmers Training and Education Programme
13	1966	FTC	Farmers Training Centre
14	1966	MCP	Multiple Crop Programme
15	1970	DPAP	Draught Prone Area Programme
16	1970	DFAP	Dry Farming Area Programme
17	1971	ICDP	Integrated Cotton Development Programme
18	1971	WVDP	Whole Village Development Programme
19	1971	SFDA	Small Farmers Development Agency
20	1971	MFAL	Marginal Farmers and Agricultural Labour Agency
21	1971-72	TADP	Tribal Area Development Programme
22	1973	HADP	Hill Area Development Programme
23	1974	T&V	Training and Visit System
24	1974	KVK	Krishi Vigyan Kendra
25	1974	TDB	Tribal Development Block
26	1975	ICDS	Integrated Child Development Scheme
26	1975	CADP	Command Area Development Programme
27	1976	IRDP	Integrated Rural Development Programme
28	1976	ORP	Operational Research Project
29	1976	SF	Social Forestry
30	1977	DDP	Desert Development Programme
31	1978	LLP	Lab-to-Land Programme
32	1978	NARP	National Agricultural Research Project
33	1979	TRYSEM	Training of Rural Youth for Self Employment

S. No.	Year	Short Name	Name of the Program
34	1980	NREP	National Rural Employment Programme
35	1980	DRDA	District Rural Development Agency
36	1980-81	TUP	Tribal Upliftment Project
37	1981	RLEGP	Rural Landless Employment Guarantee Programme
38	1982	DWCRA	Development of Women and Children in Rural Areas
39	1984-85	NAEP	National Agricultural Extension Project
40	1986-87	NWDP	National Watershed Development Project
41	1989	JRY	Jawahar Rojgar Yojana
42	1990-91	NWDPRA	National Water Development Project for Rain fed Areas
43	1998	NATP	National Agricultural Technology Project
44	1998	ATMA	Agricultural Technology Management Agency
45	2005	NAIP	National Agricultural Innovation Project
46	2005	NAREGA	National Rural Employment Guarntee Scheme
47	2009	NRHM	National Rural Health Mission
48	2009-10	ICPS	Integrated Child Development Scheme
49	2011	NRLM	National Rural Livelihood Mission

COMMUNITY DEVELOPMENT APPROACH

National Extension Services: The community development program were having limitation of resources. Hence a need was felt to expand these to bring in more and more peoples under its ambit. Therefore, the national extension service was launched in 1953 to have a wider coverage at less cost and more peoples participation.

The Decentralized Approach: A team was constituted in 1957 for the study of community projects and national Extension service and it was headed by Mr. Balwant Rai Mehta. The team recommended democratic decentralization, *i.e.* the government that derives its authority from the peoples should redistribute it to the people so that the people can plan for themselves what is best for them. The concept took the shape of Panchayat Raj in India. The Panchayat Raj envisaged a scheme of democratic decentralization with the establishment of elected and originally linked democratic bodies at the grass root level, entrusting all the planning and development functions to these bodies and providing them with adequate resources so that they can discharge their duty effectively.

Integrated Development Approach: The Integrated Rural Development Program (IRDP) was launched to cover the whole country with the objective to assist families below poverty line in the rural areas by taking up self employment ventures in a variety of activities like agriculture, horticulture, sericulture and animal husbandry in the primary sector and service and business activities in the tertiary sector. Under the IRDP program at least 30 per cent of the beneficiaries had to be women. Various programs were started under IRDP. Training of Rural Youth for Self Employment (TRYSEM) was started in 1979 with main objective to equip rural youth (18-38 years) with necessary skills and technology and enable them to take up vocations of self employment. Another scheme exclusively for women under IRDP was Development of Women and Children in Rural Areas (DWCRA). The main objective of the program was to improve the condition of rural women through the creation of income generating activities. The program envisaged formation of groups of 10-15 rural women each carrying on income-generation activities with monetary assistance from financial institutions.

Legal Right Based Approach: Right based approach of community development is the more recent approach comparing the preceding two approaches. Now, one can demand work, education, information and food as a legal right. For that we have right to work, right to education, right to information and right to food. It is the duty of the government to provide its citizens all these things. The Mahatma Gandhi National Rural Employment Guarantee Act (MGNAREGA) guarantees the right to work and ensures livelihood security in rural areas by providing at least 100 days of guaranteed wage employment in a financial year to every household whose adult members volunteer to do unskilled manual work. The Constitutional 86th amendment inserted Article 21 A in the Constitution of India; right to education that entails provision of free and compulsory education to all children in the age group of six to fourteen years as a Fundamental Right. The Right to Information Acts provides for right to information for citizen to secure access to information under the control of public authorities. Right to Food Act compels the government to provide food grain quota to five kilogram per person per family subject to a maximum 25 kg per family. The Act brings under its preview 75 per cent of the rural households and 50 per cent of urban households. The beneficiaries would receive 5 kilograms of subsidized foodgrains at the rate of rupees three per kilogram for rice, wheat for rupees two per kilogram and coarse cereals for rupees one per kilogram.

RURAL DEVELOPMENT

The term 'Rural Development' means all round development of rural areas with a view to betterment of lifestyles and standard of living in all spheres of their life. Since independence government of India has envisaged many programs in the form of planned development in the name of rural upliftment yet the conditions in the rural hinterland is not satisfactory some of the contributing factors are listed below:

Problems in Rural Development

1. People related:

- Traditional way of thinking.
- Poor understanding.
- Low level of education to understand developmental efforts and new technology.
- Deprived psychology and scientific orientation.
- Lack of confidence.
- Poor awareness.
- Low level of education.
- Existence of unfelt needs.
- Personal ego.

2. Agriculture related problems:

- Lack of expected awareness,
- Knowledge, skill and attitude.
- Unavailability of inputs.
- Poor marketing facility.
- Insufficient extension staff and services.
- Multidimensional tasks to extension personnel.
- Small size of land holding.
- Division of land.
- Unwillingness to work and stay in rural areas.

3. Infrastructure related problems:

- Poor infrastructure facilities like water, electricity, transport, educational institutions, communication, health, storage facility etc.

4. Economic problems:

- Unfavourable economic condition to adopt high cost technology.
- High cost of inputs.
- Underprivileged rural industries.

5. Social and Cultural problems:

- Cultural norms and traditions

- Conflict within and between groups, castes, religions, regions, languages.

6. Leadership related problems:

- Leadership among the hands of inactive and incompetent people.
- Malafied interest of leaders.
- Biased political will.

7. Administrative problems:

- Earlier, majority of the programmes were planning based on top to bottom approach and were target oriented.
- Political interference.
- Lack of motivation and interest.
- Unwillingness to work in rural area.
- Improper utilization of budget.

SCHEDULED TRIBE

Article 342 of the Constitution specifies tribes or tribal communities for the purpose of the Constitution are deemed to be Scheduled Tribes. Therefore, Constitution of India having no specific definition for tribe, rather, it defines tribe on the basis of certain specific characteristics, these are:

- On the basis of dialect.
- On the basis of different religion, they basically worship 'Animism' – that is worship of 'Ghost' and 'Spirit'.
- Every tribe have their chief as 'Gan Nayak'.
- They are considered to be the original inhabitants of the India.

Commission of Scheduled Castes and Scheduled Tribe in his report for the year 1952 has listed some common features of Scheduled Tribe.

- They line away from the civilised world in the inaccessible parts in the forest hills.
- Speaks the same tribal dialects.
- Prefer primitive religion known as 'Animism' in which worship of Ghost and Spirit is important.
- They are largely meat eaters.

So, tribe constitutes a group of people have a common dialect, distinct culture, definite GOD, occupy certain geographical territory, specific governing system and specific name.

Issues of Scheduled Tribes in India

- Segregation
- Identity and Culture
- Assimilation
- Underdevelopment
- Seclusion
- Problem of Development
- Land Ownership
- Exploitation of Resources
- Exploitation through Money Landers.

Tribal Sub Plan (TSP)

The TSP strategy come into existence during 5th Five Year Plan. The TSP mechanism is designed to channelize the flow benefits arising out of outlays from the general sectors in the plan of states and central minister for the welfare of scheduled tribes.

The strategy have two fold objectives :

Socio-economic development of ST and Protection of tribal's against exploitation. In order to achieve the above mentioned objectives Integrated Tribal Development Projects (ITDPs) were initially delineated in the 5th plan. Modified Area Development Approach (MADA) was identified during 6th and 7th plan.

Following considerations are kept in view:

- Formulation of appropriate need based programs for tribal areas.
- Adaptation of all the on going programs to suit the specific requirement of the scheduled tribes.
- Quantification of funds under ministry area and ear marketing a senior officer exclusively to monitor the progress of implementation of the program for the welfare of scheduled tribes.

DEFINITION OF SCHEDULED CASTES

Under Article 341 of the Constitution certain backward castes/communities suffering from untouchability and other social disabilities were declared as Scheduled Castes.

Problems of Scheduled Castes in India

Lowest Status in the Hierarchy: In the Caste hierarchy the Scheduled Castes are ascribed the lowest status. They are considered to be 'unholy', 'inferior' and 'low' and are looked down upon by the other castes. They have been suffering from the stigma of 'untouchability'. Their very touch is considered to be polluting for the higher caste people.

Education Disabilities: The Scheduled Castes were forbidden from taking up to education especially during the colonial rule of Britishers, Sanskrit education was denied for them. Public schools and other educational institutions were closed for them. Even today percentage of illiteracy is very high among scheduled castes.

Civic Disabilities: For a long time the so called untouchable castes were not allowed to use public places and avail of civic facilities such as—village wells, ponds, temples, hostels, hotels, schools, hospitals, lecture halls, dharamashalas, etc. Although the situation has changed but many incidents suggests that the practice of untouchability still prevails in many parts of the country.

Religious Disabilities: The Scheduled Castes also suffer from religious disabilities even today. They are not allowed to enter temples in many places. The Brahmins who offer their priestly services to some lower castes, are not prepared to officiate in the ceremonies of the 'untouchable' castes. They do not even bow down to the duties of these 'untouchable' castes.

No Right of Property Ownership: For centuries the Scheduled Castes were not allowed to have land and business of their own. It is only recently their ownership to the property has become recognised. The propertied people are comparatively less in them. Majority of them depend upon agriculture but only a few of them own land and most of them have small land holdings.

Selection of Occupations Limited: The Caste system imposes restrictions on the occupational choice of the members. The occupational choice was very much limited for the Scheduled Castes. They were not allowed to take up to occupations which were reserved for the upper caste people.

They were forced to stick on to the traditional inferior occupations such as—curing hides, removing the human wastes, sweeping, scavenging, oil grinding, tanning, shoemaking, leather works, carrying the dead animals, etc. These occupations were regarded as 'degraded' and 'inferior'.

Landless Labourers: Majority of the Scheduled Castes are today working as landless labourers. More than 90.1% of the agricultural labourers in India belong to the depressed classes which include the Scheduled Castes and Scheduled Tribes. More than 77.1% of the Scheduled Caste workers in rural areas are agricultural labourers.

PANCHAYATI RAJ SYATEM

The first organized effort to solve the problem of rural India was made through the Community Development Programme in the year 1952 and National Extension Service in 1953. On the completion of first five years of the CDP, the planning Commission appointed a high-ranking study committee headed by **Balwant Rai Mehta, Chief Minister of Gujarat**. This team pointed out both positive results and inadequacies in the implementation of the programme. This committee recommended Panchayati Raj.

Philosophy of Panchayat Raj: The philosophy of Panchayat Raj is deeply steeped in tradition and culture of rural India and is by no means a new concept. Panchayati Raj provides a system of self-governance at the village level. Panchayati Raj Institutions is the grass-roots units of self-government – have been declared as the vehicles of socio-economic transformation in rural India. Effective and meaningful functioning of these bodies would depend on active involvement, contribution and participation of its citizens both male and female. The aim of every village being a republic and panchayats having powers has been translated into reality with the introduction of the three-tier Panchayati Raj system to enlist people's participation in rural reconstruction.

The study team made a significant recommendation with implementation of a programme. According to it there should be effective administrative decentralization for the implementation of the programme. The decentralized administration was to be placed under the control of selected and integrated local self-government system ordinarily of 3 levels bodies from village level to block level and then to district level. This democratic decentralized system was named as **"Panchayat Raj"**. The state of Madras tried this as a pilot project as early as 1957. In 1958, Andhra Pradesh state had twenty such pilot projects. Based on the success in these it was the state of Rajasthan which became the pioneer to bring the whole state under democratic decentralization on October 2, 1959. It was implemented in Gujarat on April 1, 1963.

Some Explanations

1. **Panch**: An assembly of elders who settled the disputes within the limit of caste/customs.
2. **Panchayat**: An assembly of elected persons of the village. Village bodies were the lines of contact with higher authorities on matters affecting to the village.
3. **Democracy**: The word Democracy derived from Greek language **Democ** means the people and **Cracy** means rule of. It is leading of the people, by the people, for the people.
4. **Decentralization**: Devolution of central authority among local units close to the area served.
5. **Democratic decentralization:** This means where authority develops by the process on people's institution and act as local self-government.

Specific Objectives

1. Assistance to the economically weaker sections of the community.
2. Cohesion and cooperative self help in the community.
3. Development of cooperative institutions.
4. Development of local resources including the utilization of manpower.
5. Production in agriculture as the highest priority in planning.
6. Progressive dispersal of authority and initiative both vertically and horizontally with special emphasis on the role of voluntary organizations.
7. Promotion of rural industries.
8. Understanding and harmony between the people's representatives and people servants through comprehensive training/education and a clear demarcation of duties and responsibilities.

Three tiers (levels) of Panchayat Raj

The Gram Panchayat

Gram Panchayat is the primary unit of Panchayati Raj Institutions or local self-government. In other words it can be said that the first formal democratic institution under the directive principle in the Indian Constitution is the Gram Panchayat. It is a cabinet of the village elders, directly elected by the adult citizens of the village. Gram Panchayats are constituted considering their income, population and area. There is a provision for reservation of seats for women and Scheduled Castes and Scheduled Tribes. The panchayat has tenure of five years and is directly elected. It has income through taxes to perform its functions.

The main functions of Village Panchayat are:

1. Preparation of Annual Plans for the development of the village Panchayat area.
2. Preparation of Annual Budget of Village Panchayat.
3. Mobilization of relief in natural calamities.
4. Removal of encroachments on public properties.
5. Organizing voluntary labours and contribution for community works.

6. Maintenance of essential statistics of villages.
7. Such other development works as may be entrusted.
8. Service or developmental function, such as promotion of education, health, agriculture, etc.
9. Representative function, where the main role is to voice and represent the opinion;
10. Regulatory and administrative functions, which consists of regulating the conduct of individuals and institutions and also collection of taxes.

Sources of Income of Village Panchayat:

1. Share in land revenue.
2. Local tax.
3. Revenue earned from the settlement of shops, fisheries, etc
4. House taxes & other taxes as specified in Panchayati Raj Act.
5. Fees for providing amenities, cess, tolls.
6. Contribution and grants.
7. Fine and penalties.

Taluka/Block Panchayat

It is also known as Panchayat Samiti or Panchayat Union. This is the second tier of the administration at Taluka or Block level. It is headed by Taluka President. Block Development Officer is appointed by the Government. He functions as the leader of the Block.

The main functions of the Panchayat Samitis are planning, execution and supervision of all developmental programmes in the Block. It also supervises the works of Gram Panchayats within its jurisdiction. It has to instill among people within its jurisdiction a spirit of self-help and initiative and work for raising the standard of living. It has to support for the implementation of development programmes. It has the welfare and development activities in the fields of agriculture, animal husbandry, health, sanitation, elementary education, cottage industries and social. It has to use the village housing project funds and loans.

Zilla Panchayat

It is also known as District Development Council or Zilla Parishad. This is the third tier of Panchayat Raj functioning at district level. It is headed by Panchayat Union Chairman. District Collector leads the work with the help of District Development Officers.

Functions:

1. It works as advisory body for blocks.
2. It approves budget and plan of blocks.
3. It allots funds to the blocks.
4. Secondary education is the responsibility of this council.
5. It should advise Government in all matters relating to rural development in the district.
6. It has to review the results achieved under various items in all the blocks.

DEMOCRATIC DECENTRALISATION

It was J.S. Mill who had stated about democracy that "The only government which can fully satisfy all the exigency of the social state, where the whole people participate".

Peoples participation forms the basic of democracy. When people participate in the operation of their government in the country in larger, continuous, more active and constructive way, it is said to be nearer to democracy as a political ideal. It is democratic decentralisation which aims at associating people with the government to the maximum possible extent. The word democratic in front of decentralisation emphasises the purpose decentralisation. The purpose is to provide larger, greater and closer association of the people with the work of their own government at all levels, national, regional and more particularly local level. In a democratically decentralise system, people have got the right to initiate their own projects for local well being and they have the power to execute and operate them in an autonomous manner.

Democratic decentralisation is a centrifugal movement. Power moves from the central to the regional and local areas. It aims to entrust local organs created in local areas with powers local in character. Thus, there is devolution of authority from higher level of the government to the lower level of government. The process of decentralisation is vertical rather than horizontal.

The decentralised authority thus should be managed by the people directly or indirectly through their representativeness. The institutional machinery of democratic decentralisation is necessarily elective. Democratic decentralisation is thus a political ideal and local self government is its institutional form. In India it is Panchayat Raj Institutions which are the institutional form of the democratic decentralisation.

Some special features of Democratic Decentralization:

1. The sanctioning powers of most of the works and schemes are with panchayat samitis and standing committees.
2. Most of the functions are implemented and performed by administrative control of the Panchayat Samitis. Thus, there is a single agency at Block level for all development programmes.
3. The power and functions of the District Boards are allocated among the Parishads and the Samitis.

Importance of Democratic Decentralisation and Peoples Participation

- Decentralisation of power would make effective institutional arrangements.
- Too much concentration of and dependency on the central guidance causes delay, increase cost, reduce efficiency, limits initiatives and discourage inventions.
- The real decentralisation is where participation of people or their involvement in decision-making for their own and communities development.
- The decision-making centers should be very close to the people. This can be achieved only by well organised local institutions located close to the people.
- Through democratic decentralisation and peoples participation energies and talents of the people can be harnessed for the development purpose.
- The entire development is based in stimulating people participations in decision making. No development is possible without massive involvement of people. Therefore, maximum progress could be achieved only through maximum participation.

IMPORTANT COMMITTEES AND COMMISSIONS RELATED TO PANCHAYATI RAJ SYSTEM IN INDIA

B.R. Mehta Committee: The Panchayat were a subject of study by a number of committees and study teams starting with the B.R. Mehta Committee recommending a three tier Panchayat Raj structure.

L.M. Singhavi Committee: In 1986 the L.M. Singhavi Committee studied Panchayati Raj and suggested that Gram Sabha be the base of a decentralized democracy and Panchayati Raj Institutions (PRIs) viewed as institutions of self governance which would actually facilitate participation of people in the process of planning and development. Therefore, on the recommendation of Singhavi committee the 73rd Amendment included the Gram Sabha as the basis of the three tier Panchayati Raj.

Statutory Panchayats: The statutory panchayats were created by the law. These laws are given as follows:

Royal Commission on Decentralization (1907): These owe their origin to the Report of the Royal Commission on Decentralization. The commission had recommended the creation of village Panchayats for reducing the financial burden of the provincial governments and for extending the concept of local self government to the village level.

Mayo's Resolution (1870) and Ripon Resolution (1882): The mayo's resolution (1870) had created municipalities in the urban areas and the Ripon Resolution (1882) the district board at the district level and the rural board at the taluka/ tehsil levels, as the local self government institutions. The Royal Commission not only advocated their strengthening but also suggested creation of these at the village level as the Panchayats.

Village Panchayat Act (1912): Consequently, the government of various provinces enacted Village Panchayat Act in the second decade of 20th century. Village Panchayat Act was made in 1912 for the creation of statutory panchayat. The objective of this Act was to strengthen the Panchayats both as units of Local Self Government and as judicial bodies.

Government of India Act (1919): After the introduction of Dyarchy in provinces as a result of the implementation of the Government of India Act (1919), the local self government was made a transferred subject. Thereafter, the Indian ministers got new village panchayat Acts enacted for strengthening the Village Panchayats.

MULTIPLE CHOICE QUESTIONS

1. Blocking a wish or desire from expression is termed as
A. Denial B. Repression
C. Projection D. Regression

2. Which among the following is not a component of client case worker relationship?
A. Autonomy B. Confidentiality
C. Empathy D. Sympathy

3. _____ is the first settlement in U.K. which is associated with group work.
A. Charity organisation society
B. Neighbourhood guild
C. Toynbee Hall
D. Hull house

4. Social learning theory is associated with
A. Albert Bandura B. Julian Rotter
C. Walter Mischel D. All the above

5. Amartya Sen is associated with which of the following concepts?
A. Freedom B. Human Rights
C. Basic Needs D. Economic Rights

6. Which among the following is not a symptom of schizophrenia?
A. Paranoia
B. Vocational function
C. Auditory hallucination
D. Disorganized thinking

7. Mean difference is also called as
A. Standard error
B. Variance
C. Co-efficient
D. Correlation

8. Which of the following is an antisocial element?
A. Clique
B. Crowd
C. Organised group
D. Gang

9. The review of questionnaire with the object of increasing accuracy is
A. Coding B. Editing
C. Recording D. Decoding

10. The book entitled "Two Treaties on Civil Government" is by
A. Hegel B. John Lock
C. James Mill D. Bentham

11. The 'Employees Provident Fund and (Miscellaneous Provisions) Act' was passed in the year
A. 1948 B. 1952
C. 1961 D. 1976

12. 'Self talk', means
A. The messages that a person gives to himself/herself.
B. A technique of talking with two persons.
C. The message a person receives for himself.
D. Message received from super natural power.

13. Human Rights Day observed on
A. 1st December B. 10th December
C. 12th December D. 15th December

14. National Institute of Social Defence is situated at
A. Delhi B. Bangalore
C. Mumbai D. Chennai

15. The basic skill of active listening which is the cornerstone of effective communication is
A. making a diagnostic formulation of the client as he speaks.
B. clarify what the client relates without being paternalistic.
C. evaluate the effect that transference is having on the social worker-client relationship.
D. understand both what the client & the social worker are saying and the undercurrents of unspoken feelings between the two.

16. Which of the following is not a part of community organisation?
A. To determine the social needs of a community.
B. To integrate the specific needs of some individual members of a community.
C. To consciously do planning for meeting the needs of the community.
D. To mobilize community resources to meet the social needs of a community.

17. National Policy for children was launched in
A. August 1974 B. August 1977
C. August 1978 D. August 1975

18. Who coined the term 'Isolated nuclear family'?
A. William J. Goode
B. Murdock
C. Cooper
D. Talcott Parsons

19. Which article of the Indian Constitution provides maternity leave for women?
A. Article 40 B. Article 41
C. Article 42 D. Article 44

20. One of the following sections of IPC deals with cruelty :
A. Section 354 B. Section 376
C. Section 498 A D. Section 508

21. New Economic Policy in India is characterised by :
(a) Privatization (b) Globalization
(c) Safety Nets (d) Liberalization

Choose the correct answer using the following code :
A. (a) and (b)
B. (a), (b) and (c)
C. (a), (b) and (d)
D. (a), (b), (c) and (d)

22. Match List I and List II and select the correct answer using the codes given below :

List-I Type of Therapy	List-II Proponent
(a) Client Centred Therapy	(1) William Glasser
(b) Behaviour Therapy	(2) Carl Rogers
(c) Transactional Analysis	(3) Joseph Wolpe
(d) Reality Therapy	(4) Eric Betne

Codes :

	(a)	(b)	(c)	(d)
A.	(2)	(3)	(4)	(1)
B.	(3)	(4)	(1)	(2)
C.	(4)	(3)	(2)	(1)
D.	(3)	(1)	(2)	(4)

23. Match List I and List II and select the appropriate answer by using the codes given below :

List-I Level of Intervention	List-II Action of Social Worker
(a) Micro Level	(1) With disabled child
(b) Mezzo Level	(2) Working with Panchayat for water harvesting
(c) Macro Level	(3) Working with self help group of cancer patients

Codes :

	(a)	(b)	(c)
A.	(1)	(2)	(3)
B.	(1)	(3)	(2)
C.	(3)	(2)	(1)
D.	(2)	(1)	(3)

24. Match the items of List – I with List – II.

List-I	List-II
a. Monogamy	1. Husband marries sisters of wife
b. Polyandry	2. Women marrying brother of husband
c. Fraternal Polyandry	3. One husband one wife
d. Sororal Polygamy	4. One wife and more than one husband

Codes :

	a	b	c	d
A.	3	1	2	4
B.	3	1	4	2
C.	3	4	2	1
D.	4	3	2	1

25. One of the following is not present in single parent families :
A. Kin relationship
B. Step relationship
C. Parental relationship
D. Biological relationship

26. Human life is mostly influenced by
A. Friends B. Family
C. School D. Colleagues

27. Juvenile crime can be prevented mainly by
A. Good parenting and family support.
B. Peer pressures.
C. Unrestricted freedom by parents.
D. Over indulgence by family.

28. Match the following :

List-I	List-II
a. Health Survey and Planning Committee	1. 2007
b. Mental Health Act	2. 1959
c. Attrocities against Women Act	3. 1952
d. Hindu Code Bill	4. 1987

Codes :

	a	b	c	d
A.	4	3	2	1
B.	3	1	4	2
C.	2	4	1	3
D.	1	2	3	4

29. One of the following is not the function of a social worker in a juvenile residential institution :
A. Administration
B. Maintaining case records
C. Court hearing of cases
D. Publishing research papers

30. Jan Shikshan Sansthan (JSS) is the programme of
A. Ministry of Social Justice and Empowerment
B. Ministry of Information and Broadcasting
C. Ministry of Human Resource Development
D. Ministry of Agriculture

31. Services provided for weaker sections of the society are called
A. Community Services
B. Voluntary Services
C. Public Welfare Services
D. Social Welfare Services

32. Louis Braille Day is being observed on
A. 5th January B. 6th January
C. 7th January D. 8th January

33. Institutional Redistributive Model of Social Policy is associated with
A. Capitalist State
B. Communist State
C. Totalitarian State
D. Welfare State

34. The concept of Total Fertility Rate (TFR) means
A. The average number of children born to an adult women during her lifetime.
B. The average number of children born to an adult male during his life time.
C. The average number of children born in a family.

D. The average rate of growth of population.

35. Social Legislation attempts to
A. justice as well as social security
B. anticipate social needs
C. provide for change in social order
D. All the above

36. ______ describe the process by which a course of action is selected to deal with a specific problem.
A. Decision-making
B. Goal setting
C. Strategic planning
D. Organisational planning

37. ROI is ______
A. Return over Investment
B. Return on Investment
C. Return on Interest
D. Return on Internship

38. Industrial Disputes Act ______ provide for setting up bipartite works committees as a worker participation programme in India.
A. 1980 B. 1923
C. 1936 D. 1947

39. Assertion (A) : The divorce rate is increasing in metro cities in India due to high expectation and poor sensitivity.

Reason (R) : There is greater sensitivity to each other's needs in rural areas and the divorce rate in rural areas will remain much lower for a long time.

Select your answer from the following :

Codes :
A. Both (A) and (R) are correct, but (R) is not a correct explanation of (A).
B. (R) is correct, but (A) is wrong.
C. (A) is correct, but (R) is wrong.
D. Both (A) and (R) are wrong.

40. Assertion (A) : Education creates more sensitivity and develops self confidence.

Reason (R) : Educated women will demand more respect from society in general.

Select the right answer.

A. Both (A) and (R) are correct, but (R) is not an explanation of (A).
B. (R) is correct, but (A) is wrong.
C. Both (A) & (R) are wrong.
D. Both (A) & (R) are correct and (R) is the correct explanation of (A).

41. Urban Community Development Services in India were started by
A. American Friends Service Committee
B. Government of India
C. UNICEF
D. Ford Foundation

42. The book "Community Welfare Organisation – Principles and Practice" has been written by
A. K.D. Gangrade
B. H.Y. Siddiqui
C. Murrey G Ross
D. Arther Dunham

43. Which is the cause of poverty of small, marginal and casual workers in rural areas of India?
A. Small land holdings
B. Low productivity
C. Poor educational base and lack of vocational skills
D. All of the above

44. Match the following :

List-I (Name of the Author)	**List-II (Title of the Book)**
(a) H.Y. Siddiqui	(i) Introduction to Social Case Work
(b) S.K. Khinduka	(ii) Working with Communities
(c) Murli Desai	(iii) Social Work in India
(d) Grace Mathew	(iv) Ideologies and Social Work : Historical and Contemporary Analyses.

Codes :

	(a)	(b)	(c)	(d)
A.	(ii)	(iii)	(iv)	(i)
B.	(iii)	(ii)	(i)	(iv)

C. (iv) (iii) (i) (ii)
D. (i) (iv) (ii) (iii)

45. **Assertion (A) :** Technological advancement adds to the complexity of human society.
Reason (R) : To keep the advancement giving some of its negative implications need to be understood and dealt with.

Codes :
A. Both (A) and (R) are true.
B. Both (A) and (R) are not true.
C. (A) is not true, but (R) is the explanation of (A).
D. (A) is true, and (R) is not true.

46. **Assertion (A) :** Social worker should make an eye contact with client during interview process.
Reason (R) : Eye contact result is effective non-verbal communication.

Codes :
A. Both (A) and (R) are true and (R) is a correct explanation of (A).
B. Both (A) and (R) are not true.
C. (A) is true, but (R) is not true.
D. (A) is not true, but (R) is true.

47. **Assertion (A) :** There is no vaccine for AIDS.
Reason (R) : The AIDS virus frequently changes its genetic code.

Codes :
A. Both (A) and (R) are true and (R) is the correct explanation of (A).
B. Both (A) and (R) are true, but (R) is not the correct explanation of (A).
C. (A) is true, but (R) is false.
D. Both (A) and (R) are false.

48. **Assertion (A) :** Social Diagnosis is the important part of social case work process.
Reason (R) : It is a reflective thinking that gives direction to problem solving process.

Codes :
A. Both (A) and (R) are true and (R) is the correct explanation of (A).
B. Both (A) and (R) are true, but (R) is not the correct explanation of (A).
C. (A) is true, but (R) is false.
D. Both (A) and (R) are false.

49. The practical wisdom i.e. the ability to make right decisions in difficult circumstances, according to Aristotle is :
A. Kinesis B. Phronesis
C. Synthesis D. Diagnosis

50. The term foster care refers to :
A. Temporary placement of the child with non-biological parents
B. Permanent placement of child with parents
C. Repatriating child to the parents
D. None of the above

51. Consider the following statements and select your answer according to the codes given below :
Assertion (A) : Minority - sensitive practice requires that social worker has an in-depth understanding of the effects of oppression on minority groups.
Reason (R) : Social worker has an obligation to serve oppressed and marginalized.
A. Both **(A)** and **(R)** are true and **(R)** is the correct explanation of **(A)**
B. Both **(A)** and **(R)** are true but **(R)** is not the complete explanation of **(A)**
C. **(A)** is true but **(R)** is not true
D. **(A)** is not true but **(R)** is true

52. United Nations declared 1994 as the year of:
A. Family B. Education
C. Girl child D. Health

53. When facts are assembled, ordered and seen in relationship, they constitute
A. A Project B. A Scale
C. A Theory D. A Concept

54. The Civil Society Organizations is called
A. First sector B. Second sector
C. Third sector D. Fourth sector

55. The major theme of HDR (Human Development Report) of 2007/08 was
A. Water harvesting
B. Fighting climate change

C. International cooperation
D. Democracy

56. Functional approach in Case Work was developed by
A. Jessy Taft
B. Otto Rank
C. Gordon Hamilton
D. Talcott Parsons

57. The therapy developed by Otto Rank is called
A. Crisis intervention
B. Humanistic therapy
C. Rational emotive therapy
D. Will therapy

58. Which one of the following is the characteristic of society?
A. Non-assistance
B. Non-organisation
C. Interdependence
D. Non-difference

59. The concept of Directive Principles of State Policy was borrowed from the Constitution of
A. USA B. England
C. Ireland D. France

60. SOS villages were started by
A. Hermann Gmeiner
B. R.N. Butler
C. C. Phillipson
D. K.D. Gangrade

61. The person educated through a foreign language is sure to be unpatriotic :
A. The statement is a fact
B. The statement is an advice
C. The statement is an opinion
D. The statement is a prejudice

62. Match the following pairs :

(a) Association	(i) 't' test
(b) Dispersion	(ii) Chi-square
(c) Inference	(iii) Correlation
(d) Difference	(iv) Standard Deviation

Codes :

	(a)	(b)	(c)	(d)
A.	(iii)	(iv)	(ii)	(i)
B.	(i)	(ii)	(iii)	(iv)
C.	(ii)	(iii)	(iv)	(i)
D.	(iii)	(ii)	(i)	(iv)

63. Who classified values of social work as abstract and instrumental?
A. Kohs B. Herbert Bisno
C. Pumphery D. Philip Klein

64. Which one of the articles of Indian Constitution authorises the Indian state to make special provisions for women and children?
A. 16 B. 15
C. 23 D. 17

65. Assertion (A) : Nominal level of measurement is the lowest and most simple level of measurement.

Reason (R) : A variable is classified into several nominal sub-classes.

Codes :
A. (A) is correct, but (R) is wrong.
B. Both (A) and (R) are correct.
C. (A) is wrong, but (R) is correct.
D. Both (A) and (R) are wrong.

66. Arrange the field practicum in sequence :
A. Orientation, Concurrent field work, Observation visit, Block Placement
B. Observation visit, Orientation, Block Placement, Concurrent field work
C. Concurrent field work, Observation visit, Orientation, Block Placement
D. Orientation, Observation visit, Concurrent field work, Block Placement

67. Assertion (A) : Social work is a human rights profession.

Reason (R) : Client's problems should be solved as per his/her decision.

Codes :
A. Both (A) and (R) are wrong.
B. (A) is correct but (R) is wrong.
C. Both (A) and (R) are correct.
D. (A) is wrong but (R) is correct.

68. Which one of the following is not a correct matching?

A. Murray G. Ross – Community
B. P.D. Kulkarni – Social Policy in India
C. H.B. Trucker – Social group work
D. M.S. Gore – Social case work

69. Match the following writers with their contributions to specific areas of understanding social group.

List-I	**List-II**
(I) Simmer	(1) Leadership theories
(II) MacIver	(2) Primary group
(III) Eubank	(3) Nature of group
(IV) Cooley	(4) Collection of Human beings

Codes :

	(I)	(II)	(III)	(IV)
A.	(3)	(4)	(1)	(2)
B.	(3)	(4)	(2)	(1)
C.	(3)	(2)	(1)	(4)
D.	(3)	(1)	(4)	(2)

70. Public Interest Litigation is aimed at to protect
A. the public servants
B. the tribals
C. the women
D. the public

71. Arrange the stages of social work intervention in order.
A. Situational analysis, Need Assessment, Prioritizing, Action plan, Implementation
B. Need Assessment, Prioritizing, Situational analysis, Implementation, Action plan
C. Situational analysis, Action plan, Prioritizing, Need Assessment, Implementation
D. Prioritizing, Need assessment, Situational analysis, Action plan, Implementation

72. Assertion (A) : Social heterogeneity in the urban environment has become an important feature.

Reason (R) : The growth of urbanisation and industrialisation has dragged the people from various places in search of employment.

Choose your answer from the following :
A. Both (A) and (R) are true.
B. Both (A) and (R) are true, but (R) is not the correct explanation.
C. (A) is true, but (R) is false.
D. (A) is false, but (R) is true.

73. Assertion (A) : Social work cannot be considered as human right profession.

Reason (R) : It only deals with human problems.

Choose your answers from the following :
A. (A) is false, but (R) is true.
B. (A) is true, but (R) is false.
C. Both (A) and (R) are true and (R) is not the correct explanation of (A).
D. Both (A) and (R) are wrong.

74. Assertion (A) : There is no vaccine for AIDS.

Reason (R) : The AIDS virus frequently changes its genetic code.

Choose your answer from the following :
A. Both (A) and (R) are true, but (R) is not correct explanation of (A).
B. Both (A) and (R) are true and (R) is the correct explanation of (A).
C. Both (A) and (R) are false.
D. (A) is true, but (R) is false.

75. Assertion (A) : Drug abuse is a cognizable offence.

Reason (R) : Drug abuse is not an antisocial activity.

Choose your answer from the following :
A. Both (A) and (R) are true and (R) is the correct explanation of (A).
B. Both (A) and (R) are true, but (R) is not the correct explanation of (A).
C. (A) is true, but (R) is false.
D. Both (A) and (R) are false.

76. Assertion (A) : It is never safe to take published statistics at their face value without knowing their meaning and limitations.

Reason (R) : Published statistics usually shows the trend.

Choose your answers from the following :
A. (A) is correct, but (R) is wrong.
B. (A) is wrong, but (R) is correct.
C. Both (A) and (R) are wrong.
D. Both (A) and (R) are correct.

77. Assertion (A) : Interviews introduce more bias than does the use of questionnaire.

Reason (R) : Bias of interviewer does not affect the interview process.

Choose your answer from the following :
A. (A) is wrong, but (R) is correct.
B. (A) is correct, but (R) is wrong.
C. Both (A) and (R) are wrong.
D. Both (A) and (R) are correct.

78. Assertion (A) : There is a gap between social policy statement and the development programs.

Reason (R) : The reason is lack of political will and commitment in the formulation and implementation of programs.

Codes :
A. (A) is correct, but (R) is not correct.
B. (A) is not correct but (R) is correct.
C. Both (A) and (R) are correct, and (R) is not the correct explanation to (A).
D. Both (A) and (R) are correct and (R) is the correct explanation of (A).

79. Assertion (A) : Social work and Human rights are based on the same philosophical foundations.

Reason (R) : Both have similar values such as dignity and respect for individuals / groups / community.

Codes :
A. Both (A) and (R) are correct and (R) is the correct explanation of (A).
B. Both (A) and (R) are correct, but (R) is not the correct explanation to (A).
C. (A) is correct but (R) is not correct.
D. Both (A) and (R) are not correct.

80. Assertion (A) : Legislative measures alone can't reduce the incidence of crime.

Reason (R) : Effective implementation of the legislation does not require societal support.

Codes :
A. Both (A) and (R) are correct.
B. (A) is correct but (R) is not the correct explanation to (A).
C. Both (A) and (R) are not correct.
D. (A) is correct and (R) is the correct explanation to (A).

81. Assertion (A) : Social work as a problem solving profession can address social problems of the society.

Reason (R) : Social workers are equipped with broad based knowledge and appropriate skills.

Codes :
A. (A) is right but (R) is wrong.
B. Both (A) and (R) are correct but (R) is not the right explanation to (A).
C. Both (A) and (R) are correct, and (R) is the right explanation to (A).
D. Both (A) and (R) are wrong.

82. Assertion (A) : Democratic leadership to be successful require more time but it brings effective change in communities.

Reason (R) : Democratic leadership is process oriented and involves people's participation.

Codes :
A. (A) is correct, and (R) is wrong.
B. Both (A) and (R) are correct and (R) is the correct explanation of (A).
C. Both (A) and (R) are wrong.
D. Both (A) and (R) are correct, but (R) is not an explanation of (A).

83. Assertion (A) : Community organization leads to social action.

Reason (R) : Social action may not always leads to community organisation.

Codes :
A. Both (A) and (R) are correct.
B. (A) is correct and (R) is wrong.
C. (R) is correct and (A) is wrong.
D. Both (A) and (R) are wrong.

84. **Assertion (A) :** Gender sensitive professional social workers have better understanding of Gender Specific Issues.

Reason (R) : Professional social workers understand gender as a social construct which differentiates men and women in terms of their positions in the society.

Codes :

A. Both (A) and (R) are wrong.
B. Both (A) and (R) are correct and (R) is the correct explanation of (A).
C. (A) is correct, but (R) is wrong.
D. (A) is wrong, but (R) is correct.

85. Which one is not the approach of groupwise practice?

A. Therapeutic B. Developmental
C. Task oriented D. Ornamental

86. Spencer Hatch was associated with

A. Nilokhari Experiment
B. Firka Experiement
C. Etawah Project
D. Marthandam Project

87. Arrange the following phases of PRA in a sequential order :

I. Sharing the outcomes of PRA with stackholders
II. Situational analysis and solution designing
III. Rapport building and sensitization
IV. Preparation of micro-plans

A. II, III, I, IV B. III, II, IV, I
C. III, II, I, IV D. II, III, IV, I

88. The method of research used in census study is ________.

A. Case Study
B. Survey
C. Quasi-experimental
D. Developmental

89. A Researcher with limited understanding of the problem under study adopts ________.

A. Experimental B. Descriptive
C. Exploratory D. All of the above

90. A basic unit of analysis in a given research study is called

A. Respondent B. Sample
C. Universe D. None of the above

91. The extent of difference between population parameter and sample statistic is called ________.

A. Statistic B. Sampling bias
C. Sample error D. None of the above

92. Sub-divided bar diagram is also known as

A. Pie-diagram
B. Histogram
C. Component Bar Diagram
D. Bar Diagram

93. Match the following items given in List-I with the items given in List-II.

List-I	List-II
(i) Creative thinking	(1) Body Language
(ii) Convergent thinking	(2) Language
(iii) Synergy	(3) Novel thinking
(iv) Kinesics	(4) Responses based on reasons

Codes :

	(i)	(ii)	(iii)	(iv)
A.	(3)	(4)	(1)	(2)
B.	(4)	(3)	(1)	(2)
C.	(4)	(3)	(2)	(1)
D.	(3)	(4)	(2)	(1)

94. Match the following National institutes given in List-I with their places of functioning given in List-II.

List-I	List-II
(i) National Institute of Orthopedically Handicapped	(1) Mumbai
(ii) National Institute of Visually Handicapped	(2) Kolkata
(iii) National Institute of Nutrition	(3) Dehradun
(iv) National Institute of Hearing Handicapped	(4) Hyderabad

Codes :

	(i)	(ii)	(iii)	(iv)
A.	(2)	(3)	(1)	(4)
B.	(2)	(3)	(4)	(1)

C.	(3)	(2)	(4)	(1)
D.	(3)	(2)	(1)	(4)

95. Match the following names of the books given in List-I with the names of the authors given in List-II.

List-I	List-II
(i) An Introduction to Social Work	(1) W.A. Fried Lander
(ii) Community Organisation : Theory and Practice.	(2) Skidmod and Thakrey
(iii) Social Case Work : Problem Solving Process.	(3) M.G. Ross
(iv) Introduction to Social Welfare	(4) H.H. Perlman

Codes :

	(i)	(ii)	(iii)	(iv)
A.	(2)	(4)	(3)	(1)
B.	(2)	(3)	(4)	(1)
C.	(4)	(2)	(3)	(1)
D.	(1)	(3)	(2)	(4)

96. Match the labour legislations given in List-I with the year of enactment given in List-II.

List-I	List-II
(i) Industrial Disputes Act.	(1) 1948
(ii) Provident Fund Act.	(2) 1952
(iii) Employees State Insurance Act.	(3) 1961
(iv) Maternity Benefits Act.	(4) 1947

Codes :

	(i)	(ii)	(iii)	(iv)
A.	(4)	(2)	(1)	(3)
B.	(3)	(4)	(1)	(2)
C.	(1)	(3)	(2)	(4)
D.	(1)	(2)	(3)	(4)

97. One of the following is not an aim of social policy.

A. Balancing trade policies
B. Elimination of poverty
C. Maximization of welfare
D. Pursuit of equality

98. 'Agoraphobia' is the fear of

A. Height B. Blood
C. Crowd D. Animal

99. Scientific attitude is based on

A. Wishful thinking
B. Spiritual thinking
C. Consistent thinking
D. Devotional thinking

100. 'Concentric circle theory' is associated with

A. Peoples' participation
B. Economic status of the country
C. Hydrological system
D. Monitoring system

101. Who defined 'Statistics as the Science of estimates and probabilities'?

A. Bodington B. Bowley
C. Fisher D. Agarwal

102. Regression is

A. the measure of the average relationship between two or more variables in terms of the original units of data.
B. based on the assumption that the data being studied is normally distributed.
C. the sum of the differences of two variables.
D. deviations that are taken from an assumed mean.

103. After passing of a bill in both the houses of Parliament and after President's assent, within how many days the bill should come into force?

A. 30 B. 31
C. 60 D. None of the above

104. Determinant of population growth is

I. Family II. Marriage
III. Economy IV. Fertility

Codes :

A. I and II are correct.
B. II and III are correct.
C. III and IV are correct.
D. only IV is correct.

105. 'Sturdy beggars,' is a term used for

A. Beggars begging at religious places.
B. The able-bodied beggars

C. A class of beggars who are handicapped.
D. Beggars who beg in a particular season.

106. 'Reaching inside the silence' is a skill that refers to
A. Efforts to explore the meaning of the client's silence.
B. Efforts to explore the means to break the client's silence.
C. Efforts to deepen the client's silence.
D. Efforts to encourage client to be silent who speaks more.

107. Match the following fears with their technical names :

List-I	List-II
(a) Hydrophobia	1. Fear of heights
(b) Nictophobia	2. Fear of darkness
(c) Acrophobia	3. Fear of water
(d) Pyrophobia	4. Fear of fire

Codes :

	(a)	(b)	(c)	(d)
A.	3	2	4	1
B.	2	3	1	4
C.	2	3	4	1
D.	3	2	1	4

108. Assertion (A) : Drug abuse has been on the increase.
Reason (R) : The control of family and intergenerational communication is declining.
Codes :
A. (A) is true and (R) is not true.
B. Both (A) and (R) are not true.
C. Both (A) and (R) are true, but (R) is not the explanation of (A).
D. (A) is true and (R) is the correct explanation of (A).

109. The F-test is a
A. Parametric test
B. Non-parametric test
C. Discriminant analysis
D. Health status test

110. Match List-I with List-II and select the correct answers from the codes given below :

List-I	List-II
(I) Psycho-social theory	(1) Sigmund Freud
(II) Psychoanalytical theory	(2) Skinner
(III) Learning theory	(3) Hamilton
(IV) Behaviour Modification Theory	(4) Thorndike

Codes :

	(I)	(II)	(III)	(IV)
A.	(3)	(1)	(4)	(2)
B.	(2)	(3)	(4)	(1)
C.	(2)	(1)	(3)	(4)
D.	(1)	(2)	(4)	(3)

111. Match List-I with List-II and select the correct answers from the codes given below :

List-I	List-II
(I) Hallucination	(1) False perception
(II) Bipolar Disorder	(2) Mood disorder
(III) Dementia	(3) Anorexia nervosa
(IV) Eating Disorder	(4) Organic psychosis

Codes :

	(I)	(II)	(III)	(IV)
A.	(1)	(3)	(2)	(4)
B.	(1)	(2)	(4)	(3)
C.	(1)	(4)	(2)	(3)
D.	(1)	(4)	(3)	(2)

112. Which one of the following pairs is correctly matched?
A. Supervision and Education in charity – Jeffrey. R. Brackett
B. Supervision in social case work – Bertha Renolds
C. Learning and Teaching in the Practice of Social Work – Virgina Robinson
D. The Learner in Education for the Professions – H.H. Perlman

113. Match List-I with List-II and select the correct answer from the codes given below :

List-I	List-II
(a) Unitary approach	(i) Gandhiji

(b) Trusteeship approach — (ii) John R. Commons
(c) Systems approach — (iii) Dunlop
(d) Pluralist approach — (iv) Edward

Codes :

	(a)	(b)	(c)	(d)
A.	(iii)	(i)	(ii)	(iv)
B.	(ii)	(iii)	(iv)	(i)
C.	(iii)	(ii)	(iv)	(i)
D.	(iv)	(i)	(iii)	(ii)

114. Match the Acts given in List-I with their year of passing given in List-II :

List-I (Title of the Act)	**List-II (Year of Enactment)**
(I) The Equal Remuneration Act	(1) 1923
(II) The Employee's Compensation Act	(2) 1972
(III) The Employees State Insurance Act	(3) 1948
(IV) The Payment of Gratuity Act	(4) 1976

Codes :

	(I)	(II)	(III)	(IV)
A.	(4)	(2)	(1)	(3)
B.	(2)	(4)	(3)	(1)
C.	(3)	(2)	(4)	(1)
D.	(4)	(1)	(3)	(2)

115. Match the pairs:

(a) Mary Richmond — (i) Crisis intervention
(b) Lydia Rappaport — (ii) Social diagnosis
(c) H.H. Perlman — (iii) Group work with children in institution
(d) Giesla Konopha — (iv) Social casework : a problem-solving process

Codes :

	(a)	(b)	(c)	(d)
A.	(ii)	(iv)	(i)	(iii)
B.	(ii)	(i)	(iv)	(iii)
C.	(iv)	(iii)	(ii)	(i)
D.	(iii)	(ii)	(iv)	(i)

116. Match the pairs :

(a) Family — (i) Secondary group
(b) Managing Committee — (ii) Primary group
(c) Crowd — (iii) Clique
(d) Triad — (iv) Un-organised entity

Codes :

	(a)	(b)	(c)	(d)
A.	(ii)	(i)	(iii)	(iv)
B.	(i)	(ii)	(iii)	(iv)
C.	(ii)	(i)	(iv)	(iii)
D.	(iii)	(i)	(ii)	(iv)

117. Match the pairs :

(a) Bardoli Satyagraha — (i) B.G. Tilak
(b) Kesari & Mahratta — (ii) Vallabh Bhai Patel
(c) Women's Education — (iii) Lord Bentinck
(d) Abolition of Sati — (iv) Ishwar Chandra Vidyasagar

Codes :

	(a)	(b)	(c)	(d)
A.	(ii)	(i)	(iv)	(iii)
B.	(iv)	(iii)	(i)	(ii)
C.	(i)	(iv)	(ii)	(iii)
D.	(ii)	(iii)	(i)	(iv)

118. Match the pairs :

(a) Specific objectives — (i) Casework
(b) Confrontation — (ii) Community organisation
(c) External agent — (iii) Group work
(d) Delinquency — (iv) Deviance

Codes :

	(a)	(b)	(c)	(d)
A.	(iii)	(ii)	(iv)	(i)
B.	(ii)	(i)	(iii)	(iv)
C.	(iv)	(ii)	(i)	(iii)
D.	(iii)	(iv)	(ii)	(i)

119. Match the pairs :

(a) National Emergency — (i) 1979
(b) International Year of the Child — (ii) 1975
(c) Special Marriage Act — (iii) 1950
(d) Constitution of India — (iv) 1956

Codes :

	(a)	(b)	(c)	(d)
A.	(iii)	(ii)	(iv)	(i)
B.	(iv)	(i)	(ii)	(iii)
C.	(ii)	(i)	(iv)	(iii)
D.	(i)	(iii)	(ii)	(iv)

120. Match the Movements from List I with their Associates of List II and select correct answer using the codes given below the lists :

List-I	List-II
(a) YMCA Movement	(1) Mariezakrezewska
(b) YWCA Movement	(2) Jane Addams
(c) Settlement Movement	(3) Mrs. Kinnird and Miss Roberts
(d) Playground and Recreation Movement	(4) George William

Choose the correct answer from the following codes :

	(a)	(b)	(c)	(d)
A.	(4)	(3)	(2)	(1)
B.	(1)	(2)	(3)	(4)
C.	(4)	(2)	(3)	(1)
D.	(2)	(4)	(1)	(3)

121. The following are included in basic skills of Social Group Work :
(a) Skill in purposeful Relationship
(b) Skill in programme Development
(c) Skill in Communication
(d) Skill in Leadership

Choose the correct answer from the following code :
A. (a), (c) and (d) B. (b), (c) and (d)
C. (a) and (b) D. (a), (b), (c) and (d)

122. The objectives of Social Group Work method includes :
(a) Individualization
(b) Development of sense of belonging
(c) Development of the capacity to participate
(d) None of the above

Choose the correct answer from the following codes :
A. (a) and (b)
B. (b) and (c)
C. (a), (b), (c) and (d)
D. (a), (b) and (c)

123. The scheduled area and scheduled tribes commission was appointed in :
A. 1961 B. 1959
C. 1950 D. 1952

124. The social expectation regarding age—appropriate behaviour are called :
A. Developmental tasks
B. Developmental Indicators
C. Practice
D. Values

125. The institutional re-distributive model is linked with :
A. Totalitarian State
B. Welfare State
C. Capitalistic State
D. Communist State

126. The predominant route of transmission of HIV + in India is :
A. Intravenous drug use
B. Blood transfusion
C. Heterosexual contact
D. Homosexual contact

127. The first legislation concerning social security in India was concerned with :
A. Compensation to workmen
B. Provident fund to employees
C. Maternity benefit
D. Insurance linked to deposit

128. Panchayat Raj system was given constitutional status by :
A. 63rd Constitutional Amendment
B. 73rd Constitutional Amendment
C. 83rd Constitutional Amendment
D. None of the above

129. Municipality system was given constitutional status by :
A. 73rd Constitutional Amendment
B. 83rd Constitutional Amendment
C. 74rd Constitutional Amendment
D. 93rd Constitutional Amendment

130. What is the percentage of seats reserved for women in Panchayati Raj System at different level?
A. 30 per cent B. 33 per cent
C. 40 per cent D. 50 per cent

131. Which of the following is NOT a part of the "Panchayati Raj" Institutions?
A. Village Panchayat
B. Nyay Panchayat
C. Kshetra Vikas Samiti
D. Zila Panchayat

132. Which state was the first to make law relating to Panchayati Raj in the post-independence period?
A. Maharashtra B. Gujarat
C. Uttar Pradesh D. Madhya Pradesh

133. Urban Community Development Services Project in India was started by :
A. American Friends Service Committee
B. Govt. of India
C. UNICEF
D. FORD Foundation

134. Which one of the following was the earliest project of community development in India?
A. Sevagram project
B. Sriniketan project
C. Gurgaon project
D. Itawah project

135. Panchayati Raj Institution in India have brought about one of the following :
A. Eradication of untouchability.
B. Spread of land ownership to the Depressed Classes.
C. A formal representation of the weaker sections in village governance.
D. Spread of education to the masses.

136. Socialisation means :
A. Developing friendship with unknown persons
B. Ensuring equity in the society
C. The process of internalisation of social norms
D. The establishment of rapport with clients

137. Systematic Theory of Population is given by:
A. Robert Malthus
B. W.S. Thompson
C. C.P. Blacker
D. Frank Notestein

138. Which of the following are the main causes of social change in India?
(1) Independence
(2) Industrialisation
(3) Education
(4) Sanskritisation

Choose the correct answer from the following:
A. 1, 2 and 3
B. 2, 3 and 4
C. 1, 3 and 4
D. 1, 2 and 4

139. The practice of untouchability is abolished by the Indian Constitution in Article :
A. 17 B. 19
C. 38 D. 42

140. Who initiated the Etawah Pilot Project in the year 1948?
A. Spencer Hatch
B. S.K. Dey
C. Albert Mayor
D. Vinoba Bhave

141. Doraught Prone Area Program was initiated in the year
A. 1970 B. 1966
C. 1973 D. 1984

142. The main objective of TRYSEM Scheme was:
A. Women Self Help
B. Youth Self Employment
C. Child Development
D. Rural Reconstruction

143. Which among these is the Pioneer State to bring democratic decentralisation?
A. Gujarat
B. West Bengal
C. Maharashtra
D. Rajasthan

ANSWERS

1	2	3	4	5	6	7	8	9	10
B	A		A	B	B	B	D	B	B
11	**12**	**13**	**14**	**15**	**16**	**17**	**18**	**19**	**20**
B	A	B	A	D	B	A	D	C	C
21	**22**	**23**	**24**	**25**	**26**	**27**	**28**	**29**	**30**
C		B	C	B	B	A	C	D	C
31	**32**	**33**	**34**	**35**	**36**	**37**	**38**	**39**	**40**
D	A	D	A	D	A	B	D	A	D
41	**42**	**43**	**44**	**45**	**46**	**47**	**48**	**49**	**50**
A	D	D	A	A	A	A	A	B	A
51	**52**	**53**	**54**	**55**	**56**	**57**	**58**	**59**	**60**
A	A	C	D	B	B	D	C	C	A
61	**62**	**63**	**64**	**65**	**66**	**67**	**68**	**69**	**70**
D	A	D	B	B	D	D	D	A	D
71	**72**	**73**	**74**	**75**	**76**	**77**	**78**	**79**	**80**
A	A	C	B	C	D	B	D	A	B
81	**82**	**83**	**84**	**85**	**86**	**87**	**88**	**89**	**90**
C	B	A	B	D	D	B	B	C	A
91	**92**	**93**	**94**	**95**	**96**	**97**	**98**	**99**	**100**
C	C	D	B	B	A	A	C	C	A
101	**102**	**103**	**104**	**105**	**106**	**107**	**108**	**109**	**110**
A	A	A	D	B	A	D	D	A	A
111	**112**	**113**	**114**	**115**	**116**	**117**	**118**	**119**	**120**
B	C	D	D	B	C	A	B	C	A
121	**122**	**123**	**124**	**125**	**126**	**127**	**128**	**129**	**130**
		A	A	B	C	A	B	C	D
131	**132**	**133**	**134**	**135**	**136**	**137**	**138**	**139**	**140**
B	B	A	B	C	C	A	A	A	B
141	**142**	**143**							
A	B	D							

➤➤➤➤➤

CHAPTER

4

Family and Child Welfare

INTRODUCTION

Women constitute about one-half of the global population. They also constitute the largest group amongst the most marginalised sections of society. Women have lower status in all spheres of life whether social, economic, political or educational. The scenario is more pathetic in the developing countries like ours. Women equality is an issue of primary importance to the Welfare and progress of our nation. Therefore, we need an atmosphere which is free, fair and offers equal opportunities for all sections of the society encluding women.

STATUS OF WOMEN: GLOBAL AND LOCAL SCENARIO

Women as Workers

- Women do more than 67% of the hours of work done in the world, earn only 10% of the world's income and own only 1% of the world's property. The value of unremunerated work was estimated at about $16 billion, from which $11 billion represents the invisible contribution of women
- Women are paid 30-40% less than men for comparable work on an average
- 60-80% of the food in most developing countries is produced by women
- Women hold between 10-20% managerial and administrative jobs
- Women make up less than 5% of the world's heads of state
- 70% of the 1.2 billion people living in poverty are female.

Women as Workers in India

- Female share of non-agricultural wage employment is only 17%
- Participation of women in the workforce is only 13.9% in the urban sector and 29.9% in the rural sector
- Women's wage rates are, on an average only 75% of men's wage rates and constitute only 25% of the family income. In no Indian State do women and men earn equal wages in agriculture
- Women occupy only 9% of parliamentary seats less than 4% seats in High Courts and Supreme Court. Less than 3% administrators and managers are women.

Women and Education

- 60% of the 130 million children in the age group of 6-11 years who do not go to school, are girls
- Approximately 67% of the world's 875 million illiterate adults are women
- 3 out of 5 women in Southern Asia and an estimated 50% of all women in Africa and in the Arab region are still illiterate

- The reality of women's lives remains invisible to men and women alike and this invisibility persists at all levels beginning with the family to the nation. Although geographically men and women share the same space, they live in different worlds.

Women and Education in India

- Literacy rate of India in 2011 is 74.04%. The Male literacy rate is 82.14% and Female literacy rate is 65.46% according to Census 2011.
- Close to 245 million Indian women lack the basic capability to read and write
- Adult literacy rates for ages 15 and above for the year 2000 were female 46.4% male rate of 69%.

Women and Health

- Women account for 50% of all people living with HIV/AIDS globally
- In the year 2000, there were 80 million unwanted pregnancies, 20 million unsafe abortions, 5 lakhs maternal deaths
- 99% of these cases were reported in developing countries.

Child Sex Ratio (0-6 years)

- The child sex ratio has dropped from 945 females per 1000 males in 1991 to 927 females per 1000 males in 2001
- The United Nations Children's Fund, estimated that up to 50 million girls and women are 'missing' from India's population because of termination of the female fetus or high mortality of the girl child due to lack of proper care.

Women and Health in India

- The average nutritional intake of women is 1400 calories daily. The necessary requirement is approximately 2200 calories
- 38% of all HIV positive people in India are women yet only 25% of beds in AIDS care centers in India are occupied by them. 92% of women in India suffer from gynecological problems
- 300 women die every day due to childbirth and pregnancy related causes
- The maternal mortality ratio per 100,000 live births in the year 1995 was 440.

Crimes Against Women In India

Although efforts have been taken to improve the status of women, the constitutional dream of gender equality is miles away from becoming a reality. Even today, 'the mainstream remains very much a malestream'. The dominant tendency has always been to confine women and women's issues in the private domain. The traditional systems of control with its notion of 'what is right and proper for women' still reigns supreme and reinforces the use of violence as a means to punish its defiant female 'offenders' and their supporters. Hence it is of no surprise when the National Crime Records Bureau (NCRB) predicted that the growth rate of crimes against women would be higher than the population growth rate by 2010. The reported cases of crime against women were 2,49,270 cases in the country in the year 2012 according to the national crime record bureau.

Every 3.5 minutes, 1 crime was committed against women in India in 2002

Nearly one-third said the perpetrator had been a father, grandfather or male friend of the family.

Sexual Harassment

24,923 incidents of sexual harassment were reported in the year 2012, 121 women were sexually harassed every day, 1 woman was sexually harassed every 12 minutes, An increase of 20.6% was seen in incidents of sexual harassment between 1997-2002, Importation of girls/Trafficking, 11,332 women and girls were trafficked, 31 women and girls were trafficked every day, 1 woman or girl was trafficked every 46 minutes.

Kidnapping and abduction

38,262 women and minor girls were kidnapped or abducted in the year 2012, 40 women and minor girls were kidnapped every day, 1 woman or minor girl was abducted every 36 minutes.

Dowry Related Murders: 8,233 women were murdered due to dowry in the year 2012, 21 women were murdered every day, 1 woman was murdered due to dowry every 66 minutes.

Domestic Violence: 106,527 women faced domestic violence in their marital homes in the year 2012, 135 women were tortured by their husbands and in-laws every day, 1 woman faced torture in her marital relationship every 11 minutes; domestic violence constitutes 33.3% of the total crimes against women.

Domestic Violence: Over 40% of married Indian women face physical abuse by their husband, 1 in every 2 women faces domestic violence in any of its forms physical, sexual, psychological and/or economic.

SOCIAL AND DEMOGRAPHIC CONDITION OF ELDERLY IN INDIA

The elderly population (aged 60 years or above) account for 7.4% of total population in 2001. For males it was marginally lower at 7.1%, while for females it was 7.8%.

Among states the proportion vary from around 4% in small states like Dadra & Nagar Haveli, Nagaland Arunachal Pradesh, Meghalaya to more than 10.5% in Kerala.

- Both the share and size of elderly population is increasing overtime. From 5.6% in 1961 it is projected to rise to 12.4% of population by the year 2026.
- The sex ratio among elderly people was as high as 1028 in 1951 but subsequently dropped to about 938 in 1971 and finally reached 972 in 2001.
- The life expectancy at birth during 2002-06 was 64.2 for females as against 62.6 years for males. At age 60 average remaining length of life was found to be about 18 years (16.7 for males, 18.9 for females) and that at age 70 was less than 12 years (10.9 for males and 12.4 for females).
- There is sharp rise in age-specific death rate with age from 20 (per thousand) for persons in age group 60-64 years to 80 among those aged 75- 79 years and 200 for persons aged more than 85 years.
- The old-age dependency ratio climbed from 10.9% in 1961 to 13.1% in 2001 for India as a whole. For females and males the value of the ratio was 13.8% and 12.5% in 2001.
- About 65 per cent of the aged had to depend on others for their day-to-day maintenance. Less than 20% of elderly women but majorities of elderly men were economically independent.
- Among economically dependent elderly men 6-7% was financially supported by their spouses, almost 85% by their own children, 2% by grand children and 6% by others. Of elderly women, less than 20% depended on their spouses, more than 70% on their children, 3% on grand children and 6% or more on others including the non-relations.
- Among the rural elderly persons almost 50% had a monthly per capita expenditure level between Rs. 420 to Rs. 775 and among the urban elderly persons; almost half of aged had monthly per capita expenditure between Rs. 665 and 1500 in 2002.
- Nearly 40% of persons aged 60 years and above (60% of men and 19% of women) were working. In rural areas 66% of elderly men and above 23% of aged women were still participating in economic activity, while in urban areas only 39% of elderly men and about 7% of elderly women were economically active.
- Even in 2007-08 only 50% men and 20% of women aged 60 years or more were literate through formal schooling.
- In rural areas 55% of the aged with sickness and 77% of those without sickness felt that they were in a good or fair condition of health. In urban areas the respective proportions were 63% and 78%.

- The proportion of elderly men and women physically mobile decline from about 94% in the age-group 60–64 years to about 72% for men and 63 to 65% for women of age 80 or more.
- Prevalence of heart diseases among elderly population was much higher in urban areas than in rural parts.
- About 64 per thousand elderly persons in rural areas and 55 per thousand in urban areas suffer from one or more disabilities. Most common disability among the aged persons was loco motor disability as 3% of them suffer from it.
- In age-groups beyond 60 years, the percentage of elderly women married was markedly lower than the percentage of men married.
- More than 75% of elderly males and less than 40% of elderly females live with their spouse. Less than 20% of aged men and about half of the women live with their children.

SOCIAL AND DEMOGRAPHIC CONDITION OF YOUTH IN INDIA

Our country is said to be the youth Nation in the world as the size of the youth population (15 to 24 age group) has increased three fold during last four decades of the 20th century. It increased from 73.22 million in 1961 to 195.07 million in 2001. The projected estimations (RGI) indicate a further increase in the size of the youth population to 222.1 million in 2006 and to 239.77 million in 2011. The share of youth population in the total population in India increased from 16.7 per cent in 1961 to 20 per cent in 2001 and the projections show that it would further increase to 20.1 per cent by 2011. Both the size and share of youth population is increasing in India and it is a clear indication of bulging youth population in the country. The population of India as of March 2011 was 1.2 billion, 17.5 per cent of the global population. From 2001 to 2011, its population increased by 181 million. About 60 per cent of the population resides in rural areas.

As China and Japan and many other nations face an aging demographic profile, the youth segment of India's population is growing rapidly, and is projected to continue to do so for the next 30 years. Provided India can act quickly on health, education and employment, this demographic dividend has the potential to inject new dynamism into its flagging economy. Failure to do so, however, will result in demographic disaster.

Today, more than half of India's population is under the age of 25, with 65 per cent of the population under 35. By 2020, India's average age will be just 29 years, in comparison with 37 in China and the United States, 45 in Western Europe and 48 in Japan. This demographic trend will confer a significant competitive advantage upon India. About a quarter of the global increase in the working age population (ages 15-64) between 2010 and 2040 is projected to occur in India, during which time this segment is set to rise by 5 per cent to 69 per cent of its total population. Roughly a million people are expected to enter the labour market every month, peaking at 653 million people in 2031. As a result the IMF projects that India's demographic dividend has the potential to produce an additional 2 per cent per capita GDP growth each year for the next twenty years.

The key to transforming the demographic dividend into economic growth lies not just in having more people, but having greater numbers of better trained, healthier and more productive people. The relationship here is mutually reinforcing; India must harness the advantage of its youth to fulfil its economic potential, and in turn must generate growth in order to continue to support its growing population.

At the most basic level, India must focus on improving the overall health and well-being of its children in order to make the most of their immense potential. The Asian Development Bank estimated that 32.7 per cent of India's population lives below the poverty line of $1.25 a day (PPP), and India is home to one-third of the world's poor. At 44 deaths per 1,000 live births, India's mortality rate is high. The World Bank notes a direct link between undernourishment and impaired cognitive development, so should India fail to ensure the health and well-being of its children, its future productivity and development will be severely curtailed. With a Human Development Indicators ranking of 134 out of 187 countries, India has a long way to go, and must swiftly invest in developing the potential of its enormous human capital.

Perhaps the most crucial task India faces is equipping its burgeoning youth with education and skills training. According to India's 2011 Census, India's literacy rate sits around 74%, with significant variation according to state and gender. In this regard, India's 2009 Right of Children to Free and Compulsory Education Act is a big step towards guaranteeing a basic education for every child. Since its launch in 2010 India has witnessed some positive results, with 94 per cent of children between the ages of 6 and 14 enrolled in school, and steady improvements in terms of facilities such as toilets and drinking water.

Nevertheless, concerns regarding the implementation of the Act persist, with teacher absenteeism and large class sizes in many government schools fuelling the popularity of private institutions. Basic educational indicators across the country have actually deteriorated since the implementation of the Act in 2001, with the proportion of children in Standard V reading at a Standard II level and unable to complete basic arithmetic rising.

FAMILY IN INDIA

A perusal of varied literature on Indian society and culture, particularly generated by ethnographers, historians, Christian missionaries and subsequently by anthropologists and sociologists, suggests that the twentieth century recorded certain changes of far reaching importance in the family system under the influence of westernization, industrialization, modernization and greater population mobility across the sub-continent.

Ever since then the Indian family has progressively confronted and combated various kinds of problems and challenges, and yet India does not have any family policy per se so far; albeit the Government of India has indeed taken several useful legislative measures relating to widow remarriage, women's right to property, practice of child marriage, succession, adoption and maintenance, dowry, dissolution of marriage affecting different communities and most recently domestic violence, which have impacted the Indian family system in more ways than one. It is, however, recognized that the formulation of a single national policy given the large size and heterogeneity of a society like that of India is really a difficult task. Barriers to the creation of a comprehensive national policy in India are intricate parts of Indian ethos and ideology. This is perhaps the important reason why India has not so far succeeded in evolving a common civil code despite public demand for it through various social and political fora in the recent past. Muslims, who comprise 12.4 per cent of India's population, are opposed to the idea of a uniform civil code in the country. Anyway, in order to do that one must have a reasonably good understanding of problems that the Indian society has been facing. Here we would like to throw some light on the major problems that confront the Indian society in general and a family in particular. It is really imperative that one should understand the hurdles in promoting social protection and intergenerational solidarity for the well being of family as a social sub-system. At the outset let me move a word of caution — it is hazardous to offer a generalized view of the nature and problems of the Indian family system which have persisted over the years, as the subject is quite complicated for the reason that the Indian society is very vast and is characterized by bewildering complexity.

According to the 2001 census, India consists of 192.7 million households spread over 0.59 million villages and about 5,000 towns.

The Indian society exhibits considerable variations between regions, between rural and urban areas, between classes and finally, between different religious, ethnic and caste groups.

The Indian society is, in fact, a congeries of micro-regions and sub-cultures and differences between which are quite crucial from sociological angles.

Furthermore, the differences are also discernible with respect to the level of female literacy, sex ratio, age at marriage of girls, incidence of dissolution of marriage, household size, female workforce participation rate, marital practices, gender relations and authority structure within the family. Diversities inherent in Indian society are also reflected in the plurality of family types.

It would be noticed from the subsequent discussion that the magnitude of changes that the Indian family has experienced over a period of a century appears to be far greater than the expectations of Indian sociologists and anthropologists.

The virtual disappearance of traditional joint family from the urban scene, increase in the life expectancy of women from 23 years in 1901-10 to 65 years (it is higher than that of men by three years) in 2009,

Rise in the proportion of female headed households, decrease in the average age of household heads,

Increase in the incidence of separation and divorce, greater tension and conflicts between wife and husband, parents and sons and between brothers,

Increased freedom of marital choice, passing of child marriages,

Shrinking of kinship ties, continuous consultations between sons and parents on familial matters,

Greater involvement of females in decision making process,

Increase in the mean age at marriage of female from 13 years in 1901 to 18.3 years in 2001,

Rise in the level of female education,

Decline in total fertility rate from 4.9 in 1971 to 2.76 in 2009 are concrete and clinching evidence to suggest a whole range of changes in the family system— its structure, functions, core values and regulative norms (Singh, 2004: 129-166).

In course of these changes many new problems have surfaced, while some of the old ones, such as dowry, divorce, lack of intergenerational solidarity, discord between siblings and gender violence have got further intensified.

The passing of joint family system since time immemorial the joint family has been one of the salient features of the Indian society.

But the twentieth century brought enormous changes in the family system.

Changes in the traditional family system have been so enormous that it is steadily on the wane from the urban scene. There is absolutely no chance of reversal of this trend.

In villages the size of joint family has been substantially reduced or is found in its fragmented form.

Some have split into several nuclear families, while others have taken the form of extended or stem families.

Extended family is in fact a transitory phase between joint and nuclear family system.

The available data suggest that the joint family is on its way out in rural areas too (Singh, 2004: 134-140).

The joint family or extended family in rural areas is surviving in its skeleton or nominal form as a kinship group.

The adults have migrated to cities either to pursue higher education or to secure more lucrative jobs or to eke out their living outside their traditional callings, ensuing from the availability of better opportunities elsewhere as well as the rising pressure of population on the limited land base.

Many of the urban households are really offshoots of rural extended or joint families. A joint family in the native village is the fountainhead of nuclear families in towns. These days in most cases two brothers tend to form two independent households even within the same city owing to the rising spirit of individualism, regardless of similarity inoccupation, even when the ancestral property is not formally partitioned at their native place.

The nuclear family, same as elsewhere, is now the characteristic feature of the Indian society. According to the census of India data, of all the households nuclear family constituted 70 per cent and single member or more than one member households without spouse (or eroded families) comprised about 11 per cent.

The extended and joint family or households together claim merely 20 per cent of all households.

This is the overall picture about the entire country, whereas in the case of urban areas the proportion of nuclear family is somewhat higher still.

The available data from the National Family and Health Survey-1 of 1992-93 (henceforth NFHS) suggest that joint family does not make up more than five per cent of all families in urban areas (Singh, 2004:137).

An extended family, which includes a couple with married sons or daughters and their spouses as well as household head without spouse but with at least two married sons, daughters and their spouses, constitute a little less than one fifth of the total households.

With further industrial development, rural to urban migration, nuclearization of families and rise of divorce rate and the proportion of single member household is likely to increase steadily on the line of industrial West.

This is believed to be so because the states, which have got a higher level of urbanization, tend to have a higher proportion of single member households.

Similarly, about a couple of decades ago almost 20 per cent households contained only one person in the USA (Skolnick and Skolnick 1980: 2).

More or less, a similar situation exists in other developed countries as well, and above all, not a single country has recorded decline in the proportion of single member household during the last three decades. In fact, the tendency is more towards increase in the proportion of single member households. As the process of family formation and dissolution has become relatively faster now than before, households are progressively more headed by relatively younger people.

Census data from 1971 onward have clearly borne out that at the national level over three-fifths of the households are headed by persons aged less than 50 (Singh 1984: 86-95).

There is every reason to believe that proportion of households headed by younger persons is likely to constitute a larger proportion than this in urban areas where the proportion of extended family, not to speak of joint family, is much smaller than that of rural areas.

The emergence of financially independent, career-oriented men and women, who are confident of taking their own decisions and crave to have a sense of individual achievement, has greatly contributed to the disintegration of joint family.

Disintegration of joint family has led to closer bonds between spouses, but the reverse is also true in certain cases. For many, nuclear family is a safer matrimonial home to a woman. In bygone days people generally lived in joint families, yet familial discord never escalated into extreme physical violence or death, as we so often come across such instances in our day-to-day life and also know through national dailies, both electronic and print media. Changes in authority structure, once the authority within the family was primarily in the hands of family elders commonly known as Kartain Hindi.

The general attitude of members of the family towards the traditional patriarch was mostly one of respect. Loyalty, submissiveness, respect and deference over the household were best owed on him. These attributes also encompassed other relationships in the family, such as children to their parents, a wife to her husband, and younger brothers to their older brothers (Gupta, 1978: 72).

Within a household no one was supposed to flout the will of his elders. The father, or in his absence the eldest brother, was consulted on all important family matters like pursuing litigation in courts of law, building a house, buying and selling of property and arranging marriages, etc. The joint family did not allow the neglect or disregard of elders. The age-grade hierarchy was quite strong. Now the people of younger generation, particularly those with modern tertiary education, do not seem to show the same reverence which their fathers had for their parents or elders.

Among women, patriarch's wife was the paramount authority. In fact, women's position depended on the position of their husbands in the household. The wife of the household head or mother-in-law was incharge of the household. Her word was law or at least had the same force. Her decisions were made for the entire family and not for the welfare of the individuals in it. Young women in the family were expected to be dutiful and obedient. Self-assertion, even in bringing up their own children, was blasphemy. Widows and those spurned by their husbands were assured of the family roof, though mostly as voiceless members.

With a view to absolving themselves of responsibility now parents cleverly encourage their educated sons and daughters-in-law to take independent decision in a joint and extended family situation, leave aside urban areas, the similar situation has started to emerge in rural areas too. This is not unusual when sons and daughters tend to possess a higher level of education and a greater degree of exposure of the world outside the family than ever before. Now boys and girls, contrary to the old practice, are beginning to assert their wishes in mate selection.

A new law banning child marriage was passed in December, 2006. The law provides certain positive initiatives for the intervention of courts to prevent child marriages through stay orders. In India, the National Family Health Survey-2 found that 65 per cent of girls are married by the time they are eighteen. Child marriages are solemnized during times of festivals such as Akshaya Tritiya, Akha Teej, Ram Navami, Basant Panchami and Karma Jayanti.

According to UNICEF's 'State of the World's Children-2009' report, 47 per cent of India's women aged 20-24 were married before the legal age of 18, with 56 per cent in rural areas.

Child marriages have been prevalent in many cultures throughout human history, but have gradually diminished since some countries started to urbanize and experience changes in the ways of life for the people of these countries. An increase in the advocacy of human rights, whether as women's rights or as children's rights, has caused the traditions of child marriage to decrease greatly as it was considered unfair and dangerous for the children. Today, child marriage is usually practiced in countries where cultural practices and traditions of child marriage still have a strong influence. Although child marriages have been outlawed a long time ago, South Asia has currently the highest prevalence of child marriage of any region in the world (UNICEF,2009: 34).

In the face of rising dowry practices across the country consanguineous marriages have appreciably declined in South India in recent years. However, such marriages have remained tabooed among the vast majority of Hindus of North India. The Hindu Marriage and Divorce Act 1955 prohibits marriage among close relatives— called sapinda marriage. The sapinda relationship extends as far as the third generation in the line of mother and the fifth in the line of father. In North India not only Muslims, certain scheduled castes and scheduled tribes also tend to practise consanguineous marriages.

PROBLEMS OF CHILDREN

Children (persons aged 0-14) constitute a little over 30 per cent of the total population of the country according to the 2001 Census of India. Evidence suggests that they are quite vulnerable and their exposure to violations of their protection rights remains widespread and multiple in nature. The manifestations of these violations are very varied, ranging from child labour and child trafficking to commercial sexual exploitation and many other forms of violence and abuse. With an estimated 12.6 million children engaged in hazardous occupations (2001 Census), for instance, India has the largest number of child labourers under the age of 14 in the world. Although poverty is often cited as the cause underlying child labour, other factors such as discrimination, social exclusion, as well as the lack of quality education or existing parents' attitudes and perceptions about child labour and the role and value of education need also to be considered. While systematic data and information on child protection issues are still not always available, evidence suggests that children in need of special protection belong to communities suffering disadvantages and social exclusion such as scheduled castes and scheduled tribes, and the poor. It has been estimated that 46 per cent children from scheduled tribes and 38 per cent from scheduled castes are out of school. The lack of available services as well as the gaps persisting in law enforcement and in rehabilitation schemes also constitute a major cause of concern. The children of poor families, especially those of artists, craftsmen, and other professions are trained by their parents and elders of the family in their vocations such as weaving, tanning, sweeping dyeing, hairdressing, painting, carpentry and agriculture. A vast number of children grow up lending a helping hand to elders in their home-industries. The practice or intergenerational transfer of traditional callings more or less is still continuing. Such kids who lack formal schooling, but working and specializing in some craft or their traditional callings help them build a career.

Indeed, the poverty in India forces many parents to send their children to earn extra money. The employers who hire such children pay them paltry wages. One can see boys of poor families act as vegetable vendors throughout India. Children of construction workers help in bringing water, cleaning vessels or collecting twigs for fuel. Their parents are compelled to come to cities when monsoon fails and they cannot cultivate their lands. Children are also subjected to gender based discrimination. Discrimination against women in fact starts the day she is born. Sometimes it also starts when she is in her mother's womb as a foetus. The practice of female foeticide, despite being illegal, is vigorously practised in urban India. The girl child's right to survival, health care and nutrition, education, social opportunities and protection has to be recognized and made a social and economic priority. Along with this the basic structural inequalities that cause poverty, malnutrition and the low status of women have to be addressed, if these rights are to be ensured. Within family parents are first to practise gender based discrimination and it is the first school of learning where girls are inculcated the values of their being inferior to their brothers. Although India loves their children, still thousands of children roam the streets of major cities around the country and receive neither education, proper food, clothing, or a bed to sleep in at night. Why are these children roaming and begging in the streets? What should be done and who is willing to do something to help these poor children? A mind and heart that cares, awareness presentations through multi-media, contributions, talking and sharing information among friends, education, self-help initiatives and good old fashion kindness are all that is needed to get these kids off the streets. Basically they need five things for their living: food, clothing, shelter, medical assistance and education. Contrary to the above, there are children who belong to the well-off sections of society, but they are also not free from problems. They are facing a different kind of problem either due to lack of adequate care or attention from their working parents or due to heavy expectation from them by their parents in a fiercely competitive modern world full of uncertainties in life. In cases of working mothers, children are placed in an entirely different situation. The demands of city life are such that both wife and husband tend to remain outside their home for work even at the cost of interests of their children. Working couples are unable to give proper care and affection to their children. Obviously, latchkey children of working couples are strangers to the sense of security enjoyed by their own parents. The system of surrogate mothers or the Montessori and Kindergarten systems of schooling has proved to be a very poor substitute for family as an agent of socialization. With the diminished role of family as an agent of socialization juvenile delinquency is on the increase. In the past children enjoyed security of a kind unknown today. Growing up under the joint care of adults made them feel responsible for all the extended members of the family, besides their own parents. Now children are at greater strain than ever before because in general parents intend to accomplish those things in their life through their children what they themselves could not be able to achieve, no matter how difficult they are. Children are put under great stress and stain to score high marks at schools to be able to meet the ever-increasing challenges of fiercely competitive world of education and employment. In addition to helping their children achieve higher goals of life, women, sometimes both the parents, have to work harder with a view to attaining economic independence and maintaining a higher standard of living of their family. As stated above, there has been appreciable decline in fertility over the years. This has not been possible without recording drastic changes in the attitude of people towards the size of family and the value system of patriarchy and patriliny. Based on studies on fertility behaviour and contraceptive practices one can conclusively contend that perhaps no element of the Indian social system has experienced greater changes than the system of family during the post-independent period. This is clearly borne out by various empirical investigations. Despite considerable decline in fertility or lesser burden of children on the family, there is no improvement in the quality of care of children especially in rural areas. There hardly exists any pre-school or community centre in villages. There also does not exist even a basic facility of play ground for children. The older children have to mind the younger children at home and sometimes they are also expected to lend helping hands to their parents in the household chores as and when required. The poor children learn the expected roles of life of their own with the passage of time, while the well-off peasantries send their children to private schools (also called public schools in the Western world) in towns and cities for better schooling.

CHILD LABOUR IN INDIA

The problem of child labour is quite conspicuous to the naked eyes in India. Its prevalence is clearly evident in the form of high workforce participation rate among children, which is higher than that of any other developing country. Poverty is the prime reason behind child labour in India. Unfortunately enough, whatever the meagre income they are able to generate is absorbed by their families. Child labour is extensive with children under the age of fourteen working in carpet making factories, glass blowing units and making fireworks with bare little hands. There are at least 44 million child labourers in the age group of 5-14. More than 80 per cent of them in India are employed in the agricultural and non-formal sectors and many are bonded labourers, too. Most of them are either illiterate or dropped out of school after two or three years (Saini, 1994: 2; ILO, 1996: 7). The exploitation of little children for labour is an accepted practice and perceived by many as a necessity to alleviate poverty. Carpet weaving industries pay very low wages to child labourers and make them work for longer hours in unhygienic conditions.

Children working in such units are mainly migrant workers, who are shunted here by their families to earn some money and send it back to them. Their families dependence on their income forces them to endure the onerous work conditions in the carpet factories. The situation of child labourers in India is desperate. Children work for eight hours at a stretch with only a small break for meals. The meals are also frugal and the children are ill nourished. Most of the migrant children who cannot go home, sleep at their work place, which is very bad for their health and development. About 70 per cent of India's population still resides in rural areas and are very poor. Children in rural families who are ailing with poverty perceive their children as an income generating resource to supplement the family income. Parents sacrifice their children's education to the growing needs of their younger siblings in such families and view them as bread-winners for the entire family. Children are also compelled to work as bonded labourers. They are trapped to grow in a hostage like condition for years. The importance of formal education is also not realized, as the child can be absorbed in economically beneficial activities at a young age. Moreover there is no access to proper education in the remote areas of rural India for most people, which leaves the children with no choice. There are thousands of bonded child labourers in India. They are also mostly the children of parents who belong to scheduled castes and tribes. Young children are sold to employers by their parents to pay back small loans that they have borrowed. Such children are made to work for many hours a day over several years. Often, child labour is considered to be a 'necessary evil' in poor countries such as India for the maintenance of the family. In that context, some consider it virtuous to give a job to a child. In fact, some academics and activists campaign not for the reduction of child labour but only for a reduction in the exploitation of children. Bonded labour or slave labour is one of the worst forms of labour not only for children but also for adults. In India, bonded labour has been declared illegal since 1976 when the Parliament enacted the Bonded Labour System (Abolition) Act. However, the practice is still widespread. Children or adults are bonded in order to pay off debts that they or other members of their families have incurred. They toil all their lives and endure physical attacks that often amount to torture. The Indian government has tried to take some steps to alleviate the problem of child labour in recent years by invoking a law that makes the employment of children below 14 illegal, except in family owned enterprises. However, this law is rarely adhered to due to practical difficulties. Factories usually find loopholes and circumvent the law by declaring that the child labourer is a distant family member. Also in villages there is no law implementing mechanism, and any punitive actions for commercial enterprises violating these laws is almost non existent.

MULTIPLE CHOICE QUESTIONS

1. Which of the following is not an Indicator for calculating Human Development Index?
A. Long and Healthy Life
B. Dimension of Knowledge
C. Participation in decision-making
D. Decent standard of Living

2. 'Women's Component Plan' was initiated in which Five Year Plan?
A. 6th Five Year Plan
B. 7th Five Year Plan
C. 5th Five Year Plan
D. 9th Five Year Plan

3. According to the National Rural Employment Guarantee Act, the percentage of women beneficiaries shall be
A. 50% B. 33%
C. 75% D. 100%

4. The reason for low literacy rate of weaker section is due to
A. Continued monopolization of resources by middle and upper class groups.
B. The stronger influence of casteism in the rural areas.
C. The control of customs of the Society.
D. All the above

5. Which National Education Policy gave impetus to women's studies in India?
A. Kothari Commission 1964–66
B. National Education Policy 1986
C. Recent Education Policy
D. Education Commission of 1882

6. Which is not the form of qualitative research?
A. Case study
B. Oral history
C. Survey
D. Focus group discussion

7. Manushi is a
A. Newspaper
B. Magazine
C. Film
D. TV Program

8. The Child Marriage Act amended in .... year raised the minimum age of marriage for girls from 15 to 18 years.
A. 1986 B. 1929
C. 1976 D. 1991

9. Among the following states which one has literacy rate below 90% according to 2011 census.

A. Kerala
B. Lakshadeep
C. Mizoram
D. Goa

10. Who is the author of Book 'Discrimination'?

A. Gary Becker
B. Adam Smith
C. Marshal
D. Robinson

11. Muted group theory speaks about the Women's

A. educational status
B. occupational status
C. domination
D. silence

12. Match the items from List-I and List-II.

List-I	List-II
(*a*) Equal Remuneration Act	(*i*) 1955
(*b*) The Hindu Marriage Act	(*ii*) 1961
(*c*) The Dowry Prohibition Act	(*iii*) 1956
(*d*) The Immoral Traffic (Prevention) Act	(*iv*) 1976

Codes :

	(*a*)	(*b*)	(*c*)	(*d*)
A.	(*iv*)	(*i*)	(*ii*)	(*iii*)
B.	(*iii*)	(*i*)	(*ii*)	(*iv*)
C.	(*i*)	(*ii*)	(*iii*)	(*iv*)
D.	(*iv*)	(*ii*)	(*iii*)	(*i*)

13. What is LPG?

A. Liberal, Processing, Globalisation
B. Liberalistion, Poverty, Globalisation
C. Liberalisation, Privatisation, Globalisation
D. Low Pressured Gas

14. Women are highly concentrated in low paying jobs .... this exemplifies

A. Matriaschy
B. Sexual Harassment
C. Feminisation of Poverty
D. Institutional Sexism

15. The Integrated Child Development Scheme was initiated in

A. 2009 B. 2005
C. 2010 D. 2004

16. National Commission for Child Rights was established in the year

A. 1993 B. 2001
C. 2003 D. 2007

17. Which of the Five Year Plans stressed the need for National Policy for the empowerment of Women?

A. Seventh B. Ninth
C. Fifth D. Sixth

18. Among the following, which is not a contraced method?

A. Depo-provora B. Nor Plant
C. Emergency Pill D. IVF method

19. Which of the following is related to the term 'Employment'?

(*i*) Power to
(*ii*) Power over
(*iii*) Power with
(*iv*) Power within

Codes:

A. (*i*), (*ii*), (*iii*), (*iv*)
B. (*i*) only
C. (*ii*) only
D. (*ii*) and (*iii*) only

20. According to 2011 census which state has (0–6 years) the highest child sex ratio.

A. Kerala B. West Bengal
C. Chattisgarh D. Mizoram

21. Assertion (A): The percentage of women in the higher levels of political bodies are negligible.

Reasons (R): The money and muscle power associated with the electoral bodies inhibits women's political participation.

A. Both (A) and (R) are true, (R) is the correct explanation for (A)

B. Both (A) and (R) are true, (R) is the correct explanation for (A)
C. Both (A) and (R) are true
D. Both (A) and (R) are false

22. Assertion (A): Education of girls and women in India have reinforced gender role specially motherhood.

Reason (R): In India, women's education was neglected for many years.

A. Both (A) and (R) are true, (R) is not the correct explanation for (A)
B. Both (A) and (R) are true, (R) is the correct explanation for (A)
C. (R) is true and (A) is false
D. Both (A) and (R) are true

23. Who among the following is not an Entrepreneur?

A. Indira Nooyi
B. Kiran Mazumdar Shaw
C. Ekta Kapoor
D. Kalpana Shah

24. Masculinities and femininities are

(*i*) Gendered rather than non-gendered
(*ii*) Socially constructed rather than naturally
(*iii*) Changing across time and space
(*iv*) Based on biological determinism

Codes:

A. (*i*) only correct
B. (*iv*) only correct
C. (*i*), (*ii*) and (*iii*) are correct
D. (*i*) and (*ii*) are correct

25. Which feminist thought suggest that gender equality can be realized by eliminating the cultural notion of gender?

A. Post-modern Feminism
B. Radical Feminism
C. Neo-classical Feminism
D. Socialist Feminism

26. Among the following women who's name is closely associated with Central Social Welfare Board?

A. Dr. Annie Besant
B. Aruna Asaf Ali
C. Vijayalakshmi Pandit
D. Durgabai Deshmukh

27. Germaine Greer coined the term Female Eunuch to describe

A. The biological inferiority of women
B. The idealization of women in society
C. Castration of women by aspects of patriarchy
D. The motherhood of women

28. Equal Remuneration Act provides that

(*i*) Women and men will be paid equally for doing the same work.
(*ii*) There will be no discrimination against women at the time of recruitment.
(*iii*) The employer is bound to maintain a register of the workers.
(*iv*) There will be no discrimination against women workers in any condition of service like promotion, training or transfer.

Codes:

A. (*i*), (*ii*), (*iii*) and (*iv*)
B. (*i*) and (*ii*) only
C. (*ii*) and (*iii*) only
D. (*i*) and (*iv*) only

29. Among the following which is not an objective of Rashtriya Mahila Kosh?

A. To advise the government on all policy matters affecting women.
B. To promote the provision of micro credit to poor women.
C. To demonstrate and replicate participatory approach in the organisation of women's group.
D. To link with thrift and savings with credit.

30. Assertion (A) : The self help group of women have been found very effective in organizing and sensitizing women.

Reason (R) : The self help group of women are supported by educated women.

Codes :
A. Both (A) and (R) are true.
B. Both (A) and (R) are false.
C. (A) is true, but (R) is false.
D. (A) is false, but (R) is true.

31. The chief barriers of female education in India are :
(*i*) Shortage of female teachers.
(*ii*) Inadequate school facilities.
(*iii*) Gender bias in school curriculum.
(*iv*) Inadequate English schools.

Codes :
A. (*i*), (*ii*) only
B. (*i*), (*ii*), and (*iii*) only
C. (*iv*) only
D. (*iii*) and (*iv*) only

32. Which International Conference had the thrust on the concept of empowerment?
A. Mexico B. Beijing
C. Copenhagen D. Nairobi

33. The Department of Women and Child Development provides for the schemes.
(*i*) Short stay homes for women and girls.
(*ii*) Hostels for working women.
(*iii*) Condensed courses of education for elderly women.
(*iv*) Family Counselling Centres.

Codes :
A. (*i*), (*ii*), (*iii*) only
B. (*ii*), (*iii*), and (*iv*) only
C. (*i*), (*ii*), and (*iv*) only
D. (*i*), (*iii*), only

34. Match the following from List-I (Authors) and List-II (Books) :

List-I	**List-II**
(*a*) Pandita Rama Bai	1. Recasting Women Essays in Colonial History
(*b*) Neera Desai	2. High Caste Hindu Women
(*c*) Sangari. K	3. Decade of Women's Movement in India
(*d*) K. Jayawandana	4. Feminism and Nationalism in Third World

Codes :

	(*a*)	(*b*)	(*c*)	(*d*)
A.	2	3	1	4
B.	1	3	2	4
C.	4	2	1	3
D.	4	1	2	3

35. Which Social Reformer viewed "The subjugation of women as an instrument for maintaining Brahminical dominance in Indian society"?
A. Jyotiba Phule
B. Raja Ram Mohan Roy
C. I.C. Vidya Sagar
D. Karve

36. Assertion (A) : Education is a strong vehicle of women's equality and empowerment.

Reason (R) : Resource mobilization and management of mass education is a challenge of Indian educators.

Codes :
A. Both (A) and (R) are false.
B. (A) is true (R) is false.
C. Both (A) and (R) are true.
D. (A) is false (R) is true.

37. What is the main focus of gender budget initiatives in India?
A. Women Component Plan
B. Complimentary role for effective convergence
C. Proper utilization and monitoring of funds from various development sectors.
D. All of the above

38. What is the main reasons for women being increasingly pushed to the unorganised sector?
(*i*) Lack of the opportunity to acquire skills and training which could facilitate occupational shifts.
(*ii*) Unequal structural conditions.
(*iii*) Women have to bear the major burden of domestic chores.
(*iv*) Women lost jobs due to globalisation processes.

Codes :
A. (*i*) and (*iv*) are correct.
B. (*ii*), (*iii*) and (*i*) are false.
C. (*iv*) and (*i*) are correct.
D. (*i*), (*ii*), (*iii*) and (*iv*) are correct.

39. "If Men would.... Snap our chains.... They would find us more observant daughters, more faithful wives, ...in a word better citizens" Which of the following feminist thinkers made this statements :
A. Robert Owen
B. William Thompson
C. Harriet Taylor
D. Mary Wollstonecraft

40. Assertion (A) : The Hindu Succession Act 1956 has failed to reduce social inequalities among women.

Reason (R) : Religious traditions and customary practices came in conflict with the act.

Codes :
A. (A) is true but (R) is false.
B. Both (A) and (R) are true.
C. (A) is false, but (R) is true.
D. Both (A) and (R) are false.

41. Which is the correct chronological sequence of stages of development of feminist research?
(*i*) Research on gender as an organizing principle in all social systems.
(*ii*) Research on sex differences based on biological properties of individuals.
(*iii*) Research based on men's experiences.
(*iv*) Research on individual level sex roles and socialization.

Mark the correct sequence from the codes given below :

Codes :
A. (*i*), (*ii*), (*iv*), (*iii*)
B. (*iv*), (*iii*), (*i*), (*ii*)
C. (*iii*), (*iv*), (*ii*), (*i*)
D. (*iii*), (*ii*), (*iv*), (*i*)

42. Issue of women's citizenship relate to
(*i*) Power
(*ii*) Autonomy
(*iii*) Choice to live as free and participating citizens.
(*iv*) Politeness

Codes :
A. (*i*), (*ii*) and (*iii*) only
B. (*i*) and (*ii*) only
C. (*iii*) and (*iv*) only
D. (*i*) and (*iii*) only

43. What do you mean by 'Deregulation'?
A. Existence of private market
B. Regulations by civil society
C. Existence of safety nets
D. Government will control the markets

44. Match the items from List-I and List-II given below :

List-I	List-II
(*a*) Barkha Dutt	(*i*) Hindustan Times
(*b*) Mrinal Pandey	(*ii*) Print-media
(*c*) Aruna Roy	(*iii*) UGC
(*d*) Armaity Desai	(*iv*) RTI Act

Codes :

	(*a*)	(*b*)	(*c*)	(*d*)
A.	(*i*)	(*iii*)	(*iv*)	(*ii*)
B.	(*ii*)	(*i*)	(*iv*)	(*iii*)
C.	(*iv*)	(*ii*)	(*iii*)	(*i*)
D.	(*iii*)	(*i*)	(*ii*)	(*iv*)

45. What is not meant by Feminisation of poverty?
A. women workers excluded and secluded from higher wages.
B. work for long hours and low wages.
C. lack of property/land rights.
D. women's economic independence.

46. Assertion (A) : The challenges of women entrepreneurs are higher than men entrepreneurs.

Reason (R) : Women are restricted due to social norms and family responsibilities.

Codes :
A. Both (A) and (R) are correct.
B. Both (A) and (R) are false.

C. (A) is correct (R) is false.
D. Both (A) and (R) are correct and (R) is the correct explanation for (A).

47. Which is not the correct statement relating to women's job satisfaction?
A. Women's work is visible and recognized.
B. Women's work is invisible and not recognized
C. Sex discrimination
D. Gender division of labour

48. What is the recent gender related Index that have been developed and used by United Nations in 2010 :
A. Gender Related Developed Index (GDI)
B. Gender Inequality Index (GII)
C. Gender Empowerment Measure (GEM)
D. Inequality adjusted Human Development Index (IHDI)

49. What is the Bread Winner Paradigm?
A. Man is the main bread winner
B. Woman is the main bread winner
C. Women headed families
D. Elder people lead the family

50. Assertion (A) : The impact of globalisation and technology on rural women is negative.

Reason (R) : Women of rural areas are displaced due to upgradation of technology, automation and adoption of high-tech.

Codes :
A. Both (A) and (R) are correct.
B. Both (A) and (R) are correct (R) is the correct explanation.
C. Both (A) and (R) are false.
D. Both (A) and (R) are correct but (R) is not the correct explanation.

51. Match the following from List-I and List-II:

List-I	**List-II**
(*a*) Department of Women and Child Development	(*i*) 1975
(*b*) Integrated Child Development Scheme	(*ii*) 1985
(*c*) Juvenile Justice Act	(*iii*) 2000
(*d*) Indian Association for Women's Studies	(*iv*) 1982

Codes :

	(*a*)	(*b*)	(*c*)	(*d*)
A.	(*iv*)	(*iii*)	(*i*)	(*ii*)
B.	(*iii*)	(*iv*)	(*i*)	(*ii*)
C.	(*ii*)	(*i*)	(*iii*)	(*iv*)
D.	(*ii*)	(*iv*)	(*iii*)	(*i*)

52. 'ASHA' denotes :
A. Association of Scientific Health Acitivists
B. Association of Social Health Activists
C. Accredited Social Health Activists
D. Accredited Social Health Association

53. Which one of the following pair is not correctly matched?
A. Kishori Shakti Yojana – National Programme for Adolescent Girls
B. AYUSH – Programme to revitalise local Health Traditions
C. SWADHAR – Programme for women in difficult circumstances
D. Janani Suraksha Yojana – Programme for disabled mothers

54. Women's studies researchers viewed women as
A. objects and consumers
B. subjects and producers
C. objects and producers
D. subjects and consumers

55. Mark out the factor contributing to high maternal mortality rate
A. Antenatal care
B. Education
C. Increase in the number of working women
D. Early marriage

56. Institutional initiatives for women's issues in the post-independence period are
(*i*) Constitutional provisions and social legislations
(*ii*) The Brahmo Samaj

(*iii*) Indian Association for Women's Studies
(*iv*) The Women's India Association

Codes:
A. (*i*) and (*iii*) only
B. (*i*), (*ii*) and (*iii*) only
C. (*ii*) and (*iii*) only
D. (*i*), (*ii*) and (*iv*) only

57. Gender disaggregated data are the basis for
A. Analysis of women's work
B. Gender sensitive policy formulation and programme planning
C. Gender mainstreaming
D. Gender sensitization

58. The first Research Centre for women was established in 1974 by:
A. SNDT Women's University
B. ICSSR
C. Centre for Women's Development Studies
D. UGC

59. 'Consciousness raising' is the major agenda discussed by
A. Liberals B. Post-modernist
C. Marxist D. Radicals

60. Match the List-I (Thinkers) with List-II :

List-I	**List-II**
(*a*) John Stuart Mill	(*i*) Marxist feminism
(*b*) Jane Flax	(*ii*) Radical feminism
(*c*) Clara Zetkin	(*iii*) Liberal feminism
(*d*) Shulamith Firestone	(*iv*) Socialist feminism

Codes :

	(*a*)	(*b*)	(*c*)	(*d*)
A.	(*i*)	(*ii*)	(*iii*)	(*iv*)
B.	(*iii*)	(*i*)	(*iv*)	(*ii*)
C.	(*ii*)	(*i*)	(*iv*)	(*iii*)
D.	(*i*)	(*iv*)	(*iii*)	(*ii*)

61. Assertion (A) : Violence against women is a universal problem that must be condemned.

Reason (R) : Violence affects the lives of millions of women worldwide.
A. Both (A) and (R) are true, (R) is the correct explanation for (A)
B. Both (A) and (R) are false
C. (A) is true, (R) is false
D. Both (A) and (R) are true

62. Parivarik Mahila Lok Adalats Programme was launched in 1996 by
A. The Commission for SC/ST
B. The Human Rights Commission
C. The National Commission for Women
D. The National Law Commission

63. Women's studies finds its relevance in the ways:
(*i*) To uncover the gender discrimination prevailing in the society.
(*ii*) To mobilize women's attitude for betterment of their living.
(*iii*) To provide better jobs for women.
(*iv*) To activate the women on social and economic issues.

Codes:
A. (*i*) and (*ii*) only
B. (*i*), (*ii*) and (*iii*) only
C. (*ii*) and (*iv*) only
D. (*i*), (*ii*) and (*iv*) only

64. Arrange the chronological sequence of the laws with the year of their enactment.
(*i*) The 73rd and 74th Constitutional Amendment Act
(*ii*) Medical Termination of Pregnancy Act
(*iii*) The Equal Remuneration Act
(*iv*) Child Labour (Prohibition and Regulation) Act

Codes:
A. (*iii*), (*ii*), (*iv*), (*i*)
B. (*ii*), (*iv*), (*i*), (*iii*)
C. (*ii*), (*iii*), (*iv*), (*i*)
D. (*iii*), (*iv*), (*i*), (*ii*)

65. Assertion (A) : Empowerment of women is closely associated with women's participation in unorganized sector.

Reason (R) : Empowerment of women is related to enhancement of women's capabilities and decision.
A. Both (A) and (R) are true
B. (A) is false, (R) is true
C. Both (A) and (R) are false
D. (A) is true, (R) is false

ANSWERS

1	2	3	4	5	6	7	8	9	10
C	D	C	D	B	C	B	B	D	A
11	**12**	**13**	**14**	**15**	**16**	**17**	**18**	**19**	**20**
D	A	C	D	A	D	B	D	A	D
21	**22**	**23**	**24**	**25**	**26**	**27**	**28**	**29**	**30**
A	A	D	C	B	D	C	A	C	B
31	**32**	**33**	**34**	**35**	**36**	**37**	**38**	**39**	**40**
B	B	C	A	A	C	D	D	D	B
41	**42**	**43**	**44**	**45**	**46**	**47**	**48**	**49**	**50**
D	A	A	B	D	D	A	B	A	B
51	**52**	**53**	**54**	**55**	**56**	**57**	**58**	**59**	**60**
C	C	D	B	D	A	B	A	B	B
61	**62**	**63**	**64**	**65**					
A	C	D	C	B					

CHAPTER

5

Crime and Deviance

DEFINITION OF CRIME

Defining crime is extremely difficult. It is an act committed or omitted violation of law forbidding or commanding it and for which punishment is imposed up on conviction. Crime is an unlawful activity. It is unjust, senseless or disgraceful act or condition.

Causes of Crime: There might be several answers to why a person commits crime. Some of the reason for committing crime might be poverty, lack of employment, lack of education, social environment (if it is conducive to crime), dysfunctional family structure etc.

DEFINITION OF DEVIANCE

In a sociological context, deviance can be described as actions or behaviours that violate social norms, including formally-enacted rules (e.g., crime), as well as informal violations of social norms (e.g., rejecting folkways and mores). It is the purview of sociologists, psychologists, psychiatrists, and criminologists to study how these norms are created, how they change overtime and how they are enforced.

Norms are rules and expectations by which members of society are conventionally guided. Deviance is an absence of conformity to these norms. Social norms differ from culture to culture. For example, a deviant act can be committed in one society that breaks a social norm there, but may be normal for another society.

Deviance as a violation of social norms

Norms are rules and expectations by which members of society are guided. They are not necessarily moral, or even grounded in morality; in fact, they are just as often pragmatic and, paradoxically, irrational. (A great many of what we call manners, having no logical grounds, would make for good examples here.) Norms are rules of conduct, not neutral or universal, but ever changing; shifting as society shifts; mutable, emergent, loose, reflective of inherent biases and interests, and highly selfish and one-sided. They vary from class to class, and in the generational "gap." They are, in other words, contextual. Deviance can be described as a violation of these norms. Deviance is a failure to conform to culturally reinforced norms.

THEORIES

There are three broad sociological classes describing deviant behaviour, namely structural functionalism, symbolic interaction and conflict theory.

Structural-Functionalism

Social integration is the attachment to groups and institutions, while social regulation is the adherence to the norms and values of the society. Those who are very integrated fall under the category of "altruism" and those who are not very integrated fall under "egoism." Similarly, those who are much regulated fall under "fatalism" and those who are much unregulated fall under "anomie". Durkheim's strain theory attributes social deviance to extremes of the dimensions of the social bond. Altruistic suicide (death for the good of the group), egoistic suicide (death for the removal of the self due to or justified by the lack of ties to others), and anomic suicide (death due to the confounding of self-interest and societal norms) are the three forms of suicide that can happen due to extremes. Likewise, individuals may commit crimes for the good of an individual's group, for the self due to or justified by lack of ties, or because the societal norms that place the individual in check no longer have power due to society's corruption.

Durkheim's Basic Insight

Durkheim claimed that deviance was in fact a normal and necessary part of social organization. In 1964, when he studied deviance he stated there are four important functions of deviance.

1. "Deviance affirms cultural values and norms. Any definition of virtue rests on an opposing idea of vice: There can be no good without evil and no justice without crime".
2. Deviance defines moral boundaries, people learn right from wrong by defining people as deviant.
3. A serious form of deviance forces people to come together and react in the same way against it.
4. Deviance pushes society's moral boundaries which lead to social change.

Merton's Strain Theory

Robert K. Merton discussed deviance in terms of goals and means as part of his strain/anomie theory. Where Durkheim states that anomie is the confounding of social norms, Merton goes further and states that anomie is the state in which social goals and the legitimate means to achieve them do not correspond. He postulated that an individual's response to societal expectations and the means by which the individual pursued those goals were useful in understanding deviance. Specifically, he viewed collective action as motivated by strain, stress, or frustration in a body of individuals that arises from a disconnection between the society's goals and the popularly used means to achieve those goals. Often, non-routine collective behaviour (rioting, rebellion, etc.) is said to map onto economic explanations and causes by way of strain. These two dimensions determine the adaptation to society according to the cultural goals, which are the society's perceptions about the ideal life, and to the institutionalized means, which are the legitimate means through which an individual may aspire to the cultural goals.

Symbolic interaction

As political movements come to terms with their "terror of adolescence," the debates seem to coalesce around the suffering of those who are victims of violent crime. The fear of crime that seems to be forever increasing is a powerful personal and political emotion. Ironically, the fear of kids in Canada has been fuelled by two phenomena that are largely the result of business as usual. First, part of the problem has been the increased visibility of young people in public places. As industry "rationalizes" production by reducing employment costs, youth unemployment rises, as high as 30% in some areas in Canada. Simply put, more youth have increasingly more idle time and the work that is available is poorly paid, bereft of benefits and offers little in terms of meaningful apprenticeship. The typical employee at fast food chains is the adolescent, the typical wage is at or just above minimum wage, the work is typically hard and quite dangerous, and the typical benefits package is nonexistent. Furthermore, the building of centralized shopping centers is not done with community solidarity in mind, but is merely the result of profit considerations. That adolescents gather in such places is neither anathema to profit, nor is it discouraged by private interests. Yet the presence of youth in places such as shopping malls fuels the panic that kids are loitering with intent.

Second, people gain their images and opinions about the nature and extent of crime through the media. In Canada, much of our vicarious experience with youth crime is filtered through television. Television news, much of which teeters on the edge between fact and fiction, is highly sensational, selective to time and place, and focuses primarily on the bad. I argue below that such depictions are not based on reality, but rather on the wants of a presumed audience. All forms of news accounts, though they are mandated to be based on an objective reality, are largely based on consumer demand.

What we are left with, then, is a gulf between reality and perception. The reality is that youth are mostly disenfranchised from the democratic process at all levels of governance. They are disadvantaged in the labour market and have few services available to them unlike the adult world. When they do break the law, they victimize other youth who are like them. Furthermore, youth crime has not increased significantly, although the prosecution of youth crime has.

Sutherland's differential association

In his differential association theory, Edwin Sutherland posited that criminals learn criminal and deviant behaviours and that deviance is not inherently a part of a particular individual's nature. Also, he argues that criminal behaviour is learned in the same way that all other behaviours are learned, meaning that the acquisition of criminal knowledge is not unique compared to the learning of other behaviours.

Sutherland outlined some very basic points in his theory, such as the idea that the learning comes from the interactions between individuals and groups, using communication of symbols and ideas. When the symbols and ideas about deviation are much more favourable than unfavourable, the individual tends to take a favourable view upon deviance and will resort to more of these behaviours.

Criminal behaviour (motivations and technical knowledge), as with any other sort of behaviour, is learned. Some basic assumptions include:

- Learning in interaction using communication within intimate personal groups.
- Techniques, motives, drives, rationalizations, and attitudes are all learned.
- Excess of definitions favourable to deviation.
- Legitimate and illegitimate behaviours both express the same general needs and essential values.

Neutralization Theory

Gresham Sykes and David Matza's neutralization theory explains how deviants justify their deviant behaviours by providing alternative definitions of their actions and by providing explanations, to themselves and others, for the lack of guilt for actions in particular situations.

There are five major types of neutralization:

- **Denial of Responsibility:** the deviant believes s/he was helplessly propelled into the deviance, and that under the same circumstances, any other person would resort to similar actions.
- **Denial of Injury:** the deviant believes that the action caused no harm to other individuals or to the society, and thus the deviance is not morally wrong.
- **Denial of The Victim:** the deviant believes that individuals on the receiving end of the deviance were deserving of the results due to the victim's lack of virtue or morals.
- **Condemnation of The Condemners:** the deviant believes enforcement figures or victims have the tendency to be equally deviant or otherwise corrupt, and as a result, are hypocrites to stand against.
- **Appeal to Higher Loyalties:** the deviant believes that there are loyalties and values that go beyond the confines of the law; morality, friendships, income, or traditions may be more important to the deviant than legal boundaries.

Conflict Theory

In sociology, conflict theory states that society or an organization functions so that each individual participant and its groups struggle to maximize their benefits, which inevitably contributes to social change such as political changes and revolutions. Deviant behaviours are actions that do not go along with the social institutions as what cause deviance. The institution's ability to change norms, wealth or status come into conflict with the individual. The legal rights of poor folks might be ignored, middle class are also accept; they side with the elites rather than the poor, thinking they might rise to the top by supporting the status quo. Conflict theory is based upon the view that the fundamental causes of crime are the social and economic forces operating within society. However, it explains white-collar crime less well.

This theory also states that the powerful define crime. This raises the question: for whom is this theory functional? In this theory, laws are instruments of oppression: tough on the powerless and less tough on the powerful.

Biological Theories of Deviance

Praveen Attri claims genetic reasons to be largely responsible for social deviance. The Italian school of criminology contends that biological factors may contribute to crime and deviance. Cesare Lombroso was among the first to research and develop the Theory of Biological Deviance which states that some people are genetically predisposed to criminal behaviour. He believed that criminals were a product of earlier genetic forms. The main influence of his research was Charles Darwin and his Theory of Evolution. Lombroso theorized that people were born criminals or in other words, less evolved humans who were biologically more related to our more primitive and animalistic urges. From his research, Lombroso took Darwin's Theory and looked at primitive times himself in regards to deviant behaviours. He found that the skeletons that he studied mostly had low foreheads and protruding jaws. These characteristics resembled primitive beings such as Homo Neanderthalensis. He stated that little could be done to cure born criminals because their characteristics were biologically inherited. Over time, most of his research was disproved. His research was refuted by Pearson and Charles Goring. They discovered that Lombroso had not researched enough skeletons to make his research thorough enough. When Pearson and Goring researched skeletons on their own they tested many more and found that the bone structure had no relevance in deviant behaviour. The statistical study that Charles Goring published on this research is called "The English Convict".

DEFINITION OF PUNISHMENT

Punishment is the infliction of some kind of pain or loss upon a person for a misdeed. Punishment may take forms ranging from capital punishment, flogging, forced labour, and mutilation of the body to imprisonment and fines. Deferred punishments consist of penalties that are imposed only if an offense is repeated within a specified time.

Types of Punishment

According to Dr. Burke, there are four different types of punishment. Each has a different philosophy and objective:

- **Deterrence:** applied with the belief that an unpleasant consequence makes people think twice before repeating the behaviour. This is most effective at stopping crime that is planned or premeditated. Sometimes the goal is to deter the individual from repeating the behaviour; other times it is to deter others from engaging in a similar behaviour.
- **Retribution:** an "eye for an eye, tooth for a tooth" punishment applied with the belief that offenders should suffer similarly to their victims.
- **Restitution:** applied with the belief that offenders should repay their victim's loss in money or services.
- **Rehabilitation:** used more frequently with juveniles, it is applied with the hopes of helping the person resolve comorbidities that may contribute to crime.

The Objectives of Punishment

The overall objective of punishment is to impose some kind of penalty on an individual for violating a law or rule, in the hopes that the penalty or punishment will result in that individual not committing future violations of the laws or rules, or causing any further harm to society (Foster, 2006).

The deterrence objective of punishment is achieved by the certainty of imprisonment, which seems to have a discouraging effect on those who commit crimes or who may commit crimes. Individuals tend to avoid repeating criminal acts, or committing criminal acts altogether when the consequences are known (Foster, 2006).

The Incapacitations' objective of punishment is to protect society by imprisoning those who commit criminal acts, so those individuals no longer pose a threat to society. Therefore, society is safer because the criminals have been removed.

The Reformations' objective of punishment is to rehabilitate individuals while they are imprisoned which aids in reducing criminal activity and may even eliminate future criminal activity for some individuals. This is achieved through various programs which promote law abiding behaviour.

Correctional Services: In the field of criminal justice, correction, corrections, and correctional, are umbrella terms describing a variety of functions typically carried out by government agencies, and involving the punishment, treatment, and supervision of persons who have been convicted of crimes. These functions commonly include imprisonment, parole and probation.

A typical correctional institution is a prison. A correctional system, also known as a penal system, thus refers to a network of agencies that administer a jurisdiction's prisons and community-based programs like parole and probation boards; this system is part of the larger criminal justice system, which additionally includes police, prosecution and courts.

Causes of Juvenile Delinquency – There is no single cause or simple explanation for the development of delinquent behaviour. Juvenile delinquency takes place in various forms and vary in degree, frequency, duration and seriousness and involves different forms of specialization like drug addiction, sex offences, predatory acts etc. Delinquency like other social behaviours has complex roots.

There is no single cause of juvenile delinquency but there are many and varied causes. Basically, causes of juvenile delinquency are of three types.

- Biological
- Socio-Environmental
- Psychological, Physiological and Personal

Biological Causes:

(1) **Ocular Ailments:** It leads to irritability. It is discontent factor causing emotional disturbance and discomfort.

(2) **Nose and throat problem:** This may cause weakness and discomfort and may result in dislike of work and responsibility.

(3) **Hearing Problem:** Deafness or difficulty in hearing makes the person concerned inefficient. Inefficiency is generally weak and adversely affects his ability to work and he depends on others which may lead to anti social behaviour.

(4) **Speech Problem:** It is also found to lead to delinquency acts especially in children. A person with speech problem is pitted or laughed at in the society. Due to this, feeling of inferiority may be developed which may lead to a desire to make up in criminal acts.

(5) **Enuresis:** It involves a disorder of functions of the bladder. Sometimes it discomfort and even some time may lead to delinquency.

(6) **Irritation:** Irritation caused by ailments such, as ringworm eczema, irritation of sexual organs is also a significant factor resulting in delinquency.

(7) **Headache:** It may cause irritation of temperamental though rarely may result in some sort of out burst.

(8) **Excessive strength:** A person who is possessed excessive physical strength and his mental trait being uncultured and not

properly channelized, probability of his committing an act of offence becomes higher.

(9) **Hypoglycemia:** Hypoglycemia caused by low level of glucose in blood disturbs the mental equilibrium and affects the level of consciousness, memory and orientation.

Socio-Environmental:

(i) **Mobility:** This factor is responsible for crime causation in the society. The rapid growth of industrialization and urbanization has led to expansion of means to communication, travel facilities and propagations of views through press and platform. Migration of persons to new places where they are strangers offers them opportunity for crime as chances of detection are minimized considerably.

(ii) **Cultural conflicts:** In a dynamic society, social change is an inevitable phenomenon. The impact of modernization urbanization and industrialization in a rapidly changing society may sometimes result in social disorganization and this may led to culture conflicts between different valves of different sections of society.

(iii) **Family background :** This factor also incites or encourages the Juvenile to commit for offence/crime in society. Sutherland said that the family background has greatest influence on the criminal behaviour of offender or Juvenile. The children are apt to imbibe criminal tendencies, if they find their parents or members of they family behaving in the similar manner. Some are the factor which emanates from the family background are as under:

(a) **Family Structure:** Family is considered to be the most effective variable in socializing the child and also in serving as a source for learning various types of behaviour. The nature and structure of the family are largely responsible for carving out the personality make-up of the children. A functionally adequate family encourages growth, confidence, frankness and ability to face reality. Delinquents mostly come from functionally inadequate homes.

(b) **Child's Birth Order in the Family:** Another aspect of family structure which has often been related to delinquency is the ordinal position of the child in the family. Lees and Newson (1954) found differences among the delinquents which could be attributed to sibling position. Their study showed that intermediate children having both older as well as younger siblings were significantly overrepresented in a group of delinquents. They found that the intermediate children were attended to less by parents as compared to the oldest and youngest children which lead the intermediate children towards delinquency. The results of their study have received some support from the findings of Gluecks (1950) and Nye (1958).

(c) **Family Size and Type:** Family size has also been cited as a factor in causation of delinquent behaviour in juveniles. Delinquents are found more likely to come from larger families as compared to the smaller families.

(d) **Parent-Child Relationship:** The most important single factor in the developmental picture of children is relationship with their parents including parental behaviour. The pattern of interpersonal relationship with a family is important in shaping the inter-personal behaviour and cognition of the child.

(e) **Behaviour of Step Parents:** The behaviour of step-parents is also the main cause of delinquency. When step motherly treatment is given to the child by the step parents the child tries to run away and this also leads the child to commit offence.

(f) **Behaviour of alcoholic parents:** It is fact that the bahaviour of such parents also influences the children's behaviour. When behaviour of parents is not good and meaningful, behaviour of child would also be biased because the mind of child is impressionable. The children of the alcoholic parents are mostly found indulging in the delinquent activities.

(g) **Excessive punishment:** Excessive punishment given to the children by their parents many a time spoils the child instead of disciplining him because he may feel dejected and frustrated leading to his involvement in anti-social activities for the purpose of bringing shame to the parents.

Psychological, Physiological and Personal: The following factors could play important role in causing juvenile delinquency such as school dissatisfaction, drug-addiction, bad company, early sex experience, mental conflicts, love of adventure, sudden impulse, and physical condition.

THE JUVENILE JUSTICE (CARE AND PROTECTION OF CHILDREN) ACT, 2000

Main Provisions

- The Government of India enacted the Juvenile Justice Act in 1986. In 1989 the General Assembly of the United Nations adopted the Convention on the Rights of a Child. India ratified the UNCRC in 1992. The convention outlines the right of the child to reintegration into society without judicial proceedings where avoidable. Hence the Government, to fulfil the standards of the convention felt a need to re-write the law. Hence in 2000 the old law was replaced by the Juvenile Justice (Care and Protection of Children) Act.
- In this act a child or juvenile is defined as a person who has not completed his/her 18th year of age. It outlines two target groups: Children in need of care and protection and Juveniles in conflict with law.
- This act protects not only the rights of children, but a person's rights when he/she was a child. Meaning that if a crime or an incident took place while the person was a child, and then during the preceding the juvenile ceased to be of age the case would continue as if the juvenile has not turned eighteen yet.
- The second chapter of the Act addresses Juveniles in Conflict with Law (JCLs). This section calls for the establishment of Juvenile Justice Boards (JJBs) where the State Government sees fit. JJBs must contain a Metropolitan or Judicial magistrate and two social workers where one of the workers must be a woman. The magistrate is required to have a background in child psychology or child welfare. JCL cases can only be heard in the JJB and not by another court. The powers of the JJB can be exercised in a High court or Court of Session when an appeal has been made as part of the act.
- The state is required to set up a number of institutions where the needs and protection of juveniles may be fulfilled. For the reception and rehabilitation of JCLs the state must set up Observation Homes and Special Homes in every district or group of districts. The state may directly set up these homes or contract a voluntary organisation to do so. Observation homes are for institutions for juveniles while their proceedings are underway. After the proceedings of a particular case are complete, the JJB may decide that the rehabilitation of the child is not complete and hence place them in a Special home for no longer than three years.
- When a police officer comes in contact with a juvenile he must place the child with the Special Juvenile Police Unit (SJPU)

who must report the child to the board without delay.

- Bail is available to juveniles in all cases as long as the Board find the release of this child will not place him in any danger or in the influence of criminals. If the child is not released on bail he is only to be placed into the custody of an Observation Home.
- The SJPU are responsible for informing the juvenile's parents of the arrest, as well as inform the Probation Officer who will make the necessary enquires about the child.
- The JJB must make an inquiry into the case and if they determine the child is guilty of the crime then they may release the child after advice and counselling.
- The child can be released either to his parents/guardians or into an institution, with or without a bond.
- The Board may also make the child pay a fine (if he is above fourteen and earns) or complete hours of community service.
- A social investigation report from the probation officer is required for the child to be discharged.
- The probation officers may be required to continue a follow up of the child even after discharge.
- A child cannot be charged with the death penalty, imprisonment which can extend to life imprisonment or committed to prison for inability to pay a fine or providing a security for the bond.
- Under this act juvenile cases cannot be processed with non-juvenile cases. A juvenile cannot be rendered unfit or 'disqualified".
- Juveniles are not exposed to the media as magazines, news papers and visual media are not permitted to release the information about the juvenile. Juveniles who run away from the Observation or Special homes can be brought back without a warrant and without punishment.
- Cruelty (such as assault or neglect) towards juveniles in the home or by any person in charge of him/her is a punishable offence.
- This act also has provisions to penalize people who exploit children for a crime. A person, who employs a child in a hazardous industry, employs him/her for begging or provides a child with drugs or alcohol is liable to serve prison time and pay fines.
- Chapter III address Children in Need of Care and Protection (CNCP). In place of a JJB, CNCP cases are heard by the Child Welfare Committee (CWC).
- The Child Welfare Committee is meant to have a chairperson and four other members of whom at least one should be a woman and at least one expert in children's issues.
- The purpose of the CWC is to provide for the care, treatment, protection, rehabilitation and development of the child and in doing so uphold the rights of the child.
- The child may be brought in front of the CWC by a police officer, public servant, social worker, CHILDLINE, the child or anyone public citizen.
- The committee may commit a child to the Children's home or a Shelter home if the child has no immediately available family or support system. Like in the case of JCL, CNCP are provided with Children's Homes and Shelter Homes. The state may directly set up these homes or contract a voluntary organisation to do so.
- Shelter homes are for children whose family cannot be located or whose case has been completed. Children who come from a different area or state are meant to be transferred to an institution and CWC that is closest to his/her residence. The main aim of this system is to restore the child to his family or family environment after determining the safety of the environment.
- The fourth chapter discusses the importance of rehabilitation and social integration as the purpose of this act.

- This section discusses certain non-institutional solutions such as adoption, foster care, and sponsorship. Orphaned and abandoned children are eligible for adoption. The CWC may declare a child fit for adoption and refer him/her to an adoption agency (set up by the government) for placement.
- Foster care in this act is only for looking after infants before adoption takes place. Sponsorship programmes are to help provide supplementary educational, nutritional, medical and other services to families, guardians, and homes. After-care organisations are also to be set up to take care of children after they leave the homes.
- The last chapter of the act contains many miscellaneous provisions.

SOCIAL WORKER'S SPECIFIC ROLE IN CORRECTION

Social worker's specific role in correction is as follows:

As an Investigator: Act as the officer of the court or other quasi-judicial body to investigate and report about the offender and his social situation, contributing the results of such social observations in an appropriate and meaningful way to the making of legal decisions.

As a Supervisor: Supervise the client's social activities in such a way that violations of the conditions of his status and his success in meeting conditions are perceived and can be reported. The general control plan provided in the status is individualized according to the client's need for constructive social control. Controls are provided by the social worker in such a way that the client is supported in viably conforming behaviour and inner growth toward self control is stimulated.

As a Motivator: Help the involuntary client to handle the stress produced by the law enforcement and correctional process constructively. Become motivated to ask for and use help in the modification of delinquent and criminal behaviour. Modify his behaviour in the direction of increasingly viable conformity with social expectations.

As a Problem Solver: As the formal authority person in the delinquent or criminal's life, work with either authorities associated with the client (parents, teachers, employees, social agencies, institutional personnel) in such a way that: The problems of these authorities with the delinquent or criminal are alleviated. The activities of the authorities support the delinquent or criminal's efforts towards satisfactory behaviour. The delinquent or criminal is more soundly linked with the resources of his groups and his community.

As a Team Worker: Enact a role in a multidiscipline agency involving shared decisions and teamwork obligations in partnership with: Personnel from other professions, Personnel in the same role as his, but with other educational backgrounds, Personnel with sub-professional assignments and backgrounds, Personnel from other agencies in the administration of criminal justice, Personnel in other agencies who have served the delinquent/criminal or will do so in the future.

As a Professional: Take a responsible part in the social change of the correctional institution and in the development of the field of service of the correctional institution, contributing from his professional knowledge and experience to the determination of policy.

As a Change Agent: Contribute to developing professional knowledge of social work in corrections. The social worker helps the offender to change his offending behaviour, therefore he can relate constructively to others and become socially acceptable. This is done through working with the individual to help him to change through better understanding of himself and by tapping his own strengths and resources; and through modification of his environment to bring about a more healthy social climate in which he has to live. The social worker encourages the offender to talk about his problems, to feel about them, and to come to an insightful understanding of himself, accompanied by socially constructive behaviour.

MULTIPLE CHOICE QUESTIONS

1. Which of the following discipline does not directly contribute to Criminology?
A. Geography B. Economics
C. Sociology D. Geology

2. What type of crime is committed by a Chartered Accountant who manipulates accounts of a business corporation?
A. Smuggling
B. Cyber Crime
C. White Collar Crime
D. Money Laundering

3. Which of the following is not an economic offence?
A. Food adulteration
B. Cheating
C. Tax Evasion
D. Money Laundering

4. Which of the following is not an offence against person?
A. Rape B. Hurt
C. Cheating D. Murder

6. Match the items in List-I with items in List-II :

List-I	List-II
i. Born Criminal	a. Freud
ii. Anomie	b. Merton
iii. Sadism	c. Lombroso
iv. Differential Association	d. Sutherland

Codes :

	i	ii	iii	iv
A.	a	d	c	b
B.	c	b	a	d
C.	a	b	c	d
D.	d	c	b	a

6. Who propounded the theory of hedonism in Criminology?
A. Beccaria B. Lombroso
C. Hooton D. Sigmund Freud

7. Who among the following is associated with the Cartographical School in Criminology?
A. Joseph Gall B. Johannes Lange
C. Malthus D. Quetelet

8. Who has postulated the concept that delinquency and crime are learnt in companionship groups?
A. Merton B. Erikson
C. Sutherland D. Parsons

9. **Assertion (A) :** Fast going up migration and mobility are causing social disorganisation, juvenile delinquency and crime.
Reason (R) : Migrants are all the time concern with their survival and accept few social responsibilities.
Codes :
A. (A) is correct, but (R) is wrong.
B. Both (A) and (R) are correct.
C. (A) is wrong, but (R) is correct.
D. Both (A) and (R) are wrong.

10. Who has given this definition : "Crime is both normal and functional"?
A. Beccaria B. Emile Durkheim
C. Freud D. Lombroso

11. Rejection of goals and acceptance of means are known as
A. Ritualism B. Innovation
C. Rebellion D. Socialization

12. The name of Franz Joseph Gall is associated with
A. Body type B. Chromosomes
C. Atavism D. Phrenology

13. The first study of 'Family Tree' examining hereditary aspects of criminal tendency was conducted in which country?
A. England
B. France
C. Germany
D. United States of America

14. Who among the following has developed the concept of 'Inferiority Complex'?
A. Maslow B. Adler
C. Cattel D. Cyril Burt

15. What does the term 'Electra complex' mean?
A. Extraordinary attachment with father
B. Extraordinary attachment with mother
C. Extraordinary attachment with brother
D. Extraordinary attachment with sister

16. What is the main purpose behind an experimental research design in criminological research?
A. To describe and analyse a social phenomenon.
B. To probe and find out occurrence of crime.
C. To find out and analyse the frequency of a criminal occurrence.
D. To study cause and effect relationship.

17. For setting up a probability sample, which method is used?
A. Intelligent guess
B. Random numbers
C. Informed opinion
D. Experience and insight

18. Among the following, on which study sample interview technique cannot be used for information gathering :
A. Industrial workers
B. Track drivers
C University students
D. Nursery school children

19. What does the statistics of regression measure?
A. Difference between variables
B. Correlation between variables
C. Association between variables
D. Corresponding change in variables

20. Which one of the following is not a method of adaptation, according to Merton?
A. Retreatism B. Conformity
C. Intuition D. Rebellion

21. Assertion (A) : Visibility of crime is also a factor in determining whether a person is labelled criminal.

Reason (R) : People who live in ghetto areas are more likely to be visible in committing a crime. They are also more likely to be visible after crimes are committed because of their greater contact with public servils.

Codes :
A. Both (A) and (R) are true and (R) is the correct explanation of (A).
B. Both (A) and (R) are true, but (R) is not the correct explanation of (A).
C. (A) is true, but (R) is false.
D. (A) is false, but (R) is true.

22. Containment theory has been propounded by
A. Reckless and Dinis
B. Reckless and Sutherland
C. Sutherland and Dinis
D. Reckless and Hirschi

23. Assertion (A) : Critical criminology is a theoretical perspective in criminology which borrows from conflict perspectives such as Marxism, feminism, political economy theory and radical approaches.

Reason (R) : The focus of critical criminology is the genesis of crime and nature of 'justice' within the structure of 'class' and 'status' inequalities. Law and Punishment are viewed as connected to a system of social inequality.

Codes :
A. (A) is correct, but (R) is wrong.
B. Both (A) and (R) are correct.
C. (A) is wrong, but (R) is correct.
D. Both (A) and (R) are wrong.

24. Various sectors of Criminal Justice system are :
I. Courts II. Police
III. Prisons IV. Special Homes
Find the correct combination, using the codes given below :
A. I, II and III are correct.
B. I and II are correct.
C. II and III are correct.
D. III and IV are correct.

25. Which one of the following pairs is not correctly matched?
A. Guilty mind – Mens Rea

B. Physical act – Actus Reus
C. Eye for Eye – Lextalionis
D. Hedonism – Atavism

26. Which one of the following is correctly matched :

A. U.N. Standard Minimum Rules for the Administration of Juvenile Justice – Beijing Rules
B. Child Abuse – Crime syndicates
C. Children's home – Juvenile in conflict with law
D. Special home – Children in need of care and protection

27. The Juvenile Justice Act mainly deals with the following types of children :

I. Children in Conflict with Law
II. Children in Foreign Countries
III. Children in Need of Care and Protection
IV. Non-Resident Indian Children

Choose the correct answer, using the codes given below :

A. I and II are correct.
B. II and III are correct.
C. I and III are correct.
D. III and IV are correct.

28. Match the items in List-I with items in List-II :

List-I	List-II
i. Sutherland	a. Outsider
ii. Young A.	b. Principles of Criminology
iii. Cohen A.	c. Imagining crime
iv. Becker	d. Delinquent Boys

Codes :

	i	ii	iii	iv
A.	b	d	c	a
B.	b	c	d	a
C.	a	b	c	d
D.	c	a	d	b

29. According to Juvenile Justice Act 'begging' means

A. Soliciting or receiving alms in a public place.
B. Entering into any private premises for the purpose of soliciting or receive alms.
C. Exposing or exhibiting any soar, wound, injury deformity or disease for extorting alms.
D. All of the above

30. 'Observation Home' under the Juvenile Justice Act is established for

A. Children in need of care and protection
B. Juveniles in conflict with law
C. Both A and B of above
D. None of the above

31. Who was the Chairperson of the Commission which developed the Indian Penal Code?

A. Dr. Ambedkar
B. Lord Macaulay
C. Colonel Sleeman
D. Lord Curzon

32. Directive Principles of State Policy seek to make India

A. Democratic State
B. Secular State
C. Welfare State
D. Sovereign State

33. The concepts associated with E.H. Sutherland are :

I. Crime is learned
II. Born Criminal
III. White Collar Crime
IV. All of the above

Choose the correct combination using the codes given below :

A. I and III are correct.
B. II and III are correct.
C. I and II are correct.
D. IV is correct.

34. Which one of the following is considered as a contemporary form of crime?

A. Beggary
B. Commercial sex
C. Cyber crime
D. Dowry death

35. Which Section of the Code of Criminal Procedure deals with Victims Compensation Scheme?

A. 357(a) B. 375(a)
C. 315(a) D. 351(a)

36. The statement given by the victim, to the Court, regarding his/her victimization, its loses etc., is called
A. Restorative Justice Statement
B. Offender Impact Statement
C. Victim Impact Statement
D. None of the above

37. In India, how many prisons are functioning at present?
A. About 400 B. About 900
C. About 1400 D. About 1900

38. Who was the Chairperson of the 'All India Committee on Prison Reforms 1980-1983'?
A. Justice M.N. Venkatachaliah
B. Justice A.S. Anand
C. Justice Krishna Iyyer
D. Justice A.N. Mulla

39. What is the minimum time an offender has to spend in jail who has been sentenced to life imprisonment?
A. 7 years B. 14 years
C. 20 years D. 25 years

40. Which State in the country has the largest number of open-air jails?
A. Maharashtra B. Punjab
C. Rajasthan D. Uttrakhand

41. Which authority grants probation to offenders?
A. Police B. Prosecution
C. Court D. Jail authority

42. Which authority approves or grants "special remission" to jail inmates?
A. Central Jail Supdt.
B. I.G. of Prisons
C. Jail Minister
D. All the above

43. Among Narcotic producing countries, which one is not a part of "Golden Crescent"?
A. Afghanistan B. Iran
C. Pakistan D. Kazakhstan

44. First Information Report (FIR) can be lodged with
A. Superintendent of Police
B. Session Judge
C. Officer-in-charge of the Police Station
D. Inspector General of Police

45. Which school of thought used the concept of social disorganization in explaining juvenile delinquency?
A. Classical school
B. Positive school
C. Chicago school
D. None of the above

46. In Ramamurthy *vs.* State of Karnataka the Supreme Court of India has given direction for.
A. Juvenile justice reforms
B. Prison reforms
C. Judicial reforms
D. Police reforms

47. On whose authority, prisoners are admitted to open air jail
A. Police B. Judiciary
C. Jail Authorities D. None of the above

48. Actions that are wrong in themselves are called.
A. Actus Reus B. Mens Rea
C. Mala Prohibita D. Mala in se

49. The aggregate of all operating, administrative and technical support agencies that perform criminal justice functions is called.
A. Social Justice System
B. Civil Justice System
C. Criminal Justice System
D. Consensus approach

50. The due course of legal proceedings according to the rules and forms that have been established for the protection of private right is
A. Due process of law
B. Crime control model
C. Trial
D. Bail

51. Human trafficking is a form of
A. Hate crime
B. Organised crime
C. Violent crime
D. Property crime

52. A human male who has XYY chromosome structure is called
A. Superman B. Superhuman
C. Super female D. Super male

53. A developing intellectual approach which emphasizes gender issues in the subject matter of criminology is called
A. Labelling criminology
B. Post-modern criminology
C. Radical criminology
D. Feminist criminology

54. Who among the following is connected to critical criminology?
A. R.E. Park
B. E.H. Sutherland
C. William J. Chambliss
D. Cloward

55. In D.K. Basu case the Supreme Court has laid down guidelines regarding
A. Rape victims B. Child rights
C. Women rights D. Arrest by police

56. Match the List-I with List-II :

List-I	List-II
(a) Justice A.N. Mulla	(i) National Police Commission
(b) Mr. Dharm Vira	(ii) Committee on Criminal Justice Reforms
(c) Justice Krishna Iyer	(iii) All India Committee on Prison Reforms
(d) Justice V.S. Malimath	(iv) Committee on Women Prisoners

Codes :

	(a)	(b)	(c)	(d)
A.	(i)	(ii)	(iii)	(iv)
B.	(iv)	(iii)	(ii)	(i)
C.	(iii)	(i)	(iv)	(ii)
D.	(i)	(ii)	(iv)	(iii)

57. Arrange the following in the order in which they proceed for consideration of probation. Use the codes given below :
I. Judgement
II. Trial
III. Release on probation
IV. Successful completion or probation on revocation of probation.

Codes :
A. III, I, IV, II B. III, II, I, IV
C. I, II, IV, III D. II, I, III, IV

58. Under Juvenile Justice Act, the observation home is mainly meant for
I. Thrown away children,
II. Children in conflict with law
III. Run-away children
IV. Children whose cases are pending

Find the correct combination using the codes given below :
A. I and II are correct.
B. II and IV are correct.
C. III and IV are correct.
D. III and II are correct.

59. How many members are there in the Child Welfare Committee, including the Chairman?
A. 6 B. 5
C. 4 D. 3

60. Under Juvenile Justice Act, for whom the special home is mainly meant for?
I. Children in conflict with law
II. Thrown-away children
III. Run-away children
IV. Children whose cases are decided

Find the correct combination using the codes given below :
A. I and IV are correct
B. II and III are correct
C. III and IV are correct
D. II and IV are correct

61. At the individual level, examples for social disorganization are
A. Drug Addiction B. Alcoholism
C. Gambling D. All of above

62. Which among the following intoxicating drugs is not produced in India?
A. Charas B. Cocaine
C. Bhang D. Brown sugar

63. AloAno is an organisation meant for
A. Alcoholics
B. Drug addicts
C. Family member of alcoholics
D. Fellow drug users

64. Sub jails are mainly meant for
A. Undertrial prisoners
B. Convict prisoners
C. Political detenues
D. Children in conflict with law

65. Which Commission given below has brought out a report on Capital Punishment?
A. Police Commission
B. Law Commission of India
C. Human Rights Commission
D. Central-State Commission

66. The Act which provides for community service in India is
A. Domestic Violence Act
B. Juvenile Justice Act
C. Probation of Offender Act
D. Indian Penal Code

67. Social change means
A. change in social structure
B. change in social relations
C. change in institutional framework
D. All of the above

68. For studying habitual drug users, the most useful sampling method would be
A. Simple random sample
B. Snowball sampling
C. Cluster sampling
D. Stratified random sample

69. The first jail training school in India was established in
A. Madhya Pradesh
B. Uttar Pradesh
C. Andhra Pradesh
D. Kerala

70. Gottfredson and Hirschi's theory mainly focuses on
A. Learning B. Self-concept
C. Self-control D. Anomie

71. Which of the following is not an integrative theory?
A. Labelling theory
B. Network analysis
C. Integrated cognitive Anti-social Potential (ICAP) theory.
D. Integrated strain control perspective

72. Lie Detector or Polygraph is an aid to :
A. Investigative process
B. Correctional process
C. Rehabilitative process
D. None of the above

73. Match List-I with List-II :

List-I	List-II
(a) The principles of criminology	(i) Vold
(b) Theoretical criminology	(ii) Sue. Titus Reid
(c) Crime & Criminology	(iii) Donald Clemmer
(d) The prison community	(iv) Sutherland & Cressy

Codes :

	(a)	(b)	(c)	(d)
A.	(i)	(ii)	(iii)	(iv)
B.	(iv)	(i)	(ii)	(iii)
C.	(iv)	(iii)	(ii)	(i)
D.	(i)	(ii)	(iv)	(iii)

74. Restitution refers to
A. Victim pays money to the offender
B. Offender pays money to the victim of crime
C. State pay money to the offender
D. None of the above

75. Assertion (A) : Enrico Ferri rejected the doctrine of free will, that is, it is not the criminal who wish to act.

Reason (R) : Ferri believed that the situation actually influences the criminal's actions. He believed that crime was produced primarily by the type of society from which the criminal comes.

A. (A) is correct, but (R) is wrong.
B. Both (A) and (R) are correct.
C. (A) is wrong, but (R) is correct.
D. Both (A) and (R) are wrong.

76. Phrenology is associated with

I. Anomie
II. Fransis Joseph Gall
III. Study of heads and head casts
IV. Investigation of the bumps and other irregularities of the skull.

Choose the correct combination using the codes given below :

A. I, II, III & IV are correct.
B. II, III & IV are correct.
C. III & IV are correct.
D. IV is correct.

77. Followings are included in Robert Merton's modes of adaptation :

I. Conformity   II. Retreatism
III. Retribution   IV. Rebellion

Choose the correct combination, using the codes given below :

A. I, II & IV are correct.
B. I, II & III are correct.
C. II, III & IV are correct.
D. I & IV are correct.

78. In the year 2010 how many offences under the special and local laws were registered by the police?

A. 35–40 lakh   B. 40–45 lakh
C. 45–50 lakh   D. More than 50 lakh

79. In statistical analysis that does chi-square indicate?

A. Correlation   B. Significance
C. Association   D. Difference

80. Who among the following is eligible for the appointment of the chairman of the National Human Rights Commission in India?

A. Former Chief Justice of India
B. Former Chief Justice of High Courts
C. Former Supreme Court Judge
D. All the above

81. That aspect of law that specifies the methods to be used in enforcing substantive law is

A. Case law   B. Procedural law
C. Personal law   D. Economic law

82. Victim compensation scheme has recently been made a part of the

A. Indian Penal Code
B. Code of criminal procedure
C. Indian Evidence Act
D. None of the above

83. The partial representation of constructs like social status, power and intelligence is called

A. Measurement
B. Operational Definition
C. Variables
D. Definition

84. Which of the following statistical technique can be used to find the relationship between two dichotomous variables?

A. Regression
B. Standard Deviation
C. Chi-square
D. Mode

85. Which one of the following is not correctly matched?

A. Ensilo Femi – Positive school
B. Drift theory – Gresham Syres
C. Differential opportunity structure – E.H. Sutherland
D. Power-control theory – John Hagan

86. Which one of the following is not correctly matched?

A. Ecological theory – Ernest W. Burgess
B. Subculture theories – William A. Bonger
C. Defensible space – Oscar Newman
D. Routine Activity theory – Marcus Felson

87. A statistical index of the strength of relationship between two variables is called

A. Percentage analysis

B. Correlation coefficient
C. t-test
D. Regression

88. Lie detector/ polygraph ascertain the changes in the following :
A. Rate of heart beat
B. Rate of Respiration
C. Conductivity of skin
D. All of above

89. Historically victims (or their families) were permitted to take measures to avenge crime. This is called
I. Revenge II. Retaliation
III. Retribution IV. Rehabilitation

Choose the correct combination using the codes given below :
A. I, II, III & IV are correct.
B. I, II & III are correct.
C. II, III & IV are correct.
D. III & IV are correct.

90. The idea that humans have mental conflicts because of desires and energies that are repressed into the unconscious is propounded by
A. Eric Silver
B. Michael Milken
C. Sigmund Freud
D. B.F. Skinner

ANSWERS

1	2	3	4	5	6	7	8	9	10
D	C	B	C	B	A	D	C	A	B
11	**12**	**13**	**14**	**15**	**16**	**17**	**18**	**19**	**20**
A	D	D	B	B	D	B	D	D	C
21	**22**	**23**	**24**	**25**	**26**	**27**	**28**	**29**	**30**
A	A	B	A	D	A	C	B	D	B
31	**32**	**33**	**34**	**35**	**36**	**37**	**38**	**39**	**40**
B	C	A	C	A	C	C	D	B	C
41	**42**	**43**	**44**	**45**	**46**	**47**	**48**	**49**	**50**
C	D	D	C	C	B	C	D	C	A
51	**52**	**53**	**54**	**55**	**56**	**57**	**58**	**59**	**60**
B	D	D	C	D	C	D	B	B	A
61	**62**	**63**	**64**	**65**	**66**	**67**	**68**	**69**	**70**
D	B	C	A	B	B	D	B	B	C
71	**72**	**73**	**74**	**75**	**76**	**77**	**78**	**79**	**80**
A	A	B	B	B	B	A	C	C	A
81	**82**	**83**	**84**	**85**	**86**	**87**	**88**	**89**	**90**
B	B	C	C	C	B	B	D	B	C

➤➤➤➤➤

YOUR SPACE